Author's Preface

This special reprint edition of *Blue Guide Romania* is essentially a reprint of the first edition (2000) of the guide with a number of corrections of typographical errors.

Romania has changed out of all recognition since I first went there in 1993. Back then, people looked exhausted, the streets were lifeless and the food shops empty but for a few dusty, fly-blown goods. Now the cities are full of energy, hustle, brashness and noise, the shops are bursting with colourful products and if you so much as blink, top of the range cars mow you down on the newly-asphalted roads. Instead of desperation, you sense that things are happening and that anything is possible. The 18th century heart of Bucharest is enjoying a make-over and medieval Sibiu has been transformed as a sparkling European City of Culture. Conservation projects such as those funded by the Eminescu Trust, the Messerschmidt Foundation, Opérations Villages Roumains, Pro Patrimonio and many others, have made great strides in saving Romania's wonderfully varied architectural heritage. Added to this, smart, new hotels and bright, welcoming, family-run guesthouses have sprung up all over the place. The Carpathian Mountains are still relatively unspoilt, making this one of the most physically attractive countries anywhere in east-central Europe. Romania's superb wildlife still exists, even if the rarest animals (bears, lynxes and wolves) are under pressure from farmers and trophy hunters. It would be stupid to say that Romania has solved all its problems, that everything is fair and that everybody who lives there is happy. Daily life is full of conflicting aims, of struggles between progressives and traditionalists, between those who believe entirely in market forces and those who want to save the world with idealistic dreams, between people who have and those who don't. The great difference is that now, Romanians of all political colours can discuss their opinions in public without fear of reprisals. There is an air of confidence among younger people because those with enough money and qualifications can travel and work abroad more easily than before. And at home, slowly (often very slowly!) the infrastructure is getting back on its feet. The ghastly state-run orphanages have been closed. Above all, membership of NATO and the European Union has given Romanians the feeling that they truly belong to Europe, rather than being marginalised. Having suffered unbearable wrongs throughout their history, the Romanians developed extraordinary powers of endurance and good humour. With luck these qualities will at last bring them the rewards they deserve.

I would like to thank Maria-Cristina Enescu, Şerban Cantacuzino and Raluca Preotu for their help with the Romanian text.

Caroline Juler
January 2009

Your views on this book would be much appreciated. We welcome not only specific comments, suggestions or corrections, but any more general views you may have: how this book enhanced your visit, how it could have been more helpful. Blue Guides authors and editorial and production team work hard to bring you what we hope are the best-researched and best-presented cultural, historical and academic guide books in the English language. Please write to us by email (editorial@blueguides.com), via the comments page on our website (www.blueguides.com) or at the address given above. We will be happy to acknowledge useful contributions in the next edition, and to offer a free copy of one of our titles.

Romania

Caroline Juler

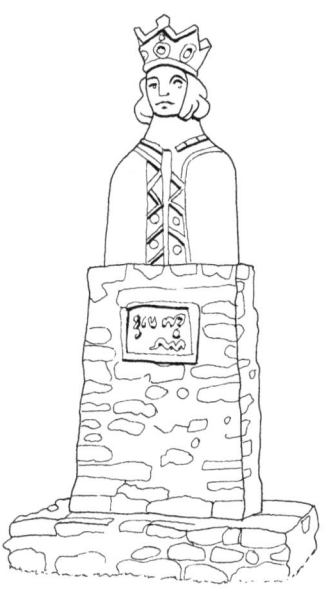

BLUE GUIDE

Somerset Books • London

1st edition July 2000
This 1st edition reprinted with author amendments 2009

Published by A & C Black (Publishers) Limited
35 Bedford Row, London WC1R 4JH

© Caroline Juler, 2000, 2009

Maps and plans drawn by RJS Associates, © A&C Black

Illustrations © Jim Urquhart

All rights reserved. No part of this publication may be reproduced or used in any form or by any means – photographic, electronic or mechanical, including photocopying, recording, taping or information storage and retrieval systems – without permission of the publishers.

The rights of Caroline Juler to be identified as author of this work have been asserted by her in accordance with the Copyright Designs and Patents Act, 1988.

'Blue Guides' is a registered trademark.

A CIP catalogue record of this book is available from the British Library.

ISBN 978-1-905131-33-4

The author and the publishers have done their best to ensure the accuracy of all the information in Blue Guide Romania; however, they can accept no responsibility for any loss, injury or inconvenience sustained by any traveller as a result of information or advice contained in the guide.

Title page illustration: bust of Prince Petru Rares, Moldovita Monastery.

Caroline Juler graduated from Oxford Polytechnic in 1978. Since then she has written two books on Orientalist painting, numerous articles for art journals and newspapers. She first went to Romania in 1993, fulfilling a lifelong ambition to see the country for herself. She was not disappointed.

Printed and bound in England by Lightning Source.

Contents

Preface 9
Acknowledgements 10

Practical information

Planning your trip 11
Getting there 16
On arrival 18
Where to stay 19

Getting around 20
Additional information 23
Food and drink 32

Background information

Romania: an historical introduction 37
Aspects of Romania 54
  The land 54
  The people 56
  Religion 60
  Visual arts 68

  Literature 84
  Music and dance 89
  Wildlife 102
  Language 104
  Further reading 109

The Guide

Bucharest

Bucharest 113
  Curtea Veche, Lipscani and
    Calea Victoriei 129
  Piața Universității 135
  Piața Universității to Piața Romană 136
  East from Piața Universității 136
  East from Piața Romană 138
  Calea Victoriei: B-dul Elisabeta to
    Piața Revoluției 138

  West of Calea Victoriei 141
  Calea Victoriei: Piața Revoluției to
    Piața Victoriei 143
  Piața Victoriei to Piața Presei Libere
    144
  South of the centre:
    Palatul Parliamentului 149
  Around Bucharest 151

Wallachia

Wallachia 155
Oltenia 160
Călimănesti and Căciulata 161
Râmnicu Vâlcea 162
Târgu Jiu 166
Drobeta Turnu Severin 169
Craiova and its museums 171

Muntenia 174
Curtea de Argeș 174
Câmpulung 178
Târgoviște 179
Pitești 181
Sinaia 183
Alexandria 187

Moldavia

Moldavia 188
Northwest Moldavia 191
Bucovina 192
Sucevița 200
Rădăuți 206
Suceava 207

Dragomirna 213
South and east of Suceava 214
Southwest Bucovina 217
Câmpulung Moldovenesc 217
Vatra Dornei 220
Neamț region 222

Târgu Neamţ 222
Agapia and Văratec 227
Războieni 230
Southern Neamţ 232
Piatra Neamţ 232
Bacău 236
East Moldavia 237
Iaşi 237

South to Vaslui 259
Southern Moldavia 261
West of the Bărăgan Plain 261
Focşani 266
Into the Vrancea mountains 269
Buzău and Râmnicu Sărat 271
Brăila 273
Galaţi 276

Maramureş
Maramureş 281
Baia Mare 293
Sighetu Marmaţiei 298
Historic Maramureş 301
The Cosău Valley 302

The Mara Valley 304
The Iza Valley 305
The Vişeu Valley 308
Borşa 309

Crişana and the northwest borderlands
Crişana 313
Oradea 313
Satu Mare 319
The Oaş Country 324

South of Satu Mare 324
Silvania 326
Zalău 329

The Banat
The Banat 333
Timişoara 336

Arad 344

Dobrogea
Dobrogea 351
The Danube Delta 354
Tulcea 355
Into the Delta 359
North and northwest Dobrogea 362
From Tulcea to Constanţa 365
Mamaia 368

From Cernavodă to Constanţa 369
Constanţa 371
Southern Dobrogea: Constanţa to
  Mangalia 378
Mangalia 380
Southwest Dobrogea: Mangalia to
  Călăraşi 386

Transylvania
Transylvania 388
Southwest Transylvania 389
Over the Mureş 392
Deva 394
Ţara Haţegului 399
Brad to Poarta Mureşului 404
North from the Arieş Valley:
  Munţele Mare, Măgura Călăţele 408
Alba Iulia 410
From Alba Iulia north to
  the Apuseni borders 416
From Turda to Cluj 418
Cluj-Napoca 419
Cluj to Nicula 432
Târgu Mureş and the Székely country
  433

Northern Transylvania 437
Bistriţa 438
Sovata 445
Eastern Transylvania 447
Miercurea Ciuc 448
Around Miercurea Ciuc:
  the Székely villages of Bazinul
  Ciucului 451
Sfântu Gheorghe 453
Southern Transylvania 455
Sibiu 456
Sighişoara 473
Braşov 478
South from Sighişoara 487
Into Wallachia: Valea Prahovei 489
Into Ţara Făgăraşului 491

Index
Index 493

Town plans
Brașov 483
Bucharest 130–131
Cluj-Napoca 425
Constanța 375
Iași 243
Sibiu 461
Sighișoara 475
Târgu Mureș 435
Timișoara 342

Area maps
The Banat 334
Crișana and the northwest borderlands 314
Dobrogea 351
Maramureș 282–283
Moldavia 188
Transylvania 390–391
Wallachia 156–157

To Anna Hulbert, who loved Romania and its horses.

Preface

'Romania is an enigma, the great mystery of the Middle Ages.' (Nicolae Iorga).

'*Codrul frate cu românul.*' ('The forest is the Romanian's friend', Romanian proverb.)

I first went to Romania in 1993, on my way to a festival of performance art in the Carpathians. Having heard about Transylvania from Eastern European friends, AnnArt, as the festival was called, gave me the excuse I wanted to see the country for myself. At the time I had not read Misha Glenny's withering description of pre-revolutionary Romania as a weird, mutant asteroid plunging its way through the communist firmament, nor seen Dervla Murphy's account of her experiences just after 1989 in *Transylvania and Beyond*. In fact, I had not delved into any of the travelogues, political, philosophical and literary analyses, or the histories, geographies and biographies which are part of the researcher's armoury. All I had to go on were the warnings of my friends in Hungary ('Romania isn't part of Europe, you know'), clichés about Dracula, vampires, and the promise of unlimited forests. So here I was, squashed into the corner of a crowded compartment on the overnight train from Budapest, on my way to a town I had vaguely heard of in connection with the Pied Piper of Hamelin.

Boisterous teenagers boarding the train at 4 a.m. put paid to any idea of sleep. Stumbling crossly into the corridor, I was soon glad that they had woken me. Within minutes I was watching the dawn break over a landscape of unbelievable perfection. As the light turned from blue to violet, pink and finally to gold I had problems in believing my eyes. Rolling meadows dotted with absurd, lollipop haystacks climbed gently into rounded hills and fell again into valleys threaded with silver rivers. Men and women in white blouses were rhythmically cutting hay with long-handled scythes. Further afield, narrow roads lined with poplars ribboned their way across the landscape, accompanied by the occasional slow-moving oxcart or a cyclist. Streams tumbled and bubbled over rocks and pebbles, the woods were full of burgeoning trees, the railway line was bordered by flowers and in the distance, majestic blue peaks strode along with us, giving the landscape continuity and depth. In that magical, misty half-light, there was not a single pylon, wire fence or, apart from the cyclist, any other sign of twentieth-century life: no grain silos, tractors or combines, no steel warehouses, street lights or impatient cars, trucks or motorbikes, nothing. Even the train seemed out of place, and when we thundered over a small bridge we frightened a horse which was pulling a cart through the tunnel underneath. Its driver had been fast asleep at the reins and got the fright of his life when his horse bolted out from the other side.

Of course not all of Transylvania is like this. But on this and following visits, I realised that my preconceptions about Romania, which had been fed by media coverage of the plight of children in orphanages and the conditions in old people's homes, the outdated and poisonous industrial plants, corrupt politicians and ethnic hatred were very one-sided. Iliescu's government must have been desperate when it hired Saatchi and Saatchi to improve the country's image, but there is a much more positive side to Romania than you could possibly guess from the almost exclusively lurid reports in newspapers and on television.

Romania is going through a difficult period of transition, like that of Britain after the Second World War. The West waits impatiently for signs of a painless segue into a market economy, as we are supposed to have seen in the Czech Republic, Hungary or Poland. Romania's situation was different from theirs, and it will take longer to recover. But young people are no longer leaving the country in droves and there are signs of initiative everywhere.

So why should you go to Romania? The straight answer is because it is one of the most beautiful of all the countries of southeast Europe. But you cannot see everything at once. If your time is limited, there are some places you should not miss. And if I could only go to one of them at a time, I would go first to the Maramureș and then to northern Moldavia (with the painted monasteries of Bucovina), followed by the Danube Delta; the Apuseni mountains; the Saxon towns and churches in southern Transylvania, the Dacian fastnesses of Sarmizegetusa and northern Oltenia—but the choice is yours!

Acknowledgements

Hundreds of people have helped me gather information for this guide, many of them giving freely of their time and expertise without expecting any reward. My thanks are due to all of them; without their support the book would never have appeared, and whatever shortcomings it has are mine.

There is not room to list everyone who deserves a mention, but I want to include Eva Gligor of Atlantic Tour, Bucharest; Mrs Mădăraș of OJT Baia Mare, and the Anglo-Romanian Bank for a donation of £100 towards my research. My thanks are also due to ambassadors Sergiu Celac and Radu Onofrei and to Mihai Gafița, Sânziana Dragoș and Dan Chiriac at the Romanian Embassy, London; Cristina Rai and Caroline Mortlock; the Făgărașanu family in Timișoara; Parasca Făt-Sabăud; Georgeta and Dumitru Iuga; Katalin Tímár; Ileana Pintilie; Judit Angel and Sándor Bartha; Marcela Gafița; Marcel and Ortensia Zahariciuc; Maria Borzan and her colleagues in Reghin; Dr Alina Ciobanel; Livia and Tudor Stoia; Sorin Iftimi and Coralia Costas; Irina Nicolău of the Muzeul Țăranului Român; Dr Corneliu Bucur and his family; Ioan and Ana Godea; photographer Kosei Miya; Jean Blajan and the Vasiliu family; Tiberiu Graur; Horea Ciugudean; Ancă Rotărescu and her husband Gabi; Dr Jennifer Scarce; Marius Mistretu; Delia Grigore; Sorin Mașca; Mihaela Danga; Vasile Ionescu; Sanda Marta; the Romanian Cultural Foundation; the monasteries of Bistrița, Agapia, Neamț, Văratec, Dumbrăvele, Putna, Moreni, Dobrovăț, and Războieni; Dan Matei and Irina Oberländer of CIMEC; Antoineta Taneva; John Nandriș; Paul Neagu; Dr Caterina Costinescu; Alexandru Matei; Ileana Shirley-Smith and Dana Berciu; Popeluc (Pete Castle, Lucy Castle-Hotea and Ioan Pop) for letting me see their musical guide to Transylvania; Lucia Duca; Nick Jukes; Manci in Codlea; James Roberts; Dr David Y. Mason; Ian Chilvers; Michael Jacobs; Iain Zaczek; Vesna Goldsworthy; Ruth Freeman.

I would also like to thank Sorin Ciutacu and his parents; Gizella Olah; Sandu Ilea; Manuna Didea; Mariana Marcelu; the Seventh Day Adventists of Gurasada; Ronald Joyce; Chris and Cristina of Exodus UK; Aki and Martin Shann. Most of all though, *Blue Guide Romania* owes its life to Kit (surely he should be Sir Kit?), for transforming an ancient Sherpa van into a reliable (and much admired) conveyance for negotiating mountain roads, and for not letting me duck out.

PRACTICAL INFORMATION

 Planning your trip

When to go
Romania's climate is officially 'temperate-continental', which means that it ranges between the extremes of very hot summers and very cold winters, when temperatures can drop lower than ⁻15°C in the mountain regions. Romania contains both alpine and low-lying coastal regions, and it is always hotter in the plains than in the mountains. In June, July and August, the hottest places in Romania are near the Black Sea coast, where average temperatures reach 24–30°C, so if you are planning a trip there, it is best to go in May or early June—and you miss the crowds as well.

Traditionally, the really cold weather starts in November and lasts until the end of March. A cauterising wind known as the *crivăţ* blasts its way south from Russia, and snow falls over most of the country, cutting off many roads. If you are planning to travel to Romania at this time of year, bring plenty of warm, waterproof and windproof clothing, even if you plan to spend most of your time in towns and cities. Hotel and domestic heating systems are not reliable, and when it freezes in the centre of Bucharest, the gas pressure regularly drops in sympathy and leaves a large number of buildings, many of which are linked up to an antiquated central system, without heating or cooking facilities.

Spring in the Romanian mountains comes between April and June, and while this is the season for wildflowers such as narcissi, it can bring torrential rain as well. The highest peaks are usually snow-covered all year round. Spring and autumn are the best times to visit the Delta, when flocks of migratory birds are on the move and the mosquitoes are bearable. In summer the mountains can trick you even if there is a drought on the plains: thunderstorms can last there for days, and this is a good time to visit Transylvanian and Moldavian churches. The mild, sunny days of autumn usually linger from early September until late October and sometimes into November, turning the mixed forests from green to a kaleidoscope of colours.

Passports and formalities
Unless you come from the USA, one of the former socialist states of Central or Eastern Europe, or from Austria, Cyprus, Mexico, Tunisia or Turkey, you will need a visa to enter Romania; this is partly in retaliation for the visa restrictions that Western European countries impose on Romanians, who find it extremely difficult and expensive to travel abroad. British visitors need a full 10-year passport, valid for six months from the date of entry. Tourist visas are single-entry and valid for 30 days; you have to use them within three months of the issue date. You can no

longer rely on getting a visa at the border or at Otopeni airport: the EU has imposed restrictions on the sale of visas which Romania may apply as well.

It is an offence to outstay your visa, but foreigners can sometimes get extensions from the *judeţ* (county) police HQ. In Bucharest you can apply at the office on the 1st floor of Str Nicolae Iorga 27 (open Mon, Wed, Fri 09.30–13.00, Tues 17.30–22.00, Thur 09.30–14.00 and 17.30–20.00, Sat 09.30–13.00). You will have to pay the fee at a CEC bank (in Bucharest this is on Piaţa Amzei); it costs US $25 plus $6 on top for same-day service. If you pay in hard currency you will get a receipt; take this back to Strada Iorga, where the staff may tell you to return in a day or two; offer a few dollars and they may act quicker. If a tourist visa is not renewed more than five days before expiry by someone wanting to stay in Romania, a fine of 300,000 lei or more may be levied.

You also need a visa if you are travelling in neighbouring countries such as Moldova, Ukraine and Serbia (where the visa is free, but unobtainable at the border). Bulgaria lifted visa restrictions on visitors from the EU in 1997, but it is wise to check all entry requirements before leaving. Passengers on the train from Bucharest to St Petersburg will need transit visas for Ukraine, Belarus and possibly the Baltic States, as well as a visa for Russia itself.

You do not need any vaccinations for travel in Romania, but it would be wise to get hepatitis A, polio and typhoid boosters if you plan to stay in remote areas without hygienic sanitation.

Tourist agencies outside Romania

Romania's Ministry of Tourism has replaced the old communist-run ONT, and its international offices are helpful. It has branches in the following countries:

Austria: Wahringerstrasse 6–8, Wien 1090, ☎/fax 1 317 3157.
Belgium: Place de Brouckere 44–46, Bruxelles 1000, ☎/fax 2 218 0079.
Denmark: Vesterbrogade 55A, Kopenhagen DK-1620, ☎ 31 246219.
France: 12 Pyramides, Paris 75002, ☎ 1 40 20 99 33; fax 40 20 99 43.
Germany: Zeil 13, Frankfurt am Main 60313, ☎ 69 295278; fax 292947, and Frankfurter Tor 5, Berlin 10243, ☎ /fax 30 589684.
Greece: 33 Vassilissis Sofias, Athens, ☎/fax 1 7251884.
Israel: 1 Ben Yehuda Street, Tel Aviv, ☎ 3 663536.
Italy: Via Torino 100, 00184 Rome.
Moldova: Ştefan cel Mare Bulevardul 151–153, Chişinau, ☎ 2 222354; fax 261992.
Netherlands: 165 Weteringschans, Amsterdam C 1017 XD, 165 Weteringschans, ☎/fax 20 623 9044.
Russia: Ulitza Dimitria Ulianova 16/2, Moscow, ☎/fax 095 1242473.
Spain: Calle General Paradinas 108 1G, 28006 M, Madrid 16, ☎ 1 564 0333; fax 562 9638.
Sweden: Vasahuset Gamla Brogatan 33, 1120 Stockholm, ☎ 8 210253/63; fax 210253.
Switzerland: 10 Schweizergasse, Zurich 8001, ☎ 1 2111730; fax 2111745.
Turkey: 7 Lamartin Caddesi, Kat 1, 8090 Taksim, Istanbul, ☎/fax 212 2568417.
United Kingdom: 83A Marylebone High Street, London W1M 3DE, ☎ 0207 224 3692.
USA: 14E 38 St, 12th Floor, New York, NY 10016, ☎ 212 545 8484; fax 251 0429.

Tour operators

The **Romania Travel Centre** can arrange flights, hotel reservations, car hire, internal flights, insurance and someone to meet you. Contact James Greig at Clayfield Mews, Newcomen Road, Tunbridge Wells, Kent TN4 9PA, ☎ 01892 516901; fax 511579; e-mail james@romtrav.demon.co.uk.

Balkan Holidays offer a number of package tours, including beach holidays at Neptun and a 'Dracula coach tour' of Transylvania that covers Sinaia, Bran and Poiana Brașov. Contact them at Sofia House, 19 Conduit Street, London W1R 9TD, ☎ 0500 245165 for brochures, 020 7543 5555 for reservations, or 020 7543 5583 for information on independent travel.

Explore Worldwide, 1 Frederick Street, Aldershot, Hants GU11 1LQ, ☎ 01252 344161 (brochure request), 319448 (reservations and dossiers); fax 343170. They operate an excellent mixed-interest programme that includes Sinaia, Bran, time on a floating hotel in the Danube Delta, together with Maramureș and the monasteries of Bucovina; about a third of the tour involves well-planned day hikes, rather than pure trekking. They have very good Romanian leaders, who lead for no-one else, otherwise a Romanian-speaking British leader.

Waymark Holidays, 44 Windsor Road, Slough, Berks. SL1 2EJ, ☎ 01753 517477; fax 01753 517016. A high-quality specialist mountain walking (and winter cross-country skiing) operator with a fine mountain-walking tour in Romania, staying in good *cabane*.

There are scores of American companies offering holidays in Romania. For a list of them contact the Romanian Embassy in Washington DC or the Romanian Tourist Office in New York. ***Questers Worldwide Nature Tours, Inc.***, 381 Park Avenue South, New York 10016, ☎ 212 251 0444/800 468 8668; fax 212 251 0890 and ***Quo Vadis, Inc.***, 288 Newbury Street, Boston, MA 02115, ☎ 617 421 9494; fax 617 421 0928; e-mail:Quovadis@usa.com.

Travellers who want to join guided wildlife tours should try **Wexas**, 45 Brompton Road, London SW3 1DE, ☎ 020 7581 4130. **Earthwatch**, 57 Woodstock Road, Oxford OX2 6HJ, ☎ 01865 311600; fax 311383; e-mail info@uk.earthwatch.org, organises conservation holidays in Romania. So does the **British Trust for Conservation Volunteers** at 36 St Mary's Street, Wallingford, Oxon OX10 0EU, ☎ 01491 839766. *Exodus Expeditions* organises 15-day treks along the Făgăraș range of the southern Carpathians, between Mount Negoiu to the west and the Bucegi massif to the east; contact 9 Weir Road, London SW12 0LT, ☎ 020 8675 5550; fax 020 7673 0779; e-mail sales@exodustravels.co.uk.

All the companies listed below are bonded tour operators with full brochure, tour report and pre-departure information services.

Snail's Pace Holidays, 25 Thorpe Lane, Almondbury, Huddersfield HD5 8TA, ☎ 01484 426259. Small group wildlife tours concentrating on birdwatching and botany. *Avian Adventures*, 49 Sandy Road, Norton, Stourbridge DY8 3AJ, ☎ 01384 372013; fax 01384 441340, perhaps the tour operator with the greatest experience of any of operating in Romania. *Sunbird*, PO Box 76, Sandy, Beds SG19 2DF, ☎ 01767 682969; fax 692481, is one of the most prestigious wildlife tour companies, with a unique programme, visiting the medieval painted monasteries in Bucovina and enjoying wildlife with a medieval ecclesiastical flavour—tailor-made for couples with combined interests. Their tour also visits the Danube Delta and the high Carpathians.

Speyside Wildlife, 9 Upper Mall, Grampian Road, Aviemore, Inverness-shire PH22 1RH, ☎/fax 01479 812498; e-mail speyside_wildlife@msn.com. Birdwatching and all-round wildllife tours, with the emphasis on enjoyment, rather than purely a long list of birds. *The Travelling Naturalist*, 1 Little Britain, Dorchester, Dorset DT1 5NN, ☎ 01305 267994; fax 265506. Birdwatching and all-round wildlife. *Wildwings*, International House, Bank Road, Bristol BS15 2LX, ☎ 0117 984 8040; fax 967 4444. *Papyrus Wildlife Tours*, 9 Rose Hill Court, Bessacarr, Doncaster DN4 5LY, ☎ 01302 530778. *Birdfinders*, 18 Midleaze, Sherborne, Dorset DT9 6DY, ☎/fax 01935 817001. *Limosa Holidays*, Suffield House, Northrepps, Norfolk NR27 0LZ, ☎ 01263 578143; fax 579251. *Gourmet Birds*, Windrush, Coles Lane, Brasted, Westerham, Kent TN16 1NN, ☎ 01959 563627; fax 01959 562906. *Ornitholidays*, 29 Straight Mile, Romsey, Hants SO51 9BB, ☎ 01794 519445; e-mail:ornitholidays@compuserve.com; website http://www.ornitholidays.co.uk. *ACE Study Tours*, Babraham, Cambridge CB2 4AP, ☎ 01223 835055; fax 01223 837394; e-mail ace@studytours.org, operate a well thought-out historical and architecture tour, covering the major monuments and much of the country, including the German fortified churches of southern Transylvania, Bucovina, Maramureş and much more.

Ibis Excursions, Ganløseparken 46, Ganløse, 3660 Stenløse, Denmark, ☎ 45 48 19 59 40 ; fax 48 19 59 45. Successful, responsibly-run small British-run birdwatching tour company.

James Roberts works as a freelance tour leader specialising in wildlife and mountains, but not ignoring the human aspects of the country. His small company organises small groups direct and can be contacted by e-mail at jameselena@netgates.co.uk. He is the author of *A Birdwatching Guide to Romania* (Arlequin Press, 1999).

A wealth of information about Romania is available on the internet. At the time of writing, http://www.info.polymtl.ca/romania offers the widest range of contacts. Hard on its heels is Romania's dynamic embassy in Washington, DC, which currently belongs to a network that posts all kinds of travel information and services to prospective visitors: access is via http://www.embassy.-org.romania, then rotravel.com. You can send e-mails to this site at romania@-embassy.org.

Tourist agencies in Romania

Tourist offices in Romania have largely been privatised, but there is a regulatory body called *ANAT* (short for Asociația Națională a Agenților de Turism din România) whose members are increasing all the time. *ANAT*'s powers are limited and not legally enforceable, and although it recommends its own rules for drawing up contracts, it cannot control prices. The main regulator is the government, which issues two categories of licence: A for international trade and B for national only. Members of *ANAT* have to pay an annual registration fee, and the organisation holds an annual competition to see which agency has attracted the most clients and the largest income. For a booklet listing their names and addresses—which are updated annually—contact *ANAT* at Str Foișorului 8, Bloc 3C, Scara 2, fl 2, ap 41, București 1, ☎/fax 01 321 1908. ANAT also publishes a monthly newssheet.

Among the agencies are *Pan Travel*, Str Tr. Grozăvescu, Cluj-Napoca 3400, ☎/fax 064 420516; e-mail pantravel@mail.dntcj.ro; website http://www.

dntcj.ro/pantravel. **Căliman Club Holidays** specialise in tailor-made tours including hiking, mountain-biking, riding, minibus trips and windsurfing; contact them at Str Florilor 1, Ap 86, 4400 Bistriţa, ☎/fax 063 231780; e-mail cit@elcom.ro; website www.elcom.ro/caliman. *Over the Wall* holidays for Link Romania are at Fam Apostol, Sat. Hârja 20, 5461 Oneşti, Jud. Bacău, ☎ 034 337813; mobile: 094 212065, e-mail roving@mic.ro.

A few of the old-guard communist-era *ONT* offices still exist, with the head office at Bulevard Magheru 7, Bucureşti, ☎ 01 120915/140759/136806; fax 120915. However, the service here is grudging at best.

For detailed information on tourism and on participatory and spectator sports, contact the appropriate ministry: Ministry of Sport, Ministerul Tineretului şi Sportului, at Str Vasile Conta 16, Bucureşti, ☎ 01 211 5555; fax 0540. The Ministry of Tourism is listed under 'Cultural organisations' on p 31.

Maps and guidebooks

Bartholomew publishes an excellent map of the whole country; the GeoCenter *Euromap* of Romania and Moldova is also good. But one of the best relief maps is the single-sheet *România*, which you can buy from large bookshops and street stalls in Romania itself. Subtitled '*Harta Fizicogeografică şi Administrativă*', it was published in 1996 for school and university use and also includes Moldova and a map of the counties. If you are travelling through Budapest on your way to Transylvania, try to pick up a copy of *Erdély*, the Hungarian map of Transylvania which shows place names in their Magyar, German and Romanian forms; you may also be able to get one from bookshops in Cluj-Napoca. An excellent new road map, published by Flamanco, is *Atlas Turistic Rutier*, available in good bookshops.

The Romanian Tourist Offices have reasonable road maps and will also supply a wealth of information and listings for visitors published by the energetic Ministry of Tourism. City maps vary greatly: Bucharest tourist agencies such as ONT can supply adequate plans, and hotels often distribute them free. Editura Anastasia produces a plan and guide to the country's churches and monasteries, called *Harta şi Ghidul Schiţurilor, Mănăstirilor*, which is available from most important religious institutions and some bookshops. As yet, there is no commercially available equivalent to British Ordnance Survey maps.

Romania Tourism, published annually by Pagini Naţionale, is a useful directory which summarises each county's main tourist attractions in Romanian, English and French. It also contains addresses and contact numbers for every conceivable service. For more information ☎/fax 01 222 3355, or write to Pagini Naţionale at Piaţa Presei Libere 1, Bucureşti. *Ghidul Turistic al României* is a similar publication, giving a wealth of information in alphabetical order by county, including hotels, museums, garages, festivals and maps of mountain paths. It is produced by Publirom at Piaţa Unirii 10, 3400 Cluj-Napoca, ☎ 064 192205; fax 199445, but at the time of writing it was only available in Romanian.

Getting there

Travel into and out of Romania is easy: there are plenty of planes, trains and buses that can take you there and away.

By air

Airlines with direct flights from the UK to Bucharest include *TAROM* (the Romanian national airline), which flies eight times a week from Heathrow and twice a week from Stansted and Manchester. It runs a 'Smart Miles' scheme that credits your air miles to an account that can be cashed in with the car-rental firm *Avis*. Both companies offer 'fly-drive' deals that cut the cost of car hire in Romania; these have to be booked through *TAROM*'s offices abroad. Discounts are available to people under 25. Contact *TAROM* in Britain at 27 New Cavendish Street, London W1M 7RL, ☎ 020 7935 3600; fax 020 7487 2913, or Terminal 2, Office Block, Heathrow Airport, ☎ 020 8745 5542; fax 020 8897 4071; in France at 38 avenue de l'Opéra, F-75002 Paris, ☎ 01 47 42 25 42; fax 42 56 43 67. *TAROM* provides charter flights from Gatwick and Manchester to Constanța in the summer and to Bucharest in the winter, valid for a maximum stay of one month. British Airways also flies direct between Gatwick and Bucharest.

KLM runs daily flights to Bucharest from several airports in Britain and often has very good offers; all involve a change at Schipol in the Netherlands. Other companies that connect the UK to Romania with one change of plane include *Air France*, *Alitalia*, *Austrian Airlines*, *CSA*, *LOT*, *Lufthansa*, *Malev* and *Swissair*. Romania is also served by *Aeroflot*, *Alitalia* and *Delta Airlines*; some Italian airlines run business flights between Italy and western Romania. The main international airport in Bucharest is Otopeni, 11km north of the city, but the airports at Constanța and Timișoara also receive international flights. Most of these airlines have offices in Bucharest.

In Britain, discounted fares are advertised in newspapers such as the *Daily Telegraph* and the *Independent* in their classified travel sections on Saturdays; the *Observer*, *Sunday Times* and *Independent on Sunday* carry the same sections on Sundays. In London, you can often find similar deals in publications like *Time Out*, the *Evening Standard* or *TNT*, the free magazine that is found outside large Tube and mainline rail stations. Some travel companies specialise in cheap fares for students and people under 26, and will sometimes sell scheduled tickets at a discount.

A new international airport is being built near Satu Mare, close to the Romanian-Hungarian border.

By rail

Travelling by train to Romania from Victoria Station in London takes about 47 hours, and standard return tickets (valid for two months) are more expensive than discounted air fares. But a standard ticket allows you to make stopovers en route, and InterRail passes valid for 15 days or a month let you travel to other countries as well. (InterRail is now available for people over 26 as well as under, although the 26+ ticket is more expensive and more limited in scope.) Once you get into the former communist countries, train travel becomes much cheaper.

At the time of writing, Romanian national railways, SNCFR (Societatea Naţională a Căilor Ferate Române) operate a wide-ranging service into and out of the country. Trains from Bucharest run to and from many European cities: Amsterdam, Athens, Belgrade, Berlin, Bratislava, Brussels, Budapest, Frankfurt, Geneva, Istanbul, Kiev, London, Madrid, Munich, Moscow, Paris, Prague, Rome, St Petersburg, Sofia, Thessalonika, Vienna and Warsaw. First- and second-class seats and sleepers are available. There are nine trains a day to Bucharest from Budapest; the ticket costs around US $65 return.

Black-market money changers frequently travel on these trains and should be avoided, but ordinary passengers may offer to change currency with you as well. You can usually tell the difference by body language.

By bus

Several European bus operators run services to and from Romania; these include Euroline from London, which stops en route in Sibiu, Arad, and Sebeş before reaching the *Hotel Dorobanţi* in Bucharest. Contact Victoria Coach Station in London, ☎ 020 7730 3466, for details of these and other services.

There are frequent buses connecting Germany and Transylvania. *Trans-Europa* picks up from Sibiu, Suceava, Târgu Mureş, Bacău, Cluj, Baia Mare, Satu Mare and Oradea four days a week, and picks up from Frankfurt, Mannheim, Karlsruhe, Stuttgart, Ulm and Nürnberg on a different four days. One-way trips take around 24 hours. For information from Germany contact *Trans Europa*, ☎ 0161 290 6861/271 7338; in Romania the same company is in Sibiu, ☎ 069 211296; fax 210364; Târgu Mureş, ☎ 065 167064; Cluj, ☎ 064 195447; Bistriţa, ☎ 063 211872; Baia Mare, ☎ 062 411043; Satu Mare, ☎ 061 711178; Oradea, ☎ 059 436613; Deva, ☎ 054 213173; Bacău, ☎ 034 170534; Iaşi, ☎ 032 143037. Prices for children up to 4 years old cost 50 per cent of the adult fare, 4–12-year-olds can travel for 75 per cent of the adult fare; up to 50kg of luggage is allowed free per person. There are also plenty of buses that connect Romania with Turkey.

By car and motorcycle

If you intend to bring a car or motorcycle into Romania, you will need to bring the vehicle's registration document, a valid certificate of insurance and a current driving licence (a green card is not compulsory, but is a good idea); you must buy your visa at a Romanian embassy. For motorcyclists, helmets are compulsory. Four-wheel-drive vehicles with strong suspension are preferable, even if you plan to use only major roads.

Border crossing points are open 24 hours a day. From Hungary the northernmost crossing is at Csenger/Petea, and going south there are entry points at Borş, Vărşand and Nădlac. Nădlac and Borş tend to be the most congested, because they are on the most popular transcontinental trucking route; Petea and Vărşand may be better. To or from the Yugoslav Republic (Serbia) the entry points are at Jimbolia and further south at Moraviţa, Naidaş and Porţiile de Fier, near Drobeta Turnu-Severin. Romania's entry points into Bulgaria are (west to east) at Calafat, Giurgiu (usually with the worst delays), Ostrov-Silistra, Negru Vodă and Vama Veche; some of these involve picturesque ferry crossings. If you are going from Romania to Moldova, the entry points are (north to south) at Albiţa, Sculeni, Sânca Costeşti and Oancea. There is only one crossing from Romania into Ukraine, at Siret, 45km north of Suceava (the entry point north of Sighetu Marmației is reserved for local people).

At the larger crossing points from the west, such as Borș and Nădlac, visitors may be stopped by young men pretending to be foreign visitors to Romania. They may ask you to change large denominations of Western money (usually Deutschmarks) saying they have no other funds and will not be able to find anywhere to stay. This is a con-trick: keep all windows closed and drive on; if you produce any money, they will grab it and escape in a car parked nearby. Watch out for people trying to open the car boot and steal your luggage; this is another trick near border crossings, while you are waiting at traffic lights.

The *AA* (☎ 01256 20123) and *RAC* (☎ 0345 333222) provide information about taking a car to Romania as well as addresses of motoring organisations inside the country. They also have European route-planning services which can organise a print-out of the most appropriate roads to take.

A non-governmental organisation, **Intelligent Transport Systems Romania**, is being set up to coordinate information about road conditions and the road system in general; by 2000 a database and website will be in operation. ☎ 0040 (0) 222 3138 or 0040 (0) 315 7566, or contact the director, Dorin Dumitrescu, on e-mail dorind@incertrans.ro or ☎/fax 0040 (0) 410 0400.

On arrival

If you are flying to Romania on your own for the first time and do not speak the language well, try to arrange for someone to meet you; tourist agencies can often help with this. Airports and railway stations are meccas for taxi touts. Agree a fee before you set off; each city has an official rate for taxis, around 400 lei per kilometre for inside its limits, and slightly more if you want to travel further. Regular express buses run from Otopeni airport into the centre of Bucharest; they are fast and pleasant and cost much less than taxis. Buy your ticket from the driver.

The Gara de Nord is Bucharest's main national and international train station. Although it has greatly improved over the last 10 years, arriving here for the first time can be harrowing: at night bedraggled street kids hang around the platforms, begging for food, and people bang into you and elbow you out of the way in a frantic rush to get their tickets and make it onto the right train. There are porters who will take your luggage and there are waiting rooms to retreat into, but the best thing to do with Gara de Nord is to leave it far behind.

Fortunately, the city's Metro system has a station here and is easy and cheap to use. You can get a ticket valid for two or ten journeys. Buses, trolleys and trams also circulate the capital and getting to know their routes takes time. In Bucharest, yellow kiosks at main street corners sell carnets of bus and tram tickets (which are interchangeable). They are open during normal business hours. You have to stamp your ticket once you board; inspectors will fine you on the spot if you travel without a valid ticket. Bucharest's trams cover some of the most picturesque routes in the city.

Some Romanian towns and cities have *Maxitaxis*, minibuses that link town centres with their railway stations.

Where to stay

Romania's hotels are improving fast, but despite privatisation there are still many that seem suspended in a communist ethos. What is certain is that independent pricing has led to fast changes in the hotel industry. The Romanian Ministry of Tourism publishes a booklet listing hotels in several European languages; ask for an up-to-date copy from the tourist office in your country.

There is a 1–5-star grading system for hotels: the only 5-star ones are in Bucharest, including the *Athenée Hilton* in Piaţa Revoluţiei. Prices for these top-grade hotels are over double those of 4-star in the capital, while a similar grade in some parts of the country costs less than a third. Hostels and lower-grade hotels are, by comparison, relatively cheap places to stay. The old system of charging foreigners six times as much as Romanians was officially dropped in 1998 but it still goes on in some hotels.

If you want to meet Romanians in their home environment, there are several options. The Belgian charity, **Opérations Villages Roumains**, was established in 1989 to counteract Ceauşescu's systematisation programme. Three thousand villages across Europe took part in a scheme to adopt a threatened Romanian village, and since then *OVR* has developed a wide-ranging programme which provides financial aid and expertise to local communities who want to help themselves. An important element in this project is the 'agro-tourism' network (*Reţea turistică*), groups of private householders who offer bed and breakfast accommodation, usually in traditional farmhouses. Guides and information about local festivals are also available. French and German speakers should contact *OVR* at their headquarters in Belgium, Rue Zénobe Gramme 57, 6000 Charleroi, ☎ 71 68 61 51. In the UK the contact address (for information only, not bookings) is The Old Dye House, Spring Gardens, Frome, Somerset BA11 2NZ, ☎ 01373 466555; fax 454442. French OVR is at Rue A Duparchy, 18 bis, 91600 Savigny sur Orge, ☎ 40 15 71 51; fax 40 15 72 30. Alternatively, you can find OVR in Romania itself; their head office is at Str Ion Raţiu 2, 2400 Sibiu, ☎/fax 069 21 18 14.

ANTREC (Asociaţia Naţională de Turism Rural, Ecologic şi Cultural) is a Romanian intitiative that offers countryside bed and breakfast, local tours and much else. Contact the head office by letter to Bucureşti CP 22–259 or ☎/fax 01 222 8322. *ANTREC* has another headquarters in the village of Bran and regional offices in most county towns. Their efficiency and willingness to help may vary enormously from place to place. It is usually better to rely on the head office rather than the local ones.

Fundaţia Eco Rural Brădet also specialises in farmstay holidays. Supported by the EU Phare fund, *FERB* has concentrated on developing 'eco-friendly' tourism in a small group of picturesque mountain villages to the north of Curtea de Argeş. Its staff are very enthusiastic and will give you every assistance. Write to the head office at 72 150 Bucureşti, CP 48–22, or send a fax to 01 223 2071.

Other alternatives include contacting the branch office of **Centrul de Creaţie Populară** (the Centre for Folk Arts) in whichever county you would like to stay in; the staff often know private householders in picturesque places who would be keen to let rooms to foreigners. In addition, the traditional method of asking for accommodation when you arrive at a monastery can also work wonders. Romanians have been famed for their hospitality since Dimitrie Cantemir's day; please don't abuse it.

Getting around

Travelling in Romania is getting easier all the time—relatively speaking—but it is still a difficult country to tour on your own. This is not because it is particularly dangerous but because the infrastructure (roads, telephones and hotels) has not had time to recover from decades of degradation and neglect under the communists. National train and bus networks cover a large part of the country, but while trains are a viable option for seeing many of the main towns and cities, most of Romania's national buses are on their last legs and long-distance journeys require stamina and a sense of humour.

By air

TAROM runs internal flights between several cities; internal flights leave Bucharest from Băneasa airport near Otopeni. For detailed information contact the company in Bucharest or at its branches in Britain, France, Ukraine or the USA (see p 16). *Aeroclubul Traian Vuia* in Arad operates an air taxi service; contact the club at Calea Bodrogului, ☎ 057 281306. You could also try *Venus Prodimpex* at Str Cuza 71, Băilești, ☎ 051 311 536. Sibiu has a private flying club.

By rail

The rail network covers a large proportion of the country, and for Westerners tickets are amazingly cheap. However, on all but the most expensive trains (which are still reasonable) the rolling stock is ancient and uncomfortable. If you can afford the extra cost, it is often better to buy a first-class ticket or go by Intercity; tickets are about three times more expensive than the standard fares. Interrail tickets are valid for Romania, and young people can get other discounts.

The official timetable, *Mersul Trenurilor*, is updated annually and runs from May to May. You can buy a copy from most main rail stations or write to the *SNCFR* headquarters: Serviciul Mersurilor de Tren, B-dul Dinicu Golescu 38, Sector 1, 70050 București (a marvellous Art Deco building)—but do not rely on the timetable without also checking for the availability of the service at the stations concerned.

There are several different categories of train in Romania: double-deckers called *trenuri curse*, coded C, are very slow, stop at every halt and generally go only relatively short distances; *trenuri de persoane*, coded P, also slow; *accelerat*, Romania's A trains; *rapid* (R); *expres* (E); and *Intercity* (IC).

The Romanian ticket system can seem Byzantine at first: you get a seat ticket as well as the ticket which proves you have paid your fare. You can buy these in advance from the various *SNCFR* offices in towns and cities or within one hour before you travel from the station itself. Main stations, such as Bucharest's Gara de Nord, have introduced a more efficient system, but wherever you plan to go, make sure to give yourself enough time to get the ticket well in advance to avoid last-minute panics. If the queues are so long that you risk losing the train, the guards on the train may accept a bribe to let you stay on board.

Intercity trains sometimes have restaurant cars, but go well provided with food and drink on the others; apart from anything else, offering your sandwiches and *ţuica* around is a great way to break the ice with your fellow-travellers. Most toilets on Romanian trains are indescribably awful, so never travel anywhere (by any means of transport) without your own supply of toilet paper.

You can expect to encounter beggars, some with terrible disabilities and deformities, on trains and at large train stations; the latter also attract pickpockets and all kinds of touts.

By bus

Local buses can be the answer when exploring remote rural areas, and tickets are extremely cheap. Go prepared for the worst but in a spirit of adventure, and you may learn things you had never dreamt of—Romanians are generally gregarious and will find a way of communicating with you, even if they cannot speak your language.

Most town and city bus stations are either next to or near the local train station; ask the staff in the booking office for times and destinations after checking any timetables outside.

By taxi

Small minibuses known as *Maxitaxis* operate in Timişoara, Iaşi and other towns, where they run along fixed routes between signposted shops. You flag them down and pay a nominal sum for travelling between the stops.

Most Romanian towns and cities have their own authorised taxi operators who use meters and comply with a fixed fee per kilometre (if you travel outside the town limits, the rate increases). If possible, agree the fee before getting in or setting off. The best solution is to phone for a taxi; numbers are provided for individual towns and cities.

'Rogue' taxi drivers have an unerring eye for foreign faces and are always waiting to hassle you clamorously at stations—they even come onto the platforms at Gara du Nord—and major airports such as Otopeni and Băneasa; avoid them and look for legitimate taxi drivers who are waiting in their cars.

By car

If you can afford it, take or hire a car to see Romania, or even buy one when you get there; the British Embassy in Bucharest can advise you what formalities apply. Getting to out-of-the-way monasteries and ancient burial sites is impossible without four-wheel-drive, although a horse would often come in handy as well. A strong camper van with high road clearance would be ideal.

Hertz and *Europcar* operate in Bucharest, at Otopeni airport and several other cities. Both firms use imported cars such as Peugeots and Toyotas, while Romanian firms like **JET Turist**, **Mercedes** and **Sebastian** may be able to offer you a humble but solid Dacia. Local rates can vary from those charged if you book from abroad, and they also vary according to season, so it is worth checking both before you decide what to do. In Bucharest *Europcar* has offices at *Hotel*

Bucureşti, B-dul Magheru 7, *Hotel Intercontinental* and *Hotel Dorobanţi*; in Timişoara at *Hotel Cardinal*, B-dul Republicii 6, and in Constanţa at B-dul Tomis 46, where the branch is only open 15 Jun–15 Sept. Hire terms can include a collision damage waiver, but you are responsible if the car is stolen; drivers must be over 21 and have a clean licence.

Surprising as it may seem, hiring a taxi for long journeys can work out relatively cheap. Taxis are regulated and have fixed rates per kilometre, depending on whether you want to travel in or out of town.

Romanians drive on the right. Many European routes go through the country and are signposted accordingly with a white European E route number on a green background as well as their Romanian national number. The Romanian highway code tells you not to toot your horn in built-up areas and to keep your vehicle clean at all times; the latter rule is hardly ever enforced. Seat belts must be worn at all times.

Romanian roads are rough at the best of times. There are motorways, but the word could be taken as a euphemism for 'free-for-all', because it is not unusual to see ox- or horse-carts trundling down the fast lane in the face of oncoming traffic. Carts are more of a hazard at night because they do not always carry lights or reflectors.

The speed limit in towns and villages is 80kph (50mph). Police can make on-the-spot fines for speeding of up to 100,000 lei. There are speed limits which apply to the cylinder capacity of the vehicle you are driving and whether you are in a built-up area or on the open road. If you have a crash, legally you must wait for the police to turn up; the legal alcohol limit for motorists is 0.00 per cent, and the penalty for being caught after you have been drinking is very severe.

Pedestrians on crossings without traffic lights have priority at all times but having said this, they take their lives in their hands. Parking is restricted in the centre of Bucharest; there are two tow-away companies in the capital, one of them engagingly called *Pantera Roză* ('The Pink Panther'). If your car has been legally towed away, you have to find the appropriate police station which deals with the area where you parked, show the duty officer your passport and car insurance documents, pay c 60,000 lei, and then go to one of the city's two car pounds. There you have to pay another 15,000 lei release fee, and you are free to go again.

Many petrol stations in Romania now advertise unleaded petrol (*benzină fără plomb*), often using its German name of *bleifrei*. By western European standards, petrol is not prohibitively expensive in Romania. It is not always possible to get high-quality fuel; 98 octane is the best, and even with this you may find your engine pinking more than usual. Diesel is also available widely.

The Romanian Automobile Club, *ACR*, has an official agreement with partner motoring clubs abroad. If you belong to one of these organisations, including the AA and RAC, you are entitled to free or cut-price technical assistance. *ACR* also runs an emergency repairs system with patrol cars, and can arrange car hire. *ACR*'s headquarters in Bucharest are at Str Tache Ionescu 27, ☎ 01 6560 2595, and Str Cihoski 2, ☎ 01 611 0408.

East Germans had Trabants and Romanians have Dacias, remodelled Renault 12s with incredibly soft suspensions, just right for the bone-breaking roads. Romanians also drive a lot of Oltcits (refashioned Citroens). For as much as it might cost to hire a car, you can probably buy one of these secondhand when you get there; your country's embassy can give advice. Parts for Mercedes and other German marques should be available from specialist garages. If you are in any doubt, make enquiries beforehand from *ACR*.

Because of lack of good public transport, hitching is many people's only option, and they expect to pay for it. All the same, never pick up anyone when you are alone unless you are sure you will be safe.

By sea and river

Romania's Black Sea ports include Constanţa, where the seafaring Greeks founded Tomis, and Sulina and Sf Gheorghe in the Delta. You can get sea passages from Constanţa to Varna, Istanbul, Odessa and Sulina; from Sulina there are passenger ships to Odessa and Sevastopol. Danube ports include Tulcea, Galaţi, Brăila, Călăraşi, Drobeta Turnu-Severin, Moldova Veche, Olteniţa, Orşova, Bechet and Calafat. Cabin cruisers can navigate up to Olteniţa, Giurgiu and Drobeta-Turnu Severin.

You can also navigate by river all the way from Rotterdam to Constanţa via the Romanian Danube–Black Sea canal. The national shipping company, which organises trips along the Danube between April to October, is *Compania NAVROM S.A.* Their contact address is Str Portului 1, Giurgiu, ☎ 046 214303; fax 311 3529. Books about navigating Romania's rivers include *Backdoor to Byzantium* by Bill and Laurel Cooper (A&C Black, London, 1997), an account of a narrowboat trip down the Danube; Claudio Magris's *Danube* (1986) is also excellent, if biased towards Romania's German minority. A recommended video is Nick Saunders's *The Black Sea Odyssey* (1995), the tale of two Englishmen who cruised a 60ft narrowboat and butty from the north of England to the Black Sea via the Danube (the butty sank near Bratislava).

By bicycle

Dervla Murphy 'did' Romania by bicycle in 1990–91, and described her exciting and unnerving experiences in *Transylvania and Beyond* (1992). She was preceded during the communist period by some intrepid Anglo-Saxons, including novelist Georgina Harding. As a minimum take spare inner tubes, repair kits and a few spokes; there are hardly any bike repair shops in the country but Romanians are amazingly ingenious, and mechanics in towns and villages should be able to mend simple faults.

Motorcycles are rare apart from mopeds, so spares may be difficult to get hold of. Bikers are restricted to 40kph (24mph) in built-up areas and 50kph (31mph) in other places. Helmets are compulsory, and as with bicycles, you must bring vital spares with you.

 # Additional information

Customs

Customs regulations state that you must declare high-value goods such as jewellery over the value of US $100, and the government forbids the importation of ammunition, explosives, narcotics and pornographic material. Foreigners can bring in up to US $50,000, although legally you have to declare amounts over US $1000 on arrival.

The state restricts the export of articles which it considers to be patrimony: this can include artworks, carpets, antiques or objects of historic value, so check on the status of anything of this kind before you buy it, and keep the receipt. Officially, you may not take more than 5000 lei out of the country.

Money

The currency in Romania is the leu (literally, 'lion'; the plural is lei), made up of 100 bani, but you will not need to worry about bani unless someone tries to slip you some instead of lei. Lei coins come in denominations of 1, 5, 10, 20, 50, 100 and 200. Banknotes include the pretty 500-lei note, which is decorated with engravings of Brâncuși's most famous sculptures, and the 1000- and 10,000-lei notes. In 1996, the government introduced a 50,000 note so as to reduce the huge wads that people had to cart around for even modest transactions. In 1989 there were 30 lei to the UK pound; by mid-2000 the exchange rate had risen to over 30,000 lei.

One traveller's essential is clean (preferably virgin) hard-currency notes. American dollars and German marks are the preferred currencies, but the British pound is fine as long as it is strong. Travellers' cheques are safer than carrying large amounts of money, but Romanian exchange houses often charge exorbitant commissions when you cash them in; banks often restrict deals in travellers' cheques to a few hours in the morning. Many of the large banks now accept credit cards, such as **Visa**, **Eurocheque**, **Mastercard**, **Diners Club** and **American Express**; some have cash machines for cardholders. Common sense dictates that you should never leave valuables or large amounts of money in your hotel room or visible in your car.

Apart from the banks, there are many licensed exchange offices in Bucharest and in other big cities; it is worth shopping around for the best rate. Black-market deals are illegal, and the police sometimes make spot checks on foreigners they suspect may have taken advantage of such offers on the street. However, beware of conmen masquerading as plainclothes police; they may pretend to fine you but are in fact trying to steal your cash. In the late 1990s the legitimate police in Bucharest reported hundreds of cases of tourists, mainly affluent-looking males, being taken for a ride in this way.

Disabled travellers

Travelling around Romania can be tricky for able-bodied people, and negotiating the uneven street surfaces in a wheelchair is work for the devil. As far as most Romanian organisations are concerned, disabled travellers either do not exist or come as a vague afterthought, although some hotels in the Black Sea coast have ramps that allow wheelchairs to get to the beach. The National Tourist Board suggests that disabled people book their holiday through a package tour operator and ask for special conditions. You could also try the **National Society for Physically Handicapped Persons** in the Primăria at B-dul Banu Manta, RO-78171 București, ☎ 01 659 3000; the **Handicapped Persons' Sports Club**, Str Vasile Conta 16, RO-70139 București, ☎ 01 211 5550/ 5095, and the **Blind Persons' Association of Romania**, Str Vatra Luminoasă 108, RO-73305 București, ☎ 01 250 6525.

Health

Romanian chemists' shops are called *farmacie* (singular); there is supposed to be one 24-hour chemist open in each town; if not, they should display an emergency number. Chemists advertising 24-hour services in Bucharest include *Farmacia Magheru*, B-dul Magheru 18, ☎ 01 659 6115, *Farmacia 20*, Calea Șerban Vodă 43, ☎ 01 336 7647 and *Farmacia 26*, Șos Colentina 1, ☎ 01 635 5010. There are non-stop pharmacies at Otopeni airport and Gara de Nord as well.

You can buy packs of sanitary towels and tampons at chemists' and shops selling household goods; they are also available from large department stores and sometimes at street kiosks and market stalls. They are still considered a taboo subject, so do not ask for them in a loud voice. Take your own condoms.

The British and American embassies in Bucharest can give you the address of an English-speaking doctor or dentist, and there are clinics in the capital that specialise in treating foreigners. Casualty and first aid stations in most localities (*stația de salvare* or *prin ajutor*) usually have ambulances. Each county capital has its own hospital, called **Spitalul Județean**, but hospitals and *policlinici* in smaller towns can be dire if you are used to Western standards of care. However, foreigners often get preferential treatment, especially if they offer to pay for it— emergency treatment is free, excluding drugs. Romanians have to pay for all but the most basic health care. ☎ 961 for an ambulance; for emergencies concerning pregnant women and children, ☎ 969 (this ambulance service is not free). The *Medisana București Medical Centre* at Str Dr Nanu Muscel 12, near the Eroilor metro station, ☎ 01 410 8643/8543/8403/8459; fax 8076, has English-speaking staff and a reputation for efficiency. Payment is in lei.

If you can afford it, take out travel insurance that allows you to be flown home in case of accident or serious illness. Drinking water taken from taps is said to be safe from the risk of hepatitis, but if you are in any doubt, buy bottled mineral water. Take precautions against diarrhoea and sunburn, too. Official figures show that Romania has 45 per cent of Europe's children and young people infected by HIV/AIDS (called SIDA in Romania). Because of this, hospitals have stopped re-using syringe needles as a matter of course, but if you use needles it would be a sensible precaution to take your own.

Romania has no poisonous insects, but in the Danube Delta and Valea Cernei in the southern Carpathians there are species of viper whose bites can be deadly. If you are travelling in these areas, get advice from your travel agent or embassy and take the appropriate serum with you. There is also a risk of certain unpleasant virus infections that can be caught from ticks. While the risk of malaria is minimal in Romania, the mosquitoes are vicious, especially in the Delta, but they are active all over low-lying regions from late spring until the first frosts of autumn.

Rabies exists in Romania and stray dogs roam most major cities, especially Bucharest, where thousands were abandoned after the 1977 earthquake. In 1997 a mass sterilisation programme for stray dogs was carried out to try and stem their proliferation.

Embassies and consulates

Romanian embassies and consulates can be found in the following countries:

Australia: 4 Dalman Crescent, O'Malley, ACT 2606, Canberra, ☎ 06 286 2343; fax 286 2433
Canada: 655 Rideau Street, Ottawa, Ontario K1N 6A3, ☎ 613 789 5345/ 3709; fax 789 4365
France: 5 rue de l'Exposition, 75007 Paris CEDEX 07, ☎ 1 40 62 22 02/62 22 04; fax 45 56 97 47
Germany: Botschaft von Rumanien, Legionsweg 14, 53117 Bonn 1, ☎ 228 555 8628; fax 680 247; Berlliner Aussenstelle der Botschaft von Rumanien, Matterhornstrasse 79, 14129 Berlin, ☎ 30 803 3018/ 3019; fax 803 1684
Ireland: 60 Merrion Road, Ballsbridge, Dublin 5, ☎ 31 668 1336/ 1147; fax 668 1582
Moldova: Ambasada României, Str București 66/1, Chișinău, ☎ 2 237 583/233 529; fax 233 469
Netherlands: 55 rue Catsheuvel, 2517 Ka, The Hague, ☎ 70 354 3796/ 355 7369; fax 354 1587
South Africa: 117 Charles Street, Brooklyn 0011, Pretoria, ☎ 12 469310/466941/462743; fax 012 466947
United Kingdom: Arundel House, 4 Palace Green, London W8 4QD, ☎ 0207 937 9666; fax 937 8069
USA: 1607 23rd Street, NW, Washington DC 20008, ☎ 202 232 3694/332 4852; fax 232 4748

The following embassies and consulates are all in Bucharest; if you ring from abroad dial 0040 1 and then the individual number; within Romania but outside Bucharest, insert 01 first.

Australia: Str Nicolae Racotă, 16–18, ☎ 666 6923; fax 212 1424
Canada: Str Nicolae Iorga 36, ☎ 222 9845; fax 312 0366
France: Str Biserica Amzei 13–15, ☎ 312 0217; fax 312 0200
Germany: Str Rabat 21, ☎ 212 2580; fax 312 9846
Netherlands: Str Atena 18, ☎ 212 2242; fax 312 7620
United Kingdom: Str Jules Michelet 24, ☎ 312 0303; fax 312 0229
USA: Str Tudor Arghezi 7–9, ☎ 210 4042; fax 210 0395

Consulates outside Bucharest:
Germany: Str Lucian Blaga, Sibiu, ☎ 069 211 133; fax 214 180
United Kingdom: B-dul Tomis 143 A, Constanța, ☎ 041 638 284; fax 638 285
USA Information Service: Str Universității 7–9, Cluj-Napoca, ☎ 064 193 815

Crime and personal security

☎ 955 in emergencies. Every county has its own police service. Always ask to see ID if you are accosted by someone claiming to be a police agent in plain clothes, and check it carefully before agreeing to do anything.

There is a lot of talk about car crime in Romania, fuelled by stories of Gypsies who steal expensive foreign cars and sell them abroad. These may be alarmist, but if you leave your car out overnight in a large town or city, it is wise to remove the windscreen wipers (although this trick is on the decline, because selling them is far less profitable than it used to be) and take all valuables with you.

Generally speaking, the risks to travellers are exactly the same as they are in richer countries, and the rule is to use common sense: be careful about giving lifts to hitchhikers (although hitching rides is standard practice), do not flaunt money or jewellery, use a money belt, and if anyone asks to see your passport or wallet (for currency checks), ask to see their ID and credentials before doing so. Never change money on the street unless you are with Romanians who know the law and the score.

Opening hours

Banks open during weekdays 08.00–12.00. In towns shops are open 10.00–18.00; the hours in the country are 08.00–16.00. Most shops and offices close on Sunday and museums on Monday. Bakeries often open at 06.00 and close in the afternoon or late at night. Some shops close for lunch during the week. Open-air markets are open on Sunday mornings and close around midday.

Public holidays and annual festivals

National Romania Day is on 1 December; other public holidays include Christmas Day and 26 December, Good Friday and Easter Sunday and Monday, and 1 May. A cornucopia of folk art, music and dance festivals occur throughout the year: for an up-to-date list of what's on, contact the Village Museum in Bucharest, or Centrul de Creație Populare, which has branches in every county town. Details of other festivals can be found through tourist agencies, the Ministry of Culture (see p 31) or the annual guide *Ghidul Turistic al României*.

Telephone and postal services

The communications company Siemens has contracted to lay a line of optical fibres across Romania, but until this is completed using the national phone network can be a frustrating business.

Rural villages sometimes have old-fashioned exchanges where an operator plugs the lines into a board; some villages only have one phone among the total population. Calls made through the operator are charged a fixed rate for three minutes (minimum); if you are dialling from a private house, you may have to go through the operator to get an international line.

In large towns and cities, orange card phones allow you to make calls wherever you want, while the blue phones accept 50- and 100-lei coins as well as cards. In Bucharest, there are still some old blue call boxes with dials that only take 20-lei pieces. You can receive calls of up to three minutes on public phones. Bucharest's main 'Telephone Palace' is on the corner of Str Matei Millo and Calea Victoriei.

Most large post offices (sometimes signposted PTTR) and some hotels sell magnetic phone cards (*cartela telefonică*) for 20,000 or 40,000 lei (hotels may charge a commission). Sales staff should check a card for you before you walk away, but if the card does not work at first, try rubbing the magnetic contacts.

If you need an English-speaking operator abroad, ☎ 01 800 4444 (***British Telecom***), 01 800 4288 (***AT&T USA Direct***), 01 800 1800 (***MCI Worldwide***) or 01 800 0877 (***Sprint***). Call Romanian directory enquiries on ☎ 930. Other Romanian phone services include train enquiries (952), taxis (953) and road and traffic information (954).

The Romanian for 'stamp' is timbru (plural *timbre*). Delivery times for cards and letters to Western Europe are four and six days; ordinary post to North America takes about 7–20 days. Poste Restante services are available from the post office (*poştă*); post is kept for one month. Collection times are Mon–Fri 07.30–20.00 and Sat 07.30–14.00. If you have to collect a package that has arrived from abroad, expect some irritating formalities: staff have instructions to open parcels when you collect them to check what is inside. Some large post offices operate a fax service; these are usually efficient and cheap. In Bucharest the main post office (open 07.30–19.30) can be found at Str Matei Millo 10, near the Telephone Palace. **DHL** and other express delivery services have branches in some large Romanian cities.

Newspapers and magazines

Romania's equivalent to a newspaper of record is *Adevărul* ('The Truth') which supports the opposition PDSR party (ex-communist), while *România Liberă* ('Free Romania') stands behind the democratic coalition. *Evenimentul Zilei* ('The Day's Event') is a popular daily; its editor, Ion Crişoiu, moved to Ion Raţiu's *Cotideanul* in 1998. Most Romanian newspapers can be found on-line. A number of newspapers have their own websites, including *Curentul*: http:/www.curentul.logic-net.ro or redactia@curentul.kappa.ro for e-mail.

Romanians are fascinated by current affairs, and by far the most popular reviews are those which carry political comment; literary and historical magazines come second. Look out for *22*, *România Literară* and *Orizont*. Romania's version of *Private Eye* is *Academia Caţavencu*, a satirical weekly founded by Mircea Dinescu. Hungarian-language newspapers include *Romániei Magyar Szó* and *A Hét: Deutsche Zeitung* is also available, and other ethnic minorities, such as Jews and Armenians, have their own publications. English-language newspapers and magazines published in Romania include *Nine O'Clock*, the *Romanian Economic Observer* and the *Romanian Business Journal*. Outside Bucharest, Timişoara is a thriving centre for literary and political publications.

Multimedia

A number of publishers have produced videos and CD-Roms on Romania's popular tourist areas, including the famous painted monasteries. A selection of these is on sale at the **Muzica** store on Calea Victoriei, Bucharest, and other well-stocked bookstores; some museums and art galleries sell them as well.

Time

Romania local time is 3 hours ahead of GMT in summer (from the last Saturday of March to the last Saturday of September) and 2 hours ahead the rest of the year. To find the correct time ☎ 958.

Tipping

Unless specifically prohibited, tipping waiters and waitresses is an accepted practice in restaurants.

Public toilets

Take your own toilet paper with you. Public toilets (*toalete* or *WC*) are improving greatly and you don't always have to take your life in your hands. The Ladies staffed by Romany in the little town of Sebiş, do exist. When ethnographer Irina Nicolău asked a peasant farmer if she could use his WC, he looked at her in amazement and replied, 'Why do you need a toilet when you have the entire countryside at your disposal?' (or words to that effect).

Male and female cubicles are indicated by pictograms or by '*Doamne*' (women) and '*Domni*' (men)—the coy '*Fetiţe*' (little girls) and '*Fii*' (little boys) are sometimes used. In emergencies, you may be able to use toilets in restaurants and cafés if you are not a customer there.

Electric current

At time of writing Romania uses 220V, 50Hz AC, and although this can vary according to local suppliers it is reliable enough for most small appliances, such as hairdryers, shavers and small laptop computers. You will need a European plug or an adaptor with two round pins.

Local customs and etiquette

Although Romanians are invariably warm, open and tolerant of foreigners and their eccentricities, they are not as extrovert as, for example, the Italians, and in general they value modesty. Though not stiff or prudish, educated and older people behave with old-fashioned courtesy and even surprising formality, and expect children to be courteous to their elders and to mind what they say.

When a Romanian man greets or says goodbye to a woman, he will often kiss her hand but will keep his eyes down unless he is sexually interested in her. Many people greet each other by a kiss on one cheek, then the other, regardless of whether they are men or women. However, overt fondling and displays of affection can be frowned upon, particularly outside urban areas.

When invited to a private home, take flowers for your hostess, and offer to take off your shoes upon entering; you may be offered outsize slippers to wear instead. (See p 32 for the etiquette of eating and drinking.)

Many people smoke like chimneys in Romania, but it is not considered good manners to light up when other people are eating; however, this rule is often broken in restaurants.

Charities

After the first flush of compassion that was stirred up by heartrending scenes in Romanian orphanages, many charities have pulled out of the country while others have only recently arrived. For an up-to-date list of charities based in Britain, write with a SAE to the **Romania Information Centre**, The University, Southampton SO9 5NH, ☎ 01703 551328; fax 593939. RIC also publishes a newsletter which is extremely useful.

Link Romania, established in 1990, raises money to rehouse street children in Iaşi and other major cities. **Link** hires out space in its trucks that is not occupied by humanitarian aid. Its sister organisation, **Over the Wall**, arranges sponsored events and tours of Romania. For further information, see their advertisement at the back of this book.

Sporting and leisure activities

With its vast mountains and wide plains, Romania offers almost unlimited scope for sporting or activity holidays. There is skiing and potholing in the Carpathians, horse-riding across the Transylvanian plateau, diving for Greek ruins and even flying, not to mention the opportunities for travelling by steam train. Non-governmental organisations such as **Romsilva** control many of the country's excellent nature reserves as well as hunting, fishing and shooting rights. To find out more, contact a travel agent or the Ministry of Tourism in Bucharest (see p 31).

The **Napoca Cyclotourist Club** is an independent, non-governmental organisation that offers information on cycle tours, mountain-biking, 'environment hiking', mountaineering, climbing, skiing, caving and paragliding. Contact them at Str Septimu Albini 133, Ap 18, 3400 Cluj-Napoca, ☎/fax 064 142953; e-mail cicloturism@mail.cjnet.ro. For information about caving and speleology, contact the **Institut de Speologie** at Str Clinicilor, PO Box 58, 3400 Cluj-Napoca, ☎/fax 064 195954, or its sister organisation which goes by the same name, at Str Frumoasa 11, 78114 București 12, ☎/fax 01 211 3874; e-mail sconstantin@pcnet.pcnet.ro.

Hiking/sporting tour operators based in Britain include the **British Trust for Conservation Volunteers**, the **Cyclists Touring Club**, **Exodus**, **Footprint Adventures** (who specialise in birdwatching) and **Naturetrek**. As already mentioned, **Link Romania**'s subsidiary **Over the Wall** organises individual tailor-made tours by train, Land-Rover or on foot to beautiful mountain regions as well as sponsored treks in Romania. Write to Link House, 59/61 Lyndhurst Road, Worthing, West Sussex BN11 2DB, ☎ 01903 529555; fax 529007; e-mail fundraising@linkrom.org. (See also general information on tour operators on pp 13–15.)

For steam-train enthusiasts, **Ronedo Tours** runs several trips a year, mainly on Transylvania's narrow-gauge track on the three remaining forestry railways. They are at B-dul Decebal 59, Ap 1, Piatra Neamț, ☎ 033 231870; ☎/fax 231306; e-mail ronedo@decebal.ro.

The state-owned **SNCFR** urges you to escape from the world by taking their trips in steam trains: **CFR** is based at B-dul Dinicu Golescu 38, Sector 1, București, ☎ 01 637 4481; fax 223 0671, e-mail vbota@central.cfr.ro. It recommends two trips in particular: Câmpulung Moldovenesc–Vama–Moldovița. This 36km tour takes 90 minutes, departing from Câmpulung Moldovenesc railway station and finishing at Moldovița narrow-gauge station. The engine is one of the 50 series and the first-, second- and third-class carriages are over 100 years old. The Brașov–Întorsura Buzăului tour, also 36km, again lasts 90 minutes. Embark at Brașov, and arrive at Întorsura Buzăului. The steam engine is a 150-series steam locomotive; the train comprises first- and second-class carriages. There may be a restaurant car on this service. SNCFR can organise custom-made tours including return rail or air travel from England. There is a direct rail service between Paris and Bucharest.

Travel agents specialising in these tours include: **Atlantic Tur**, Calea Victoriei, Bucharest (see p 116); **Romsteam Aldo**, B-dul Burebista 7, Bl L4, Ap 1, Piatra Neamț, ☎ 033 236119, fax 033 231431, e-mail romsteam@decebal.ro; and **S. C. Mondo Tur**, Str 1 Decembrie 11, Deva, ☎/fax 054 212162.

Crafts

Romania's predominantly rural economy has engendered a tradition of fine craftsmanship. Typical handmade products range from sheepskin waistcoats, embroidered blouses and flat-weave carpets, to gorgeously decorated Easter eggs, metalwork, musical instruments, pottery, carved wooden spoons and cheese moulds and much else. Far-sighted ethnographers saw the value of preserving this heritage back in the 1920s when the first folk arts and crafts museums were established, but the industry now faces a stark choice: adapt to a market economy or perish.

This situation may be of little interest to the visitor, but even if you are only looking for an inexpensive souvenir it does make a difference where you buy it. Most handmade craft items are sold in dedicated crafts shops, but their quality may vary enormously. If you do not want to be disappointed and you have time to research what you want, there are organisations that are designed to help you. They also aim to promote and develop Romania's traditional crafts so that they can make a real contribution to the country's economy while helping to foster a sense of national identity.

The joint Anglo-Romanian team of Caroline Mortlock and Cristina Rai established *Fundaţia Meşteşuguri Români (Crafts Foundation Romania)* in 1997, to promote collaborative projects between traditional craftspeople and avant-garde artists. It can be contacted at OP 1 CP 204, Bucureşti, Romania, ☎ 01 771 4280; fax 221 5317; e-mail craftsro@fx.ro.

In many areas traditional cottage industries are supported by *Centrul de Creaţie Populară*. You can contact this organisation's headquarters in Piaţa Lahovari, Bucharest, ☎ 01 659 5185, but there is a branch in every county. Its staff should be able to help you find the best craftsmen in that area so that you can visit their workshops. The centres can also give information on local or regional crafts and music festivals.

In 1992, the Astra Museum in Sibiu organised a national academy of 'master craftsmen' (Academia Meşteşugărilor) and will give you the names and addresses of people who produce what you are looking for. Twice a year the museum holds a large crafts fair in Sibiu, and Muzeul Satului in Bucharest organises similar events throughout the year. County and local ethnographic museums can also be extremely helpful, and you can buy pottery and kitchen utensils in Romanian markets and often by the roadside as well.

Cultural organisations

The following are all in Bucharest unless otherwise indicated.

American Cultural Centre: Str J. L. Calderon 7–9, ☎ 01 210 1602
British Council: Calea Dorobanţilor 14, ☎ 01 210 0314
French Institute: B-dul Dacia 77, ☎ 01 210 0224, and B-dul Copou 26, Iaşi, ☎ 032 147 900
Goethe Institute: Str Henri Coandă 22 ☎ 01 210 4047, and Casa de Cultură F. Schiller, Str Batiştei 15, ☎ 01 211 3229
Spanish Institute (Institutul Cervantes): Str Paris 34, ☎ 01 212 1354
Ministry of Tourism: Str Apolodor 17, ☎ 01 410 7174; fax 312 2345
Ministry of Culture: Piaţa Presei Libere 1, ☎ 01 223 1530; fax 223 4951; for details of festivals etc., ☎ 01 222 8320

Romanian Cultural Foundation (Fundația Culturală Română): Aleea Alexandru 38, ☎ 01 633 3121/6018

Women travellers

Travelling alone is no more dangerous for a woman than in many Western European countries (and sometimes it feels much less so). The same advice applies to women as it does to men. If you are being harassed by strangers, the phrase 'Lasați-mă în pace!' usually works; if not, shout 'Poliția!' When visiting some churches you may be asked to cover bare arms and legs.

Food and drink

One of the first Romanian cookery books was published in the 13C, and a copy was lodged in the little hill church of Ieud in Maramureș. By the 19C Romania's cuisine had become cosmopolitan, reflecting both the tastes of the various dominant powers that had had a stake in the country and the growing influence of France. A mixture of Islamic, Greek and Slavonic dishes served to make Romanian cooking lighter than in Slav countries: dumplings are a rarity, but *sarmale*, stuffed cabbage leaves, are part of the staple diet.

As Romania carved out an identity of its own, cooking played an important role. During the 19C it was regarded as a subject for serious discussion, so much so that in 1841 the future revolutionaries and statesmen, Mihail Kogălniceanu and Constantin Negruzzi, collaborated on a recipe book containing some 200 dishes. At the same time, Bucharest tried to emulate Paris, that inspiration for iconoclasts and epicureans alike, and during the early 20C Romania's capital earned an enviable reputation for its cafés and restaurants.

Shortages of everything but the most basic foodstuffs during Ceaușescu's regime left the population all but starving: Romanians used to joke that they had been better off in the Second World War! Romanian restaurants can be disappointing places. But wherever you go you will be invited to share a meal with Romanians in their own houses, and home-made dishes are a world apart.

Phanariot Greeks introduced the habit of eating appetisers, called *meze*. These are still popular and can comprise a bean salad, baked aubergines, a salad of raw carrots and tomatoes, and a variety of cheeses or sausages and ham.

Romania's great unofficial national dish, which the visitor either loves or hates, is *mămăligă*. This is a boiled cornmeal porridge which can be enlivened with cheese, meat or, more excitingly, squid. It is usually served with *smântână* (sour cream), which gives it a much-needed bite, and, if you are lucky, a fresh salad.

Meat is unavoidable in Romania: *mititei*—skinless sausages made entirely with pork meat—are common in old-fashioned bistros, where they come with a dollop of mustard and wedges of white bread. Another traditional staple is *ghiveci*, meat stewed with vegetables or quinces. *Ciorba de burtă* (belly pork soup) will probably not appeal to fastidious Westerners, but other soups made from meat stock can be extremely good. They are often garnished with a hot chilli pepper, to be chewed separately if you dare!

Romania's oriental heritage shows up in the love of grilled beef (*carne de vacă*) and lamb (*miel*) available on most restaurant menus. Chicken (*pui*) and duck (*raţă*) are less common in restaurants, but Transylvanians like chicken cooked with tarragon or dill and sautéd in wine and peppers. Potatoes and pasta are widely used as stomach-fillers. In restaurants, meat portions are sometimes sold by their weight, so be careful that you get what you want.

Vegetarians will have to look hard to find anywhere that caters for them imaginatively, and the position is even bleaker for vegans, but if you ask for the *meniu de post* (fasting menu without meat) you can often find some delicious choices. But in season, markets always have a good supply of green and root vegetables (*legume*, *verdeşuri*), fruit (*fructe*), nuts (*nuci*) and honey (*miere*). 'Lacto-vegetarian' restaurants, where you could buy omelettes and other simple fare, are becoming a thing of the past.

In villages and small towns, bread (*pâine*, pronounced 'pweeneh') is often baked fresh twice a day; made without preservatives, it quickly goes hard, and most varieties are unleavened. Wholemeal bread is becoming more popular, but is still hard to come by except in big towns; loaves are called *graham* after an American agronomist who introduced the mixture to eastern Europe. Sweeter breads are also available and bakeries (*brutării*) often sell *cozonaci*, traditional Easter cakes that have plums in them; they can also be marbled with chocolate.

When I went shopping for milk (*lapte*) in a village near Sibiu I was told roundly, 'We don't have milk because we don't keep cows.' This was true during the communist regime, but since parcels of land have been given back to their previous owners most smallholdings have a cow, and if you stay with a farming family you will be offered delicious, warm, fresh unpasteurised milk ladled out of a bucket. Many of the older-style *alimentări* (food shops) still consider milk a luxury item, but you can generally always get some in large town supermarkets and delicatessens. The fashion is dying out, but for many years you could always buy drinking yoghurt, which made a refreshing alternative; it came in small, irregular bottles of thick, chunky glass. *Brânza* is the usual name for curd cheese, while *caşcaval* is the stiffer, yellower variety, closer to cheddar.

Ritual foods play an important part in religious celebrations: after a funeral, mourners eat *colivă*. This is a pudding made of wheat or barley soaked for 12 hours in water and mixed with walnuts, vanilla essence and the alcohol of your choice; it is then cooked in a casserole and eaten cold with yoghurt or sour cream.

Sweet dishes from France include *clătite*, pancakes filled with cottage cheese or jam, or omelettes served with a fruit sauce. *Dulceaţă*, a sweet preserve of fruits, nuts and rose petals, is the delicious Romanian form of sherbet. It is normally offered to guests as a special treat and is eaten reverently from a spoon with a glass of cold water and a Turkish coffee. A favourite snack is *plăcintă*, a sweet or savoury flaky pastry turnover, but fast-food restaurants are supplanting traditional foods and in Bucharest it is considered chic (and expensive) to go to **McDonalds**.

Individual regions also have distinctive foods: the Danube Delta is famous for its varieties of fish, such as sturgeon, sterlet, mackerel, sardine and the ubiquitous catfish. Transylvanian cuisine reflects the tastes of Austro-Hungary and of the German community that settled there for 800 years; it is characterised by the use of sour cream and paprika, though not in the quantities found in Hungarian food. One of southern Moldavia's culinary delights is a maroon-skinned onion shaped like a ninepin, which is equally delicious cooked and raw in salads.

One of the most entertaining introductions in English to Romanian cooking is Lesley Chamberlayne's *The Food and Cooking of Eastern Europe* (Penguin, London, 1989).

Drink

As an aperitif or pick-me-up, and to welcome their guests, Romanians drink twice-distilled *ţuică* or thrice-distilled—and much stronger—*palincă* or *horincă*, all of which are made from plums. The best kinds are very smooth and give a tremendous kick if you are not used to them; downing them in one gulp, if you can bear it, is probably better than taking genteel sips. Sensible to the last, Romanians would never dream of travelling without taking their own food and drink with them: for one thing, it is expensive to buy snacks en route, and the choice is not inspiring. A train journey is considered a convivial event and Romanians always share their provisions with strangers; I once travelled with a man who had a four-litre can full of *ţuică* for contingencies just such as these. Wine, one of Romania's greatest potential exports, is covered on pp 35–36.

In Transylvania you may come across springs of mineral water (*apă minerală*). In Timişoara you can fill your own bottles from the piped spring in Piaţa Unirii. The waters of Borsec and other eastern Transylvanian springs have been exploited for commercial use and are available in bottled form. Romanian villagers also swear by their home-made fruit and herb teas, which are said to aid digestion.

Etiquette

If you refuse what a host offers you to eat or drink, this will often be taken as modest dissimulation, the proper reluctance of a guest who really means to say 'yes' (like prospective princes, who had to hide from their supporters on the day of their coronation); eventually you are expected to take it. But if you cannot or do not want to drink alcohol, or have another reason for rejecting the proffered item, say so firmly, and ask for an alternative. If you do accept, leaving a drink unfinished in your glass is thought to bring bad luck to your hosts—and the more you leave, the worse it is. You will disarm any frosty host or hostess after eating their food if you say '*mulţumesc pentru masa!*'

Useful terms and phrases

'*Poftă bună!*' is the Romanian equivalent of '*Bon apetit!*'.

'*Roşii vostri nu sunt buni! Sunt stricaţi!*' is a useful phrase when presented with split or ageing tomatoes in the *piaţa* (marketplace). It means 'Your tomatoes are blemished' and shows that you are not prepared to be cheated—substitute with other items as appropriate. Fruit and vegetables are often blemished when you buy them this way, but spots do not necessarily mean they will taste bad. One of the ironies of the country's agriculture is that most small farmers cannot afford insecticides, herbicides and fertilisers, making them—ostensibly—ideal producers of healthy, organic food.

'*O jumătate de pere, vă rog*' means 'I'd like half a kilo of pears'. Romanians often truncate the word and say '*O jumate*' instead. '*Un sfert*' is a quarter.

I don't eat meat	*Nu consum carne*
I like it very much	*Îmi place foarte mult*
It tastes bad, I don't like it!	*Gusta rău, nu-mi place!*

fresh vegetables	*legume proaspete*
fruit	*fructe*
fish	*peşte*
grocery shop	*băcănie*
butcher's	*măcelarie*
pork	*porc*
ham	*şuncă*
sausage	*salam*
dairy	*lăptărie*
yellow cheese	*caşcaval*
curd cheese	*brânză*
soup	*supă*
salad	*salată*
ice cream	*îngheţată*
hot/cold	*cald/rece*
sugar	*zahar*
salt	*sare*
tea	*ceai*
wine	*vin*

Romanian wine

In one of his *Letters from the Black Sea* Ovid wrote, 'I am surrounded by barbarians... who can down buckets of wine at a sitting.' Drinking wine is still a way of life in Romania, and many people make their own.

> ### *The first Romanian wines*
> Coins and jewels depicting grapes have been found in Thracian graves dating from the 4C BC, suggesting that wine-making in Romania goes back at least this far. The earliest known document to mention wine in Romania dates from 1C BC, when a historian called Columella described three vines which we know today as Cabernet Sauvignon, the white Feteasca Albă and Gamay Beaujolais. Feteasca Albă is said to be the first true Romanian grape, but opinions differ as to whether it came here from the northwest through Transylvania or with the Romans when they started colonising Dacia in the 2C AD.

Commercial vineyards have existed in Romania since the 17C, and even though practically all the vineyards were wiped out during the 1880s phylloxera epidemic many of Romania's great labels, such as Cotnari, Dealu Mare, Nicoreşti, Niculiţel and Odobeşti, come from these ancient estates. Since the 1989 revolution about 80 per cent of the country's plantations have passed into private hands, and just under half of these are in now in some form of industrial cooperative.

Romania's climatic conditions favour many different types of wine, from dry, sparkling whites to rich, purplish-reds heavy with the aroma of liquorice. Traditional fermentation-methods do without chemicals of any kind, and this often means that you can drink them without suffering a hangover. The main problem with exporting Romanian wine to date has been the lack of standard-sized bottles.

Following the trail of Romania's vineyards can take you across some fascinating regions, from the ancient terracing of Seini (27km northwest of Baia Mare) through Transylvania and Wallachia as far as the Dobrogean coast. In Moldavia, the easternmost vineyards are Cotnari and Huși, which lie close to the River Prut.

If you want the latest information on Romanian wine or to hire specialist guides, consult the Catedra de Viticultură și Vinificație at the Universitatea de științe Agronomice, B-dul Mărăşti 59, 71331 București, ☎ 01 222 3700. *The Wines of Romania* by M. Macici provides an excellent introduction (an English edition was published in Bucharest in 1996).

Romanian wine is becoming more widely available in the UK, where large chain stores such as *Sainsbury's*, *Tesco* and *Waitrose* have woken up to its quality. Two firms that specialise in Romanian wines are Halewood International Ltd, The Sovereign Distillery, Huyton Industrial Estate, Liverpool L36 6AD, t 0151 480 8800; fax 489 0690, and The Sovereign Winery, Roberttown Lane, Liversedge, West Yorkshire WF15 7LL, ☎ 01924 410110; fax 410041.

BACKGROUND INFORMATION

Romania: an historical introduction

Romania's history is colourful but complicated. The country as we know it came into being in 1918 after a long struggle for unity between a group of small, neighbouring principalities which shared the same language, background and religion. Romania's rulers have had to pit themselves against powerful aggressors from all points of the compass, and internecine jealousies, intrigue and double-edged diplomacy have all played their part in its evolution as a nation state.

Prehistory

During a visit to the USA in 1993, President Ion Iliescu told an audience, 'As you all know, Romanians are the descendants of ducks who came from the trucks.' What he meant was that the Dacs came from the Tracs which is only slightly less funny. But Iliescu was right: Romania lies within the Carpathian-Balkan region of southeast Europe which was once populated by Thracians, an Indo-European people who migrated there from Asia in the third millennium BC and mixed with the indigenous population. About 2000 years before Christ, a distinctive Thracian subgroup emerged in what is now Romania. The Greeks called these people Getae, but to the Romans they were Dacians. Herodotus called them 'the fairest and most courageous of men' because they believed in the immortality of the soul and were not afraid to die. Peaceful, frugal and ascetic, the Dacians worshipped a deity called Zamolxis who may have been a real person.

But who were the first peoples in the land we know as Romania? In 1978 a potholer who was exploring the limestone caves at Cuciulat in the Someş Valley discovered the lively sketched outlines of a horse. Research has shown that it was probably painted in the Upper Pleistocene epoch, in other words more than 10,000 years ago. Together with other sites at Ileanda-Perii Vadului and Buşag, near Baia Mare, the cave represents the earliest known examples of human settlement in what is now Romania. Collective habitations from the Neolithic Age have been found at Hăbăşeşti, near Iaşi, and at Truşeşti, both from c 2000 BC, and at Pietocle and Blejeşti in the Danubian plains near Bucharest, vestiges of spacious Stone Age dwellings have emerged from mounds of ash. Inside many objects had survived intact, including vases, silex tools, figurines and items of clothing. From c 1200–1100 BC up to the 4C BC, the Caucasian Koban culture had an impact on Romania as well.

Many cultures flourished in the transitional period between the Stone and Copper Ages. Outstanding among these civilisations were the Cucuteni people, named after a large fortified settlement and burial site at Cucuteni in Moldavia. Excavations at this site brought to light a singularly attractive style of pottery which is decorated with striking abstract patterns. The Cucuteni knew how to grow crops, and they also built sanctuaries and temples and endowed their dead with finely wrought gold; their precise religious beliefs are still a mystery, but they corresponded to the spiritual culture of southeast Europe as a whole.

At the start of the first millennium BC, groups of Cimmerians invaded the Dacians' territory several times, and tribes from the Hallstatt-Illyrian and Italic-Villanovan cultures came from the west. In the 7C BC Scythians of Iranian descent introduced excellent craftsmen into eastern Romania, and in the late 4C BC, Celts from the La Tène civilisation arrived, helping to orientate the Dacians further towards the west. The Dacians assimilated all these influences without being submerged, and in 514 BC, when King Darius of the Persians crossed Dobrogea on his way to quell the Scythians, Dacian armies were the only Thracian tribes strong enough to resist him. Alexander the Great invaded the Danubian plains as well, but after capturing a Dacian town in 335 BC, he left after 24 hours, never to return.

Western-style civilisation in Romania developed significantly when Miletan Greeks founded communities along the Dobrogean coast in the 7C BC. Present-day Constanţa and Mangalia both owe their existence to the Greeks, and the fascinating archaeological site at Histria near Lake Sinoe was once Istria, for a while the most important centre of the Greek-speaking world on Romanian territory. The Miletans introduced building skills which they passed on to their 'barbarian' neighbours: there is some evidence to suggest that latter-day Dacians adopted Grecian-style fortifications in their mountain fastnesses. Greek imports also included fine pottery and oils, which they exchanged for Dacian slaves, as well as cereals, honey and wax.

Dacian art

Craftsmen from this region created marvellous designs which drew upon eastern and western influences. Some of the artefacts taken from Dacian tombs in what is now Dobrogea show a knowledge of Grecian, Persian and Scythian motifs. An eight-legged stag whose antlers merge with birds' heads was stamped onto the silver beakers found at Agighiol (now in the Metropolitan Museum of Art, New York) and Rogozen (both mid-4C BC). Savage predators stalk the gilded, silver and bronze armour which accompanied Thraco-Getic warriors on their way to the afterlife at the Iron Gates, Peretu and Coţofeneşti, while their greaves show Medusas' heads. Some of the helmets have 'double eyes', a pair of false eyes impressed in the metal above the warrior's own eyes, presumably to frighten his adversaries with the threat of supernatural powers.

Another fascinating dimension to Romania's prehistory emerged with the discovery of the Gundestrup Cauldron in 1891. This lovely chased silver bowl, decorated with elephants, lions, dolphins, stags, snakes, griffins, hunters and deities, was found in Jutland and has been dated to the period c 150 BC–150 AD. Experts differ, but the consensus of opinion is that it was made by Thracian or Dacian craftsmen who were in touch with many different cultures. The figures around the bowl include soldiers in Celtic helmets and a representation of the Asiatic goddess Hariti with her hair surrounded by birds.

Dacian pottery also has a distinctive character and, like other forms of Dacian culture, such as clothing and building styles, its designs have been assimilated into present-day Romanian folk art.

Dacian rulers

The first known Dacian king was Dromichaetes, who fought the Macedonians and took the tyrant Lysimachus prisoner in 292 BC. One of his successors, Burebista (r. 82–44 BC), united the Dacian tribes under one 'empire' which reached from Moravia (now in the Czech Republic) to the Bug River in the north, to the Balkans and the Tisa Rivers in the south and west. Burebista must have been an impressive personality: Pompey considered him worth having as an ally, and in 44 BC Julius Caesar was about to mount a campaign against Burebista when he was murdered by Brutus.

The ruler of Dacia in its final years was Decebal (r. 87–106 AD). He extended Burebista's fastness at Costeşti in the southern Carpathian foothills into a complex of forts and sanctuaries called Sarmizegetusa. Among the separate precincts set aside for secular and religious activities were the markers for a calendrical system that was unique in the ancient world. Decebal was fascinated by the Roman settlements in Moesia (most of modern Serbia and parts of Bulgaria) south of the Danube, and led his men across the river on raids which caused a great deal of irritation in Rome. After unsuccessful attempts to keep the Dacians in check, the Emperor Domitian came to an agreement which allowed Decebal Roman expertise and money in return for a promise that he would stay at home.

The Roman period

The Emperor Trajan took a different attitude. An outstanding soldier and powerful leader, he regarded Domitian's treaty as a humiliation which had to be redressed. Trajan's expedition to the Carpathians was fuelled by the added incentive of gold and salt which the mountains reputedly held in unlimited supplies. Trajan's reign spelt the end of an independent Dacia. After quelling the Pannonian Plain (the future Hungary) and the Banat in AD 98, he set his sights on Decebal's kingdom. His campaign lasted for seven years, starting with the First Dacian War of 101–102 AD. At the same time, Decebal sent emissaries to the Parthian king of Petra, in the hope of building a defensive alliance in the east. But although he failed to penetrate Dacia's hill forts at first, the end was in sight when Trajan ordered a gigantic bridge to be thrown across the Danube, allowing cohorts to tramp into southern Oltenia with enough supplies to last for a concerted effort. After refusing to capitulate, Decebal lost his kingdom in the Second Dacian War of 105–106 AD. He stabbed himself to death in Sarmizegetusa rather than face defeat.

Relations between victor and vanquished did not remain hostile: Dacians in the Maramureş (which remained part of Free Dacia) sold salt to the garrison towns, and examples of Daco-Roman pottery show that they learnt from each other as well. Roman Dacia covered most of present-day Romania, while the Dobrogean coast belonged to another Roman province, Scythia Minor. Dacians continued to inhabit Romanian territory, and their Thracian kin survived in the Carpathians until the 10C.

During their 170 years of occupation, the Romans imported their own laws and building styles along with demotic Latin, which became the basis for the modern Romanian language. They also brought vines which provided the foundation stock for many of the country's excellent vintages. Trajan called in additional support from his garrisons in Syria and Lebanon, and these soldiers brought their favourite Oriental cults with them: bronze statuettes of Jupiter

Dolichenus and the Palmyran god, Sol Hierobulos, have been found in Transylvania, and archaeologists have discovered Mithraic symbols here too. In the 1980s, gold tokens and votive inscriptions dedicated to gods and goddesses of healing were salvaged from the Roman baths at Sângeorgiu Băi near Deva, which was the base of a Romano-British auxiliary unit. Roman ruins lie strewn all over Romania as though they had been left there casually the day before: some of the finest are to be found at Sarmizegetusa Ulpia Traiana, south of Deva; at Drobeta Turnu-Severin on the Danube; at Porolissum, north of Zalău, with its superb oval theatre, and in Cluj-Napoca. Roman gold mines have been partially excavated at Roșia Montana and other sites in the Apuseni.

Repeated attacks by Goths, Carpae and free Dacians from the north persuaded Aurelian to withdraw in 271–272. But while the army and civil servants marched back over the Danube into Moesia, veteran legionaries who had been given estates as a reward for long service stayed behind with other camp followers to tend their farms and vineyards. Funeral tablets show that Dacians and Romans intermarried and Daco-Romans became the nucleus of the proto-Romanians, romani, or Vlachs as they were known to the medieval Saxon world. Roman fortresses were maintained along the northern bank of the Danube even after the occupying forces had left. Along the Black Sea coast, Romano-Greek cities would be absorbed into Eastern Rome after Constantine's miraculous conversion to Christianity and the foundation of his holy city, Constantinople, on the ruins of Greek Byzantium.

The great migrations

Over the next millennium, Asiatic and Turkic tribes flooded into Romanian territory, usually to devastating effect. Indigenous romani were either absorbed by the interlopers or took refuge from them in the mountains. Along with Dacian, Greek and Roman blood, modern Romanians can trace their ancestry to Goths, Huns, Avars, Gepids, Slavs, Cumans, Magyars, Pechenegs and Tartars, until in the 14C their Romanian-speaking forebears were strong enough to establish independent principalities in Moldavia and Wallachia. However, archaeology has yet to trace the exact movements of the romani during this period.

Threatened by invading nomads, the Roman Empire went into a state of crisis, and its borders fluctuated with bewildering rapidity. Constantine annexed the southern Danubian plains which Aurelian had relinquished 50 years earlier, and in 395, Dobrogea was incorporated into the newly created Eastern Roman Empire under its leader, Flavius Arcadius. Shortly afterwards the Christian church organised its teachings into their 'correct' or 'Orthodox' form, and established five Apostolic Sees, in Constantinople, Rome, Antioch, Alexandria and Jerusalem. The earliest known records of churches in Romania date them from the 4C and 5C; most were in Dobrogea.

Avars destroyed the Greco-Roman coastal cities in the early 7C, at roughly the same time as they were repulsed from the gates of Constantinople by the legendary intervention of the Holy Virgin. Shortly afterwards, Turkic Bulgars established a khanate along Romania's littoral when they spread south into Bulgaria, allegedly giving Dobrogea its name. Two Romano-Bulgarian brothers, Ivan Asen (r. western part 1186–96) and Peter Asen (r. eastern part 1186–97), created the Second Bulgarian Tsarate as a breakaway Christian state in the 12C. Incorporating Dobrogea, the Asens' kingdom stood independent of the

Byzantine Empire and helped to spread Orthodoxy throughout the Slavonic and Greek-speaking peoples of southeast Europe.

Archaeologists have found signs of sedentary communities in Romania during the migration period, but physical evidence for the continuation of the Daco-Roman population is scarce. Administrative formations which adopted the Slavonic names of *cnezate* and *voivodate* covered much of Transylvania and some of the Danubian plains, while regions called *ţări* (lands) came under the control of individual 'dukes'. These were well established by the time of the Hungarian invasions, and the leaders, Gelu, Glad and Menumorut, whose domains occupied much of western Transylvania at the time, fought courageously but in vain to save their independence.

Hungarians in Transylvania

In c 800, Magyar nomads looking for fresh, fertile country to provide for their expanding population began riding east from the Hungarian plain into the Banat and Transylvania. With their superior fighting ability, Magyars would come to dominate the whole plateau; in the year 1000, King Stephen I (r. 997–1038) adopted Christianity and used this as an excuse to conquer the 'pagans' of Transylvania who refused to adopt Catholicism. His reign marked the beginning of a thousand years of Hungarian influence in Transylvania, which only officially came to an end with the Treaty of Trianon in 1920.

As the Hungarians pushed further east, Vlachs and Pechenegs took to the forests and mountains. Some of them eventually crossed over the Carpathians, taking their flocks with them. By the 10C Hungarian-speaking border guards from a Turkic tribe called the Székely (Szeklers) were living in central Transylvania but when King Geza II (r. 1141–62) issued his 'invitation' to northern European colonists during the mid-12C, the Székely moved east to make way for Flemings, Walloons and Saxons, who received both land and privileges in return for their military support. King Endre II (r. 1205–35) issued a further call to northern European 'guests', among them Teutonic Knights on their return from Palestine. Endre hoped that the Knights would extend his borders into the plains between the Carpathians and the Black Sea.

In 1241–42, 'devil's horsemen' under the command of the Mongol general, Batu Khan, swept across Transylvania, destroying everything in their path; contemporary estimates held that they left 99 in every 100 people dead. After this and a succession of Ottoman attacks, the Saxons strengthened their villages, creating extraordinary fortress churches, more like miniature citadels, to which the whole community could flee when the alarm was sounded. Many of these marvellous buildings are still there, especially around Sibiu, Sighişoara and Mediaş in the Saxon strongholds of southern Transylvania.

The greatest threat to medieval Hungary came from Ottoman Turkey. Two of Transylvania's legendary heroes, Iancu de Hunedoara (János Hunyadi in Hungarian) (r. 1446–56) and his son, Matei Corvin (Matyás Corvinus) (r. 1458–90), spent most of their adult lives thwarting the ambitions of successive sultans who thrust their way into Europe during the 14C and 15C. Iancu de Hunedoara beat Mehmet II in Bulgaria during the Long Campaign of 1443–44, and as royal governor he joined the Albanian ruler, George Scanderberg, in an effort to defeat the Turks at Kosovopolje in 1448. Eight years later he threw the Turks back from Belgrade. Matei Corvin, who was born in Cluj, was another accomplished military leader who teamed up with, but later imprisoned the Wallachian prince Vlad III (Dracula), during one of the many tortuous political reversals that characterise the relationship between medieval Hungary and its Romanian neighbours. Corvin was also famous for introducing Renaissance ideas into Hungary and Transylvania.

Medieval Hungarian laws treated peasants as second-class citizens and enslaved them along with the Roma: most peasants in Transylvania were ethnic Romanians or Gypsies. As followers of the hated Orthodox church, they were also regarded as 'schismatics', to be suppressed or, at best, barely tolerated. Ethnic Romanians who supported Hungarian military campaigns were encouraged to convert to Catholicism and adopt Magyar-sounding names, and many did so rather than suffer social and economic deprivation. But Hungarians and Romanians protested together against feudal injustices, notably in the Bobâlna Uprising of 1437–38, the Doja Rebellion of 1514, and in 1784, when Horea, Cloșca and Crișan led an uprising against the nobles. All three revolts were savagely crushed.

Transylvanian history becomes fragmented after the Turks gained control in 1541; Hungarian nobles retained large estates in the region long after this period and produced some excellent leaders, such as the enlightened Prince Gabriel Bethlen (r. 1613–29), while Magyar scholars founded universities. During the Reformation, which spread to Transylvania in the early 17C, Catholics in Transylvania came under vicious attack: Catholic clergy were hounded from sanctuary and many of their churches were burnt down. Luther's teachings gained ground in the region thanks to its influential, German-speaking population, and many Hungarians converted to Protestantism as well, founding the Hungarian Reformed Church.

The northern European settlers put down strong roots in Transylvania: when the influx tailed off in the mid-14C most of southern Transylvania and much of its remaining area were said to be inhabited by 'Saxons', a collective term adopted because the Germans were in the majority. Their industriousness and powers of self-determination won them considerable respect. As well as building fortified towns and founding wealthy guilds, they organised themselves into a 'university' which functioned as a virtually independent polity within Transylvania. Germans still refer to the region as the Siebenbürgen, after the seven most important centres of the region. 800 years after they first arrived, Transylvanian Germans started returning to their ethnic homelands. From 1980, Ceaușescu gave them a chance to escape the wretchedness of his communist regime by blackmailing Bonn into paying him for their release.

Relations between Hungary and Romania hang largely on the question of nationalist claims to Transylvania. This issue has been kept alive by politicians when most of the population would rather live and let live. By the late 18C Transylvania contained more Romanians than Magyars, but even after its separation from Vienna in 1867, the Hungarian government ignored Romanians' requests for national recognition and refused to let them open their own schools. Hungarian nationalists claim that the Magyars came to Transylvania before the Romanians because the Romans slaughtered or removed the entire indigenous population when they left Dacia in 271–72. And after a thousand years of occupation, the Hungarians feel they have a natural right to the province and its considerable wealth. There are several factors which prompt Romanians to feel this is unjust, and these have often been ignored by the Western press. One of the most potent of these is the fact that in 1940, the Fascist dictatorships of Germany and Italy gave northern and eastern Transylvania back to Horthy's Hungary in the infamous Vienna Award. During the next four years Magyar soldiers inflicted horrific atrocities on the indigenous population and deported thousands of Jews to death camps.

Shortly after the 1989 revolution trouble between ethnic Hungarians and Romanians flared again and in 1992, Romanian smallholders from the isolated Gurghiu Valley drove into Târgu Mureș with scythes and other improvised weapons. Acting on a rumour that the Magyars intended to annex Transylvania, they attacked the headquarters of the Hungarian nationalist party, and several people were killed. Meanwhile Romania's post-revolutionary government allowed Hungarians and other ethnic minorities to educate their children in schools where lessons were taught in their own language. Transylvania's largest university, Babeș-Bolyai in Cluj, runs parallel classes in both languages for all subjects. But the Magyars want a completely separate university, where classes will only be taught in Hungarian. Taken to its logical extreme, this would be a step on the way to creating a mini-Hungarian state within Romania. Tensions between the two communities eased visibly when the governments in Bucharest and Budapest supported each other's application to join NATO. But when Romania was rejected from the first rank of NATO candidates in 1997, a number of Romanian politicians on both sides of the ethnic divide saw this as an excuse to raise the age-old problem of Transylvania once more.

The foundation of Moldavia and Wallachia

Between the southern Carpathians and the Danube lies Wallachia. Romanians also know it as Țara Românească, the earliest independent Romanian principality, which came into being in the mid-14C after a boyar named Basarab defeated the Hungarian king, Károly Róbert, at the Battle of Posada in 1330. As Basarab I (r. 1330–52) he formed marital alliances with the royal houses of Orthodox Bulgaria and Serbia, creating a psychological as well as a physical barrier between his lands and the Catholic territories to the north.

In 1359 a Metropolitan Bishop was installed at the royal court of Curtea de Argeș in Wallachia. A few years beforehand, Bogdan of Cuhea and a band of loyal followers escaped from Hungarian-held Maramureș and crossed the Prislop Pass to Moldavia. Here Bogdan declared himself an independent prince, replacing the puppet rulers installed by the Magyar kingdom earlier in the century. Soon afterwards, in the reign of Alexander the Good in the early 15C, Moldavia also gained an Orthodox bishopric. Membership of the Orthodox church brought both regions within the Byzantine commonwealth, and when the empire collapsed they became a refuge for the Orthodox elite and a repository of its wisdom. Vasile Lupu (Basil the Wolf, r. in Moldavia 1634–53), regarded himself as a latter-day Byzantine emperor and lived accordingly.

While they shared a common faith, these neighbouring Romanian countries fought each other as fiercely as they resisted the Poles, Hungarians and Turks. Michael the Brave (Mihai Viteazul) (r. 1593–1601) united them with Transylvania in 1600–01, and there were other short-lived attempts to bring the three Romanian principalities together. But it was not until 1859, when nation

> **Mircea cel Bătrân (Mircea the Wise)**
> 'The bravest and most clever of the Christian princes', Mircea (r. 1386–1418) earned the respect of his western allies when he defeated Bayazet the Thunderbolt in 1395. As Prince of Wallachia, he strengthened the chain of fortresses along the Danubian plain, improved the country's military and administrative systems and signed defence agreements with Hungary and Poland. In 1396, while struggling to oust an Ottoman usurper from his throne, he lent his support in the disastrous crusade to Nicopolis. Arrogant Catholic knights led by Sigismund of Luxembourg and Jean de Nevers ignored his advice, and the Christian army was decimated as a result. But Mircea survived to intervene in the Turkish war of succession, and his astute combination of threats and diplomacy almost certainly saved Wallachia from becoming an Ottoman pashalik.

alism had become a central issue in European politics, that Moldavia and Wallachia were joined as the nation of Romania.

Under leaders such as Alexandru cel Bun (Alexander the Good) (r. 1400–32) and Ștefan cel Mare (Stephen the Great) (r. 1457–1504) Moldavia encompassed land to the east of its present-day borders, in what is now the Republic of Moldova and the Soviet Republic of Transnistria. Romanians called this region Bessarabia because is used to belong to the Basarab family. It still contains the ruins of magnificent fortresses built by Moldavian princes to defend the country from the Ottoman Turks. In 1941 Bessarabia was annexed by the Soviet Union, and is now an independent country in its own right. Similarly, the part of northern Moldavia which is known as Bucovina was once twice its present size and encompassed the Ukrainian city of Černovci (Romanian Cernăuți).

Turkish influence

Moldavians and Wallachians fought like the devil to maintain their independence, but in 1415 Wallachia was forced to accept Turkish suzerainty. But unlike its Bulgarian and Serb neighbours, and Hungary later on, Wallachia did not become a pashalik; instead, the country was allowed to elect its own native princes in return for an annual tribute. The same concession was given to Moldavia when in 1456, weakened by internal conflicts, it too accepted nominal vassalage and agreed to pay a tribute.

Islamic rule was naturally abhorrent to the Christian countries of central and eastern Europe, but until the mid-17C, when the Ottoman Empire began its long decline, the conditions imposed by the Turks were relatively civilised. Providing the tribute money and goods kept rolling in, subject states were ruled under a *pax Turcica* which allowed them to worship as they liked. While Moldavia, Transylvania and Wallachia elected their own princes (although they needed approval from the Porte—the seat of government—usually bought with gold), this gave strong and independent leaders the chance to form secret ties with European Christian powers. Eventually this situation caused a backlash; ferocious border raids organised by the vengeful Turks traumatised Wallachia throughout the 17C and 18C, fears of losing both revenues and prestige eventually provoked Ahmed III and his Grand Vizir to impose direct rule. Greek-speak

> ### Ștefan cel Mare (Stephen the Great)
> According to Mircea Eliade, Ștefan (r. 1457–1504) was the greatest Romanian ruler ever known. Small of stature and sober in his ways, he won 38 of his 40 battles, warding off predatory armies from Hungary and Poland before turning his energies against the Turks. Ștefan firmly believed that recapturing Constantinople from the Muslims and recreating the eastern Holy Empire were his God-given destiny. With that aim in mind, he started a Moldavian crusade. But Ștefan depended on financial help from his western allies, and when that failed to materialise there were years when he was forced to pay the Ottomans a tribute in both money and kind. When the Hungarian and Polish kings concluded peace treaties with the Turks, Ștefan was isolated, but he never gave up his belief in Moldavia's crucial role as a bastion of Christianity.
>
> Ștefan's brave deeds and modest character appealed to early 20C nationalists who hoped their young country would assume an important place in the world. Intellectuals of Eliade's stature saw him in this context, but under Romania's communist ideology Ștefan's name became synonymous with the kind of monolithic and one-dimensional heroes who can only inspire ridicule. Recent attempts to re-read his personality and reign have revealed a vicious enmity between Ștefan and his cousin, Vlad III (Dracula) of Wallachia, and the fact that he impaled some of his victims and traded in Gypsy slaves. But separating Ștefan from the propaganda that surrounds him still leaves him as an impressive if slightly less perfect figure.

ing princes from the Phanar district of Istanbul were installed on the thrones of Moldavia in 1711 and Wallachia in 1716.

The Phanariots were often greedy and weak, but a few, such as Nicolae and Constantin Mavrocordat, and Alexander and Constantin Ipsilanti, introduced reforms in land distribution and helped to abolish slavery. Their record is not one of pure sainthood, however, because along with these improvements they could be extremely harsh; Constantin Mavrocordat, for example, ordered prostitutes to be starved to death. Phanariots could be eccentric as well: Nicolae Mavrogheni (r. 1786–90) taxed the rich to help the poor—but also ennobled his horse. In 1821, as a result of Tudor Vladimirescu's uprising and the Greek War of Independence, the Phanariots in Moldavia and Wallachia were ousted in favour of native princes.

As Ottoman Turkey grew weaker, European powers gathered like vultures to fight over the spoils of its empire, which included the Romanian principalities. Conflicts between Habsburg Austria, Tsarist Russia and the Ottomans spilled over into Romanian borders from the late 18C until 1878, when the country became involved in the Russo-Turkish war. In return for considerable sacrifices while fighting for Russia, Romania gained international recognition of its independence in 1880, officially ending over 400 years of Turkish rule. But even after this date, an Ottoman enclave survived on the Danubian island of Ada Kaleh, forgotten by diplomats until it became part of Romania during the First World War. Dobrogea, Constanța, Mangalia and Babadag still contain mosques from the Ottoman period, and there are smaller Turkish communities along the Black Sea coast where women continue to wear baggy *shalwar* trousers as a matter of course.

Habsburg influence

Throughout the 16C, the Habsburgs tried to extend their dominions into eastern Europe and the Balkans. Eventually, in 1689, they 'liberated' the unwilling Transylvanians from the Turks, gaining the Banat and part of Crişana soon afterwards. A rule of enlightened absolutism ensued under a series of governors appointed by the Viennese court. The Habsburgs pursued a vigorous counter-reformatory campaign, spearheaded by Jesuit priests who built Catholic churches and established schools and colleges in many of the most important towns and cities. Alternative religions were tolerated to a limited degree, but Orthodox priests were anathema, and many perished.

As an inducement to convert, the Austrian authorities introduced a compromise between the Orthodox and Roman Catholic churches in the form of a new church called Greco-Catholic or Uniate. Originally devised as a way of uniting the divided churches during the wars with the Turks, Greco-Catholicism demanded that its followers recognise the Pope as their supreme head. It also required that they include the *filioque* clause in the Nicene Creed ('*filioque*' means 'and the son'; at the time, the Orthodox church did not believe in the dualistic, two-person nature of God, whereas the Catholic church did), that they use unleavened bread in the mass, and that they recognise the existence of Purgatory. In all other respects the services and liturgy were identical to traditional Orthodox practise, being conducted in Slavonic.

A large number of Romanians joined the new church because it conferred material as well as social improvements to what was basically a second-class status, and Greco-Catholic priests were paid the same level as Catholic ones. Greco-Catholicism is still very popular in Transylvania, especially in the Maramureş. In addition, leaders of the church, such as Bishop Inochentie Micu-Klein, succeeded, at least for a while, in bringing Romanian concerns to the notice of the Habsburg regime.

In the first half of the 18C, the Habsburg authorities invited a new wave of colonists to improve the land in the border regions of the Banat and Crişana. Many of the newcomers were veterans from Austrian campaigns, and while most came from German-speaking areas, they also included Spaniards and Italians. Whatever their origins, they came to be known as Swabians; their tasks included draining the Timişoara marshes.

Once absolutism had been established, Empress Maria Teresa (r. 1741–80) became more enlightened. Both she and her successor, Joseph III (r. 1780–90), set about improving the lot of serfs in Transylvania. Unfortunately, their reform policies came too late to avoid bloody uprisings. In 1784, a young peasant called Horea complained about the conditions of Romanian serfs to the Viennese court. At the time over three-quarters of all farm workers in Transylvania were ethnic Romanians who had no political representatives of their own. When his demands were ignored, frustration boiled over. Horea and two fellow peasants, Cloşca and Crişan, led attacks on landowners' houses, killing the nobles or forcing them to convert to Orthodoxy. The rebels wanted to abolish feudalism, but their actions brought a terrible revenge: in the winter of 1784, all three leaders were captured and brought to Alba Iulia. Horea and Cloşca were crushed on the wheel and dismembered, pieces of their broken bodies being displayed around the streets as a warning to others. Crişan committed suicide in prison. After their deaths Joseph III brought serfdom to an end in Transylvania, and peasants gained the right of free movement.

At the same time, the Habsburgs were involved in the carving-up of Poland with Tsarist Russia. In 1775, they annexed a part of northern Moldavia ignoring the protests of Moldavia's prince Grigore Ghica, who was throttled for his pains. The Habsburgs called the land Bucovina after its thick beech woods, and used it as a corridor between their new acquisitions in Galicia and Transylvania. The northern half of Bucovina was taken by the Soviet Union during the Second World War, and today it is part of Ukraine.

The Habsburgs influenced generations of Transylvanians by educating them in Western ideas and art; they also built magnificent Baroque citadels, such as the ones in Alba Iulia and Arad, and erected fine churches. The palaces of the Habsburg governors in Cluj and Sibiu are among the most splendid examples of Baroque architecture in Transylvania.

The rise of Romanian nationalism

In the wake of the 1784 Horea uprising, a group of ethnic Romanian intellectuals founded the Scuola Ardeleană (Ardelean School), which was dedicated to raising awareness of Romanian culture and political ambitions. Centred around Cluj and Sibiu, the nationalist movement concentrated on educated Romanians to respect their own language and achievements. The ending of Phanariot rule gave a fillip to nationalist ambitions in Moldavia and Wallachia, but the movement only got fully under way after the revolution of 1848–49, when a number of gifted students returned from self-imposed exile in France to demand self-determination and liberation from Russian occupation and Turkish suzerainty.

In Transylvania the situation was more complicated: what began as a Hungarian revolt against Habsburg rule turned into a vicious civil war. Ethnic Romanians at first supported the Magyars but turned against them when their charismatic leader, Avram Iancu, voiced his suspicions of Hungarian intensions. Encouraged by the promise that Vienna would look favourably on their demands, the Transylvanian Romanians helped to undermine the Hungarians' struggle for independence. The Habsburgs called on Russia to help them suppress the revolution and conceded nothing whatever to the Romanians. In the aftermath of the revolution, there were moves to reconcile the conflict between Hungarians and Romanians in Transylvania.

Although the revolution was crushed, it sowed seeds of change. During June and September 1848, Wallachian liberals set up a provisional government that promised radical reforms. Among these were the extension of civil and political rights and an economic system that would encourage entrepreneurs and give the majority of the population—dispossessed peasants—a fair deal. The 'forty-eighters' also envisaged the creation of a greater Romania which would comprise the Romanians of the Habsburg and Russian empires.

While Ottoman Turkey, Austria and Russia put down Romania's '1848', Russia and Turkey were still at loggerheads over their Black Sea possessions, in which Romania played a significant part. Napoleon III weighed in on Turkey's side when the Tsar claimed the right of protection over Orthodox monasteries in the Near East; the conflict led to the Crimean War. One result of the war was greater international awareness of Romanian claims to self-determination. In 1859, Moldavia and Wallachia elected the same prince, Alexander Ioan Cuza, to be their joint leader, forming the basis for what came to be known as the Old Kingdom. In the next few years, dynamic and far-sighted politicians such as

Mihail Kogălniceanu and C.A. Rosetti helped to introduce more improvements, among them Kogălniceanu's abolition of Gypsy slavery, while the wealth of the dedicated Greek monasteries, which by then owned a quarter of all the country's land, was converted into state property.

Societies such as Junimea (Youth), founded in Iași in 1863, promoted ethnic Romanian culture as opposed to imported Western ideas. Junimea believed in fair redistribution of land; one of its outstanding members was the great Romantic poet, Mihai Eminescu (1850–89). In 1901 another nationalistic group formed around the magazine *Sămănătorul* (*The Sower*). This organisation was also dedicated to agrarian reform and to educating the peasants. Its main driving force was Nicolae Iorga (1871–1940), one of the country's finest and most prolific historians. Iorga dedicated his life to building an image of Romania as a highly cultured civilisation that was a rightful heir to Byzantium.

Modern Romania

In 1866 Romania's government invited Prince Karl of Hohenzollern-Sigmaringen to be their head of state as Prince Carol I. While the young Catholic prince knew little about the country, he was well connected and on good terms with the Prussian leadership and Napoleon III. And in spite of his strong ideas on duty, he held liberal views. Carol I ruled as king of Romania from 1881 until his death in 1914. This was the longest reign in the country's history, and in many ways the most successful. As sovereign, Carol was the most important political figure in the country; he had powers of veto on all parliamentary decisions.

Between his accession and the communist takeover in 1947, Romania experienced a rapid modernisation, and while its governments were dogged by corruption and factional struggles, they did introduce a number of important democratic reforms. In 1921, nearly 2,500,000 subsistence farmers were given over 6,000,000ha of land, mitigating some of the frustrations that had led to the peasants' revolt in 1907. Oil exploration began in the Danube plains in 1895, grain production increased dramatically, and young people started moving to the towns and cities. On a cultural level, Romania looked towards Western Europe rather than Ottoman Turkey or Russia, and by the mid-19C men in Moldavia and Wallachia had relinquished their Oriental caftans in favour of European dress, one reason being, allegedly, that Romanian women were more attracted to Russian soldiers, who wore tight uniforms, than their own menfolk, who were always tripping over their skirts!

Carol's German connections made him reluctant to bring Romania into the First World War on either side, and for two years the country maintained an armed neutrality. But in 1916, with Carol's nephew Ferdinand installed as king, Romania declared war on Austria-Hungary, with the declared intention of gaining Transylvania. After decisive victories at Mărăști, Mărășești and Oituz in 1917, Romanian and Russian troops contained the German advance on the Eastern Front, and an armistice was signed at Focșani six months later. Supported by thousands of Romanians living in North America and by the governments of France, Great Britain and the USA, Transylvania became part of Romania in 1918. Bessarabia had already voted to join the union, and Bucovina added its voice to the movement later the same year. Except for its southern tip, Dobrogea had been part of Romania since 1878, and after the Second Balkan

War of 1913, Romania won this part as well, including the attractive sea port of Balcic. (Bulgaria regained Balcic and the area to the south in 1940.)

Creation of România Mare, or 'Greater Romania', engendered confidence and optimism, and between the two world wars the country experienced a brilliant period. Intellectuals such as Nicolae Iorga, Mircea Eliade and Nae Ionescu inspired belief in Romania as a dynamic country with an invincible spirit. Exciting innovations in architecture, increases in industrial output and improvements in technology, as well as massive cereal exports made Romania one of the wealthiest and forward-looking nations of Europe. In the 1930s, economic progress was hindered by the Great Depression, and the accession of the playboy king, Carol II, had disastrous results for the country's political stability. Having rejected his claim to the throne in 1925, Carol won the support of a group of political and military leaders and returned from exile in secret, flying into Alba Iulia one night in the summer of 1930. On his arrival in Bucharest he forced the Regency Council to resign, and proclaimed himself king in place of his nine-year-old son Michael.

To use a common Romanian term, Carol was not a 'serious' king. He was both vain and authoritarian, and he surrounded himself with yes-men, wasting huge amounts of money on new uniforms for himself and his guard, and fulfilling to perfection the image of a Ruritanian despot. In a reign marred by jealousy, profligacy and paranoia, his most positive contribution was the establishment of a fund which aided various cultural initiatives, including the excellent Village Museum in Bucharest. He also rebuilt the royal palace in Piața Revoluției.

During this period Romania was in its political infancy, and governments came and went with bewildering rapidity. Far-sighted foreign and domestic policies were held up by internal bickering, corruption was rife and power tended to be concentrated in cliques. Independent political groups such as the National Peasant Party, led by Iuliu Maniu, had to contend with a king who meddled in government, and they withdrew, too frightened or disorganised to provide effective opposition. In 1927, a young university graduate from Iași called Corneliu Codreanu founded a movement which he called the League of the Archangel Michael. Also known as the Legionary Movement, it encompassed a hotchpotch of ideas which were based loosely on those of intellectuals who wanted to give Romania a strong and united identity. Codreanu whisked up support by riding around the countryside on a white horse, impressing a largely illiterate peasant population with his good looks and sincerity. But whereas Iorga and Ionescu believed in settling differences through debate, Codreanu sanctioned violence. He was also an anti-Semite.

Initially, Carol gave his outward support to the Legionary Movement, but he was envious of its leader's popularity and in 1938 he ordered Codreanu's secret assassination, along with 13 of his followers. In the same year, Carol abolished all Romania's political parties and proclaimed a royal dictatorship. A few months later, the king had 252 members of the Legionary Movement murdered. Without Codreanu's moderating guidance, the Legionaries took refuge in Nazi Germany, where they fell prey to Fascism. Western governments showed little interest in Romania's plight and, frightened of losing more of his country's territory to the USSR, Carol tried negotiating with Hitler. In September 1939, Romania declared its neutrality in the war between Germany and the Soviet Union.

The Legionary movement already held anti-Semitic views, but collective hatred of Jews grew out of all proportion when Romania was forced to cede Bessarabia (now the Republic of Moldova) to the Soviet Union in 1940. Jews were blamed collectively for aiding the annexation, just as they were blamed for the rise of communism in Romania itself.

Having corrupted and weakened his country, Carol abdicated by popular demand in 1940. He escaped as dramatically as he had come, with soldiers firing shots at his departing train, leaving his 18-year-old son, Michael, in his place. With Michael's agreement, Romania was placed under the charge of Marshal Ion Antonescu and joined the Second World War on Germany's side in June 1941. Romania had little choice of war-partner: no help was forthcoming from the Western Allies, and the USSR had just taken nearly a third of its territory. Germany was the only country that could help Romania regain Bessarabia.

Antonescu was an ambivalent character whose career is currently undergoing reassessment. The kindest view is that he was an independent and strong leader who played along with Germany's demands as long as there was no better alternative. He professed anti-Semitism but, in defiance of Nazi ideology, found ways of protecting many of the Jews who lived in Wallachia, southern Transylvania and Moldavia. Even so, after Romania recovered northern Bucovina and Bessarabia, thousands of Jews from other regions, mainly northern Moldavia and Bessarabia, were deported to camps in Transnistria across the Dniestr River. They represented just under half the entire population of Jewry in Romania. Allegedly, Antonescu ordered the deportations to give the Jews protection against reprisals from Romanians and the Nazi death camps. But in the chaos which surrounded the entire operation, they were treated little better than animals.

Secret negotiations between Romania's opposition leaders and the Allies gave King Michael the support he needed to arrest Antonescu in 1944. Shortly afterwards Romania joined the Allies' war effort, signing an armistice with the Soviet Union in September of the same year. This amounted to an unconditional surrender, and Romania's fate was sealed at the Yalta Conference when Churchill, Roosevelt and Stalin agreed to leave central and eastern Europe in Soviet control. In December 1947, King Michael was blackmailed into abdicating and Romania was proclaimed a People's Republic.

Romania under communism

A complete picture of this period has yet to be drawn. Socialist ideas began taking effect in Romania in the 1850s and 1860s, when trade unions were formed in Transylvania. In 1921, a fully-fledged communist party was established on the Soviet model, only to be made illegal three years later. During the late 1940s Soviet-style communism gained control over every part of Romania's political life, leaving the country powerless to act on its own initiative. Elections held in 1946 were rigged in favour of the Bloc of Democratic Parties (the communists), which gained over 79 per cent of the vote. Critics of the new regime were imprisoned or sent to near-certain death on the Danube-Black Sea canal scheme. In the early 1950s, as Paul Goma's book, *Din Calidor* (*My Childhood at the Gate of Unrest*) relates, Stalin had thousands of Romanians deported from Bessarabia to Siberia. Only a few returned. And in a similarly effective alienation campaign, three southern counties of Bessarabia were given to the USSR so as to ensure control of the Danube mouth (they are now part of Ukraine).

Between 1947 and the late 1950s, Romania's government followed the

Kremlin's directives, nationalising all commercial enterprises with little or no regard for regional or local needs. After the popular uprisings in Hungary and Poland, party secretary Gheorghe Gheorghiu-Dej began taking a more independent line, and the 1960s were a period of liberalisation. Students were encouraged to travel abroad, and artists could express themselves freely.

In 1965 Nicolae Ceaușescu succeeded as Secretary-General of the Romanian Communist Party. At first he continued the relaxed policies of his predecessor, gaining worldwide approval by refusing to send troops to crush the Prague Spring. He also allowed Romania's Jewish community to join the World Jewish Congress. Ceaușescu's independent leadership began to take a megalomaniac turn in 1971 after his visit to North Korea. From then on, he made himself and his family the focus of a personality cult, and although Romania signed commercial agreements with the USA and Canada, the country spiralled off course. Defying Moscow, Ceaușescu determined to repay Romania's entire foreign debt so that he should be beholden to no-one. In doing so, he impoverished his people still further by exporting most of Romania's agricultural produce and cutting down on domestic supplies of heating and lighting; his government even stipulated the amount of food a person could eat (in terms of calories and proteins), and he forced families to have at least three children. Unable to feed or clothe their babies, young mothers abandoned their children to state-run orphanages that were little better than dumping grounds.

The secret police service, the Securitate, extended its networks into every part of Romanian society; even priests were recruited as informers. All contacts with foreigners had to be reported to the police, and privately-owned typewriters had to be registered. Lack of investment in new machinery meant that agricultural work had to be done by hand, and the workforce was supplemented by soldiers, students and factory labourers. At the same time, vast and underfinanced industrial projects, such as the Cernavodă nuclear power station, were initiated for the sole purpose of glorifying Ceaușescu's name.

By the mid-1980s Ceaușescu's isolationist tactics had become apparent to the rest of the world; he ignored Gorbachev's calls for *perestroika* and devised a plan which would destroy nearly half of Romania's rural villages, replacing these ancient communities with identical 'agro-industrial centres'. (Ceaușescu was executed after only a handful of villages had been destroyed.)

Protests, although risky, were not unknown. Up until the 1960s, there had been pockets of resistance to the communist leadership in the Făgăraș mountains, the old home of the 19C nationalist rebels, Frația. In 1977, 35,000 miners in Valea Jiului went on strike for better pay and conditions. When they took a member of the Central Committee hostage, Ceaușescu promised reforms. But as soon as they went back to work, reprisals began and lasted for the next few years. In the same year, c 200 people joined the Goma Movement, which sent open letters to the leadership complaining about the regime. Ten years later a workers' meeting held in Brașov to protest against massive job losses spilled onto the streets; it was put down by the army and Securitate. University lecturer Doina Cornea wrote an open letter protesting against the rural systematisation scheme in 1988, and six former party bosses made their disapproval of Ceaușescu's policies known the following year.

1989 and after

Encouraged by reports of the popular uprisings in Poland, Czechoslovakia and East Germany, Romanians took matters into their own hands. A rumour that an outspoken Hungarian priest, László Tökés, was about to be arrested in Timişoara triggered a spontaneous revolt in the city on 15–16 December 1989, and during the next few days the unrest spread across the country. But the focal point of the revolution was Bucharest, where on 21 December workers and students publicly defied a bewildered Ceauşescu, who fled by helicopter with his wife Elena from the roof of the Party headquarters in Piaţa Revoluţiei. The army initially supported the Ceauşescus, but turned against them when it saw the strength of popular will. Captured and executed on 25 December after a summary trial, the couple were buried in a Bucharest cemetery in separate, unmarked graves.

Standing ready in the wings were Ion Iliescu and a cadre of opposition figures; apparently they had been waiting for a chance to take power as soon as the dictator was removed. Iliescu was an experienced politician with a good track record in environmental matters, but his critics tar him with the same brush as Ceauşescu. There is still a lot of room for conjecture about what really happened before and after the 1989 revolution. From 1990 events unfolded rapidly: Iliescu took charge without a mandate, forming an interim government called the National Salvation Front, with Petre Roman as his Prime Minister. A mass demonstration in January called for (and apparently won) the abolition of the Communist Party, but Iliescu revoked the decision the next day. Historic political groups such as the National Peasant Party and the National Liberals were resurrected, and Iliescu called elections in May. Voters endorsed his presidency by 85 per cent, but students unhappy with his style of government began agitating for Iliescu's resignation.

Between April and June 1990, hundreds of students gathered in Bucharest's university square, Piaţa Universităţii, while behind the scenes, thugs used harassment and threats to silence anyone they suspected of causing trouble. A consensus of opinion believes they were Iliescu's men, but it is possible that they were acting for the Securitate. Whoever they were, 100,000 young people fled the country as a result, blaming Iliescu as the cause. During the sit-ins, the President made a television appeal, calling for the nation's support in saving Romanian democracy. The press later reported that hundreds of miners from the Jiu Valley went to the capital in response, beating up and in some cases killing the students, and damaging buildings in a rampage around the city. But here again, it is difficult to distinguish fact from fiction. Was one or other faction of the Securitate involved in manipulating the public perception of what happened in June, 'framing' the miners, or Iliescu, or both? As with so much of Romania's recent history, the full story has yet to be told.

Pools of unrest bubbled over in Transylvania, where Hungarians were suspected of trying to annex the region to Budapest. Romany communities also became targets of violent attacks. In 1993 the government introduced a law officially recognising its 17 ethnic minorities, appointing a representative councillors to each group in the Ministry of Culture. Romania's new constitution, promulgated in 1991, declares that all Romanian citizens should be treated with equal respect and that national minorities should be allowed free 'expression of identity'. There are laws stipulating that minorities should have their own schools. In contrast, Romania's laws on sexual minorities are still reactionary:

homosexuality is an offence, and until very recently it was a taboo subject for discussion.

The economy

At the end of 1989, of the ex-Warsaw Pact countries only Albania was in a worse economic situation than Romania. Ceauşescu's policy of paying off all international loans was in sharp contrast with other Comecon countries, whose debts were written off. The impact of the war in former Yugoslavia also had a devastating effect, because Romania depends on the Danube as a trade route and on hydroelectric power generated by Serbia. The first post-Ceauşescu governments were slow to introduce structural reforms, and the country's urban, telecommunications and transportation infrastructure were in need of urgent repair. Inflation rose sharply until 1994, when it dropped to 62 per cent. Industrial output fell and unemployment also rose, stabilising at 9.5 per cent in 1995. Since then unemployment has been steadily rising, and reached 1,000,000 (out of a total population of 23,000,000) in 1998.

Iliescu's attempts to attract foreign investment met with limited success, but in 1995 Romania regained its Most Favoured Nation status with the USA. Although foreign companies have shown interest in doing business in certain geographical areas, notably Bucharest and Transylvania, Romania as a whole has failed to attract foreign direct investment; major companies such as Palmolive and Daewoo are there because of low wages, while exports are concentrated on labour-intensive and low-technology goods, such as textiles, footwear and furniture. Overall, Romania's economic performance has differed greatly from that of other former communist countries which are candidates for the European Union.

After 1989, land from collective farms was given back to its former owners so that households received up to 10ha of agricultural land and 1ha of forest. This has resulted in a fragmentation of agriculture which inhibits efficient development. While nearly half the population still lives in rural areas, young people are moving into the towns and cities, leaving the old to work small plots for their own and their immediate family's use. Few of them can afford machinery, which is why Romania's countryside looks so picturesque, but that is scant comfort to the smallholders. Natural disasters, such as the severe summer flooding which has affected Romania for several years running, make regenerating Romanian agriculture all the more problematic. During August 1998 and in the spring of 2000 whole counties in Moldova and Transylvania were devastated by flood, and several hundred people lost their lives.

Romania's velvet revolution

In 1996 Romanians voted Iliescu out of office, bringing a peaceful end to a harrowing period of communist rule that stretched back 50 years. Replacing Iliescu came university lecturer Emil Constantinescu, leader of Convenţia Democratică Română, the Democratic Convention. Described as a coalition of coalitions, the CDR's most influential element is the National Peasant Party–Christian Democrat bloc, a conglomerate of two separate parties. Former union boss Victor Ciorbea was appointed Prime Minister and began an energetic programme of reforms, which included rapid privatisation of industry in line with the European Union's directives for candidate countries. Even so, by July 1997 none of the major banks had been privatised. If anything, Ciorbea's government tried to achieve too much and no-one could agree on the priorities. Taking responsibility for the resulting chaos, Ciorbea resigned in March 1998. He was replaced by Radu Vasile who ceded the role to Mugur Isărescu in December 1999. President Traian Băsescu was re-elected for a second term in 2004.

In 1997, Romania was refused membership of the EU on the grounds that it did not comply with the economic and civil rights requirements set by Brussels. It also failed to get into NATO, which many Romanians see as an essential protection from future invasion. Many people feel let down by Western Europe, and are resentful that the West does not give them more help. But Romania does belong to other international economic organisations, among them the Union of Balkan States (although the government has so far vetoed its constructive proposals) and BSEC, the Black Sea Economic Co-operation (CEMN in Romanian). This organisation was founded in 1992 with 11 member states, including Turkey, Russia, Ukraine and Georgia. A parliamentary assembly and a bank have been established, and there are moves to transform BSEC into an international body. At the moment the individual nations involved seem noticeable more for their differences than for their shared aims. Part of its rationale for membership is that Romania hopes that pipelines carrying oil from the Caspian Sea will come its way and not pass through Russia.

Romania's political culture is still in its infancy, and in the country at large there is an ingrained distrust of the parliamentary process: after all, it was the people who broke down communism, not the politicians. With few outlets for public opinion during the communist period, there is no tradition of discussion, and confrontation comes more easily than debate.

How do Romanians now regard 1989? After the euphoria and frustrations of the early 1990s, there is a general agreement among government leaders that the revolution has been over-politicised. Iliescu, who was elected to the Senate after his defeat in 1996, still talks of his role in the ousting of Ceaușescu, but rumour has it that he himself is being investigated by the security services which he helped to set up. A very public sacking of former communists in government posts took place soon after Constantinescu gained power, and trials of army members implicated in killings which took place during the 1989 revolution are now going ahead. Securitate files are being opened to the people they targeted, but perhaps the most optimistic sign for the future is that Romanians themselves are becoming bored with the subject and want to move on.

ASPECTS OF ROMANIA

The land

Sweeping through the country in a great arc shaped like a nose, the Carpathians have given Romania its identity. Their name comes from the Dacian tribe whom the ancient Greeks called Karpathos-Horos—the Carpi—and Romanians still think of themselves as a mountain people rather than steppe-dwellers.

While they cannot compete with the Alps (the tallest peak is Mt Moldoveanu at

2544m), the Carpathians were glaciated, and in the Făgăraş and Retezat ranges to the south there are glacial lakes and moraines created when the ice melted c 10,000 years ago. Around Transylvania, the mountains formed Europe's longest volcanic chain—the only remaining volcanic lake is Lacul Sfânta Ana, north of Braşov. To the west, in the range called the Apuseni, they were once rich in gold and silver. Copper and salt are still mined in Transylvania, and the rocks yield marvellous crystals. Romania's mountains also contain some of Europe's last remaining wilderness: in the Călimani range of the eastern Carpathians you can walk for several days without meeting another human being. By contrast, eastern and southern Wallachia and parts of southeast Moldavia and Dobrogea are formed by rolling plains of dark, fertile chernozem soil that gives way further east to chalky steppe. Dobrogea is a case apart: separated from the rest of Romania by the Danube on its final northern fling to the sea, it is bisected by a low, stegasaurean spine of hills, the Măcinilui, which are even older than the Carpathians, and the Delta's reed beds attract thousands of migratory birds each year.

At 238,391 sq km, present-day Romania is roughly half the size of France. It comprises several regions which remained politically separate until an awakening nationalist consciousness brought them together in the 19C and early 20C. For Westerners, the most evocative of these areas is the former principality of Transylvania, the high plateau concealed within the Carpathian bend and isolated from the west by the Apuseni. To the southwest of Transylvania lies the Banat, or more precisely part of historic Banat, another self-contained area bordered by the Mureş to the north, the Danube to the south and the Tisa to the west. Seeing its potential, the Viennese court brought in loyal settlers who drained the marshes and turned the flatlands into a bread basket. Today the region is shared by Romania, Hungary and Serbia. Scenically, Romania's share has come off best because to the east it extends to a luxuriant and unspoilt landscape of hills and woods. North of the Mureş, the Hungarian *puszta* peters out in Crişana, where three rivers called Criş converge on their way west from the Apuseni. Continue north, and you come to a county named for its principal town of Satu Mare; together with Crişana, this area was once known as Partium, a border country dividing Hungary and Transylvania during the Turkish and Habsburg occupations.

Drive east from Satu Mare to Cluj, and the road crosses into the Apuseni by a route used since Dacian times to bring salt from the Transylvanian plateau. On the western side of the pass the road cuts through Silvania, the Wood Land which is a prelude to Transylvania proper. Beyond that lies another historically self-contained area, the Maramureş. Tucked out of easy reach between a spur of the Carpathians and its main spine, the Maramureş contains a group of strikingly beautiful valleys where life continues much as it did in the 1930s. In 1922, northern Maramureş was ceded to Czechoslovakia, severing two-thirds of the old region from its Romanian roots.

The old principality of Moldavia touches the Maramureş's eastern borders. It is known to Romanians as Moldova and should not be confused with the Republic of Moldova, which lies beyond the Prut River, further east. Moldavia joined with Wallachia to become the United Principalities of Romania in 1859. In ancient times, the Siret Valley provided a corridor into Wallachia from the Ukrainian steppe for migrating tribes who poured down between the mountains and the Black Sea from central Asia. The Republic of Moldova and the strip of

Ukraine to its south once belonged to Romanian Moldavia; together they were known as Bessarabia. Moldavia also contained Bucovina, a piece of land named after its luxuriant beech woods and annexed by the Habsburgs in 1784 while they carved up the spoils from a defeated Poland with Tsarist Russia. Northern Bucovina is now in Ukraine, but Černivci was the Moldavian city of Cernăuți; the southern half of the region is famous for the painted monasteries commissioned by Stephen the Great (r. 1457–1504) and his son, Petru Rareș (r. 1527–38 and 1541–56). Apart from this, Moldavia is known for its wines and its mountain resorts.

In the Middle Ages, Moldavia met the principality of Wallachia at the Milcov and Siret Rivers, although later the border moved a few kilometres further south. The name means the land of the Vlachs and is a foreign appellation; Romanians know the region as Țara Românesca, or together with Moldavia as the Old Kingdom, from the time when they united to become Romania. Wallachia comprises two traditional regions: Oltenia to the west of the Olt River and up to the Carpathians, and Muntenia to the east. Most of Wallachia, including the capital Bucharest, consists of flatland or steppe which has been exploited for agriculture, oil and in some places wine. Wallachia stretches south and east to the sandy Danubian plains, but in the Carpathians it has a mountainous rim of spectacular beauty. Romania has 200 km of sea coast and joining the littoral its landscape is a strange but fascinating mixture of woodland and pasture, low hills, steppe, wetlands and wild dunes.

The people

In 1992 the official census counted 23,000,000 people in Romania. About half of these live in cities, and officially just over 2,500,000 belong to 17 ethnic minorities. Of these the largest group are the Romany. In reality probably account for about 10 per cent of the total population, although government statistics say there are only 400,000 of them. 1,600,000 ethnic Hungarians live in Transylvania, with the highest concentration in the eastern counties of Covasna and Harghita, where their ancestors, the Székely, settled in the 10C. The Magyars' UDMR party has representatives in parliament. Romanian nationalist and anti-Magyar sentiments tend to fluctuate with the state of the economy; since Romania's failure to enter NATO in 1997, the country has withdrawn into itself and anti-Hungarian voices have become more noticeable. Some of the Hungarians' demands for education in their own language have been met, but this is still a contentious issue.

Most of the ethnic German population has abandoned its traditional strongholds in Transylvania and the Banat, leaving just under 120,000 people behind. There are also 65,000 Ukrainians, 45,000 Russians (who live in the east), and nearly as many Serbs in the Banat and Crișana, along with around 18,000 Slovaks. Of the 760,000 Jews recorded in Romania between the two world wars, there are around 9000 left. In addition, some 7000 Armenians live in Romania. In 1993, the government established a special department in the Ministry of Culture to protect the identity of Romania's minorities, all of whom are guaranteed equal rights under the constitution.

The Romany

As Romania moves shakily from a command to a market economy, Gypsies (properly known as Romany but usually called *ţigani*) have been singled out as scapegoats for every conceivable ill. Vicious racial attacks in 1991 and 1992 left several of them dead and many of their homes burnt to the ground; to date, the perpetrators have still not been brought to justice.

Tradition has it that the Romany left northern India in the 10C and 11C to escape the rigid caste system. Some were employed as musicians by a Persian king but, frustrated by their fecklessness, he condemned them to wander the earth for evermore. When they arrived in eastern Europe, the Gypsies were enslaved, many of them in the Romanian principalities. In 1385 *voivode* Dan I of Wallachia confirmed the gift of 40 Romany families which his uncle had made to Vodiţa monastery a few years previously; a hundred years later, Prince ştefan cel Mare brought more than 17,000 Romany from Anatolia to work on his estates in Moldavia.

Vătraşi or settled Gypsies owned by boyars or monasteries were especially vulnerable to exploitation: they and their children became chattels who could be sold, exchanged or given away, and they were treated like animals. Wandering Romany were called *lăiesi* and paid an annual fee to the state. Persecution of both groups continued without restraint until the early 19C, when humanists such as Mihail Kogălniceanu campaigned with great eloquence for their freedom. As this coincided with cheap grain imports from north America, few boyars objected. Officially liberated in 1856, the Romany had begun to move westwards and into northern Europe a few decades earlier; by the 1880s they had reached the USA.

During the Second World War, over 20,000 Romany were deported to Transnistria along with the Jews of Bessarabia; many died. Under the communist government Gypsies fared better: even though they were discouraged from travelling, illiteracy among children fell dramatically, as it did in the population at large. Today Romania's Gypsies constitute the largest ethnic minority in Europe. Most have a home in one place, although about 200,000 spend at least half the year as nomads. Traditionally they are divided into about 40 distinct tribes which are equal in status. These include the *argintari* (silverworkers), *boldeni* (flowersellers), *căldărari* (tinkers and coppersmiths), *curara* (sievemakers), *fierari* (blacksmiths), *lovari* (horse dealers) and *lăutari* (musicians). Stradivarius is said to have learnt to make violins from the Gypsies, and poet Vasile Alecsandri immortalised a Romany musician who played at the court in Iaşi.

Romany language and customs have close affinities with Hindu culture, and while the Romany are universally misunderstood and condemned by the *gadjé* (their term for non-Gypsies), they observe strict ideas of propriety. Everything is either clean or unclean: in bodily terms, anything from the waist upwards is regarded as clean, while everything below the waist is not. Gypsies eat with their hands because cutlery can carry disease; married women always wear their hair in a scarf.

Most of the country's Romany live in Transylvania under the command of two rival 'kings', larger-than-life characters who are reputed to be immensely rich. Both of them are based in Sibiu. A common complaint about the Transylvanian Romany is that they have taken over and trashed the lovely farmhouses abandoned by the Saxons; when driving around towns and cities, you can expect to be plagued by little children demanding money for cleaning your windscreen—or just demanding money.

Voices raised against Gypsies always repeat the same shibboleth: '*Furau și non lucrează*' ('They steal and do no work'). While this is true of many Roma, there are some who have set up legitimate businesses, while others take an active part in Romanian politics. Some of the country's brightest intellectuals are of Gypsy origins. Sadly, attempts to bring Romany into an arena for constructive discussion are often beset by their own reluctance to change. But writers such as Isobel Fonseca, whose *Bury Me Standing* (1996) looks in depth at the history and position of Romania's Roma, and Alexander Fraser, author of *The Gypsies* (1992), are the latest in a distinguished line of scholars who have tried to bridge the gap which separates Romany from the rest of the world's population. In Romania, young ethnographer Delia Grigore has learnt the Gypsies' language and is a welcome visitor to the large Romany community that lives in Giurgiu, south of Bucharest.

In the maize fields east of Sibiu, Gypsies from Craiova camp under neat tents of plastic sheeting to make bricks out of local clay. And during autumn, around Bucharest you will come across strings of Romany caravans returning home after their summer's work, pots and pans rattling as they go. Sometimes *argintari* set up their portable anvils in markets and on street corners. Take them an old silver spoon, and they can fashion a wonderful ring or a brooch. Love them or hate them, the Gypsies bring colour and vivacity to everything they do. You can find out more about annual Gypsy festivals from a tourist office or the Ministry of Culture.

The Jews

Jews came to Romania with the Romans; more arrived after the Jewish Khazar empire collapsed, and others came in the 14C and 17C, when they were expelled from Hungary and Poland. They separated into two distinct communities, the Yiddish-speaking Ashkenazim, who congregated in Bucovina and Maramureș, and the Ladino-speaking Sephardim, who headed for the Danube. Most, however, settled in the areas of Bucovina and Bessarabia.

Treated with respect under the Turks, the Jews were alienated by Romanians and suffered horrendous casualties during the peasant uprising of 1907. Problems continued when Bessarabia and Bucovina were returned to Romania after the First World War. As the Iron Guard became more Fascist the Jewish population faced increasing dangers, and hundreds were butchered during one night of terror alone. Over half of Romania's Jews were handed over to the hostile powers of Hungary and the Soviet Union during the Second World War. The largest group, which numbered nearly 280,000 in 1930, lived in Bessarabia, northern Bucovina and the Herța region (between Bucovina and Bessarabia). Just under half withdrew into the USSR when Germany and Romania advanced into Bessarabia in 1941. Of the remaining half, at least 100,000 were deported to Transnistria where, despite the assurances of military dictator Marshal Antonescu to the contrary, they were treated like beasts. Conservative estimates show that 54,000 perished. Ironically, although Romania had a tradition of anti-Semitic legislation dating back to before the First World War, Jews were safer there during the Nazi period than they were in Hungary, Poland, Czechoslovakia and the Baltic States.

Antonescu's ambivalent policies with regard to Romania's Jewry are discussed briefly on p 50; his willingness to listen to pro-Semitic voices makes it difficult to condemn him out of hand. Throughout his regime, 1940–44, Antonescu was lobbied with some success by Dr Wilhelm Felderman (1882–1963), the tireless champion and president of Romania's Jewish community. Felderman spoke in defence of Antonescu at the latter's show trial in 1946 before he himself was forced to resign under violent pressure from Jews in the new communist order. He fled from Romania shortly afterwards. Further purges against Jews took place when foreign minister Ana Pauker was executed in 1952.

From 1947, Chief Rabbi Moses Rosen maintained a perilous balance by developing close links with the USA. Using his considerable skills as a negotiator, he argued for the continuation of Romania's Most Favoured Nation Status in return for exit visas. He died in 1994. At the same time, American governments gave financial aid to Romania's Jewish population. Ceaușescu allowed Jews to emigrate to Israel in return for large cash payments, and over 300,000 had left by 1989. Today, most major cities have a synagogue, and Bucharest's Yiddish theatre is the only one of its kind in eastern Europe; however, anti-Semitic attitudes are still rife.

Aromani, Moldovans and Transdniestrians

In northern Greece, Macedonia and Albania there are communities of ethnic Romanians known as Aromani (in English, Aromanians). They have preserved their language and many elements of ancient Romanian culture. Technically, the Aromani of northern Greece speak a dialect known as Megleno-Romanian and those from the Adriatic speak Istro-Romanian, although the latter has largely died out. Herbert von Karajan came from an old Aromanian family, and so does the well-known actor and Culture Minister, Ion Caramitru. Names starting with Cara- are always Aromanian.

In the Moldovan Republic, 64 per cent of the country's 4,500,000 inhabitants are also ethnic Romanians, but their language, Moldovan, was Russified by the Soviet Union from 1924 and remains subtly different to the Daco-Romanian spoken in Romania itself. Just under half the population of neighbouring Transdniestr, across the Bug River, are Moldovans, but the tiny republic remains stubbornly communist, and while the official language is Moldovan, it is written with a Cyrillic alphabet. Ukraine has a small population of ethnic Romanians who were 'left behind' when the Soviet Union annexed Bucovina and when northern Maramureș was absorbed into Czechoslovakia.

Armenians

Armenians, who belonged to the first Christian state, founded in 301, were persecuted by Orthodox Christians because, like the Copts and the Ethiopians, they were monophysites who refused the Chalcedonian confession of 451 which admitted Christ's humanity, and would not accept the person of Christ in two natures. As a result they were excommunicated, and when the Byzantines captured their capital, Ani, in 1045, and the Tartars invaded in the mid-13C, thousands of Armenians fled to the coastal areas of the Black and Caspian Seas. Most of them settled in the Crimea, where they established trading posts that allowed them to move into Russia, Poland and the Romanian lands.

In Moldavia they quickly made themselves indispensible, working as diplomats, interpreters, advisers and most of all businessmen who traded in carpets and glass. Their greatest sphere of influence was along the Mare Drum Tătăresc, the Great Tartar Road, which connected the Black Sea to the Baltic. Their most important eastern European centre was the Polish city of Lvov, where they established a bishopric. In 1401, the Armenian Archbishop Ohanes Nasredinian founded the church at Zamca, and between 1401–35 the Armenian community helped to stabilise the rule of the Moldavian prince Alexandru cel Bun. By the early 16C Armenians in Suceava were powerful enough to be granted leadership of the city council for one year in two and from 1572–74 the Armenian John the Brave was voivode.

Tolerated because of their prodigious skills, Moldavia's Armenians were officially regarded as pariahs by the Orthodox church, and Armenian priests figure among the heretics awaiting the Last Judgment at Voroneț.

Religion

Romania is a part of Europe, but its culture is strikingly different from many Western countries. The differences can be bewildering because, outwardly, people dress and behave in the same way as they do in the West. Adding to the confusion are the assumptions that many Westerners make about Romania before they even arrive. These are often based on the literature created by Western European, and especially British, writers who, from Byron onwards have seen Romania as part of the Balkans, with all the romance, disparagement and fear that this implies. It is not easy to adapt to Romanian culture, where hard-and-fast rules are never laid down, but one of the best ways to gain an understanding is to appreciate how Romanians feel about their religion.

Religion plays an integral part in the lives of many, if not most, Romanians. 1992 census figures claimed that over 86 per cent of the population belonged to the Orthodox church. In terms of per capita numbers alone, only the Russian church has a larger following, but historically Romanians have always felt closer to their church, having been converted by choice, not by force. Catholics and Protestant minorities, such as the Hungarian Reformed Church, are well represented in Transylvania, but Transylvania's Greco-Catholic community has dwindled to a sixth of its former size since it was banned by the communists in the late 1940s.

Under communism, Orthodoxy became the official religion of the Romanian Socialist Republic. This left the Patriarch in an ambiguous position, and priests were said to have worked as informers; but by the same token, Orthodox clerics were among the thousands of opponents to the regime who were sentenced to work on the deadly Danube–Black Sea canal scheme.

Ceaușescu, whose attitudes were nothing if not schizophrenic, maintained close links with certain monasteries while closing scores of others. As his megalomania grew, he hated any rival sources of influence, and using the 1977 earthquake as his excuse, he moved or bulldozed over 20 churches to make way for his 'restructuring programme'. Since 1990, most of the remaining foundations have reopened and many are thriving.

History

Romania's links to the Eastern church go back to the Byzantine period. After the Great Schism, which caused a rift between Constantinople and Rome in 1054, Latin-speaking Catholics and Greek-speaking Orthodox refused to countenance one another. They were divided by language as well as theological, doctrinal and political differences which were only (temporarily) resolved when the Ottoman Turks threatened to destroy Christendom altogether. When Sigismund of Luxembourg organised the disastrous crusade to Danubian Nicopolis in 1396, he grudgingly accepted the aid of 'schismatics' from Wallachia. But the only Catholic knight to take notice of their sensible battle plan was the French baron, Enguerrand de Coucy.

Early Christianity

Romanians will often tell you that they were born Christians, by which they mean that their ancestors were naturally predisposed to a Christian way of life, thanks to the Dacians' belief in the immortality of the soul. Historical documents tell a similar story. The 4C historian Eusebius of Caesarea records that Romanians' predecessors were baptised by St Andrew when he came to the lower Danube and the Black Sea coast. Tertullian went further and stated that the Scythians and Dacians converted to Christianity in 196 AD. We know that a group of Geto-Dacians visited Jerusalem before 270, and the first known missionary to Dacia was Wulfila, who came from south of the Danube to preach the Gospel in Gothic and Latin.

The Roman emperor Diocletian persecuted Jesus's followers along the Danube from Dobrogea to Pannonia in present-day Hungary. In 304, martyred Christians included Bishop Ephrea of Tomis (now Constanța) and priests and deacons from Axiopolis (Cernavodă), Dinogetia and Noviodunum. All these places are in Dobrogea, known then as Scythia Minor.

When the Heruli destroyed the western empire in 476, Rome's imperial insignia were sent to Constantinople. In the following century, Justinian (r. 527–65) tried to recover Rome's lost territories in western Europe, pushing his borders north to the Danube as a bulwark against the incoming Slavs. During this period, Bishop Valentinian of Dobrogea corresponded in Latin with the Pope while maintaining close contacts with the Patriarch of Constantinople. But the Byzantine Empire lost the Danube provinces in 602 when the Avars attacked, leaving Dobrogea as its sole possession on Romanian soil. Byzantium had to relinquish Dobrogea 80 years later.

After the Battle of Silistra in 971, the Byzantine frontier extended once again to the lower course of the Danube. It remained there until two Romano-Bulgarian brothers, John and Peter Asen, stirred up a revolt among Balkan peasants which resulted in the formation of the independent Vlacho-Bulgarian tsarate of 1185–86. Except for a few brief periods, the Byzantines never regained Dobrogea. Tsar John Asen II incorporated Dobrogea and southern Wallachia into the Bulgarian patriarchate of Trnovo, and from that period Bulgarian monasteries became an important influence on Romanian Orthodox doctrine and aesthetics. In 1235, John Asen formed an anti-Catholic alliance with John Vatatzes of Nicaea; a century later, this gave the impetus for the formation of Moldavia and Wallachia as independent Orthodox *voivodates*.

Romania's first churches

As in the rest of southeast Europe, the earliest Christian services held in what is now Romanian territory took place in private. This happened from the second half of the 1C AD. The first known church in Romania, dating from Constantine's reign, was built at Piatra Frecăței in Tulcea county, northern Dobrogea. In the following century a basilica was built with a side atrium in the Syrian style at Callatis (present-day Mangalia).

Archaeologists have traced the foundations of 4C churches in Niculițel near Tulcea and Densuș in southwest Transylvania, while a 4C Christian votive tablet has come to light at Biertan. Other early churches, from between the 4C and the 6C, have been identified in Celei and Cenad, while 5C and 6C basilicas are found in Dobrogea at Constanța and on the site of the Dacian citadel of Sucidava. At Basarabi near Constanța you can visit cave basilicas that were cut into the rock some time between the 9C and the 12C. Traces of 12C Byzantine churches have also been found at Niculițel near Tulcea.

Romania's first Metropolitan churches or bishoprics were founded before 1359 at Câmpulung, Turnu Severin and Curtea de Argeș. In Moldavia the first church officials came from Kiev. When the Romanians tried to promote a native priest to the Metropolitanate of Suceava they fell foul of Constantinople, because the Patriarch wanted Greeks in charge. Deadlock was only averted with the accession of Alexandru cel Bun in 1400 and a new, more tolerant attitude in the Byzantine capital. Romania's close relationship with Mount Athos dates from the 14C; the Wallachian monastery of Dionisie was founded on the Holy Mountain in the 1520s.

Monasticism in Romania

Until the early 17C, Romanian Orthodox priests celebrated the liturgy in Middle Bulgarian, a form of Old Slavonic. This was due to the country's monastic traditions which were established by monks of Slav origins, such as Nicodemus the Athonite (d. 1406). Half-Serb and half-Greek, with firsthand experience of the contemplative life on the Holy Mountain, Nicodemus had a network of contacts ranging right across the Orthodox world. He came to Wallachia in the 1370s, and although he was not the first Athonite monk to be appointed to the Wallachian see, he was the true founder of Romanian monachism.

The practice of contemplation known as 'hesychasm' involved continuous internal chanting of a single prayer, 'the prayer of the heart', to induce an ascetic, mystical frame of mind. Encouraged above all by the monks on Mount Athos, it was a decidedly anti-Latin phenomenon and belonged mainly to the reactionary days of the 14C. Hesychasm was introduced into the principalities by Nicodemus and by itinerant artists and architects from the Adriatic and the Black Sea regions; another important source were ethnic Romanian monks who trained at the secluded Bulgarian monastery of Paroria in the Balkan Mountains. When Paroria closed down in c 1350, its didactic role was assumed by Kilifarevo near Trnovo.

Links between the principalities and Orthodox centres abroad remained close until 1863, when foreign-owned monasteries lost their rights to Romanian soil.

Romanian patronage of the Orthodox church abroad started when Vladislav I of Wallachia sponsored the Athonite monastery of Koutloumos in c 1371. Some 50 years later the Moldavian prince, Alexandru cel Bun, helped to fund the monastery of Zogrof on Mount Athos. (Zogrof is now in Bulgarian hands.) When the Byzantine Empire fell to the Turks, thousands of Greek monks fled from the Near East to Romania, where they could pursue their religious practices in relative peace. With the Romanian princes' blessing they founded monasteries, but the income they generated was sent to their mother churches. For this reason, Moldavia and Wallachia were known as the church's milking cow.

Monasteries and convents in Romania usually welcome visitors, but you may be asked to pay a nominal fee for taking photographs. You will probably come across another type of monastic establishment called a *schit*, from the Greek '*skitos*'. In English it is called a skete. Sketes are usually smaller and less formal than the cenobitic monasteries; they range from large monastic villages to organisations which are run by as few as five or six people, and they are often devoted to agriculture or crafts.

The Armenian church in Romania
During the early years of Christianity, clerics argued over the intricacies of theological doctrine at a series of Ecumenical Councils. In the fourth of these, held at Chalcedon in 451, bishops from the Oriental and Near Eastern churches broke away from the main body of Orthodoxy, refusing to accept that Christ could be both the Son of God and fully human at the same time. After this they were called Monophysites or Non-Chalcedonians. Among the Monophysites were the antecedents of the Armenians who settled in Romania and built monasteries and churches of their own. Fifteen of these churches are still standing, among them the Armenian Cathedral in Bucharest (1781), which attracts a large proportion of Romania's 7000 Armenian inhabitants.

Wallachia's bishoprics
In 1359, Jakinth of Vicina in Dobrogea became the first Metropolitan of Wallachia. His official seat was in the capital of Curtea de Argeş. In 1516 the Metropolitanate moved to Târgovişte, and in 1661 the bishop was installed in a palace in Bucharest. The Wallachian See had authority over most of Transylvania's Orthodox as well, but in 1391 Peri Monastery, in what was then part of Maramureş, became an exarchate, gaining the right to train its own monks. Until its demise in the early 18C, Peri was responsible for all the Orthodox Christians in Maramureş as well as parts of northern Transylvania.

Orthodoxy in Transylvania
Things were more complicated for the Orthodox in the Catholic regions. Those who belonged to the Eastern church were treated as second-class citizens. A Catholic rule of 1271 forbade them to build churches in stone, and although this rule eventually lapsed, the Habsburgs continued to persecute Orthodox priests when they invaded Transylvania in 1689.

A period of uncertainty, caused by a split between Transylvanian and Wallachian bishops, left the principality without an Orthodox spiritual leader for over a century. During this time, the Serbian church took charge of the Romanian Orthodox from its base in Timişoara. However, in 1868 Bishop Andrei Şaguna re-established the Romanian church in Transylvania and four bishoprics were established, with seats in Arad, Oradea, Caransebeş and Cluj-Napoca.

The new Byzantium

Ottoman sultans allowed their subject nations religious freedom as long as they caused no trouble. Romania's association with the Orthodox church rose to its height between the 16C and the 18C, while the principalities were Turkish vassals. 16C *voivozi* such as Petru Rareş, Petru Şchiopu and Şchiopu's Wallachian contemporary, Alexandru II Mircea, went on pilgrimages to Sinai and Jerusalem, endowing chapels with money and splendid gifts, which included silver and gold, ceremonial swords, embroidery and illuminated books.

The 17C prince, Vasile Lupu, exercised a considerable influence over the Orthodox world at large. Lupu came to power in Moldavia at a time when the patriarchates of Constantinople and Mt Athos were bankrupt. He became their principal supporter, not only inviting Greek monks from Antioch and Jerusalem to found churches in Moldavia, but also supporting monastic foundations abroad, including all the Athonite monasteries. Lupu became so important to the church that during the 1640s matters of doctrine were decided at his court in Iaşi and not in Istanbul. He also established presses where ecclesiastical and secular books were printed in several languages, including Romanian, and he encouraged dialogue between intellectuals and theologians in Moldavia and the Near East. Lupu thought of himself as a latter-day Byzantine Emperor, a belief he shared with the members of several other princely families, the Cantocuzinos, the Mavrocordats, the Morazis and the Sturdzas and Constantin Brâncoveanu among them.

After the union of Moldavia and Wallachia, the Patriarch of Constantinople recognised the Romanian Orthodox Church as an autonomous body. When Transylvania and the other provinces joined Romania in 1918, the church was radically reorganised and the Metropolitan of Wallachia, Miron Cristea, was raised to the status of Patriarch. Today there are four metropolitan bishops in Romania; they have responsibility for the church in the Banat, Moldavia and Bucovina, in Oltenia and in Transylvania, while the Patriarch looks after Muntenia and Dobrogea.

The Greco-Catholic church

When the Austrians conquered Transylvania they offered Orthodox Romanians social and economic inducements to join the Greco-Catholic or Uniate church. This religion, originally devised as a means of reconciling the Roman Catholic and Orthodox churches at the Council of Florence in 1438–39, introduced four key changes from traditional Orthodoxy. These points were recognition of the primacy of the Pope, inclusion of the *Filioque* clause in the Creed, the acceptance of the state of purgatory, and the use of unleavened bread in the mass. While Orthodox clergy denounced the changes and advised their followers to refuse, the solution proved a popular one, because it brought material benefits to the lives of many who were poverty-stricken.

On a minor level, the adoption of a Catholic viewpoint caused changes in both the iconography and style of mural painting, creating a particularly vibrant period of Transylvanian church art. More importantly, the Greco-Catholic church became a force for radical change in Transylvania's nationalist movement, and one of its bishops, Inochentie Micu-Klein (c 1692–1768), devoted his life to establishing the rights of Romanians under Habsburg rule. By 1948 there were 1,500,000 Greco-Catholics in Romania. But the communist leadership forced them to reunite with the Orthodox church, and their numbers have dwindled to one-sixth of their former size.

Inside an Orthodox church

Orthodox churches are meant to embody heaven on earth. This is the reason why they are often very dark inside, with small pinpoints of light entering from high in the cupola windows. Such an atmosphere is intended to inspire awe and encourage worshippers to direct their thoughts and prayers upwards to God.

The layout is basically the same as in Greek or Russian Orthodox shrines. At the west end is a narthex, or entrance, representing the wider world. People who have not been baptised may watch services through the open narthex doors. Next comes the naos, or nave for the baptised congregation. Monastery churches often have an extended narthex to accommodate the lay congregation during important services. At the east end is the apse, containing a sanctuary with the altar. The sanctuary represents heaven and is usually separated from the rest of the interior by the icon screen. As its name suggests, the screen carries rows of icons held in a wooden matrix. The screen is often gilded and can be dazzlingly ornate.

Icons have a very special meaning: although from a Western aesthetic the figures can seem abstract and stiff, they are meant to convey the sense that the painted saint is a living being. Celebrants can find a direct path to God through contact with the icon's eyes. Romanians often place icons of a saint inside their homes; this does not mean that they venerate a particular saint but that he or she represents the panoply of saints and the Holy Family.

In the centre of the screen is a pair of ornate doors. These are the Royal or Imperial Doors, symbolising the passage of the divine into the world. They are only opened during services, when the officiating priest walks between the naos and the sanctuary. On either side of the Royal Doors there may be two other doors which are used when services are not in progress.

Some churches have a choir gallery. The external doors into the narthex are usually kept open during services to allow non-believers to look inside, but no-one except the priest is allowed into the sanctuary, which contains the altar, holy books, candelabra and containers for holy bread, such as a chivot, and reliquaries. Outside, near the west end, you will often find two metal cabinets containing burning candles: these are for the *vii* and *morții*, the living and the dead. (See also Wall paintings in Romanian Orthodox churches on pp 66–67.)

Religious services, festivals and customs

Orthodox services are usually elaborate rituals involving a great deal of symbolism. Candles, incense and rich vestments all play their part in what can be a very theatrical performance. The liturgy in an Orthodox church can last for several hours; it is spoken and sung without accompaniment. During the service the congregation stands, although a few chairs or benches are provided around the walls. But the atmosphere is rarely sombre, and people come and go freely without embarrassment.

Services in monasteries take place every day, and are based around three daily prayers: Matins, Vespers and Compline. The main service of the week is held on Saturday evening, when the Sabbath officially begins, and the holy day ends on Sunday evening; there is no obligation to go to church on Sunday. In Orthodoxy, the Nicene Creed is spoken in its original form, without the *Filioque* clause. Saints are singled out for special veneration, the most important being the Virgin Mary. As in other Orthodox countries, priests can marry but monks and bishops are expected to remain celibate. A remarkable facet of religious life in post-communist Romania is that certain priests have taken to becoming hermits, reviving an early medieval custom that is almost unheard-of elsewhere in the modern Christian world.

As soon as you enter a church it is considered polite to cross yourself while facing the icon screen, and most Romanians buy a candle and place it near the icon of their choice. Some priests insist that women wear decorous clothing which covers the whole body including the upper arms and thighs, but even if they do not, it creates a good impression if you remember these rules. Many Romanian women cover their heads with scarves when they go into a church. You hardly ever see segregation between men and women any more, but some older, rural churches have a women's area, called a pronaos, between the west entrance and the naos. But Orthodoxy still follows some ancient laws which can seem very outdated. For example, women are not allowed into the sanctuary and there are no women priests. Traditionally, women are not allowed into a church when they are menstruating or immediately after childbirth. Remarriage is allowed in the Orthodox church. Funerals are complex affairs involving celebrations and feasts at fixed periods for up to seven years after the person has died; during the funeral service, coffins are left open for mourners to kiss the dead. Romanians in general spend a lot of time celebrating the lives of family members and friends who have died. These extended grieving rituals (some of which are described below) can be truly impressive and surely help to soften the blow.

Burial rites and folklore

It may shock Western visitors to see bodies in uncovered coffins being carried to a church for a burial service. This practice is common to all Orthodox countries. It is a sign that the church encourages a close relationship between the living and the dead.

One of the most striking examples of this is the ritual known as the 'Wedding of the Dead'. This ancient ceremony was once widespread throughout Europe but now probably survives only in Romania. If a young person dies before marriage, the burial service includes a 'wedding' ceremony: a girl is married to Christ and a boy to a symbolic 'wife' in the form of a sapling. Ritual verses are chanted by the female relations of the dead child. There are many other folkloric beliefs involving trees: the ancient poem *Miorița* associates death with a cosmic wedding to the earth, the sky and the trees.

Feasts and blessings for the dead person are held after the initial burial service. These rites continue at regular intervals for seven years. At this point the relatives exhume the bones and bless them before reburying them for ever. This ceremony is called *pămâna*. After the reburial the family holds a feast with special, symbolic food, and everyone in the village is invited to share it.

At one stage during the feast some of the dead person's personal belongings, such as clothes or handkerchiefs, are placed in a tree beside the table in case he or she may want them. It also helps the family to come to terms with losing someone they love in a gradual and remarkably positive way.

Weddings comprise a civil and separate church ceremony, and celebrations will often go on for two or three days. Traditionally, a member of the bride or bridegroom's family places two trees outside the girl's front door on the day of her wedding, although this happens less often in towns. In country areas the participants still wear traditional embroidered, homespun clothes, and a local Romany or village band will often play at the wedding feast.

Orthodox Easter (Paştele)

Easter, which is celebrated about a week after the Catholic and Protestant Easter, is the most important festival in the Orthodox calendar. It is taken very seriously and older people often fast during the week beforehand. Thursday is the traditional day for painting hens' eggs in symbolic colours, among which red commemorates Christ's blood. Food plays an important part in the celebrations, and women make special dishes such as *sarmale* (stuffed cabbage leaves), *cozonac* (a marbled cake or bun) and *pasca* (a Moldavian cheese bun). After a midnight Mass the previous night people spend Easter Day with their families and eat their painted eggs.

Christmas and New Year (Crăciun şi Anul Nou) *and name days*

The period leading up to Christmas is usually quite sober and used to be a time of fasting. Now women prepare for the celebrations by cleaning their homes, buying presents and finding a Christmas tree. If there is one, the family pig is killed, surrounded by *ţuica*-drinking onlookers; sometimes the pig is anaesthetised with *ţuica* too. On Christmas Eve country people go carol-singing, and groups of Romany musicians play in city streets. No marriages may be celebrated until after the New Year.

Christmas festivities last for the full 12 days, including a boisterous New Year's Day when Romanian villagers give their colourful folklore full rein. In Sighetu Marmaţiei, carol-singers gather from all over the country to parade through the streets in their traditional costumes.

Romanians also celebrate on the saint's day that corresponds to their given name. They go to church in the morning and hold parties for their friends afterwards. Once again, this is just a way of stating their faith; it is not to do with singling out any particular saint for praise or distinction.

Mărţişor

On 1 March, women and girls are given *mărţişor*, an amulet or charm tied with red and white thread which symbolises love and the joy of spring. *Mărţişori* can be a flower or a little animal; tradition says that the recipient should wear hers until she sees the first flowering tree, then hang it on a branch.

Other religious festivals

Important saints' days include St Gheorghe on 23 April, Ss Constantin and Elena on 21 May, Sts Petru and Pavel (29 June), St Maria (15 August), St Dumitru (26 October), Sts Mihai and Gavril (8 November) and St Nicolae (6 December).

Pre-Christian rituals

In Romania's rural areas, organised religion has a fascinating relationship with pre-Christian myths and folklore. Wayside crosses called *troiţe* mark the edge of a village or a crossroads where, according to superstition, evil spirits lurk in wait for travellers.

Rites of regeneration still have their influence in the celebrations traditionally held for New Year, when young men dress in terrifying masks and animal costumes. And in some villages, day-to-day activities such as housebuilding would not be complete without killing a cockerel and pushing a cat out of a window to make sure that Satan leaves with it. To this day in some rural areas, there are 'wise' women who know how to make healing charms. While the Orthodox church does not condone the custom, it encourages the charm-makers to come to church to have their work blessed.

Shamanism was practised widely until at least the 19C, and places connected with shamanic beliefs still exist. They include certain rock formations high in the mountains.

Visual arts

Religious art and architecture

From the Middle Ages until the mid-19C, the Orthodox church played a dominant role in Romanian art. Byzantine styles of architecture and painting were introduced from the cosmopolitan ateliers of Constantinople, either directly through Greek artists who travelled to the provinces, or filtered through the Slavic lands of Bulgaria and Serbia. The Frankish invasion of Constantinople in 1204 also drove artists and craftsmen to seek refuge in neighbouring Orthodox countries. The Paleologan emperors who regained the Holy City for the Byzantines encouraged a new flowering in mosaic and wall-painting, Ideas spread to the Orthodox countries of eastern Europe beyond Constantinople's borders and continued to be a source of inspiration until the Turks conquered the Byzantine capital in 1453.

Wall paintings in Romanian Orthodox churches

With special thanks to Sorin Iftimi and Anna Hulbert

Romanian Orthodox churches are often decorated with colourful murals. Sometimes the paintings cover the entire interior wall surface, the vaults in the ceiling, and, even, as in the famous painted monasteries of Bucovina, the exterior walls as well. Where they have survived, the effect can be very striking. But it can also be bewildering, especially where there are scores of individual scenes jostling for your attention. This essay introduces the themes which were repeated in every medieval church, with special emphasis on the Bucovinan churches, which have the most beautiful fresco cycles of all.

It is generally accepted that the murals in churches of the 15C, 16C and 17C were there for a didactic as well as a devotional purpose. It is often though that they were meant to show people who could not read or understand Slavonic what the Church wanted them to believe. In c 600 Gregory the Great sent a letter to Bishop Serenus in Gaul in which he stated, 'It is one thing to worship a picture, it is another by means of pictures to learn thoroughly the story that should be venerated. For what writing makes present to those reading, the same picturing makes present to the uneducated... because in it the ignorant see what they ought to follow... wherefore... especially for the common people, picturing is the equivalent of reading.' Fresco painters helped worshippers to identify individual saints and other holy personages by adding labels. But these were usually written in Slavonic, or in Romanian transcribed with Slavonic letters. Nowadays, the labels are often too faint to read, but the fact that they were there at all suggests that it was not only the illiterate who were supposed to take note.

Although the painting in some of the smaller Romanian village churches may have a cartoon-like quality, the frescoes you can see in the painted monasteries are fascinatingly complex representations of the Bible stories and the hierarchy of the Christian Church. At their most basic, they illustrate important episodes in the Old and New Testaments and the lives of important saints; they also show which saints and martyrs should be remembered on each day of the year. Although the frescoes can be very attractive, they are not mere decorations, nor are they naïve. In fact they are often subtle pieces of propaganda designed to persuade spectators to a particular point of view, and they were sometimes highly political.

The murals are a vital part of the church, which was itself seen as a dynamic entity representing Heaven on Earth. They complement the icons, which are often movable, and they follow a classic scheme that evolved during the Byzantine period.

The painting style in these frescoes is neo-Byzantine. By comparison with Renaissance art, the figures seem doll-like and the buildings and landscapes out of scale and illogical. Early Renaissance painters such as Duccio and Giotto learnt their skills from Byzantine models, but Byzantine art remained true to the spiritual realities rather than objective or naturalistic ones. Once you are used to the pictorial language of Byzantine painting the chances are that you will see that the frescoes in Romanian medieval churches are full of emotion and drama, but that they also burst with vitality and individualism, charm, wit and humour.

Romanian Orthodox wall paintings follow several basic rules. The first of these is that the higher a figure is on the wall, the closer he or she is to God. After God and Christ, the Virgin is the most important personage; she is also the Patron Saint of Romania and, like God and Christ, she often appears in several places at once and in many different guises. Scenes illustrating Heaven are always shown with a white background; scenes from the Earth ('after the Fall') have a blue background.

In 15C and 16C Moldavian churches, the wall paintings were carried out in fresco. The artists concerned made their pigments from minerals, using special recipes which included natural preservatives such as rennet and extracts from cow hide. They also used a lot of gold leaf. In the Maramureş and other regions where painters worked on canvas laid on wood, the colours were sometimes made from plants as well. Later, especially in the 19C and early 20C, church murals were carried out in oils. These are far less durable than fresco, and in many cases the wall paintings made in this medium are disintegrating.

Interior wall paintings

When you walk into a Romanian Orthodox church, you may pass through an open or closed porch, known as a *pridvor*. This area is often painted throughout, with frescoes covering the vaulting and the walls. The scenes may include part of the Menologion (the Orthodox calendar), showing the saints who are celebrated on each day of the year. And because it was the first point of entry, this part of the church was chosen as an appropriate place for The Last Judgment. The combination of dire warning and sweet encouragement was meant to focus the mind of the congregation before they entered the sacred space.

The pronaos (pronaosul)

This chamber was once reserved for female worshippers, who were not allowed too close to the sanctuary. Now there is far less segregation of the sexes, but traditionally women still pray on the left-hand side facing the altar and men on the right. Paintings in the pronaos, also known as the exonarthex, are devoted to martyrs and saints. On the vault you will see an image of the Virgin modelled on the early Byzantine Vlachernitissa icon. This is one of the most ancient images of the Mother of God. She has her arms raised in a gesture of invocation, with Jesus in her arms. A circle of archangels surrounds her. At Moldoviţa and Humor she is protected by a second ring of prophets from the Old Testament. On the pendentives are the figures of the Four Penniless Doctors: Cosmin, Theophanes, Joseph and John of Damascus. If the pronaos has two vaults, the second one shows the Baptism of Jesus or the Holy Trinity.

The upper register in the pronaos is framed by the arches of the vaults. The paintings in these spaces show the seven ecumenical councils: the Council of Nicaea (325) on the east side; the Councils of Constantinople (381) and of Ephesus (431) on the south side; the Councils of Chalcedon (451) and Constantinople (553) on the west side above the entrance, and the Councils of Constantinople (680) and Nicaea (787) on the north side.

The lower register is divided into two sections. One shows the life of the patron saint accompanied by medallions of saints and martyrs, and the other features the Menologion. Sometimes all the 365 saints are shown, otherwise only a selection appears. At Humor, the Menologion consists of saints for three months (September to November), while at Dobrovăţ the cycle is complete and appears in the tomb chamber. At Moldoviţa the Menologion shows saints for six months of the year (September to February) in the pronaos, while the remaining six are shown in the tomb chamber.

If the Menologion is complete it usually covers the naos and overflows into the porch. Added to this cycle, the pronaos contains Christian martyrs undergoing a full and vivid range of tortures: decapitation, burning at the stake, drowning, being broken on the wheel, pelted with rocks, crucifixion and being roasted on the spit.

The burial chamber (gropniţa)

This chamber is found only in Moldavian churches which were designed to be royal burial places. It always comes between the pronaos and the naos, and is seldom painted, with exceptions at Humor, where the frescoes show the life of the Virgin, and Suceviţa, in which the murals illustrate the life of Moses.

The naos (naosul)

This area corresponds to the nave in a Catholic or Protestant church; it is where the priest and the choir stand to chant the liturgies; it usually contains one or more special icons, and of course the icon screen and the Imperial doors. Two ornately carved seats may also stand on either side of the naos between the side apses and the west wall: these were traditionally kept for the bishop and the reigning prince. If there is a vault or tower over the naos, it contains the most important images. Christ Pantokrator (Christ Omnipotent) appears in the cupola above three to five registers which are contained within the angles of the vault: these contain Seraphim or Hierophim; standing Angels; Prophets; Apostles and sometimes the Athonite theme of the Divine Liturgy, which shows Jesus leading a church service assisted by angels, opposite the Imperial doors. You can see this scene in the naos at the monasteries of Dobrovăț and Sucevița and in the churches of Sf Gheorghe and Sf Dumitru in Suceava.

The four pendentives of the vault contain the figures of the four Evangelists, Luke, Matthew, Mark and John, or their symbols.

To the north and south of the naos wall are two semicircular spaces created by the vaults of the side apses. From the 16C it was customary to show the Crucifixion in the north conch while in the south you could find either the Descent of the Holy Spirit (Sf Duh in Romanian), the Holy Trinity, or, dating from the 17C, the Birth of Jesus.

Paintings in the southern apse and the west wall of the naos are always devoted to The Passion. The individual scenes comprise the Prayer on the Mount of Olives, the Garden of Gethsemane, the Betrayal, Judas's Kiss, Jesus with St Anne, Jesus with Pontius Pilate, Peter denying Jesus, the Repentance and Death of Judas, the Way to Golgotha, Simon leading the Cross, the Removal of Jesus's clothes, Nailing Jesus to the Cross, Joseph of Aramathea walking towards Pilate, the Descent from the Cross, Peter bowing his head beside the Pietà.

Below this group comes the lowest register of the naos. This contains images of military saints. The northwest wall of the naos often shows the figures of the Holy Emperor Constantine and Empress Helen, while the southeast side is generally resereved for votive portraits of the donor and his family, although there are many exceptions to this rule. Traditionally, the donor and his family stand to the left of Christ who is seated on a throne; the donor offers a model of the church as a symbolic gift to Christ while some holy personage intercedes between the two (usually this will be the saint to whom the church is dedicated). These paintings are fascinating because if they are intact they show the original shape of the church in question. From the 17C the wall above the columns or the dividing wall between the naos and the pronaos contained the scene of the Dormition of the Virgin.

In the naos you may also find the 24 scenes illustrating the Akathistos. In Moldavian painted churches this occurs more often on the exterior walls and is explained below.

The icon screen (Iconostasul)

Although this is not technically a mural, the screen carries some of the most visible and important images in the church. Icon screens developed during from the early Byzantine period, when a low chancel was the only barrier between the altar and the congregation in the naos. During the 9C a higher screen called a *templon* was introduced, providing a doorway into the sanctuary. This was only opened during services. The *templon* developed from the arrangement in Sf Sofia in Constantinople, whereby 12 marble columns hid the sanctuary from the naos, imitating the façade of a Greek temple. The 12 columns represented the 12 Apostles. A simplified wooden version evolved from this, with four columns symbolising the Four Evangelists. The wooden *templon* hid the altar from view, increasing the spiritual distance between the 'temporal' and 'heavenly' parts of the church. Icon screens still have this function today.

By the time Stephen the Great began to endow churches, the *templon* had evolved into an elaborate screen with central doors (the Royal doors) and two side doors. Large icons hung between all three openings, and smaller icons in hierarchical sequence were arranged in rows above the doors. Originally the icons on the screen were movable, but by Stephen's day they were fixed. They were an integral part of the liturgy, being venerated and censed during the ritual.

Some icon screens are sculpted to imitate a Jesse Tree or Tree of Isaiah which represents Jesus's forebears. Isaiah is shown asleep at the bottom of the composition. The Romanian system follows the iconographic layout devised in the Russian Orthodox Church during the 15C and 16C. Sometimes in Romanian, the iconostasis is called a *catapeteasma*. Strictly speaking this is a curtain hiding the altar from the congregation. The *catapeteasma* was originally used in the Judaic cult.

The lowest row of the icon screen shows four figures who alternate with the doors into the sanctuary. From the left, they are Jesus Pantokrator; the Mother of God with the Christ Child; the patron saint of the church in question, and finally St Nicholas, or sometimes John the Baptist or the Archangel Michael. The painting of the Mother of God is modelled on the Hodigitria icon which was supposedly created by St Luke and used to hang in the Hodigitria Church in Constantinople.

Above this come *Prăznicarele*, the Romanian name for the 12 icons showing the most important religious festivals during the Orthodox calendar. These are the Birth of Mary; the Angel Gabriel bringing Mary the news of Jesus's Birth; the Birth of Jesus; the Baptism of Christ; the Transfiguration, when Jesus appeared to his disciples on top of the mountain with the prophets Elijah and Moses (called *Schimbarea la față* in Romanian); the Entry into Jerusalem; the Crucifixion; Jesus's Descent into Hell; Doubting Thomas; the Resurrection; the Whitsuntide or Pentecostal remembrance of the dead (called *Rusaliile* in Romanian, after the wicked spirits which must be prevented from creating havoc); the Adoration of the Virgin.

The third register is devoted to the Deësis. This comes from the Greek for 'prayer' or 'request for forgiveness'; in Romanian it is called *cinul*. It shows Jesus enthroned, with Mary and John the Baptist on either side, and the most important saints asking Christ's forgiveness for the sins of true believers. On either side of the Deësis are icons showing the 12 Apostles. At the top, a cut-out image of the Crucifixion crowns the whole assembly.

The sanctuary (sanctuariul)

The sanctuary is the little room behind the icon screen at the east end of the church. It contains the altar and more than any other part of the church, it represents Heaven on Earth. On the walls, the Virgin with the Infant Jesus takes pride of place. She hovers overhead immediately above the altar. On either side of the Virgin are two angels, and below these figures is a frieze of Seraphim (heads of angels with eight wings apiece). Below this there is usually a small Gothic style window. In the recess above the window you will find the Adoration of the Lamb, sometimes replaced by Christ in a Chalice, an image which came into Romanian usage from Serbia during the reign of the Serb king, Stephen Dušan (1331–55). Two more angels stand on the left- and right-hand sides of this image.

To the left of the window are two scenes: the one at the extreme left is the Last Supper. Next to it comes Christ Sharing Bread with the Apostles. To the far right of the window is Jesus washing Peter's feet, and next to that, Christ Sharing Wine with the Apostles. At the bottom, under the window and around the curving apse wall come figures of bishops, including the Three Hierarchs of the Orthodox Church, Basil the Great, Gregory the Theologian and John Chrysostom.

Sometimes other themes such as the Anastasis (Jesus descending into Hell), and the Virgin's Stake (an ancient symbol of her virginity) may be substituted.

There may also be paintings in the Proscomide, a niche designed to carry cult objects. The images often include Abraham's Sacrifice and Jesus in Compassion, seen in his tomb or accompanied by the Virgin Mary. In the diaconicon, where the priests keep their vestments, are paintings of deacons or a bishop.

The exterior paintings: east and side apses

With special reference to Suceviţa and other 16C Bucovinan churches

The Prayer of All Saints (*Cinul* in Romanian) covers the surfaces of all three apses. Usually, there are four or five registers but at Suceviţa there are seven. They show a hierarchical sequence of saints and holy people converging on God, Christ and the Virgin. The main axis of the Prayer, which contains the most important figures in the Prayer, occupies the central 'frames' on the eastern apse wall, forming a vertical line from top to bottom. Looking at the top of this central frame, you will usually see God the Father enthroned between two kneeling angels. On either side, forming an orderly queue around the top of the walls of the north and south apses, is a row of seraphim. Normally Jesus Emanuel (the Blessing Christ) comes below God, flanked by a register of angels on both sides. Under Jesus, in every case you will find an image of the Virgin sitting on her throne with Christ on her lap and two angels at her arms. Rushing towards her on either side come 54 prophets.

Below this, on the fourth register, you will find Jesus on his throne, between the Virgin and John the Baptist, accompanied by two angels. To the left and right of this composition are 70 apostles, led by Sts Peter and Paul and ending with some of the early deacons. The fifth register usually contains the symbol of the Eucharist, the Lamb of God; if not, it will show the Infant Jesus in a cup with two seraphim watching over him. Processing towards these figures are 61 bishops including the Three Hierarchs.

Row seven coincides with the sanctuary window; on either side of this come 70 martyrs, each of whom carries a small cross. The bottom row features either John the Baptist or the patron saint of the church in question. Heading towards them are 92 figures comprising female saints, anchorites, Stylites, hermits and confessors. At less splendid churches, the Prayer is usually compressed into four registers.

The south wall

The Tree of Jesse (*Arborele lui Ieseu*) usually occurs on the south wall. It is often one of the most attractive compositions in the painted churches because each scene is framed by a circular pattern of curling acanthus or, more rarely, vine fronds. It starts at the bottom with the figure of the Jesse, who is shown sleeping beside the stem of the tree. Above him come six ancient kings of Israel and Judah: David, Solomon, Rehoboam, Joshua, Manasseh and Joachim. They are shown in ascending chronological order so that the earliest kings are at the bottom. On either side of the stem, flanking the kings, are the 12 tribes of Israel.

Sometimes, as at Voroneţ and Sucevița, the Tree throws religious logic to the winds and encompasses ancient literary and philosophical personalities who were pagans. You can find Apollonius, Solon, Thucydides, Socrates, Plato, Aristotle, Sophocles, Philon, Plutarch, Sibyl, Homer and several others who are even more unlikely fellow travellers of Christianity, including Aristophanes. The official reason for their inclusion in the iconography is that their writings and beliefs helped to brace the Old Testament prophets. You usually encounter these figures on the lower registers.

Imnul Acatist (the Akathistos Hymn), means 'hymn sung while standing' and may celebrate any important saint, but this particular hymn celebrates the Virgin. The paintings comprise 24 scenes coinciding with the 24 strophes of the hymn. The original version was composed in the 6C by the Syrian monk, Romanos the Melodion. It was expanded in later centuries to incorporate the legendary Siege of Constantinople, during which the Virgin protected the city from the Persians and Avars in 626. Individual scenes include the Burning Bush, which is a symbol of virginity, and the Virgin seen as a town, symbolically protecting her inhabitants. Wider paintings along the bottom register show the Siege of Constantinople, interpreted more topically as the Turkish attack of 1453, and the Stake in Flames. This scene shows one of the most popular symbols of Mary's virginity. The 'stake' is represented as a pile of rocks crowned with a large bouquet of red flowers. Pictured in a medallion set against the flowers are the figures of the Virgin and Child. The Akathistos can also appear in the Naos.

West wall or exonarthex

The Last Judgment is shown on the west entrance or on the walls of the porch, deliberately 'in your face' as you enter the church. Usually it shows God the Father as the Ancient of Days at the very top where the Gates of Heaven are open. Around God on a white band are the signs of the zodiac. Two angels are preparing to wrap them up showing that time has run its course and the old universe is about to disappear. Below this register comes Christ enthroned within an almond-shaped mandorla, surrounded by angels and 12 Apostles. Beside him stand the Virgin and John the Baptist: the scene is a Deësis.

The next register down shows the *hetymasia* or Seat of Judgment, represented by a vacant throne with a Bible. A dove and a cross lie on its seat. To the left and right are the kneeling figures of Adam and Eve. They have returned from Hell to implore Christ to have mercy on their descendants. To the right of the throne is a group of good people including prophets, bishops and martyrs, led by St Paul. On the left hand side is a group of unbelievers, led by Moses. Here you can often see Jews, Turks, Tartars, Armenians, Arabs, Persians and sometimes Roman Catholics (as at Moldoviţa).

Below this, in the centre of the composition the disembodied Hand of God holds the balance. Souls are being weighed in little parcels while devils empty sacks of sins to weigh down the scales in their favour—they don't stand a chance! Processions of the chosen and the damned appear on either side: on the left, going up, on the right, going down. St Peter is waiting for the good people in the Garden of Eden, where the Virgin sits on her throne. To her side stands the 'good villain', the first soul received in Heaven, carrying a cross. The three patriarchs, Abraham, Isaac and Jacob, sit in the shade of the trees, holding the souls of good people to their breasts.

On the right-hand side of the next row down sinners are being flung into the Styx, the fiery river of Hell which flows from Christ's feet. The river grows wider as it runs closer to Hades. Valleys of fire are swallowing a multitude of the Damned, identifiable as Licinius, the Prophet Mahomed and various Roman emperors who persecuted Christians. Judas and Caiaphas are waiting at the mouth of Hades, and Satan is there too, with a cup in his hand, maniacally riding a two-headed monster. If you look at the version at Voroneț you will see many other intriguing details.

Secondary themes (north and west walls)

One of the less important themes often found on the outside walls is that of Genesis. It is usually painted on the top row of the north wall of the pronaos, as at Voroneț and Sucevița, or on the west wall, as at Arbore and Moldovița. Genesis is divided into three main sections: the Creation of Earth and Heaven, Adam, the Garden of Eden, Eve, and the Naming of the Living; the Temptation: Adam, Eve and the Serpent; the Gaining of Knowledge; Adam and Eve's surprise at finding themselves naked; the Expulsion from Heaven; the Punishment: Adam at work ploughing the land; the Birth of Abel; Cain and Abel; Eve spinning and rocking her children to sleep, and many others.

At Voroneț, Humor and Sucevița, you can find an apocryphal theme, called *Zapisul lui Adam* (Adam's Contract), which comes from Balkan folklore and the Bogumil Heresy. Adam is shown signing a document which recognises that the Earth and the dead people of the Earth belong to the Devil; he does this so that the Devil will leave him alone. The contract was torn up by Jesus when he descended into Hell, thereby liberating mankind from the Devil's grasp.

Another secondary theme is the Heavenly Customs Post (*Vămile Văzduhului*), which is related to a popular legend about the First Judgment. The story comes from the Life of St Basil the New and tells of an old woman who worked as St Basil's servant. When she lay dying, she was forced to stop on her way to Heaven and face the Devil 24 times. Each time the Devil tried to tempt her with a different sin. The painting shows a tower with 24 storeys, each one bearing the name of a sin and guarded by its own devil. At the top of the tower stands a simple wooden ladder, up which only those people who have successfully resisted the devils may climb to Heaven. You can find versions of this scene at Voroneț, Humor, Moldovița and Arbore. Otherwise you may find the Ladder of Virtue.

The Ladder of Virtue (*Scara Virtuților*) is an unusual theme in Orthodox iconography. In Romania the only known versions occur at Dobrovăț, Râșca, Sf Ilie in Suceava and at Sucevița, where the painting, though faded, is exceptionally fine. Apart from this, the only known fresco versions are on Mt Athos in the monasteries of the Great Lavra and Dochiariu. The theme is also connected with the First Judgment after death. At Sucevița, the ladder has 30 numbered steps corresponding to the number of years Christ lived on Earth and the 30 monastic virtues. On each rung the name of a sin or a virtue is inscribed. Fifteen monks are climbing the ladder, encouraged by 52 angels. At the top Christ is receiving the figure of St John Climacos into Paradise. A further nine monks are shown falling into the mouth of Hades. In Hades a monster with three huge green heads is waiting to devour them. The story of the Ladder of Virtue was first elaborated in the 7C by St John Climacos or Climax (known as Sf Ioan Sinaitul in Romanian), the abbot of St Catherine's Monastery on Mt Sinai. It was not until the 11C that his story became popular in illuminated manuscripts; the first known icon of the Ladder of Virtue was painted in the 12C.

Finally, you will be able to identify the Return of the Prodigal Son (*Întoarcerea Fiului Risipitor*), with its familiar scenes showing the son parting from his father, throwing his inheritance away, his contrite return and the celebratory feast at which his father ordered the 'fatted calf' to be killed. Apart from this there are usually scenes illustrating the lives of saints. Favourite saints are Nicholas, who has 24 scenes and appears on the south walls of Humor and Voroneț on the right-hand side; the Virgin with her parents (at Moldovița on the north wall, halfway along the left-hand side), John the New (at Voroneț, Humor and St George's in Suceava), and George (at Voroneț, to the left of the entrance into the church on the south wall, and at Arbore, on the left-hand side of the external niche).

Erminia and the Podlinnikii: *the instruction manuals*

In Romania, painting styles evolved according to local, conditions, personalities and needs, as well as to the current interpretation of certain themes which the bishops wanted to emphasise. Painters used pattern books which conformed to the classic models of Byzantine iconography, but they did not copy them slavishly. One of the best-known examples of this is in the Akathistos cycle, where painters updated the 626 Siege of Constantinople to 1453 to give it contemporary relevance to Moldavia's long-running struggle against Ottoman domination.

Painters could consult two pattern books, one originating from Mt Athos and the other from Russia. The Athonite manuals were known in Romanian as *Erminia* (Hermenaea in Greek) and date back to the 16C; the first printed versions appeared in Romania at the start of the 19C.

The *Erminia* told painters how they should treat scenes from the Old and New Testaments. These included the Life of Christ according to Matthew's Gospel, the Life and Acts of the Virgin, the most important saints and *Sinaxarul* (the martyrs associated with each month of the year). Details were precise and allowed little leeway for invention. Prophets, for example, were always shown barefoot, in long robes, with a coat thrown over their shoulder supported by one of their arms. Bishops must have beards, shoes and a coat ornamented with squares or crosses. As well as this, they must hold a cross and a holy book. At the lower end of the scale came Stylites. They were represented by figures who were partially hidden behind a schematic column. The lowest rung of all was reserved for martyrs, who had no beards but wore short tunics and tall boots. The manual also told the artists where each scene should go according to what kind of ceiling it had.

Apart from this, the *Erminia* gave advice on the preparation of materials and brushes, the proportions of the human body, and made suggestions as to how to paint tricky areas such as faces, hair and beards. They also contained a special prayer to the Virgin which the artists were urged to say before they began work, and prayers for the painters themselves. But the Erminia did not give any guidance on painting the outside walls. This is where Moldavian painters, set free from the rules handed down from Mt Athos, came into their own.

From Russia came *Podlinnikii*, meaning 'originals' or 'models'. These corresponded to the Greek *Erminia* but had their own specifically Russian characteristics as well. Both Greek and Russian models circulated in Romania, where they were adapted to suit local needs. Neither the Bulgarians nor the Serbs used *Podlinnikii*, even though they were ethnic Slavs.

Romanian bishops did not insist that painters should follow the manuals until the late 19C. Before that, they were used as a helpful guide which had the advantage of age and authenticity: the models and recipes they recommended had been handed down from the earliest known Byzantine sources. Using them ensured unity between churches in the entire Orthodox space. On the other hand, the *Erminia* encouraged the conservatism which is one of Byzantine art's main features. Their very existence worked against experimentation and emotional realism which developed in Roman Catholic art. Instead they laid emphasis on the expression of spirituality and symbolism.

Transylvania

The earliest Catholic churches in Transylvania were Romanesque in design. In the 13C French Cistercian monks invited into the province by the Hungarian monarchy brought Gothic architecture, and this became the most popular style for religious buildings until Renaissance and Baroque ideas began to filter through from the West in the 17C and 18C. Because of an edict which forbade Orthodox Romanians to build in stone, most early churches were of timber and have long since been destroyed. Their successors were the beautiful wood-built churches of northwest Transylvania and Maramureş. These extraordinary buildings show the receptivity and skill of local carpenters, who absorbed Gothic and Baroque elements while creating individual designs of their own. Constant refinements led eventually to masterpieces such as the 18C church at Şurdeşti.

Southern Transylvania is famous for its Saxon citadel churches, which were built to withstand attacks from Tartar and Turkish armies as well as from marauding Transylvanian nobles. More citadels than churches, with thick perimeter walls and impressive watchtowers, some of them were large enough to accommodate the entire parish and its livestock. Fine examples of these fortresses are to be found at Prejmer and Hărman near Braşov, and at Biertan near Sibiu, but there are scores to choose from, even though many are falling into disrepair.

Transylvania has a sprinkling of attractive Hungarian churches, too, most of which are now Reformed (Protestant). Some of these are charmingly, if simply, decorated: the most striking feature is often a wooden cassette ceiling, which is either painted or tiled, as in the magnificent church at Huedin and in the villages of Satu Mare and Sălaj counties in northwest Transylvania, which used to belong to great land-owning families such as the Bánffy and Wésselenyi. Here you can also see the stone pulpits and fonts of sculptor David Sípos, whose 'floral style' became famous throughout the principality in the late medieval and Renaissance periods.

Icons

Icons were introduced into the Romanian principalities by Greek painters from Constantinople. In Romania, icons fulfill the same purpose that they do elsewhere in the Orthodox world, providing portable shrines which can be worshipped at home, and as a means of direct communication with the divine. Romanian women often decorate individual icons with embroidered towels, but in churches they are also displayed on an icon screen (called iconostasis or *catepeteasma*) that separates the naos from the sanctuary. A strict hierarchical system governs which saints and church elders should go where, and icons showing the Virgin and Child and Christ are always placed beside the Royal Doors. Above this register, the most important figures are shown at the top, with lesser personages lower down.

Some icons were credited with miraculous powers. In the mid-17C, the Virgin of Nicula in Transylvania was seen to weep for 12 days without stopping.

Demand for replicas of the original outstripped supply, and the monks hit on a clever solution, using glass instead of wood and founding a cottage industry to mass-produce the images. This started a trend that inspired other regional schools. Needing much less preparation than wood, glass icons are painted in a much freer and more naive style, and at their best they are wonderfully cheerful and decorative. Today, they are regarded as a form of folk art, and painters such as Georgeta Iuga in Baia Mare and Nicolae Suciu (d. 1997) in Cincu, near Făgăraș, have generated an international market. While most scenes show popular saints or representations of the Last Judgment, contemporary painters create secular paintings as well. The National Art Museum and the Peasant Museum in Bucharest hold fine collections of Romanian icons, showing regional variations.

Moldavian churches

In the early 15C, stonemasons in Moldavia began to develop a new type of church. Tall and slender, it combined a Byzantine ground plan with steeply-pitched, shingle roofs which fanned out at both ends. Between the apse and naos roofs stood a tall tower with a conical cap. At the base of the cupolas two or more superimposed squares formed a star pattern similar to those seen in Islamic buildings. Gothic-style patterning around the door and window frames showed a Western influence, but these buildings were unique to the region and their design came to be known as the Moldavian style. It is possible that the masons modelled their churches on the highly individual timber churches which indigenous carpenters built in Carpathian villages. Later on, Italianate Baroque styles from Poland and Russia replaced the Moldavian style, and in the 19C neo-Classical art from Russia eventually submerged the Moldavian tradition.

Moldavian frescoes

Highlighted by the wonderful painted monasteries of Bucovina, Moldavian fresco painting evolved into an identifiable national school which reached its apogee in the 15C and 16C. Pressures from foreign aggressors as well as internecine rivalries put Romanian princes on their mettle, and with the imminent threat of a Muslim conquest, leaders such as Ștefan cel Mare and his son, Petru Rareș, saw themselves as embattled guardians of Christendom. Both rulers founded monasteries (Ștefan established one for each of his 38 victories) and encouraged a tremendous flowering of local skills. Several of the monasteries had schools for book illumination and embroidery, which produced wonderful work, but the most famous artistic activity was fresco painting.

Moldavian frescoes fall into two main phases. The first reached its peak by the late 15C, and is illustrated by the restrained and introspective scenes painted by monks in the churches at Pătrăuți, Sf Ilie, Bălinești and Popăuți. The second phase developed during the next century, when teams of lay painters retained by the royal courts travelled around Bucovina, covering the external surfaces of monastery walls with frescoes that illustrated important themes such as the Deësis (the heirarchy of Heaven), the Akathistos (the hymn to the Blessed Virgin Mary) and the Last Judgment. Woven into these glorious tapestry-like paintings was a pugnacious political message designed to give the peasants new heart in their fight against the Turks. At the time, the official church language was Slavonic, which few of the lay population could read; paintings were an accessible alternative and had the advantage that many people could 'read' them at once. The artists used standard pattern books, but they were extremely skilled, and their work is full of vigour and spirit; in some cases they even introduced new compositions. Compared to the 15C murals, these frescoes were more flamboyant and ornamental. Known everywhere as the painted monasteries, they include Voroneț, Humor, Moldovița and Sucevița.

Wallachia

Wallachia has at least one Greek-style cross-in-square church that may date back to the 12C, but after the fall of Constantinople, Bulgaria and Serbia provided the models for the country's religious buildings. Serbian art was especially influential. The expansionist policies of the Serb King Milutin in the early 14C encouraged a burst of church building and attracted Greek émigré craftsmen, who developed new styles of painting and architecture. Combining Italianate with classical Greek and Seljuk motifs, they created elegant, trefoil churches which, like Calenic, were concentrated in the Morava Valley. This style was unique to northern Serbia and it spread over the border into Wallachia, where Serbian Athonite monk Nicodim built superb monasteries at Cozia and Tismana.

Even though Orthodoxy was frowned on by the Hungarian authorities in Transylvania, Byzantine influences spilled across the Carpathians where they merged with Romanesque styles, as at the 13C and 14C churches of Densuș, Strei and Gurăsada and the (since destroyed) 13C monastery of Peri in Maramureș.

This colourful mix of cultural styles continued to influence Wallachian art and architecture over the following centuries. But in the late 17C and early 18C, enthusiastic patrons such as Șerban Cantacuzino (r. 1678–88) and his successor Constantin Brâncoveanu (r. 1688–1714) encouraged artists to develop their own national style. Like the Moldavian churches, this turned out to be a synthesis of eastern and western influences together with indigenous forms. Known as *stilul Brâncovenesc*, the Brâncovenesque style or Romanian Baroque, it spread right across the artistic spectrum, and was used in secular as well as religious buildings, and in decorative arts such as metalwork and embroidery.

Brâncovenesque architecture can be identified from its arcaded columns and in panels of densely-carved, vegetal scrollwork, which contrast strikingly with plain walls. Examples of the style include the Hurezu monastery in Oltenia and the reconstructed monastery at Sâmbătă near Făgăraș in southern Transylvania; you can see a secular form of Brâncovenesque architecture at the lovely princely houses of Mogoșoaia and Potlogi near Bucharest.

Castles, mansions and farmhouses

Medieval castles were built for strength rather than beauty, and of those that have survived, such as the ruined citadels at Suceava, Râșnov and Rupea, it is their ruggedness that strikes you before their elegance. One notable exception to this rule is the extraordinary fortress at Neamț, whose huge, rough-cast walls were constructed so skilfully that they appear to be absolutely straight.

In Transylvania, the castles of Hunedoara and Bran were built along sheer ridges according to medieval Hungarian custom, while the fine Renaissance fortress of Făgăraș resides comfortably in the middle of the town. Transylvanian-born Matei Corvin (r. 1458–90) introduced Renaissance culture into Hungarian court life when he married an Italian princess. One of his 17C successors, Gabriel Bethlen (r. 1613–29), built several palaces and town houses that absorbed Renaissance elements into Transylvania's existing architectural language.

Baroque art and architecture came late to Transylvania. Introduced by the Jesuits who proselytised for the Catholic Church and by the military who administered the province, it appeared in religious and secular architecture, notably in the colossal citadels constructed in Arad and Alba Iulia to designs by Sébastien Vauban (1633–1707).

By the late 18C, Habsburg officials such as Samuel Brukenthal preferred a less formal version of the Baroque. Brukenthal built a splendid mansion and gardens in the little town of Avrig before moving into his elegant Sibiu residence, and both houses used Baroque with vernacular elements. These include the softly sloping mansard roofs that were a feature of medieval Saxon towns. Governor Bánffy commissioned an equally magnificent palace in Cluj-Napoca, and landowning families such as the Wésselenyis (in Jibou), the Telekis and the Keménys commissioned fine Baroque houses which reflected their status and wealth.

With the raising of Hungarian national awareness in the late 19C, architects such as Ödön Lechner (1845–1914) and Károly Kós (1883–1977) designed a number of public buildings in Transylvania that reflected an attractive synthesis of Jugendstil, Oriental and indigenous influences.

Sturdy Saxon farmhouses dating back to the 18C can be seen in towns and villages all over Transylvania. With their colourful façades and strong, protective walls, they give the region a special character. Sadly, many of these attractive buildings are falling derelict since the German-speaking population decided to leave en masse.

Across the mountains in Wallachia, most of the medieval palaces are in ruins. They would have been decorated in a mixture of western and oriental styles. Minor nobles of the 17C and 18C often lived in *cule*, fortified houses which also combined Islamic and Western features.

During the 18C and early 19C, Phanariot Greeks introduced houses modelled on their homes in the western quarters of Istanbul. They were built with steeply overhanging eaves on four sides of an interior courtyard. With the Phanariots came *hans* (inexpensive inns and eating places) and Ottoman-style kiosks.

Modern Romanian architecture

By the 1830s urban architecture was beginning to respond to French influences, and neo-Classical and neo-Gothic styles became de rigueur along with the French language and idioms. While French architect André Lecomte du Nouÿ (1844–1914) restored and reshaped medieval churches across Moldavia and in Wallachia, Ion Mincu (1852–1912) developed a new national style which came to be known as neo-Romanian. Mincu's formula was much the same as that of the Brâncovenesque architects two centuries earlier, but he took more notice of Romania's heritage. Meanwhile Gustave Eiffel (1832–1923) designed a steel-framed hotel for the centre of Iaşi, and engineer Anghel Saligny (1854–1925) experimented with reinforced concrete.

The accession of a forward-looking, German-speaking king, Carol I, gave a fillip to building as well as the other arts. After his death in 1914, modern ideas continued to flood into the capital, borne on a wave of enthusiasm for a new national consciousness and the creation of Greater Romania. Avant-garde architects such as Marcel Iancu (1895–1984), Horea Creangă (1892–1943) and G.M. Cantacuzino (1899–1960) created functionalist designs, and in the 1930s Bucharest was turned into a garden city.

Vernacular buildings

Romania's folk architecture is a whole subject in itself. To get an idea of its variety and charm, visit one of the country's excellent ethnographic museums, such as the Village Museum in Bucharest, or those in Sibiu, Cluj-Napoca or Cârţisoara near Târgu Jiu. Different regions have their own particular characteristics, dictated by climate and the availability of building materials as much as by aesthetics and superstition.

The earliest known domestic houses to use timber were modelled on the classical *megaron*, a one- or two-roomed dwelling surrounded by a courtyard. In the Maramureş and many parts of Transylvania, Romanian and Székely villagers still mark the entrance to their farmsteads with formidable wooden gates which are pieces of sculpture in their own right. Sometimes these gates measure 4–5m high, and they are decorated in a variety of styles which coincide with regional as well as ethnic tastes. In the Maramureş these decorations include twisted rope motifs, while the Székely prefer gates with floral patterns, rosettes and slim, vertical palisades. In some cases the gates have a row of pigeon boxes along the top.

Folk architecture in Romania is pregnant with symbolism, and one of the most picturesque beliefs relates to the verandah. Called different names in different localities, the verandah signifies a halfway stage between the internal and external self, a spiritual as well as a physical transition from public to private life. More practically, the verandah allows you to survey the distance without being too visible yourself, an important consideration in Romania's troubled past. Made of wood which can be carved into herringbone patterns, barley-sugar twists or straight and slender rectangular poles, Romanian verandahs have been an inspiration to artists, most famously to the sculptor, Brâncuşi.

Building a new house still entails braving superstition: before the family can sleep in the building they have to kill a cockerel and push a cat out of a window, symbolically letting Satan out with the animal. In the Danube plains, some people built their houses literally half into the ground to make them less visible to potential enemies. On the door posts are fixed apotropeic figures, such as stylised horses' heads, to ward off evil spirits.

Traditional Romanian farmhouses are still often made of wood, with two or three separate buildings that house sleeping and guest rooms in one, a kitchen and bathroom or washroom in another, and larders and pantries in another, with animal and store barns as well. Builders used to pride themselves on never using metal nails to make joints, and the corner-joints of timber buildings can be constructed in many different ways; the carpenter's art has its own mythology in Romania.

Modern vernacular building has run wild; it is now fashionable (and warmer) to have a brick villa on two or even three storeys, with an arched balcony on one floor. Zinc often replaces tiles as roofing material because it is cheaper, and in Moldavia you can see zinc roofs fashioned into exuberantly Baroque forms, the guttering and roof ridges decorated with geometrical or floral motifs.

Roma who have grown wealthy often build amazing palaces: no expense is spared, and every inch of space is decorated. These mansions are usually protected by elaborate metal fences and railings; Gypsies have become used to being pariahs in their own country. Between Bucharest and Constanţa an enterprising fan of the American soap opera *Dallas* has built a replica of South Fork Ranch. In contrast, some villagers have retained their traditional building styles, using wood shingles not only for the roofs but also for the walls.

Balance wells are simple but attractively sculptural structures that consist of a tall, upright pole and a long crossbar balanced in its fork. They are still common in rural parts of Romania, and are known as *fântâni cu cumpână*.

Modern painting and sculpture

Romanian painting and sculpture changed radically with the introduction of Western—predominantly French—ideas. Reflecting this energetic cultural growth, fine-art academies and art museums were opened in the mid-19C, notably in Bucharest and Craiova. Carol I was an enthusiastic collector, whose acquisitions (mainly of Old Masters) formed the nucleus for Romania's National Museum of Art in Bucharest.

Theodore Aman (1831–91) was the father of modern Romanian painting. As the director of Bucharest's art academy and a keen nationalist he wielded great influence, encouraging painters such as Nicolae Grigorescu (1838–1907), Ion Andreescu (c 1851–92) and other young students to study abroad. Grigorescu is Romania's most famous 19C progressive painter; after teaching himself to paint icons which he sold by the roadside, he spent several months with the Barbizon group in the Forest of Fontainebleau. He is best known for pastoral scenes featuring ox-carts in panoramic landscapes, but he was capable of a deep emotional realism. Theodor Pallady (1871–1956) and Ştefan Luchian (1868–1916) belonged to the next generation; together with Iosif Iser (1881–1958), Nicolae Tonitza (1886–1940) and Ion Ţuculescu (1910–62), they introduced a fine brand of post-Impressionism and early abstraction, and their work is represented in many public collections around the country.

Modern Western-style sculpture began with Frederick Storck (1872–1942), but his work was superseded by the extraordinary vision of Constantin Brâncuşi (pronounced Brencoosh) (1876–1957), who revolutionised the art form not just in Romania but in the whole Western world. Brâncuşi's much-publicised walk from Bucharest to Paris was carried out in stages (he went by train whenever he could afford it), but the sculptor kept his base in France for the rest of his life, returning to Romania only eight times. The three pieces—**The Column of the Infinite**, **Table of Silence** and **Gate of the Kiss**—can still be seen in Târgu Jiu, near Brâncuşi's birthplace where they have recently been restored and their settings redesigned.

Bucharest's intellectual circles included architect, painter and former Dadaist Marcel Iancu (1895–1984), who returned from Zurich in 1920 to shock the public with an exhibition of his latest post-Cubist pictures. Avant-garde artists and writers joined the group which formed around Iancu's magazine, *Contimporanul*, and its sister publications, the Dadaist review, *75 HP*, and *Punct*. Surrealist Victor Brauner (1903–66) also cut his teeth in Bucharest before moving to Paris in 1930. Other progressive artists included Transylvanian-born Hans Mattis Teutsch (1884–1960), whose bold woodcuts reflected his interest in the work of the German Expressionists.

Art under communism

Artists who were active in the 1950s could rely on state patronage and privileges if they toed the party line; Ion Bitzan (1924–87) and Sorin Dumitrescu both benefitted from this situation while creating their own highly individual art in private.

Favourable conditions persisted from 1965–71 during Ceauşescu's Romanian Spring, when artists were positively encouraged to absorb Western influences as a flood of magazines, exhibitions and information poured into the country. Artists were allowed to travel, study and exhibit abroad. Painters Horea Bernea (b. 1938), Ana Lupaş, Wanda Mihuleac and Károly Elekes and sculptor Napoleon Tiron (b. 1953) built their early careers in this atmosphere. So did sculptor Paul Neagu (1938–2004), who left for London in 1967. Neagu has made a successful career in England, where his students have included Anish Kapoor.

But from 1972 Ceauşescu set Romania on an increasingly weird trajectory, forbidding contacts with the West and modelling himself on dictators Kim Il Sung and Muammar Gaddafi. Artists had to produce what they were told, and if they would not, they risked being ostracised by the all-important Artists' Union, the only organisation in a position to confer commissions. Despite this, some of the painters and sculptors who had experienced the 1960s thaw formed unofficial groups which gave each other mutual support. They were able to hold individual or group exhibitions or carry out 'actions' which had the advantage of being temporary and therefore less likely to attract the attention of informers. A number of radical artists expressed themselves using prohibited means such as performance, conceptual and land art; among these were the ethnic Hungarian artists Miklós Onucsán, László Újvárossy (b. 1950) and Anikó Gerendi from Oradea.

Transylvanian Hungarians could take advantage of their nationality by crossing the border into Hungary, where cultural life was far less circumscribed by authority. They could also stay in touch with the outside world through Hungarian and Yugoslav television broadcasts. The focus for the Romanian avant-garde remained in Transylvania during the 1970s and 1980s; in 1981 Imre Baász organised a show called 'Medium 81', which attracted artists across Transylvania with a shared interest in innovative media that were completely ignored by official channels. From his base in Târgu Mureş, Károly Elekes compiled *Fifth Season*, a volume containing poetry and reproductions of work by artists aged between 20 and 35. These Transylvanian initiatives were bolstered by a group of about 15 young graduate artists who gathered around Elekes and the philosopher Vilmos Ágoston. They took the collective name Mamu (short for Marosvásárhely Műhely—Marosvásárhely workshop—Marosvásárhely being the Magyar name for Târgu Mureş). From 1978–84 they experimented with progressive media, inspired by their contacts with artists in Hungary and by the writings of progressive critics. Polish initiatives such as the Krákow graphic biennales and avant-garde theatre also provided fresh air and encouragement to the stifled artists who laboured under Ceauşescu's heavy-handed regime.

By the mid-1980s, attacks on Hungarians and other minorities in Romania proved that the communist dictator was trying to wipe them out. Mamu split up, and several of its members moved to the artists' colony of Szentendre near Budapest. Of those who stayed behind, some continued to experiment. In Sf Gheorghe, a small town north of Braşov, Imre Baász (1941–91), Gusztáv Ütő and his wife, Pálma Szigeti, created a biennial of their own which was specifically designed to bring ethnic Hungarians and Romanians together. After the 1989 revolution, this group started a performance art festival called AnnArt, which takes place each July with an increasingly international list of participants.

Post-revolutionary artists in Romania found themselves bewildered by the lack of external support: when the barriers with the West came down they found apparent indifference and felt that the ground had been pulled from under their feet. During the early 1990s they went through a transitional period, trying to come to terms with their past, present and possible future. Their attempts have been helped by initiatives from the Soros Foundation, whose imaginative exhibitions in Bucharest and elsewhere have allowed innovative artists to reflect on their own and their country's situation. And with growing confidence artists such as multimedia artists Alexandru Patatics (b. 1963) from Timișoara, conceptualists Dan (b. 1961) and Lia Perjovschi (b. 1961), Teodor Graur (b. 1953) and Sándor (b. 1962) and József Bártha (b. 1960) have been able to exhibit abroad and find an international voice, as have Rudolf Kocsis (b. 1963), who works out of Arad and Sorin Vreme (b. 1963) from Timișoara.

Film

Romania's film industry is producing some interesting work. More details about it can be obtained from Fundația Dakino, which holds an annual film festival. The foundation can be contacted at Str. Aurel Vlaicu 147, Bloc 20, Scara 1, Etaj 7, Ap. 29, Sector 2, București, ☎/fax 01 211 0782. A number of films have looked back at the events surrounding the 1989 revolution and its consequences, among them *Requiem for Dominique*, produced in France, and *Vulpe Vânător* (*Hunting Fox*); other notable films include *Gadjo Dilo*, *Oglinda* (*The Mirror*) and *The Stone Wedding*.

Literature

In its spoken form, the Romanian language was identifiable by the 10C. Its Latin roots were recognised by Italian humanist Poggio Bracciolini in his *Disceptationes Conviviales* of 1451. The first known example of written Romanian is a letter from a resident of Câmpulung Muscel to a Saxon in Brașov in 1521, containing information about Ottoman troop movements.

Until the 17C the Orthodox church conducted its liturgies in Slavonic, and religious texts appeared in Slavonic or Greek. Confusingly, some liturgical texts were also transcribed into Romanian using Cyrillic rather than Latin characters; you can see examples of this phenomenon in the Greek-Catholic churches of Maramureș. Medieval and Renaissance princes commissioned histories to lend prestige to their reigns: these include the 1504 *Chronicle of the Days when Moldavia was Founded by the Will of God*. Written in Slavonic, the book is a mine of information about feudal Romania; some of its passages were dictated by Stephen the Great.

Romania's first printing shop was opened in Brașov by the Saxon scholar, Johannes Honterus (1498–1549), in 1535. Honterus was a keen follower of the Nuremburg humanists and promoted Lutheran teachings throughout Saxon Transylvania. Transylvania's ethnic Romanians gained confidence from the German initiative, and shortly afterwards, printed gospels with parallel texts in

Slavonic and Romanian appeared in Sibiu and Brașov. In 1559, St Nicholas's church in the Schei (Orthodox) district of Brașov opened a school in which lessons were taught in Romanian. From this period, philosophical, historical and religious texts appeared in all three principalities.

In mid-17C Moldavia, Prince Vasile Lupu (r. 1634–53) funded a printing press to encourage the diffusion of Orthodox texts both at home and abroad. Books were published in Greek, Slavonic and in some cases, Arabic. One of Lupu's successors, Dimitrie Cantemir (r. 1710–11), wrote the first novel in Romanian, *Istoria Ieroglifica* (*The History of the Hieroglyph*), and his *Descriptio Moldaviae* (*Description of Moldavia*, 1706–17) gives a fascinating insight into 18C Moldavian life. A Moldavian boyar, Ion Neculce, left another valuable source of information in his 1743 chronicle and in *O Seamă de Cuvinte* (*A Couple of Words*), which comprises 46 historical legends. Romanian replaced Old Slavonic in religious and official documents during the 17C.

Bishop Inochentie Micu Klein (1692–1768) wrote a brief history of his people in 1778; it was one of the first publications of the Scuola Ardeleana, the Transylvanian or Ardelean School, a group of intellectuals who wanted to educate their co-nationals and give them a sense of identity. Over the next 30 years the Scuola Ardeleana produced school textbooks, grammars, more histories and the heroic-comic poem of Gypsy folklore, *țiganiala*, by Ion Budai-Deleanu (1800). The School's work was continued by the more actively nationalist Asociațiunea Transilvană pentru Literatura Română și Culturală Poporului Român, (Transylvanian Society for Romanian Literature and Popular Culture, or ASTRA), founded in Sibiu in 1861.

Folk literature

Romania's folk literature evolved through a powerful oral tradition. Narrative poems with fantastic, heroic or moralistic themes were passed from generation to generation. In some areas the practice survived until the late 19C and early 20C. Among these tales were *Cântecele Pețirii*, 'the courting songs', which include apocryphal subjects such as *The Song of the Sun's Wedding*, *Chicory*, *The Chief Magistrate and the Swans*, *St Vineri* (*St Friday*) and the most famous of all Romania's folk ballads, *Miorița* (*The Ewe Lamb*).

Creating a national identity

In 1852, playwright and novelist Vasile Alecsandri (1821–90) published a booklet which contained 17 'popular poems' that he claimed to have transcribed from authentic, indigenous sources. They included a version of *Miorița*, a tale of self-sacrifice and devotion which was taken as an allegory for the fate of Romanians throughout history.

While Romania's *nouveau chic* steeped themselves in French novels, Romania's foremost 19C Romantic poet, Mihai Eminescu (1850–89), believed the influx of Western ideas to be an abomination. Eminescu, whose real name was the Slavonic 'Eminovici', became passionately involved in the nationalist cause. As part of his campaign he travelled around Romania collecting local words and phrases which he compiled into a new, specifically Romanian literary language.

Eminescu's contemporary, Ion Creangă (1839–89), shared a love of indigenous Romanian culture. Creangă specialised in rewriting folk stories with a lively and humorous twist. His *Tales of My Childhood* has become a classic and is still taught in Romanian schools. Playwright Ion Luca Caragiale (1852–1912) was another outstanding 19C writer. Caragiale made his name by satirising the pretensions of urban society.

Experimental literature in the early 20C

Innovations in early 20C Romanian writing were influenced by French Symbolist poetry and later by Constructivism and Italian Futurism. Ion Minulescu, Adrian Maniu, Ion Vinea, and two of the co-founders of Zurich Dada, Tristan Tzara (1896–1963) and Marcel Iancu (1895–1984), all contributed to the rich and varied body of experimental work which was created in Bucharest in the years 1900–32.

Another inspirational figure was Urmuz (1883–1923), a savagely destructive proto-Surrealist who began publishing his 'bizarre pages' in 1907. Urmuz (whose real name was D. Demetrescu-Buzău) dedicated his entire life to art. When he decided he had no more to say he killed himself. Urmuz was idolised by generations of anarchic Romanian writers, especially the Romanian Surrealist group, which formed its own fully-fledged programme in 1940.

During the 1920s, the best new writing appeared in *Contimporanul*, founded by Vinea and Iancu (1922–32), *75 HP*, a Dadaist review which had only one issue (1924), and *Punct*, published 1924–25. In 1924, Vinea edited an 'Activist Manifesto to Youth' which rejected the art and literature of the past and heralded the 'great industrial activist phase'.

Early 20C mainstream literature

Liviu Rebreanu (1885–1944) created the modern Romanian novel. The son of a village schoolteacher, he was imprisoned in Hungary for criticising the Magyar authorities. He made his name with the novel *Ion* (*John*, 1920) which focussed on the problems of land tenure. Rebreanu was a realist and researched his subjects with meticulous care. Two other novels, *Pădurea Spânzuraților* (*The Forest of the Hanged*, 1922), and *Răscoala* (*The Uprising*, 1932) examine the plight of ethnic minorities in the last days of the Habsburg Empire. Nostalgia for Romania's dying folk culture was expressed movingly by Marthe Bibescu (c 1887–1973) in *Izvor: Land of Willows* (1923).

Mihail Sadoveanu (1880–1961) was another leading novelist who eulogised traditional village life; his best known books include *Baltagul* (*The Hatchet*) and *Creanga de Aur* (*The Golden Bough*). Sadoveanu collaborated with the communist regime. Tudor Arghezi (1880–1967) studied theology before becoming a writer whose work has been compared to that of Lorca. He wrote poetry and prose.

Nicolae Iorga, Constantin Noica and Nae Ionescu (1890–1940)were the leading philosophers and historians of the day. Iorga (1871–1940) was a staunch nationalist. He published 1000 books and 12,000 articles. Among them were his 11-volume *Istoria Românilor* (*History of Romania*, 1936–39) and a history of the Ottoman Empire, published in German. Iorga was a politician as well as a writer, and he was Prime Minister from 1931–32. His downfall came from supporting Carol II's royal dictatorship and helping to bring Corneliu Codreanu to trial. In a brutal retaliation, he was murdered by members of the Iron Guard.

Literature under communism

In 1948, many outstanding writers and academics were banished from academic life. These included essayist and philosopher, Lucian Blaga (1895–1961), Gheorghe I. Brătianu (1898–1953), historians Constantin C. Giurescu (1901–77), P. P. Panaitescu, and Victor Papacostea (1900–62). Some intellectuals were sent to prisons such as the notorious Sighet jail, where they died of starvation. Others were condemned to work on the Danube–Black Sea canal project. Simultaneously, new writers emerged to promote the interests of communism. Among them were Petre Dumitriu (b. 1924), who defected to the West in 1960 at the height of his success. Dumitriu described his collaboration with communism as a 'pact with Mephisto'. In France, he wrote several polemical novels describing the nightmare of life under Romania's totalitarian regime. They included *Doomsday Encounter* and *Incognito* (1962).

During the first few years of Ceauşescu's regime, the cultural climate thawed and some writers were able to create valuable work. But this window of opportunity snapped shut in 1971; writers who were brave enough to defy Ceauşescu's dictatorship included the Bucovinian novelist, Paul Goma (b. 1935), satirist Mircea Dinescu (b. 1950) and essayist Andrei Pleşu. Pleşu became Foreign Minister in the coalition government elected in 1996. Marin Sorescu (1936–1996) overcame communist oppression with irony. His first volume of poetry was *Singur Printre Poeţi* (*Alone Amongst Poets*, 1964); this was followed by plays and more verse, and in 1983 a volume, *Selected Poems*, was published in English by Bloodaxe Books, (PO Box 1SN, Newcastle-upon-Tyne NE99 1SN, ☎ 01434 240500, fax 240505; e-mail editor@bloodaxebooks.demon.co.uk). Two further books by Sorescu, *The Biggest Egg in the World* was published by Bloodaxe in 1987, and *The Crossing* in 1999. Hailed as 'the funniest poet writing behind the Iron Curtain' and 'Romania's comic genius', His work is still enormously popular and new English translations of his work are in preparation. Other writers who maintained their integrity under communism included Mircea Dinescu, author of *Exile on a Peppercorn*, and Maria Banuş, who made her stand in the book *Demon in Brackets*.

The myth of the pure Romanian peasant was born in the 19C, but became debased during Ceauşescu's rule. In 1975, the Central Committee's Department of Propaganda devised a biennial festival called Cânterea al României (Song to Romania). Cânterea was meant to create 'the widest framework for the intensification of cultural and educational activities, for the participation of the mass of the people in the development of the homeland's new spiritual assets'. The festival re-used the title of a prose poem by Alecu Russo (1819–59), emphasising the links between the present leadership and the revolutionary spirit of 1848. Its key features were patriotism and hero worship, and it comprised mass displays on political, scientific and cultural themes by people from all ages and areas of Romanian society. Participation was more or less compulsory if you wanted to keep your job.

Folklore, as well as folk music and dance, played a prominent role (Ceauşescu had made an impassioned speech praising the folk heritage of the Maramureş in 1974), but it was stereotyped to conform to Party needs. In 1985, over 3,500,000 people took part in Cânterea al României, which had become an encomium dedicated to one spectator, 'the most beloved son of the people', Ceauşescu himself. Consequently, although the rural idyll still holds strong (it is, after all, an important part of the tourist economy), many Romanians regard the whole 'folk' phenomenon with mistrust. That said, writers and artists could get good, independent work past the censors, many of whom were writers themselves and sympathetic to the cause. But although references to the oligarchy had to be veiled, plays which poured satirical scorn on Romania's rulers were extremely popular. In a different area, Cânterea helped Romania's traditional folk song and dance groups to survive: an example is the little troupe of school children from Sârbi and Budeşti, neighbouring villages in Maramureş. Thanks to the exposure it gained under Cânterea the group now has an international reputation which allows the children the experience of travelling abroad, something that is impossible for most of their schoolmates.

Writers in exile

The Surrealist vein was taken up by Eugene Ionesco (1909–94), who invented the Theatre of the Absurd. Born in Slatina to a Romanian father and a French mother, Ionesco spent his childhood in France but returned to Romania during the 1920s. He made his literary debut in 1927, and in 1934 his book *Nu* (*No*) won a Royal Academy prize. Ionesco was an active member of Bucharest's anarchic, bohemian circles, arguing through the night with contemporaries Emil Cioran and Mircea Eliade at Bucharest's famous Capşa Restaurant. In 1941, Ionesco left Romania for good and settled in France, where he became a writer of 'anti-plays'. His first was *La Cantatrice Chauve* (*The Bald Prima Donna*, 1950), which satirises bourgeois society, inspired by the emptiness and cliché-ridden conversations he found in an English phrase book. Its success encouraged him to continue; other well-known plays are *The Chairs*, *The Lesson* and *Rhinoceros*, all of which fuse farce and tragedy with an atmosphere of nightmarish unreality. They can also be extremely moving. His plays were banned in Romania under the communists, and after his death Ionesco's daughter refused to allow them to be produced there because of the country's poor human rights record.

Philosopher and historian Mircea Eliade (1907–86), achieved world renown for his work on the history of religions. He became a guru in his own right. At first an enthusiastic supporter of Corneliu Codreanu, he realised how ugly the League was becoming and was arrested in 1938. He then became a diplomat. Eliade moved to France after the Second World War, and later took a teaching job at the University of Chicago. In his 20s he was fascinated by Oriental spiritualism and studied yogic philosophies in India. He wrote prolifically; the three-volume *The History of Religious Ideas* is a synthesis of his most important writings.

A conviction that the world is absurd drove Emil Cioran (1911–95) to evolve a bleak anti-philosophy that resulted in bright and breezy titles such as *A Short Account of Decomposition*, *Syllogisms of Bitterness* and *The Inconvenience of Having Been Born*. Cioran himself was born in the village of Răşinari near Sibiu in the southern Carpathian foothills, where his father was an Orthodox priest. Like Eliade and many other young intellectuals of his generation, Cioran supported the anti-Semitic League of the Archangel Michael, and after studying in Berlin he gave way to a xenophobia of which he was later extremely ashamed. His first book, *Pe Culmile Disperării* (*On the Summits of Despair*), won him an Academy prize in the same year as Ionesco's *Nu*. In the late 1930s Cioran moved to Paris, where he lived for the rest of his life. His work is written with impeccable style and is eminently readable.

Because of their location close to Romania's borders with former Yugoslavia and Hungary, western cities such as Timişoara and Arad were more open to independent writers; Timişoara had a tradition as a centre of diverse, multi-cultural opinion, and ethnic German, Hungarian, Romanian and Serb writers could find publishers here. The Timişoara-based magazine, *Orizont*, was founded in 1948 and is now the second largest literary review in Romania, with a circulation of around 5000.

Contemporary writers

Since 1989, Romanian publishers have been keener to promote the work of foreign writers in translation rather than supporting their own. This leaves the field open for magazines such as *România Literără* and *Orizont*, both of which encourage contributions from new writers. The cultural and political weekly *22* has a younger and sharper image, publishing the likes of Lucian Boia (b. 1944) and H-R. Patapievici. These two historians have helped to separate fact from fiction in Romania's past. The Soros Foundation also encourages Romanian writing.

Up-and-coming poets, such as Romulus Bucur (b. 1956) from Arad and Moldovan Iulian Fruntaşu, have also been published in English. Bucur's *Love and Courage* (1995) won him widespread recognition in Romania, and his *Ditties* (1998) is available as a pamphlet from Slow Dancer Press (☎ 020 4735 5964), as is Fruntaşu's *God's Ear*. To date, Forest Books (☎ 020 8529 8470; fax 524 7890; e-mail brenda@forest.demon.co.uk) is the largest English publisher of Romanian writers. Other sources of Romanian literature in England are Peter Jay's Anvil Press (☎ 020 8469 3033; e-amil anvil@cix.compulink.co.uk).

Romania also has a tradition of excellent theatre; look out for productions by the National Theatre of Craiova and by the Hungarian National Theatre in Cluj-Napoca. Producers Andrei Şerban (who lives in the USA) and Alexandru Darie are both well-known in their field, as are the Paris-based playwright Matei Visniec, who is strongly influenced by Ionesco, and the film and theatre director Livu Ciulei. Ciulei staged one of the finest productions of Enescu's *Oedip* ever performed and he now often works in the USA. His films include *Văluvile Dunării* (*The Danube Waves*, 1963) and an adaptation of Rebreanu's *Pădurea Spînzuraţilor* (*The Forest of the Hanged*, 1965).

Music and dance

With special thanks to Sorin Ciutacu, Robert Garfias, Sanda Marta, Jöri Murk, Costel Puscoiu, John Nandriş and Brad White.

'Music and laughter are the cure for all ills.' Romanian proverb.

Yehudi Menuhin said that Romania was the most naturally musical nation in the world. From any other source, you might dismiss such praise as hyperbole, but Lord Menuhin was taught to play the violin by George Enescu and knew what he was talking about.

It isn't hard to find evidence for Romania's musical affinities. Listen to the pan-flute riffs of the Gypsy band, Taraf de Haidouks, and you will hear free-flowing, quicksilver notes that imitate birdsong, unmistakeable if you play one while listening to the other. Or visit a monastery when the *toaca* is beaten to call the brothers or sisters to prayer. A *toacă* is a plank of wood about 4m long suspended between two uprights and played with a pair of wooden hammers. During the Middle Ages, it was used as a means of calling the population to war. It could hardly be a simpler instrument, but the best practitioners are real artists who create music with a dynamic rhythm and shape. Stay at the monastery while the service gets under way, and feel the hairs on your skin prickle when the plainsong starts.

If you approach a sheepfold unannounced, you will be spotted from far off and a voice will sing out, '*Pe cine căutați?*' ('Who are you looking for?'). Even Romanian dogs are musical: according to 19C novelist Ion Creangă, they say 'humhum'.

The roots of Romanian music can be traced back to the 7C BC, when Greeks from Miletos settled on the Black Sea coast and began trading with indigenous Thracians. Musical instruments appear in Dacian art and archaeologists have discovered that Dacian ceremonies often had a musical accompaniment. Dacian music was both monodic (for a single voice or instrument) and polyphonic (harmonic lines for many voices or instruments). The epic poems such as *Miorița* which have been handed down orally through the generations may stem from stories which Thracian shepherds told each other on the long transhumance, and the soulful melodies which shepherds traditionally play on the *caval* (flute) are probably just as old. When Dacia was being converted to Christianity, Byzantine chants percolated into the country from Constantinople.

Music with a specifically Romanian identity began to develop in the Middle Ages. Several medieval codices mention a round dance called the 'Wallachian Dance', and in 1490, during the reign of Stephen the Great, the Putna monastery opened a school for liturgical music which ran for nearly a century. The Putna school was the most influential of its kind in the Romanian principalities, but there were others such as the Transylvanian Counterpoint school, which had branches in Bistrița, Brașov, Sibiu and Sighișoara.

In the 16C and 17C, monasteries and royal courts at Bucharest, Alba Iulia, Suceava and Iași encouraged the study of Renaissance and Baroque music. Individuals such as 17C composer Ioan Căianu, Dimitrie Cantemir (1673–1723) and Anton Pann also helped to develop Romanian music during this period. Ioan Căianu collected folk tunes, and his short compositions have survived in a few beautiful fragments which have been fleshed out by Doru Popovici (Căianu's scores are kept at the Teleki Library in Târgu Mureș); Dimitrie Cantemir was a connoisseur of folk and ceremonial music, and at his little house in Râmnicu Vâlcea, Anton Pann created a huge archive of musical folklore as well as writing music for religious and secular audiences.

In periods of prosperity, Western-style concert ensembles and musical troupes visited Transylvania and the Banat, while in Bucharest, Oradea, and Timișoara *cappella* and *collegium musicum* groups were formed. Although cultural influences travelled from east to west as well as vice versa, Western and Central European music had its greatest impact in Habsburg-controlled Transylvania and the Banat. Pieces by Mozart were heard in Timișoara only five years after their first performances in Vienna. Superb Baroque music was written by ethnic Hungarian and Saxon composers during the 17C; most of their scores are kept in the Batthanyeum Library in Alba Iulia.

Samuel Brukenthal, Habsburg Governor of Transylvania in the late 18C, thought music was an essential element of the cultivated mind. With the encouragement of his wife, Sofia, Brukenthal started a programme of twice-weekly chamber concerts which took place in the elegant white-and-gilt drawing room of his Sibiu palace. The Brukenthals' guests came by invitation only and comprised the Transylvanian élite such as Princess Cantacuzino and Count Ceri. Fired by lofty intellectual ideals and surrounded by the highest possible contemporary taste, with the muses looking down benignly on their gatherings from gilded frames, the Brukenthals' circle aspired to nothing less than Parnassus. They listened to Bach, Haydn, Joseph Kuhnau and Mozart. Brukenthal was in tune with Enlightenment ideals, but in Transylvania he was ahead of his time and his efforts to raise the level of culture affected only the privileged few. However, his passionate belief in the civilising effect of classical music eventually bore fruit and chamber concerts became fashionable across Transylvania.

Romania's birth as a nation brought about a sea change in all the arts. Westernisation was seen as the key to freedom and progress, not only in politics and economics but in culture as well. The Ottoman Empire was dying a lingering death that paralysed its territorial possessions, and ambitious Orthodox Romanians no longer set their sights on Istanbul (Constantinople) as their privileged forebears had done. Those who were rich enough travelled to Paris, Berlin and Rome, or to Kiev and St Petersburg, which were also more Western in outlook than Turkey. Many young and radical Romanians who took part in the nationalist rebellions fled to the West to escape imprisonment, and a large number waited out their exile in France.

After unification and the subsequent accession of a German prince, Western cultural influences became even more prevalent. However, even when they trained abroad, the most original composers of the later 19C identified closely with Romanian folk music. In 1847, on the eve of the revolutions that helped to change the map of Europe, Franz Liszt toured Moldavia stirring cultural exchanges. Johannes Brahms travelled around western Transylvania and the Banat in the late 1860s, with his favourite violinist, Johann Joachim in tow. German composer Alexander Flechtenmacher wrote the national anthem, *Hora Unirii* (National Ring Dance), in 1848. Romanian musicians were in touch with the nationalistic ideals that swept across Europe and they made their own contribution to the revolutionary music of the day.

In 1833 a Philharmonic Society was founded in Bucharest. This was quickly followed in Iași with a new School of Music and Drama. Besides departments for theatre, literature and instrumental music, these academies offered singing and ballet classes. In 1836, pupils of the Bucharest Philharmonic Society performed Rossini's *Semiramis*; this production was followed a few years later by the staging of Bellini's *Norma* in Iași. Both schools aimed to create a national literature and dramaturgy, and although they were short-lived, other institutions took their place. The Iași Conservatoire opened in 1860, and its Bucharest rival began taking students soon afterwards. A new Romanian Philharmonic Society was founded in 1868. Timișoara's privately-funded Philharmonic Society was established in 1871 and became a state enterprise in 1947. In 1888 the philanthropist Constantin Exarcu started a public subscription ('Give a leu for the Atheneum') so that he could build a concert hall in the centre of Bucharest. The Atheneum is a magnificent building with a Greek-style portico, a circular auditorium and an interior that is covered with murals and gilt. Recently restored, it is still the capital's smartest concert hall.

George Enescu

Enescu (1881–1955) is generally considered to be Romania's greatest 20C musician. He was phenomenally talented, combining the gifts of virtuoso violinist, cellist and pianist with those of conductor, composer and teacher. Enescu was born in Liveni, a village near Dorohoi in northeast Romania, the last and only surviving child of Costache and Maria Enescu. When he was three Enescu's parents moved to nearby Cracalia, where the young George watched performances of country dancing at the local manor. He put his first violin together from roofing shingles and began composing music in 1886. Folk tunes figured in his earliest work. One of his first compositions was an arrangement of the Gypsy melody, *Am un Leu* (*I have a leu*), a theme which he used later in *Romanian Rhapsody 1*. By this time composer Eduard Caudella (1842–1924) recognised his prodigious talents and advised Enescu's parents to take him to Vienna. In the autumn of 1888, the Enescu family duly set out for the Habsburg capital and seven-year old George enrolled at the Vienna Conservatoire.

Enescu graduated from the Conservatoire in 1893 and went to Paris the following year. His tutors at the Conservatoire were Jules Massenet and Gabriel Fauré, and his fellow students included Maurice Ravel and Jean Roger-Ducasse. In 1898 Enescu performed *Poema Română* (*Romanian Poem*) for the first time. Folk tunes also made their presence felt in his unfinished *Romanian Suite in G minor* and most famously in the *Romanian Rhapsodies no. 1 in A major* and *no. 2 in D major*, which Enescu completed in 1901. The folk connection continued when he collaborated with Queen Elizabeth of Romania, alias poetess Carmen Sylva, by setting several of her romantic verses to music. The queen took Enescu under her wing and he made frequent visits to the royal palace at Sinaia. He also wrote arrangements for *doine*, the archetypal Romanian folksongs.

Enescu made his début as a conductor in 1923 and was appointed to the New York Philharmonic in 1937 and 1938. As a composer he was immensely prolific, creating over 300 works during his student years alone. Sadly, many of his pieces have been lost because he never felt the need to write them down. As a result he published relatively little. In 1939 Enescu married Princess Maria Cantacuzino, who brought him the magnificent Cantacuzino Palace on Bucharest's Calea Victoriei. But these surroundings were too grand for Enescu and he preferred to live and work in a couple of small rooms in the gardens. These have been turned into a memorial museum; the palace has become the headquarters of Romania's Musicians Union.

Yehudi Menuhin had his first violin lessons with Enescu while visiting Paris in 1927. He studied under Enescu again the following year, this time in the beautiful Carpathian resort of Sinaia. At the end of 1931 the two musicians played Bach's *Double Concerto* (Menuhin and Enescu on violin) and was the first of many collaborations between them. Enescu was also a friend of Erik Satie, and he met the virtuoso pianist Dinu Lipatti in 1935. In 1931 Enescu finished his first and only tragic opera, *Oedip* (*Oedipus*). The opera received its French-language premiere in Paris five years later; the first performance of *Oedip* in Romanian took place in 1958.

A handful of 19C composers stand out. One of these is Ciprian Porumbescu (1853–83), who was born at Șibot in north Moldavia. By far the most idealistic of all Romania's 19C composers, Porumbescu lived according to his Romantic beliefs. He modelled his operetta *Crai Nou* (*The New Moon*) and his *Balada for Violin and Piano* on tunes he had heard being played by village bands. *Crai Nou* was produced for the first time in 1882, but Porumbescu's promising career was short-lived. An unhappy love affair drove him to write his famous *Ballad of Ciprian*, but he was arrested soon afterwards on suspicion of being an anarchist and died after spending several years in jail. Gavriil Musicescu and Eusebiu Mandicevski were among the other excellent Moldavian musicians from the same period.

Enescu and Porumbescu were not the only Romanian composers to draw on folk music. Almost all Romania's 19C Classical composers found inspiration from this source, and many others have done since then.

Béla Bartók (1881–1945) was born in Sânnicolau Mare (Nagyszentmiklós in Hungarian and Grosssanktnikolaus in German) to the west of Arad and close to Romania's present-day western border with Hungary and Serbia. Bartók's interest in the indigenous music of eastern European led to the establishment of one of the world's most important folk music archives in Kecskemét, Hungary, and his importance in the development of modern Western music needs no introduction here.

Other famous Romanian musicians from the 20C include composer and conductor Constantin Silvestri (1913–69). Silvestri was principal conductor of the Bucharest Philharmonic before defecting to the West. He died in London aged 55 at the peak of his career. Ionel or Jonel Perlea (1900–70) became Intendant of the Bucharest Opera between 1929–30 and 1934–36. After the Second World War, Perlea conducted orchestras in Italy and then at the New York Metropolitan Opera, where he made a brilliant début in 1949 with *Tristan und Isolde*.

German conductor Bruno Walter (1876–1962) started his career at Timișoara in 1898, and the protean Herbert von Karajan (1908–89) was the son of an Aromanian whose family (the Caraion) moved to Vienna during the 17C. No discussion of 20C conductors would be complete without Sergiu Celibidache (1912–96). Born in Roman, northern Moldavia, Celibidache studied piano in Iași and Bucharest and later spent eight years at the Music Hochschule in Berlin. He was conductor of the Berlin Philharmonic between 1945 and 1952, and went on to conduct orchestras in Stockholm, Stuttgart and Munich, at La Scala in Milan and La Fenice in Venice. A popular figure with audiences and students alike, he taught in Germany, France, Italy and the USA and was awarded many honours, including the prestigious Maximilian Order of Germany. Celibidache was a great interpreter of post-Romantic music, his particular favourites being the work of Anton Bruckner and French Impressionist composers such as Debussy and Ravel. George Costin (b. 1955) from Baia Mare and Camil Marinescu (b. 1964) from Bucharest are among the younger generation of Romanian conductors who have made names on the international circuit.

20C virtuosi

Dinu Lipatti (1917–50) came from a wealthy musical family. He was so gifted that he made his public début as composer and pianist at the age of four. Lipatti won second prize at the Vienna Piano Competition in 1934 and then moved to Paris, where his mentors included Alfred Cortot and Nadia Boulanger. From that period his fame as a pianist spread rapidly, and Lipatti performed in Germany and Italy as well as in Paris. Poulenc was a great admirer of his, saying that Lipatti possessed a 'divine spirituality'. Lipatti's playing combined charm and pathos with great intellectual power. His brilliant career came to an untimely end after he contracted leukaemia, and he died when he was only 33.

Pianist Radu Lupu was born in 1945. He studied with Florica Musicescu (who also taught Lipatti) and later spent seven years at the Moscow Conservatoire, where his most famous tutor was Heinrich Neuhaus, who had trained the Russian piano players Richter and Gilels. Radu Lupu gave his first public recital at the age of 12 with a programme consisting entirely of his own compositions. In 1966 he won the Van Cliburn Competition and he came first at the Leeds Piano Competition in 1969. Hailed as an artist who single-handedly turned the tide of modern piano playing, he has made some excellent recordings. Among his finest recordings are Beethoven's *Emperor Concerto* and the Schubert *Sonatas*.

Romanian opera

The first Romanian opera was performd in 1772, when Livio Cinti's 'operists' travelled through Bucharest on their way to Sibiu. Soon afterwards Italian, French and German opera companies toured Romania, and these were joined in the early 19C by others from Russia, the Balkans and the Near East. These companies staged operas by Sacchini, Paisiello, Cimarosa, Salieri, Grétry, Dittersdorf and Mozart (*Die Entführung aus dem Serail*). The main operatic centres at this time were Sibiu, Cluj, Oradea, Timişoara, Arad, Iaşi and Bucharest.

In the first half of the 19C, one of the most active troupes was that of Johann Gerger from Braşov. In 1818, the Cişmeaua Roşie theatre mounted his productions of *Idomeneo*, *Die Zauberflöte*, *L'italiana in Algeri* and *La Cenerentola*. Angelica Catalani's Italian troupe came to Bucharest and Braşov in 1821, providing the impetus which established the Italian opera in Bucharest. This was the first permanent lyric theatre in Romania, opening in 1843. A number of Romanian ensembles also presented short operatic seasons in Bucharest, Timişoara, Cluj, Braşov, Sibiu and Iaşi.

George Stephănescu (1843–1925) was the driving force behind the operatic movement in Bucharest. Stephănescu graduated from the Bucharest and Paris Academies of Music, and in 1877 was appointed conductor of the National Theatre Orchestra. While training singers at the Academy of Music he raised the profile of the National Theatre, extending its repertoire from vaudeville and musical comedy to opera. Stephănescu's own operas included *Petra*, composed in 1902. His contemporaries at the Bucharest Opera were Mauriciu Cohen-Linaru (*Mazeppa* and *Insula florilor*) and Eduard Caudella (*Olteanca*, 1880 and *Petru Rareş*, 1900)

In 1902, the opera section of Bucharest's National Theatre was forced to close through lack of funds. Enthusiastic singers kept opera alive by forming independent societies and they staged regular performances, even when the capital moved to Iaşi during the First World War. In 1921 the first state-run Romanian Opera came into being. It opened with performances of *Löhengrin* conducted by George Enescu.

After the Second World War, eight new opera and ballet theatres were created in Romania, and in 1953 the Bucharest Opera moved into a larger theatre with a thousand seats. More than 150 premieres have been staged here, and every year the opera's repertory has grown. It has an excellent company, and its productions are well worth seeing.

The Romanian Opera in Cluj-Napoca opened in 1919. It was the brainchild of tenor Constantin Pavel, Italian conductor Egisto Tango, composer Tiberiu Brediceanu and the brilliant Wagnerian baritone Dimitrie Popovici-Bayreuth.

Operas by Romanian composers began to be performed at the end of the 18C. They included the comic German-language pieces, *Das Freudenfest zu Tunis* (first performed in 1795), *Die Fürstengrille* (1796) and *Die Einquartierung* (1796) which were performed in Sibiu and Brașov. The earliest operas by a Transylvanian composer, Anton Hubaček, were staged in Sibiu (1795) and Brașov (1796). Hungarian-language operettas by Ioan Pátko and Josef Chudi were sung in Cluj. The performances were often embellished with ballets and intermezzos involving Romanian folk dance.

Romanian opera made great leaps forward in the period between Romanian Independence and the Second World War. Performances were dominated by works such as Dimitrie Cuclin's *Traian and Dochia* (1921) and *Agamemnon* (1922), Sabin Drăgoi's *Năpasta* (*The Calamity*, 1927), Constantin Nottara's *La drumul mare* (*On the Highway*, 1932), Alexandru Zirra's *Alexandru Lăpușneanu* (composed 1930–44), *O noapte furtunoașă* (*A Stormy Night*, 1934) by Paul Constantinescu (1909–63), Nicolae Bretan's *Horia* (1937), and most strikingly, Enescu's *Oedip* (first performed in 1936). In the finest pieces, composers drew on ancient and modern Romanian melodies, combining these with modern harmony and orchestration. In *Oedip* Enescu used the recitation style of traditional ballads.

Romania has produced many fine opera singers from the 19C onwards. Elena Teodorini (née de Mortun, 1857–1926) became one of the finest mezzo-sopranos in the world. Mentioned in the same breath as Adelina Patti and Dame Nellie Melba, she was born in Romania and began her musical studies when she was six. At 14, she started training at the Milan Conservatoire and made her début at La Scala three years later, when she played Valentine in Meyerbeer's *Les Huguenots*. Besides Lucretia Borgia and La Gioconda, Valentine became one of her star roles and she was fêted by Enrico Caruso.

Elena Teodorini established a Romanian Music Academy in Paris, and in 1925 Queen Marie of Romania invited her to give a gala performance to celebrate the state visit of future Japanese emperor Hirohito. In 1997, the London-based Elena Teodorini Foundation was established with Sir Paul Getty as its president. The Foundation's aim is to encourage opera and ballet, award scholarships to young musicians and dancers, and to re-edit Teodorini's 1903 recordings onto CDs. For more information contact Dr Florin Popențiu, The Elena Teodorini Foundation, 344 Westbourne Park Road W11 1EQ, London, ☎ 020 7221 6746, or send him an e-mail at Fl.Popentiu@city.ac.uk. Alternatively you can write to Woodfield House, Tangier, Somerset TA1 1BL or ☎ 0182 345 000; fax 0182 334 003.

Hariclea Darclée (1860–1939) came from Brăila in Moldavia and made her début at the Paris Opera in *Faust*. She was an immensely popular soprano, especially in Italy, and sang in public until she was 58.

Traian Grozăvescu (d. 1927) was a renowned tenor. He was born in Lugoj and sang many times in Vienna. Having performed many tragic roles, his own life came to a dramatic end: he was killed by his jealous wife after a series of extramarital affairs.

In the second half of the 20C at least two Romanian singers have become household names, and a third is on her way. Ileana Cotrubas was born in Galaţi in 1939 and made her first public appearance as a soloist with the Children's Chorus on Radio Romania. Her sweet voice and gentle personality endeared her to audiences all over the world. She retired in 1989.

Soprano Angela Gheorghiu (née Burlacu) was born in 1965, the daughter of an engine driver from the Moldavian town of Adjud. Discovered at the Bucharest Music Academy, she became famous overnight when she sang Violetta in *La Traviata* at Covent Garden in 1994. Her portrayal was so bewitching that the BBC dropped its scheduled programmes to broadcast the opera live.

Ruxandra Donose is a mezzo-soprano who has received critical and popular acclaim around the world. In 1992 she received rapturous notices for her Varvara in *Katya Kabanova* at the Vienna Staatsoper. Since then, Donose has performed in the USA and the Glyndebourne Festival.

The Bucharest company Electrecord has issued recordings of operas from the standard European repertory and of several Romanian works.

Perennial Romania (IMCD 1109) is a CD of Romanian Classical music played by the Orchestra Naţională Radio. It contains pieces by George Enescu, Ciprian Porumbescu, Paul Constantinescu, Sabin Drăgoi, Constantin Dimitrescu, Marţian Neagra, and Theodor Rogalski. The CD is published by Intercont Music and is available from most good music shops throughout Romania. For more details about this and other recordings of Romanian music, write to Intercont Music, Str Pantelimon 111A, Bucureşti, Sector 2, ☎ +40 (0) 1 250 8242; fax 250 8369.

Romanian ballet
Romania has corps de ballet in Bucharest, Cluj and Constanţa.

Romanian folk music
As you would expect from a country which has been occupied and settled by so many different ethnic groups throughout its history, Romania's folk music is extremely heterogeneous. Romanian folk tunes blend Slavonic, Hungarian, Greek, Jewish, Armenian, Turkish and Tartar as well as autochthonous melodies. In Transylvania ethnic Hungarians have had a profound influence on the region's folk music, whereas there is a noticeably Serbian flavour to the traditional music of the Banat. Jewish *klezmer*, folksongs from the *shtetls* of Bessarabia, have been absorbed into the music of northeast Romania, and the Oriental character of Romania's folk music becomes ever stronger as you travel further east.

Best-known of all Romania's folksongs are the *doine* (plural of *doină*), semi-improvised, rhythmically free and passionately expressive songs. They are often associated with the Roma, but although the *cântec de pahar*, the 'song of the glass', and the romantic *cântecele de dragoste* (songs of love and yearning) are a favourite of Romanian Gypsies, they are not a Gypsy preserve.

Robert Garfias studied the Romanian *doină* during the 1970s and 1980s, a time when it was politically tactless to suggest that Romanian music should have any foreign origins at all. Working cleverly around these restrictions, Dr Garfias developed fascinating theories about the connections between Islamic and Romanian music. As he says, considering that the Romanian lands were subjected to 500 years of cultural influence from the Ottoman Turks and Phanariot

Greeks it is hardly surprising that their music should sound the same. But it is also possible that the origins of these traditional songs date back to the period when Thracian shepherds were putting their own epic stories to music.

Romanian folk music started to attract attention abroad during the 19C. During the last years of the 19C and the early years of the 20C new forms of popular music came into being in Romanian cities, particularly Bucharest and Craiova. Greek, Turkish and Armenian traditions played an important part in these city songs, mixing with the Romany *cântec de dragoste*.

Gypsy music

Gypsy music is usually faster and more energetic, ornamental and Oriental than the folk music played by non-Roma. Gypsies have their own favourite forms of the *doina*, such as the *cântec de pahar* and *de dragoste* and the epic ballad, *cântec bătrânesc*, which is usually only performed by *lăutari* or Gypsy minstrels. Another specifically Romany song is the *ca pe lunca*, which is associated with the Danube plains: the word *lunca* means the plains. In Romany performances these songs usually follow an instrumental Turkish *tachsim*.

When Gypsies were freed from slavery in the 1860s, many of them migrated to the larger cities and settled in enclaves in the outskirts. These enclaves were known collectively as *mahale*, a word imported from the Phanariot district of Istanbul more than a century before. In these *mahalale* or suburbs, new variants of urban pop music evolved. The best can be interesting, but most of the cheap 'Gypsy' music of this kind is frenzied and discordant and so irritating that it seems to have been designed on purpose to induce nothing more uplifting than a headache.

Clejani which lies to the south of Bucharest on the Danube is a Romany community from which many fine Gypsy musicians have emerged. They include the well-known band, Taraf de Haidouks. It used to be a tradition that country weddings would be accompanied by a Romany band. Romany bands generally use a range of instruments that comprises a 20-pipe panflute (called a *nai* or *muscal* in Romanian), cembalom (hammered dulcimer), accordion, fiddle and bass. The pipes are traditionally played as a substitute for the second fiddle.

Romany folk musicians

Today the most famous exponents of the high-pitched urban Gypsy singing style are women, notably Gaby Lunca and Romica Puceanu. This type of vocalisation has no known precedent in Romanian folk music, but is not unusual in old Greek or Turkish popular music. Fănică Luca (d. 1968) was the most famous male exponent of the style in Romania as well as being a celebrated nai player.

The 12-piece Taraf de Haidouks (which translates roughly as the Band of Outlaws) is one of Romania's best-known Gypsy ensembles. With ages ranging from the twenties to the seventies, they come from the large Romany community at Clejani near the Danube in southern Wallachia. Taraf de Haidouks use traditional instruments including fiddles and accordions, but they are also great vocalists and are renowned for electrifying audiences with their spontaneous energy. In 1991, Taraf reached number 1 in the European World Music Charts with *Musiques des Tziganes de Roumanie* (Cram World 2 CD) and they did equally well with their second album, *Honourable Brigands, Magic Horses and Evil Eye*

(Cram World 13 CD) in 1994. One of their latest releases is *Dumbala Dumba*, which was recorded in 1997. Assisting Taraf on this album are several guest musicians, including singers from Mârsa who use a distinctive call-and-response style, and the Ursari, who are descended from the Gypsy bear tamers who used to roam the Balkans. Taraf took part in *Latcho Drom*, a film about *lăutari* (traditional Gypsy musicians) which won several awards at Cannes.

Damian Draghici-Luca (b 1970), great-grand-nephew of Fănică Luca, is an internationally known panflute player. He has performed and recorded since the age of 10 and has studied jazz in Boston. Damian Draghici-Luca has played with the New England Romanian Ensemble.

Folk instruments

If you visit some of Romania's ethnographic museums such as Muzeul Lemnului in Câmpulung Moldovenesc or the little museum at Lupşa near Cluj, you will find a selection of weird and wonderful instruments. Many of these are no longer used, but the spirit of improvisation lives on in folk music today. Village song-and-dance bands use bellows, open-ended drums, cembalom and at least 14 different kinds of pipe, including the panflute and all its subgroups, and five sorts of *buciumi* (alphorns). Stringed instruments include the contrabass and, in some areas of the southern Banat, the tambura, a type of Serbian mandolin. If you are touring the Banat you may also come across players of the taragot, which looks like a clarinet and sounds like a saxophone. Romany musicians traditionally use the fiddle and accordion with vocals.

The Romanian panflute

Of all the instruments used in Romanian folk music the panflute is probably the oldest. It is certainly the most romantic. Known in various forms and by different names all over the world, the panpipes are mentioned in Greek legend.

In Classical Greek literature, the name of the instrument was *syringa panos*, and it was said to be characteristic of the people who lived north of the Danube in present-day Romania. In Romanian folklore there are ballads that are similar to the legend of Pan and Syrinx. They include the legend of *The Cuckoo and the Turtle-dove*, and *The Blackbird and the Thrush*.

In his poem *Tristia*, written while he was exiled in Tomis (Constanţa) on the Black Sea coast, Ovid describes the panflute he saw being played by shepherds. Thracian shepherds almost certainly used the panpipes as well as alphorns during the biennial transhumance between summer and winter pastures. During the Middle Ages, panpipes are described in documents such as the early 16C *Textbook of Prince Neagoe Basarab's Teachings for his son Teodosie*. A variety of panpipes called a *tevniţă* was used by musicians to the Romanian royal courts. The *nai* and *muscal* are mentioned by the historians Dimitrie Cantemir, Anton Pann and Dionisie Fotino. In the 18C church in Ostrov there is a painting of a panflute with seven pipes.

Costel Puscoiu believes that Romanian panpipes are a combination of the *syringa panos* and the Oriental *muscal*, from which some Romanian pipes get their name. The term *ney* in Persian, Arabic and Turkish means 'a reed pipe', and the Persian words *Nay mus* mean 'the pipes of Pan'. There are similar words in Persian, Arabic and Turkish, linking *miskal, musikar*, and *musiqal* or *musqal* with the ancient panpipes.

A primitive instrument called a *fifa* (fife) still exists in the Gorj region of Romania. There the instrument is a closed pipe of 12 to 15 cm (5 to 6 inches) in length, and is used by women who can play melodies of three, four or five tones with a special chromatic technique.

The evolution of the classic panpipes began after the Second World War, and is still continuing. Their use in modern Classical music is increasing, and passages for the *nai* have appeared Anatol Vieru's symphonic piece *Clepsidra II* (*The Sandglass*, 1972), in Gheorghe Zamfir's *Panpipes Concerto* and *Rhapsodie du Printemps* (1981), and in *The Panpipes Concerto* (1986) by Jore Haanstra.

Gheorghe Zamfir

A farmer's son who came from a village about 60km north of Bucharest. Zamfir was discovered by Swiss music lover and folklorist Marcel Cellier when he visited Bucharest. Cellier arranged a meeting with Zamfir and his tutor, Fănică Luca, and later broadcast the recordings he made of Zamfir's playing on his radio show, 'From the Black Sea to the Baltic'. Cellier dedicated hundreds of his weekly broadcasts to panflute artists, bringing Zamfir and his Romanian contemporaries to a wider audience. In 1969 Cellier invited Zamfir to Switzerland and surprised him by playing Romanian *doina* on a church organ. Zamfir was so enchanted that he joined in with his soprano pipes. The two instruments sounded good together and this was the start of an international concert career. Since then Zamfir has recorded scores of albums devoted to sweetly haunting compositions of Romanian folk music and Classical melodies. He has also written for films, notably *Picnic at Hanging Rock*. His releases include *Solitude* (1973), *Lonely Shepherd* (1984) and *Songs of Romance, Volume 1* (1997). Zamfir reached no. 4 on the UK charts in 1976 with a traditional *Doina De Jale*. Many of the world's greatest musicians have fallen under the spell of Zamfir's *nai*: they include Yehudi Menuhin and James Last.

Panflute players

In 1843, 13 professional panflute players were registered with the musicians' association in Bucharest. Between the two world wars, Romanian panpipes players became even better known and travelled widely in Europe. The panflute revival came about after the war, when Fănică Luca, who had performed at the Paris World Fair of 1937 and the New York World Fair of 1939, made his concert tours of France, England, Poland, Egypt, China, Russia and the United States. Fănică Luca was attached to the Experimental Folk Orchestra—now the Barbu Lăntaru Orchestra—of the Folklore Institute in Bucharest. In 1949, with the Folklore Institute's help, he started teaching the pipes to students. In 1953 his class moved to the Music Lyceum, and he continued to teach until he died. Fănică Luca's work produced wonderful results. Thanks to his efforts a whole generation of Romanian panflute players has appeared in the West, among them Gheorghe Zamfir, Damian Draghici-Luca, Simion Stanciu 'Syrinx', Nicolae Pîrvu, Constantin Dobre, Radu Simion, Damian Cirlanaru and many others.

For those who want to know more about the panflute, some of the world's finest players have formed a network on the Worldwide Web. Go to the panflute.com webpage or contact the Dajoeri panpipe Craft and Schools, Wildenbühlstrasse 53, 8135 Langnau a/A, Switzerland, ☎ +41 1 7133606; fax +41 1 7133633; e-mail info@dajoeri.com.

Nicolae Pîrvu teaches the panpipes as an official subject at the Hilversum Conservatory in the Netherlands. Hilversum is the only college in the world which awards a teaching and a soloist degree in the instrument.

Romanian folk dance

Traditional Romanian dances are usually ring dances, or *hore*, from the ancient Greek *chora*. The earliest evidence of these dances or ritual dance formations on Romanian soil are the Neolithic pottery figures. Archaeologists have found them arranged in circles of alternating male and female figures inside ceramic vases and other vessels.

Country dancing in Romania is an occasion for dressing up in your best clothes. Some dances such as the *bărbatesc* are for men and others are for women, but most *hore* are for both sexes: in the *sârba* men and women alternate in the circle, with their hands on each other's shoulders. In the *brâu* (belt) the participants form a long line like a conga, holding on to the waist of the person in front. The *învârtita* is a dance for couples who spin furiously around each other, stamping as they go.

In the south of Romania and some areas of northern Bulgaria, there is an ancient ritual involving dance, dramatic plays, fighting and healing, called the *Căluş*. It takes place only at *Rusalii* (Whitsuntide or Pentecost). Coming 50 days after Orthodox Easter, this is the traditional period when people mourn their dead and when, according to Romanian folklore, evil spirits are abroad. The long winter is over and householders mark the transition by cleaning their homes and farmers by starting to work in the fields. *Rusalii* and *Căluş* both denote this symbolic period of regeneration when man must try to impose his will over nature for the coming year. For this reason, *Căluş/Rusalii* imposes certain restrictions, and during the week of Pentecost no-one may wash themselves or their houses, or climb trees. If anyone breaks these taboos, they are said to be possessed (another meaning of *Rusălii* is wicked spirits) and must be ritually healed by the *Căluş*. At the same time, the dance protects the village from the evil spirits and, like the English Morris dance, it is also a fertility rite, designed to ensure a good harvest in the year to come.

Ritual *Căluş* is dying out. But a mixture of dance and mime, and the steps of the dancers are accompanied by a band playing *vioara* (violin), *cobza* (lute) and *chitara* (guitar), and sometimes cembalom and accordion too. In the past the *Căluş* bands played *cimpoieri* (bagpipes) and small wooden flutes. If you want to know more about the folklore surrounding *Căluş*, Gail Kligman's book, *Căluş: Symbolic Transformation in Romanian Ritual* (University of Chicago Press, 1981) is by far the best source of information available in English. It has a foreword by Mircea Eliade.

Folk music festivals

On the first Sunday of August the Olt Songs festival brings together famous Romanian and foreign folk music bands who perform at the Village Museum in Râmnicu Vâlcea, Oltenia.

Each July, a group of villages in Maramureş plays host to Maramuzical, a celebration of Moroşeni music and dance which incorporates a crafts fair as well. Song and dance workshops, street concerts and improvised 'music cafés'are organised to create a festive atmosphere so that everyone can join in. Trips on the Vişeu de Sus narrow gauge railway are included. For more information and reservations contact Opération Villages Roumains (OVR), Bd Zoé Drion 1, B-6000 Charleroi, Belgium, ☎ +32 71324527; fax +32 71284078; e-mail ovri@win.be, or Association Echanges-Roumanie BP 249, 42173 St Just - St Rambert, France, ☎ +33 4 77364435; fax +33 4 77558053. Maramuzical has its own administrative headquarters in Botiza, ☎/fax +40 62 334233, and you should also be able to get information from Asociaţia Ţara Maramureşului, 4926 Vadu Izei, judeţ Maramureş, ☎/fax +40 62 330171, or Fondation Rurale en Roumanie (OVR), ☎/fax +40 69 212184.

Contemporary folk and jazz musicians

Maria Tănase who died in the 1960s was generally considered to be the finest Romanian folk singer of her day. The Maramureş-based band, Iza, is an internationally known folk group which specialises in the special song and dance music of this region. Lead singer Ion Pop (Popica) forms a third of the Anglo-Romanian band, Popeluc.

Muzsikás is an ethnic Hungarian group who have made a speciality of promoting Transylvanian music. They have produced several excellent albums, the finest of which include *Maramaros, the Lost Jewish Music of Transylvania* and *Blues for Transylvania* (both available as CD or cassette).

Damian Draghici-Luca, great-grand-nephew of Fănică Luca and one of the world's leading panflutists, has formed the orchestra Gypsy Feelings. For more information, write to Damian Draghici-Luca, Rue du Pélican 6, Boîte 29, B-1000 Bruxelles, Belgium.

The New England Romanian Ensemble, directed by Tom Pixton, has been presenting annual concerts of Romanian music in the Boston area of Massachusetts since 1994. Each member of the ensemble is active in traditional music of diverse origins. In 1998, the New England Romanian Ensemble was featured in the Cambridge Revel's winter solstice celebrations in Cambridge, Massachusetts, and they have played with the Zdravets Balkan Music Ensemble.

Quasi Essentia is a Classical folk band based in Holland comprising panflutist Jos Aerts and guitarist Paul van de Heijden: for more details about their concerts and albums contact Jos Aerts at Tjiestplein 23, 5271 XL St. Michielsgestel, Netherlands, ☎ +31 (0) 73 5944009; e-mail josaerts@wxg.nl.

Transylvanian saxophonist Nicolas Simion started recording Romanian folk music in 1992. Simion fled from communist Romania in 1989, arriving in Vienna with hardly any luggage besides his favourite possessions: copies of Mihai Eminescu's poems, recordings by George Enescu and photographs of Constantin Brâncuşi's Column of the Infinite. He dedicated pieces to Enescu and Brâncuşi in his 1997 album, *Back to the Roots*. *The Unfinished Column* was inspired by Brâncuşi while *Prélude à l'Unisson* is based on a theme taken from Enescu's *Suite d'Orchestre*, opus 9. *Back to the Roots* is available on TUTU CD 888 170.

In the summer of 1999, American bass player Steve Wolownik and friends organised The Road-Diner, a Balalaika and Folk Dance Camp which offered a chance to learn as well as listen to Eastern European music and dance. Tuition was given in playing balalaikas, *domras*, cembaloms, tamburas, *gajdas*, *tupans* and many other folk instruments from Central and Eastern Europe at large. For information on future programmes, contact Steve at PO Box 203, Mt. Laurel NJ 08054, USA, or e-mail wolownik@mtlaurel.lib.nj.us. Details of similar events may be found by logging onto http://www.eefc.org/ on the internet.

The DOINA Foundation for Romanian ethnography and folklore at Aarhuispad 22, 3067 PR Rotterdam, The Netherlands, ☎ +31 10 421 86 22; +31 10 455 60 65, organises dance and culture tours around Romania.

Romanian rock music

After the 1989 revolution, 1970s band Phoenix rose from the ashes with several albums that combine folk music with rock. Their songs are very appealing, but for a sharper cutting edge, try getting hold of CDs by Sarmelele Reci (*Cold Stuffed Cabbage*), who write scathingly iconoclastic lyrics criticising Romanian political and social mores to music that parodies a range of different Western pop and rock styles. Sarmelele Reci's music is distributed by East Art in Bucharest (☎/fax 01 320 0201), and English translations of their lyrics are available. Râmnicu Vâlcea holds the Constellations Rock Festival at the beginning of December.

Wildlife

Romania harbours some of Europe's rarest mammals. Most notably, they include brown bears, wolves, wild boars and lynx; Carpathian stags, roebucks and roe deer, chamois and moufflons, European hares, wild cats and martens are also to be found. According to recent figures, over 6000 bears and c 2000 wolves roam the Romanian mountains; ironically, the bears have escaped predation by man thanks to Ceaușescu's policy of reserving them all for himself. Both bears and wolves are shy of people, but it is possible to get close to the wolves safely by joining a tour organised by the Carpathian Wolf Project. Set up in the 1990s, the project tracks individual animals with the help of radio transmitters implanted in the cubs soon after birth. Several specialist tour companies can arrange wolf-tracking tours (see p 14). Bears, lynx and wolves are protected under CITES (the Convention on the International Trade in Endangered Species), although the Romanian government still permits hunting of bear and lynx with a special licence. An autonomous organisation called Romsilva controls most of the forest land, including many nature reserves, and holds the rights to hunting and fishing.

Birds flourish abundantly in the Carpathians and the Delta. Among the species that live in the beech woods on the lower slopes are titmice, grey and little owls, goshawks and jays, red-backed shrikes and nutcrackers. Higher up in the common spruce you can find black and larger spotted woodpeckers, mountain cocks and crested tomtits. Above the treeline are plovers, larks, common creepers, mountain, golden and grey eagles and grey vultures. There are wetland reserves near the River Olt where you can see lesser spotted eagles, ferruginous ducks, storks, terns and marsh harriers.

The most spectacular area for birdwatching in Romania, however, is the Danube Delta, where some 300,000ha of continuous reedbed attract sedentary species and migratory birds from all over the world: pygmy cormorants, white pelicans, herons and egrets are easy to spot on the water during the summer months, while glossy ibis, grebes, orioles and nightingales inhabit nearby mixed woods of oak and willow. Further inland, stone curlews and calandra larks live alongside rollers and several species of predatory birds.

It is not only the birds that make the Delta special. Located between the northern steppes and the Mediterranean, it attracts animal species from both areas. Ecologists believe that as a result, new species may be created here, but water and air pollution from the Odessa region and the consequences of Ceaușescu's mammoth drainage programme both pose serious threats to the Delta's natural habitats. Attempts to save them have provoked some action. In 1992 the Danube Delta was designated as a biosphere of world importance, and shortly before his death, Jacques Cousteau helped to found a conservation research station on the Sf Gheorge channel.

Some parts of the Carpathians are relatively free of pollution, and fish such as trout and umber still flourish in mountain rivers and streams. The rare huck can be found in the Bistrița, Vișeu and Tisa rivers, and this species has been introduced into Crișul Repede, the Mureș, the Cerna and Someșul Mic. Near Brădet in the southern Carpathians are the last few relics of a prehistoric fish which Romanians call *asprete* (*Romanichtys valsanicola*). The most famous fishing area is the Delta region, which supports dwindling quantities of freshwater and salt water fish.

In the southern Carpathians there are salamanders and adders; Aesculapius's vipers, and horned vipers (*Vipera cornata*), which can kill a human within minutes, live in the forests of northern Oltenia in Valea Cernei and the surrounding mountains, in southwestern Transylvania and the eastern Banat. There are also deadly snakes in some parts of the Delta and in southern Dobrogea near the Bulgarian border. Lizards inhabit the alpine regions, and in the coastal meadows near Mangalia there are wild tortoises. On Mt Domogled, near the Danube and the spa of Băile Herculane, is a reserve where both plants and animals have a Mediterranean character; it also has turtles. Vivid butterflies and beetles also flourish in the mountains. If you are walking in the forests, watch out for ticks, which, like vampires, love warm human blood and can transmit extremely unpleasant diseases. Changes in farming practices mean that Anopheles mosquitoes are on the increase in Romania. But their numbers are not yet of any significance and do not pose a threat to people.

Two-thirds of Romania is covered by trees, nearly half of them 'climax' forest in the eastern Carpathians. On the lower slopes you will find beech woods which, as you climb higher, give way to spruce, birch and juniper. Many of the forests have been untouched except for relatively small-scale logging operations, which are done in the eastern Carpathians with the help of narrow-gauge railways, shutes and rafts. Elsewhere, families gather their own timber in the time-honoured manner with horse and cart; along with the 10ha of land that was given back to peasant farmers after 1989, the government conceded 1ha of forest. Most of the woodland is controlled by non-governmental organisations such as Romsilva. Many homes, especially in rural areas, still rely on wood-burning stoves for heating and cooking. Collecting wood by cart can take several days, and villagers often go in a convoy, returning along main roads through the night. A plan by the government to let the Malaysian company Samling exploit limited areas of the Carpathians for systematic, industrial logging purposes is currently under appraisal. This would almost certainly spell disaster for Romania's forests.

The drastic cutbacks which Ceauşescu imposed on Romanian farming have had a beneficial effect on the country's wild plants; you only have to travel by train in spring or summer to marvel at the variety of colourful flowers by the tracks. In the Retezat National Park alone there are 900 recorded species. The Bucegi massif harbours rhododendron, bilberry and edelweiss, white ivy, lad's blood (*Nigritella rubra*) and yellow crosswort.

Around the steep cliffs of Piatra Craiului you can find the Piatra Craiului pink (*Dianthus callizonus*), the Cross of Hercules (*Hepatica transilvanica*), and mountain poppy, as well as stork's bill and rocket. Filbert trees, black-leafed eglantines, lilacs and pines clothe the hillsides of Mt Domogled along with white, vanilla-scented Carthusian pinks, carnation and devil's bite (*Scabiosa banatia*). Other rarities to look out for in the mountains are yellow spotted gentian (*Gentiana punctata*), lady's shoe and varieties of saxifrage. In spring the meadows of Transylvania come alive with wild narcissi, while later on cornflower and autumn crocus cover the fallow ground.

In 1995, the European Year of Nature Conservation, the Romanian and Swiss governments collaborated on a scheme to encourage more awareness of environmental issues in schools. Two new protected zones, Scărişoara cave and the Slătioara forest, were created, and pupils from a school in Bucharest cleared an area of the Retezat mountains as well as establishing paths and unblocking the magnificent Tamina waterfall in Piatra Craiului near Braşov. In the same year, young enthusiasts from international action groups helped to clean up the resort of Lacu Roşu, north of Gheorgheni, while other youngsters cleared routes through the Cheile Nerei (Nera Gorges) in Caraş-Severin county in the southwest. In Alba Iulia the Albamont Club has concentrated on saving special sites in the Apuseni mountains in western Transylvania, including the Cheile Turzii and Cheile Rămeţilor.

Language

The Romanian language has evolved from demotic Latin, which was introduced when the ancient Romans occupied Dacia between 106 and 270 AD. During its early development, it absorbed elements from other immigrant tongues, especially Slavonic. Thracian and Greek have left their imprint as well. Thracian tribes, who are known to have survived in the Carpathians until at least the 10C AD, gave many words to Romanian shepherding terminology. Modern Romanian also contains words and phrases from Turkish, Hungarian, French, German and even English. During the 19C and early 20C, the educated classes preferred French as their second language. Transylvanian Romanians often learnt to speak or at least to understand German, while a knowledge of Russian was compulsory during the communist era. Today, English is more popular because it is seen as a passport to a career abroad.

If you already speak French or Italian and can remember your school Latin, you will find Romanian easy. *Teach Yourself Romanian* by Dennis Deletant and Yvonne Alexandrescu (Teach Yourself Books, London, 1997), is an excellent beginner's course; it comes with a cassette tape.

Nouns and prepositions

Romanian nouns have three genders: masculine, feminine and neuter. Adjectives and pronouns always agree with the gender of the noun. The indefinite article, 'un' for masculine and neuter, and 'o' for feminine words, comes before the noun; neuter nouns take the feminine case in the plural. However, the definite article is added to the end of the noun: '-ul' for masculine and '-a' for feminine words. When you want to use plural nouns with the definite article, endings become more complicated because there are several irregular forms: masculine and neuter nouns usually take the endings '-i' or '-le'. Word endings also incorporate genitive and dative cases, as in 'a României' ('of/to the Romanians').

Romanians also use the vocative case for men's and women's names and titles, adding an '-e', as in 'Bună ziua, domnule', ('Good afternoon, sir').

'La', 'a' and 'al' are forms of 'to' and 'at'; 'towards' is generally expressed by 'spre'.

Verbs

To be:
Eu sunt
Tu ești
El (or ea) este
Noi suntem
Voi sunteți
Ei (or ele) sunt.
The negative form becomes 'eu nu sunt' etc.

To have:
Eu am
Tu ai
El (or ea) are
Noi avem
Voi aveți
Ei (or ele) au.

Verbs can also be reflexive, as in to go:
Eu mă duc
Tu te duci
El (or ea) se duce, etc.

To wish, to ask for:
Eu doresc
Tu dorești
El (or ea) dorește
Noi dorim
Voi doriți,
ei (or ele) doresc

To want:
Eu vreau
Tu vrei
El (or ea) vrea
Noi vrem
Voi vreți
Ei (or ele) vor.

It is usual to drop the pronoun unless you want to emphasise it.

Pronunciation

Pronouncing Romanian words is straightforward; the emphasis usually comes on the penultimate syllable. The letters 'â' or 'î', which are identical, are pronounced like a short, strangled 'ieu' sound at the back of the throat; it looks far harder than it is. The original form of the letter is 'â', replaced by 'î' when it comes at the beginning of a word; during Gheorghiu-Dej's regime, 'î' was used all the time, in line with the general Russification of Romanian culture ('România' became 'Romînia'). After the 1989 revolution, the 'â' was restored, but many old maps and road signs still use the communist spelling. A single '-i' at the end of a word is usually silent, as in the village of Desești and 'scuzați' (sorry). 'E' at the start of a word is pronounced like 'ye' in Slavonic, as in 'eu' ('I') which sounds like 'yeu'.

Other unusual letters are ț (ts) and ș (sh), while 'ă' is pronounced 'er', as in 'vă rog' (please). As in Italian, 'ce' and 'ci' sound like the soft English 'che', as in 'ceai', and 'chi' as in 'cicatrice'; 'ge' is pronounced 'j', while 'ch' is hard, as in 'chip' ('face'). Romanians often elide their syllables so that 'ea' almost becomes 'a', as in 'Biserica domnească'. There are a number of regional dialects, called *graiuri*, which often use words unheard of elsewhere.

Greetings

By and large, Romanians are friendly and open, and no-one will mind if you make mistakes with the language; most people will be impressed if you only try a few halting words. Older people particularly appreciate being addressed in the correct way. It is usual to shake hands when you meet someone and when saying goodbye. When a man is introduced to a women, he will probably kiss her hand, strictly avoiding her eyes—eye contact can mean he is interested in a sexual relationship. Typical greetings include 'Săru' mâna' ('I kiss your hand'), used by boys and men to older women; 'Sănătate!' ('Good health!') is a friendly salutation to equals and older people whom you know well. 'La revedere' ('Goodbye') has many informal variations, including the lovely phrase 'Vă pup' ('Kiss, kiss'), 'Pa pa' ('Bye bye') and 'Drum bun', which means 'Have a good journey', literally 'Good road'.

'Good morning' before 10.00 is 'Bună dimineață'; after 10.00, use 'Bună ziua'; 'Good evening' is 'Bună seara', and 'Good night' is 'Noapte bună'. You'll often hear people saying 'Bună' on its own, which covers most eventualities. When you want to ask a stranger for information, begin by saying 'Nu vă supărați...', which means literally 'Don't get angry...' It is also respectful to use the form 'dumneavoastră' rather than 'voi' to a man or a woman you are meeting for the first time.

Useful phrases

Greetings and orientation

Where are you from?	De unde sunteți/sânteți (pronounced the same)
My name is...	Mă numesc...
I'm English/American/French	Sunt englez/american/francez
I'm an Englishwoman/an American woman/a Frenchwoman	Sunt englezoiacă/americană/franțu zoiacă
Do you speak English?	Vorbiți englezește?
Would you speak more slowly, please?	Vorbiți mai rar, vă rog
I'm sorry/Forgive me	Iertați-mă
Excuse me	Scuzați-mă
Yes	Da
No	Nu
I don't understand	Nu înțeleg
Would you write it down, please?	Puteți să notați, vă rog?
What's the time?	Cât e ceasul?
It's a quarter to twelve	E douăsprezece fără un sfert

I would like to speak to...	Doresc să vorbesc cu...
I would like a book of tickets/ a telephone card for 20,000 lei	Doresc un carnet/ o cartelă telefonică al douăzeci de mii
I want to send a fax/letter	Vreau să trimit un fax/o scrisoare
Please...	Vă rog...
Thank you	Mulțumesc
We thank you	Mulțumim

Getting around

Where is the train station/Metro/ bus station?	Cum merg spre gara/metroul/ stația de autobuz?
Where can I find petrol/a hotel/ an exchange house?	Unde pot să găsesc benzina/un hotel/ casa de schimb?
When is the next/first/last train?	Când este următorul/primul/ultimul tren?
When does the train leave/arrive?	Când pleacă/sosește trenul?
Go straight ahead	Mergeți drept înainte
To the left/right	La stânga/dreapta
Up to the crossroads/traffic lights/ corner	Pâna la intersecție/semafor/colț
Are you on foot?	Mergeți pe jos?
Where can I buy a ticket?	De unde iau un bilet/tichet?
How much is it?	Cât costa?
I have no money	Nu am bani
I want to hire a car	Vreau să închiriez o mașină
We would like to see the Făgăraș mountains	Am vrea să vedem Munții Făgărașului
Do you know where the priest's house is?	Știți unde se află parohia, vă rog?
Is the church open?	Este deschisă biserica?
Yes, the church is open but it's forbidden to take photographs	Da, biserica e deschisa, dar nu este permis să se facă fotografii
Is it far?	Este departe?
I can't find it	Nu pot să găsesc
Would you show me on the map?	Arătați-mi pe harta, vă rog?
Is it OK?	Este regular?

Emergencies

I have an urgent request, I need a doctor	Am o rugăminte urgentă, trebuie să găsește un medic
I need... a chemist's/the police	Am nevoie de... o farmacie/poliția
I need repellent/spray for insect bites	Am nevoie de unguent/spray contra muscăturii insectelor
I feel ill/The child is sick/ My daughter has had an accident/ where is the hospital?	Mi-e rău/Copilul este bonav/ Fata mea a avut un accident/ unde este spitalul?
I've lost my passport/luggage	Am pierdut pașaportul/bagajul
Do you have any sticking plaster/ tampons, please?	Aveți leucoplast/ tampoane, vă rog?

Dealing with harassment

I'm waiting for... a friend/ my husband/the menu	Aștept... un prieten/ soțul/meniul
It's annoying, stop that at once	Este supărător, opriți imediat
Leave me alone!	Lasă-mă în pace!

Eating out and finding accommodation

I'm hungry/thirsty	Mi-e foame/sete
Let's go to the café/a restaurant	Mergeți la cafenea/un restaurant
Is that the price per person?	Prețul acesta e per persoana?
Is that the total price?	Acesta e prețul total?
It's too expensive	E prea scump
Do you have something cheaper?	Aveți ceva mai ieftin?
I would like the bill, please	Doresc plata, vă rog
I'd like a beer	Doresc o bere
I want to have a wash	Vreau să mă spăl
Where is the WC/ lavatory?	Unde este WC/toaleta?
The lavatory is broken!	Toaleta este stricată!
Have you got a room for two, please?	Aveți o camera pentru doua persoane, vă rog?
Does it have one bed or two?	Are un singur pat, sau două?
Does the price include breakfast?	Prețul acesta cuprinde micul dejun?
The room is very noisy	Camera este foarte zgomotoasă
Has it got hot water?	Are apă caldă?
I'm happy	Mă bucur
Wonderful!	Minunat!

For food and drink, see pp 32–36.

Numbers

one	un	eleven	unsprezece
two	doi (or două if they are feminine)	twelve	doisprezece
		thirteen	treisprezece
three	trei	fourteen	paisprezece
four	patru	fifteen	cinsprezece
five	cinci	sixteen	șaisprezece
six	șase	seventeen	șaptesprezece
seven	șapte	eighteen	optsprezece
eight	opt	nineteen	nouăsprezece
nine	nouă	twenty	douăzeci
ten	zeci	one hundred	o sută
		one thousand	o mie

Days of the week

Monday	luni	Friday	vineri
Tuesday	marți	Saturday	sâmbătă
Wednesday	miercuri	Sunday	duminică
Thursday	joi		

Further reading

History, opinion and travel

Almond, Mark, *The Rise and Fall of Nicolae and Elena Ceauşescu* (Chapmans, London, 1992).

Antal, Dan, *Out of Romania* (Faber & Faber, London, 1994).

Behr, Edward, *Kiss the Hand You Cannot Bite: the Rise and Fall of the Ceauşescus* (Hamish Hamilton, London, 1991).

Beza, Marcu, *Roumanian Chroniclers* (Free Roumanians National Committee, London, 1941).

——, *Origin of the Roumanians* (Free Roumanians National Committee, London, 1941).

Boner, Charles, *Transylvania: its Products and its People* (Longmans, London, 1865).

Căndea, Virgil and Cornelia, *Transylvania in the History of the Romanians: Heritage and Continuity in Eastern Europe* (1983).

Cantemir, Dimitrie, *The History and Decline of the Ottoman Empire* (1734).

Cioran, Emil, *A Short History of Decay* (Arcade Press, 1998).

——, *Anathemas and Admirations* (Arcade Press, 1998).

——, *Tears and Saints* (Arcade Press, 1996).

——, *Précis de Composition* (Paris, 1949).

——, *Syllogisms of Bitterness* (Paris, 1952).

——, *The Temptation to Exist* (Paris, 1956).

——, *Ecartèlement* (Paris, 1979).

Craven, Lady, *Voyages de Milady Craven à Constantinople par la Crimée en 1786* (Paris, 1789).

Deletant, Dennis, *Ceauşescu and the Securitate: Coercion and Dissent in Romania* (Hurst and Co, London, 1996).

——, *Communist Terror in Romania: Gheorghiu-Dej and the Police State* (St Martin's Press, London, 1999).

——, *Romania under Communist Rule* (The Center for Romanian Studies, Iaşi, 1999).

——, *Studies in Romanian History* (Editura Enciclopedica, Bucharest, 1991).

——, and Sorescu, Marin, *Vlad Dracula the Impaler: a Play* (Forest Books, London, 1989).

Drysdale, Helena, *Looking for Gheorghe: Love and Death in Romania* (Sinclair-Stevenson, London 1996).

Eliade, Mircea, *The Romanians: a Concise History* (Roza Vintorilor, Bucharest, 1992).

——, *Autobiography 1907–37: Vol. 1, Journey East, Journey West* (University of Chicago Press, Chicago, 1992).

——, *Autobiography 1907–37: Vol. 2, Exile's Odyssey* (University of Chicago Press, Chicago, 1988).

——, *The Romanians: a Concise History* (Editura Athena, Bucharest, 1995).

Fermor, Patrick Leigh, *Between the Woods and the Water* (John Murray, London, 1988).

Florescu, Radu R., *Essays on Romanian Romania* (The Center for Romanian

Studies, Iași, 1999).

Georgescu, Vlad, *The Romanians, a History* (Tauris, London, 1991).

Gerard, Emily, *The Land Beyond the Forest* (W. Blackwood and Sons, Edinburgh and London, 1888).

Glenny, Misha, *The Rebirth of History* (Penguin, London, 1993).

Goldsworthy, Vesna, *Inventing Ruritania* (Yale University Press, New Haven and London, 1998).

Goma, Paul, *My Childhood at the Gate of Unrest* (Readers' International, London, 1990).

Harding, Georgina, *In Another Europe* (Sceptre, London, 1989).

Hitchins, Keith, *Rumania 1866–1947* (Clarendon Press, Oxford, 1994).

Hlihor, Constantin and Scurtu, Ioan, *The Red Army in Romania* (The Center for Romanian Studies, Iași, 1999).

Huntingdon, Samuel P., *The Clash of Civilizations and the Remaking of World Order* (Simon & Schuster, New York, 1997).

Iorga, Nicolae, *History of the Romanians, Vols 1–11* (1936–39).

——, *Histoire des Relations Roumaines* (Semne, Bucharest, 1995).

——, *History of Romania* (AMS Press, 1925).

Kaplan, Robert D., *Balkan Ghosts* (Papermac, London, 1994).

Latham, Ernest H. Jr (ed.)., *Miorița: An Icon of Romanian Culture* (The Center for Romanian Studies, Iași, 1999).

McNally, Raymond, and Florescu, Radu, *In Search of Dracula: a True History of Dracula and Vampire Legends* (Robson, London, 1997).

Martinas, Dumitru, *The Origins of the Changos* (The Center for Romanian Studies, Iași, 1999).

Michelson, Paul E. (ed.),*The Revolution of 1848 in the Romanian Lands, An Introduction and Guide* (The Center for Romanian Studies, Iași, 1999).

Murphy, Dervla, *Transylvania and Beyond* (Arrow, London, 1993).

Nagy-Talavera, N.M., *Nicolae Iorga: a Biography* (Center for Romanian Studies, Iași, 1998).

Ogden, Alan, *Romania Revisited: On the Trail of English Travellers, 1602–1941* (The Center for Romanian Studies, Iași, 1999).

Pakula, Hanna, *Marie, Queen of Romania* (Phoenix Giant, London, 1996).

Phillimore, Mrs Lion, *In the Carpathians* (Constable and Co., London, 1912).

Pop, Ioan Aurel, *Romanians and Hungarians from the 9th to the 14th Century: the Genesis of the Transylvanian Medieval State* (Fundația Culturala Romana, Cluj-Napoca, 1996).

Porter, Ivor, *Operation Autonomous: with SOE in Wartime Romania* (Chatto & Windus, London, 1989).

Rady, Martyn, *Romania in Turmoil* (Tauris, London, 1992).

Retegan, Mihai, *In the Shadow of the Prague Spring: Romanian Foreign Policy and the Crisis in Czechoslovakia, 1968* (The Center for Romanian Studies, Iași, 1999).

Roberts, James, *Guide to the Mountains of Romania* (Cicerone, Oxford, 1999).

Sitwell, Sacheverell, *Romanian Journey* (Oxford University Press, Oxford, 1992).

Treptow, Kurt W. (ed), *A History of Romania* (Center for Romanian Studies, Iași, 1996).

——, *Vlad III Dracula: The Life and Times of the Historical Dracula* (The Center for Romanian Studies, Iași, 1999).

——, and Ionescu, Mihail E. (eds), *Romania and Euro-Atlantic Integration* (The

Center for Romanian Studies, Iași, 1999).
Verdery, Katherine, *Transylvanian Villagers* (University of California Press, Berkeley, 1983).
Zub, Alexandru, *Reflections on the Impact of the French Revolution 1789, de Tocqueville, and Romanian Culture* (The Center for Romanian Studies, Iași, 1999).

Art, architecture and folklore

Andreesco, Ioana, *Où Sont Passés les Vampires?* (Paris, 1996).
Barca, Ana, and Dinescu, Dan, *The Wooden Architecture of Maramureș* (Humanitas, Bucharest, 1997).
Beza, Marcu, *Byzantine Art in Roumania* (Batsford, London, 1940).
Buxton, David, *The Wooden Churches of Eastern Europe* (Cambridge University Press, Cambridge, 1986).
Calame, François (ed), *Charpentiers au Travail: le Bois en Europe* (Editions à Die, Paris, 1993).
Celac, Mariana, et al (eds), *Romania in the 1930s: Architecture and Modernity* (exhibition catalogue, Bucharest, 1996).
Eliade, Mircea, *De Zamolxis à Gengis Khan: Etudes Comparatives sur les Religions et le Folklore de la Dacie et l'Europe Orientale* (Bibliothèque Historique, Paris, 1970).
——, *La Colonne sans Fin* (University Press of America, Lanham, 1984).
——, *The Sacred and the Profane: the Nature of Religion* (Harcourt Brace, New York, 1968).
——, *Shamanism: Archaic Techniques of Ecstasy* (Princeton University Press, Princeton, 1972).
Giurescu, Dinu C., *The Razing of Romania's Past* (Architecture, Design and Technology Press, London, 1990).
Kligman, Gail, *The Wedding of the Dead* (California University Press, Berkeley, 1986).
Machedon, Luminata, and Schoffham, Ernie, *Romanian Modernism: the Architecture of Bucharest 1920–1940* (MIT Press, Cambridge, 1999).
Mansel, Philip, *Constantinople, City of the World's Desire* (Penguin, London, 1997).
Mihăilescu, Popescu and Panzaru, *Paysans de l'Histoire* (Bucharest, 1992).
Miya, Kosei, *La Roumanie des Quatre Saisons* (exhibition catalogue, Musée de l'Homme, Paris, 1997).
Mulligan, Tom, 'Hungary, Romania, Yugoslavia: the Fine Arts and the Boundaries of Change' in Aulich, James, and Wilcox, Tim (eds), *Europe without Walls: Art Posters and Revolution 1989–93* (Manchester City Art Galleries, Manchester, 1993).
Runciman, Stephen, *The Great Church in Captivity* (Cambridge University Press, Cambridge, 1968).
Treasures from Romania (exhibition catalogue, British Museum, London, 1971).

Religion

Beza, Marcu, *The Romanian Church* (SPCK, London, 1943).
Eliade, Mircea, *The History of Religious Ideas*
Ware, Timothy (Bishop Kallistos), *The Orthodox Church* (Penguin, London, 1993).
——, *The Orthodox Way* (Mowbray, Oxford, 1987).
——, *The Akathistos Hymn to the Most Holy Mother of God* (Ecumenical Society of the Blessed Virgin Mary, Oxford, 1987).
——, 'Act out of Stillness': the Influence of 14th Century Hesychasm on Byzantine

and Slav Civilization (Hellenic-Canadian Association and the Society of Metro Toronto, Toronto, 1995).

Classics of Romanian literature

Caragiale, Ion Luca, *The Lost Letter and Other Plays* (Lawrence and Wishart, London, 1956).
Creangă, Ion, *Recollections* (Dent, London, 1930).
——, *Tales and Stories* (Abbey Library, London, 1933).
Ghyka, Matila, *The World Mine Oyster* (Heinemann, London, 1961).
Treptow, Kurt W. (ed), *Selected Works of Ion Creangă and Mihai Eminescu: Classics of Romanian Literature, Vol 1* (East European Monographs, Boulder, 1991).
Zamfirescu, Duiliu, *Sasha* (A.M. Philpot, London, 1926).

Plays

Ionesco, Eugène, *Plays, Vols 1–12* (John Calder, London, 1958–88).
——, *Les Chaises* (Gallimard, Paris, 1996).

Fiction

Tzara, Tristan, *La Coeur à Gaz* (GLM, Paris, 1946). For other references, see pp 87 and 89.

Fiction by non-Romanian writers

Bailey, Paul, *Kitty and Virgil* (Fourth Estate, London, 1998).
Bellow, Saul, *The Dean's December* (Penguin, London, 1982).
Bradbury, Malcolm, *Rates of Exchange* (Vintage, London, 1990).
Brownjohn, Alan, *Long Shadows* (Dewi Lewis, Stockport, 1997).
Manning, Olivia, *The Balkan Trilogy* (Mandarin, London, 1994).
Von Rezzori, Gregor, *Memoirs of an Anti-Semite* (Vintage, London, 1991).

Some of these books are no longer in print. Apart from trawling the internet and secondhand bookshops, asking your local library or obtaining a ticket for the British Library, you could try ordering them from **Eastern Books**, 125A Astonville Street, London SW18 5AQ (☎/fax 020 8871 0880), or **Beaumont Travel Books**, 31 Museum Street, London WC1A 1LH (☎/fax 020 7637 5862).

THE GUIDE

Bucharest

It has been called Paris of the East and Babylon of the Apocalypse. An American guide book describes Bucharest as 'that Gotham from Hell'. But the city once had 365 churches, one for every day of the year. Bucharest has been controversial for centuries, but unless you come here in the height of summer, when temperatures can reach 40 degrees or more, it is neither the hell hole nor the sink of iniquity that—a mostly Western—literature and some first appearances might suggest.

Like most vibrant cities, Bucharest is a mixture of things that will delight and annoy, horrify, stimulate and comfort you though not necessarily in that order. What remains of 'old' Bucharest ranges from 16C monasteries to a host of adventurous buildings created between the two world wars. If your taste runs to the classical, a ten-minute walk from Ceaușescu's Assyrian-style palace brings you within sight of gracious 19C apartments built for the city's long-dead nobility, financiers and captains of industry. True, these vestiges of individuality are more striking because there are so few of them, but they prove that Bucharest can give as many pleasant surprises as it deals you nasty shocks.

Since Ceaușescu put his stamp on the city, more than 20 churches have been moved or destroyed. Worse than this, the megalomaniac dictator ordered a large chunk of central Bucharest to be razed, causing thousands of people to lose their homes. His changes broke the rhythm that held the capital together. They also caused chaos: one result of his 'systematic restructuring' was that a large section of the capital's water pipes were cut without being sealed. They have still not been repaired, so that every year countless gallons seep away unused. Few capital cities have pretty outskirts, but the ways into Bucharest are grimmer than most—mile after mile of dreary apartment blocks line many of the roads into the centre. As if this were not bad enough, in summer the streets are thick with gritty dust that gets into eyes and throats: contact lens wearers beware. The streets are pockmarked with craters that never seem to get filled. When it rains the craters become great lakes of oily water. Open manholes lie in wait for unwary walkers and blind people. Say your prayers at pedestrian crossings... But did we ever say that travelling in Romania was going to be easy?

In March 1977 an earthquake measuring 6.5 on the Richter scale devastated Bucharest. The disaster left 1500 dead and thousands homeless. It also gave Ceaușescu an excuse to push forward his plans for redesigning the city centre. In 1971, while he was still to outward appearances the maverick communist beloved by the West, Ceaușescu visited Pyongyang. He was terribly impressed. Kim Il Sung's North Korean capital was a monument of self-glorification, and Ceaușescu wanted the same. Between 1977–89, an area covering 10,000ha to the south of the Dâmbovița canal was flattened. Before it was destroyed, this part of Bucharest resembled the old district of Lipscani, a marvellous blend of patrician mansions, coaching hotels and oriental pavilions, of inns with hidden courtyards, hilltop monasteries, little squares and welcoming cafés. Ceaușescu replaced this friendly scene with the concrete canyon that is B-dul Unirii, leading to the jewel in his megalithic crown, Palatul Parlamentului. He had scores of historic buildings pulled down or moved, regardless of whether or not they were actually damaged. It was a rape which provoked Bucharest architect Gheorghe Leahu to lament, 'we feel like strangers in our own town'.

Westerners who have not been here often remark that Romania seems loath to shrug off Ceaușescu's legacy, implying some deep-seated laziness. It is so much more complicated than that. Helena Drysdale has described the Romanians as 'an old people, old and sophisticated'. Centuries of evading domination and destruction by the rival powers of Ottoman Turkey, the Slavs, Hungarians and Habsburgs has made them skilful at obfuscation and, from some perspectives, passive—the 'mioritic' syndrome in its negative sense (see p 263 for the *Miorița* legend). It has also made them romantic dreamers. But such generalisations are always dangerous, however useful they may be. Until you come here it is hard to appreciate how much physical and emotional damage Ceaușescu caused. As Mark Almond explained, 'Romanians are well aware of how much they have inherited from the Ceaușescu regime and how difficult it is, with the best will in the world, to purge the moral degradation from their souls.'

Ceaușescu obliterated many other historic districts, including Sebastian, Alexandria, Ispirescu, Brâncoveanu and Văcărești. During his reign of madness, one-fifth of the old city, including 22 churches and monasteries, disappeared. Churches such as Mihai Vodă and Schitul Maicilor, which had the misfortune to lie on the edge of the civic centre, were shorn of their outlying buildings, undermined, lifted onto huge rollers and dumped on waste land. Other shrines, such as Sf Ion Nou and the Italian church, are suffocated by apartment blocks built virtually on top of them.

The dictator's systematisation had a far more shocking impact than any previous modernising programmes, and it was done without public consultation. Having said all this, when I stayed in Bucharest for the third time, in 1995, I met Romanians who told me they liked Palatul Parlamentului. It was hard to tell if they meant it sincerely or if they were tired of hearing their city derided. After all, similar horrors are not totally unknown in other European cities.

In her *Balkan Trilogy*, the English novelist Olivia Manning describes late 1930's Bucharest as a decadent city in a no man's land between east and west. Her portrayal, seen through the eyes of her unhappy heroine, was brilliant but prejudiced by her own experiences of living there on the eve of war, and by her failing marriage. Sacheverell Sitwell travelled around Romania at the same period, and in *Romanian Journey* he gives a much more sympathetic view of the capital. The view of Bucharest as a marginal place that stands between oriental and occidental cultures is a legacy of the Romantic period. It is prevalent in British writing about the Balkans as a whole, and it dies hard.

Ten years before Olivia Manning arrived in Romania, the Bucovinian writer Gregor von Rezzori found it possible to indulge his sexual fantasies here much as Flaubert had done in Egypt 70 years before. Derek Patmore gives us a deferential glimpse into Bucharest's high society in *Invitation to Romania* (1939), showing no sign that this privileged world was on the verge of collapse. At a party given by the Sturdzas, he was enchanted to see parrots chained to the branches of trees and surprised to find that the house was a modern villa which contained a collection of paintings by Rouault. In *Romania Revisited*, published in 1999, Alan Ogden pieces together fragments of the gracious and cultivated atmosphere which permeated pre-1940 Bucharest. Ogden's book echoes the leisured, gentlemanly tones of Sitwell's and Patmore's travelogues; one can imagine him drifting around the country in an open tourer and tapping his cigarettes on a silver case as he admires the bra-less beauty of Romanian women. Looking back on the brilliance of 1930's Bucharest and the daring deeds of British spies who parachuted into Romania during the Second World War, Ogden dismisses the following 50 years as a period of anti-culture. But if the Soviet-style regime crushed Romania's intellectual and artistic sensibilities, Bucharest continued to have a cultural life of some kind, albeit spasmodically and with difficulty. Censorship did not destroy all creative, independent thought, and during the bleakest days of Ceauşescu's rule people would queue all night to buy tickets for the latest satirical plays. Bucharest exercised a fascination over the West even during the communist period, although its image was often a negative one. It was one of the cities that inspired Malcolm Bradbury's *Rates of Exchange* (1983), a novel about an unnamed eastern European capital which turns out to be much more exotic than its unpromising appearance suggests.

As it recovers from decades of physical and cultural starvation, Bucharest is opening out again. A friend told me that immediately after the Revolution, even Coca-Cola awnings were welcome because they showed that the doors to the West had opened. Ten years after the Revolution new bars, cafés and kiosks have opened, and the cream of Bucharest's chic saunters along Calea Victoriei window-shopping as if they had all the time and money in the world. Superficially at least, the city is flexing its aspirational muscles. Superficially, because Romanian women have a knack of looking wonderful on a budget tiny by Western European standards. But shocking contrasts remain. Many of the people who live here today do not have hot running water, and some have to make do without heating in winter. On the edge of the city, in suburbs such as Colentina and Floreasca, Romany families live in ghettoised shanty towns. They are feared and resented by their *gadjé* neighbours, but the Gypsy women in their flamboyant traditional clothes contribute a great deal to Bucharest's picturesque character, as they have done for centuries.

Practical information

 Tourist information
ONT Carpaţi at B-dul Magheru 7, ☎ 614 0759/1138/4058; fax 312 0915, is a hangover from the communist period and still claims to be the city's main tourist information centre; its chain-smoking assistants may deign to help you, but only if you go to the right desk—which is difficult because they are unmarked. Services offered here include organising hotel accommodation and rooms in private houses, tours of the city and regions, and car hire. You can also change money and travellers' cheques and get cash on *Visa/Master Card* and *Diners' Club*. Business hours are Mon–Fri 08.00–19.00 and Sat 08.00–14.00.

Alternatives include the nearby *Agenţie de Turism Patriot*, ☎ 337 4475, which arranges car hire, hotel rooms and trips to the Black Sea. *BTT* at Str D. I. Dobrescu 4–6, ☎ 613 3841,

312 1890; fax 312 0126, is orientated towards group travel for young people.

If you are driving, *Touring ACR (Automobil Clubul Român)*, near Piaţa Romană at Str Stanislav Cihoschi 2, ☎ 211 0410; fax 211 4366, can also help with hotel reservations and private accommodation; you can get free city maps here too. The staff act as agents for *Eurodollar* hire cars and are geared to helping foreign motorists. The office is open Mon–Fri 08.00–20.00, Sat 08.00–15.00 and Sun 08.00–14.00. ACR's head office is at Take Ionescu 27, ☎ 650 2595; fax 312 0434; it specialises in package tours and caravan holidays. ACR also has branches in most large towns and cities, although I found the managerial staff in Bucharest singularly uninterested in helping me.

Tourist offices and travel agencies are regulated by *ANAT* at Str Foişorului 8, Bloc 3C Scara 2, Ap 41, ☎ 321 1908. How much control it can really exercise is a matter of opinion, but the following travel agencies have a good reputation. *Atlantic Tours* at Calea Victoriei 202, ☎ 312 7689, 650 2848; fax 312 6860; e-mail atlantic@kappa.ro or www.kappa.ro/clients/atlantic, is a family firm that arranges tours of the city and the country on an individual and group basis; one of its specialities is an excursion by steam train. The Atlantic staff can also book visits to Palatul Parlamentului. *Continental Tours* at Calea Victoriei 56, ☎ 312 4342; fax 312 0134, rents Avis cars. *Dacia Tours* at B-dul Magheru 1-3, ☎ 210 4568/4547; fax 210 4515, is an agent for most international and national airlines. *Marshal Turism* at B-dul Unirii 20, ☎ 410 5304; fax 312 4657, is Romania's sole agent for American Express. It has a branch at B-dul Magheru 43, ☎ 659 6812, 650 2347; fax 223 1203; e-mail office@marshal.eunet.ro; website www.romania.eu.net/clients/marshal.

The doyenne of agrotourism in Romania is Maria Stoian of *ANTREC*, short for Asociaţia Naţională de Turism Rural Ecologic şi Cultural. *ANTREC* won European funding to get established in the early 1990s and now has a country-wide network of private householders willing to accept paying guests. This is what agrotourism means in Romanian. If you want to stay with a family in one of Bucharest's outlying villages, contact the head office on ☎ 222 4462; ☎/fax 222 8322, or write to PO Box 22–259, Bucureşti; *ANTREC* also has a city office at *Lar Tours*, Str Ştirbei Vodă 2-4, ☎ 615 3276/3206.

Visas

Bucharest's city hall, where you can make enquiries about visa problems, can be found at B-dul Kogălniceanu 27 near the Cismigiu Gardens. It is a splendid neo-Romanian construction from 1910 by Petre Antonescu (1873–1965).

Getting around
By train

The city's main train station is **Gara de Nord**, which serves most national destinations and all international ones, at B-dul Gării de Nord 2, ☎ 223 0880/0455. A few local trains that run between Bucharest and towns such as Braşov, Craiova, Piteşti, Sibiu, Suceava, Timişoara arrive/depart from **Gara Basarab**, an unwholesome station on the northwestern edge of Gara de Nord, ☎ 637 5705. Trains to and from Giurgiu use **Gara Progresul**, on the southern outskirts of the city via tram 12, ☎ 685 63851, 223 0660 internat 153 or 135. Local trains serving Snagov and a handful of seasonal trains to/from Mangalia and Cluj-Napoca use **Gara Băneasa**, on the northern edge at Şos Bucharest-Ploieşti, ☎ 223 0880 internat 3537. Some local services between the capital and Cernica and Constanţa use **Gara Obor** east of the centre, ☎ 635 0702, 223 0880 internat 152 or 238. You can book tickets in advance at the main CFR office at Str Domniţa Anastasia 10–14; for journeys within Romania go to the hall on the ground floor; international tickets are sold on the first floor. Both offices are open Mon–Fri 07.30–19.30 and Sat 08.00–12.00.

By bus

Buses to Western Europe leave from the northern end of Calea Dorobanţilor; companies operating services between Romania, Germany and Western Europe include *Atlas Reisen*, Str Ankara 4, *Double T*, Calea Victoriei 2, and *Touring* at Str Sofia 26. All of these firms have offices abroad; or ask for information at a travel agent. Domestic buses between Bucharest and other Romanian cities leave from/arrive at Calea Griviţei, outside *Hotel Nord*. There is a good bus network around the city, and the trolleys and trams are not bad either; buy tickets in advance from yellow kiosks and validate them on board. Some bus stops show route maps.

By metro

Bucharest's underground system, the metro, has three lines and is by far the most reliable form of public transport. Trains run 05.00–23.30; you can buy magnetic tickets for 2–10 journeys. Expect to be serenaded heartrendingly by Romany women and children begging for money. Maps of the metro are available from travel agencies.

By taxi

Metered taxis cruise the streets and wait at taxi ranks; they also congregate at railway stations and in front of large hotels. Choose a licensed cab (they have a registration number printed in white on black on the door) if possible; if you use an unmetered taxi, agree a price before you set off. ☎ 953 or 941 to call a taxi by phone. For travelling from Otopeni into the city, there is an excellent bus service (no. 783) connecting the airport and the **TAROM** building in central Bucharest. It leaves every 30–60 minutes throughout the day, and at the time of writing a single ticket costs a mere 1750 lei. Keep a tight hold of your luggage if you do not want to be shanghaied by the unlicensed cab drivers in the arrivals hall. Licensed cabs wait in line outside.

Airports

Bucharest has two commercial airports, **Otopeni**, which is reserved for international flights, ☎ 212 0122; fax 312 2744; and **Băneasa** for internal travel and flights to Kiev, Sofia and the Republic of Moldova, ☎ 633 0030; fax 210 5687. Both can be reached from the main Bucharest–Ploieşti road: Otopeni is 16km from the city centre, and Băneasa c 8km from the centre.

Airlines operating services in and out of Romania include:

Aeroflot, Str Biserica Amzei 29, ☎ 615 0314, 614 8972.

Air France, B-dul N. Bălcescu 35, ☎ 312 0086; fax 312 2395.

Air Moldova, Str Batistei 5, ☎ 312 1258; fax 312 0822.

Alitalia, Str Batistei 4, ☎ 210 4111/2; fax 210 4109.

Austrian Airlines, B-dul N. Bălcescu 7, ☎ 614 1221; fax 312 8391.

Balkan Air, Str Batiştei 9; ☎/fax 312 0711.

British Airways, B-dul Elisabeta 3, ☎ 303 2222.

Delta Airlines, B-dul D. Cantemir 1, Sc. 2, Et. 6, ☎ 323 4458; fax 323 2735.

Jaro International, Şos Bucharest–Ploieşti 14–22, ☎ 212 2273; fax 312 9758.

KLM, B-dul Magheru 41, ☎ 312 0149.

Liniile Aeriene Române, Str Ştirbei Vodă 2–4, ☎ 615 3206; fax 312 0148.

LOT, B-dul Magheru 41, ☎ 659 2575.

Lufthansa, B-dul Magheru 18, ☎ 650 4074; fax 312 0211.

Malev, Str G. Enescu 3, ☎ 321 0427; fax 312 0428.

Romavia, B-dul D. Cantemir 1, ☎ 311 1055; fax 311 1051.
Swissair, B-dul Magheru 18, ☎ 312 0238 internat 39; fax 312 0240.
TAROM: for information and bookings to do with international flights go to Str I. Brezoianu 10, on the first floor of the CFR building at Str Domniţa Anastasia 10–14, ☎ 615 0499, open Mon–Fri 08.00–19.30, Sat 08.00–12.00; internal flight information is available from Str Buzeşti 59–61, ☎ 659 4185/4125, open Mon–Fri 07.30–19.30, Sat 07.30–13.00.
Turkish Airlines, B-dul Bălcescu 35A, ☎ 311 3210.

Car hire

Avis, *Europcar* and *Hertz* all have offices at Otopeni airport. Phone *Hertz* (0040 1) 337 2910; *Europcar* (0040 1) 312 7078; or Avis (0040 1) 210 4344, but you can arrange car hire through ACR and some travel agents as well.

Petrol stations

There are 24-hour petrol stations in most districts, and at Şos Bucharest 2, Şos Colentina 262, Şos Chitilei km 9.7, on Calea Dorobanţi, at the intersection of Şos Pantelimon and Catelu, on Splaiul Independenţei, at km 36 on the Piteşti road, at on Str Tudor Arghezi near the *Intercontinental Hotel*. Most petrol stations sell unleaded petrol and diesel.

Parking

You can pay to leave your car opposite the royal palace in Piaţa Revoluţiei (near the Atheneum); there is an underground car park near Universităţii, and one called Ciclop, but this is very expensive. Street parking is controlled; watch out for towing-away signs and the *Pink Panther* trucks that do the deed.

Additional information
Money

Changing money in the capital should not be a problem as long as you avoid transactions on the street. There are plenty of exchange houses in central Bucharest; most of them open early and close late. Make sure you take only virgin or very clean notes; cashiers will not change foreign notes that are damaged. If you have travellers' cheques, it is best to cash them at a bank because exchange houses generally charge a hefty commission; the same applies if you use your credit card to cash money. Some banks, such as *Bancorex*, *BCIT* and *Bancă Agricola*, will not cash travellers' cheques after 12 noon. *Bancorex* has a branch overlooking Piaţa Victoriei at Calea Victoriei 155 and another at B-dul Bălcescu 11 (open 08.30–14.00); *BCIT* is at Şos Nicolae Titulescu 1 and Str Doamnei 12 (open 09.00–14.30), and *Bancă Agricola* can be found at Str Lipscani 27 and Str Smârdan 3; the latter has a strikingly handsome, Eclectic façade. There are ATM cashpoints at *Bancă Agricola*; *Bancă Comercială Română* at B-dul Elisabeta 5; *Bancă Naçională* at Str Doamnei 8, and at *Banc Post*, B-dul Magheru 1-3 beside the *Blue Moon* night club.

Telephones and postal services

Bucharest has blue pay phones that take 20 lei pieces and orange phones, for long-distance calls, that take 100 lei pieces or cards. For international calls use a hotel, one of the train stations, or the Telephone Palace on the corner of Calea Victoriei and Str Matei Millo. You can also send faxes from here. Bucharest's area code is 01.

The main **post office** is at Str Matei Millo no. 10, 2 minutes' walk down the hill from the telephone palace on the right-hand side. You can easily miss it because it is very small.

Film developing

There is a person-operated photomat in

the Piaţa Romănă metro station. Camera shops that will develop films include *Agfa Film*, B-dul I. C. Brătianu 35; *Foto Studio Classic*, Str Doamnei 21, ☎ 315 5277, which has a photo studio and can make passport photos; *Fuji* at Piaţa Romănă 9 on the corner with B-dul Magheru, and at Calea Moşilor 241; *Kodak* at B-dul Magheru 8-10, and Calea Moşilor 257. There is a Kodak developing centre in the entrance of the *Ambassador Hotel*. Few Romanians use slide film when they are on holiday, and Bucharest is about the only place in the country which has commercial slide-processing facilities.

Laundry services

Nufărul at Calea Moşilor 274 and many other branches, is open Mon–Fri 07.00–20.00, Sat 09.00–13.00. It does not take bags but charges per item. *Nuf Nuf* at Calea Şerban Vodă 76 is open 24 hours, and offers coffee and TV while you wash your own socks.

Health services

For medical emergencies, ☎ 961 for an ambulance or 969 for the special ambulance service (for pregnant women or women with small children). First aid in hospitals is free, but all other medical services have to be paid for. The city centre has a number of 24-hour chemists.

Clinics and hospitals

The American Medical Centre, Str Dragoş Vodă 70,☎ 210 2796; fax 210 4923; *Batiştei Clinic*, Str Batiştei 27, ☎ 315 1643, open Mon–Fri 08.00–18.00, Sat 08.00–14.00; *Biomedica International*, Str Mihai Eminescu 42, ☎/fax 211 7136, open 08.00–21.00, 24-hour emergency ☎ 230 4570/092 33 8383, reservations for private rooms in the Florească Hospital, ☎ 230 7843/230 8901; *Emergency Clinic Hospital*, Calea Florească 8, ☎ 230 0166, open 24 hours; for gynaecological problems, the *Marie Stopes Foundation* (aka Mary Stopps), B-dul Mărăşeşti 90, ☎ 330 1536/330 2585, open Mon–Fri 08.00–18.00, Sat 08.00–14.00; *Medicover*, 24-hour medical centre, Calea Plevnei 96, ☎ 310 4411/310 4056/310 4197/310 4198/310 4199; fax 310 4022, with another branch at Str Eugen Lovinescu 16, ☎ 223 4931/223 4932; fax 222 7352; emergency ☎ 310 4040/310 4007/310 4008; *Unirea Medical Center*, B-dul Unirii 57, bl E4, Tronson 1, has a 24-hour emergency service for members only, open Mon–Fri 08.00–20.00, Sat 09.00–14.00, ☎ 327 1188/327 1189; fax 327 1195, general practitioner service at Str Batiştei 9, ap 31, ☎/fax 211 5942.

24-hour ambulance service. *SOS*, serving Bucharest's Emergency Hospital and the Elias Hospital pediatric department, is based at Str Leon Vodă 19A, Sector 4, ☎/fax 330 9594, ☎ 675 2195, emergencies ☎ 976.

24-hour pharmacies. *Farmadex*, Calea Moşilor 280; *Sensibiu*, Calea Dorobanţilor 65.

Dentists. *Biodent*, Piaţa Amzei 10–22, Sc D, Ap 9, ☎ 312 3752; *Dent-A-America*, Str Varşovia 4, ☎ 212 2608/212 2826; *Dentatek*, Str Brezolanu 44,☎ 310 1637/315 1693, closed Sun; *Dental Corporation International*, St. G. Demostone 21, ☎ 410 9390; fax 232 2897, closed Sun.

Opticians. *Eba Optics*, Str Ion Câmpineanu 20, ☎ 315 4688; *German Optik*, B-dul Unirii 17; *Opticris*, B-dul Unirii 17; *Optinova*, B-dul Unirii 5.

Street crime

Rumours that the Russian mafia has arrived in Bucharest are not to be taken lightly, but street crime in the capital is no more dangerous than in many other Western cities. But be careful of pickpockets and purse snatchers, especially when using public transport. Gangs of thieves have a favourite trick that involves surrounding a (usually) female target on a crowded bus and making a slit in her shoulder bag so that the contents fall out. As passengers scramble to get off or on at a stop, the thieves can make off with valuables before the victim has time to protest or even realise what has happened.

Never agree to change money on the street, and be wary of anyone in plain clothes claiming to be a policeman who wants to see if you are carrying foreign cash. Do not reach for your wallet or passport, even if they produce an ID card. Real policemen wear uniforms. If they continue to hassle you, shout 'Poliţia!', or swear loudly in your own language. As in any unknown city, it is wise to look purposeful, as though you know where you are going. It is also sensible not to wander around parks late at night. If you need to contact the police urgently, ☎ 955.

Where to stay

***** *Crown Plaza Flora*, Str. Poligrafiei 1, ☎ 224 0034, fax 224 1126; *Intercontinental*, B-dul Nicolae Balcescu 4, ☎ 310 2020, fax 312 0486, e-mail inter@starnets.ro. **** *Lido*, B-dul Magheru 5–7, ☎ 314 4930, fax 312 6544; *Majestic*, Str. Academiei 11, ☎ 312 1967, fax 310 2799, e-mail majestic@starnets, ro; *Bucureşti*, Calea Victorieri 63–81, ☎ 312 7070, fax 312 0927.
*** *Ambassador*, B-dul Magheru 8–10, ☎ 315 9080, fax 312 3595; *Capitol*, Calea Victoriei 29, ☎ 315 8030; *Dorobanţi*, Calea Dorobanţi 1–7, ☎ 211 5484, fax 210 0150.
** *Astoria*, B-dul Dinicu Golescu 27, ☎ 637 7640, 638 2690; *Banat*, Piaţa Rosetti 5, ☎ 313 1057, fax 312 6547. If you are looking for a bed at the lower end of the price range *Villa Helga*, a hostel at Str. Salcamilor 2, ☎/ 610 2214, e-mail helga@rotravel.com is highly recommended.

Food and shopping

Western-style supermarkets and delicatessens are springing up all over the city centre, but one of the most enjoyable ways to buy food is at one of the many open-air fruit and vegetable markets. One of the largest and most central of these can be found behind Leahu and Urum's 1960s *Unirea* department store on the northeast corner of Piaţa Unirii. Often crowded, the market is open Mon–Sat 06.00–20.00 and Sun 06.00–12.00. Bucureşteni say that the most exclusive open-air stalls can be found in Piaţa Amzei, a pretty square surounded by neo-Baroque and Jugendstil houses between Calea Victoriei and Str Mendeleev, 5 minutes' walk south of B-dul Dacia; the market has a rural atmosphere and traders here often have time for banter; do not be afraid to haggle. This is also a great place to browse among intriguing pots of honey. There are bakers', butchers' and supermarkets close by.

Restaurants

Eating out in Bucharest can be expensive, but if you are looking for atmosphere as well as quality, try the *Doina Restaurant* in Ion Mincu's classic neo-Romanian building at Şos Kiseleff 8, *Velvet* at Str Ştirbei Vodă 2–4, *Casa Oamenilor de Ştiinţă de Vară* at Piaţa Lahovari 9 (known as COS, this is popular with the city's intellectuals) or *Il Gattopardo*, housed in the Writers' Union at Calea Victoriei 115. You would not be wasting your time if you went to the *Doi Cocoţi* on the way north out of town at Şos Bucureşti-Târgovişte 6. *Nan Jing* at Str Gheorghe Manu 2 is Bucharest's oldest and finest Chinese restaurant. Other recommendations include *Bistro Ateneo* and *La Taifus*, *Casa Veche* (at Str. G. Enescu 15–17, ☎ 312 5816), the *Gogosaru*, *Four Seasons* (☎ 311 2887) and the expensive *Terrace* at the *Café de Paris*;

Mamma Mia on the north side of Piața Kogălniceanu, *La Soiseau* on Șos Kiseleff, *Casa Domnească*, *Casa Română*, *The Golden Horn*, specialising in Turkish dishes, and *Da Vinci's* (behind the main university building). *Carul cu Bere* at Str Stavropoleos 5 is modelled on a 19C Bavarian *bierkeller*, decorated with elaborate, gilded murals showing hunting scenes, and a lot of chunky wooden furnishings.

Fast-food restaurants, such as *Spring Time*, *Pizza Hut*, *TGI Friday* and the inevitable *McDonald's*, can be found around the centre; *Sheriffs* on B-dul Brătianu also serves good fast food. The underground pizzerias beside Universității metro station are also worth remembering if your blood sugar runs low. Another good place for a quick snack is the little shop that serves fresh *plăcinte* (flaky pastries with sweet or savoury fillings) over its counter in the wall on the northeast corner of Str General Berthelot and Str Popatatu.

 Entertainment

Bucharest has several 'art' **cinemas** that specialise mainly in old films: these include *Cinematica* (the old *Eforie*) at Str Eforie 2, and *Union* at Str Ion Câmpineanu 21, near the Crețulescu church. The *Prima Club* on the fourth floor of the National Theatre building at B-dul Bălcescu 2 shows good-quality films during the summer, and you can soak up some classics of French cinema at the *French Institute* on Wednesday evenings. Other cinemas are *Cotroceni* at Str Cotroceni 9 (metro Eroilor); *Patria* at B-dul Magheru 12–14. Films change every Friday; foreign-language films have Romanian subtitles. Excellent concerts of classical music are held at *Ateneul Român* at Str Benjamin Franklin 1 on the edge of Piața Revoluției, ☎ 615 0026. For up-to-date information, try website www.pcnet.ro and look in the weekly Bucharest guides.

Romania deserves its reputation for marvellous **theatre** productions. *Teatrul Național* (the National Theatre, ☎ 614 7171) has the best reputation, but try the *Sala Izvor* at Teatrul L. S. Bulandra at B-dul Schitul Măgureanu 1, at the southern end of the boulevard. During Ceaușescu's rule, it put on plays that were as close as anyone could get to criticising him in public without risking jail. *Rapsodia Română*, the folk theatre, is at Str Lipscani 53, and *Teatrul de Operetta* at B-dul Bălcescu 2, ☎ 313 6348.

For **classical music** try the magnificent *Ateneul Român* (*The Atheneum*) at Str Benjamin Franklin 1 on the edge of Piața Revoluției, ☎ 315 6875; *Opera Română* often puts on excellent productions at 70–72 B-dul Kogălniceanu, ☎ 313 1857. Then there is *Sala Radio*, headquarters of the long-established Romanian Radio Society. It has two concert halls at Str General Berthelot 60–64, ☎ 314 6000, and performances start at 21.00.

Books and periodicals

Immediately after the 1989 revolution a flood of newspapers and journals hit the stands. Their publishers' euphoria was soon curtailed by what looked like deliberate censorship through a government-imposed shortage of newsprint. Today you can again buy any number of newspapers and magazines; some of the central newsagents sell foreign papers as well. The national daily, *România Libera*, was one of the official mouthpieces of the communist regime but now belongs to a foreign proprietor. Not to be confused with *The Free Romanian* founded by Ion Rațiu, who returned to Romania in 1990 after 50 years in exile to stand as a candidate in the 1990 elections. The charismatic Rațiu, who made a fortune in London as a property developer and shipping magnate, stood for the National Peasants' Party. Like Iliescu's other opponents, NPP supporters were harassed during the campaign by the National

Salvation Front and the offices of *România Liberă* were destroyed in a mysterious fire. An English-language edition of the paper is published weekly. *Adevărul* is the nearest thing Romania has to a paper of record; other heavyweight newspapers include *Evenimentul Zilei*, *Curentul* and *Cotideanul*.

A good read if you know Romanian is the adventurous *22*, a critical review which has articles on politics and art. Named after the revolution on 22 December 1989, *22* attracts respected commentators such as Andrei Pleşu and some of Romania's sharpest critics such as H.-R. Patapievici and Lucian Boia. For the more satirically minded there is *Academia Caţavencu*, roughly equivalent to France's *Canard Enchaîné* or Britain's *Private Eye*. Caţavencu was founded in 1992 by Mircea Dinescu; the title comes from 19C playwright I. L. Caragiale, who made his name by exposing his fellow countrymen's social vanities. Dinescu played a leading role in the 1989 revolution and is currently president of the Writers' Union.

Other, more serious-minded, reviews to look out for are *Dilema*, published by Fundaţia Culturală Romană and edited by Pleşu; it features articles on philosophy and ethnography and has its own website:http://www.netside.net/romanian_lobby/dilema.html or http://www.sfos.ro/culture/dilema. *România Literară*, published on Tuesdays, is one of the country's oldest literary warhorses: it was founded in 1855 during the nationalist struggle. The magazine encompasses a wide range of views, some of them anti-Hungarian. *Orizont* was founded in 1948 and is now the second largest and second most important literary review in Romania, with a circulation of around 5000 (*România Literară* has 8000). Because of the economic sanctions suffered by all Romanian publications after Iliescu came to power, it has had to cut down from weekly to fortnightly issues.

There are bookshops around the university and in Victoriei. **Humanitas**, a publisher which produces academic and literary titles, has a shop at Calea Victoriei 20, facing Hotel Bucureşti. For new, secondhand and antiquarian books in English and other non-Romanian languages, try **Librări Noi** at B-dul Bălcescu 18. **Librărie Mihai Eminescu** and the **Universitate Populară Ioan I Dalles** bookshop (known to everyone as *Dalles*) are next door to each other on the corner of Regina Elisabeta and Academiei: *Dalles* is a good source of secondhand art books. Other options include **Fundaţia Cărţii Librărie** at B-dul Lascăr Catargiu 3, which has a good selection of phrasebooks, dictionaries and guides. The **French Institute** at B-dul Dacia 77 also sells a range of French books and magazines, while **Euromedia**, at Str General Berthelot 4, has German-language editions. A number of English-language newspapers and guides are published in Bucharest itself; the best places to look for these are in big hotels. *Romania Turism: Pagini Naţionali* is an annual directory containing addresses of tourist and government organisations in the capital as well as Romanian, French and English guides to individual counties.

Organisations such as the **British Council** (at Calea Dorobanţilor 14) and the **French Institute** have excellent libraries which take daily newspapers from all over Europe. You can also read at the library of the **Romanian Academy** in Calea Victoriei (the entrance is opposite the Casino Victoria, a few metres north of the crossing with B-dul Dacia). Take your passport and a letter of introduction. The **Soros Foundation** is financed by Hungarian billionaire George Soros as part of an initiative which covered all the former eastern bloc countries. The Foundation supports a wide range of cultural and social organisations and is an excellent source of information on contemporary artists and exhibitions. It has a good library as well.

History of Bucharest

A settlement existed on the city site before the 14C, and it was strengthened by Mircea cel Bătrân (Mircea the Wise, r. 1386–1418) when he built a chain of citadels across the Danube Plain to protect Wallachia from the Turks. The earliest-known documentary evidence about Bucharest comes in 1459, when Mircea's grandson, Prince Vlad III (r. 1456–76), known as the Impaler, built a fortified palace. It was a promising choice because the settlement lay at the crossroads of two important routes linking Wallachia with the outside world. At the same time, Bucharest also stood midway between the Danubian forts of Giurgiu and Silistra and the princely residences of Târgoviște and Curtea de Argeș.

In 1453, just six years before Vlad built his Bucharest palace, Constantinople fell to the Ottoman Turks, bringing to an end 1100 years of Byzantine rule in eastern Europe. As a result, medieval Bucharest became a refuge for Byzantine culture in exile, developing as a religious centre long before it became a recognisable town. Wallachia's princes negotiated a measure of freedom from Ottoman interference by paying the Turks a hefty annual tribute. And while the Sultans went on to capture Belgrade and Budapest and finally (with reluctant help from Wallachia) to attack Vienna, Bucharest flourished because it stood on the only viable trade route linking western Europe with the Near East. Bucharest became the leading city of Wallachia in 1659, after Târgoviște was partially destroyed by Turkish and Tartar armies.

Wallachia's tempestuous history threw up some strong personalities. Some of them, like Mihai Viteazul (who united Moldavia, Transylvania and Wallachia 1599–1601), Șerban Cantacuzino (r. 1678–88) and Constantin Brâncoveanu (r. 1688–1714), have entered Romanian mythology as heroic proto-nationalists. They also commissioned buildings in Bucharest.

The Cantacuzino family can trace its origins to 14C Byzantine emperor John VI Cantacuzinos; after the conquest of Constantinople, John's descendants sought refuge in Christian territory rather than give up their faith. One branch of the family took root in Wallachia in the early 17C, and another settled in Moldavia. Cantacuzinos rose to positions of influence in both principalities, where they engaged in fierce competition with other boyars. Their greatest rivals were the Băleni family, whose members Șerban Cantacuzino systematically eliminated once he was on the throne.

Șerban Cantacuzino built the royal palace and monastery at Cotroceni after surviving an attempt on his life and his reign continued to exemplify Wallachia's tortuous politics. As an Ottoman vassal he owed allegiance to the Ottoman Sultan, but he also formed secret alliances with the German Emperor, the Russian Tsar, the King of Poland and the Pope. He was forced to support the Turks during their 1683 siege of Vienna, but he managed to aid the Habsburgs at the same time. Șerban Cantacuzino has also gone down in history for commissioning the first Romanian-language edition of the Bible.

Brâncoveanu was called *Altân bey* (the Golden Prince) by the Turks because he behaved like a latter-day Byzantine emperor. As well as building beautiful palaces at Mogoșoaia and Potlogi and endowing magnificent churches, he introduced liberal fiscal reforms and widened Bucharest's roads. He also encouraged artists to develop the style of building and ornamentation now known as Brâncovenesque. A.M. Del Chiaro, a Florentine historian who worked as secretary to Constantin Brâncoveanu, commented that if a new plan to enclose Bucharest with a circular city wall was followed, the houses of its 50,000 inhabitants would look lost because there were so few of them. These homes belonged mainly to merchants, craftsmen and labourers, and each household had its own garden of fruit trees. They made the city look very pretty. By 1774, Bucharest had 25 hotels or inns, each of them built in a Turkish style. Brâncoveanu's beheading was instigated by his uncle, Constantin Cantacuzino, whose son, Ștefan, reigned briefly 1714–15—shortly afterwards, Ștefan and his father were executed by the Ottomans.

In 1716, the Turks imposed direct rule over Wallachia, installing Greek-speaking princes from the Phanar district of Constantinople. Known as Phanariots for this reason, their main task was to ensure that tributes were paid promptly. But there was no system regulating the principalities' obligations to Istanbul, and in practice the Phanariots often proved weak or greedy. There were exceptions: Nicolae and Constantin Mavrocordat, Alexandru and Constantin Ipsilanti and Nicolae Mavrogheni all introduced radical reforms.

19C Bucharest witnessed an upsurge of national consciousness. Young intellectuals keen to see an end to Ottoman rule sought inspiration and support in western Europe. Many of them went to France and took part in the revolution of February 1848. They then returned to inititiate their own '1848' at home. At the same time, princes such as Gheorghe Bibescu (r. 1838–48) introduced French-style architecture and city planning. This transformed Bucharest into a cosmopolitan capital which came to be known as 'a little Paris of the East'.

Romania's emergence as a modern state inspired a huge outpouring of creative energy that continued to change the face of Bucharest. It was bombed during the First and Second World Wars, but the interim period saw exciting developments in both building and design. But most of these advances were abruptly curtailed by the Stalinist policies that were introduced when the communists came to power.

The architecture of Bucharest

The Ministry of Culture lists some 5000 historic buildings in Bucharest alone. Among these are 16C and 17C churches, 18C villas, 19C apartment blocks and early 20C factories. There are churches everywhere, some of them sandwiched incongruously between tower blocks or shoved onto building sites, a few resplendent in Byzantine-style courtyards, and others, such as the monastery of Plumbuita, tucked away in sleeping suburbs.

According to architect Dana Harhoiu, the oldest surviving masonry buildings are churches and monasteries from the mid-16C. Harhoiu believes that Bucharest developed according to a symmetrical plan modelled on the ideal Renaissance city. Medieval churches here were located at the centre of their parishes; in Bucharest the parishes accumulated snowball fashion but also in concentric rings. Certain churches stood on points which converged to an *axis mundi*, the city's heart. Contrary to popular opinion, Harhoiu claims that the dead centre of Bucharest was not Mircea Ciobanul's 1559 princely church in Curtea Veche, but another shrine, Sf Gheorghe Vechi (Old St George's). This church was erected shortly afterwards for one of Prince Mircea's councillors, a boyar named Bălăceanu. Sf Gheorghe stood on the site of the town's first Orthodox bishopric and beside the junction of the city's two main transcontinental access roads, Calea Moșilor and Calea Călărașilor-Splaiul Independenței. It also stood near the spot marked out as the city's official bull's-eye, kilometre 0. Sf Gheorghe Vechi was burnt to the ground in the Great Fire of 1847, but Harhoiu believes it must have been an important building because at one time the church also housed the Princely Academy.

Inspired by the Crusades, imaginary maps of the holy city of Jerusalem proliferated in European literature during the Middle Ages; some of these plans showed a circle cut into four equal sectors by two diagonals; others showed a series of concentric circles sliced by eight diagonals which were connected at their outer edges to form a star-shaped city wall. And even though the Crusaders proved that the real Jerusalem was very different, the notion of the ideal city persisted into the Renaissance when Italian artists such as Filarete and Leonardo da Vinci refined these theories still further, making direct links between art, spirituality and mathematics. Filarete's architectural treatise was translated into Latin on the orders of Hungarian king, Matei Corvin. A copy of the manuscript has been found in Russia. It could easily have been seen in the Romanian lands as well.

There is some evidence to show that Bucharest's early town planners shared these ideals. Dana Harhoiu has plotted the circles and diagonals and found that a remarkable number of existing and demolished churches conform to the scheme. According to her, this geometrical plan survived more or less intact until the 19C.

Most houses in medieval Bucharest were made of wattle and daub over timber frames, a technique still used in some rural areas; stone and brick were reserved mainly for churches and noblemen's houses. By the 17C the skyline was punctuated with watchtowers and scores of neo-Byzantine cupolas.

Șerban Cantacuzino built his princely residence and monastery on a country estate to the west of Bucharest. Cotroceni became the most important royal palace in Wallachia, and while nothing remains of the church, part of the handsome brick shell of Cantacuzino's 17C palace has survived in a faithful copy.

The Phanariot Greeks who came to live in Bucharest imported a new concept of housing. Their two-storey buildings were modelled on homesteads and inns in the Christian quarters of Istanbul. They had deeply overhanging eaves, and were built around rectangular courtyards. On the street side, windows were often enclosed behind shuttered balconies. At the back of each property there was usually a plot of land where members of the household cultivated fruit, vegetables and flowers. These dwellings were modelled on houses in the Christian quarters of Constantinople, and several of them remain in Bucharest.

Another idea which the Phanariots introduced to Bucharest was the *maï-*

dan. Designed as open spaces for social interaction and markets and fairs, these areas were located beyond the existing city limits, often near a church, and each one had a fountain in the centre. *Maïdan* can be found right across Asia, but several of these *terrains vagues* (as the French call them) were constructed along Calea Moșilor. In 1869, artist Amedeo Preziosi painted a spirited watercolour of the *maïdan* used for Târgul Moșilor (the Ancestors' Fair); the picture is part of a large collection of his Bucharest scenes held by the National Art Museum.

Early 19C Bucharest witnessed a sea change from Oriental to Western culture. A graphic illustration of this can be found in the neo-Classical rotunda built for the Ghica family as a chapel on their estate near the city's northeastern limits. Inside Capela Ghica Tei are two portraits; one shows Grigore IV Ghica (r. 1822–28) and the other his brother, Alexandru (r. 1834–42). Grigore wears a caftan, while only ten years later Alexandru is dressed in the tight-waisted jacket, waistcoat and trousers of western Europe.

Gheorghe Bibescu (r. 1838–48) was a weak ruler who was accused of pandering to the Russian consul. But he also loved France and helped to diffuse French fashions in the capital. Thanks to him, elegant boulevards such as Kiseleff were created in the northern sectors of the city, and he financed several parks modelled on French designs. They included the Cismigiu Gardens. Ironically, his shortcomings as a ruler drove many young Romanians to seek exile in Paris, where they joined forces with the revolutionaries of 1848 and eventually chased Bibescu off the throne.

The man in charge of redesigning Bucharest later in the century was engineer and architect Grigore Cerchez (1850–1927). Cerchez had seen Haussman's Parisian transformations at firsthand. He introduced two new axes on the lines of Haussman's 'great crossroads'. One of these ran north–south along present-day boulevards Catargiu, Magheru, Bălcescu and Brătianu, and the other went east–west from Kogălniceanu, Regina Elisabeta, Carol I and Pache Protopopescu to Gara de Est. Cerchez also made radical changes to the northern sector of the city, extending the existing axes of Kiseleff, Aviatorilor and 1 Mai into three fan-like boulevards.

Cerchez was one of several planners who made the city look more dignified. But while their alterations smoothed out some kinks, the new system left much of the existing street network alone. Inevitably some buildings were sacrificed: for example, in the new financial district at the southern end of Calea Victoriei, the 17C monastery of Sf Ioan cel Nou was pulled down to make way for Paul Gottereau's CEC building, and in 1912 the old monastery church of Sărindar gave way to the ornate military headquarters, Cercul Militar. Fundamental changes also took place at Piața George Coșbuc, to the southwest of Piața Unirii. This oval square with its radiating streets was built in 1893 on the site of a pond, and all the surrounding houses were cleared to make way for it. At the same time the Dâmbovița River was canalised through the city centre.

19C building in Bucharest was nothing if not varied, but it is possible to identify four main styles. neo-Classicism is exemplified in the superb Palatul Ghica-Tei (1822), Josef Heft's National Theatre (1846–52) and the University Rectorat (1869) designed by Alexandru Orăscu; the Gothic Revival is shown in Konrad Schwink's Șuțu Palace (c 1833) and the French

> ### Ion Mincu (1852–1912)
> Born in Focșani on the border between Wallachia and Moldavia, Mincu studied in Bucharest and Paris, where the Society of French Architects gave him a scholarship to travel in Spain, Italy and Greece. Attracted by Art Nouveau, he developed a specifically Romanian brand of the style inspired by elements of medieval vernacular and religious architecture which he found in his native country. His neo-Romanian style incorporates Byzantine and Islamic motifs such as arcaded verandahs, lancet arches and roofs modelled on watchtowers; typically, his buildings are asymmetrical and contrast richly decorated areas with areas of plain wall. Mincu had many imitators, but his most famous designs include Casa Lahovari (1886), now the Dr I. Cantacuzino Hospital in Piața Lahovari, Casa Monteoru (1889), now the Writers' Union building on the corner of B-dul Dacia and Calea Victoriei, and the Buftea Restaurant (1889–92), now the Doina, just south of Arcul de Triumf in Șos Kiseleff. In 1906 Mincu restored the Stavropoleos Church.

Eclectic style in Gottereau's CEC building (started in 1895). But the most interesting of these new trends was the neo-Romanian style, whose champion was architect Ion Mincu.

After the First World War, Romania enlarged its territory, gaining Transylvania, northern Bucovina, Bessarabia and Dobrogea. The new state enjoyed one of the healthiest economies in Europe; it also avoided the worst effects of the 1929–33 depression. Adventurous patrons, new technology and tax breaks created conditions that encouraged innovative design, especially in building. Heavily ornamented academicism gave way to a clean and simple style which, in the words of architect Duiliu Marcu, 'satisfied both the eyes and the brain'.

Leading architects from Romania's dynamic modernist period include Horia Creangă (1892–1943), Marcel Iancu (also spelt Janco), and his brother Iuliu. Other names to look out for are Duiliu Marcu (1886–1966), who designed the existing Gara de Nord and the surrounding area including austere the Ministry of Transport building which faces the station, and Piața Eroilor; Octav Doicescu (1902–81), whose 1932 Rest House for the Gaz-Electra Company near Snagov Lake still stands, and G.M. Cantacuzino (1899–1960), author of the Crissoveloni Bank and other fine buildings. All these architects were involved in plans to redesign the capital as a garden city. However, the crisp and airy buildings they created have fallen into a state of such neglect that they are unrecognisable. And sadly, their vision of a constructivist utopia is sometimes confused with that of the Soviet-style architects who came after them.

In 1935 a team of architects and engineers, including Duiliu Marcu and G.M. Cantacuzino, devised a new master plan which came into being three years later, completing the ring road and the north–south and east–west axes, and establishing residential, industrial and green zones. The northern edge of Bucharest became a Garden City and the Colentina River was diverted into a series of artificial lakes that flow into one another in a series of loops from west to east.

> ### Marcel Iancu (1895–1984)
> A Romanian of Jewish origins, Iancu was born in Bucharest. He studied architecture in Zurich, where in 1916 he co-founded the Dada movement with Hugo Ball and fellow Romanians Tristan Tzara and Ion Vinea. An idealist by nature, he wanted to create a synthesis of abstract painting and architecture, and to dissolve the barriers between fine and applied art. After visiting Paris, he returned to Romania in 1922 and electrified the public with a show of his latest post-Cubist paintings. Iancu enthused other young artists with his avant-garde ideas and founded the arts review *Contimporanul*. The magazine carried articles on a wide range of creative activities, not just architecture. It was a great success and its contributors included Hans Richter, Hans Arp, Kurt Schwitters, Theo van Doesburg and several other leaders of progressive European art. Iancu organised the first international *Contimporanul* show with Max Mary and Ion Vinea in 1924. The exhibition brought together Paul Klee and Arthur Segal with Brâncuși, Victor Brauner, Matthis Teutsch and many others, placing Romanian artists firmly on the map of vanguard culture. In 1926, Iancu designed the first modernist buildings in Bucharest: tenement housing in Str Trinității and Imobilul Herman Iancu at Popper Street 55. As he grew more experienced his style became more innovative, maturing into the simple outlines and playful surfaces of his 'white cubes'. For an example of this phase of his work, head east along B-dul Dacia to Str Silvestru (beyond Piața Galați) to no. 75, his Villa Jean Juster (1931). Iancu fled to Israel in 1941; in Tel Aviv he became a member of the New Horizons group, and in 1953 he established the famous artists' colony at Ein Hod.

Under the early days of the communist leadership, new state buildings conformed to the Russian model. One of the first and most striking examples is Casa Scânteii (House of Sparks) from 1956, which towers over Piața Presei Libere on the city's northern outskirts. (Scânteia was the name of a socialist underground newpaper founded in 1932.) The last was the hardly less Stalinist Palatul Parlamentului, then called Casa Popurului, which Ceaușescu scheduled for a grand opening in August 1990.

Ceaușescu's *sistematisarea* (systematisation) of nearly half the country's rural villages had only just begun when he was executed. The only places badly affected were the outskirts of Bucharest, including northern hamlets such as Otopeni, and Bălătești, near Mogoșoaia, where the inhabitants were given a few hours' notice to quit their homes. At first sight, the 'agro-industrial centre' at Bălătești does not look bad. But the flats were thrown up in such a hurry that they had no central heating and in some cases no running water.

Curtea Veche, Lipscani and Calea Victoriei

Bucharest's most picturesque quarter can be found in Lipscani between B-dul Bălcescu and Calea Victoriei. **Curtea Veche** (the Old Princely Court) stands near the junction of Str Franceza (formerly Str Maniu) and Șepcari, containing truncated pieces of wall and arcaded buildings that were created for *voivode* Mircea Ciobanul (Prince Mircea the Shepherd, r. 1545–52) and his successors between 1545–59. It was destroyed in 1767, but beside the ruins stands Bucharest's oldest church, the chunky **Biserica Domnească**, completed in 1591. Altered, restored and rebuilt many times, this royal church was modelled on the triconch Serbian basilicas of the Morava Valley, with a deeply recessed cupola and rich geometrical detailing on the cornices. The west door is framed by Brâncovenesque scrolling, which was a later addition and contrasts strikingly with the severity of the building as a whole (this is a 1915 copy of the carving that was commissioned by Prince Ștefan Cantacuzino in the early 18C). Although it is badly damaged, you can still see the handsome Byzantine

Bucharest's parks and gardens

Apart from the Botanic Gardens, which were founded in 1860, the city is surprisingly well endowed with green spaces. Most of these appeared in the 19C, but were by no means the first—Wallachian princes were keen on gardens from the days of Mircea Ciobanul. In c 1600 the princely court in Bucharest employed a team of gardeners, and Matei Basarab (r. 1633–54) was known for the beautiful flowers which his wife, Princess Elena, used to augment with seeds that came from far-away Brașov. Constantin Brâncoveanu maintained these horticultural traditions in his formal, Italianate garden, which was kept in trim by 20 men. Some boyars preferred informal English styles, and by the early 19C a visiting Hungarian nobleman could remark that every Wallachian prince either cultivated a garden or built a manor.

Public gardens in Bucharest date from the early 19C, when Prince Gheorghe Bibescu commissioned Austrian landscape gardener Carl Friedrich Wilhelm Meyer to design the Kiseleff Gardens, complete with artificial lake and rocks. The unkempt vestiges of this park can be found between the southern ends of B-dul 1 Mai, Șos Kiseleff and B-dul Aviatorilor. After the revolution of 1848, Meyer began work on Grădina Cismigiu in the city centre. This lovely park, which is probably modelled on the Parisian Jardin des Plantes, replaced an area of stinking marshland that belonged to the Ottoman water inspectorate.

A distinctly French influence can also be seen in Parcul Carol, laid out in 1906 by E. Redont to coincide with the Romanian International Fair. Parcul Carol formed an integral part of the new Inter district to the southwest of Piața Unirii. It was also close to Bucharest's first railway station, Filaret, inaugurated in 1869. The little-known Grădina Ioanid is more oriental, with sinuous pathways and variegated beds. It is near the crossing of B-dul Dacia and Str Polonă; entry is via Întrarea Ioanid, on the northeast corner of Piața Gheorghe Cantacuzino. It stands on the site of a former maïdan amongst a cluster of private villas.

130 • BUCHAREST

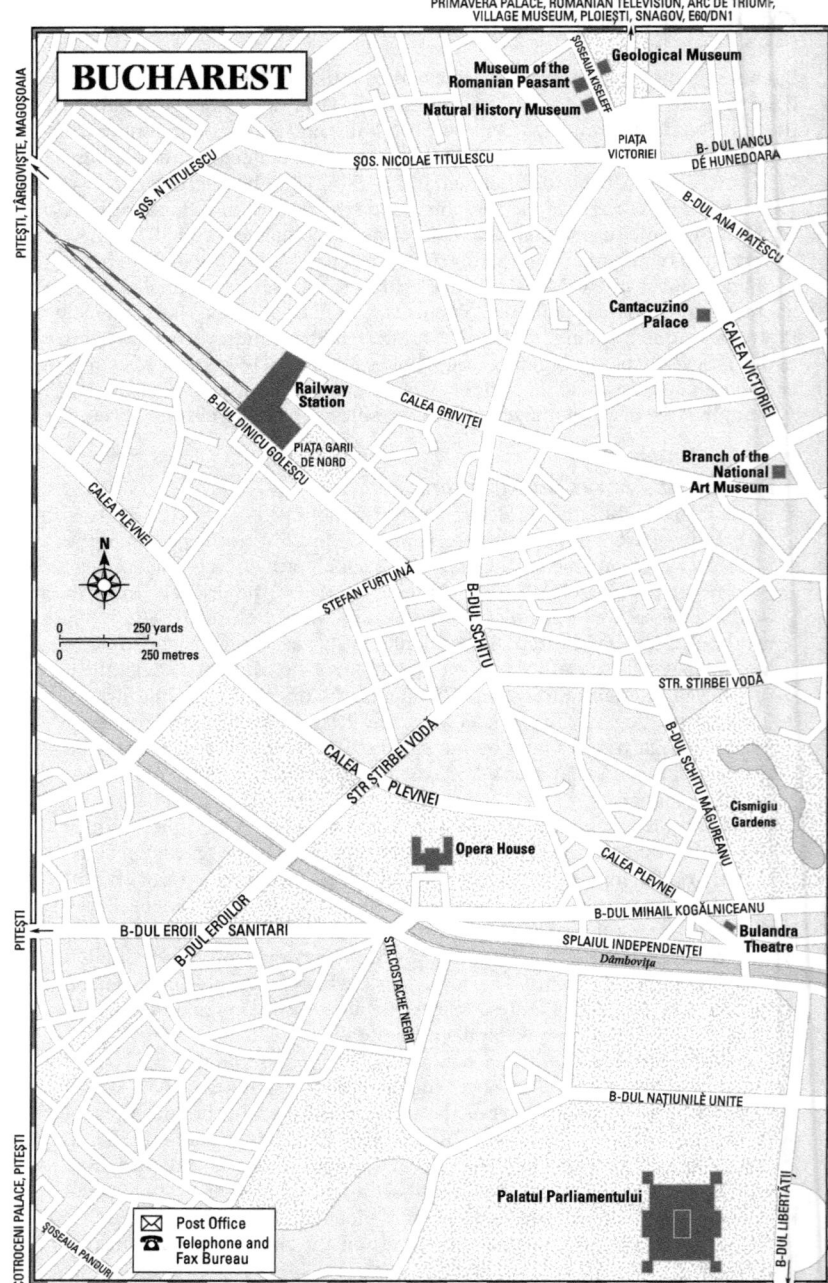

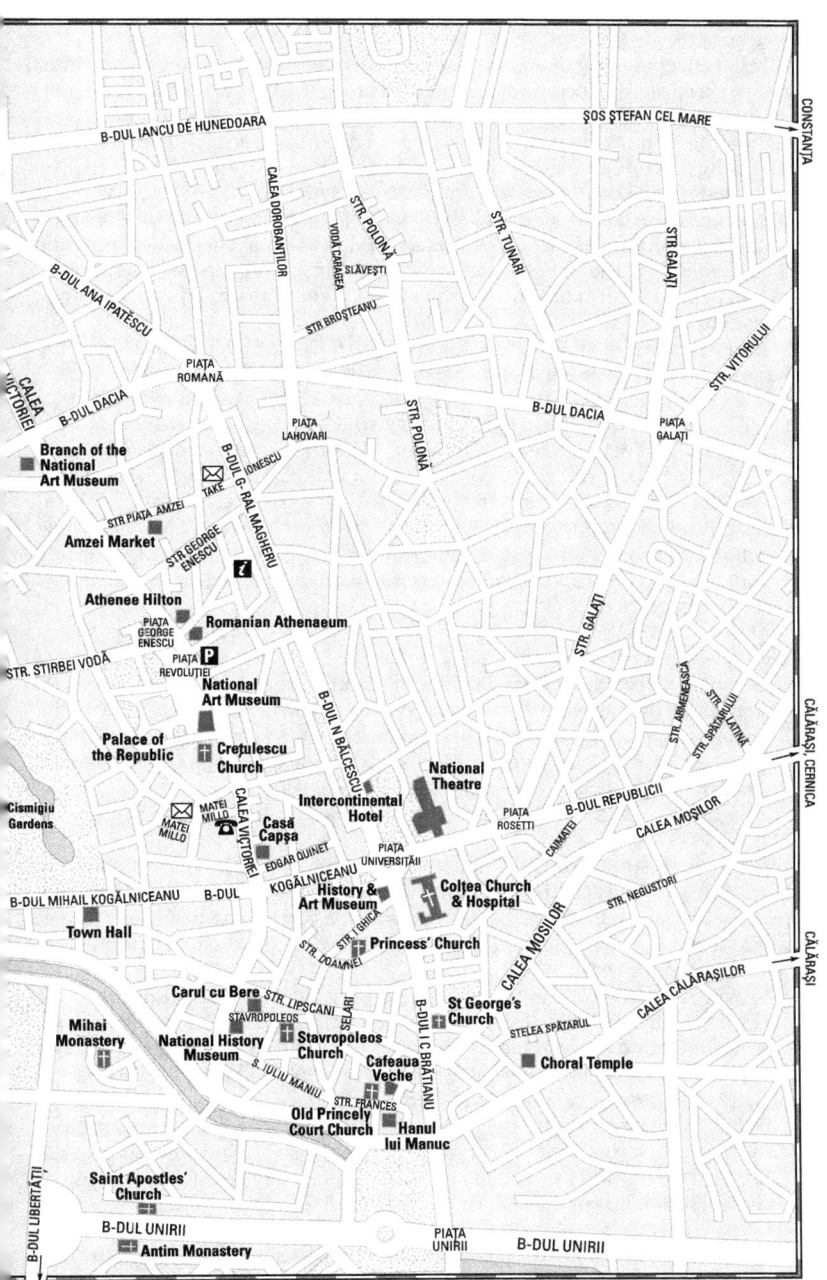

patterning of alternating brick and plaster that once covered the entire external wall surface.

Inside, the **painting** dates from three periods: on the upper walls of the southern *proscomidia* (the niche where wine and bread are blessed) you can see fragments of fresco from the reigns of Mircea Ciobanul and his sons. To the left and right of the entrance you may also be able to make out pieces of mural commissioned by Ştefan Cantacuzino when he had the church restored in 1715. The main body of the church was decorated in 1852 by E. Lecca and Miţu Popp in a disappointingly flat neo-Classical style. Mircea Ciobanul and his wife Doamna Chiajna are shown to the left of the door into the altar; Ştefan and his Lady Păuna appear on the right; these portraits were inspired by the 1715 murals. I. Mihail painted the inside of the cupola in 1935. The church and court are open Tues–Sun 09.00–17.00.

At the bottom end of Şepcari, at Str Franceza 64, stands *Hanul lui Manuc*, the largest and best preserved of Bucharest's travellers' inns. It was bought in 1808 by a wealthy and influential Armenian called Emanuel Mânzaiau (1769–1817), better known as Manuc Bey, who four years later was a signatory of the Russo-Turkish treaty by which Bessarabia was ceded to Russia. Constructed around an oblong courtyard, Hanul lui Manuc has the solid defensive walls and attractive two-tier galleries that were characteristic of caravanserais all over the Ottoman Empire. It was restored in the 1960s and now functions as a hotel and (supposedly) upmarket restaurant. Do not eat here because the service is appalling, but it is worth buying a beer just to soak up the Oriental atmosphere.

Close to Curtea Veche, at the junction of Str Poştei and Str Stavropoleos, stands the superb **Stavropoleos Church**. Founded in 1724 for a small community of Greek monks, its name means literally the Church of the City of the Cross. Its design shows the blend of Ottoman and Western elements that was typical of the Brâncovenesque style; the *pridvor* (porticoed entrance verandah) is particularly striking, and some of the interior murals were painted during the reigns of the Phanariot prince, Nicolae Mavrocordat (r. 1715–16 and 1719–30). Left in ruins during the 19C, this lovely little church was restored in 1906 by architect Ion Mincu.

Opposite, at Str Stavropoleos 5, is *Carul cu Bere*, a neo-Gothic bierkeller that opened in 1879. Inside, the cavernous vaulting and baronial decorations show mixed German and English parentage, and the restaurant has a menu that would tempt the most voracious carnivore. But while the decor is entertaining, the food is overpriced.

Nearby stands G.M. Cantacuzino's neo-Classical **Chrissoveloni Bank** of 1925–27, blending successfully into the 19C buildings on either side. This was one of Cantacuzino's early, more conservative designs; in the 1930s he became far more radical, creating startlingly simple, cube-like villas and hotels for the Black Sea resorts of Eforie Nord and Mamaia.

Follow Str Stavropoleos to the right and you enter Str Smârdan; turn left and the next junction you come to brings you into the heart of **Lipscani**, Bucharest's oldest commercial district. Str Lipscani is a long street that crosses Calea Victoriei and B-dul Brătianu, but the quarter becomes most interesting between these two arteries.

Lipscani gets its name from the *Leipziger* merchants who once brought their goods to sell here. Together with the surrounding streets, Smârdan, Şelari (saddlemakers), Covaci (ironmongers), Şepcari (capmakers) and Gabroveni (merchants from the Bulgarian town of Gabrovo), this is the antithesis of *centru civic*. Instead, Lipscani offers an absorbing warren of alleys, courtyards and squares where you can buy imitation designer jeans, Italian-made fake-fur Russian hats, sunflower seeds, wooden spoons and sewing thread. Theoretically, it is possible to get anything you want here, but it is equally fascinating to wander around and enjoy Lipscani's exotic atmosphere. This is also where, if you are lucky, you may find nomadic Romany silversmiths who specialise in rings and brooches. These craftsmen still set up pitches on pavements and street corners all over Romania, just as countless generations of their ancestors must have done before them.

At Str Covaci 16 you will find the charming façade of *Cafeneaua Veche*, Bucharest's oldest surviving café, which was mentioned in a document of 1781. Look out for **Hanul cu Tei** at Str Lipscani 63, the 1855 Hotel Fieschi at Şelari 9 with its spiral staircase (seen best from Str Soarelui), and Curtea Sticlarilor at Şelari 11, where glass is still made; across B-dul Brătianu, Str Patriei contains another survivor of Phanariot Bucharest, **Hanul Patria**, with its long line of windows; traders used to hawk their wares in the inner court paved with river stones.

Cross B-dul Brătianu into the continuation of Str Lipscani, and to your left stands **Sf Gheorghe Nou**. Constantin Brâncoveanu founded this church in 1699; after he and his sons were executed and buried in Istanbul, his wife Maria had her husband's corpse exhumed in secret and reburied here in 1720. A statue of Brâncoveanu by Karel Storck stands in the churchyard. After the Great Fire of 1847, many houses around the church were destroyed; the area was later cleared and turned into a public garden, but traces of the old street network were preserved.

A few minutes' walk south at Str Sfânta Vineri 9 stands the Jewish **Choral Temple**, and Bucharest's largest **synagogue** is 150m further south at Str Mămulari 3; inside is a museum of Jewish history, open Wed and Sun 09.30–13.30. Bucharest's Jews suffered horrific persecution during the Second World War and thousands were deported to concentration and death camps in Germany, Poland and Transdnistria.

A few minutes' walk further north along the east side of Brătianu brings you to **Biserica** and **Spitalul Colţea**. The monastery church with its lovely *pridvor* (porticoed entrance) was completed in 1698 for *spătarul* (sword-bearer) Mihail Cantacuzino, who had founded the monastery of Sinaia a few years before. Inside, the ornate icon screen of gilded limewood and the friezes and doors are fine examples of Brâncovenesque carving. Part of the monastery's endowment was a hospital which opened in 1704; Spitalul Colţea grew from a single-storey house with a handful of beds into the majestic building that now surrounds the church on three sides. The current neo-Classical edifice dates from 1888 when B-dul Brătianu was extended. On the asphalt outside the grand courtyard a number of white stone slabs mark the place where Turnul Colţea, the church's 18C watchtower, stood.

Walk back along Lipscani into **Calea Victoriei** and turn left; on the opposite side of the street you will see the imposing **CEC building**. This is the headquarters of Romania's Casă de Economi şi Conseminaţiuni (or *caisse d'épargne*), founded in 1864 and the one bank that was allowed to do 'business' during the communist period. It is a handsomely domed, eclectic structure by French architect Paul Gottereau (1843–c 1904), built 1894–1900. CEC stands on the site of a 16C monastery, Sf Ioan cel Nou. From the late 19C, this area was the heart of Bucharest's banking district. Next to it is the smart new Financial Plaza; the shiny, new glass-and-steel **Bancorex building** at the southern end of Calea Victoriei looks exciting from the street, but it towers over the 19C houses like a giant oil drum, ruining the view from the south side of the canal. This is a great shame because Bucharest does not have that many pretty panoramic views to choose from. Cross to the other side of Victoriei to explore Pasajul Villacrosse and Pasajul Macca, two elegant semicircular pedestrian alleys roofed with glass and wrought iron.

Str Mihai Vodă was named after the monastery of Mihai Vodă which used to stand here. The church, founded by Mihai Viteazul before 1591, and Baroque gate tower were dragged to a building site across the Dâmbovița and are now secreted between apartment blocks on Str Sapienței (to reach it, walk down the alley from Splaiul Independenței 7). The church has been sensitively restored and looks well, even though its former position was certainly more magnificent and it has been shorn of its surrounding buildings. The wooden icon screen and gallery, and the Baroque stone carving around the west entrance, are lovely. Petre Antonescu's neo-Romanian State Archive building, which was part of the monastery, was pulled down and the hill on which the whole ensemble once stood was completely flattened. Follow Independenței further east and turn right into Str Sfânți Apostoli to see another fine church that was virtually obliterated during the 1980s, the 16C Sf Apostoli, at no. 33A.

Facing the CEC at Calea Victoriei 12 is another grand edifice with a long colonnade of Ionic pillars. Until 1970, when it became the National History Museum, this was the city's main post office. It was designed by Alexandru Săvulescu in the French Renaissance style, and opened in 1889.

A tiny alley called Str Biserica Doamnei leads off the right-hand side of Calea Victoriei on the corner with Str Doamnei to **Biserica Doamnei** (the Princesses' church). Almost completely enveloped by surrounding apartment blocks, this is a charming shrine founded by Doamna Maria and her husband Șerban Cantacuzino in 1683; some fragments of indecipherable 17C fresco remain inside its very black interior.

Opposite the southern end of Calea Victoriei, in Piața Senatului (another square which has acquired an official name that no-one knows), squats the charming little white church of **Sf Spiridon Vechi** (Old St Spiridon's). Started in 1747, it was pulled down by Ceaușescu's demolition squads in 1987 but has been rebuilt using some of the original materials, thanks to the National Bank of Romania. Its wall paintings were done in 1996 and constitute some of the finest modern Byzantine art to be seen. A few yards away is **Biserica Sf Apostoli Petru și Pavel** (the church of Sts Peter and Paul). Matei Basarab placed the foundation in 1636. This is another Ceaușescu survivor, a doughty building with several nice touches: Ștefan Cantacuzino paid for some of the stone ornamentation in 1715 (see his inscription above the attractive main entrance, which includes the Wallachian emblem and the Byzantine eagle). The interior is almost totally black and there are some nasty cracks in the walls and ceilings, but the magnificent iconostasis glints seductively in the gloom. On the roof the twin

> ### Armenians in Wallachia
> Armenians came to Wallachia from 1453, after the fall of Constantinople. Monophysite Armenians were welcomed by Romanian princes because they brought both riches and excellent diplomatic skills. Armenians settled in Pitești, Ploiești and Craiova as well as in Bucharest, and some converted to Catholicism. The size of their population fluctuated wildly, because between 1895 and 1915 they suffered terrible massacres in Turkey. Today there are some 7000 Armenians registered in Romania, but most were assimilated into the general population long ago and have lost touch with their language and their separate identity. There are 22 Armenian churches left in Romania, although some of these are in ruins; the largest single group can be found in Suceava. In Bucharest you can buy two Armenian newspapers, *Ararat* (in Romanian) and *Norg Iani* (New Times) published in Armenian with a Romanian abstract.

towers are decorated with handsome mouldings. Next to the church is a picturesque priest's house, and both buildings stand in a small cottage garden that is almost surreal in its incongruity.

Piața Universității

One of the best places to find maps and secondhand books is next to the university buildings on the west side of Piața Universității. The stalls are open every day, and the fast-food restaurants in the nearby underground shopping mall are also worth keeping in mind. Bucharest's university was founded in 1864 shortly after the city became capital of the newly-united principalities. The Rectorat building, with its entrance on B-dul Regina Elisabeta, stands on the site of the 17C Academy of Sf Sava.

A few metres to the north is a little square with a fountain; this was nicknamed Tiananmen in memory of the students who died here during the 1989 revolution and its aftermath when Iliescu summoned Jiu Valley miners 'to defend democracy' in June the following year. In the centre of the boulevard is another group of simple memorials. The fading graffiti in Chinese characters covers an end wall of the **Faculty of Architecture** beside the little square. Grigore Cerchez conceived this building in 1912, and it was completed five years later. Dedicated to Ion Mincu, it is a superb homage, combining Islamic and Renaissance motifs that hark back to the Brâncoveanu period with a sense of real gravitas. Its rooftops frame the frivolous McDonald's logo on Bălcescu like a rebuke. Nearby is G.M. Cantacuzino's witty solution to inner-city housing needs of 1936: an elegant, crescent-shaped block with an elongated dome like a turban at either end.

Teatrul Național (the National Theatre) at B-dul Bălcescu 2 was designed in the 1970s by a group of architects who had to rework the building several times before Elena Ceaușescu gave her approval. This ought to condemn it, but the row of tall arches along its façade is actually quite attractive. It stands on the site of Joseph Heft's fine neo-Classical theatre which was destroyed during the Second World War.

On the southwest corner of Brătianu and Regina Elisabeta stands the **Muzeul de Istorie şi Artă al Municipiului** (Municipal Museum of History and Art), which focusses on Bucharest's own history. It is located in the former Şuţu Palace, a neo-Gothic mansion conceived by Konrad Schwink for Costache Grigore Şuţu, a *postelnic* or court official and councillor to the prince. The building, with its splendid *porte-cochère*, was finished in 1833 and its owners were famous for the lavish parties they threw here. The Şuţu family were Phanariots and produced a couple of princes: Mihai Şuţu ruled in Wallachia 1783–86, 1791–93 and 1801–02, and in Moldavia 1792–95 and 1819–21, and Alexandru was prince of Moldavia 1801–1802, *camaicam* (regent) of Wallachia June–August 1802, and prince August–October 1806 and 1818–21. There is some reason to believe that Alexandru was killed deliberately to make way for a native Romanian royalty. In 1921, the house was transformed into the museum. Recently restored, it contains modern Romanian art, documents and photographs relating to the city's history and an extensive library. It is open Tues–Sun 09.00–17.00.

Turn left along Regina Elisabeta towards Calea Victoriei, and in a few metres you come to Str Ion Ghica, a side road containing **Biserica Studenţilor**, the stygian Students' Church dedicated to Sf Nicolae. A few minutes further south on Str Doamnei stands **Biserica Rusească**, the Russian Orthodox Church, complete with corkscrew domes.

Piaţa Universităţii to Piaţa Romană

Following the modernisation of Bucharest in the 19C, some downtown areas underwent even more radical changes between the First and Second World Wars. Some of the most dynamic new buildings appeared along the central axis which runs from Piaţa Romană down Magheru, Bălcescu and Brătianu boulevards to Piaţa Unirii. Many of these edifices were designed for commercial enterprises, but one of the earliest was Horea Creangă's Aro apartment building on B-dul Magheru and Cinema Patria (1929–31), quickly followed by Rudolf Fraenkel's office block (1934–35) and the Hotel Ambassador (1935–36) by Arghir Culina at Magheru 8. Boulevards Bălcescu, Brătianu and Magheru are named after leaders of Wallachia's 1848 revolution. Shrouded by apartment blocks at Bălcescu 41 stands the red-brick 1930's Italian church.

These buildings set the style for modern apartments along arterial roads such as B-dul Iancu de Hunedoara and Şos Ştefan cel Mare, and in some of the new residential districts on the outskirts, such as Colentina, Floreasca, Rahova and Pantelimon, all of which were built between the First and Second World Wars.

East from Piaţa Universităţii

For a taste of 'unknown' Bucharest, stroll east from Universităţii along B-dul Carol I past Piaţa Rosetti and turn right into Str Armenească. This was once the focal point of the city's **Armenian quarter**. The Armenian Orthodox Cathedral at B-dul Carol 43 was built in 1781. Dedicated to the Archangels Michael and Gabriel, it attracts one of the largest congregations of any church in the capital.

A museum dedicated to the Armenian community is located inside the church. Open Tues–Sun 10.00–16.00.

From here it is a short step to Str Spătarului where, at no. 22, is the **Pallady Museum**, ☎ 211 4979. Theodor Pallady (1871–1956) was a Post-Impressionist painter of considerable strength. This collection contains many of his paintings and drawings acquired in the early 20C by the Raut family. Arranged as though it were still a private home, the museum is housed in Casa Melic, one of the city's oldest Phanariot-style residences, dating from 1760. It stands back from the road in a pretty garden and has been beautifully restored. Children's art workshops are held in one of the balcony rooms.

Continue walking to the east to find more of the old, pre-Ceaușescu Bucharest: the maze of streets between Calea Moșilor and Calea Călărași is fun to explore on a Sunday morning when few people are about; Str Țepeș Vodă also evokes the old city. This area also contains a number of innovative buildings from the 1920s and 1930s, a period when Bucharest's artists and intellectuals were keen to modernise the city along Western lines. Several of the houses in this area were designed by Marcel Iancu. To avoid disappointment, please remember that many of them have been neglected.

Turn right down Str Caimatei just past Piața Rosetti (heading away from Brătianu), and at no. 20 you will reach **Imobil Clara Iancu**, which Iancu built for his wife in 1931. This is a four-storey 'cube' financed by Iancu himself; he probably ran his Office for Modern Studies on the top floor. The building contains one flat on each floor; garages and service rooms were installed slightly below ground level.

Further afield at Str. Negustori 27 stands Iancu's Villa Jean Fuchs (1927–29). Within the structural severity of this classic white cube, Iancu uses the play of light on different forms and surfaces to create striking effects. Villa Fuchs also has a roof garden.

Another fine Iancu house can be found at Întrarea General Ipătescu 4. Heading away from Brătianu, at the junction where Calea Moșilor turns north (left) from B-dul Carol, follow Moșilor to the left and turn first right into Olari; head left into Str Gen. Ipătescu, and then immediately right into the close. Iancu designed no. 4 for Poldi Chapier in 1929. Chapier was a personal friend—they were at school together and belonged to a literary circle called Simbolul (The Symbol). Here again Iancu uses the shape and position of windows, balconies and doors to articulate a flat surface. And while you are here, look at Str Olari 23, a family house which Iancu designed between 1931 and 1935. This is an unusually well-preserved and austere example of Iancu's work; no alterations have been made since it was built and it still contains original furniture and interior decoration.

The city's first **modernist buildings** were Iancu's work. Enthusiasts can find two of his earliest houses at the entrance of Întrarea Maior Avram Zenovie near the eastern end of Unirii, a long hike from Universității. Walk southeast from Piața Rosetti, cross Piața Coposu, head east along Str Matei Basarab, turn right down Str Traian, left into Maximilian Popper and left again into Întrarea Zenovie. In order to try out his ideas, Iancu had to rely at first on family commissions; the alley was developed by his father. Nearby at Str Maximilian Popper 55 is another experimental Iancu house, Imobilul Herman Iancu, dating from 1926.

East from Piața Romană

In the part of the city that fits between B-dul Magheru and Str Galați, and between B-duls Dacia and Ștefan cel Mare, you can find graceful and secluded quarters that the ravages of history have left intact. Behind wrought iron and palissade fencing there are villas of majestic, if decaying, elegance built by nobles and requisitioned by commissars; here you will find the pink villa that seems far too frivolous to be the British Embassy.

B-dul Dacia contains some handsome villas from the late 19C and early 20C. Walk east along Dacia and left into Calea Dorobanților, and you pass the lemon-coloured neo-Baroque building that houses the British Council. Turn right into Str Broșteanu and left into Caragea Vodă, formerly Str Boierilor (Boyars' Street), which is full of aristocratic mansions; beside nos 9–15 stands a superb Panhovskaja tree from Turkmenistan. Between here, Str Polonă and Aurel Vlaicu street lies another pocket of old Bucharest, part of which dates back to the 18C.

Calea Victoriei: B-dul Elisabeta to Piața Revoluției

Calea Victoriei is one of Bucharest's most graceful streets. As a thoroughfare it dates from 1692, when Constantin Brâncoveanu cut a road allowing him to reach Curtea Veche from his palace at Mogoșoaia. It was originally known as Podul Mogoșoaia (Mogoșoaia Bridge) because it was layered with wooden tree trunks to keep carriage wheels from sinking into the dirt. Podul Mogoșoaia became Calea Victoriei in 1878 after the Romanian war of independence.

Walking north from Regina Elisabeta, you will see a rich mixture of buildings, public, private and commercial. On the left-hand side is the neo-Classical Cercul Militar designed in 1912 by Dumitru Maimarolu, Victor Ștefănescu and Ernest Doneaud. A gigantic wedding cake of ornamented stone, it replaced the monastery church of Sărindar. Facing Cercul Militar at Str Edmund Quinet 1 is the *Capșa Restaurant* which opened in 1845. During the 1920s and 1930s Capșa became the city's smartest café, talking shop and trysting place. Today Capșa has been refurbished and reopened as an expensive hotel.

At the northern end of Calea Victoriei is the **Muzeul Național de Istorie a României** (National History Museum), ☎ 615 7056, the country's best endowed history museum. Apart from superb Sarmatian and Scythian figures—and the famous Neolithic 'Thinker' from Hamangia in Dobrogea—showing the breadth of Romania's prehistoric culture, its attractions include a basement full of finely-wrought gold and a plaster copy of Trajan's Column. The gold collection contains fascinating Scythian and Cucuteni pieces, including a ceremonial helmet with false eyes, and beautiful medieval cloisonné jewellery. The main museum is open Tues–Sun 10.00–17.00; you can visit the Argintăria (silver objects section) separately.

Set back from the road on the right is Teatrul Comedia; walking a few metres further north brings you on the left to the Art Deco **Telephone Palace**, still exciting after years of depression. The building and its phone system (then one of the most advanced of its kind) were funded by the American company IT&T in 1933. Louis Noecke and Roy Waters designed the tower, which soars to 53m and is decorated with dynamic technophile reliefs. To make national or international calls or send a fax, use the entrance a few metres down Str Matei Millo; you can buy phone cards and send telexes from here too.

On the corner of Victoriei and Str Ion Câmpineanu stands the neo-Baroque *Hotel Continental*. As you enter Piaţa Revoluţiei, you will see

The Hamangia Thinker and companion

the slim red-brick **Biserica Creţulescu** on your left. The church was commissioned by *clucerul* (court tax collector) Iordache Creţulescu and his wife Safta, a daughter of Prince Constantin Brâncoveanu, in 1722. Fragments of late 19C frescoes by Gheorghe Tattarescu can be seen inside; the church was restored in the 1930s but suffered badly during the fighting of December 1989. Overlooking the church stands another apartment building, designed by G.M. Cantacuzino in 1936.

Beside Biserica Creţulescu is a **bust of Corneliu Coposu**, President of the National Peasant Democratic Party (PNŢCD) from 1989 and of the Democratic Convention (CD) 1992–93. Coposu (1914–95) was a disciple of Peasant Party leader Iuliu Maniu, and in 1947–64 he went to prison rather than give in to pressure from the Securitate. Hailed as a champion of moral values, Coposu maintained his independent stance during Iliescu's presidency. His death in November 1995 was mourned by hundreds of thousands, and during his funeral central Bucharest came to a virtual standstill.

Palace of the Republic

Dominating Piaţa Revoluţiei is the former **royal palace** and **Palace of the Republic**, part of which now contains the **Muzeul Naţional de Artă al României** (National Art Museum), Calea Victoriei 49–53, ☎ 615 5193, 312 4327; fax 312 4327. The original residence, dating from 1815, belonged to Prince Dinicu Golescu. King Carol II is said to have found pigs foraging around the old mansion and had it rebuilt from scratch between 1930–37.

Closed for several years because of damage caused in December 1989, the museum is struggling to maintain the 2000 paintings and 500 sculptures for which it is responsible. Its holdings of Romanian religious art are particularly fine; some of the objects—icon screens, Royal Doors, crosses and fragments of frescoes—have been rescued from buildings that were destroyed by Ceauşescu, but there are also lovely icons showing the influence of Greek and Slavonic painters who fled to Romanian lands after Constantinople fell to the Turks. Its main subject areas comprise medieval and modern Romanian art, European painting and sculpture from the 15C to the early 20C, European decorative art from the 16C to the 1930s, Oriental decorative art from Turkey to Japan, and

19C and 20C prints and drawings (including Japanese prints). One of its lesser-known holdings is a collection of exuberant watercolours by the Maltese Orientalist, Count Amedeo Preziosi (1816–82). His paintings of Bucharest give fascinating insights into how the city looked in the mid-19C.

Founded in the present-day Peasant Museum in 1912, the collections were moved to the royal palace in 1948. Some of its wide-ranging pieces were requisitioned from the aristocracy, and it contains a group of over 130 paintings that once belonged to Carol I. The king had excellent taste, and with good advice and the right contacts he bought wisely and well: most of his collection came from the connoisseur and Prussian consul Felix Bamberg between 1879–89. Among Carol's paintings were a *Crucifixion* by Jacopo Bassano, *Haman Begging Esther's Pardon* by Rembrandt and El Greco's stunning *Betrothal of the Virgin*. On his death, the king left his gallery to the state, stipulating that it should never leave the country.

Anastasie Simu, who opened his own museum of European art in 1910, was above all a lover of French Impressionist paintings and acquired works by Monet, Pissarro, Renoir, Signac and Sisley (since the revolution his collection has been rehoused in a new location, at Mihai Obedenaru 3). The National Art Museum shows how eclectic Romanians were in their taste and how financial restrictions limited their scope on the international art market. Other highlights include Domenico Veneziano's *Madonna and Child*, Maineri's *Good and Ill Omen*, an early *Annunciation* by Tintoretto and marvellous portraits by Rubens and Vigée-Lebrun.

According to official figures around 100 paintings were lost during the fighting in 1989, and while the building's exterior has been restored a large part of the museum's collection lies rotting in the basement. Because of this, there is a move to sell off some of the less valuable works to raise money to save the rest. Open Wed–Sun 10.00–18.00. For information on the latest shows and to browse the virtual gallery, contact the museum's website, www.itc.ro/museum.

Facing the Biserica Crețulescu is the former headquarters of the Central Committee of the Communist Party, now home to the **Senate**. Ceaușescu delivered his final public speech from a balcony here and Iliescu's National Salvation Front took the building over immediately afterwards. Beside it to the left stands the burnt-out shell of the Securitate archive building; a mass burning of incriminating documents took place shortly after the 1989 revolution, but the remaining files have been opened for public scrutiny.

Next to it as you walk north is the Central University Library, founded by Carol I to a design by Paul Gottereau and opened in 1895. This building was gutted during December 1989, but has now been restored. On the opposite side of the square and behind the art museum is the saucer-like dome of Sala Palatului. Love it or hate it, this is a classic of its time; it was designed by Horia Maicu, Tiberiu Ricci and Ignace Șerban in 1963 to house state celebrations.

On the north east corner of Piața Revoluției stands Bucharest's most prestigious concert and exhibition hall, **Ateneul Român** (the Romanian Atheneum), a bijou equivalent to London's Albert Hall. It was conceived by diplomat and philanthropist Constantin Exarcu, and was created by French architect Albert Galleron from a mélange of styles modelled on the Erectheion in the Acropolis in Athens and the Sybil's Temple in Tivoli. The building was completed in 1888 after a public collection when people were asked to 'give a leu for the Atheneum'. Inside, a gloriously over-the-top mixture of gilt and stucco celebrates the arts of music, painting and sculpture. This is the place to hear classical music in the capital; the resident orchestra is the George Enescu Philharmonic.

Across the street, on the corner of Victoriei and Clemenceau, rises the newly-refurbished *Athenée Hilton* (formerly the *Athenée Palace Hotel*).

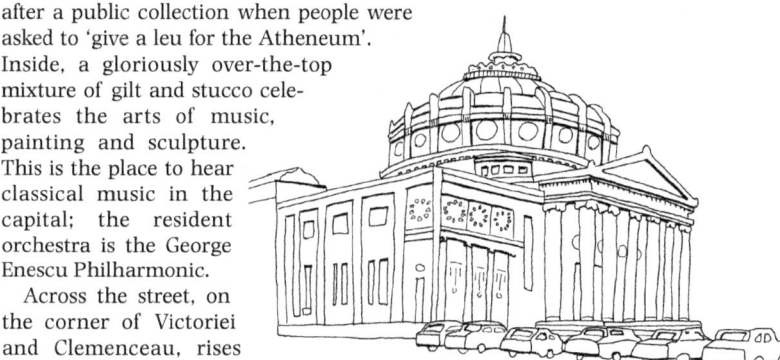

Ateneul Român

The hotel was immortalised by American journalist Baroness Waldeck when she came here in the 1930s and found it a hotbed of intrigue and corruption. Hotel staff had a field day, working not only for a paranoid Carol II (who even set spies on his mother) but also for British Intelligence and the Gestapo. In the early 1950s, rooms were fitted out with bugs and phone taps to keep a watch on suspicious visitors.

Head right from the centre of Revoluției along Str C.A. Rosetti for the **Theodor Aman Museum** at no. 8. This is worth seeing for the house, which Aman (1831–91) helped to design and decorate himself, as well as for the modest collection of his paintings and murals. Completed in 1869, it is one of the few 19C mansions in Bucharest to have retained a true period feel. Aman helped to found the Romanian Academy of Fine Arts and became its first director. His painting is extremely romantic and reflects his deeply patriotic interests, commemorating many of the battles and political confrontations that have entered the country's mythology. Open Tues–Sun 09.00–17.00.

West of Calea Victoriei

Follow B-dul Regina Elisabeta west of Calea Victoriei, or turn left between the Crețulescu Church and the National Art Museum, and in 5–10 minutes you come to the **Cismigiu Gardens**. These were the inspiration of Prince Gheorghe Bibescu and are among the oldest public parks in Bucharest. Popular with young and old alike, the gardens are split into two main sections, one formal and the other romantic. You can hire canopied rowing boats on the lake for next to nothing, and if you come here after dark you may see men playing lively chess tournaments by torchlight.

Cotroceni Palace

Walk to the west along the extension of Regina Elisabeta into B-dul Kogălniceanu, and in 10 minutes you will reach the 1953 Opera House. From here cross the river and take a bus or trolley to the magnificent and well-guarded Cotroceni Palace.

Cotroceni functions today as part museum, part presidential residence; for centuries it was a royal palace and it has a fascinating, if complicated, history. It is said to have been named after the place where Șerban Cantacuzino took refuge in 1678 after rivals got wind of his attempted coup: the Romanian verb *a cotroci* means to hide. In any case, Șerban founded a monastery here in 1679–81 which he dedicated to the Assumption of the Virgin; he also built a princely residence in the monastery grounds. His successors continued to live here, turning the monastery into one of the wealthiest religious foundations in Wallachia.

In 1802 an earthquake destroyed part of the royal houses, together with the cells and the bell tower, but the church took the brunt of the damage. Rebuilding lasted until 1810. New murals replaced the earlier frescoes; no one knows whether they followed the original cycle or not. Disaster ensued again in 1821, when the monastery was burnt down following Tudor Vladimirescu's anti-Phanariot uprising. This time repairs took much longer because they were hampered by Russian troops who were stationed here after the Russo-Turkish war of 1829. During the revolution of 1848–49, Cotroceni monastery and palace were commandeered by the Turkish army; several leading Romanian revolutionaries, including Nicolae Bălcescu, Dimitrie Bolintineanu and the Golescu brothers, were imprisoned in the monastery. 1848 also saw the church used as an arsenal.

Ceaușescu ordered the remains of Șerban Cantacuzino's lovely church to be pulled down in 1984. Apart from fragments which are preserved elsewhere (some of the frescoes are being restored at the National Art Museum), all that remains is the outline of its trefoil naos and apse and rectangular narthex, surrounded by chestnut trees.

After Prince Ioan Alexandru Cuza was elected ruler of the joint principalities in 1859, Cotroceni Palace became a royal summer residence. In 1862 it was altered by architect Scarlat Beneș, and Carol I and Queen Elisabeta stayed here until they moved into the centre of Bucharest. The palace was transformed in the late 19C when the main building was enlarged for Prince Ferdinand and his wife, Marie of Saxe-Coburg-Gotha. In preparation for their arrival, Paul Gottereau designed a new palace based on the richly-ornamented French eclectic style then fashionable in Romania. But Gottereau preserved some of the medieval residence by incorporating its vaulted, brick-lined kitchen, refectory and cellars into the ground floor and basement. He also used some of the fluted 17C columns from the princely court to enclose the remaining monks' cells in the east wing. Gottereau's alterations were completed in 1895.

Further changes were made when Princess Marie commissioned Grigore Cerchez to add a neo-Romanian wing to the north side of the new palace, near the former medieval court. Cerchez's design comprised two pavilions with decorative balustrades modelled on Constantin Brâncoveanu's monastery at Hurezu in Oltenia. The plan was carried out in 1913–15, during which period Ferdinand and Marie acceded as King and Queen of Romania. Marie introduced many of her own touches, notably a Norwegian-style drawing room lined with wood.

After Ferdinand's death in 1927 Marie inherited Cotroceni, and when she died it was used by her son, Carol II, and grandson Michael. But in 1940 the palace was shaken by an earthquake and evacuated; seven years later Michael was blackmailed into abdicating. Shortly afterwards, most of the valuable furniture and books left in Cotroceni disappeared; they were either stolen or destroyed. In the years 1949–76 the palace became the headquarters of Romania's Pioneers (a communist youth movement). The 1977 earthquake caused more damage, prompting the government to turn Cotroceni into a museum-cum-hotel for high-ranking officials. Meanwhile repairs, which had continued in a desultory fashion since the 1940s, were systematically reorganised. Hundreds of conservators devoted their time to tracing and making replicas of the missing furniture. Their work came to an abrupt end in 1988 when the increasingly megalomaniac Ceaușescu expressed his displeasure at being overshadowed by so much illustrious history. With his execution the building entered a new and happier phase, opening as the Cotroceni National Museum in 1991. Two of the royal saloons were fitted out specially in Louis V and Louis VI style for a visit by Queen Elizabeth II, which was scheduled for 1990; history decreed otherwise.

You can visit the Cotroceni museum and some of the royal apartments by appointment, ☎ 637 4611; fax 312 1618. Visits are free on the first Tuesday of every month. The street entrance is an unprepossessing doorway at 37 Șos Cotroceni. Guided tours are available in a range of European languages, and the museum sells an excellent guidebook.

Nearby, in what was once part of the monastery grounds, lies the scruffy but charming **Grădina Botanică** (Botanic Gardens). The gardens opened in 1860 and now cover 17 ha; you can visit the botanical museum and greenhouse as well. The gardens are open Tues–Sun 07.00–20.00, the museum and greenhouses Tues, Thur and Sun 09.00–13.00.

On your way back into the city centre, take a detour along Str Dr Clunet (south from B-dul Eroii Sanitari, one block east of the crossing with B-dul Eroilor), where at no. 14 you can visit the delightful **memorial museum** dedicated to painter Dimitrie Ghiața and his wife, the decorative artist, Aurelia. Located in their former home and studio, the collection consists mainly of their own paintings, drawings and textiles. ☎ 615 8730.

Calea Victoriei: Piața Revoluției to Piața Victoriei

From Piața Revoluției, Calea Victoriei begins to open out, and the further north you go the more gracious its houses become. Turn right along Enescu to see some recently restored mansions. Take the left turn into Mendeleev, at the next crossing head left again and you will come to **Piața Amzei**. This is the home of one of Bucharest's smartest open-air markets, which used to be the place to find oranges and grapefruit when they were unobtainable elsewhere. The north side of Amzei is lined with patrician houses, many of which have private gardens; on the corner of Str Biserica Amzei and Str Christian Tell is a Jugendstil house which once belonged to Maria Mihăescu, Bucharest's first woman cyclist, who was known as Mița Biciclista.

On the right in the courtyard of no. 120 are the offices of the progressive political and literary review, **22**, named after the outbreak of the Revolution in Bucharest on 22 December 1989. On the left-hand side, at no. 111, is **Muzeul Colecțiilor de Artă**, the excellent Art Collections' Museum, ☎ 650 6132. Since 1989 some of the holdings, such as the Zambaccian collection, have been restored to their original locations in villas around the city and opened to the public as well. Downstairs in the basement is **Galerie Catacomba**, which holds excellent exhibitions of contemporary art.

The Writers' Union is housed in a splendid mansion on the southwest (left-hand) corner of Dacia and Victoriei, built by Ion Mincu for the Monteoru family in 1889.

Walking north from here brings you to the **Cantacuzino Palace**, unmistakable from its wrought-iron and glass *porte-cochère* in the shape of a giant clam. The house was designed by I.D. Berindei, architect of the Culture Palace in Iași. Inside is a small museum dedicated to composer George Enescu, who inherited the mansion on his marriage, ☎ 659 7596, open Tues–Sun 10.00–17.00. It is also the headquarters of the Romanian Musicians Union; on the top floor the Soros Foundation has information on many of the country's innovative and up-and-coming artists; there is also an excellent library here. In the garden behind the main palace is the smaller town house which Enescu preferred to use as his home; it has been left much as it was when he died and makes a charming contrast to the grandiose villa next door. Concerts are frequently held in the Cantacuzino Palace; phone for details.

Cantacuzino Palace

Piața Victoriei is a huge road junction and driving across it for the first time takes some nerve. If you are sightseeing on foot, watch out for currency sharks who offer to change money on the street and their colleagues who pose as policemen (see pp 119–120).

On the right-hand (northeast) side of Piața Victoriei is **Palatul Victoria**, a stern-faced government building created by Duiliu Marcu in 1938; during the communist period it was used as the Presidency of the Council of Ministers. It is now reserved for various government departments. In 1996 someone had the zany idea of wrapping it in a bright red Christmas ribbon—a great improvement! Facing it on the west are the Natural History Museum and a few metres further north, the Museum of the Romanian Peasant (see below).

Piața Victoriei to Piața Presei Libere

Two main arterial roads, Șoseaua Kiseleff and B-dul Aviatorilor, head north from Victoriei. Both were built during the restructuring of Bucharest organised by engineer Grigore Cerchez in the 1880s. Together with B-dul 1 Mai they fan out from Piața Victoriei like the spokes of a wheel. With its abundant parks, the area between Kiseleff, Aviatorilor and Calea Dorobanților contains some of the city's smartest and most secluded quarters; it is also a favourite location for foreign embassies, many of which are housed in the residences of former Romanian nobles.

> ### Pavel Kiseleff
> The man who gave his name to Şos Kiseleff was a Tsarist general who between 1829–34 created and supervised the Organic Regulations. This bizarrely named document was a new constitution which the Russians granted to Moldavia and Wallachia at the Treaty of Adrianople of 1829. The Regulations gave the principalities some freedom from the crumbling Ottoman Porte and were another step along the way to independence. Kiseleff was exceptionally forward-looking: during his five-year stint in Wallachia he improved conditions for peasant farmers and carried out reforms in public health.

The **Muzeul de Istorie Naturală 'Grigore Antipa'** (the Natural History Museum) stands at no. 1 on the southern end of Şos Kiseleff. Antipa was a naturalist who made his name by researching the life cycle of fish in the Black Sea and Danube Delta. The collections were begun by the St Sava Academy in 1834, and this building opened in 1908. It is worthwhile but terribly dingy, and restoration is likely to continue for several years. Open Tues–Sun 09.00–17.00.

Muzeul Ţăranului Român

At no. 3 stands the imposing Muzeul Ţăranului Român (the Museum of the Romanian Peasant), ☎ 650 5360. Thanks to its director Horia Bernea (1938–2000), who is also a well-known painter, the museum gains everything by being individualistic and whimsical; in 1995 it was winner of the European Museum of the Year Award. Inside, it looks more like an art gallery than a didactic institution. Bernea's influence makes itself felt from the painted backdrops to individual displays and the flair with which objects are presented to the handwritten information sheets with their freehand sketches, and even to the decoration of the ladies'—the handiwork of Dr Irina Nicolau. Information is presented on handwritten sheets illustrated by freehand sketches, and the exhibits are displayed in attractive clusters that emphasise their aesthetic qualities; there are few labels. Holdings include 18,000 pieces of pottery from 100 different centres, 20,000 examples of national dress from all over the country, and 10,000 carpets, decorative towels and wall hangings, not to mention glass icons, furniture, magnificent *troiţe* (crosses placed at the edges of villages or at crossroads) and gateways as well as photographs and films detailing fast-vanishing customs of rural life. Inside one of the galleries there is also an incredibly fragile-looking timber church, minus its roof.

Muzeul Ţăranului Român grew out of a modest textile museum founded in the 1870s; in 1906 this became the National Museum of Fine, Decorative and Industrial Arts, only to be renamed six years later as the National Art Museum. In this year Carol I laid the foundation stone of N. Ghica-Budeşti's present building, which stands on the site of the former Mint and the Mavrogheni Palace. Designed to resemble a monastery with its loggias and massive central watchtower, the museum shows the influence of Ion Mincu's neo-Romanian style. It was only completed in 1941. Expoziţia de Artă Ţărănească, the new ethnographic museum, was inaugurated in 1931. Envious communists 'liberated' the museum at the height of its success in 1953, when the exhibits were sent to Palatul Ştirbei in Calea Victoriei; Ghica-Budeşti's majestic building was turned into the Museum of the Communist Party History and Revolutionary Democratic Movement. At the back, facing B-dul 1 Mai, stands an **18C wooden church** (one of six that museum staff have rescued from almost certain decay), overlooked by a relic of the totalitarian period, a *Proletcult* mosaic. Open May–Oct, Tues–Sun 10.00–18.00; Nov–Apr, Tues–Sun 09.00–15.00.

Opposite is a splendidly didactic **Geological Museum** containing a room of beautiful crystals from the Carpathians. The museum is part of the university and visits are by appointment only; ☎ 650 5094, fax 312 8444.

At the corner of Mincu and Aviatorilor you will find the **Hrandt Avakian Collection** in a fine old mansion at Str Ion Mincu 19. The house has been recently restored.

On the east side of B-dul Aviatorilor, embassies and government institutions stand in leafy side streets. The area was a favourite with communist party bosses, and it has an exclusive feel right through to Calea Dorobanților. Walk along Str Zambaccian to no. 21A, a lovely pavilion-like building that contains the **K.H. Zambaccian Museum**. Modelled on vernacular architecture such as the fortified *cula* houses of Oltenia and on Islamic styles, the house was designed by C.D. Galin specifically to house the collection; both the house and artworks were donated to the state in 1946; open Tues–Sun 09.00–17.00. Krikor Zambaccian (1889–1962) was a wealthy Armenian businessman who acquired paintings and sculptures by leading Romanian artists; his collection includes works by Ioan Andreescu, Nicolae Grigorescu, Ștefan Luchian and Gheorghe Pătrașcu, as well as some landscapes, portraits and still lifes by leading French painters of the 19C and early 20C, among them Romantics such as Corot and Delacroix and early modernists such as Cézanne, Bonnard, Renoir, Matisse and Picasso. In 1978 Zambaccian's paintings, drawings and sculptures were transferred to the Art Collections' Museum; they were restored to their original location in 1996.

The K.H. Zambaccian Museum

Halfway along B-dul Aviatorilor a Soviet-style stone angel towers over the traffic. In September 1997 this well-known landmark was incorporated into a new work by contemporary sculptor Paul Neagu, who unveiled a gigantic **bronze disk** in the centre of Piața Charles de Gaulle. Called Crucea Secolului (Cross of the Century) because it is pierced with holes in the shape of a cross, the disk forms a visual pivot linking the angel and the nearby Arc de Triumf. Neagu contrasts the motion of the traffic, which travels anticlockwise around the square, and the sun, which moves in the opposite direction. At the same time he emphasises the difference in the shape of each monument: the verticality of the angel, the horizontality of the arch and the roundness of the disk. (Piața Charles de Gaulle used to be Piața Aviatorilor; it was renamed to mark the visit of French president, Jacques Chirac, to Bucharest in 1997.)

Beside Piața Charles de Gaulle stands the seven-storey **Imobilul Bazaltin**, which Marcel Iancu conceived in 1935. Although it has been much altered since then, it was an imaginative idea, combining the headquarters of a road construction company with three residential flats. Building regulations forced Iancu to keep part of his design below a certain height; he overcame this restriction by dividing the plan into two levels so that the highest part stood well back from the road.

Joining Piața Charles de Gaulle from the southeast is Calea Dorobanților. Supposedly named after medieval settlers from Brabant, this road contains the offices of Romanian television. **RTV headquarters** has an emotive significance for Romanians. In December 1989, revolutionaries forced their way into the station and broadcast the news that Ceaușescu's government had fallen. Its walls are still scarred by bullet holes, and in front of the entrance is a modest wooden cross commemorating those who were killed here at that time.

Turn northeast from Piața Charles de Gaulle, walk to the end of B-dul Primăverii, and at no. 50, on the right-hand corner with B-dul Mircea Eliade, you will find the Ceaușescus' former villa, **Palatul Primăverii**. Today it is shared by the Russian embassy and various other government departments; if you want to see inside you have to brave gun-toting Russian guards. Further along Mircea Eliade, at no.1, is **Clubul Ilie Năstase**, Ceaușescu's private health club which is now open to the public Tues–Sun 12.30–16.00 and 20.00–24.00.

Turning left along Piața Charles de Gaulle brings you to the **Arc de Triumf**. Constructed from concrete and granite and modelled on the triumphal arch in Paris, it commemorates the creation of Greater Romania between the declaration of unity in 1918 and its ratification at the Treaty of Trianon two years later. Portraits of King Ferdinand and Queen Marie decorate the southern face, while the inscriptions record the names of battles fought by Romanians during the First World War. An earlier monument, reputedly made of wood and cardboard, was erected here in 1878 to mark Romania's independence from the Ottoman Turks. In 1922 this was replaced by a shoddy timber arch just in time to mark Ferdinand's triumphal entry into the capital as the first king of Greater Romania. Eventually enough money was found for the present arch, which Petre Antonescu (1873–1965) created in 1935–36. To the northwest of the Arc, on nearby Str Câmpina, stands the imposing **Casin** church.

Muzeul Satului

Continue north a few metres along Șos Kiseleff between the trees of Parcul Herăstrău and turn first right at no. 28 for Muzeul Satului (the Village Museum), ☎ 617 1732/5959, 222 9100. If you do not visit any other museum in Bucharest, you must come here. Located on the banks of Herăstrău Lake and covering over 14 ha, the museum was conceived as a bigger and better version of the open-air museum in Cluj (see p 426). Today it is one of the largest of its kind in Europe, comprising around 300 vernacular buildings from all over the country. These include timber houses and farm steadings but there are also wind and fulling mills, oil and grape presses, trellised maize stores, a primitive ferris wheel and three churches. Many of the buildings were brought here in pieces while some are copies of the originals; the oldest houses date back to the 17C. In addition, the museum hosts events throughout the year, notably crafts fairs and demonstrations of traditional song and dance.

Behind the project from the start was ethnographer Dimitrie Gusti, who became its first director when Muzeul Satului opened in 1936. The opening was scheduled to coincide with 70 glorious years of Hohenzollern rule in Romania, and King Carol II visited the building site nervously to make sure it would be ready on time. Royal pressure made itself felt a few years later too, when some of the Bessarabian houses were pulled down to make way for the Elisabeta Palace (*see below*). In 1940, after Bessarabia and northern Bucovina fell to the USSR, refugees from these areas were housed in the museum. During the communist period the buildings were allowed to deteriorate and Muzeul Satului was only saved by devoted curators. In September 1997 an arsonist set fire to three of the oldest timber houses; many more were destroyed as a result but they have been rebuilt from new.

Gusti wanted his museum to emphasise the social and environmental aspects of rural life. Because of this, Muzeul Satului mirrors as closely as possible a living village, with clusters of houses linked by winding paths. Until recently it had its own flock of sheep and a donkey that grazed between the homesteads. Still seen as Romania's greatest cultural showcase and a source of passionate national pride, the museum is often requisitioned for state functions; it also hosts a number of annual or biennial crafts fairs and folk music and dance festivals, and there are celebrations here on traditional feast days such as Mărțișor, Christmas Eve and New Year's Day.

Muzeul Satului is open May–Oct, Tues–Sun 09.00–20.00; Nov–Apr, Tues–Sun 09.00–17.00. It is served by buses 331 and 131 from Piața Lahovari; trams 41, 3 and 4, or by metro to Piața Charles de Gaulle.

Plans for a new research centre, conservation laboratory and lecture halls have been put in cold storage until finances allow; it is likely that before this happens, Muzeul Satului will merge with the National Peasant Museum down the road. You can hire boat trips around the lake. Beside Muzeul Satului is the Mediterranean-style **Elisabeta Palace**. Built in 1937, today it is used as a conference centre and residence for visiting heads of state, but it also functions as a hotel and restaurant. The long gallery contains some fine paintings, ceramics and furniture. The palace was built for Princess Elisabeta, Queen of Greece and sister of Carol II.

Herăstrău Lake is the westernmost of a group of reservoirs that stretch across the north of the city as far as the Colentina district and beyond. You can walk beside them the whole way.

Piața Presei Libere is dominated by the former communist press building, **Casa Presei Libere** (House of the Free Press), where the editors of all the city's journals and radio stations were corralled under one roof. Before 1990 it was known officially as Casa Scânteii (House of the Spark), and a bronze statue of Lenin stood in front of its main entrance. Lenin was removed after the 1989 revolution and ditched in the grounds of Mogoșoaia Palace (see pp 151–153). Casa Presei Libere now contains the Ministry of Culture. To the west of the square is Bucharest's **World Trade Center** exhibition building, together with smart hotels catering for businessmen.

On the road towards Otopeni airport, beside Băneasa railway station off Șos Bucharest, are two museums, **Muzeul de Artă Populară Minovici** (the Minovici Museum of Folk Arts) and **Muzeul de Artă Veche Minovici** (the Minovici Museum of Ancient Art). Located at Str Dr Nicolae Minovici 3, the folk art section can be found in a fortified house built in 1905 and modelled on a 17C Oltenian cula: it contains a country-wide selection of indigenous arts and crafts, while the Museum of Ancient Art focuses on 15C and 16C Western art. Nicolae Minovici (1868–1941) was a physician and philanthropist who founded the Romanian ambulance service. He was also an enthusiastic amateur anthropologist: the Museum of Folk Art was his idea, and he designed the mansion specially to house his collection, which opened to the public in 1915. The Museum of Ancient Art across the garden was founded by his nephew. Both museums are open Wed–Sun 09.00–17.00.

About 8km to the northeast of the city centre, at Str Plumbuita 58, you will find **Mănăstirea Plumbuita**. Petru Vodă cel Tânăr (Peter the Young, r. 1559–68) founded the monastery, and the buildings were expanded by Alexandru II (r. 1568–77) and his son Mihnea Vodă Turatul (r. 1577–83). During the Turkish invasion of 1595, it was damaged by troops following Sinan Pasha, and when Matei Basarab confronted Radu Vodă here in 1632, he rebuilt the monastery as a sign of gratitude for his victory, adding a palace for good measure. In 1848 some of the revolutionary leaders were incarcerated at Plumbuita.

The church has a trefoil plan with a *brâu* (sculpted cord motif) separating its upper and lower walls. Because its side apses are skewed the interior of the naos is not square; inside, on the side walls of the pronaos and naos apses there are odd pieces of fresco from the time of Alexandru. The first printing press in Bucharest was set up here in 1570 to produce psalm books, gospels and service orders. Some of the ancillary buildings are fascinating; in the northeast section of the perimeter wall, the kitchen, called a *cuhnea*, was constructed in the reign of Matei Basarab and is the oldest of its kind in Wallachia. In the early 1990s the monastery's abbot was a practising sculptor who ran a series of workshops for lay craftspeople, specialising in textiles, wood and metal. Nearby on the lakeside, at Str Doamna Ghica 5, you can visit Palatul Ghica Tei with its lovely neo-Classical chapel.

South of the centre: Palatul Parliamentului

The bare wasteland created by Ceauşescu's megalomania has begun to grow skin, and among the monochromatic blocks of flats and offices, several attractive churches lie hidden. **Mănăstirea Mihai Vodă** may be surrounded by buildings that reduce its scale and may have lost its outer walls, but it is still a magnificent church. Its western door is especially pretty: it has a frame of gracefully carved stone featuring phytomorphic motifs and a pair of very smug-looking lions face each other at ground level.

Nearby on the south side of Piaţa Naţiunile Unite (the old Piaţa Senatului) and opposite the southern end of Calea Victoriei stands the little white church of **Sf Spiridon Vechi**. It was founded in 1747, demolished in 1987 and completely rebuilt, using much but not all of the original material, in 1992. Inside, the church has been painted throughout with new neo-Byzantine frescoes and is really magnificent. Close to Sf Spiridon Vechi is another brave relic of Bucharest's past: **Sf Apostoli Petru şi Pavel**. The church was founded in 1636 by Matei Basarab on the site of a wooden church. Şerban Cantacuzino embellished and extended it in 1715. His inscription is mounted above the west entrance, where you can also see the Wallachian emblem and the Byzantine eagle. This attractive Orthodox church is in a parlous state: its walls are cracking and the frescoes are soot black, but some of the external decoration is lovely.

Five minutes' walk from here, in Str Apostoli, the neo-Byzantine **Domniţa Bălaşă** church rises smartly from the formal bushes and walkways of its well tended garden. It has been damaged several times by earthquakes, but owing to thorough restoration, the church has a tight glamour that makes it seem sharper and more urban than the other nearby shrines. A startling mix of ochre and green stripes decorate the outside, and it is one of the most popular places for weddings in the entire capital. Doamna Bălaşă was a daughter of Constantin Brâncoveanu, and her statue stands in the garden.

One of Bucharest's most notorious landmarks, **Palatul Parlamentului**, (also known as Casa Poporului) dominates the west end of B-dul Unirii. Conceived by a young, unknown architect called Anca Petrescu who won the competition to design *centrul civic*, it is an ugly pile of artificial stone covering 265,000sq m and rising to 84m high, competing with the Pentagon in size, but not elegance. The five underground storeys contain lead-lined bunkers and access to an electric light railway in case the dictator should need to escape in a hurry. No expense was spared on its decoration, and Ceauşescu intended Casa Poporului to be his home, power base and fortress, and probably his mausoleum as well. Entirely without character, the façade is pierced by hundreds of windows which Bucureşteni say used to follow them around wherever they went, like spies.

As its name implies, Palatul Parlamentului is now used as the parliament house and for conferences and exhibitions. Tours of the building are available from various travel agents, including *Atlantic Tour* (see p 116). If you walk to the northeast of Palatul Parlamentului along Staicovici, Pasteur and Lister streets next to B-dul Eroii Sanitari, you will find another pocket of old Bucharest mouldering gently on the edge of one of the main routes in and out of the city.

Standing on a promontory to the southeast of Palatul Parlamentului is the attractive **Catedrala Patriarhiei**, the Patriarchal Cathedral and palace. Once visible from most parts of the city centre, Ceauşescu tried to blot it out by building apartment blocks in the way. The Romanian Orthodox church was a puppet of the communist government, and this may have been why the building survived at all. You can enter the cathedral precinct from either end of Str Coşbuc. The Byzantine-style church was begun in 1654 by Prince Constantin Şerban (r. 1654–58) and finished by Radu Leon (r. 1664–69), when it became the Metropolitan's official seat. Its handsome *pridvor* is decorated with fluted columns; only one original painting remains: an icon of Saints Constantin and Elena above the entrance to the pronaos. To the east of the church stands a beautifully proportioned *clopotniţa* (bell tower) commissioned by Constantin Brâncoveanu; the oldest bell was cast in 1888. The bell tower was restored in 1959. Three lovely 16C and 17C stone crosses inscribed in Slavonic characters stand beside the church.

The vaulted cellars on the south side are all that remain of Constantin Şerban's original monastery buildings; they date from 1658 while the rest of the palace complex has undergone many alterations, notably in 1793 after a fire, and in 1875. Bishop Miron Cristea became the first Patriarch of Romania in 1925. Bordering the Patriarchate to the south stands **Camera Deputaţilor** (Chamber of Deputies) in the former parliamentary building of 1909.

In Str Antim, between the Cathedral and Palatul Parlamentului, you will come across the splendid **Mănăstirea Antim**, another impressive Brâncovenesque complex. It was completed in 1715 to designs planned by its founder, Antim Ivireanul, who was Metropolitan of Wallachia. Antim himself sculpted the frames around the church's west doors and the icon screen.

Walk from the Patriarchate down towards Piața Unirii and turn right into Str Bibescu Vodă; from here it is a 10-minute trek across another arterial road, B-dul Cantemir, and into Str Radu Vodă to see the **monastery** built on a mound here by the prince of that name in 1615. A few minutes' walk further south along Radu Vodă brings you to the junction with B-dul Mărășești; cross into Str Bucur and Splaiul Unirii to find the early 18C **Biserica Bucur**. Standing on a mound with its porch enclosed by rickety glazing, under its quaint mushroom dome it is a forlorn little church. It seems all the sadder after all the hype that surrounds its legendary role in the founding of Bucharest. In the 18C the Bucur church was used as a *bolniță* (sanitarium) by the monks of Radu Vodă and in 1909–10 it was restored by Grigore Cerchez. Women wearing trousers may be refused entry, and opening hours are somewhat random.

The tale of Bucur

Legend has it that the city was founded by a shepherd called Bucur. Bucur means 'joy' in Romanian and the story, committed to paper by a Franciscan monk in 1761, appealed hugely to Romanian nationalists who saw it as a symbol of the city's spiritual significance—like the legendary ballad of *Miorița* (*The Ewe Lamb*), it provided a romantic link with their ancient pastoral origins. In his *Profetism Românesc* (*Romanian Prophecies*), the great religious historian Mircea Eliade (1907–86) went so far as to see Bucur as a 'connoisseur of signs' who was 'predestined to recognise that the place had a cosmic energy'.

Opposite the east end of the Bucur church is a branch of the canal; across the canal to the left stands the new National Library building.

2.5km to the south, on the northwestern edge of Parcul Tineretului (the Youth Park), is the **Belu Cemetery**, in which are the graves of Mihai Eminescu, Gheorghe Gheorghiu-Dej and Mihail Sadoveanu, among others; the adjoining Heroes' Cemetery was a children's playground before being requisitioned by the authorities as a burial ground for people killed on the streets during the fighting in December 1989. It is still an emotive place to visit.

Around Bucharest

Mogoșoaia Palace is at Str Constantin Brâncoveanu 18, outside the ring road to the northwest of the city, c 14km from the centre. If you are driving, follow Calea Griviței, B-dul Bucharest Noi and Șos Bucharest–Târgoviște, the main route for lorries going to Ploiești. Alternatively catch bus 460 from the centre or take the early-morning Snagov train from Gara de Nord; some trains from Gara de Nord to Galați also stop at Mogoșoaia. Mogoșoaia's grounds are open Tues–Sun 10.00–18.00; guided tours in English and French are available free of charge. You can eat inside the complex at Restaurantul Mogoşoaia, Str Valea Parcului 1, open from Tues–Sun 10.00–23.00.

The palace is one of the most sublime 18C buildings in Romania. Meaning literally Mogoş's wife, it was commissioned by Constantin Brâncoveanu for his son Ştefan and completed in 1702. The Brâncoveanu family had to relinquish the estate 12 years later when the Grand Vizir of Ottoman Turkey had Constantin, Ştefan and his three brothers executed in Istanbul. On their deaths the palace was converted into an inn. During the anti-Phanariot riots of 1821 a large part of the complex was burnt down, and Russian soldiers raided the building in 1853. Towards the end of the 19C the palace passed to the Bibescu family, who were distantly related to the Brâncoveanus.

Prince Gheorghe Valentin Bibescu gave Mogoşoaia to his wife, Marthe in 1912. Marta Bibescu, also known as Marthe Bibesco, (1886–1973) was a highly cultured historian and novelist who spent much of her life in France. She was devoted to Romania and its people, and this was expressed in her tragic novel *Isvor: Land of Willows* (1922). She also took a great interest in her husband's old family home and commissioned two architects, the Venetian Domenico Rupolo and the Romanian G.M. Cantacuzino (1899–1960), to restore the whole ensemble. Rupolo had recently built the Pescheria in Venice, and there are certain similarities between his designs for the fish market and those for the guest house. Marthe Bibescu was eventually driven out by the Stalinist regime and left Mogoşoaia to her daughter. In 1956 the palace was handed over to the state and turned into a museum. Ceauşescu closed it down and requisitioned the furniture. After this final insult the buildings were left to rot, but repairs carried out in the early 1990s have made it fit to visit once more.

Inside the museum is a collection of silver, embroidery, icons and wooden sculpture, along with traces of fresco, Islamic decoration and a cellar with a fine vaulted ceiling. But the exterior is more interesting. Although it has been altered far beyond the original building, the spirit of Brâncoveanu's style remains, a perfectly integrated mix of Palladian, Islamic and vernacular Romanian architecture originating in Venice, Constantinople and Wallachia. Walk around to the lakeside, and you will find a beautiful Venetian-style *loggia*, while overlooking the main courtyard is a balcony graced by the characteristic phytomorphic carvings of the Brâncoveanu style. Counterbalancing all this delicate ornamentation are the severe lines of the palace itself. On the left-hand side of the courtyard as you enter is a new wing which used to belong to the Writers' Union. In the grounds you may come across the broken remains of Lenin, or at least of his statue, which used to stand outside Casa Presei Libere in Bucharest.

Brâncoveanu's little **church**, dedicated to St George of the Meadow, stands on the drive, just outside the palace gates. It was built of brick in 1688 and decorated by a team of Greek painters. Candle smoke and incense have virtually obliterated their work, but in the upper registers of the pronaos you may be able to see the seven ecumenical councils, while the lower registers contain other saints and portraits of the founder and his family. Constantin Brâncoveanu is shown with his wife, Maria, his four sons and seven daughters, all wearing royal dress. The icon screen is another typical Brâncoveanu design, but the only original icons are those showing the prophets and the Crucifixion. In the centre of the sanctuary dome is a painting of the Virgin with the little church of Biserica Doamnei below her.

Concerts, workshops and temporary exhibitions are often held in the palace kitchens to the right of the main gate; these are organised by the National Cultural Centre, which promotes regional art events; ☎ 223 4689, 668 4990.

40km west of Bucharest on the DJ 401A you will reach **Potlogi**, where Constantin Brâncoveanu built another beautiful palace in 1698.

The **Căldăruşani Monastery**, in the countryside c 40km north of Bucharest, was one of a chain of religious foundations strung across the Wallachian plains by Matei Basarab (r. 1632–54). It is a splendid collection of buildings, now badly in need of restoration. The monastery was famous for its icon-painting school, one of whose students was Romania's foremost Impressionist, Nicolae Grigorescu (1838–1907), who spent several months here as a trainee in 1855. Buses from Bucharest come within 1.5km of Căldăruşani, and some trains from Gara de Nord–Galaţi stop at Greci, 2km from the monastery.

The woodland, lake, church and monastery of **Snagov** are part of a popular leisure spot that lies c 40km north of Bucharest. Drive north past Otopeni and keep going until you see the signs for Snagov. The lake is some 18km long and surrounded by villas that are tucked discreetly away in the dense trees. In the lake stands an island where a succession of royal princes built and then added to a monastery church. The first known church at Snagov was founded by Mircea cel Bătrân in the 11C. Dan I (r. c 1383–86) added a monastery in the 1380s, and in 1453 the timber church was pulled down and replaced with a masonry version. Unfortunately, the new stone church sank in the lake. In 1456, at the start of his second tumultuous reign, Vlad III Ţepeş (Dracula) ordered fortifications to be erected around the monastery. With the foresight born of long experience, he also built an escape tunnel, a prison and torture chamber and a bridge to the lake shore. At the same time, he founded a new stone church and bell tower. Vlad's prison served as a penitentiary for Nicolae Bălcescu and other revolutionaries from 1848. It lies in ruins behind the church. Like its predecessors, Vlad's church did not survive the test of time, and another was erected between 1517–21. This is the present-day church, and it is one of a handful of Romanian buildings protected by UNESCO's world heritage programme. Its Royal Doors, sculpted in 1453, belong to the earlier building and are among the finest medieval woodcarvings in Wallachia. Legend says that Vlad's decapitated body was buried in front of the iconostasis after his assassination in December 1476, his head being sent as a gift to Sultan Mehmet II. When the grave was opened in the 1930s it was empty. Men and women who are indecently dressed may not be allowed inside the church.

Boats to the island can be hired more or less year round from the *Dolce Vita* restaurant. The return trip is on a motor boat with room for up to six passengers, and the more of you there are, the cheaper it is. Dining at the *Dolce Vita* is a lot more expensive, but in warm weather you can eat out on its floating stage. When the lake freezes over you can hire skating equipment from the hotel.

Nearby stands **Palatul Snagov**, an Italian Renaissance-style residence which Prince Nicolae built in the early 20C. Today the Palace is used as an hotel, conference centre and restaurant by guests of the state. Ceauşescu reserved the nearby Villa no. 10 as his personal summer house, hence the excellent condition of the road. If you are wealthy, famous and ghoulish enough you can stay here.

Ţigăneşti skete (monastic village) lies on the other side of the E60 close to the second turn-off for Snagov from Bucharest, c 13km further north than the first. The monastery stands in Ciolpani *comuna*. 150 nuns live here, pursuing a picturesque but tough existence raising livestock and growing fruit and vegetables. Instead of cells they live in colonnaded bungalows that lie around the church, each with its own garden. The nuns also run a farm and a textile workshop, using jacquard looms which were imported from Germany in 1936. Ţigăneşti has supplied Romania's Orthodox clergy with ceremonial clothes for 50 years. In 1992, an Anglo-Romanian team set up a restoration project in the monastery to save precious books and manuscripts which had been damaged during the Revolution and the communist period. Ţigăneşti's neo-Classical *catholikon* was founded in 1812, but the monastery probably dates from the mid-17C. It was originally built for monks. Nuns were transferred here from Bucharest in 1805. Murals in the church interior were painted in 1812 and restored in 1929, and it has a striking Last Judgement in mosaic. The cemetery church dates from 1817 and was painted in 1880. In the museum are precious religious books and manuscripts, including a 1693 *Gospel Book*.

Cernica monastery has an idyllic setting on an island in Lacul Cernica, 14km to the east of Bucharest. Head out towards the east-bound DN3 to Feteşti and Constanţa, and before you reach the ring road, turn south at signs to Cernica, Budeşti and Olteniţa. The monastery was commissioned by Governor Cernica Ştirbei before 1608 and became one of Romania's most important seminaries. In 1815, Archimandrite Gheorghe ordered the old church of Sf Nicolae to be replaced; his successor Calinic built another church alongside the first. This was dedicated to Sf Gheorghe and was completed in 1838. Calinic also restored the fortress and founded a school of religious painting here. The late-19C painter Gheorghe Tattarescu painted frescoes in one of the chapels. The monastery was closed down during the Second World War; it reopened in 1995.

Wallachia

Wallachia forms a corridor between the Danube and the Carpathians. Starting a few kilometres west of Orşova in the west, it stretches over 100km east of Bucharest, where the Danube forms another natural barrier as it flows north to the Delta. Wallachia is richly endowed with beautiful buildings, especially its Orthodox monasteries; among the other attractions are its ancient potters' villages, and it is also a great wine-producing area. And if the Danube plains do not have much going for them in terms of picturesque landscapes, the hill country which fringes the mountains to the north can be spectacularly lovely. This is especially true of Oltenia, the western part of Wallachia, where the slopes are cloaked in deciduous forests full of beech and birch.

History

Wallachia's name comes from 'vlach', 'blach', 'wallach' or even 'iflak', medieval German or Slavonic terms which have been used, at first disparagingly, since the Middle Ages to describe the Latin-speaking peoples of southeast Europe or foreign peasants in general. 'Welsh' and 'Walloon' come from the same root. But the people who live here call the region Muntenia, the mountain country, or Ţara Românească, the Romanian country, just as they have always called themselves *români*. The ancient Romans themselves crossed Wallachia on their way to destroy the Dacian strongholds in 106 AD. They left traces of a magnificent bridge which spanned the Danube near Orşova and there is some documentary evidence to show that Daco-Roman culture continued to flourish in pockets along the Danube basin after the Romans left in 270. This was a period of serial migrations from Asia. Avars, Cumans, Gepids, Goths, Pechenegs, Slavs and Visigoths were among the tribes who came and went or intermarried in Wallachia, and no-one knows for certain what demographic transformations took place after Aurelian's withdrawal.

Moldavia and Wallachia were the last south-eastern European countries to fall under Byzantine influence. By this time the Empire was already in decline and the Romanians took their religion from the southern Slavs. Church Slavonic remained the liturgical language until the late 17C. The Vlacho-Bulgarian tsarate held lands north of the Danube until the early 1200s. Meanwhile, Hungarian kings were establishing strongholds in Transylvania, forcing a large population of Cumans into Wallachia. In 1233 King Endre II of Hungary claimed sovereignty over the Cumans, hoping to extend his influence across the southern Carpathians. With the help of the Knights of St John, the Hungarians later controlled Oltenia, but only briefly. After the Tartar invasions of 1241–42, Wallachia passed into Mongol hands. During this period, Wallachia's first ethnic Romanian dynasty began to gain power.

Legend has it that the first prince of Wallachia was *descălecatul* Radu Negru, a Vlach from Ţara Făgăraşului who crossed the mountains in 1290. (*Descălecat* is the theory of the foundation of the Romanian principalities. It says that the original voivodes came down from the Carpathians, where they are supposed to have retreated during the barbarian invasions of the early Middle Ages.) Negru founded his capital at Câmpulung and endowed an

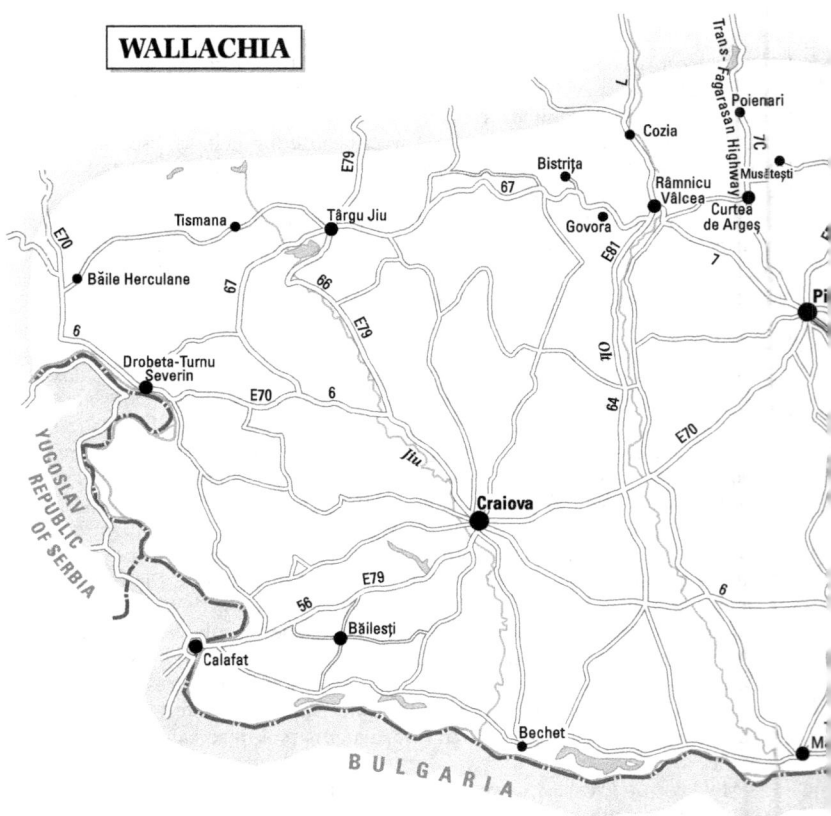

Orthodox monastery near the town. His successor, Basarab I, founded one of the great Wallachian dynasties. By forming alliances with the Bulgars and Serbs, Basarab I (r. c 1310–52) gave his country a firmly Orthodox identity.

However, in the early 14C Wallachia found itself under Hungarian suzerainty, paying tributes to a state which was an avowed enemy of the Orthodox world—Magyars had taken part in the 1204 crusade against Constantinople. In 1330 King Károly Róbert of Hungary (Charles Robert of Anjou) led an army into Wallachia via the Danubian town of Severin. Determined to crush 'our prince of Wallachia' for his defiance, the king chased Basarab to Poienari. Here, having run out of food, the Magyar sovereign had a change of heart and Basarab was able to forge a peace with Hungary which lasted until Károly Róbert died. It was then that the independent principality of Wallachia emerged, and the first Metropolitan of Wallachia was appointed by the Patriarch of Constantinople at Argeș in

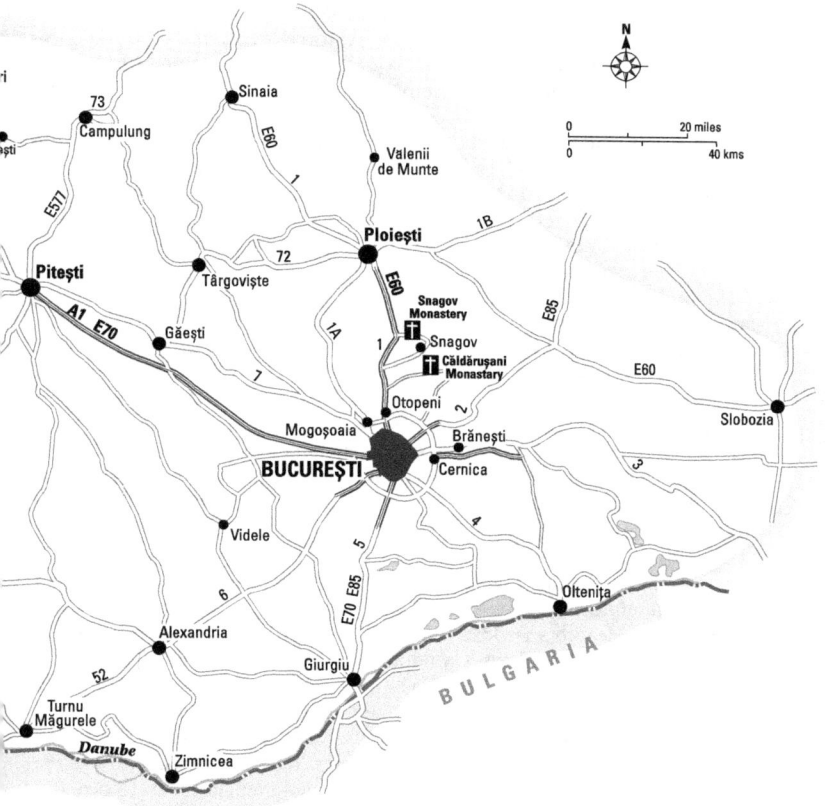

1359. Another Metropolitanate was established shortly afterwards at Severin on the Danube. At that time, the Argeş bishop had authority over the Transylvanian see as well.

Despite this understanding with Hungary, life did not get easier. In 1391 Wallachia paid its first tribute to the Ottoman Sultan on the understanding that the country would remain loyal to the Turks in return for a measure of independence. Even so, Wallachia's princes had to fight tooth and nail to maintain their freedom. Sandwiched between warring superpowers, they spent their lives playing one neighbour off against another. It was a game of viciousness and duplicity.

One of Wallachia's most famous princes was Vlad Dracula, the doe-eyed Impaler whose cruelty became a European legend. Born in c 1427, at 13 years of age he was sent by his father as a hostage to the court of Sultan Murad II. His brother, Radu cel Frumos (Radu the Handsome), went too, currying favour by becoming the Sultan's catamite. In 1447 Vlad's father and elder brother were buried alive.

After his release, Vlad spent years in exile, nominally a Turkish princeling. As Vlad III, he became prince of Wallachia three times, in 1448, 1456–62 and 1475. During these periods his regime ran on the simple rule that he would torture and kill anyone who offended him. He had people 'ethnically cleansed' in their hundreds: a favourite ploy was to invite those who annoyed him to a feast and then murder them. His nickname, Țepeș, comes from the Romanian word for 'stake'. Impaling was not unique to Romania (for a comparison read Ivo Andric's *Bridge over the Drina*), but Vlad was an expert. The victim was laid flat on the ground while a stake was battered into the rectum with a hammer. With the stake planted in the ground, offenders would then be left to die in agony.

Having at first bribed the Sultan to leave him alone, Vlad found it more advantageous to turn against the Turks and offer his support to Hungary. For a while, he relied on support from the Saxons of southern Transylvania, allowing them in return to trade freely in Wallachia. But in the 1450s the Saxons backed a rival claimant to his throne, and he withdrew their privileges. When the Saxons took no notice he went on a raid to Transylvania and ransacked their towns and villages. He also impaled some of Brașov's citizens—the numbers vary from hundreds to 40, according to which source you consult—and a German woodcut inspired by this event shows him enjoying a hearty meal in front of his victims.

His most celebrated exploits were directed against the Turks in 1461–62. Having refused to pay tribute to the Sultan, Vlad attacked the Ottoman fortresses along the Danube and in what is now northern Bulgaria. On one occasion he stole into a Turkish camp at night with a small force and slaughtered thousands in their beds. On another he received the Sultan's envoys by nailing their turbans to their heads. When the Turks retaliated and marched on Wallachia he outmanoeuvred them by scorching the land in their path. Further on, towards Târgoviște, Vlad impaled 20,000 Turks planting the stakes together, so that they resembled a grisly forest. This sickening sight broke the nerve of the already exhausted and demoralised Ottoman army, and it fled. But Mehmet II was not put off so lightly and eventually drove Vlad off the throne.

The Saxons also wanted revenge. Vlad was arrested by Matei Corvin on the pretext of a forged letter that implicated him in a Turkish plot to overthrow the Hungarian king. The Magyar sovereign held him as a prisoner at Visegrád, and would present him to visiting Turkish emissaries as a warning of what could happen to them if they misbehaved. In 1475, Vlad was reinstated in Wallachia with the king's help, but his final reign lasted only a month: rival claimants had him assassinated and his beheaded body was buried at Snagov monastery near Bucharest.

Significantly, no paintings of Vlad have been found in Wallachian churches. But his terrible reputation outlived him; in 1462 a German manuscript appeared publicising his monstrous deeds, and this was followed by many more, published in Germany and Russia. A few portraits of Vlad survive. The earliest is a copy of a 15C original and now hangs in Ambras Castle in the Tyrol. There is also a miniature in the Kunsthistorisches Museum, Vienna, while he appears as the personification of evil in a painting of St

Andrew's Martyrdom (c 1470) in the Viennese Belvedere. But the Ambras portrait is the most telling. It shows a thin face with wide eyes and a stocky neck, which tallies exactly with the written description of the Impaler made by a papal legate who saw him in Visegrád.

The Turks eventually gained the upper hand in Wallachia in the 15C. Instead of turning it into a pashalik they let the principality appoint its own leaders, extracting large annual tributes instead. Transylvania and Moldavia were allowed similar freedoms, while Bulgaria, Hungary (including the Banat from 1552) and Serbia were kept more closely at heel. Lebanon was the only other country which retained its own rulers and institutions while it was a

The Dracula legend

The connection between the real Dracula and Bram Stoker's vampire is tenuous but persistent. Rising from the dead to terrify the living, vampires have long been part of eastern European folklore, and were eagerly assimilated by Western writers keen to transform the Balkans into a region of terrifying lawlessness.

In Romanian, vampires are called *strigoi*. Stoker's villain was a Székely. This would make him a descendant of the mysterious Khabaro-Turkic tribes who defended Transylvania's medieval borders and spoke a Hungarian dialect that was written with runic characters. But Vlad the Impaler was a Vlach, descended from the Basarabi family. He was also a cousin of Ştefan cel Mare, Moldavia's saintly medieval prince. His name, Dracula, means 'son of Dracul'. His father, Vlad Dracul, was initiated into the Order of the Dragon, an exclusive body created by King Sigismund of Hungary to honour those who showed extreme valour against the Turks. Vlad Dracul was also a terrifying character, and 'the devil' (which also translates as *dracu*) would have been an appropriate soubriquet. But the debate rumbles on. Ironically, philologists have seen a connection between *dracu* and *drag*, the Romanian/Slav word meaning 'dear' or 'precious'! The last living descendant of Vlad III is Count Vlad Dracula Kretzulescu. He owns a castle in Berlin and is known for being kind to bats...

Nationalist and communist propaganda has generated a pantheon of medieval heroes whose deeds are supposed to have set Romania on the path to independence. Among the most enduring figures in this pantheon are the two cousins, Vlad Dracula and Ştefan cel Mare, who was called the Athlete of Christ because of his energetic battles against the Turks. But in 1473, Ştefan told his people that 'Wallachians are to us what the Turks are' and seemed to trust the Poles more than his kinsmen over the border to the south. According to historian H.-R. Patapievici, Ştefan's conflict with Vlad 'verged on the pathological'. He goaded Mehmet II to invade Wallachia while Dracula responded by sending half his army to guard the Moldavian border, leaving the other half to cope with the approaching Turks; Vlad then rode off to Chilia 'to square accounts with Ştefan'.

During the communist period, Vlad was hailed as a harsh but just lawgiver, and this view of his character persists alongside the more familiar image, diffused by German and Russian folktales, that he was a monster. As late as 1991, Romanian historians were presenting him as a key figure in the evolution of the country's independence.

Turkish vassal. When the Ottoman Empire began to fall apart, the Turks mounted savage raids into Wallachia and in certain cases the *voivodes* and their families were beheaded for refusing to convert to Islam. But even during the 16C Pax Turcica of Suleiman I, when the empire was at its height, Moldavian and Wallachian princes had to pay the Porte crippling tributes. These caused enormous hardship.

Life was often brutish and short, and the political wind was always capricious. Wallachia's folklore is studded with ballads about men forced to become outlaws so as to escape persecution by their own nobles as well as by foreign foes. Given the instability of the times, it is remarkable that any cultural life existed in Wallachia at all. But under princes such as Matei Basarab (r. 1632–54), Șerban Cantacuzino (r. 1678–88) and Constantin Brâncoveanu (r. 1688–1714), the country gained some of its finest churches and monasteries.

Romanian nationalism, sparked by Mihai Viteazul in the early 17C, became an increasingly irritating thorn in the Ottomans' side. By the early 18C the Turks were so desperate to keep hold of the two Romanian principalities that they installed their own leaders from the Phanar district of Constantinople. The Phanariots were mainly of Greek extraction and, with some notable exceptions, they were universally hated. They were finally expelled after Tudor Vladimirescu's uprising in 1821. Some 40 years later Moldavia and Wallachia were united under the new state of Romania, with its capital in Bucharest.

OLTENIA

After it turns south near Sibiu, the Olt River slices through the Carpathians at Turnu Roșu, and heads for the Danube through country that was once strewn with Stone, Bronze and Iron Age settlements. On its way it carves Wallachia into unequal halves: Oltenia to the west, and Muntenia, 'the mountain country' to the east. Muntenia is much larger, but Oltenia has just as much to offer.

Drive south on the E81 from Sibiu and you pass to the left of the river **Câinenii Mici**, a village famous for its vernacular houses and rustic post-Brâncovenesque church. Biserica Sf Nicolae (constructed 1733–69) is worth seeing for its interesting wall paintings, which can be found on both the interior and exterior surfaces. In c 26km further south of the village, the road west past Brezoi into the **Lotru (Outlaw) Valley** brings you eventually into spectacular countryside, and if you have the appropriate maps or a guide who knows the terrain, you can hike for miles in the splendid mountains on either side. On the east bank of the Olt in the village of Călinești and 84km south of Sibiu, stands Cornet skete. You will find it near the railway station. Cornet was founded in 1666 during the reign of Matei Basarab. In 1741 and 1835 artists painted neo-Byzantine frescoes on the interior surfaces of its curtain wall.

Voineasa, 40km to the west, is an attractive resort with several 1- and 2-star hotels and a number of tourist villas. Mysteriously, *Hotels Brădițor* (✩✩), *Lotru* (✩✩), *Lotrițor* (✩), *Poenița* (✩), *Vidruța* (✩) and *Voinesița* (✩) are all listed with the same address and telephone number: Str M. Eminescu 1, ☎ 050 735084. The same address and phone number are also used for some 3-star villas, the train booking office, a restaurant, disco, billiard hall and electronic games saloon.

Alternatively, for something with more character, contact ANTREC in Bucharest (see p 116) or one of the tourist offices in Râmnicu Vâlcea.

The monasteries of Oltenia

Some 60km south of Sibiu, the E81 brings you to **Cozia**, the site of a beautiful 14C monastery named after a nearby mountain. The word *cozia* is related to a Slavonic word for goat, while *cozi* is a Turkish term for walnut: take your pick, because both interpretations are appropriate. Today the monastery buildings are split in two by the E81. The monastery church lies to the left, near the river, while Radu Paisie's elegant *bolniţa* (infirmary church, 1542) stands on the other side, deliberately set apart on a hill to itself. Make time to see this as well because it is extremely elegant in its own right.

The original complex was completed in 1390, but only the main church has survived from this period. Built by Serbian architects for Prince Mircea cel Bătrân (r. 1386–1418), it is modelled on the lovely monasteries of the Morava Valley. Beautifully proportioned to look both slender and strong, it has a trefoil plan and a long rectangular narthex that was once crowned by a tower. The exterior walls are a feast of decorative tiles, filigree latticework, clustered colonnettes and strongly articulated blind arcades, showing the combined influences of Classical Greek and Islamic designs. The ocular windows high up in the walls are typical of late-medieval Serbian churches, while the ogive arches come from Turkey and the plaited crosses are also from Classical Greece. Here and there you can see the Byzantine double-headed eagle, borrowed to add an imperial lustre. An open *pridvor* or porch was added during the reign of Constantin Brâncoveanu (1688–1714). Inside, the pronaos has some fine 14C paintings while the frescoes in the naos and altar were added in the early 18C. The icon screen is also Brâncovenesque.

The Serbian style was introduced into Wallachia by an Athonite monk called Nicodemus. He founded several monasteries under Mircea's protection, among them Tismana in Oltenia, Vodiţa near Drobeta Turnu Severin and Prislop in the Haţeg country of southwest Transylvania.

Călimăneşti and Căciulata

Cozia is close to the spas of Călimăneşti and Căciulata, a few kilometres to the southwest. The two villages have long since run together into one, forming a long string of buildings that stretches for several kilometres along the road. They are still popular, as can be seen from the number of hotels that line the main through road. The sulphurous waters were exploited by the Romans; Napoleon III liked taking them too, but he had his supplies transported to Paris. Nearby lies Ostrov, a river island that was once a retreat for anchorites.

Practical information

☎ **code**
050

Getting around
By train The railway which runs between Piatra Olt and Podu Olt has a station at Călimăneşti.

Where to stay
Try **Hotel Traian** (✩✩✩) at Calea lui

Traian 953 in Căciulata, ☎ 750521, or the less picturesque but probably more comfortable *Motel Tour-Imex* at 1079 Călimănești-Căciulata, ☎ 751179, or the *Complex Turistic* at Str Calea lui Traian 418 in Căciulata, ☎ 750270.

Post office

The main post office is at Calea lui Traian 409 in Călimănești.

Râmnicu Vâlcea

Some 28km further south lies the county town of Râmnicu Vâlcea. An unostentatious place in an attractive setting, it has plenty of historic churches. The oldest is the 15C **Biserica Cetățuia**. In 1529, Radu de la Afumați and his son, Vlad, were assassinated here by boyars trying to claim the country back from the Ottomans. **Biserica Paraschiva** is a fine example of mid-16C architecture, and Râmnicu's **Episcopal Cathedral** is impressive too, although nothing remains of its original 16C buildings. The existing cathedral church dates from the 19C and contains murals by Gheorghe Tattarescu. You may also like to visit the **memorial house** dedicated to the writer, Anton Pann, at Str Stirbei Voda 18. But nothing in Rimnicu compares with the cluster of monasteries that lie a short drive to the west in the foothills of the Munții Căpățînii.

Practical information

☎ code

050

Tourist offices

Agenția de Turism a Sindicațelor can be found at Calea lui Traian 176, ☎ 735402; *BTT* is at Piața Ștefan cel Mare 4, ☎ 738720; *Euro Tour* is at Str Gabriel Stoianovici 7, ☎ 739748; and *Seytour* is at Str N. Bălcescu 15, ap 1, ☎ 746298.

Getting around

By train The station is on Str Cozia; *CFR*, the train ticket office, is on Calea lui Traian, ☎ 734650.
By bus This is at Str N. Bălcescu, ☎ 732674.
By car *ACR* has an office in Râmnicu at Str Ana Ipatescu S3, ☎ 733140. For **car repairs** and servicing, try *Hery* at Str Fabricii 14, ☎ 745603, or *RP Integral*, Str Mihaescu 80, ☎ 734750, which also has a car wash; alternatively, ask ACR for help. **Petrol stations** can be found at Hery, Str Fabricii 14, and on Calea lui Traian and Str Mihaescu.

Where to stay

Hotel accommodation includes *Hotel Hery* (★★) at Str Fabricii 14, ☎ 745603, and there is another 2-star hotel in the *Complex Turistic Alutus* at Str Praporgescu 10, ☎ 736601. Failing these, try *Motel Riviera* (★★) at Calea lui Traian 346, ☎ 742489.

Post office

The main office can be found at Str Tudor Vladimirescu 6, ☎ 736910.

Money

There are banks at Calea lui Traian 1–5, 150, 158 and 188, and at Str General Magheru 4. Exchange houses include one on Tudor Vladimirescu 168, *Edmond* at Str Mareșal Ion Antonescu 168, or *Seytour Exchange* at B-dul Bălcescu 15.

Police

For help, contact the *prefectura* at B-dul Tudor Vladimirescu 72, ☎ 730802.

Medical help

Try the hospitals at Calea lui Traian 331 or Str Magheru 54, or you may have better luck contacting the **Cabinete Medicale** such as *Dr Tuca Nicon* at Calea lui Traian 203, ☎ 744718, *Omnimed* on Calea lui Traian 209, ☎ 741562, or *San Dubinciuc* on Calea lui Traian bl 12, ☎ 715154. Advertised **pharmacies** include *Brajan* at Calea lui Traian 209, and *Farm-Mixt* at Str Ana Iputescu 8.

Regular events

Vâlcea county has a number of regular events. These include the Ceramics fair at Hurezu from around 6–8 June; the Folklore Festival in Vaideeni around 21–22 June; the popular youth music festival in Bujoreni at Muzeul Satului in July; the Folklore Festival at Calimaneşti in the first few days of August, and the Folk Dance festival, *Braiul de aur*, at Barbateşti, which takes place on or around 8 September. If you want more precise details about any of these events, or are looking for local craftspeople, contact *Centrul Judeţean de Creaţie Popularu*, B-dul N. Bălcescu 26A, ☎ 737820.

In Râmnicu itself there are a **concert hall**, the *Filarmonica Ion Dumitrescu*, on Calea lui Traian, ☎ 732956, and a **theatre** named after Anton Pann at B-dul Vladimirescu 39, ☎ 737320. There is an **art museum** at Str Antonescu 29 and a **history museum** at Calea lui Traian 159.

From Râmnicu Vâlcea turn left onto the DN67 for Târgu Jiu, and after c 15km take a left down a side road for the monastery of **Govora** (c 1km). This simple trefoil church with its tall cupola stands inside a curtain wall, reminding you that it was once heavily fortified. Its features include an open porch and polygonal apse, while the windows are encased in lovely carved frames. It was built and had already been destroyed once before 1488, when Vlad Călugărul had it repaired, and during the reign of Radu cel Frumos (Radu the Handsome, 1495–1508) it became an influential cultural centre. Famous for its 17C printing press, Govora monastery developed still further in the 18C, when Constantin Brâncoveanu had the church rebuilt and frescoed. Further alterations were made in the 19C, and it was restored again in the 1950s.

Mănăstirea Bistriţa stands c 40km west of Râmnicu Vâlcea and c 6km from the pretty medieval village of Costeşti, in the hills to the right of the DN67. The monastery was founded by boyars from Craiova sometime before 1496, but suffered at the hands of Mihnea cel Rău (Mihnea the Bad, r. 1508–09), who attacked it when the Craioveşti became too arrogant. On their return from refuge in Transylvania the boyars rebuilt the church, but the entire building was replaced in the 19C. All that remains of their massive structure is the *bolniţa*, the hospital church, which was completed in 1521 and restored by Brâncoveanu, who added one of his favourite porches and some frescoes.

Continue heading north, and after 5km you come to **Arnota**, a monastery founded in 1633 by Matei, one of the great Basarab dynasty. Legend has it that shortly before he became Prince of Wallachia, Matei hid in some caves near here after escaping from the Turks, and built the church to thank God for his survival. Its fat towers and undulating porch roof make it less elegant than Cozia, but it is charming all the same.

Hurezi monastery

A few kilometres further west towards Târgu Jiu, the DN67 brings you to the village of Horezu. Turn right here and head into the hills for Hurezi monastery, Prince Constantin Brâncoveanu's most impressive foundation. Brâncoveanu was a leader of the Byzantine revival, and he maintained close links with all the important centres of Orthodoxy. In doing so, he infuriated the Sultan and was eventually beheaded for refusing to convert to Islam. Brâncoveanu was a great supporter of the arts, and under his patronage a distinctive style was born. Known as the *stil brâncovenesc*, the Brâncoveanu style, it was a synthesis of vernacular Romanian, Islamic and Venetian art and it pervaded architecture, stone carving, silverwork and embroidery. You can recognise Brâncovenesque buildings by their round-headed arcades (often in two storeys), and by the floral, heraldic and zoomorphic motifs which animate carvings around door and window frames. Other elements include columns with neo-Corinthian capitals and pierced balustrades that look like filigree. Another characteristic is the attractive contrast between highly decorated and plain areas.

The complex at Hurezi was finished in 1697. It comprises a spacious rectangle with, on the south side, a royal residence, an abbot's house, a bell tower and a library, and on the west, a *trapezium*, a chapel, a watchtower and monks' cells. The main church, completed 1691–94, was the work of a Greek mason, Dionisie, and the Romanian masters who brought Hurezi up to date with an elaborate Brâncovenesque porch. Two tall, helmeted cupolas of almost equal size dominate the roof, the larger supported by four massive arches and Byzantine pendentives. The main body of the church is a crisp rectangle, while the east end is softened by three circular apses so that overall it looks like a casket. The exterior walls are decorated with blind arcades containing roundels, and a marble border separates the upper and lower storeys. Above the entrance are the arms of Wallachia and the Cantacuzino family. Inside, the decor is sumptuous, comprising a splendid timber ceiling and icon screen. The Byzantine frescoes are superb and should be enjoyed at leisure: they include wonderful portraits of Wallachia's leading medieval dynasties, the Basarab, Brâncoveanu and Cantacuzino families, as well as scenes from Mount Athos.

Some of the villages around Hurezi are famous for their *olari*, families of potters who practise skills handed down by their ancestors. Many of these potters live in desperate conditions and their traditional skills are dying out. They make a variety of kitchenware and toys and flutes decorated in white, brown and grey, and sometimes green. Their designs are very lively and incorporate symbolic animals, for instance cockerels and fish, as well as geometric patterns. The old women who traditionally prepare the earthenware for firing scrape the images into the surface with traditional tools such as cows' horns and goose feathers.

A side road to the south of Horezu village brings you to **Măldărești** in c 4km. This is the site of two magnificent *cule* or fortified houses. The earlier *cula* is the Greceanu house, which dates from the early 18C, while its brother, the Duca, was built in 1815. Both are now ethnographic museums and are well worth visiting for their appealing architecture and layout. Contact the tourist agencies in Râmnicu Vâlcea for details (see p 162).

Buildings like these were erected to protect tenant farmers from murderous Ottoman and Tartar raids which shattered Wallachia's peace from the 1650s. The architectural historian Sherban Cantacuzino compares the *cula* to a Border castle, a type of 16C English fortified farmhouse that had similar origins. *Cule* were introduced in the late 17C, and provided shelter for the farmer's livestock as well as his family. Originating from walled enclosures, they developed into three-storey fortresses with room for animals and storage on the ground floor, a cellar above and living quarters at the top. Typically, the upper floors were inaccessible from inside the ground floor rooms; instead, there was an external staircase built into the wall, which allowed the inhabitants to repel intruders more easily. But the Oltenian *cula* combines strength with style: around the top floor is a spacious arcaded verandah which allowed the owner both to look out for enemies and enjoy the view. The walls are often a massive 1m thick, and the staircases are made of solid oak. Outside, the houses are usually covered in dazzling white distemper. This type of building is not unique to Romania; there are examples in Bulgaria and Serbia as well.

Before leaving Râmnicu Vâlcea for western Oltenia, drive south on the DN64 towards Drăgășani. At Băbeni (c 16km) turn right for Frâncești, and signs should point the way for the church called **Dintr'un Lemn**. The name, which means 'from a single piece of wood', comes from a legend that the monastery church was built by a shepherd using a single tree trunk. Raised for Preda Brâncoveanu in the early 17C, it was burnt down in the early 19C, but its replica is pretty and there is an interesting masonry church here too. Its beauty lies in the proportions of the porch and the carving around doors and windows. The church retains some original features, although the frescoes, porch, main entrance, window frames and pronaos tower are later additions. In the north side of the enclosure is an attractive, balconied abbot's house while opposite is an attractive loggia; both were built by Prince Ștefan Cantacuzino.

The hilly road from Râmnicu Vâlcea to Târgu Jiu crosses several rivers. It also passes at 55km the monastery of Polovragi. The church was built by Radu cel Frumos in 1470 at the mouth of the Cheile Olțetului and has some fine early 18C murals. Turn right in the village for a track to **peștera Polovragi**, a cave in the limestone massif which is said to have been inhabited by the Dacian god, Zamolxis. Since 1984 it has been managed as a natural monument; open Tues–Sun 09.00–17.00.

Continue along the country road from Polovragi, and after 20km you reach Crasna, from where you can hike to the top of Mount Parâng and cross over into the Lotru Valley. The climbing is relatively easy for an experienced mountaineer, but the path markings are not always to be relied upon; do not explore this area without a guide.

Târgu Jiu

This is an unappealing industrial town on the edge of the Jiu Valley mines. But it was here in 1937–38 that Constantin Brâncuși (1876–1957) supervised the installation of a group of sculptures that have become famous all over the world.

Practical information

☎ code
053

Tourist offices
These include *Ademig Tours* at Str Sanivesti bl 9, ap 10, ☎ 240106; *Aurum* at Str Unirii-Siret bl 8, ☎ 215385; *BTT* at Str General Tell 27, ☎ 212456; *Sind România* at Str Victoria 2, ☎ 212056.

Getting around
By train The station is at Str Republicii 2, ☎ 242263, and the CFR booking office can be found at Str Unirii bl 2, ☎ 211924.
By bus The bus station is just south of the train station, off Str Titulescu.
By car For **car servicing** and repairs, try *Coral Service*, Str Dobrogeanu Gherea 18, ☎ 219012, or *Diasintex*, Str Lului 85. *ACR* has an office at Str Victoriei bl 1, ☎ 214563. There are several **petrol stations** on Calea Bucuresti, B-dul Teodoroiu, Str Jiului and Str Victoriei.

Where to stay
Hotel Gorj (✭✭) has lots of rooms, telephones and exchange facilities in a modern block at Calea Eroilor 6, ☎ 214814. *ANTREC* boasts an office in town, tel 216964, but do not be surprised if you get no reply. As usual, it is more reliable to contact the head office in Bucharest (see page ••••). Alternatives include *Hotel Parc* (✭✭) at B-dul Brâncuși 10, ☎ 215981, and *Hotel*

Sport (✭✭) at B-dul Brâncuși 7, ☎ 214402.

Eating out
Places to eat around the county include *Pestera Muierilor* (the Women's Cave) at Baia de Fier or *Fântana lui Cosbuc* at Balesti. In town, try *Sohodol* at Str 30 Dicembrie 2, *Lider*, a pizzeria at Calea Eroilor 17, or the *Gorj* at Calea Eroilor 6. Otherwise, you can eat in the hotels.

Post office
The main post office is at Str Traian 1, ☎ 211119.

Money
There are banks at Str Vladimirescu 17, Str Traian 28 and bl C1, Str Magheru bl 2A2B4, and Calea Eroilor 17.

Police
Contact the *prefectura* at Piața Victoriei 2–4, ☎ 212017.

Medical care
The *Spitalul Județean* is at Str Progresului 18, ☎ 243315. A **dental practice** can be found at Str Unirii bl 7, ap 1, ☎ 219650. For **pharmacies**, try *Elido* at Calea Severinului 6; *Farmador* at Str Unirii bl 2, *Farmastell* at B-dul Ecaterina Teodoroiu 49, *Gențiana Farm*, also on B-dul Teodoroiu, and *Secofarm* at Str General Tell bl C2.

Regular events
Târgu Jiu is the county town of Gorj. Regular events around the county include an annual pottery fair at

Tismana and a vine planting festival called Serbarile Dealului at Runci, both in March; a shepherds' festival at Novaci in May; a folkloric festival at Runcu in May; a festival dedicated to Tudor Vladimirescu, the leader of the 1821 uprising, at Pades, in June; an open-air sculpture summer school dedicated to Brâncuși in July; a crafts fair and exhbition at Polovraci; a song and dance festival at Tismana in August; a festival to mark the transhumance in September at Baia de Fier, and a popular and folk music festival in Târgu Jiu itself during November. For more details, contact the tourist offices or *Centrul de Creaţie Populară* at Str Vladimirescu 36, ☎ 213710.

The **County History Museum** on Str Geneva suffers from the current malaise common to all Romanian cultural institutions, and desperately needs more funding; the **art museum**, 400m west on Str Stadion, although very small, is interesting; open Tues–Sun 09.00–17.00.

Brâncuși's famous installation comprises three separate pieces, one of which, *Coloana fără Sfârsit*, the *Column of the Infinite*, was erected in Parcul Tineretului, a wide, open space to the west of the town centre. It was designed as a memorial to Romanian soldiers who defended the town from the Germans during the First World War. The Column is made of 15 steel 'beads' threaded onto an iron core and soars to 30m high. In spite of its great height, when you stand back from it to see the piece as a whole, it seems to float above the ground, fulfilling Brâncuși's wish to make it work as a complete sculpture and as part of an infinite entity at the same time. Like all Brâncuși's most successful work, it is both simple and complex. It is also suprisingly moving, and rates as one of the most unusual and exciting war memorials in Europe, and certainly of modern times. The Column is deeply embedded in concrete and thanks to this, it failed to budge when an armoured tank tried to pull it down in the 1950s. Its striking profile of double pyramids is a motif which Brâncuși had been exploring repeatedly since 1918—you can see the same pattern on traditional grave posts and slender veranda pillars in many rural areas of Romania. In 1996, the Column was taken down for repairs and it should be reinstated by November 2000.

Brâncuși's other two other public sculptures stand nearer the town centre, in a small public park beside the Jiu River. They were both installed a short time after the Column, although no-one knows exactly what Brâncuși had in mind when he made them. The table, known as *Table of Silence* (*Masa Tacerii*), is made of local Banpotoc stone and is surrounded by 12 hemispherical stools. Brâncuși did not give the piece a name; its present one was adopted as the most suitable of several alternatives which other people have attached to it since it was made. On either side of the avenue to the east stand two rows of cuboid benches leading to Brâncuși's travertine arch known as *Gate of the Kiss* (*Poarta Sărutului*).

The Table and Gate stand on an east-west axis which extends to the Column, passing through an Orthodox church which is visible from the Gate. Theories as to the meanings, sources and symbolism of the Gate abound: one says that the top slab is modelled on a Romanian dowry chest; others say that the Kiss is the Kiss of Death. Abstracted versions of his famous Kiss motif are inscribed around the top slab and on all four faces of each pillar. This motif originates in his wonderfully tender sculpture of the same name from c 1908, which now resides in the Art Gallery of Craiova (see p 173). Curiously, there is another small table made by Brâncuși and then discarded in the park; here it is called *Masa festivă* and it has six little stools around it.

Nearby is the bridge held by Romanian soldiers during their gallant defence of Târgu Jiu in the First World War. If you walk around the centre of town, in the main square you will come across another monument which is interesting by comparison with Brâncuși's pieces. It commemorates the heroism of Ecaterina Teodoroiu. Born in 1894, she disguised herself as a man so she could fight during the First World War. She was made a sub-lieutenant in recognition of her courage, but was killed in battle in 1917. The memorial dates from the 1960s.

12km north of Târgu Jiu, to the right off the E79 to Petroșani, lies the village museum of **Curtișoara**. This has a superb collection of traditional houses—including a handsome 18C *cula*—that contain furniture, decorations and household objects typical of Oltenian village life. The museum is open Tues–Sun 08.00–17.00.

Brâncuși's birthplace at **Hobița** has been turned into a memorial house, open Tues–Sun 09.00–17.00. Take the minor DN67D west from Târgu Jiu, and you reach Peștișani in c 25km. Hobița is a continuation of this village; turn left at the first junction. Brâncuși was born in a traditional three-room house with a veranda, a cellar and an ancient wooden gateway. The property was moved wholesale from its original position some years ago, and the interior decoration is not original, but the house contains photographs and letters documenting the sculptor's life.

Return to Peștișani and turn left. About 10km further west, as you pass the Sohodol gorges, the road brings you to **Tismana** village. The name has Thracian origins and means a 'place fortified with walls'. Turn right into a mountain road, and soon you come to a **monastery** built into the side of a tree-covered cliff face and surrounded by rills and waterfalls. This idyllic setting is where the monk Nicodim established one of his three Wallachian foundations in the 14C. The main church, completed in 1377, is a stunning piece of Serbian-style architecture. The murals in the tall narthex make a powerful impact because they cover the entire wall space. They were painted in 1564 by an artist called Dobromir from Târgoviște. The frescoes in the main body of the church were restored in the 18C and are not nearly so striking. Repairs were carried out to the church fabric in the mid-17C.

For a while in the 14C, Tismana was the seat of the Metropolitan of Wallachia. The former monastery is now a working convent and around the courtyard stands an attractive rectangular block of sturdy fortress walls, comprising nuns' cells, a refectory, painting studios and a museum of cult objects. Monks from Tismana were trained as craftsmen and artists on Mount Athos, and some of their work is on display here. The museum also contains some of Romania's oldest embroideries. Roman bricks embedded into the floors of both churches indicate that there may have been a Daco-Roman fortress on the site long before the monastery was built. Brâncuși's father used to look after the monastery's estates. Northwest of Tismana on Mount Cioclovina are two sketes (monastic villages or hamlets where the monks or nuns live separately during the week and meet for services, and possibly meals, at weekends), which are worth a visit if you have time. Tismana village is the terminus for a narrow-gauge railway which serves woodcutters in the mountains.

Places of interest between Târgu Jiu and Drobeta Turnu Severin, 45km to the southwest, include Glogova, Motru and Broşteni, ancient villages where you can see fine **vernacular houses** and **traditional pottery**. To reach them from Tismana, return to the DN67D and turn right and then left beside the Motru River, or you can take the more reliable DN67 southwest from Târgu Jiu, which brings you directly to Motru.

Drobeta Turnu Severin

This town has the ruins of one of the largest Roman fortresses in Romania. These comprise baths, an altar, living accommodation for the troops and store houses.

Practical information

☎ code
052

Tourist offices
Try *BTT* at Str I.G. Bibigescu 4, ☎ 315 31; *Drobeta* at Str Decebal 41, ☎ 314103; *Mehedinţi* at Str Avram Iancu, ☎ 319191; and *Sind România* at Str Maresal Antonescu, ☎ 326725.

Getting around
By train The railway station is at Str Dunării 1, ☎ 311336; the CFR railway ticket office is at Str Decebal 41, ☎ 313117.
By bus The bus station is across Str Dunării from the railway station.
By car For **car services** and repairs try *Service Club Auto* at Str Mihai Viteazul 15, ☎ 226315, or contact *ACR* at Str Alexandru Barcacila B1, ☎ 315134. **Petrol stations** are at Str Smârdan 17, Calea Timişoarei, Calea Craiovei, Str Cicero 124, and B-dul Cernei 69.

Where to stay
The town has two 2-star hotels, the *Severin* at Str Eminescu 1, ☎ 312074, and the *Traian* at B-dul Vladimirescu 174, ☎ 311760. *ANTREC* has an office here, ☎ 220833.

Eating out
Try *Cicero* at Str Traian 129, *Casa Mehedinţeana* (which has dishes specific to the county) at Str Cantemir 1, and the *Chimsee Shop* pizzeria at Str Tudor Vladimirescu.

Post office
The main post office and a telephone office are next to each other at the west end of Str Decebal.

Money
There are banks at Str Aurelian 44, B-dul Carol 1, no. 55, and Str Dimitrie Cantemir 6.

Police
Try the *prefectura* at Str Traian 69, ☎ 311217.

Medical care
Contact *Hen Farm* medical centre, Str Traian 221, ☎ 311911, or *M&M Contuz* medical centre, B-dul Vladimirescu 167, ☎ 227693. **Pharmacies** include *Farmacia 54* on B-dul Vladimirescu, ☎ 312866.

Regular events
Drobeta Turnu Severin is the county town of Mehedinti. Regular events around the county include the Festival of the Lilies, with regional folk

songs and dancing at Ponoarele in May and *Sărbatoarea florilor de tei* (the Festival of the Lime Flowers), celebrating local folk song and dance, at Batlanele in June. There is another folk music festival for young people in October. Contact the local *Centrul de Creaţiei Populară*, at Str Republicii 5, for more details, ☎ 318035.

At Drobeta Turnu Severin are remains of the great bridge which the Greek architect Apollodorus of Damascus built across the river in 103–105 AD. Trajan commissioned the bridge after an unsuccessful attempt to quell the Dacians in 101–102, and it gave him the edge he needed. The Dacians submitted in 106 after the legionaries had marched north along the Olt Valley and surrounded them from the north and east. The bridge was an impressive structure and very advanced for its time. Twenty four-ribbed pillars straddled the river in pairs at 52m intervals. Each pillar was 45m high (excluding the base) and 18m wide, allowing men and supplies to cross the river in record time. The Romanian side was protected by a garrison stationed in Drobeta fortress. Today all you can see of the bridge are the pillars at the Romanian end encased in protective housings.

Apart from this, Drobeta is a sprawling industrial city that is best avoided unless you want to hire river boats; ask for details at the tourist offices. 35km west of here, at Orşova, is the Djerdap hydroelectric dam which grieved Patrick Leigh Fermor by flooding the spectacular Iron Gates gorges. Follow the river west from Orşova and you come to more fascinating fragments that mark Trajan's progress into Dacia. At Cazanele Mici, 9km west, you can see Trajan's tablet which commemorates the construction of a road here in 104. It was built into the side of the vertical rock, and you can still see the holes that held the transverse supports. There is a Roman sundial here as well. Continue a further 4km to Cazanele Mari for the most impressive section of the gorges.

From Orşova, head 13km north on the E70 and then turn right for 3km to reach the old-world spa of **Băile Herculane** (Herculean Baths) with its lovely porticoed and frescoed casino and graceful hotels. While the outskirts of the town are full of high-rise hotels, the centre is like something out of a Ruritanian fantasy, bearing the marks of an elegant Habsburg past. If you like doing things in style, you could stay at the *Hotel Cerna* (*The Black Hotel*) on Str 1 Mai, ☎ 055 560436. This is a striking 1930s-style building with wings that flank a Moldavian-style tower, with modernist and Islamic motifs thrown in for good measure. Appropriately for its name, its façade is a dark grey.

Enclosed by steep crags and forested cliffs on either side, the old centre has a very romantic atmosphere. Under the modern *Hotel Român* on Str Română 1, you will find a Roman bath which has been turned into a very small but pleasing museum. If you cross the Cerna River (the Black River) from the main access road, you will find steam wells, classical statues and a pergola, and people treating themselves to inhalations of sulphuric vapours. Technically, Băile Herculane belongs in the Banat region, but you can take a spectacular road beside the Cerna (Black) River northeast into the Mehedinţi mountains. Alternatively, driving north to Caransebeş or northwest to Anina are two equally attractive options into the Banat, with its almost unbelievably pastoral countryside.

Craiova and its museums

Craiova is an old but unlovely city, eviscerated by modern planners in the name of progress. It has a population of around 300,000, most of whom have to live in ghastly apartment blocks. But it has some saving graces, one of which is its museums.

Practical information

☎ code
051

Tourist offices
Try *Eurotourist* at B-dul Titulescu bl 18, ☎ 193447; *Alexion Comtours* at Str Mihai Viteazul 7, ☎ 411815; *Alfa si Omega* at Calea București bl 13B, ☎ 412900; *BTT Oltenia* at Str Grivița bl 4, ☎ 417358; *Mapamond* at Str Lyon 2–4, ☎ 415071.

Getting around
By train The station is at B-dul Republicii, north of the centre. The *CFR* train ticket office is at Calea București 2, ☎ 411634. *TAROM* also has an office at Calea București 2, ☎ 411049.
By bus Craiova has two bus stations: the northern one, by the railway station on B-dul Republicii, serves major destinations, and the other one, 5km south of the centre, serves villages to the south.
By car **Car repairs** and servicing can be found at *Service Auto Ray*, Calea București 179–181, ☎ 163437. There is a **car wash** at *Exocom*, Calea București 191, ☎ 124632. *ACR* has an office at Str Grivița Roșie bl 2–4, ☎ 416166.
Petrol stations can be found on Calea Severinului, Calea București, Cartier Românești, Str Ștefan cel Mare, Str Caracal, Str Ungureni, Str Unirii, Str Bibescu, and Str Bucovat.

Where to stay
There is one 4-star hotel, the *Jianu*, at Str Bibescu 16, ☎ 417257. Alternatively, *Hotel Jiul* (✮✮✮) is at Str Bibescu 1–3, ☎ 415655, and *Hotel Parc* (✮✮✮) is at Str Bibescu 16, ☎ 417257. Another 3-star motel, the *Han Craiovita*, is on Str Prelungirea Severinului, ☎ 187217.

Eating out
Eating houses with speciality menus include *Flora* at Str Mihai Viteazul 4–6, which serves Oltenian dishes, *Olga Matrimex* at Str George Enescu 2 (Italian), and *Tolo Impex*, B-dul Carol I, 26 (also Italian). Fast-food restaurants include *Cronos Com*, Str Grivita Roșie 25, *Latof Com*, Calea București bl C17, and *Saff Trading Pepperoni*, Str Lipscani 17. Craiova has two internet cafés, *Cisnet* at Calea București Lapus T9–N14, ☎ 143333, www.cisnet.ro, and *Inter Caffenet*, Calea București bl A24, ☎ 416667.

Post office
The main post office is at Str Unirii 88.

Money
Banks and exchange houses include *CEC* at Str Sf Dumitru bl 1–3–5, and *Vega Exchange* at Str Lyon 3–4.

Police
Local police can be contacted through the *primaria* at Str Cuza 15, ☎ 416235.

Medical care
Craiova has **hospital clinics** at B-dul Antonescu 60, Str Brâncuși 3, and Calea București 126; there is a **dental surgery** at Calea București 147, and an

ambulance service at B-dul Antonescu 60, ☎ 133910. There are three **pharmacies** in town: *Elfarm* at B-dul Republicii 52, *Esculap* at Str Nicolae Titulescu bl A7, and *Trei F* at Calea Bucureşti bl 17B.

Regular events

Craiova is the county town of Dolj. Regional events include the festival of popular customs in Cernateşti in March; the international Shakespeare festival in Craiova in April; the contemporary music festival in Craiova in May; Romanian folk music festival Maria Tănase in August; theatre festival Elena Teodorini in September, and another international music festival in Craiova in November. **Centrul de Creaţie Populară** at Calea Unirii 85 should be able to give you specific details, ☎ 124844.

Craiova is justly famed for its **theatrical productions**, and if you can catch the national company at home, you should. *Teatrul Naţional* is at Str A.I. Cuza 11, ☎ 415363. The *Filarmonica Oltenia* is based at Calea Unirii 22, ☎ 412334. There is also a children's puppet theatre at Str Cuza 11, ☎ 412473.

Sports facilities

Craiova has a trotting circuit in Parcul Poporului; the Electroputere football club is based at Str Stadionului 1, and there is a swimming pool at Str Lipscani 22.

Parks and gardens

These include Grădina Mihai Bravu at Str Brestei 14, Grădina 1 Mai/A.I. Cuza at Str Cuza 7, and Parcul Românescu at Str N. Românescu 1.

Craiova is Wallachia's second city after Bucharest. While the outskirts are depressing, its centre has a few elegant buildings, some of which have been turned into excellent museums and art galleries.

Craiova started out as a Roman camp under Trajan, and between the 15C and 18C it flourished as a regional capital ruled by governors called *bani*. One of them was Mihai Viteazul, who united the three Romanian principalities in 1600.

Modernisation began in the late 18C, when a number of fountains were installed to extend the town's drinking water. Some of these have survived, notably on Str Iancu Jianu and in Piaţa Chiriac.

The oldest extant building in Craiova is the fine, two-storey **Casa Baniei** (the Bans' Residence), which is now the Ethnographic Museum at Str Matei Basarab 16; open Tues–Sun 10.00–18.00. It was completed in 1699 by Constantin Brâncoveanu, who replaced a 16C house belonging to a boyar family. The ground floor rooms are vaulted with bricks and there are balconies on the first floor. The museum contains a fine collection of traditional peasant clothes and domestic tools; note particularly the lovely Oltenian carpets, which incorporate bird, flower and animal motifs unique to this region.

The **Metropolitan Cathedral** next door shows what the French architect André Lecomte du Nouÿ made of a Byzantine church. The previous building, dating from 1652, was destroyed by an earthquake, and in 1889 Lecomte du Nouÿ was asked to design a replacement. While it is nothing like its predecessor, the present building is very grand. You can compare it with another of Lecomte du Nouÿ's restorations in Holy Trinity Church, at Str Ion Maiorescu 9, and further afield in the Bishops' Church at Curtea de Argeş (see pp 176–177).

During the late 19C many buildings were erected here by foreign as well as Romanian architects. They show the then current fashion for eclectic, and especially French academic, designs. Among these are the former Jean Mihail palace at Calea Unirii 15, which now houses the **Muzeul de Artă 'Theodor Aman'**, open Tues–Sun 10.00–17.00. Designed by Paul Gauttereau and completed in 1907, it is a splendid neo-Renaissance and neo-Baroque building with marble halls, a grand staircase of Carrara marble and domed ceilings. Theodor Aman was an influential history painter who helped to found the Academy of Fine Arts in Bucharest. In 1908 his brother founded a public library in Craiova (at Str M. Kogălniceanu 9) and donated a group of Theodor's paintings to the city. These became the nucleus of the museum's collection. Its holdings now include a wide range of European and Romanian art from the 16C to the 20C, but it is known best for a small cabinet of Brâncuși's early sculptures.

Brâncuși studied industrial design in Craiova before joining the Bucharest Fine Arts Academy. He went to Paris in 1904, and settled permanently in France. But he returned to Romania eight times and maintained links with experimental art groups. His works here include a realistic bronze *Cap de băiat* (*Head of a boy*) from his Rodinesque period, a female torso in marble from c 1907 and the first known stone version of *Sărutul* (*The Kiss*) from c 1908. To find out more about Brâncuși's studies in Craiova, visit the Muzeul Constantin Brâncuși at Str Brâncuși 11; the largest collections of his work are in Paris and the USA.

Muzeul Olteniei at Str Madona Duda 4, a few hundred metres west of Calea Unirii, focusses on Oltenia's history from the Paleolithic era to the present. There is another section of the museum at Str Popa Șapca 4. Oltenia is sprinkled with archaeological sites from the Stone Age to Roman times, and excavations carried out in the 1930s showed that the region was a microcosm containing information relevant to the whole of southeast Europe. The museum has a famous Thraco-Getic treasure as well as jewellery and ceramics influenced by Byzantine art. Open Tues–Sun 10.00–18.00. There are also the Museum of Ethnography at Str Matei Basarab 4, and the National Theatre Museum at Str A.I. Cuza 11.

Much of Craiova was wrecked by the restructuring that took place during Ceaușescu's regime. Many of its fine old private houses disappeared for no other reason than that they got in the way. Lucky survivors include the Town Hall at Str Cuza 7, the Prefecture at Str Unirii 19, and courthouses at Titulescu 14 and Str Brestei 16. Among the 18C churches still standing are Biserica Sf Ilie, with its Brâncovenesque carvings, at Str 24 Februarie 2, Biserica Sf Gheorghe Nou at Str Păltiniș 15, and Biserica Obedeanu (another former Brâncovenesque building) at Str Brestei 1.

If you have time to explore the countryside around Craiova, visit **Mănăstirea Bucovat**, about 5km west along the DN55. It was built between 1506 and 1512, and on its walls is a painted chronicle that is the only one of its kind in Wallachia. Further south, near the Jiu River at Sadova, stands a monastery of the same name; dating from the 15C, it was rebuilt in turn by Matei Basarab, Constantin Brâncoveanu and several others. The 18C Cula Poienarilor at Almaj is worth seeing. There is a ruined Roman camp at Racari, and Neolithic and Bronze Age remains from the Coțofeni culture (3rd millennium BC) can be found at Coțofenii de Jos.

If you cross the county border to the east towards Slatina, Piatra Olt lies south off the DN65. About 15km to the south stands the 16C monastery of **Brâncoveni**.

Matei Basarab lived here in 1640, and Constantin Brâncoveanu rebuilt the complex in 1699.

Some ruins of a Roman town called **Romula** can be seen spread around a site at Resca, located south of Brâncoveni towards Caracal. This too was built over a former Dacian town called Malva. In Caracal itself is a ruined 16C mansion from the time of Mihai Viteazul.

Further south, at **Corabia** there is a museum devoted to the area's fascinating prehistory. Corabia is the site of a Geto-Dacian citadel called Sucidava, which became an important Roman settlement. Later still it was a centre of the Romano-Byzantine civilisation.

About 30km to the north east of Caracal, near the villages of Nicolae Tițulescu, Valeni and Seaca off the DN6, is **Rezervația Boianu**, the country's main reserve for bustards (*dropii* in Romanian). There are other nature reserves near Topana and Optașani, and at Poboru and Spineni.

MUNTENIA

This part of Wallachia, the Mountain Land, stretches east from the Olt River to Călărași, and its northern edge meets Moldavia to the north of Buzău and Brăila. Like Oltenia, Muntenia covers a wide range of landsapes from mountains to steppe and river plain, but the most attractive places are to be found in the Carpathian foothills. These include the old capitals of Curtea de Argeș, Câmpulung and Târgoviste, and the Prahova Valley.

Curtea de Argeş

To reach Curtea de Argeș from Râmnicu Vâlcea, drive 32km south towards Pitești and visit the charming 15C monastery of **Cotmeana** on the way. It stands at the end the village of Cotmeana; double back to the right of the E81 after descending the pass. Alternatively, you can take a shortcut via the DN73C to the west of Curtea, turning left in Aldești.

Practical information

☎ **code**

048

Travel agent

Try *Posada* at B-dul Basarabilor 27–29, ☎ 711801.

Getting around

By train Curtea de Argeș has a railway station on Str Albești in the centre of town.

By bus The bus station is just south of the railway station on Str Albești.

By car Romania's main motoring organisation, *ACR*, has an office at Str Basarabilor bl E13, ☎ 714505.

Where to stay

Hotel Posada (✰✰) at B-dul Basarabilor 27–29, ☎ 711800, has 130 rooms and exchange facilities, plus a restaurant. There is a 1-star hotel called *Sadim* at Str Negru Voda 36. The Sân Nicoara **campsite** at Str Plopiș 13 has two stars.

Post office

The main post office and telephone office are at Calea Basarabilor 21.

Money

For money changing, try *Hotel Posada* at B-dul Basarabilor 27–29, or *Bancă Comercială Romană* on Calea Basaribilor. Pitești, about 28 kms drive away, has around 12 banks, many of them in B-dul Republicii.

Police

The county police has its headquarters in Pitești in B-dul Republicii, ☎ 623100; there is a small police station in Curtea de Argeș on Calea Basarabilor.

Regular events

During the year, Argeș county (county town Pitești) hosts several folklore and music festivals. In April, Costești holds *Narcisa de aur* (The Golden Narcissus) folk music festival, which is followed in May by another at Corbi caled *Rapsodia Pastoreasca*. *Doina Vâlsanului* is a traditional folklore get-together at Galeș near Brăduleț. During the third week in July, Pitești holds an international choral music festival dedicated to D.G. Kiriac. Early August is the time of another international folklore extravaganza, while a few days later you can visit the celebrations which traditionally surround the transhumance, *Coboara oile de la munte*, at Albestii de Argeș. In September there is a folk music festival inspired by the legend of Master Manole, and a large crafts fair takes place in Pitești. All dates and venues can be confirmed by Centrul de Creație Populară, at B-dul Republicii 52, Pitești, fax 219080.

The *Muzeul Municipal* is on Str Sân Nicoara 1, open Tues–Sun 09.00–16.00.

Curtea, which simply means 'the court', was the capital of Wallachia from the late 13C to the mid-15C. It has two fine churches. **Biserica Domnească Sf Nicolae**, known locally as Sân Nicoară, is a lovely, sturdy little cross-in-square church standing in the town centre beside the ruins of the princely court. Although it was modelled on the Comnenian churches of the 12C and 13C, no-one knows who built it or when. Estimates of its date vary from the 12C to the mid-14C; dating is difficult because the church has undergone numerous alterations, the most extensive in the 1600s. Outside, it is decorated with alternating courses of brick and stone in the Byzantine mode, but this is so understated that the walls look as though they have been stripped. It also has an extended eastern arm which is unusual for its period.

Apart from its pleasing shape, the church has a fine set of interior frescoes. The iconography of these paintings follows the rules laid down in the *Erminii*, the Byzantine manual to which all Orthodox artists had to conform. They are similar to Paleologan mosaics in Istanbul, specifically those in the Church of Christ the Saviour and to paintings in the Church of Sts Peter and Paul in Trnovo. But the handling here is finer, being both sure of itself and highly individualistic, the scenes larger and bolder than those that may have inspired them. All the inscriptions are in Slavonic. Historian Nicolae Iorga took this to mean that the murals in Sf Nicolae were painted by a Greek artist accustomed to working in the Balkans.

In the narthex, the Deësis shows a portrait of Prince Vlad I Vlaicu (r. 1364–77). He wears a Western crown, rather than the Imperial Byzantine one that Slavic rulers often adopted to lend themselves greater prestige. In the same section is a painting of the ecumenical synods who met to thrash out questions of dogma after the church became legitimate. The narthex also contains scenes from the life of St Nicholas. All of these are excellent. In the apse you can see the Legend of the Virgin (including the Dormition and the Transfiguration), the prophets, a Pantokrator and an Adoration of the Magi, while the sanctuary is presided over by paintings of Sts Roman and Stephen, bishops, a tabernacle and the Holy Communion. The church has 14 tombs, many of them containing the remains of royal or noble personages; according to Iorga, one of the coffins revealed the remains of Prince Basarab himself, adorned with marvellous gold and silver jewels. On a sarcophagus near the southwest pillar is a carving of a richly-dressed male skeleton, while another tomb bears a Tree of Life and a 12-pointed star. These are just a few of the fascinating emblems found here that are connected with Wallachia's ancient aristocracy.

The Episcopal Church

Head north along Calea Basarabilor out of town for c 1km to see the 16C **Episcopal Church**, which stands in a monastery garden to the right of the road. It was founded by Prince Neagoe Basarab (r. 1512–21), probably on the site of the existing patriarchal church. A development of the princely church at Dealul Monastery near Târgoviște (see pp 180–181), it has a Moravan (Serbian), trefoil plan, and the outside is covered from top to bottom with extravagant ornament. The twin barley-sugar cupolas are unique to Romania (you can see later versions at the Orthodox Cathedral in Turnu Măgurele on the Danube), but also look for the birds with bells in their beaks around the cornice. There are many other charming details. The decoration is divided into two halves split by a stone girdle that encircles the church. Above this device, there are delicate rosettes within blind arcades, while below the patterning is contained within rectangular panels surrounding narrow windows. Many of the motifs are Islamic in origin.

Surprisingly slim in elevation (especially from the east end), the building was inspired by the monastery at Dealul, and its design has been attributed to the legendary Master Manole. A story goes that the master mason walled his wife inside the church to make sure that it would last, and that when the *voivode* saw his magnificent work, he was so jealous of it that he blinded Manole and imprisoned him and his assistants on the roof to ensure that they would never create a finer monument for anyone else. Wife-walling was a common, if regrettable, practice in eastern Europe; it was a hang-over from the pre-Christian belief that every valuable work of art needed a sacrifice. Nearby stands the little wooden shelter that protects Master Manole's Fountain, marking the spot where Manole is said to have fallen to his death from the roof.

Unusually, the narthex has been enlarged to form a square that is much bigger than the naos. It has a central bay or nave flanked by 12 pillars and ambulatories on either side. Several kings and queens are buried here, but the frescoes are listless 19C copies of Paleologan paintings and are very disappointing when compared to the real thing. Some of the original murals, painted by Dobromir of Târgovişte in 1526, were rescued by the National Gallery of Art in Bucharest. The monastery museum has a fine collection of embroidered vestments, illuminated manuscripts and silverware.

The monastery was burnt down in the mid-19C, leaving the church badly damaged. In the 1870s, French architect André Lecomte du Nouÿ carried out what he believed was a scrupulously authentic restoration. Elsewhere, as at Trei Ierarhi in Iaşi and other Moldavian churches, his 'scientific' rebuilding had unhappy results, but luckily almost the only signs of his influence here are the garish metal roofs of the cupolas.

13km east of Curtea de Argeş on the DN73C, the village of **Musăteşti** is a centre for a special type of red pottery that has been made locally for centuries, and for a small ethnographic museum. Both are worth seeing if you are exploring the area.

Do not miss the chance to take the **Transfăgăraşanu Highway**, constructed in the 1960s, which crosses the mountains into Transylvania immediately to the north of Curtea de Argeş. On the way, c 25km from the town, you pass what little is left of Poienari Castle, built by Vlad Ţepeş (Dracula) on the site where Wallachia's founder, Basarab I, defeated King Károly Róbert of Hungary in 1330. To get to the top involves a steep climb, but the view from the top is wonderful. On its way to the summit, the road makes a series of graceful loops before plunging vertiginously into Transylvania on the other side. But if possible ask for advice at one of the cabins beside the road before you cross the pass because it is often blocked with snow, even in late spring and early autumn.

From Curtea de Argeş drive northwest to Câmpulung, an earlier Wallachian capital. The most attractive route entails threading your way 40km across the mountains, but again, it is easier to get there via Piteşti, turning north onto the E574 for 52km. If you want to spend a day or two in the mountains, there is a group of villages between Curtea and Câmpulung which are keen to welcome foreign tourists. They comprise **Brădet**, which has a lovely 15C wooden church that is a replica of Cozia Monastery, **Brăduleţ**, and **Galeş**, where you wll find an excellent village museum. For more information about what these communities have to offer, contact *Fundaţia pentru Dezvolţare Durabilă Eco Rural Brădet* (*The Brădet Foundation for Sustainable Development and Eco-tourism*, or *FERB*) at 72250 Bucureşti, CP 48-22; fax 01 223 2071, to arrange accommodation and local tours. This is a beautiful, alpine area and is famous, among other things, for a prehistoric fish, *Romanichtys valsanicola*, which lives in the stream above the Vâlsan accumulation lake. Called *asprete* in Romanian, it is an endangered species and can be found only within a 10–12km stretch of the river.

Câmpulung

Câmpulung is one of the oldest cities in Wallachia, famous for the nearby monastery of Negru Voda.

Practical information

☎ code
048

Tourist office
Muscelul at Str Negru Voda 117, ☎ 812400, can arrange accommodation and tours of the region.

Getting around
By train Câmpulung is at the end of a line that branches from the main Bucharest–Piteşti route. The Câmpulung Nord station is on Str Nicolae Leonard.
By bus The bus station is on Str I.C. Frimu.

Where to stay
Hotel Unic (✫) is at Str Juramantului 2, ☎ 811687; the 'agrotourism' organisation, *ANTREC*, has a local office at Str Republicii 35, ☎ 842230, fax 822492, but try its head office in Bucharest first.

Money
CEC is at Str Nicolae Leonard bl A10, ☎ 811217.

Known to have existed by the early 13C, Câmpulung was fortified by Teutonic Knights from the Transylvanian Bârsa Land. Their castle was destroyed in 1225, when Endre II of Hungary ejected the Knights for dealing with the Pope behind his back. At the same time, the town had a large Saxon population that maintained close ties with Braşov. In c 1330, Câmpulung became Wallachia's first capital. An autonomous Orthodox Metropolitanate was established here before the Patriarch in Constantinople officially recognised the Wallachian See. The bishop had authority over the eastern church in Transylvania as well. Later, both capital and bishop moved to Curtea de Argeş to be further from the border with Hungary. Look for the 14C **Biserica Bărăţia** at Str Negru Voda 116, and for Biserica Domnească (founded by Prince Petru Şchiopu) and **Biserica Subeşti**, both of which date from the mid-16C.

Near the Biserica Bărăţia, at Str Negru Voda 64, is the sturdy old monastery of **Negru Vodă**. Said to have been founded in 1215 by *voivode* Radu Negru, it was completed by Nicolae Alexandru Basarab in the mid-14C. Inside the church is the tomb of a Western knight, Lavrencius de Longo-Campo, who was buried here sometime before 1300. Presumably he either gave or got his name from the town.

Drive to **Jidava**, 4km from Câmpulung, to see the ruins of a Roman camp built in the time of Septimus Severus (r. 193–211). It has been well preserved and covers an area of c 10,000sq m. The landscape along the road between Câmpulung and Braşov is extremely beautiful.

Suslăneşti, 6km south of Câmpulung, has a paleontological reservation famous for its fossilised fish and trees. About 21 kms to the south of Câmpulung on the DN73, at Mihaeşti, is a **forest reserve** containing fine examples of exotic trees, including Caucasian pine, Turkestan elm and Virginia juniper.

Lereşti, c 8km north of Câmpulung on the DN734, is a 'tourist' village that has received support for its local cottage industries; it is a centre for traditional textiles. The houses here are built in the style of the Muscel region, with veranda pillars made of Albeşti limestone.

Târgovişte

Head 66km south along the D73A from Câmpulung for Târgovişte. Although its old, rambling centre has been gutted to make way for shopping precincts and flats, here and there you can still see attractive vestiges of the medieval town.

Practical information

☎ code
045

Tourist information
BTT at Str Victoriei bl H1, ☎ 634224; *Nest-Com* at B-dul Libertăţii 7, ☎ 614643.

Getting there
By rail The railway station is at B-dul Castanilor 2. The *CFR* ticket office is at the same address, ☎ 611554.
By bus The bus station is c 1km west of the town centre and the same distance north of the train centre, off the roundabout north of Str Constantin Brâncoveanu.
By car For **car service** and repairs, *ACR* has an office at B-dul Libertăţii bl C4, no. 2, ☎ 615566.

Where to stay
Târgovişte is not well endowed with places to stay, but *Hotel Valachia* (✩✩) at B-dul Libertăţii 7, ☎ 634491, and *Phoenix Muntenia* at Str Unirii 20B, ☎ 634325, are both central.

Eating out
Try *Casa Dâmboviţeana* at Calea Domneasca 240, *Casa Domneasca* at Str Arsenalului 14, and the restaurant in *Hotel Valachia*.

Post office
The main post office and telephone office are on Str Ion Radulescu; there is a smaller post office on the south side of Str Victoriei.

Money
CEC is at Str Fântanelor bl B2, *Agricola* at Str Avram Iancu 5, *Comercială Română* at B-dul Victoriei 3, *Internationala a Religiilor* at B-dul IndependenÏei 3, *Bankcoop* at Str Revoluţiei bl C8, and *România Exchange* at Str Libertăţii 7.

Regular events
Târgovişte is the county town of Dâmbovita. During the year there are a number of festivals. The one with the highest profile is the international folklore festival, which takes place in August in various towns and villages around the county. In 1990 the village of Cornatelu began celebrating its 500-year-old market with a *Miorița* festival; each subsequent year it has grown in size and scope. *Miorița*, literally the Ewe Lamb, is a ballad or poem describing the selflessness of a Moldavian shepherd in the face of his neighbours' jealousy. The song/poem is thought to have been created sometime in the Dacian period and has been passed down to this day by oral tradition, with a little help from keen

nationalists in the 19C. Many variations exist, but the basic theme is the same wherever it occurs. 'Miorița' is known all over southeast Europe, wherever Romanian-speaking peoples have congregated, including the Greek peninsula, Bulgaria and the Ukraine, and the festival attracts folk singing and dance groups from all these countries. If you are around at the end of June, you could catch Dragaica, a pre-Christian folk festival at Baleni. In October there is a theatre festival called Crizantema de Aur. Check for details with *Centrul de Creație Populară* at Str Gen Grigorescu 15, ☎ 613112.

Complex Muzeal Curtea Domnească at Calea Domnească 221 contains the fascinating ruins of the princely court and church (see below). There is also a small **archaeology museum** at Str Stelea 4, and a **history museum** at Calea Domneasca 232. The **Writers' and Printing Museum** at Str Justiției 3–5 charts the history of printing in Romania from 1508, but it is a very sad place. **Muzeul Gheorghe Petrescu** at Str Baraţiei 24 houses a collection of post-Impressionist pictures by this painter (1872–1949). They are of very minor interest compared with the murals in the princely church. All museums are open Tues–Sun, usually 09.00–17.00.

Târgoviște (pronounced Tergovishtay, with the emphasis on the second syllable), was the capital of Wallachia between 14C–17C. Its princes kept a strong military presence here. **Curtea Veche**, the princely court at Calea Domnească 221, beside Str Nicolae Bălcescu, is half in ruins, but what is left is well worth seeing: the complex comprises a superb cross-in-square church with fine interior wall paintings, sturdy palace walls and a watchtower used by the soldiers of Vlad Țepeș (Dracula) to keep an eye out for enemies. **Turnul Chindiei** (the Sunset Tower), as the tower is called, was rebuilt in the 17C and has been transformed into a museum detailing Vlad's exploits; climb to the top for a bird's-eye view of the town. The 16C **princely church** shows the signs of a budding Wallachian style, with three slender cupolas roofed by faceted cones instead of the rounder towers with helmet-like caps that you see in Greek and Macedonian Byzantine churches. Its open porch was also an innovation. Inside, there are frescoes celebrating the life of prince Matei Basarab (r. 1632–54), and a screened gallery behind which the *voivozi* and their families used to attend the liturgy. Matei Basarab was a brilliant leader. As well as maintaining a relative stability in the region he was a keen patron of the arts. This is one reason why the church here was so well-endowed. It is contemporary with the Patriarchal Church in Bucharest (see p 150). The complex is open Tues–Sun 09.00–17.00.

Walk 500m south to the corner between Str Stelea and Str Bălcescu to see **Mănăstirea Stelea**. Built by Basarab's Moldavian contemporary, Vasile Lupu, to mark an entente between the two principalities, this is a fine 17C church that combines Gothic and Wallachian elements in the typical Moldavian style. Note the coloured discs and the 'star' bases to the cupolas. These are created by a second square that is superimposed diagonally over the first set of squinches, a system that could be extended indefinitely, making the towers narrower as they rose upwards.

Drive 4km northeast of Târgoviște to find the lovely proportions of **Dealul monastery church**. Dealul simply means The Hill, on which it stands. It was completed in 1500 and is made of ashlar blocks whose smooth surfaces contrast attractively with panels of low-relief 'tapestry' carving on the dome bases. Dealul represents a definite development away from the Serb trefoil churches to a more recognisably national style, and it became a prototype for many other Wallachian shrines of the 17C and 18C, the most spectacular of which is the Episcopal Church in Curtea de Argeş (see pp 176–177). By the 16C Dealul was functioning as a skete, run by monks who worked separately during the week and came together only for the Sabbath and other feast days. Today Dealu is a cenobitic convent.

Some 22km to the southwest of Târgovişte on the road to Găieşti, is the charming little monastery church of **Cobia**. Multicoloured, glazed bricks cover the entire surface of its exterior walls. Three tall, thin cupolas cluster together on its roof, and around the cornice are a row of ceramic discs showing the signs of the zodiac, another popular decorative device on Romanian Orthodox churches. Cobia dates from the 17C and has recently been repaired by a team of Bulgarian masons. Nicolae Iorga used to like coming here to hold seminars with his students.

Piteşti

42km west of Găieşti and linked the 114km to Bucharest by the E70 motorway, Piteşti is the county town of Argeş. Although it is a bustling industrial centre with little charm, it can make a good short-term base for exploring the surrounding area. With c 185,000 inhabitants, Piteşti has grown from a small village first mentioned in 1388 into one of Romania's most important centres for industry.

Practical information

☎ code
048

Tourist information ¶
Travel agents include *Best International*, Str Traian 14, ☎ 222400; *BTT*, Str Craiovei, zona centru, bl 13, ☎ 221299; *Maro*, Str Zmeurei, bl PS2, ap 1, ☎ 213500; and *Toros Trans*, Str Victoriei 16, ☎ 221050.

Getting there

By train Piteşti has two stations: **Nord** on Calea Brasov, ☎ 635400, and **Sud** on Str Garii, ☎ 540341. The *CTR* booking office is at Str Domnia Basala 13, ☎ 630565.
By bus Again, there are two: **Autogara Piteşti Nord** on Str George Cosbuc, and **Autogara Piteşti Sud** on Str Târgul din Vale, ☎ 217749.
By car For **car repairs** and servicing, try *ACR*, Str I.C. Brătianu, bl A1, ☎ 623542; there are **petrol stations** at km 3 and 4 from Piteşti on the Piteşti–Bucharest road.
By taxi Try *Confort*, Str Ţepeş Vodă 11, ☎ 222900; *Dinamic Piteşti*, Str Exercitiu, bl PD7, ap 13, ☎ 222600; and *Nova Taxi*, Str Deposilitor 10, ☎ 643999.

Where to stay
Hotel Muntenia (✩✩✩), Piaţa Muntenia 1, ☎ 625450; fax 214556, has 269 rooms, accepts VISA, and has an exchange desk. Others include *Hotel Star* (✩✩✩), Calea Bascov, ☎ 630240, and *Hotel Carmen*, B-dul Republicii 84, ☎ 222699.

Eating out
For specifically local dishes, try *Rehona*, Str N. Bălcescu 54; other eating places

include *John Club*, B-dul Republicii 110 and the ubiquitous *McDonald's*, also on B-dul Republicii, near the southern railway station. Among the pizzerias are *Hothouse*, Str Dumbravei 9, *Number One*, Str Ana Ipătescu 7, and *Piaţa Italia*, B-dul Republicii 11.

Post office

The central post office is at Str Victoriei 15, ☎ 632526.

Money

Banks include *Banca Agricola*, Str Intrarea Victoriei 1; *Banca Comerciala Ion Tiriac*, B-dul Republicii 71; *Banca Comercială Româna*, B-dul Republicii 38; and *Banca Natională României*, B-dul Republicii 67. Among the **exchange houses** are *ACR*, Str A.C. Brătianu, bl A1; *Adriatica*, Str Brătianu 24; *Apex*, Str Victoriei; *BIFF*, Str Victoriei 3; or try *Hotel Muntenia*.

Police

The *Inspectoratul Judeţean de Poliţie* is on B-dul Republicii, ☎ 623100.

Medical care

The **county hospital**, *Spitalul Judeţean*, is at Aleea Spitalului 1, ☎ 222398. There is a **surgery** at Calea Bucureşti, bl 1B, ☎ 624489, and **dental surgeries** at Str Griviţei 15, ☎ 680782, and Str Crinului 7, ☎ 680782. **Pharmacies** include *Farmacia Eva*, Str Unirii 5, *Farmacia Miraculum*, Str Pietei, Complex 1, and *Farmacia Mona*, Str Crinului 15.

Museums

Galeria de Arte Modernă (the Modern Art Gallery) is at B-dul Republicii 33, *Galeria de Arte Naivă* (the Naïve art Museum) at Str Victoriei 89, and *Muzeul Judeţean* (the County Museum) at Str Armand Călinescu, ☎ 633543, open Tues–Sun 10.00–18.00. Further afield, the pianist *Dinu Lipatti's memorial house* is at Leordeni in Ciolceşti village, and writer *Liviu Rebreanu's memorial house* is in Valea Mare, near Stefăneşti.

Heading east of Piteşti along the DN7, at 9km you come to a turning signposted to the **Complex Muzeal Goleşti**. Remains of this 17C manor are still visible, and there is a beautifully decorated church dating from 1646. The Golesti were boyars, and some of their descendants played an active part on the revolutions of 1821 and 1848. The complex also contains a history and ethnographic museum and a Turkish bath: installed between 1784–1807, it is the only complete bath of its kind in Romania. In the nearby **Muzeul Pomiculturii si Viticulturii** (Fruit Tree and Vine-growing Museum) can be found 150 vernacular farm buildings from Argeş county.

A further 11km east along the DN7 is the village of **Topoloveni**, famous for traditional crafts including ceramics and rug weaving. For details contact Centrul de Creaţie Populară, B-dul Republicii 52, Piteşti, ☎ 048 219080.

Return to Târgovişte and take the DN71 north for Sinaia and the Prahova Valley; the road brings you through beautiful scenery on the way to the tallest mountains in Romania.

Sinaia and neighbouring **Buşteni** are holiday resorts and make excellent bases for trips into the Bucegi mountains. Buşteni has a lovely position at the feet of Mount Caraiman and makes an excellent base if you want to explore the massif.

This is the best starting point for expeditions to Piatra Arsa, Jepii Mari and Jepii Mici, to Caraiman itself, Costila and for Urlătoarea, the Roaring Cascade. At the top of Caraiman is a huge cross that commemorates Romanians who died fighting in the First World War. Bușteni also has a cable car up to the Bucegi plateau. It is the third longest in Europe.

Sinaia

Sinaia, clinging to the hillsides and cloaked discretely in conifers, is altogether more upmarket than Bușteni. It was named by the 17C boyar Mihail Cantacuzino, who founded a monastery here after a pilgrimage to Mount Sinai and the Holy Land. The town grew up around the church, and in the late 19C Romania's first king built a castle in the forests nearby. Royal patronage endorsed Sinaia's upper crust credentials and encouraged some of Romania's wealthiest and most important personalities to build grand villas here too. Today, signs of its former grandeur are not obtrusive and give the town a pleasant and relaxed atmosphere. Staying here should not be a problem because there are scores of hotels and villas.

Practical information

☎ code

044

Tourist agencies

These include *Event 2000*, at 12 B-dul Carol 1, ☎ 312898, *Luxor Turism*, B-dul Carol 22, ☎ 314051; and *Hertz*, Str O. Goga 9–11, ☎ 310426.

Where to stay

Take your pick from the hotels along B-dul Carol I or look for something with more character near the castle. At the top of the range are villas such as *Brazi* (✩✩✩✩), Str Cuza Vodă 24, ☎ 313851, and *Cocora* (✩✩✩✩), Str O. Goga 9, ☎ 312051, while the most expensive hotels include the oddly named *Economat* (✩✩✩), Str Peleșului 2, ☎ 311151, *Furnica* (✩✩✩), Str Furnica 50, ☎ 311850; the magnificent Secessionist-style *Palace* (✩✩✩), Str Goga 4, ☎ 312051, and the *International* (✩✩✩), Str Avram Iancu I, ☎ 313851. On B-dul Carol there are the *Caraiman* (✩✩), at no. 24, ☎ 310234; *Montana* (✩✩), also at no. 24, ☎ 312751; *Paltinis* (✩✩), at no. 47, ☎ 314651, and *Sinaia* (✩✩), at no. 8, ☎ 311551. Near Castle Peleș at Str Furnica 1 stands the charming *Intim* (✩), ☎ 314555, *internat* (extension) 127, a former holiday villa with a magnificent double staircase leading to its front door; and there are also unstarred villas and mountain cabins which generally charge far less than the hotels. Details about how to book some of these cabins and villas can be obtained through *Alpin SA*, at Str Carol I, no. 12, ☎ 313398; fax 314251. If you want to stay in a private, family setting, contact *ANTREC*'s local office, ☎ 174682; fax 192977; however, as always with *ANTREC*, it is better to contact the head office in Bucharest first (see p 116).

Sinaia is a good base for **winter skiing**; the season usually lasts from December to February, and there are 12 pistes varying in difficulty from blue to black; the longest is 11km. For more details contact *Societatea Palace*, Str Octavian Goga 11, ☎ 312051; fax 313555.

Scores of footpaths lead into the mountains from Sinaia; if you want a guide, ask at one of the tourist agencies or hotels.

Framed by beautifully landscaped woodland 5km northeast of the town centre, **Peleș Castle** has become one of Romania's most popular tourist attractions; open Wed–Mon 09.00–15.00. The castle itself was built in two stages between 1875 and 1914, partly as a summer palace for King Carol I and Queen Elisabeta, and partly as a national museum. Viennese architect Wilhelm Doderer and his assistant Johannes Schulz completed the first phase in 1883, but Karl Liman, who worked here from 1896, gave the castle into its grandeur and monumentality. One of the designers' innovations was a sophisticated hot-air central-heating system. The castle is modelled mainly on the German neo-Renaissance, although the interior comprises a wide range of influences, and the complex contains two smaller palaces, Pelișor and Foișor. Pelișor was a favourite residence of Queen Marie, and its sumptuous interior shows her love of Art Nouveau.

Peleș has three floors with the main, public apartments on the ground and first floor. They consist of an impressive weapons' museum with assegais and Oriental krisses fanned triumphantly around the walls in the colonial style, and a series of halls, studies and reception rooms decorated according to different regional or period fashions. These comprise Gothic, German Renaissance, Florentine and Turkish designs—one room has a Moorish decor inspired by the filigree latticework walls in the Alhambra in Granada. Oppressively dark woodcarving and stained glass predominate in the first two floors, but the third storey shows the lighter and more modern touch of Queen Marie. Later, Ceaușescu wanted the castle as his private residence, but was put off when his advisers informed him that the walls were full of potentially poisonous spores.

Altogether more graceful than Peleș Castle is the late-17C **Sinaia monastery**, which stands on Str Mănăstiri above the town centre. There are two churches here, the earlier one stands in a separate courtyard to the west of the later building commissioned by Carol I. Wallachia's links with Mount Sinai go back to 536, when the Emperor Justinian founded St Catherine's monastery with the help of Vlach masons. In 1576 Alexandru Mircea built a chapel there dedicated to St John the Baptist, and Prince Petru Șchiopu saw Sinai as a possible refuge in case of exile. Mihai Cantacuzino, who founded this monastery, was the brother of prince Șerban and commander-in-chief of the Wallachian army. He made his pilgrimage to the Holy Land in 1682, taking his mother, Elena, and 200 riders. A small museum housed in what were originally monks' cells shows some of the monastery's valuable icons, silverware, vestments and books; the whole complex is open Wed–Sun 10.00–18.00.

Masivul Bucegi ~ the Bucegi massif

A national park containing several nature reserves to the northwest of Sinaia and reached by cable car from Bușteni, the Bucegi massif is known for its stunning, panoramic views and strange rock formations. They are like chthonic

Queen Elisabeta and Queen Marie

The wives of Romania's two first kings were fascinated by Romania and did their best to encourage its development. Outsiders by birth, they also appreciated the individuality of its folk art traditions which those more familiar might have taken for granted. Elizabeth von Wied (1843–1916) married Carol in 1869 when he was already Prince of the newly united Romania. She threw herself into her job, founding social support programmes, organising orphanages and establishing schools for the blind. She also devoted herself to promoting the Romanian crafts industry, and introduced folk costumes into certain forms of court dress. Under her pen name, Carmen Sylva, she wrote books on Romanian legends as well as poetry, short stories and nursery rhymes.

Her successor, Marie (1875–1938) was a daughter of Alfred, Duke of Edinburgh and the former Grand Duchess Marie Alexandrovna of Russia. Queen Victoria was her grandmother. Marie was very beautiful, and after her marriage to Ferdinand in 1893 she became enormously popular with the Romanians, for whom she represented a kind of living legend, a Princess Diana of her day. During the First World War she volunteered as a Red Cross nurse and established hospitals for the wounded. Marie used her influence after peace was declared, to make Western governments recognise Romania's territorial claims at the Treaty of Versailles. At a special coronation ceremony at Alba Iulia in 1922, she wore a costume inspired by Byzantine and Romanian vestments which had been copied from wall paintings in Romanian churches. She travelled widely in Europe and the USA, using her energy and charm to raise awareness of Romania's existence on the international stage.

Her 'fairytale' existence has provoked contemporary historians to deconstruct the myth that has grown up around Marie, but her reputation as something Romanians are glad to be proud of remains intact. Dorothy Parker immortalised her in a bittersweet quatrain: 'Oh, life is a glorious cycle of song,/A medley of extemporanea;/And love is a thing which can never go wrong,/And I am Marie of Roumania.'

deities, and include the famous Babele de Bucegi, which resemble old ladies having an eternal chat. The massif is a haven for wild flowers such as orchid and mountain pink, and brown bear, black goat and capercaillie also live here. Its tallest peaks include Mounts Omu (2505m), Coștila (2498m) and Caraiman (2326m). Bușteni is the best place for access to Piatra Arsă, Jepii Mari and Jepii Mici as well as Mounts Caraiman and Coștila, and for Urlătoarea, the Roaring Cascade. Many footpaths lead into mountains from Sinaia; ask at one of the hotels or tourist agencies if you want a guide.

The southern Prahova Valley

From Sinaia, break your journey southwest to Bucharest by stopping at **Breaza**, c 21km on the E60, to see its ethnographic museum. It has excellent collections of local textiles, costumes and wood crafts, displayed in a typical Prahovian dwelling at B-dul Republicii 317. In **Câmpina**, a further 5km southwest, visit Nicolae Grigorescu's memorial house at Str 23 August 166, which contains over 100 paintings and drawings by Romania's leading Impressionist. Make a detour by heading 9km south, turning left to Baicoi and then 19km north to **Brebu**, the monastery and palace developed by Matei Basarab and Constantin Brâncoveanu. The palace has a fine collection of art and tools illustrating life in the two princes' reigns.

Dealul Mare

The countryside to the north of Bucharest is a desolate place, scarred with oil refineries and the results of Ceauşescu's attempts to eradicate village life. To east and west of the petroleum city of Ploieşti lies a weird landscape of endless maize and cabbage fields rising into hills where the trees have been replaced with a sparse forest of derricks. But between Ploieşti and Buzău, and to the north of the main oilfields, the country is famous for its vineyards. Known locally as Dealul Mare, they produce superb red wines. This is also where some extraordinary prehistoric treasures have been found, notably the extraordinary Mother Hen and her Chickens, a gold chalice shaped like a chicken with seven cups as her chicks. Said to be made by a Visigoth, it is kept in the National History Museum in Bucharest (see p 138).

The Teleajen Valley

This is a beautiful and often less crowded alternative route between Ploeşti and Braşov. As an extra detour take the side road to the west 6km to the north of Vălenii de Munte on the D1A to **Slănic** (c 14km), a traditional town famous for its salt workings. There are two museums here, one devoted to the salt trade, called Colecţia 'Museul Sării', at Str Slănicul 5, open Tues–Sun 08.00–16.00, and the other, housed in a late 18C chalet at Str 23 August 9, is a gallery of contemporary Romanian sculpture, 'open seasonally'.

Another alternative to the D18 is to turn right 2km north of Vălenii de Munte and take the scenic route to Buzău. This road is flanked by several fine churches, among them the monasteries of Cârnu and Ciolanu.

About 22km north on the road from Vălenii de Munte to Braşov, **Mânăstirea Suzana** is an attractive convent with wooden buildings in a picturesque setting on a forested mountainside. It also has a museum specialising in 18C and 19C religious art, including some fine glass icons from the Nicula, Făgăraş and Olt schools. There are rooms set aside for female tourists. Open summer 08.00–20.00, winter 09.00–16.00.

The Danubian towns

Compared to the mountains nearby, the Danubian plains to the south of Bucharest are not especially attractive, but there are interesting things to see here all the same. One of the largest Romany communities in Romania can be found in the industrial city of **Giurgiu**, on the Danube 64km south of Bucharest. On the opposite bank, the Bulgarian city of Ruse spews out pollution, so it is not a place to hang around in. Travel back towards the west along the Danube and you enter Teleorman county.

Alexandria

This is the Teleorman county town, south west of Bucharest, with c 59,000 inhabitants.

Practical information

☎ code
047

Tourist offices
Travel agents that may be able to give information on local services include *BTT* at Str Libertăţii bl A7, ☎ 322671; *Sind România* at Str Independenţei 16, ☎ 312021, and *Vedea* at Str Libertăţii 245–249, ☎ 312903.

Getting around
By train Alexandria has a railway station and CFR office for booking tickets at Str Libertăţii 220, ☎ 325684.
By car For car **servicing** and repairs try *Federal Coop* at Şos Turnu Magurele 6, ☎ 315368, or contact *ACR* at Str Libertăţii bl A4, ☎ 321456.

Where to stay
Hotel Parc (✯✯) is at Str Libertăţii 220, ☎ 312901.

Eating out
Inter is a pizzeria on Calea Bucureşti, and there are a couple of restaurants on Str Libertăţii.

Money
Banca Agricolă is at Str Ion Creanga 53, *Banca Comercială Româna* at Str Dunarii 75, *Bankcoop* at Str Brâncoveanu 50, and *CEC* at Str Bucureşti 59.

Medical care
The **county hospital** is at Str Libertăţii 1, ☎ 312505. There are **pharmacies** at Str Libertăţii 202 and Str Dunarii 222.

Regular events
In November there is a song and music festival in Alexandria. For details, contact *Centrul de Creaţie Populară* at Str Dunării 178, ☎ 313861, or the travel agencies.

Teleorman is a Cuman name meaning Forest of Madness; today it is hard to envisage, but in the early Middle Ages people often lost their way in its dense oak woods. Neolithic remains have been discovered at Dulceanca and Blejesti, while important Getic treasure from the 5C–3C BC was found at Peretu. 4C BC Daco-Getic pieces have also come to light at Zimnicea. There are signs of Roman camps at Putineiu and Islaz, and of a powerful fortress called Turris near Turnu Măgurele, dating from the 2C AD. Constantine the Great built a citadel on its ruins. Mircea cel Bătrân built a medieval fortress over this.

In **Dadu** village is a monastery founded in 1646 by the *vornic* Dragomir. (A *vornic* was the most important official in the medieval court.) There are some fine murals inside. Turks occupied this part of Wallachia from 1417 till 1829, when it became part of the Ţara Românească again. At **Turnu Măgurele** is an Orthodox cathedral with twisted barley-sugar towers like the ones on the Episcopal Cathedral at Curtea de Argeş.

A lot of excellent writers came from this region. Marin Preda was one of them, and his memorial house is in **Silistea** near Roşiori de Vede. In the same town is a museum dedicated to the victims of the 1907 smallholders' uprising; open Tues–Sun. **Roşiori de Vede** also has a 2-star hotel, the *Roşiori*, at Str Oltului 1, ☎ 047 460850.

Moldavia

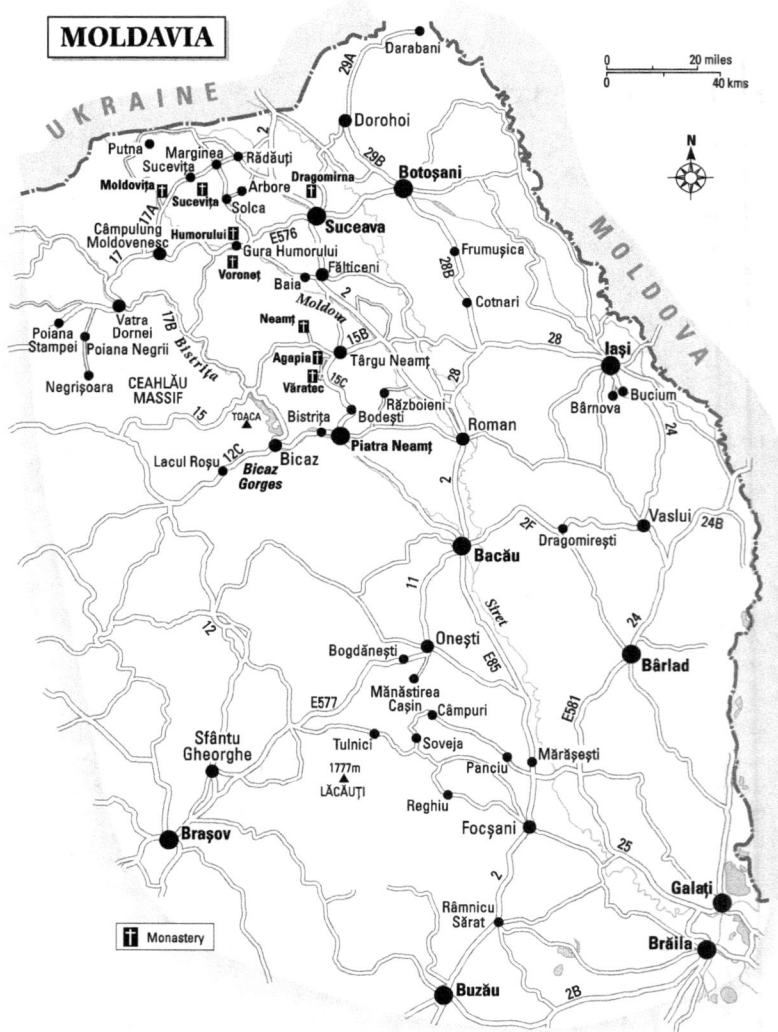

N-oi uita vreodată, dulce Bucovina
Geniu-ti romantic, muntii în lumină
Văile-n flori
Râuri resătânde printre stânce nante
Apele lucinde-n dalbe diamante
Peste câmpii-n zori.

I shall never forget sweet Bucovina,
Your romantic genius, the mountains in light
Valleys in flower
Rivers springing from high rocks
The waters shining like fine diamonds
Over the dawn meadows.

From *La Bucovina* by Mihai Eminescu, translated by Cristina Rai.

Geographically, Moldavia is a continuation of the Ukrainian steppe which lies between the Carpathians and the Black Sea. Moldavia is traditionally the most hospitable region of Romania. Writing in the 18C, Dimitrie Cantemir gave a vivid picture of the lengths to which local nobles would go to entertain guests; refusing to dine alone, they would send out their servants to search the highways for foreign travellers with whom they could share their tables—and presumably the latest news from abroad. The warm spirit which inspired this custom has not entirely died out, but today it is largely carried on by monasteries and convents. Here, providing they contribute to their board and lodging and respect the tranquillity of the house, foreign visitors may still be welcome as bringers of information from the wider world. Moldavian wine has a well-deserved reputation for excellence: the vintages of Cotnari and Odobești fortified kings before they went into battle. According to the same tradition, the Moldavians are said to be natural poets, preferring the contemplation that flourishes from long hours spent tending sheep to practical, possibly violent activity. Whether this is true or not, Mihai Eminescu (1850–89) was one of many famous Romanian writers and thinkers who were born in the principality. Moldavia was also the birthplace of the country's leading 20C composer, George Enescu (1881–1955), and of one of its most prolific historians, Nicolae Iorga (1871–1940). Life here goes at a slower pace than in Westward-looking Transylvania.

Together with the Moldavians' generosity and the picturesqueness of their rural lifestyle goes a grinding poverty that some blame on laziness and others on chronic bad luck. At the end of the 1990s most smallholders in the plains could not afford to buy seed for their next year's crops, and although this problem was not exclusive to Moldavia, farmers here were hit particularly badly.

Events of the past century have taken their toll on Moldavia, but the country has a splendid history, and this may help it to create a better future. Ask any Moldavian to name their most famous historical figure and they will come up with Stephen the Great. Long forgotten (if he was ever recognised) in the West, his image is still revered in Romania as a defender of the (Orthodox) Christian faith. Stephen, known in Romania as Ștefan cel Mare (r. 1457–1504), spent his entire reign protecting Moldavia's borders against invasions. These came mainly from the east but sometimes from Poland and Hungary as well. He is remembered in Moldavia not only as a hero who helped keep Western Europe safe from

Muslim domination, but also as a man of high culture who encouraged the greatest artistic flowering the country has ever seen.

Moldavia is still suffering from the effects of collectivisation, while many of its people yearn for the stability which they had under communism. Across the mountains in Transylvania, life is noticeably more advanced: there are more tractors and fewer horse-drawn vehicles. There are superficial differences which are nonetheless striking when you see them for the first time: during the blazing summers, Moldavians cover their heads with handkerchiefs or battered hats while the Transylvanians protect themselves with smart straw hats.

History

Asiatic tribes once swept through Moldavia on their way into Europe, but its ethnic Romanian identity begins with Dragoș (r. 1352–53), the prince whose legendary fight with an aurochs symbolises the principality's struggle for self-determination. An aurochs's head was incorporated into Moldavia's coat of arms, but it was Dragoș's successor, the Maramureș-born Bogdan I, who founded an independent principality here in c 1359. Moldavia's princes became adept at fending off greedy neighbours: Ștefan cel Mare, Petru Rareș, Vasile Lupu (Basil the Wolf) and Dimitrie Cantemir are among the brilliant leaders who withstood the threat of invasion by the predatory leaders of Poland, Hungary and Russia, all of whom wanted to extend their influence on the pretext of keeping the Turks out of Europe. Ștefan cel Mare won 38 out of his 40 battles, and in recognition of God's universal power founded a church after each one, whether he was victorious or not. The Pope called him an 'Athlete of Christ' because of his successful efforts to hold the Ottomans back from the threshhold of western Europe—but failed to give him any material support.

Between the mid-16C and 1821 Moldavia became an Ottoman vassal. But as in Wallachia, the Turks let the country control its own internal affairs and elect its own princes, until the terror of losing his empire drove the Porte to install Phanariot rulers from Istanbul. As in Wallachia, the church played a crucial role in holding the principality together both spiritually and culturally. This worked vice versa: in the 17C Prince Vasile Lupu regarded himself as a latter-day Byzantine emperor and became the mainstay of all the beleaguered Orthodox monasteries in the Near East. At one point Lupu was supporting all the monks of Mount Athos. Orthodox polemics reached fever pitch in the 17C and a famous Synod was held in Lupu's capital, Iași, instead of Constantinople.

The 17C saw a dynamic surge in Moldavia's cultural awareness: the Renaissance spirit permeated royal and ecclesiastical circles and awoke a real sense of curiosity about their own, Romanian identity. Contacts were established with scholars from all over Europe, especially neighbouring Poland, at the same time as Moldavia's age-old relationship with the Orthodox church brought a huge influx of Greek priests, on their way to visit churches in Russia or seeking refuge from the Ottoman regime and support for their own theological point of view. The cultural traffic flowed from east to west and north to south, from the Catholic to the Islamic world and back again. While there were Jesuits in Moldavia (at Cotnari), privileged Moldavians went to study in Constantinople or to Western universities such as Padua, as they had done for centuries. Devout Moldavians often made pilgrimages to holy places in the Near East, leaving expensive gifts such as illuminated Gospels, jewelled caskets, crosses and embroideries. Many of these can still be seen in the museums and libraries of the Orthodox monasteries at Jerusalem, Antioch, Mount Sinai and on Mount Athos to this day.

Visionaries such as Metropolitan Petru Movilă of Kiev, and Vasile Lupu, set up printing presses in Iași, just as their contemporaries did in Bucharest, Râmnicu Vâlcea, Snagov and Târgoviște. These presses helped spread religious tracts in Arabic, Greek, Latin and even Turkish, but they were soon used for the translation of foreign histories and even novels into Romanian. When the Sultan blew the whistle on Moldavia in the early 18C, Greeks from the Phanar district of Istanbul replaced Moldavia's princes and all pretence of self-government came to an end.

Today, Moldavia's eastern reaches no longer meet the sea. Instead they come to an end at the River Prut facing the Republic of Moldova, once known as Bessarabia, on the opposite bank. Bessarabia fell into Russian hands in 1812 and was handed back to Romania after the First World War; the Soviet Union annexed it in the 1940s and today, as Moldova, it ploughs its own furrow. Confusingly, Romanians use the name 'Moldova' for their own province and for the Republic. Moldavia's southern edge joins Muntenia to the north of Buzău and Brăila, while to the west the mountains form a administrative as well as a physical barrier with Transylvania.

Moldavian architecture developed some unique forms, among them the mixture of Gothic, Byzantine and Renaissance elements you can see in many of the medieval churches here. This combination of eastern and western influences came to be known as the Moldavian style, but vernacular wooden churches may have played an important part in its genesis as well. The finest churches are tall and slim, with shingled roofs that splay out from the walls forming a weathershield and providing shade as well. Many of them have a single spire which stands on a star-shaped base. Instead of the helmet-shaped caps which cover the towers of Byzantine churches in Greece and Macedonia, these Moldavian cupolas have steep conical roofs. Doors and windows are framed with interlaced patterns copied from Hungarian Gothic stonework, but the ground plan is usually trefoil or triconch, modelled on Wallachian churches. This style of building has great beauty, and during the Middle Ages it was adopted by many of the monasteries that were built on Mount Athos. Fine examples of Moldavian architecture can be found at the monasteries of Neamț (see pp 224–225), Putna (see pp 204–206), St George's in Suceava (see p 210), Bistrița (see pp 235–236), Dragomirna (see pp 213–214) and the Princely Church in Piatra Neamț (see p 233), but there are many others, often in places that are far from the usual tourist routes.

NORTHWEST MOLDAVIA

Northwestern Moldavia comprises two regions that stand out for their natural beauty: Bucovina and Neamț. Bucovina lies in the northwest corner of Moldavia. Originally it was about twice its present size, stretching across today's border with Ukraine. The whole of this area was annexed by the Austrians in

1775, and it was they who gave it the name *Das Buchenland*, which means the land of beech woods. Romanians converted this into Bucovina. To the west, present-day Bucovina joins Transylvania along the ridge of the Carpathians while its principal city, Suceava, lies in the eastern part of the region.

BUCOVINA

There is plenty to see in Bucovina, but if you are short of time head for the **painted monasteries**. Many of the medieval monasteries, painted and unpainted alike, are protected by UNESCO. But quite apart from their physical beauty, they represent the most striking remains of the Christian Orthodox mysticism that flourished in Bucovina during the Middle Ages. Hermitages, sketes and cenobitic monasteries were so numerous and attracted so many of the leading religious thinkers of their day that Bucovina has been compared with Mount Athos as a centre for spirituality and learning. There was a long period in Athonite history when most of its monasteries were supported wholly by Moldavian princes, and to this day you can find manuscripts and gifts on Athos which testify to the close relationship between them.

Apart from this, there is the architectural evidence which shows how widely Moldavian churches influenced Athonite buildings. Several Moldavian religious foundations had their own schools of illumination, embroidery, weaving, mural and icon painting, and later of printing.

'Painted churches' is the term generally used to refer to churches which are frescoed on the outside. The churches were covered in paintings from top to bottom, although only a handful survive in anything like their original state. The painters were usually local priests or monks, although some were teams of lay artists who travelled a circuit repeating and subtly developing the iconography laid down by the Orthodox church. Sometimes they made daring innovations, leaping between western and eastern traditions or introducing bold new themes, as at Sucevița monastery. **Voroneț** (pp 195–198, **Humor** (pp 198–199), **Moldovița** (pp 199–200), **Sucevița** (pp 200–202) and **Arbore** (pp 203–204) are the most famous painted churches. The monastery at Putna originally had external frescoes, but these were lost when the church was destroyed and they were never replaced. You can see all these buildings in a day, but Bucovina deserves your attention for at least a week, if not more.

The regional capital of Suceava has several hotels which provide decent **accommodation**, but Rădăuți and Câmpulung Moldovenesc are equipped for tourists as well. There are excellent hotels and pensions in more rural locations as well, and you can always fall back on *ANTREC* (see p 116). Some travel agents and tour operators have an arrangement with monasteries and convents; if you turn up at a monastery like a medieval traveller without booking in advance, there is always a chance that it will take you in, and at some of the popular tourist sites, local householders offer bed and breakfast. Agents from hotels often base themselves at these places and may approach you first. As everywhere in Romania, the tourist network is in its infancy and no guarantees can be given as to the level of comfort you will receive. Having made this disclaimer, I have found many excellent places to stay in, although I often found them by word of mouth rather than in official lists.

While you are in the area, do not miss the fortified monastery of **Dragomirna** (see pp 213–214) or the lovely little painted church founded in 1470 by Ştefan cel Mare at **Pătrăuţi** (see p 214), both of them a few kilometres to the north of Suceava. Western Bucovina has breathtaking alpine landscapes brimming with wildlife, and apart from its remote villages and monasteries, there are several mountain resorts which offer climbing and winter sports. At **Rădăuţi**, the stud which was founded by the Habsburgs to breed Arab and Ghidran horses now offers guided trail-riding holidays around the mountains. The main centres for tourist agencies, accommodation, changing money and other practicalities are to be found in the towns of Suceava, Câmpulung Moldovenesc, Rădăuţi and Vatra Dornei.

Crafts and ethnography

Bucovina contains several distinct ethnographic groups, each of which has brought its own culture to the region. Among these have been Armenians, Jews, Greeks and Germans, and in the mountains bordering Ukraine there are remnants of Celts and Thracians, such as the red-headed Huţul people who live in scattered pockets around Obcinile Bucovinei. Their name may have come from a Slavic tribe known (in Romanian) as the *ulici*. Another theory holds that the Huţuls (or *Huţani* as they were known in Romania) got their name from the Pocuţia mountain region of northwest Bucovina which was their original domain. Time and politics have blurred their edges, but if you travel through the region you will quickly get a feel for the differences in vernacular building styles between the north and south and appreciate the contrast with Saxon houses in neighbouring Transylvania. The design and decoration of houses, tools and clothes vary from area to area if not between villages.

Designs and materials were often dictated by practicalities as much as aesthetics, but the results are often very beautiful: imagine the skill, patience, love and sheer pride in one's work that it takes to cover a sheepskin waistcoat with delicate embroidery or to sew thousands of tiny, multicoloured beads onto a 15cm-wide leather belt. Surprisingly, while it is customarily the women who spin and weave, this fine needlecraft was man's work: women do not have enough strength in their fingers to push the needles through thick leather. You can see particularly gorgeous examples of these embroidered waistcoats at Nicolae Popa's museum in Târpeşti near Târgu Neamţ (see p 224) or in the ethnographic museums in Suceava, Rădăuţi and Câmpulung Moldovenesc. But the *cojocar* (waiscoat maker) and his skill have virtually died out, although you can still find tailors producing a workaday version of the sheepskin waistcoat without embroidered embellishments. One such craftsman is Toader Popescu, who works with ancient treadle sewing machines in the village of Bâlca, a few kilometres north of Vicovu de Jos on the road between Rădăuţi and Putna. His house number is 395; ask for directions in the village when you get there.

If you are interested in studying the variations in traditional patterns and styles, the ethnographic museums will be happy to provide the answers either in the form of books on the subject, although these tend to be rather dry, or by putting you in touch with their experts. Alternatively, contact one of the national organisations, such as *Fundaţia Meşteşuguri Români* in Bucharest (see p 31) or the county branch of *Centrul de Creaţie Populară* in Suceava Str. I.v. Viteazul 5, ☎ 030 221096.

If you want to buy carpets, pottery and the like, you will find plenty of choice at the summer season stalls which stand beside the most famous painted monasteries, on the road through the Bicaz Gorges east of Lacu Roșu, or in museum shops. There is an excellent crafts shop next to the pottery workshop in Marginea. Romanians are generally not interested in preserving their old traditions, no matter how astonishing these seem to Westerners. One sad phenomenon of the influx of Western-style tourism is that villagers all over the country have been persuaded to sell their national costumes for a pittance to passers-by, thereby virtually giving away their heritage. Some of these beautiful objects are over a hundred years old and irreplaceable. But the trade in 'renewable' crafts such as carpets, pottery and embroidery, is growing too. Do not buy the first thing you see unless you are sure it is what you want.

If you are interested in ceramics from Bucovina, there are important centres at Cacica, Marginea and Rădăuți. There are carpet-weaving enterprises at Ciocănești and Cârlibaba. If you want to buy new examples of popular dress, try visiting Cârlibaba or Vama. At Dorna you will find interesting examples of local, vernacular architecture. Some of the woodworkers of Fundu Moldovei specialise in making wind instruments.

Local festivals

Suceava county is rich in folk festivals. If you are there in March, go to **Păltinoasa**, which celebrates folk music and dance at the *Comori de suflet românesc*. Men's ring dances are the subject of the festival at Emil Bodnăraș in early April. Marginea, which is a centre for a special type of black pottery that has evolved from Dacian models, has a potters' fair in early May. A special old people's festival takes place in Bâlca during June. In early June there is another folk music and dance festival at Pădurea Arbore, and at around the same time, the people of Horodnic gather to celebrate their traditional dances. Towards the middle of June, Straja holds a festival of traditional wedding customs. Later in the same month Putna monastery holds a special service connected with the end of the fast period, while Sadova holds the important event of *Strânga oilor*, in which all the village ewes are milked together to gauge how much milk and cheese the shepherds must distribute in the year to come. In July there is a national competition for classical music in Suceava, and in August there is Arcanul, an international folklore festival held in Rădăuți. In the last week of August hosts Hora la Prislop, celebrating folk music and dance. For more details of all these activities and others, contact **Centrul de Creație Populară**, Str I. v. Viteazul 5, Suceava, ☎ 030 221096, or ask at one of the ethnographic museums or a tourist agency.

Natural beauties and wildlife

Suceava county's principal ranges are Munții Rarău, Giumalău and Călimani. The first two massifs can be found north of the Bistrița Valley; their highest peaks rise gently to 1653m and 1857m respectively. They comprise karstic areas of relatively soluble rock marked by ridges, gorges and canyons, as well as special geological and forestry reserves. A network of footpaths covers a large area of the mountains, making hiking both easy and pleasant. Take local advice or hire a guide before exploring any paths for the first time.

By contrast the Călimani mountains are wilder and more majestic, with the highest peak, Vârfarul Pietrosul Călimanilor, at 2102m. They are the largest volcanic range in the Romanian Carpathians, and are geologically the youngest mountains in the country. *Romsilva*, the government agency that controls the nature reserves, tries to conserve what is left of this region's rare alpine animals and plants as well as regulating hunting and fishing. If you are lucky you may see bear, wolf, lynx, mountain stag and *căprioara*, the little deer which is prized for its meat, but the first two are becoming increasingly rare. Bisons, which are thought to be the closest living descendants of the ancient aurochs, are bred in a reserve near Neamț monastery. At the other end of the scale, Moldavian forests are still inhabited by the tiger salamander. You may see these spectacular amphibians when they emerge after rain. Their yellow spotted skin shines like patent leather. In the summer, ponds and waterlogged ditches teem with courting frogs who sing about rivets all night long. And then there are the crickets. As if that were not enough, there are also multitudes of wild flowers in shades ranging from white to electric blue and a dark, velvety purple that is almost black. Travelling on foot, or bike or horseback through the mountains of Bucovina can be a wonderful experience, but it should be a sobering one as well: this is a wildlife paradise, but only because human beings have not yet had the chance to destroy it.

Gorges, valleys and rock formations
It is always fun to find your own favourite places in a new country, but here are some suggestions. Travelling c 20km northeast of Vatra Dornei on the DN17B, you reach **Cheile Zugrenilor**, which contain 160ha of strange rock formations and spectacular waterfalls. To the north of this and c 14km south of Câmpulung Moldevenesc is a region called **Pietrele Doamnei** where you find another striking collection of 'sculpted' rocks and wild landscapes. The 1643m peak of the same name is close to the Rurău mountain hut and also forms part of a nature reserve. A few kilometres due east lies the forest reserve of **Slătioara**, on the eastern slopes of Rurău. This is one of the oldest secular woods in Romania; some of the trees—including spruce, pine and beech—are over 400 years old. Along the terraces of **Poiana Stampei**, 18km southwest of Vatra Dornei on the DN17, lies a reserve that specialises in rare flowering plants, inclicing the carniverous *Roua cerului* (Heaven's dew).

The Bicaz gorges are strictly speaking in Transylvania, but they are as easy to reach from the Moldavian side of the mountains. Exploring Bucovina's forested mountains is not easy without a reliable guide. As yet, Romania has nothing like the British Ordnance Survey maps, and although many paths are marked the signs are not always reliable, or frequent enough to prevent you getting lost. If you want to go into the mountains, take a compass and if possible find someone who knows the way.

The painted monasteries
Although each monastery and convent has its own way of doing things, visitors should bear in mind that some items of clothing can give offence. Some churches will actually bar entry to women wearing revealing or short-sleeved tops, and to men or women wearing shorts. Women are not allowed into Daniil's Hermitage at Putna at all, and they cannot go into the sanctuary of an Orthodox church unless they are given permission by the priest.

Voroneț is said to be the most beautiful of all the painted churches in Bucovina. It has a wonderful set of external paintings, almost all of which are complete. The monastery can be found at the southern end of Voroneț village, and is signposted as you drive west out of this town, c 5km south of Gura Humorului and 40km west of Suceava on the D17. Just c1km before you enter Voroneț on the road from Gura Humorului there is a **campsite** that also has a few rooms for the night and a restaurant. You can camp by the river at Voroneț, but there are no piped water or lavatories.

Beyond Voroneț an alpine valley of pine trees and flower-filled meadows disappears seductively into the mountains, where a traditional *stână* (sheepfold) survives alongside a sprinkling of smart new chalets. The church has a triconch plan based on the Serbian model, but its buttresses, and the frames around doors and windows are Gothic, probably copied from Transylvania, in the true Moldavian style. It has a shingled roof that seems to swirl outwards like a dervish's skirt. In fact the roof is a separate structure which sits over the inner masonry roof of the church like a canopy, helping to protect the paintings from the weather. No-one knows where this building style originated, but it may have evolved at least in part from the vernacular wooden houses that have existed in Romanian lands from as long ago as the 10C, and probably much earlier.

In 1487 Ștefan cel Mare promised he would build a monastery here if he could force the Turks back across the Danube. His vow was made to his spiritual confessor, the monk Daniil, and the church went up the following year on the site of Daniil's hermitage. Ștefan was in good church-building mode because he built another at Feleac, near Cluj, and Pătrăuti monastery, north of Suceava, in the following year.

The external paintings were commissioned by Metropolitan Roșca and carried out between 1547–50. These and many of the other well-known mural cycles were the work of lay painters employed by Ștefan's son, Petru Rareș (r. 1527–38 and 1541–46).

At Voroneț a beautifully orchestrated *hierarchy of saints* (the Prayer of All Saints, known in Romanian as *Cinul*) occupies the line of vertical panels at the extreme east end of the church, while on either side a hierarchichal pairing of saints, martyrs and monks makes its way eastwards to share in the glory. Each figure occupies a compartment of equal size, and the compartments are arranged in six tiers. Even though the scenes are carefully regimented, seen together they give the impression of an eager procession hurrying towards God.

Occupying much of the southern wall like an Oriental carpet is a lovely **Tree of Jesse**. This represents Christ's family tree, and he appears in the top centre, above his antecedents. Individual scenes are encased by the curling fronds and buds of the tree which form a gentle rhythm against a gorgeous blue background. The pattern looks like a vast carpet. Alongside the Jesse Tree, showing Christ's pre-Christian antecedents, you can see the early prophets and Greek philosophers, such as Plato with his coffin and bones. Somewhat mystifyingly, the anarchic Aristophenes also makes an appearance, and there are Sibyls here as well. Saints and prophets are identified by white scrolls containing descriptions of their qualities and prophecies, and all the main protagonists are labelled in Cyrillic lettering.

Another major theme here is the Akathistos hymn (literally 'sung while standing'), 24 scenes celebrating the life of the Virgin. One of the most lively scenes illustrates the occasion in 626 when an icon of the Virgin saved Constantinople from an attack by the Avars and Persians. When Serge the Patriarch paraded the icon around the city walls, a storm of stones and fiery rain suddenly burst out of nowhere and destroyed the enemy. Afterwards a new verse was added to the Akathistos to celebrate the victory. Technically there are many Akathistos hymns, but in the context of the painted monasteries, this one is the most famous. It was composed in the 6C by a Syrian monk called Romanos the Melodion. The present version was completed in the 8C. The text contains 24 strophes and is written in flowery Greek. It glorifies Mary's deeds as well as elaborating her symbolic power over the Church.

The Mother of God has a very important role in the Romanian Orthodox Church. She is venerated as the 'Joy of health' and 'a mountain whose height surpasses the thoughts of men, a bridge which unites the earth and sky, Mother of the stars without end'. The Marian Akathistos is traditionally sung in stages on the five Fridays of Lent leading to Holy Week, but it may be heard whenever the presiding priest so wishes. On the last Friday the whole Akathistos is performed at one service. It takes about three hours. At Voroneț, the episodes pictured on the walls are taken from the text, but there are some differences between the Athonite and the Moldavian versions: for example at Humor and Moldovița Strophe 22 shows an anastasis (Christ's descent into Hell), while on Athos (and at Sucevița monastery) it shows Christ tearing up his contract with Adam. Among her many guises the Virgin appears here as an inviolable, walled town.

St George also makes a dramatic appearance on the south wall to the left of the door, where he undergoes his numerous tortures with a debonair lack of concern. In the bottom registers he disposes of the dragon, while an admiring public applauds him safely from some battlements and a princess ties her jewelled girdle to the dragon's neck to symbolise his submission.

The closed wall of the exonarthex provides an ideal surface for the grand finale of the **Last Judgment**. At the very top, in a circular frame shaded by the eaves and heralded by seraphim and angels, Christ sits in judgment immediately above the Almighty, who is framed in another circle. Below him is another **Deësis**, in which Christ is seen in a mandorla flanked by apostles. Christ's empty throne, the *hetymasia*, stands directly beneath. His purple robe lies on the seat, symbolising the wait for his second coming, with Adam and Eve as suppliants on either side. Below this the drama increases. On the left are tight clusters of virtuous men and, interestingly, holy women, their heads framed in clouds of gold. They are hustling each other like so many commuters on the underground in their eagerness to enter the Garden of Paradise, which is symbolically painted against a white background to show its spiritual, heavenly status. (Earthly scenes from after the Fall have a blue background.) Among the throng waiting to enter the Garden are Islamic Turks and Orthodox Jews. On the right, on the wrong side of the scales of justice, the sinners are being harangued by Moses, who is shown admonishing them with his scroll. They make a fascinating crew, for here, labelled for identification, are the heretics in their correct ethnic dress: Armenian priests wearing pointed cowls, swarthy Persians with batons in their turbans, Ethiopians, Tartars and Turks and schismatic Catholics.

While curly-tailed devils play naughty tricks with the scales that weigh human sins, the Angel of Vengeance pokes the damned into a mighty River of Fire. To the right of the river, the land and sea spew up their dead after the Resurrection: the Sea, pictured as a female goddess, sits prettily on a dolphin, and all kinds of weird animals and fish are shown to represent the sea as well. To the left of this on the bottom register a scene shows the death of a just man. His spirit is received by the Archangel Michael and then wafted to sleep by King David playing his *cozba* (a type of mandolin).

These paintings had a thinly veiled political purpose. They were created at a period when Moldavia was almost constantly at war with the Ottoman Empire, and here, as in many of the oldest wooden churches all over Romania, the painters substituted the contemporary enemy for the historic one. These schemes were a real challenge for the artists, because nothing on this scale had been attempted in Moldavia before. The results showed an astonishing outpouring of local talent, and the painting at Voroneț is exceptionally fine. Four of the monasteries were painted within 12 years of each other and their cycles, probably taken from pattern books, are almost identical. Given these restrictions, it is fascinating to compare the variations which occurred between them. The figures are finely modelled, with expressive faces and a real sense of purpose, giving the lie to the belief that Byzantine art is stiff and cold, and the Last Judgment is crammed with dramatic incident: nobody could remain unmoved by such scenes, even if they did not understand all their implications.

The striking blue background for which Voroneț is famous was made from azurite, although traces of lapis lazuli have been found as well. Contrary to received wisdom, none of the colours here or at any of the other painted monasteries are made from vegetable dyes, because fresco contains lime which destroys vegetable pigments. The walled enclosure which surrounds Voroneț church is a modern addition which was built to help protect the building and the painting from the elements.

The Habsburgs closed Voroneț monastery down in 1785, and it only became a religious community again in 1991. Even now it is technically a small skete, managed by five nuns who also run an icon painting studio. The monastery *hram* (name-day feast) is held on St George's Day, 23 April. Voroneț has given its name to two 16C illuminated manuscripts, the *Voroneț Codex* (*The Deeds of the Apostles*, now in the Bodleian Library, Oxford) and the *Voroneț Psalter*.

Beyond Voroneț to the south, an alpine valley shrouded by fir brings you deep into the mountains. A traditional *stână* (sheepfold) survives here opposite a sprinkling of smart new chalets. If you ask in the village, someone may be able to introduce you to the shepherds who make curd cheese from sheep and goat milk in the traditional way.

From Gura Humorului, take the road to the north 4km for **Humor** village and turn left in the village where indicated by the historic monument sign. The painted parish church (it was never a monastery) stands c 200m down this road, a short distance past the new Orthodox church. During the tourist season villagers often wait by the entrance to offer rooms in their houses. In the churchyard, you can climb into the massive defence tower commissioned in 1641 by Vasile Lupu. Together with the church and bell tower, this is all that is left of the mini-citadel founded here by Petru Rareș and his chancellor, Teodor, in 1530.

The **frescoes** at Humor were painted in 1535. They are dominated by reds (the colour of red brick) and ochres on an indigo background: these colours were cheaper and therefore not as durable as the ones used at Voroneț, and the scenes are less clear. There is a fine *Deësis*, an *Akathistos* in which the Virgin is shown among throngs of angels, and a *Liberation of Constantinople* (on the bottom register of the west end of the south wall). The Last Judgment is inside the exonarthex, or porch; this is the earliest known example of an open church porch in the principality.

The Liberation of Constantinople is a spirited piece of anti-Ottoman propaganda masquerading as the 7C siege, in which Turkish cannons are exploding with terrible force and the capital of Byzantium is a fine, battlemented Moldavian town enclosing portraits of Petru Rareş and his wife, Elena. The interior paintings at Humor are also excellent, and the iconostasis contains four 15C icons from a church founded by Alexandru cel Bun (1400–32). Another narrative shown in this fresco cycle is the life of St Nicholas, seen here healing, giving bread to the needy, riding out a storm and demolishing a tree infested by demons. As at Voroneţ, villagers often wait by the entrance to offer rooms to travellers and visitors.

Return to Gura Humorului and take the E576 to the west for Moldovita. On the way you pass Molid (Spruce) and after 16km enter Vama, named after the customs post that once operated here. Overshadowed by the peaks of Runcu Foşii (1015m), Buzău (812m) and Tomnatec (1302m), there is good hill walking and climbing nearby. The town of Vama is run-down, but full of charm. It was once known for its bracing atmosphere: poet George Vâlsan wrote that Vama's pure air hits you in the face like iced water.

Immediately past the road bridge in Vama turn right alongside the Moldoviţa river for Vatra Moldoviţei. Once here, follow the signs for **Moldoviţa monastery** (36km from Gura Humorului). This is a beautiful valley where orchards and pastures roll languorously along the gentle mountain slopes. The church stands in a fortified quadrangle complete with flower borders, shingle-hatted well and a museum, open Tues–Sun 10.00–18.00.

Nuns now manage the monastery, which is dedicated to Buna Vestire (the Holy Virgin), with a *hram* on 25 March. The original 14C church stood c 500m east of the present one, at the point where the Ciumârna and Moldoviţa Rivers meet; this church was founded and fortified by Petru Rareş in 1532. Three defence towers once protected the east side of the curtain walls. Moldoviţa's frescoes are as fine as those at Voroneţ, but here the dominant colours are the reds and an iridescent green: the colour may have been made from locally-mined copper. Highlights include an exuberant **Liberation of Constantinople**, with the

Moldoviţa monastery

best-preserved examples of exploding cannons and maddened Turks. Petru Rareş and his wife are shown here too, standing next to a model of the church. Look out for the cycle showing the life of *Sf Ioan cel Nou* (St John the New), a Greek merchant from Trabzon who was murdered by Muslims for converting to Christianity. He became Moldavia's patron saint until relegated to second position by Sfa Paraschiva (see p 244). The open exonarthex here protects what remains of a superb *Last Judgment*.

Frescoes cover the inside of Moldoviţa as well. The exonarthex contains murals of military saints, including St George, with Sts Demetrius and Mercurios below him, all on sprightly horses, with a painting of the Emperor Constantine at the Council of Nicaea. In the narthex are paintings of the seven ecumenical councils, while the squinches contain the four hymnographers. There is also a bewildering profusion of calendrical subjects in multiple registers. A tomb containing the remains of the bishop founder lies in a niche in the pronaos, surrounded by the figures of holy women, a *Deësis* and narrative paintings of saints' lives. Walk into the naos for a striking donation scene, featuring Petru Rareş with his wife and children wearing Western crowns and processing around the walls in descending order of size. Painted with great sensitivity, they are shown presenting a model of the church to Christ while the Virgin intercedes on their behalf. Christ is dressed as the Great High Priest, signalling that the Byzantine Empire no longer exists.

Suceviţa

Retrace your route south from Moldoviţa village, then turn east at Vatra Moloviţei and follow the road 34km northeast, which winds through spectacular hairpin bends over the mountains to Suceviţa. Allow a couple of hours to cover the distance because the road is often broken up. The beauty of Suceviţa convent has as much to do with its magnificent position as its architecture. Another fine Moldavian-style building, it stands on the valley floor near the Suceviţa River surrounded by forested mountains. The church itself is enclosed by a massive rectangular curtain wall with a pointed tower at each corner and an equally impressive gatetower. Dedicated to Învierea Domnului (the Resurrection), it was founded by the Abbot Gheorghe Movilă and his brothers and built between 1584–86. The mural cycle was completed in 1596, and was the last of its kind in Bucovina. The best view of the church and the surrounding fir-clad mountains is beside the cross at the top of the conical hill which stands beside the monastery.

The church has a tall tower on a triple star base and separate conical roofs over the east end; the two doors at the west end are modelled on a Wallachian design, the only striking difference with other Moldavian churches. As at Humor, the colours were not of the highest quality, and in many places the background blue has faded to a drab, charcoal grey. But on the outside walls it is the copper-based green that stands out.

As usual, the spiritual highpoint is at the east end, where the **holy hierarchy**, descends in the accepted order through an unprecedented seven registers, from the Ancient of Days surrounded by Seraphim at the top to monks and skeletal ascetics at the bottom. Among these pious figures are emaciated hermits and stylites who were pioneers of Christianity in the mountains and deserts of the Near East. The *Jesse Tree* on the south side incorporates elements from the Akathistos, and here you can see signs of Russian influence from over the border as well. A schematic, Russian Orthodox church with five onion domes is the setting for a fine painting of St Andrew's vision of the Virgin's Protective Veil. Andrew saw the Mother of God speading her cloak over the congregation in Constantinople's Hagia Sofia, and he him-

Suceviţa monastery

self appears to the right-hand side. Below the Virgin is the figure of Romanos the Melodist, who composed the original Akathistos and was famous for setting the liturgies to music. This theme is part of the Marian Anthems that the monks of Suceava would expect to sing. On the bottom register are scenes that have spilled over from the Tree of Jesse; they include paintings of the Virgin as the Patroness of Constantinople and of Suceviţa. The painters, identified only as Ion and Sofronie, crammed as many figures as possible into the fresco cycle and some of the scenes are difficult to read, but they also introduced some new ideas which are very striking.

The star attraction at Suceviţa is the **Ladder of Virtue** which covers part of the north wall. The Ladder was inspired by the vision of St John the Sinaite, and is a breakthrough in more sense than one: the composition is based on a diagonal rather than a horizontal axis and the subject is rare, not only in Romania, but in Orthodox iconography as a whole. It represents the First Judgment of the soul after death and shows the struggles of individual monks to make the journey to Heaven. Sliced dramatically in two by the diagonal ladder, the top half of the composition is filled with hosts of angels flying in formation like a Busby Berkeley swimming team, while the lower one shows unfortunate monks who have not made the grade falling headfirst into the jaws of Hell. Complacency is dangerous, the fresco warns, and even those nearing the end of their journey cannot afford to be complacent. Each bar of the ladder shows alternately a vice or a virtue, with Charity at the top. Here, Christ leans out of a window of Heaven to welcome people in. Among the few known precedents for this image of the Ladder of Virtue are an icon and an illuminated manuscript in St Catherine's Monastery on Mount Sinai.

Next to the Ladder is a Genesis cycle, showing further attempts by mortals to enter the Garden of Paradise.

The **Last Judgment** on the west wall was left unfinished, so the story goes, because the unfortunate artist responsible for it died after falling through the scaffolding. The iron 'ox-collar' hanging by the gate is a prayer gong or *toacă*, which the nuns beat to announce services. In most churches and monasteries around Romania the *toacă* is made of a single plank of wood which is two or three metres long. In the Middle Ages the *toacă* was used to summon men to battle. Played vigorously and fast, with two wooden hammers in the traditional way, it still sounds more like a call to arms than a call to prayers.

As you enter the church you pass through the exonarthex (porch) which is adorned with a Last Judgment, a Christ Pantokrator, and a series of pictures that celebrate the arrival of St John the New's relics at the Court of Alexandru cel

Bun. The walls of the pronaos, burial chamber and naos are also covered with a glorious profusion of painted scenes, each episode encased in its own frame. Some of the themes, such as the Tent of Confession in the Sanctuary, are based on Wallachian rather than Moldavian iconography. Passages from the life of Christ can be found in the naos, and here there are three fine landscape scenes taken from Genesis incorporating flowers such as wild pinks and poppies which are found nearby. A votive picture shows the family of the donor and a model of the church as it looked when new. In the *gropniţa* (burial chamber) the paintings concentrate on the Life of Moses and feature more local touches: Jews with pointed hats and animals such as dogs and pigs. On the pronaos walls are paintings from the lives of Sts Nicholas and George, while other sections are devoted to the Synods and the Calendar.

Please note that you are not allowed to use flash photography inside the church, because the light can damage the colours. This is a rule that applies to many monasteries containing precious frescoes, but especially to the ones that are now officially protected by UNESCO.

The Movilă family had strong Polish connections. They produced many distinguished clerics, among them the famous Petru, Metropolitan of Kiev, who was a moving force in the reign of Prince Vasile Lupu. Visit the monastery museum and you will find more examples of their cultural influence and wealth: embroidered shrouds (*epitaphion*) decorated with seed pearls and gold thread, icons and lay portraits.

Sucevița has an excellent new **hotel** which is five minutes' drive along the track which heads into the mountains opposite the convent gates. Turn left off the asphalt road beside the tourist shops and parking space as you arrive from Moldovița. The hotel is at no. 172, reached across a bridge on the left. It is a chalet built by Dumitru and Frida Avram on the proceeds of working as *gastarbeiter* in Germany. Prices here are comparable with those which you would pay at a decent bed and breakfast in Britain, and the Avrams can provide rooms with full and half board; there is also constant hot water, still a luxury in many Romanian homes, a bar and a disco room, and a fishing lake is also in preparation. Contacting the Avrams to book your room involves the tortuous process of dialling the Sucevița exchange and asking for their number, 105; alternatively you can arrange your stay by letter, writing to Str Bercheza 172, com. Sucevița, jud. Suceava, or simply turn up and take pot luck. Children and animals are welcome, both within reason.

Head east through Sucevița village, and 3km further on you come to **Marginea**. Both villages are strung out along the main road and seem to go on for ages; the main road also acts as a social focus, and children play in the verges or tend their cattle here, so watch out for them and for chickens and geese dicing with death in front of your wheels. Marginea is famous for its unglazed **ceramics** made from a clay which turns a deep, charcoal black on firing. This type of pottery is based on ancient Dacian designs. The pots are fired once in wood-burning kilns using the reduction technique (without oxygen). They are then decorated with sharp, round stones and burnished to let the patterns stand out. You can visit the pottery's workshops; look out for the entrance opposite a metal sign in the shape of a pot and a banner across the road saying 'Ceramica'. The factory is open

Mon–Fri 09.00–17.00. Alternatively, contact *Centrul de Creaţie Populară*, Str I.V. Viteazul 5, Suceava, ☎ 030 221096.

There is a gift shop in the workshops and another, selling some fine examples of local weaving, embroidery and more varieties of pottery, to the left of the drive as you go in. This little crafts shop also sells traditional clothes from the Bucovina region, including beautiful felt coats for women, and sheepskin waistcoats and jackets embroidered with multicoloured flowers and geometrical motifs. Think before you buy them, because these clothes are often irreplaceable; they were made decades ago by people whose skills have already died out. Such items cannot be made commercially and are non-renewable.

The monastery church at **Arbore** is c 6km along an unmetalled road to the southwest of Rădăuţi and 33km from Suceava. Turn south in Marginea, following signs to Gura Humorului, and turn left in Clit or Solca. Arbore has no places to stay, so do not plan to finish your day here. Founded by Luca Arbore, one of Ştefan cel Mare's generals, and built within five months during 1503, the church is another trefoil building in the Moldavian style but it varies interestingly from the norm: the deeply recessed arch at the west end was designed to house the bells (these now have a separate bell tower above the entrance to the churchyard). Arbore church has spectacular **paintings** on its south and west walls. They were carried out in a mixture of oil colours, casein from cow's milk, and gold leaf, by Dragoş Coman of Iaşi (Dragoşim Zugravul). Traces of these pigments were found in a makeshift stone palette which lies in the churchyard. Apart from a little overpainting, few of the murals at Arbore have ever been retouched. Luca never saw them completed because he was beheaded along with two of his sons, having been falsely accused of treachery. The painting cycles on the outside of the church took 40 years to complete.

Dragoş was familiar with Western art, and at Arbore he combined Byzantine and Renaissance styles: for example, in the arch at the west end, where the paintings have survived best, he showed guests at the Feast of St George with their backs to the viewers, and broke through the rigid framework of the individual scenes by showing the dragon stretched between two separate frames. Both concepts were foreign to Byzantine art. His inclusion of St Christopher carrying the Christ child on his shoulders is also unusual in Moldavian art.

On the west wall, in the niche beside which services for the dead are usually celebrated, Dragoş painted a series of vivid 'miniatures' like a larger version of an illuminated manuscript. The top register shows the Holy Family on the flight into Egypt and the Massacre of the Innocents. Below this are scenes from the Life of the Virgin, followed lower down by episodes from Moses's story. The lowest bands contain the Siege of Constantinople, updated to reflect contemporary fears about the Turks, rather than the Persians who were the original aggressors. To the right of the apex of the arch are scenes from Genesis which include Adam ploughing and Eve spinning.

The south wall contains eight registers devoted to scenes from Genesis and the Lives of the Saints. The Last Judgment is badly damaged, but must have been a strong and imaginative composition: what remains is of excellent quality and, in a raking light, you can see some of the incised underdrawings that were made before the paint was applied. Note the parcels containing souls who are being weighed in the balance, and the lush, exotic vegetation in the Paradise Garden.

The blue used on the exterior walls is an azurite, derived from copper carbonate, and is fading to a tell-tale malachite green. In the churchyard are two heavy stone slabs which were used as palettes: traces of pigment corresponding to the frescoes have been found in the hollows on their surface. Two restorers from Bucharest have begun the slow business of cleaning the paintings inside the church, which were badly damaged by fire in the 17C and 18C. Their work has already had wonderful results. In the pronaos, which also functions as the burial chamber, you can see the tombs of Luca Arbore and his Polish wife, Iuliana, each one decorated with unusual Gothic stonework that bears a strong Polish influence.

The icon screen at Arbore dates from about the same time as the church itself. It is heavily encrusted with smoke, but the paintings underneath are intact, preserved by the very grime which obscures them. Lead used in the original roof was stolen by the Turks who wanted it to add to their arsenals. A manor belonging to the Arbore family used to stand to the south of the church, and the remains of a tunnel linking the house with the church have been found. Arbore comuna takes its name from Luca Arbore's father. He was a guardian of Neamț citadel and bought land here from Prince Bogdan III.

If you have time, continue a few kilometres west towards **Solca**, which has a fine early-17C church commissioned by another Moldavian general in order to enhance his estate. Like many religious foundations, it commands a strong position at the head of a valley, but this one was designed specifically to hold a garrison. Gunpowder was stored in its cellars instead of ecclesiastical treasures, and the walls were pierced by arrow slits. The church is tall and heavily buttressed, with an octagonal Moldavian belfry on a double-star base. The Austrian architect Karl Romstorfer carried out restorations here in 1902 and was responsible for the garish modern tiles on the roof. The tomb chamber is empty, but above its semicircular vault is a little cache where the church's treasures could be hidden for safety. The original iconostasis was moved to Dragomirna, and the present one, by local sculptor Epaminonda Bucevschi, dates from 1895.

Return to Rădăuți and head c 20km northwest to see Ștefan cel Mare's most important foundation, the monastery of **Putna**. The drive to the village is quite spectacular because en route you will see the Carpathians forming a barrage in the west, emphasising how important they were as a barrier to invasions from the north and east. Romania's present-day border with Ukraine is only a few kilometres from here. On the way to Putna you pass the village of **Vicovu de Jos**. While you drive through it, have a look at its wooden houses with their handsome shingled roofs.

After saving Chilia from the Turks in January 1465, Ștefan laid Putna's foundation stone the following year. It stands on the site of an earlier, wooden monastery established by Alexandru cel Bun. It is sometimes credited with being Ștefan's first church, but this was in fact the monastery of Runc, founded in 1457 to the southeast of Piatra Neamț, near Buhuși in Bacău county.

Chronicler Ion Neculce tells us that Ștefan fired an arrow into the air to decide where the altar should stand. Putna church has a typical trefoil plan with an extended west end, making it look long, thin and elegant. A strong *brâu* motif encircles the whole body of the church, helping to counteract its vertical thrust

Ștefan's churches

Although the exact number of his churches can vary according to which sources you read, Ștefan cel Mare commissioned at least 38. Some of these lie within present-day Ukraine and the Moldovan Republic, and there is another at Feleac, near Cluj-Napoca. While Runc was his earliest foundation, the church at Pătrăuți (1487) was the first to manifest the distinctive architectural style usually associated with his influence. One of the most fascinating parts of this is the way in which the cupola is raised on oblique arches so that from underneath it looks as though the tower is carried on a star pattern, or a square inscribed diagonally within a square. Pătrăuți also has the satisfying dimensions of the Moldavian-style churches: a high roof and a ration of wall height to width that makes it look particularly slim. Inside is an original mural showing The Way of the Cross, and there is some external painting on the west wall. Sf Ilie church near Suceava (1488) has a similar conformation, with the addition of powerful buttresses.

Other churches from Ștefan's reign that have the same vaulting system include Sf Ioan in Vaslui (1490), the church in Bacău (1491), Sf Gheorghe in Hârlău (1492), Sf Nicolae in Iași (1491–92) (see p 248), Sf Nicolae in the Monastery of Popauți near Botoșani (1496), where the original wall painting and bell tower survive in good condition. There are also Sf Ioan in Piatra Neamț (1498; see p 233) and in Dorohoi (1495). All are worth seeing, but the most impressive from the point of view of its external and internal dimensions is the great monastery church at Neamț (1497) (see pp 224–225).

Other, lesser-known churches built by Ștefan include Sf Michael in Războleni (1496) and the monastery of Dobrovăț; this latter was Ștefan's last foundation, built 1503–04, and contains a full set of lovely but faded wall paintings commissioned by his son, Petru Rareș. None of the churches he founded received external murals in Ștefan's reign; where they occur, most were carried out during Petru's reign.

and make the building seem grounded. Instead of an entrance at the west end there are lateral doors into the narthex, and a single, polygonal tower on the roof decorated with crude floral motifs alternating with twisted columns. Blind arcading surrounds the outer walls. In the narthex is a small apse containing small scenes that show the official feasts for every day of the year.

Putna was an important foundation, not just because Ștefan lavished money on it and was buried there, but because of its excellence as a centre for manuscript illumination and embroidery. The museum contains exquisite shrouds and painted books from the monastery's superb collection of religious artefacts. One of these is a silk shroud made in 1477 by the Tartar princess, Maria of Mangop, who was one of Ștefan's wives. The portrait emphasises her striking, Asiatic features. In another, she wears a pall decorated with Islamic and Persian motifs which may have been introduced into Romania by Armenian merchants. There are also several illuminated manuscripts, one of which contains the only known portrait of Ștefan made during his lifetime. It is a miniature which the monk Nicodim painted in his *Tetraevanghelul* (Gospel book) of 1473. There are also maps showing other churches that he founded. The museum is housed in the main administration building, open Tues–Sun 10.00–18.00 in summer, 09.00–17.00 in winter.

On a hillside to the east of the monastery you can visit **Chilia lui Daniil**, the little rock church that Ștefan's spiritual confidant, the hermit Daniil, hollowed out from a boulder and made his home. Follow the sign which points to the right about 1km after you return to Putna village. But remember that women are not allowed inside. The mid-14C wooden church is set back from the road to the right as you drive from the village to the monastery, which is the oldest of its kind in Moldavia. It was built for Prince Dragoș at Volovaț in 1346, but Ștefan dragged it to its present place a century later.

Cabana Turistică Putna (also known as Complexul Putna) stands in its own grounds to the right of the road at the west end of Putna village on the way to the monastery. There is a signboard by the roadside, but you could be forgiven for missing it. The hotel looks like a Hammer House of Horror, and as you might expect from such an unlikely building it is a survival from the communist period. It has rooms which can accommodate up to eight people at a very reasonable rate but if the gloominess of its interior puts you off staying the night, you could try eating here instead: the mauve and yellow restaurant on the ground floor serves extremely good, fresh food, even though the choice is limited. There are a bar and disco in a separate building.

Rădăuți

43km northwest of Suceava, this is a small town with an interesting history. It is a pretty place, with some fine neo-Baroque buildings in the centre and a flourishing fruit and vegetable market. To find this, drive out of town along Str Ștefan cel Mare and turn right at the little church on the right-hand side of the street. Beware of pickpockets here: Rădăuți attracts a large number of Roma, and while it is unfair to blame them exclusively for all thefts, stealing is a part of their culture.

Practical information

☎ code

030

Tourist information

Complex Nordic is at Piața Unirii 67,
☎ 461598.

Where to stay

Try *Hotel Azur* (✯✯) at Calea Cernăuți 29, ☎ 464718.

The **Bogdană church** at B-dul Bogdan Vodă 4 is the oldest masonry church in Moldavia. It was founded by *voivode* Bogdan I (r. c 1359–c 1365) in 1346, and was rebuilt in 1468. The church is a simple basilica and very black inside, but its architecture combines a Romanesque plan with elements of Byzantine and Cistercian Gothic.

At Piața Unirii 63, a mid-19C building on the on the corner with Str Ștefan cel Mare houses the modest but attractive **Muzeul Tehnicii Populare Bucovinene** (the ethnographic museum), open 08.00–19.00 in summer, 08.00–18.00 in

> **Kuty pottery**
> Kuty can be easily recognised by its colours, which are almost always a combination of yellow, white and light bluey-green. The first centre of production, based at Kuty in Galicia, was founded in 1715 by Armenians from Moldavia. After Habsburg armies captured Bucovina and Galicia, Kuty designs spread across both provinces. Its origins lie in Byzantine art and the ancient ceramics of Suceava. Decoration includes fantastic, zoomorphic motifs and geometrical patterns as well as more naturalistic plants and animals and cheerful peasant scenes featuring musicians, markets and fairs. The images are scratched in the clay by the sgraffito technique.

winter. This is the oldest museum of its kind in Bucovina, and it is sad that no funds are available for brightening it up because it has a superb collection. Here you can see examples of locally produced Kuty pottery and wonderful objects made by hand which have been polished to a dark sheen through constant use.

Today, the most celebrated Kuty potters are the Colibaba family. Marcel and Florin Colibaba learnt their skills from their grandfather, Constantin (1900–75), who was acknowledged as a master during his lifetime. To arrange an appointment to see the brothers at work, contact *Centrul de Creaţie Populară*, Str I. V. Viteazul 5, Suceava, ☎ 030 221096, or *Fundaţia pentru Meşteşuguri* in Bucharest (see p 31). They have a workshop inside the Ethnographic Museum.

Follow the road south from the Bogdană church (Str Bogdan), and on the edge of the town limits, to the right of the road behind a row of fir trees, stands **Herghelia Rădăuţi**. This is a stud specialising in Shagya Arab and Ghidran horses. It was founded by the Habsburgs, but medieval documents show that Bogdan I kept 18 breeding horses here in the 14C. As part of a drive to attract more funds to the stud, the director has established a series of trail rides around the mountains. Some of these incorporate visits to the painted monasteries, and accommodation can be arranged in Rădăuţi and outlying villages. The Arabs and Ghidrans are not suitable for beginners, although the stud has some quieter, *semi-grei* (heavy) horses, and some ponies for small children. For more details and a list of trails and prices contact the director, Vasile Tratin, at Herghelia Rădăuţi, Str Bogdan Vodă 114, ☎ 464529, or phone him at home, ☎ 464562. It will help if you speak German or Russian if not Romanian.

Suceava

If you are starting out in eastern Bucovina, the industrial city of Suceava would make a practical, if not particularly attractive, base; it is the county town, with 117,000 inhabitants.

Practical information

☎ code
030

Tourist information
Bucovina Estur at Str Ştefan cel Mare 24, ☎/fax 223259, open Mon–Fri 09.00–17.00, Sat 09.00–15.00, is efficient and enterprising. The company can organise tailor-made tours and book hotels and bed and breakfast accommodation; it also has a currency exchange desk and car hire facilities, and offers a translation service.

Getting around
By train Gara Suceava at Str Nicolae Iorga 7 serves as the main link with the rest of the country, but there are also **Suceava Nord**, at Str Gării 2, and **Gara de Vest**. All three are located in the industrial centre to the north of the river. The *CFR* booking office is at Str Bălcescu 8, ☎ 214335, open Mon–Fri 07.00–20.00.
By bus **Autogara Burduieni** is on Str Gării, ☎ 297493, and **Autogara Suceava** is on Str Vasile Alecsandri, ☎ 216089.
By plane Suceava airport is to the east of the town on the DN29 road to Dorohoi, Salcea and Dumbraveni. *TAROM* has an office at Str Bălcescu 2, ☎ 214686.
By car For **car repairs** and servicing, *ACR* has an office at Str Nicolae Bălcescu 8, ☎ 210997, or try *Cooperativa Meşteşugurească*, which also has a car wash, on Şos Falticenilor, ☎ 213684, or *IATSA Suceava* at Calea Cernauti 114, ☎ 213510. **Petrol stations** can be found at Str Rulmentului, Str Falticenilor, B-dul 1 Mai, Str Cernăuţi and Str Botoşani.

Where to stay
Suceava has a handful of hotels of varying quality: *Hotel Suceava* (✶✶) at Str Nicolae Bălcescu 4, ☎ 521079; fax 214700, and *Hotel Balada* (✶✶) at Str Mitropoliei 3, ☎ 223198; fax 520087; e-mail balada@suceava.iiruc.ro, are both central. Other 2-star options include *Hotel Arcasul*, Str Mihai Viteazul 6, ☎ 210944; *Hotel Bucovina*, Str Ana Ipatescu 5, ☎ 217098; and *Hotel Gloria*, Str Vasile Bumbac, ☎ 521209; ask *Bucovina Estur* which they can recommend. If you prefer to find accommodation in a private household, contact the local branch of *ANTREC* at Str Lucian Blaga 9, ☎ 374238/374038; fax 374238/522883, or try the head office in Bucharest (see p 116).

If you are driving between Suceava and Gura Humorului on the DN17, there is a bright, new, ranch-style hotel at the 18-kilometre marker near Ilişeşti, about halfway between the two. Called *Pensiunea Baladă Obcinilor*, it has 18 rooms with hot and cold running water, a good restaurant and a large room designed for special events. The hotel stands about 1km away from the road along a track, but is clearly signposted. ☎ 094 632488, or 030 216726.

Eating out
If you are looking for a snack, Suceava has two branches of *Country Pizza*, one at B-dul 1 Dicembrie 1918, bl AT, and the other at Str George Enescu 21. Otherwise, choose one of the hotels or ask at the travel agents.

Post office
The main post office is at Str Dimitrie Onciul 1, ☎ 204262.

Telephones
PTTR (the 'telephone palace' Bălcescu and Str Meseriaşilor) is on Str Eminescu at the corner of Str Bălcescu and Str Meseriaşilor.

Money

Banc Post is on Str Nicolae Bălcescu; *Banca Comercială Ion Tiriac* at Str Ion Gramada 5; *Banca Comercială Româna* at Str Ștefan cel Mare 31; and *Bancorex* at Str Dimitrie Onciul 2. **Exchange houses** include *Bucovina Estur* (see Tourist information above) and *Bucovina Tourism* at Str Nicolae Bălcescu 2.

Police

Poliţia Municipului has its headquarters at B-dul 1 Mai 19, ☎ 213137.

Medical care

There is no hospital in Suceava (the nearest one is at Vatra Dornei); **pharmacies** include *Elmedica* at Str Universităţii 38, and *Farmacia No 1* at Str Nicolae Bălcescu 2, ☎ 217285.

History

Excavations at Scheia, in Suceava's western outskirts, have unearthed Dacian remains from the 2C and 3C AD. Written records about the town date from the 13C, and in 1375 it became the fourth capital of the Ţara de Sus (the Upper Land), succeeding Rădăuţi, Baia and Siret. The three towns were all important as royal bases in their time, and sometimes simultaneously because Moldavian princes liked to move their courts from place to place. During the Middle Ages, Suceava was a major trading and customs point for merchants from neighbouring Poland, as well as from Russia, the Balkans, Turkey and Asia. There are 17C records of English and Scottish traders based in Bucovina and Bessarabia.

There are a handful of interesting sights that put Bucovina's history in context. Curtea Domnească, the 14C Princely Court in the town centre, consists of Sf Dumitru, a 16C Moldavian-style monastery church founded by Petru Rareș, and the ruins of the court built by his father, Ștefan cel Mare. Both men were important figures closely connected with the painted monasteries. The freestanding bell tower (1561) bears the Moldavian crest, an aurochs's head surrounded by a sun, moon and star.

The Moldavian aurochs

The aurochs is an extinct form of bison which roamed central and eastern Europe during the Middle Ages; it was huge: sometimes over 3m at the shoulder and highly prized for its meat. Several noble houses used the animal's head in their coat of arms, including the Pernstejn family of Moravia (now in the Czech Republic). The story goes that Moldavia's legendary founder, Prince Dragoș, chased a mighty aurochs over the hills from Poland and killed it by a river (said to be in the gorge of Strâmtura Roșie) after a titanic struggle that lasted from dawn till dusk—hence the celestial bodies on the coat of arms. Dragoș's dog, Molda, died during the fight, and he named the Moldova River after her.

Muzeul Etnografic (the Ethnographic Museum) is housed in the attractive Hanul Domnesc, an attractive wood-framed building at Str Ciprian Porumbescu 5, open Tues–Sun 10.00–18.00 in summer; 09.00–17.00 in winter. The collection comprises local textiles, furniture and masks.

Muzeul Naţional al Bucovinei (the National Museum of Bucovina), Str Ştefan cel Mare 33, is less inspiring but has some nice pieces of Dacian pottery. ☎ 216439; websites obs.usv.ro or lab2-23k.ici.ro/Museums; e-mail mnbsv@assist.cccis.ro. There is a Natural History Museum, **Secţia de Ştiinţele Naturii**, at Str Ştefan cel Mare 23 to the north. Both open Tues–Sun 10.00–18.00 in summer; 09.00–17.00 in winter.

Muzeul Satului Bucovinean (the Museum of the Bucovinan Village), near Palatul Cetăţii de Scaun (the Citadel), has opened recently and has a fine collection ranging from the 17C to the 20C. The Casa Roşie, which houses the museum's offices, is particularly attractive and shows what can be done if you marry traditional furnishings with modern technology.

Follow the path for the **Citadel** which heads away from the city centre down into a wooded valley and up a steep hill (turn left from the main north–south road just past the right turn into Suceava's central business area), but keep straight on instead of turning left past the equestrian statue of Ştefan which stands at the top of the hill. Open Tues–Sun 10.00–18.00 in summer, 09.00–17.00 in winter.

Mănăstirea Sf Ioan cel Nou (the Monastery of St John the New), along Str Mitropoliei, has one of the largest Orthodox churches in Moldavia. Dedicated to Sf Gheorghe, it was founded by Bogdan III in 1514 and replaced the Mirăuţi church as the Metropolitan Cathedral. Although it is roofed in garish modern tiles, its roof profile has been restored to its original shape with a scoop around the cupola. It also has an elongated nave which is a Moldavian speciality, and incorporates a pronaos or tomb chamber for the relics of Sf Ioan, as well as a naos, narthex and exonarthex.

The frescoes at Sf Gheorghe are refreshingly original and include fine paintings of the Pantokrator and the Evangelists: St John the Baptist is shown unconventionally with wings, floating among the prophets. The iconography is a mixture of styles, suggesting that the Old and New Testament themes were executed at different periods.

The Princely Court ~ Curtea Domneşti/Cetatea de Scaun

Suceava was always better known as a military stronghold than as a cultural or spiritual centre, and the Princely Court was its focus. You can reach the bastioned hulk of this castle through the park opposite the main square. Cross the bridge into the woods and follow the path up the steps to the huge 1977 equestrian statue of Ştefan. From here the route is not well marked and it is easy to get lost in the woods: go straight past the statue and turn left beside the chain link fence which encloses the museum of vernacular architecture, and follow the path until you reach the café. The citadel stands to the left of that. It takes about 20 minutes to walk here from the centre of town. From the ramparts you get a great view of the town and the Mirăuţi church across the valley. Open Tues–Sun 10.00–18.00.

History

The citadel, also known as the Scaun (Throne), was founded in c 1388 by *voivode* Petru I Muşat (r. 1375–91), who moved the capital from Siret to Suceava. Originally rectangular with towers at each corner and halfway along the walls, the citadel was strengthened and altered by Alexandru cel Bun, but Ştefan cel Mare virtually rebuilt it, adding a moat and c 2m thick curtain walls supported by ten buttresses. Ştefan also built six square bastions.

Sultan Mehmet II captured Constantinople in 1453 and in the following year started battering at the gates of eastern Europe. The Moldavians resisted gamely until the mid-16C, but paid their first tribute to the Porte in 1456. The Turks were not their only enemies: in three separate years, the principality paid tributes to the Sultan and the King of Poland, and in 1475 Ştefan was in fee to the Magyar sovereign as well. When the Ottomans finally gained control of Moldavia they allowed it to elect its own princes. (They came to the same arrangement in Wallachia, which succumbed a few years earlier.) Not until the Phanariot Greeks were installed in the early 18C did the regime change, while neighbouring Hungary, Serbia and Bulgaria were turned into pashaliks. Nobody knows why the Romanian lands were so favoured.

The citadel was proof against Sultan Mehmet II in 1476; his second terrible (and unsuccessful) attack came in 1485, after which Ştefan had the square bastions enlarged to incorporate circular extensions to provide more effective protection against artillery.

Cetatea de Scaun was a link in the chain of seven citadels that protected Moldavia's eastern borders. Most of these massive fortresses lie in the present-day Republic of Moldova or Ukraine, and some have disappeared. But once they strode across the country from Chilia in the Delta, through Suceava and north to the giant fortress at Hotin.

The Turks tried in vain to destroy Suceava citadel which survived until 1673, when janissaries blew it up. Even so, much of the three-storey keep and the outlying chambers remains, and what was left of the Scaun became a symbol for the Romanian struggle for independence from the Habsburgs.

Christ's athlete

Prince of Moldavia 1457–1504 and one of Romania's oustanding heroes, Ştefan launched the principality into a golden age. Styled 'the Great' because he won 38 out of his 40 battles, he endowed churches or monasteries in practically every year of his reign: it was his way of showing his gratitude to God for preserving his life, and the churches went up whether he lost or won. Ştefan owned vast estates, including the vineyards of Cotnari where delicious dessert wines are made. He supported schools of architecture, painting, calligraphy and embroidery. His successors, Bogdan the One-Eyed and Petru Rareş, continued the practice of founding churches after their battles.

Pope Sixtus IV called Ştefan the 'Athlete of Christ' in recognition of his strenuous efforts to hold back the Ottoman army. This soubriquet may only have been lip service, because the pontiff did not lift a finger to help him. In stature, Ştefan was small (a little over 5ft), and according to the chronicles he was sober in demeanour. He was also a brilliant strategist who used guerrilla warfare to outwit his enemies. He treated traitors and other wrong doers with harsh justice: he had to dispose of a treacherous half-brother

> before he could take the throne, and he needed to act decisively. Impaling was one of his methods of retribution. Ștefan also dealt in slaves, and many of his serfs were Gypsies whom he imported to work on his estates. Despite his reputation for sobriety he had at least four wives and several mistresses, but the most important of his wives from a political point of view was Maria of Mangop, a Tartar princess from the Crimea. Portraits of Ștefan are usually copied from a 14C painting which shows him with long blond hair, flaring moustaches and a fierce expression. The only picture known to have been made of him during his lifetime is a miniature in a 1473 book of Gospels kept at the monastery of Putna. It shows him kneeling in prayer, an amiable expression on his round, apple-cheeked face: not the kind of features that we normally associate with giant-slayers.

A path from the citadel to the northwest reaches **Biserica Mirăuți** (the Mirăuți Church), the oldest church in Suceava. Petru Mușat founded the church in the 14C; restored in the 17C and 19C, it is decorated with polychrome tiles. It was Suceava's first Metropolitan Cathedral, and was where Moldavia's early princes were crowned. The façade is decorated with blind arches and a sawtoothed cornice sandwiched between thick cable mouldings. The pattern, called a *brâu*, symbolises everlasting life. Below the eaves there are frescoes of saints dating from the 19C.

To the northwest of the city, in Str Armenească on the Zamca plateau, stands a beautiful ruined **citadel church** founded by Suceava's once-powerful Armenian community.

Armenians in Suceava

Armenians arrived in Moldavia in the 9C. They made themselves indispensible, working as diplomats, interpreters, advisers and most of all businessmen who traded in carpets and glass. Their greatest sphere of influence was along the Mare Drum Tătăresc, the Great Tartar Road, which connected the Black Sea to the Baltic. Their most important eastern European centre was the Polish city of Lvov, where they established a bishopric. In 1401, the Armenian Archbishop Ohanes Nasredinian founded the church at Zamca, and between 1401–35 the Armenian community helped to stabilise the rule of the Moldavian prince Alexandru cel Bun. By the early 16C Armenians in Suceava were powerful enough to be granted leadership of the city council for one year in two and from 1572–74 the Armenian John the Brave became voivode.

Tolerated because of their prodigious skills, Moldavia's Armenians were ostracised by the Orthodox Church because they were monophysites, and Armenian priests figure among the heretics awaiting the Last Judgment at Voroneț.

Dragomirna

No visit to Bucovina's monasteries would be complete without seeing Dragomirna. Located c 9km north of Suceava, it is a Renaissance building of truly astonishing proportions. Standing 42m high and 9.6m wide, its length is equal to its height. This makes it look impossibly tall and thin, an effect enhanced by the restrained pattern of blind arcading and sheer walls that have hardly any buttressing. Architecturally the church and the surrounding complex of cells, refectory, museum and *stareția* (the abbess's offices and lodgings) are a daring refinement of the Moldavian style that began to take shape 150 years before. All the elements are here, including the neo-Byzantine ground plan, Gothic detailing and Moldavian floral stonework around doors and windows. These pretty touches offset the sternness of the building without compromising its virility: plainness and ornament complement each other in perfect harmony. This effect is unique to Romania, and rare here too: only at Mogoșoaia Palace near Bucharest do you find its equal. This is all the more amazing when you realise that the walls themselves are made of rough-cast stone: from a distance they look like dressed ashlar blocks.

Dragomirna monastery

Half way up the walls is the cable motif (*brâu*) which girdles the entire body of the church and subtly counterbalances the verticality of the walls, helping to 'ground' the building in the mind's eye. Some historians think that the pattern evolved from the skuamorphic *funie* (rope) which was traditionally carved around wooden churches in Maramureș and northern Transylvania, a throwback to a time when such churches were held together with rope. In those areas, the rope motif represents the infinite nature of God's kingdom. Here the *brâu* consists of three 'strands' symbolising the Trinity and the union of Romania's three ancient principalities, Moldavia, Transylvania and Wallachia. It is continued inside the church, around arches and window frames.

The interior of the church is also impressive, with tall arches and vaults which have the solemnity of Hagia Sophia in Istanbul. There are wall paintings in the naos which are inscribed in Romanian using Slavonic characters, and a fine Baroque iconostasis which comes from the medieval church at Solca.

History

Dragomirna monastery was built by Metropolitan Crimca and the Stroici family between 1602 and 1609, shortly after Mihai Viteazul had unified the three Romanian-speaking countries. Crimca was a highly educated man and a practising artist, and he established a famous miniature and icon-painting school here. Legend has it that Prince Ștefan Tomșa, the patron of Solca monastery, was so jealous of Crimca's craftsmen that he chased the unlucky bishop and attacked him with a mace. Crimca managed to reach Dragomirna but died soon afterwards; the monastery was eventually completed by Prince Miron Barnovschi (see pp 248–249). The monastery's name means 'love of peace'. Unusually it remained open under the Communists as a convent and has a community of ten nuns.

Before Dragomirna was built, princes were the only people who had the right to erect towers on Moldavian churches. But here the voivode waived the rule, and as a mark of gratitude Crimca and his co-founders constructed a particularly fine cupola on a triple star base, ornamented with tapestry-like stone carvings. At the west end the church has a curious polygonal exonarthex. Surrounding the church are a handsome gate tower and cells, built in 1627 by Barnovschi.

Dragomirna has an excellent museum and a smaller church in the Wallachian style. It is now a working convent, and women tourists can stay here overnight by prior arrangement. Open daily 09.00–17.00. Visitors are asked to dress with decorum. There is a well from which you can take drinking water next to the church.

Ştefan cel Mare's monastery of **Pătrăuţi** is a short drive from here. Go back to the DN2, and turn right at the signposted turning 5km further north. The church has been under restoration for a number of years and conservators have uncovered several layers of plaster in their attempts to find the original frescoes; all the wall paintings were painted over during the communist period. Only a small section of murals can be seen, at the west end of the exterior walls, and although the fragments are charming they are likely to remain shrouded in scaffolding for some time yet. A handsome wooden bell tower stands in the churchyard beside a path where roses sweeten the summer air. Inside the church the painting is smoke-blackened, but it is possible to make out some of the smart geometric patterning that decorates the walls. Pătrăuţi has a large population of Roma; if you want to avoid being waylaid by them, behave as little like a foreign tourist as possible.

SOUTH AND EAST OF SUCEAVA

This part of Bucovina is not as beautiful as the mountains, but if you are travelling through it, there are interesting places to see. On your way south, a few kilometres along the main road to Fălticeni near Horodniceni, a sign to the right tells you in Romanian and Armenian characters that there is an **Armenian monastery church** near here. If you follow the track by car and then on foot for c 4km you will see it outlined majestically against the skyline.

Continue through Fălticeni and take the small country road southwest for Baia, and you will reach another historic site. 8km southwest of Fălticeni, **Baia** was once one of Bucovina's first medieval capitals and later became a thriving commercial centre; now it is a backwater on nobody's tourist itinerary. Vestiges of a paleolithic settlement and an ancient earthwork have been discovered here, but there is nothing to see of them; instead Baia contains two fine churches from the period of Ştefan the Great and his son Petru Rareş.

During the early Middle Ages, Baia was called Moldova because the Moldova

River flows nearby. Some historians think that the principality gained its name from the town. Baia, coming from a Thracian word, means mine in Romanian, and this area was exploited for its minerals and precious metals, including gold and silver. In 1339 Baia was mentioned in contemporary documents as the largest city to the east of the Carpathians. Between the 14C and the 16C Baia throve: contemporary sources mention forges, mills, distilleries, oil presses and furnaces for melting raw minerals. Baia began to decline in the 17C when the principality's main trade centres moved towards the southeast.

Dominican missionaries built a church here in the 13C, and a Franciscan church is mentioned in 1377. Alexandru cel Bun founded a Catholic cathedral at Baia in 1410; at the time it was the largest in Moldavia and its ruins are still visible beside Caminul Cultural (the Romanian equivalent of the village community centre).

Ştefan cel Mare gained a decisive victory at Baia at the start of his reign. In the winter of 1467, King Matei Corvin of Hungary invaded Moldavia with one of the few regular armies deployed in Europe at the time. After looting and burning villages en route for Suceava, he and his troops halted at Baia. Matei let his troops pillage the city, but on the night of 15 December a small party of Ştefan's men arrived in secret, separated into three groups and set fire to Baia with the Magyars in situ. They killed over 12,000 Hungarian soldiers and Matei Corvin received an arrow in his side, but one of Ştefan's boyars let him escape. Some of Ştefan's cohorts hid in a large ash tree, which stood on the site of the church which he built afterwards as a sign of gratitude to God for his success. **Biserica Albă**, the White Church as it is known, stands on the outskirts of Baia to the northwest, near the road to Sasca Mică. Men and women passed the stone for its construction from hand to hand in a human chain that stretched all the way to Râşca.

The existing church, which like its predecessor is dedicated to St George, is an early 20C copy of the original, which was allowed to fall into ruin. It is a fine building with a rectangular plan, a narrow elevation and the unusual vaulting system describing a star pattern that was introduced in Ştefan's reign. The side apses are semicircular but inscribed within the thickness of the walls, so that inside the plan is triconch. Care was taken to replace the furnishings with authentic copies, and the oak stalls and wooden icon screen are all made in the traditional way, with joints instead of nails. The tower, rebuilt in brick, is octagonal. In the church walls you can see the shell holes made by bullets fired during the First World War. Some pieces of lintel and carved masonry from the original church were used to rebuild the perimeter wall, some of which had in any case remained intact. Next to the church in the priest's reception rooms is a romanticised and stereotypical portrait of Ştefan cel Mare which shows him in the role of military hero, with long blond hair and a no-nonsense frown.

In the centre of Baia, close to Caminul Cultural and partly enclosed by a fence of tall trees, is a **painted church** commissioned by Petru Rareş. It was completed in 1532 on the site of another church founded by Petru's father, Ştefan cel Mare, which in its turn was built over the foundations of an even older church. Original frescoes cover both the interior and exterior walls, but the exterior murals are very faint, there are cracks in the wall fabric and the paintings inside have been rotted by fungus. But even though they have deteriorated badly, you can still make out a faded image of the Siege of Constantinople on the south wall. Inside is a votive portrait of Petru Rareş, his wife Doamna Elena, and one of their children.

From Baia, turn right in Praxia and follow the signposts through Bogdăneşti for **Râşca**, another fine monastery which stands in a beautiful rural setting. You will be able to see its twin towers long before you arrive. Bogdan I founded a wooden church here in the 14C, and Ştefan cel Mare's son Bogdan cel Orb (Bogdan the One-Eyed) ordered a new monastery here after Tartars razed the existing one in 1510. The existing church and fortified walls were endowed by Petru Rareş during his second reign, after he returned from Transylvania, where he had taken refuge from Suleiman the Magnificent. Petru set about restoring the monasteries which the Turks had plundered and burnt, and in 1540 he asked Bishop Macarie of Roman to reconstruct the church at Râşca. The new church was completed two years later. Macarie was one of the finest scholars of his day. Following the murder of Ioan cel Cumplit in 1574, the monks fled, having hidden the church bells in a nearby lake. A period of 40 years passed before the monastery became functional again, but in 1677 Metropolitan Dosoftei placed Probota and Râşca under the protection of the Patriarch of Jerusalem. This situation was revoked in the mid-19C.

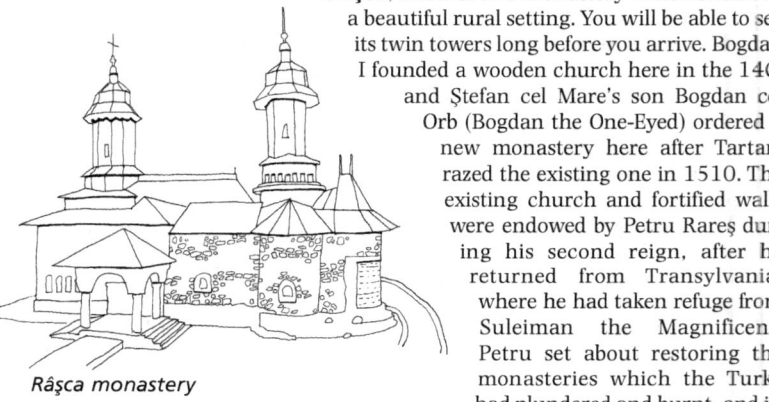
Râşca monastery

A Greek painter called Stramatello Cotronas carried out the original external frescoes in 1552, and the surviving fragments cover about half of the southern façade. They comprise a Ladder of Virtue, a Last Judgment and scenes from the life of St Anthony. The murals were restored in the early 19C. Inside the church, the frescoes have been overpainted but traces of the original work are still visible in places. They are richly embellished with gold leaf, making the interior feel very sumptuous. The finest passages can be found in the sanctuary, where they celebrate the life of St Nicholas, and in the naos. A High Court official called Costea Băcioc added a splendid Wallachian-style exonarthex to the south side of the church between 1611–17. Other changes were made in the 1820s. There is a Slavonic *pisanie* (dedicatory inscription) over the porch.

Râşca has a community of 35 monks. The church, which has UNESCO protection, is dedicated to St Nicholas, whose *hram* is celebrated on 6 December. Râşca is the name of the stream that runs nearby. Visitors are asked to wear decent clothing when they enter the monastery.

From Râşca monastery a forest road leads across the mountains to Neamţ monastery. The journey takes about five hours but is not well marked.

20km north of Paşcani and 28km east of Fălticeni stands the monastery of **Probota**, which Petru Rareş endowed in 1530. It stands on the site of two earlier churches in the western outskirts of Gulia village, to the south of Dolhasca. It was Petru's first commission and is a splendid fortified building with wall paintings both outside and in. These have not lasted well, probably because when they were carried out in 1532 when the technique was in its infancy. What remains has recently been beautifully restored. When they were new, the frescoes must have been stunning.

On the outside walls you can see traces of the original themes: *cinul* (the Prayer of All Saints, or Deësis) at the east end, a Siege of Constantinople and a Jesse Tree. In the porch there are still a few patches of the earliest Last Judgment mural to be found in any Moldavian church, which was introduced by Grigore Roşca, the scholar priest who was the Abbot of Probota and a cousin of Petru Rareş and who later oversaw the paintings at Voroneţ. In the naos, the murals showing the Synods and the Calendar are original, but the votive portraits of Petru, Doamna Elena and their son Iliaş have been altered twice.

Probota is mentioned as having a functioning church in 1391 and 1398; before this there was a hermitage here. Ştefan cel Mare built the core of the existing church as a burial place for his mother, Doamna Oltea, and his first wife, Princess Evdochia of Kiev. Two of Moldavia's earlier princes, Petru I Muşat and Alexandru cel Bun, were smitten by this pretty location, and both of them built churches nearby. Some remains of Alexandru's stone church can be seen beside the Probota stream. Between 1527–30, Metropolitan Roşca carried out Petru Rareş's instructions for building the existing monastery church.

Roşca turned the monastery into a dynamic cultural centre, and in later centuries it attracted many other religious savants, including Gheorghe Movilă, Teodosie Barnovschi and Metropolitan Dosoftei. In 1550, Princess Elena and her sons ordered a 6m-high defensive wall, defence towers and ramparts to be raised around the church. The princes' residence and the bell tower stand in the northwest corner. Prince Petru, Elena and several of their children were buried at Probota. The name of the monastery is Slavonic and means brotherhood.

SOUTHWEST BUCOVINA

Places to see here include **Câmpulung Moldovenesc**, which lies in a narrow valley below the Rarău massif, the hills of **Obcina Feredeului** and the **Giumalău mountains**. Head for the **Tihuţa Pass** into Transylvania for fine panoramic views and, if you like, a 'genuine Dracula experience': this is the place where Bram Stoker chose to locate his fictional monster's castle, and the *Hotel Dracula* promises to provide everything the Dracula enthusiast could want. To the southwest lies **Vatra Dornei**, an attractive alpine resort. Its name comes from the Dorna (Whirlpool) river, which joins the Bistriţa Aurie (the Golden Bistriţa) here, and it stands on the ancient Geto-Dacian settlement of Docirana.

Câmpulung Moldovenesc

Considerably smaller than Suceava, this resort town lies 630m above sea level and is surrounded by spectacular scenery. It would make a pleasant base for tours of this part of Bucovina.

Practical information

☎ code
030

Tourist information
For *Bucovina Tours* ☎ 311581, or try *George Turism* at Calea Bucovinei 13, ☎ 312963; fax 522922.

Getting around
By train The main station is at Str Gării 2, ☎ 312507, and **Gara Câmpulung Est** is on Calea Bucovinei, ☎ 311102. The *CFR* booking office is at Calea Transilvaniei 2, ☎ 311103.
By bus The bus station is at Str Alexandru Bogza 1, ☎ 312551.
By car For **car repairs** and servicing, try *Ing Service* at Str Trandafirilor 4, ☎ 312884, or *Service Automobile Dacia* at Calea Transilvaniei 60, ☎ 311659.

Where to stay
Hotel Dersicom is at Calea Bucovinei 141A, ☎ 313371, and *Pensiune Minion* (✰✰✰) is at Str Dimitrie Cantemir 26B, ☎/fax 311581. If you want to stay in the nearby Rarău massif, you may find room in *Cabana Rarău*, a mountain hut equipped for tourists, ☎/fax 312441; you may also be lucky experimenting with private enterprise. The Director of Muzeul Lemnului, Dr Zahariciuc, has a **mountain villa** that stands in a large and beautiful meadow to the north of town. There is no road to the house, but it has room for up to 16 people, ☎ 311387, 314796; fax 311818.

Eating out
These include *Bradul* at Calea Transilvaniei 40, *Dersi Com* at Calea Bucovinei 141, and *Doua Stele* at Str Alexandru Bogza 6.

Post office
This is in the centre of town, on the corner where Calea Transilvaniei becomes Calea Bucovinei.

Money
The *CEC* bank is at Str Dimitrie Cantemir, bl 31.

Police
Contact the *primăria* at Str 22 Decembrie 2, ☎ 312325.

Medical care
The *Diana* **pharmacy** is at Str Alexandru Bogza 4.

Museums
Muzeul Arta Lemnului is at Calea Transilvaniei 10, ☎ 311378, open Tues–Sun 09.00–16.00. This has a fascinating collection of wooden tools, musical instruments, folkloric cult objects and a handful of vernacular buildings, all but ruined by the dingy setting.
Colecția de Linguri de Lemn Ioan Țugui is at Str G. Popovici 1, ☎ 311315, open Tues–Sun 09.00–16.00. This is a collection of wooden spoons that bear an uncanny (and much-researched) likeness to the decorative spoons once made in rural Wales.

Its name meaning literally long field, Câmpulung is one of the oldest towns in this part of Moldavia. Together with Vatra Dornei (see pp 220–212) it was the hub of a mini-republic called Țara Dornilor, whose inhabitants won the right to make their own laws by protecting the principality's borders with Transylvania. In his *Descriptio Moldaviae* of 1716 Dimitrie Cantimir wrote admiringly that the villagers obeyed no-one but themselves. Câmpulung lay on an important trade route between Transylvania and Moldavia, and the people of Țara Dornilor grew rich on the profits from sending their produce far afield. During the 16C the town was at the heart of Moldavia's struggle to resist the Poles, Tartars and Turks. Campaigns were organised here by Petru Rareș in 1529 and 1542, and by Alexandru Lăpușneanu in 1556 and 1597. Self-determination only ended when the Austrians invaded Bucovina in 1774.

Today, Câmpulung is an unassuming and pleasant town. The weekly open-air **market** usually attracts many people from the surrounding villages and sometimes from across the Ukrainian border. Apart from the fun of browsing through the stands and makeshift stalls, you may also meet Huțul people who speak a Slavonic dialect and live in scattered pockets around the mountains to the north.

Some 35km to the northwest of Câmpulung in the Mestecăniș Mountains stand the long barns of **Herghelia Lucina**, the only stud in the world which specialises in purebred Huțul ponies. The main stud buildings consist of functional sheds and barns strung out along a slight depression on a glorious open plateau 1500m above sea level. Around them are several thousand hectares of pasture hedged in by pine woods on several sides. Ukraine is only 15km away.

To reach the stud from Câmpulung Moldovenesc, you will need a 4WD because during the last third of the journey the metalled road gives way to very uneven track and rotten bridges. Take the E576 in the direction of Borșa and Vatra Dornei, and turn right past Pojorâta for Fundu Moldovei. In c 19km you reach Brează, at which point the road disappears. Continue north through Brează de Sus and Benia; the single track to Lucina heads left just before you reach Moldova Sulița village; two imposing rocks on either side of the track mark the entrance to the drive. From there, ask for directions in the villages. There are buses from Câmpulung to Moldova Sulița, the nearest village to Lucina, from where you would need to ask the stud to pick you up in its 4WD. Contact the director by phone, ☎ Suceava 5, or write to him at Herghelia Lucina, Com. Moldova Sulița, jud. Suceava. You may also be able to arrange a visit through Muzeul Lemnului in Câmpulung (see above). Alternatively, any good travel agent should be able to help you.

You can hire a pony by the hour or by the day; if you decide to trek for a day or more, you must also hire a guide. There is a guest house at Lucina, but its plumbing is primitive, to say the least. If you want to stay here, it would probably be more suitable to camp or use a camper van. The 1990s have not been kind to Lucina and the stud's future is hanging in the balance.

Lucina and the Huțuls

Herghelia Lucina was founded in the early 19C during the Habsburg occupation of Bucovina, as one of the Empire's many attempts to improve the animal husbandry and agriculture of its new provinces. Lucina made a good choice because the pastures here are rich in minerals and wild herbs. Huțul ponies were a natural choice for development because of their adaptability as draught and riding animals. Not only are they hardy and strong, they are also sure-footed and, according to a research paper published in the 1950s, 'gentle, docile, prudent and seldom pretentious'.

Thanks to the Habsburgs' intervention, Huțuls were crossbred with Arabian horses from 1856. Several other crosses have been tried since then, including with the Romanian *greu* (heavy horse). Today there are three main strains of Huțul. They are good-looking little animals, rarely measuring over 14 hands. The Arabian influence still shows in their dished profiles. Most are dark brown, the colour of moleskin, and some have the lighter muzzles associated with Exmoor ponies. Huțuls are still the preferred breed for local draught animals—they can pull up to five times their body weight. Walk through any of the surrounding villages, and you will see them trotting smartly along the road. They get their name from the Huțul people who inhabit the mountain ranges between Romania and Ukraine.

Vatra Dornei

The third largest town in Suceava county, Vatra Dornei lies in a stunning position among the mountains. Although it is best known as a skiing resort, it would be another good base for hikes through the mountains in summer.

Practical information

☎ code
030

Tourist information
Bucovina Vacance Tour is at Str Republicii 5, ☎/fax 373709.

Getting around
By train The station is at Str Gării 1, ☎ 371333.
By bus **Autogara Vatra Dornei** is on Str Oborului, ☎ 371252.
By car For **car repairs** and servicing, try *Nig Supercom* at Str Mihai Eminescu 34, ☎ 371411.

Where to stay
Hotels include *Hotel Bradul* (✭✭) at Str Republicii 5, ☎ 373921; fax 371778; *Hotel Bucovina* (✭✭) at Str Republicii 5A, ☎ 374205; fax 374206; *Hotel Călimani*, also at Str Republicii 5A, ☎ 373921; fax 371778; *Vila Casa Pop* (✭) at Str Runc 2, ☎ 373528; and *Vila Rarău 5*, ☎373709. *ANTREC* has a branch office at Str Lucian Blaga 9, ☎/fax 374238; fax 522883.

Post office
The main post office is on Str Mihai Eminescu, ☎ 373030; fax 373313.

Money
Banca Comercială Română is at Str Mihai Eminescu 45; *Banca Română pentru Dezvoltare* at Str Luceafarului 18; *Bankcoop* at Str Negrilești 6; and *CEC* at Str Mihai Eminescu 42.

Police
The station is at Str Dornelor 18, ☎ 371131.

Medical care
The town **hospital**, *Spitalul Orașenesc*, is at Str Mihai Eminescu 14, ☎ 371821, and a **surgery**, *Cabineta Medicală Gabimed*, is at Str Republicii 21, ☎ 372573. **Pharmacies** include *Cesalpina* at Str Republicii 5, ☎ 374141, and *Valeriana Farm* at Str Mihai Eminescu 19, ☎ 371937.

Vatra Dornei has two museums: the **Muzeul de Etnografie** (Ethnography Museum) is at Str Mihai Eminescu 17, ☎ 371485, while the **Muzeul de Ştiinţe Naturale** (Natural History Museum) lies c 300km south across the river, at Str Unirii 3. Both are open Tues–Sun 10.00–18.00 in summer, 09.00–17.00 in winter. The town **theatre**, *Teatrul Ion Luca*, is at Str Gării 2, ☎ 373736.

Around Vatra Dornei

20km to the east of Vatra, beyond the village of Sunători, is the geological and botanical reserve of the **Cheia Zugrenilor gorges**. Southeast of Vatra Dornei, at the mouth of the Neagra Sărului river, you can visit some ancient **mountain villages**, including Saru Dornei, Panaci and Coverca. Paltiniş col offers marvellous views of the Bistriţa and Călimani ranges. The road south from Saru Dornei splits into two halves. One leads to the southwest, finally petering out at Gura Haiţii. The other travels intermittently to Panaci, continuing as tracks to higher mountain villages. Further south still, there are paths leading southwest into Transylvania and the wild expanses of the Călimani mountains close to Mount Pietrosu (2100m), through which you can walk for several days without meeting another soul. If you want to explore this area from the western side of the mountains, you may be able to hire a guide by contacting the Ethnographic Museum in Reghin (see pp 442–443). This is one of Romania's great wildernesses and, magnificent as it is, you can easily get lost, so be prepared.

Lake Bicaz and Cheilele Bicazului (the Bicaz Gorges)

At the northern end of the vast accumulation lake of Bicaz is a crossroads where the DN15 and DN17B meet. The road goes 86km northwest to Vatra Dornei and 43km southwest to Borsec, a Transylvanian spa town where a popular Borsec mineral water is produced. Alternatively, go 46km northeast to Târgu Neamţ (German Town), a useful focal point for visiting several monasteries in beautiful surroundings, while Piatra Neamţ is 43km southwest of Târgu Neamţ.

Take a right turn at the south end of Lake Bicaz for a switchback road that threads its way dizzily along 10 spectacular kilometres of the Cheile Bicazului, passing **Lacu Roşu** (Red Lake). Come here if you want to buy good-quality Romanian textiles, pottery, basketwork and woodwork. During the tourist seasons there are lots of stalls by the roadside on the way up to Lacu Roşu, competing to sell goods at (when last checked) ridiculously low prices. Lacu Roşu is surrounded by mountain peaks and is a mecca for walkers and climbers, and there are several hotels and pensions here, including *casă turistica* and the *cabana Suhard*. The lake's name comes from the pinkish alluvial clay that surrounds it. In 1838 a landslide from from nearby Mount Suhard drowned the fir trees, whose rotting stumps poke eerily from the surface of the water. For a few pence, you can hire a fibreglass dinghy for a row around the lake. At **Pângaraţi** you can visit a monastery founded by Alexandru Lăpuşneanu in 1560. The **Ceahlău Massif** also attracts climbers: its highest peak, Mount Ceahlău (1900m), is a marvellous, craggy finger that dominates the landscape. The mountain is a reserve for protected plants such as Ladies Slipper, edelweiss and yew.

Despite Alexandru Vlahuţa's description of it as 'a melancholy pasture, overshadowed by firs', **Durău** is a beautiful resort on the west side of Lake Bicaz, with a convent decorated by the modernist painter Nicolae Toniţa (1886–1940) between 1935–37. The convent is definitely worth visiting. It was closed during the communist period, but in 1990 the nuns returned and Durău has become an international centre for religious conferences. The complex also contains a modest art museum and another church, founded by the Cantacuzino family.

NEAMŢ REGION

Neamţ, meaning German, takes its name from the Teutonic Knights who established a base here in the early 13C. It is the name of a county, as well as an ethnographic area, that adjoins Bucovina to the south. **Piatra Neamţ** is the county's administrative centre, an unpretentious provincial town which has a lot to recommend it. Like Bucovina it contains some exceptional medieval monuments, among them the marvellous **citadel** and **monastery** near Târgu Neamţ. Scenic highlights include the area between **Valea Oantului** and **Pângarati**; **Pângărăcior to Vaduri**; **Viişoara** to **Gârcina**; **Dumbrava Roşie** to **Piatra Şoimului**; **Valea Almaşului** and the **Bistriţa valley**. Spend a few days here if you can.

Regular events The county town of Piatra Neamţ hosts four annual festivals. In January there is a festival of folklore and masks; in May there is an international theatre festival; a beer festival takes place July–August; and another folklore festival is held in August. On the first Sunday in August, a Sailor's Day service is held in Bicaz Port, and later in the same month there is a special celebration and service of Mount Ceahlău. A national writing competition, dedicated to Mihail Sadoveanu, takes place in early November. For details contact *Centrul de Creaţie Populară*, Str Ştefan cel Mare 18, Piatra Neamţ, ☎ 033 214026; fax 231888.

Târgu Neamţ

Heading south from Suceava, 31km to the south of Fălticeni a road heads off from the DN2 for Târgu Neamţ. The town is an industrial centre whose population increased dramatically after 1971, and it has few facilities for visitors. However, it does make a focal point for visiting some lovely churches to the north and west.

Practical information

☎ **code**
033

Tourist information
Tours Arcadia is at B-dul Eminescu bl M9, ☎ 662043.

Getting around
By train The station is signposted from the bus station.
By bus The bus station is on Str Cuza Voda.

Money
Banca Comercială Ion Tiriac is at Str Mihai Eminescu bl M11.

Shopping

As you drive west along the main street of Târgu Neamț, past the signpost to Cetatea Neamț you will come to a row of shops and parking spaces; behind these, open during weekdays, is a square containing an open-air fruit and vegetable **market** and several **shops** selling meat, cheese, chocolate, washing powder and other essentials for the intrepid traveller.

Mihai Eminescu enthusiasts may want to visit **Casa Memorială Veronica Micle** at Str Ștefan cel Mare 34. This is the home of the Romantic poet's sweetheart. Veronica Micle was a poet in her own right as well as being a woman of great beauty. Married very young to a man she did not love, she and Eminescu conducted an archetypally tragic love affair in the Romantic mode, and she committed suicide soon after he died of syphilis. Open Tues–Sun 09.00–17.00. However, apart from writer Ion Creangă's old school at Str Ștefan cel Mare 37, which has become an **ethnographic museum**, open Tues–Sun 10.00–18.00 in summer, 09.00–17 00 in winter, and a huge **hospital**, Spitalul Orășenesc, founded in 1852, the town holds very little else of interest.

Neamț Citadel and monastery

Before you shake the dust of Târgu Neamț from your feet, c 2km to the north of Târgu Neamț, impressive on the side of a hill stands Cetatea Neamțului (Neamț Citadel). Although clearly a ruin, its walls are virtually intact, and from a distance the fortress looks both sturdy and forbidding. Closer to, as you walk across the man-made causeway that allows you into its colossal interior, it sustains this impression, but you become aware of its elegance as well. Cetatea Neamț is, superlatives aside, one of the most striking medieval citadels in Romania. Built for prince Petru I Mușat (r. 1382–87), on Culmea Pleșului, the citadel towers over the surrounding countryside. The bridge was designed so that enemies could be catapulted into an *oubliette* below, but the trap has long since been dismantled. Any engineer worth his or her salt will marvel at the sheer audacity which created this building. Bringing the stone here must have taken weeks, and then, without any mechanical assistance, the masons raised walls of such breathtaking sheerness that from a distance they appear to be made of dressed stone—in fact, they are rough-cast.

Ștefan cel Mare raised the old walls and added four circular bastions at the north end. After the Battle of Războieni in 1476, Mehmet II laid siege to Neamț citadel, but it proved too strong even for him. The Sultan's Italian secretary recorded that the Moldavians refused to negotiate with the Turks and bombarded them mercilessly with artillery fire. In 1691 a small group of peasants held it from Jan Sobieski and his Polish army. Open Tues–Sun 10.00–16.00.

Ion Creangă's Cottage and Nicolae Popa's Mask Museum

Ion Creangă belonged to the same charmed (or doomed) circle as Mihai Eminescu and Veronica Micle, and he grew up nearby. Drive south from Târgu Neamț, taking the left-hand turning at the main crossroads after the bridge, and on the way through the neighbouring village of **Humulești** you will pass the little cottage in which Creangă grew up. It costs almost nothing to go inside, and even if you are not interested in Creangă's career, doing so will show you the interior of a typical and very compact 19C peasant home.

Continue on the same road until you reach Grumăzeşti, and take the sharp left fork in the village. About 3km beyond this, a turning to the right beside an isolated house brings you into **Târpeşti**. The turning comes just after a sign saying Petricani—if you pass the sign to Boiştea, you have gone too far. Drive over the bridge in Târpeşti, follow the road round a bend and take the left turning signposted Muzeu Nicolae Popa. Take the left-hand fork at the other end of the green, and keep right until you reach the end of the road. The entrance is through a traditional wooden gateway to the right of the parking area. The **Popa Museum**, open every day 09.00–19.00, is a private ethnographic, art and archaeological collection. Being less didactic than most of the county museums, it is also more idiosyncratic, and in many ways a lot more attractive.

In the 1960s a bored Nicolae Popa tried his hand at modelling the clay figurines he had seen archaeologists excavating at the Neolithic site near his village. When he heard them complaining that all their finds were damaged, he secretly put some of his own figurines in the excavation site. The rest, as they say, is history. His successful deception led to a career in sculpture and then into mask-making, which has earned him an international reputation. His stone carvings are jokey representations of Dacian figures, and he has a great affection for Brâncuşi's sculptures, so much so that he has carved his own version of *The Kiss*. Nicolae is now in his eighties and has given up making masks for the ritual pageants that take place at New Year. If you visit the museum you will see examples of his own masks and of many other colourful costumes that feature in the New Year's rituals, showing how Romanians have interwoven pagan folklore with Christian religious practices.

At **Vânători-Neamţ**, 6km to the west, is the memorial house of writer Mihail Sadoveanu, open Tues–Sun 10.00–18.00. 6km further west of Târgu Neamţ on the DN15B, and 4km down a signposted side road to the right lies **Mănăstirea Neamţ**. Before you reach the turning, an isolated roadside *han* offers excellent if unimaginative meals and nearby, well signposted, after you turn right among the fir trees and head down hill for Neamţ, is a special reserve for *zimbri* (bison).

Neamţ is the oldest monastery in the principality and a highpoint of Moldavian church architecture since the 1960s, when it was carefully restored. It was originally a simple skete founded by Petru I Muşat, but Alexandru cel Bun rebuilt it in the 15C and established a printing workshop and a library here, both of which greatly added to the monastery's renown. Today Neamţ owns the largest conventual library in Romania, containing around 18,000 books. Ştefan cel Mare altered the church still further. In commemoration of his defeat of Poland in 1497, his architects extended the nave to the east by expanding the bay in front of the apse and adding a tomb chamber between naos and pronaos.

The plan fuses two styles of church building that had been current in Moldavia since Bogdan built his basilica in Rădăuţi (see p 206) and Petru Muşat commissioned the Serbian trefoil plan for his church at Siret: here the basilica and trefoil merge, so that the exterior looks Western and the interior Byzantine, with a vast central space enclosed by clusters of apses and crowned by pendentives and domes. The size and grandeur of the enlarged church set the standard for 16C monasteries across Moldavia, although here the *gropniţa* is not yet separated from the naos by a wall. You can see the results of this new concept at Bistriţa and some of the Bucovina monasteries (Humor, Putna, Sf Gheorghe in Suceava and Suceviţa). Neamţ's open porch (exonarthex) was added to the pre-existing west end of the pronaos. The Gothic-style windows show a debt to western Europe, while the triangular pediment at the west end is a 19C afterthought.

The church is huge, with an overall length of over 40m, making it only a fraction smaller than Sf Gheorghe in Suceava. The church and arcaded cells stand in a fortified quad, an attractive mix of period statements in warm-coloured stone. A late-18C church dedicated to Sf Gheorghe abuts the east perimeter wall. In the pathway leading from the entrance to the church a stone marks the spot where, in the early 1990s, a monk noticed that some of the slabs had inexplicably been raised. Archaeologists who dug underneath found the bones of a man thought to have been Paisie Velicikovschi (1722–94), an abbot of Neamț who was canonised for his outstanding dedication to the monastic life. Sf Paisie de la Neamț, as he is also known, became a monk while studying on Mount Athos. Inspired by the ancient wisdom of the Holy Mountain, he came to Moldavia in 1763. A few years later he settled at Neamț, where he translated many important religious texts into Romanian. Among them was the Jesus Prayer which hesychastic monks chant to themselves all day long. Paisie Velicikovschi is regarded as one of the greatest abbots Romania has ever known.

Neamț's reputation as a centre of religious teaching owes a lot to the school of calligraphers and miniature painters which Gavriil Uric founded here in the 16C. You can see examples of its delicate work in the museum. Chroniclers Macarie and Eftimie also lived in the monastery, and Veniamin Costachi's printing press, which became part of the highly regarded Trinitas Press of the Metropolitanate of Moldavia, began its life here in 1808. Apart from the monastery museum and library, treasures from the church at Secu are also kept here, in a separate museum open Tues–Sun 09.00–18.00.

Next to the monastery quadrangle stands a seminary which has produced many of Moldavia's greatest religious leaders. The monastery church is dedicated to the Ascension, commemorated with a special service 40 days after Orthodox Easter. Neamț celebrated its 500th anniversary in 1999. Neamț also owns a great deal of land around the monastery and has its own vineyards at Cotnari. Not far away are the satellite hermitages of Vovidenia, Icoana and Pocrov, emphasising the fact that Neamț is a very important spiritual centre for this region. Many Romanians are sceptical about the role of the Orthodox church in view of its ambiguous position during the communist period, but as an outsider it is hard not to be impressed by the sobriety and dedication with which Romanian monks and nuns conduct themselves.

Visitors may stay at Neamț by agreement with the *stareț* (abbot), but all lay people are asked to remember that this is a place of retreat and not a hotel. There is a tap from which you can take drinking water in the church courtyard, and during the summer there is a little stall outside selling Fanta and beer. At Neamț as at many of the more popular monasteries, Romany women and children tend to congregate around the entrance, where they will beg you very appealingly for money or clothes.

Secu, Sihăstria and Sihla

The monasteries of Secu and Sihăstria and the Sihla skete are also connected to Neamț. They lie to the south of Neamț, tucked away in the majestically forested mountains called Munții Neamțului. Drive west on the DN15B towards Pipirig and turn left down an unasphalted road as you enter the village of Leghin. Follow the forest road into the mountains; the religious houses are signposted, but they are intentionally remote and it is easy to get lost. It may take an hour or more to reach Sihla by car. You can take an ordinary car up these roads, but they are designed for horse-drawn logging waggons and a 4WD might be more suitable. You may come across black-robed monks working with tractors in the mountains. The monasteries support themselves through farming and forestry, and although they live an ascetic life the monks have to work hard as well. If you are walking or using a mountain bike, take food, drink, insect repellent and a compass; it might also be wise to take some camping gear in case you have to sleep out overnight. It is a tough but rewarding climb. The views from the clearings are superb and you will be travelling through mixed forest with a fascinating and complex ecosystem that has not (yet) been destroyed by mindless exploitation. These mountains, and the mountains of this part of the Carpathians in general, are probably the closest thing to Paradise that Europe has to offer.

Secu monastery, dedicated to the Beheading of the Prophet John the Baptist, lies 16km west of Tărgu Neamţ. Nestor Ureche, a distinguished magistrate and the father of chronicler Grigore Ureche, endowed the monastery together with his wife, Mitrofana. He founded a stone church on the site of a former wooden hermitage called Zosin. Today the monastery has four churches. The largest is also the oldest and the most interesting. Completed in 1605 during the reign of Ieremia Movilă, it has been altered and extended several times since then: a porch was added in the 18C and during the early 19C, it gained a new altar, diaconimum and a smaller porch at the west end. In 1850 all the interior murals were restored. Outside, the original walls and towers were altered in the mid-17C, when Vasile Lupu was on the throne. Its murals were redone in 1850. A 17C paraclis (chapel or winter church) and two smaller churches from the 18C and 1832 respectively stand nearby. A fortified wall surrounds the paraclis. There is a museum containing many pieces from Secu's old treasury; these include pieces of intricately embroidered vestments and mid 17C Slavonic manuscripts.

Sihăstria, which lies 4kms to the south of Secu, is a much larger community. Today it houses 110 monks, about twice as many as Secu and Neamţ.

Archbishop Ghedeon of Huşi founded a wooden hermitage here between 1730–34; it stood on the foundations of a mid-17C skete. In 1821 followers of revolutionary leader Tudor Vladimirescu hid out at Sihăstria, and the church was burnt to the ground by Ottoman soldiers who were sent to hunt them down. The existing stone church was built as a replacement by Dometian, the Abbot of Neamţ, in 1824, along with the two towers which help to make Sihăstria look like a fortress. During the late 19C, after 40 years of neglect the monastery was restored again in 1910. Another fire damaged the cells and one of the chapels in 1941.

Standing in a pretty forest clearing 3km to the southwest of Sihăstria, **Sihla** is even more isolated. It functions as a skete or monastic village and is looked after by four monks who come together for religious services but otherwise live separately. Sihla was probably founded in the 16C, but it was certainly in existence

> **Father Cleopa**
> Sihăstria's fame rests largely on the reputation of Părintele (Father) Cleopa, a man of such single-minded saintliness that his death in December 1998 inspired obituaries in two British national broadsheets. Born to a family of poor small holders near Botoșani in 1912, at the age of 17 Ilie Cleopa entered Sihăstria monastery with three of his brothers. During the communist period, Părintele Cleopa was persecuted for refusing to turn away pilgrims. In 1956, rather than face imprisonment or worse he hid in the houses of two sympathetic peasants, and only came out at night to avoid being seen. Between 1958 and 1964 he retreated into the forests between Poiana Largului and Pipirig, where he lived in an underground den. A friendly woodcutter was the only person who knew where he was. Once a month the woodcutter would bring Cleopa a sack of potatoes, and he learnt to live on one a day. As the communist regime loosened its fanatical grip Cleopa returned to Sihăstria, where he devoted himself to a life of prayer, writing and preaching. He was a spellbinding speaker and became a living legend, someone Romanians could look up to with respect and love. After the 1989 revolution he attracted thousands of pilgrims to Sihăstria, and his name was put forward for canonisation.

before 1741. The main church, dedicated to the Birth of John the Baptist, sits in a meadow on the brow of a hill, 1000m above sea level. It was rebuilt in wood by the *egumen* of Secu monastery in 1813.

100m away under a rock face stands a smaller wooden church known as **biserica dintr'un lemn** because it was cut from a single fir tree. It was endowed by Aga Ionița Pașcanu Cantacuzino in 1763. Nearby is a **cave** in which a saintly lady from Sihla called Theodora lived for 60 years during the 17C. Her relics are enshrined in the Pecerska Monastery in Kiev, where she is known as St Theodora of the Carpathians. She was made a saint by the Romanian Orthodox Church in 1992. Sihla had to close down under the communists, but it reopened in 1991. You can reach Sihla from the southern side of the mountains as well. The forest road passes Agapia convent.

Agapia and Văratec

From Târgu Neamț head west along the DN15B towards Pipirig and Borșec; c 6km west of Târgu Neamț, take the country road that is signposted left for Agapia and Văratec.

Agapia is another fine old monastic institution, which stands at the head of a narrow alpine valley, ensconced between steep protective hills. With its gleaming white towers and fortress walls it rises from the encroaching wilderness like the medieval idea of a city of light, humbling the little cottages that cling to it and discouraging frivolous thoughts.

Technically there are two convents called Agapia, but one is a small skete in the hills c 2km away. Medieval manuscripts trace the origins of this older church, **Agapia Veche** or Agapia din Deal (Old Agapia or Agapia on the Hill), to the mid-

14C, when it was founded by a hermit called Agafie. Doamna Elena, the wife of Petru Rareș, endowed a skete here in 1527, but its remote position eventually forced the monks to move down the valley. The first skete has long since disappeared; all that remains of the distant past is a little belfry endowed by Anastasia, the wife of Duca Vodă, in the late 17C, while parishioners built the present church at Agapia Veche in 1935.

Its younger sister, **Agapia Nouă** (Agapia din Vale), opened as a monastery in the mid-17C. Nuns came here for the first time in 1803, and the convent is now one of the largest communities of its kind, housing over 500 sisters. Its main church is a mishmash of styles, but stands in a pretty courtyard garden surrounded by a quadrangle of handsome verandahed buildings containing the *stareția*, refectory, cells, carpet-weaving workshops and a museum. The church is dedicated to the Archangels Michael and Gabriel, and was blessed in 1647; its neo-Classical façade dates from 1823. Major alterations transformed the church and cells between 1858–62, when the young Nicolae Grigorescu (1838–1907) decorated the entire church interior, including the icon screen. Grigorescu was Romania's leading Impressionist, but his work at Agapia dates from before this period and seems very conventional. It was also carried out in oils, which are not nearly as durable as fresco. By the mid-20C they had deteriorated badly, but they were restored in the late 1990s.

There are three other 19C churches scattered around the convent. One of them is a timber **bolniță**, a hospital church. The convent **museum** contains some fascinating fragments from the 17C iconostasis, some attractively simple oil paintings showing the convent in the surrounding countryside, a number of gorgeous flat-weave rugs and some icons by Grigorescu. Photography is not allowed in the museum, which is open 08.00–17.00.

Exempt from the closures of the communist period, Agapia's nuns wove carpets for the Ceaușescus' megadrome in the centre of Bucharest. Today the **textile workshops** mainly produce carpets, wall hangings and rugs for religious purposes, but they do have commercial sales and visitors are welcome. The designs fall into two distinct types, the large, fluorescent pink roses on a black background which are popular in churches across Romania, while the traditional ones have geometrical designs in more muted, natural colours.

A picturesque village of **wooden houses** stands outside the walled enclosure, their paintwork attractively faded by the sun and their balconies drenched with flowers. The houses were once colonised by members of Moldavia's sharpest literary and artistic set. Mihai Eminescu, Ion Creangă (1839–89), Alexandru Vlahuța (1858–1919), Ion Luca Caragiale (1852–1912), Julia Hașdeu and Calistrat Hogaș (see p 234) retreated here during the summer months to soak up the mountain air and tranquil atmosphere. You can visit Vlahuța's charming **Casa Memorială**, which contains paintings by Grigorescu and Pallady, plus all the paraphernalia that breathes life into the past. Vlahuța wrote one of the earliest monographs about Grigorescu, which was published in 1910. Open Tues–Sun 09.00–17.00.

Văratec nunnery stands a few kilometres further south in another commanding, if less exclusive, position. With a membership of over 600, it has become one of the largest convents in the world. Abbot Paisie Velicikovschi of Neamț gave his blessing to the original, wooden hermitage which a group of sisters founded here between 1781–87. Văratec was later converted into a skete and then, as its numbers grew, into a convent. The wooden church was replaced by the existing masonry church between 1808–12, but painting and decoration continued until 1841. Like the big church at Agapia it has neo-Classical elements, but these are synthesised with a traditional Moldavian style which includes a line of neo-Byzantine blind arcading under the eaves. Its windows have discreet Brâncovenesque borders incorporating Islamic-style arches and are decorated with floral motifs. It has also curious cylindrical twin towers crowned by tall helmet-shaped cupolas and a porch with a pointed onion dome. But whatever you think of the dazzling white church, it is the garden, surrounding and softening it with its pools, pergolas, tall shrubs and trailing plants that makes Văratec so special.

Apart from the museum, which contains some fine old icons and carpets, and a small shop selling pretty rugs, painted eggs and guides to the convent, Văratec has **studios** for carpet-weaving, embroidery and icon-painting. Sister Elefteria, who runs the painting studio, speaks excellent English; with the Abbess's permission, she may be willing to explain her techniques, which are based on traditional Byzantine practice. Many of the nuns take it in turns to work in the studios, and they also do the farming, milking and gardening that help to maintain the convent as a self-sufficient organisation. There is a guest house here, but it is normally reserved for the Bishop; foreign visitors who want to stay at Văratec should apply to the Abbess. Guided tours are available in several European languages; ask at the entrance if you want one. Women must wear skirts below the knee if they want to visit the church and the museum; wraparound skirts are provided.

Many of the sisters live in the village, sharing traditional one-storey houses with their own gardens. Their life may seem idyllic but in fact it is extremely tough, demanding total dedication and an ability to function with only a few hours sleep every night.

The marble **tomb** of Eminescu's lover, the poetess Veronica Micle, stands in the convent cemetery. In his poem *Călin* Eminescu described *pădurea de argint* and *codri de aramă* (the silver forest and woods of bronze) that cloak the hills just above Văratec. They are still inviting, and if you climb up through the village behind the convent there are forest roads which bring you across the mountains to the south and east.

Follow the road south from Văratec and you reach **Bălţăteşti**, a health resort and spa whose sulphurous and iodine rich springs are used in the treatment of many ailments, including rheumatism, skin complaints, breathing and gynaecological problems. Salt from the springs is bottled so that you can use it in baths at home.

Drive south through Crăcăoani and cross the Cracău stream to the south and you will see signs to **Horaiţa**, a monastery founded in 1725. Its church was replaced in 1867 with the amazing building with eight spires that you see today. Horaicioara Hermitage stands c 1km away. Both are well worth a detour.

Războieni

To the southeast of Târgu Neamţ and far from the beaten tourist track, the magnificent convent of Războieni stands in a pastoral setting that resembles Victorian prints of rural England, except that the stately trees in the meadows are acacias instead of elms. But this is the edge of the Moldavian Plain, and at night you can see lights from across the Prut in neighbouring Moldova. In spring the swooping, liquid song of the bee-eaters and the sound of cuckoos and woodpeckers making merry can seriously interfere with polite conversation.

You can reach Războieni by road from two main directions. From the north–south E85/DN2 between Roman and the turning to Paşcani, drive west along the country road through Tupilaţi and over the Moldova River. Keep heading west until you reach Războieni de Jos, which is c 9km from the E85. When you get there, turn right at the *primăriă* (town hall) and ask for *mănăstirea* (the monastery/convent). Before you leave the E85 on the way to Războieni you may come to a place called Hanul lui Ancuţa (Ancuţa's Inn). This is one of the oldest resting places for travellers in the country; it has been there for centuries.

Alternatively, if you are coming from Bălţăteşti and the northwest, continue south through Bodeşti to Dobreni (c 20km) and after another 6–7km you should reach a left turn signposted for Ştefan cel Mare, which brings you across the Cracău stream and through Girov. Turn left in Girov for Ştefan cel Mare, and you should come to Războieni in 10km shortly after passing a lake on your right. Turn left at the *primăriă* and follow the road through the village to the right. This area is not well signposted and has few natural landmarks. Consult your map before setting out, and be prepared to stop and ask the way.

Războieni church towers over a perimeter wall that was built for defence, but is now little more than a gentle reminder of the demarcation line between the fields, which the nuns work for themselves, and the churchyard garden with its scattering of pretty trees. An impressive, pagoda-like gatetower guards the front entrance to the convent, but there is no sense in which Războieni is a fortress now. Its sisters take an active part in village life, and the only thing the nuns ask of visitors is that they should respect the atmosphere of peace within their walls.

The church is an austere and lovely example of Moldavian architecture from the time of Ştefan cel Mare. In fact it was founded by Ştefan after one of his most devastating campaigns against the Turks. It has no tower; the one added by 19C restorers was taken away during the communist period so that the church now looks almost exactly as it did in Ştefan's day.

History

Six months after Ştefan cel Mare used clever guerrilla tactics to rout the Ottomans from Podul Înalt near Vaslui, an army of 200,000 Turks returned to Moldavia. Ştefan had only 16,000 men at his disposal, and these were mainly boyars and *răzeşi* (yeomen) because the peasants were too busy to leave their fields. His requests for help from Western Europe fell on deaf ears. Overwhelmed by the sheer size of the Ottoman force, he made a final stand on top of a wooded hill beside the Albă stream hill about 6km to the east of the convent. The place is marked today by a simple cross, and fragments of brick and pottery have been found on the site of Ştefan's makeshift fortress.

On 26 July 1476, Turkish soldiers attacked the Moldavian encampment. They slaughtered almost all of Ștefan's men but he escaped at night, turning defeat into victory another day. The bodies of his loyal followers strewed the meadows for miles around, and their whitened bones lay there for decades afterwards as proof of their courageous sacrifice. The valley and the river which runs through the battleground are said to have been called Valea Albă and Pârăul Albă for this reason, but the names were there beforehand.

Returning here in 1496, Ștefan founded the church and the monastery as a memorial to the dead; the church itself stands on the bones of his men, and the monastery was called Războieni after the battle. The village grew up around it.

Above the entrance to the west end of the church a stone slab bears Ștefan's personal memorial to the Moldavians who died fighting for him at Valea Albă. It is a poignant document, couched in simple, dignified Slavonic that has the power to bring his grief vividly to mind. There is a Romanian translation in the *starețía* which faces the east end of the church.

Războieni is a poor village, and the convent's farmland borders a rundown lunatic asylum. The piteous and ear-splitting yells of its inhabitants will probably be the only thing that disturbs an otherwise idyllic experience. On a clear evening you can see lights of towns and villages in the Moldovan Republic, across the plain to the east.

Ștefan cel Mare's inscription

The *pisanie* (founder's inscription) above the west end of Războieni church contains one of the longest and most impressive statements that Ștefan left behind him. John Nandriș has made this translation: 'In this era of the holy and loving Christ, I Lord Stephen, by the grace of God Lord of the land of Moldavia, son of Prince Bogdan, in the year 6984 [1476 in the Byzantine calendar], in the 20th year of my reign, the powerful Emperor Mahomet [Mehmet II] rose up with all his eastern power, and Lord Basarab, called Laiotă, and all his followers, came with me. And the Turks came to destroy and lay waste the land of Moldavia. And they arrived here, at the place known as White Stream. And we, Lord Stephen, and our son Alexandru, came out and faced them as the sheepdog comes out to defend his fold, and we waged a great war against them, on the 26th day of July. And it was God's will that the Christians should be defeated by the pagans and a great multitude of Moldavian men fell there. At the same time, the Tartars also attacked Moldavia from the east.

'And for this reason, I, Stephen, built this temple sincerely in the name of the Archangel Michael, with the prayers of the Lady Maria and my sons Alexandru and Bogdan and in memory of all those right-thinking Christians who perished here. This I did in the year 7004 [1496], in the 40th year of my reign.'

(Laiotă was one of Ștefan's supporters from Wallachia; after this campaign he betrayed Ștefan, who went after him and killed him.)

SOUTHERN NEAMŢ

25km south of Târgu Neamţ as the crow flies, the metropolis of Piatra Neamţ nestles at the foot of a crag on whose summit Teutonic Knights built a fortress in the 13C. Wooded hills also help to soften its hard edges, so that the severely restructured city has an unpretentious charm.

Piatra Neamţ

A great change has taken place here since the 1989 revolution: then Piatra Neamţ was grim and desperate, but now it is a bustling town whose optimism shows in the posters advertising theatre and concerts, and the boutiques and bright delicatessens that line the shopping streets. Take a mid-morning capuccino and sticky cake at the terrace café near *Hotel Ceahlău*, and you can imagine yourself in a Mediterranean mountain resort.

Piatra Neamţ has several interesting museums as well as a fine 15C church and at least one more than adequate hotel. Twenty minutes' drive away stands the monastery of **Bistriţa**, a wonderfully venerable Moldavian-style church in an equally splendid setting. At **Bâtca Doamnei** near Piatra Neamţ are the remains of a Dacian citadel called Petrodava, which Ptolemy mentioned in 106 BC. Vestiges of massive walls, a sanctuary and dwelling houses have been found on this site.

Practical information

☎ code
033

Tourist information
AS is at Str Mihai Viteazul 4, bl 11, ☎ 231790; *BTT* at B-dul Republicii bl A2, ☎ 214686; *Dosoftei-Mioritic Tour* at Piaţa Ştefan cel Mare bl C2, ap 37, ☎ 231575; *Forum* at Str Eminescu 10, ☎ 233190; and *Sind România* at Str Petru Rareş 27C, ☎ 222550.

Getting around

By train The station is at Piaţa Mareşal Antonescu 1, ☎ 210941. The *CFR* booking office, which shares the same phone number, is at Piaţa Ştefan cel Mare bl C5.

By bus The bus station is beside the train station, at Str Bistritei 1.

By car For **car repairs** and servicing, *ACR* has an office at Str Traian bl S1, ☎ 215535, or try *Bosch Service Tutuianu* at Str Oltenei 8A, ☎ 632070. **Petrol** is available from *Oil Supermarket* at Str Gen. Dascalescu 401.

By taxi ☎ 953.

By plane *TAROM* has an office on Str Alexandru cel Bun.

Where to stay
The three main hotels are *Ceahlău* (✫✫) at Piaţa Ştefan cel Mare 1, ☎/fax 233559, *Central* (✫✫) at B-dul Republicii 26, ☎ 216412; fax 214532, and *Pietricica* (✫✫) at Str Alexandru cel Bun 27. All of these should be able to give tourist information. *ANTREC* may be able to find you a bed in a private farmhouse; ☎ 212890 *internat* 228. but if you have no luck try the head office in Bucharest (see p 116).

Eating out

Hotel Ceahlău has an excellent restaurant which serves the typically meat-based menu preferred by most Romanians; ideal for carnivores, the food is fresh, beautifully cooked, served with a smile—and there is plenty of it.

Post office

This is at Str Alexandru cel Bun 21.

 ## Money

CEC is at Str Ozana 2, bl M1, and *Banca Comercială* is at Str Eminescu bl M1. The *Hotel Ceauhlău* at Piaţa Ştefan cel Mare 1 has an **exchange desk**. Do not be put off by *Nasty Change*'s name; this exchange desk inside a delicatessen a few metres from the *Hotel Ceahlău* offers very competitive rates and takes sterling as well as other hard currencies.

Police

The station is on Str Tesatoarei, ☎ 216050.

Medical care

In an emergency ☎ 961; the town **hospital** and **polyclinic** are at B-dul Traian 1. There is a *Farmavit* **pharmacy** at Piaţa Ştefan cel Mare 111, ☎ 212666.

 ## Shopping

Piatra is well equipped for basic food shopping; for the fashion-conscious, there are also smart shoe shops and boutiques, and if you ask at *Hotel Ceahlău*, you will be able to find someone who does shoe repairs.

 ## Other activities

On the south side of Piatra Neamţ, at the foot of wooded hills across the railway tracks, is a **sports complex** which contains a swimming pool, running tracks and a hippodrome. You may be able to book **rides** from the hippodrome into the surrounding hills.

The historic centre of Piatra Neamţ survives in a few fine but beleagured buildings, most of them huddled together like shorn lambs in Piaţa Libertăţii. Ştefan cel Mare founded **Biserica Sf Ioan** (St John's Church) in 1491. Dominating Piaţa Libertăţii and standing above a small municipal park and the town's main shopping streets, it once formed part of a group of court buildings. These have all disappeared, except for the **watchtower**, which was completed in 1499, and some cellars. The church is very handsome and is decorated in the Byzantine style, with courses of brickwork alternating with stone. Its interior walls are dark and what painting there is is uninteresting. Nearby in the same cultural enclave stand two **museums**, one devoted to fine art and the other to ethnography. They are both modest but worth seeing if you are curious; the art museum is housed in the kind of fine, Neo-Brâncovenesque building that is characteristic of late-19C and early-20C municipal architecture in Moldavia. Its holdings include some pleasantly modernistic rural scenes by Dimitrie Ghiaţa (1888–1942) and a few striking portraits by Nicolae Toniţa (1886–1940). Both museums are open Tues–Sun 10.00–18.00.

A few minutes' walk from Piaţa Libertăţii brings you into Str Dr Ernici, which contains two **synagogues** side by side. From Sf Ioan, head past the *primăria*, town hall) on your right, and turn right up the cobbled hill. The older synagogue, lower down the hill, has some fascinating wall paintings showing Piatra in former times. Jewish people who wish to trace forebears who fled from northern Moldavia during the 20C pogroms may find that the caretakers are willing to help them by looking at cemetery archives. Restorations are being carried out here.

If your taste leans towards **churches**, there are several interesting ones in the outskirts of Piatra Neamţ: these include the wooden church at **Văleni**, which had an influential painting school in the 16C and 17C; the churches at **Vânători** (1776) and **Sărata** (1780); the **Cozla** skete (1769) and the 18C stone churches in the **Doamna** and **Dărmăneşti** quarters. But apart from Sf Ioan in Piatra itself, the finest church in the vicinity is the monastery church at Bistriţa.

The **Museum of History** at Str Mihai Eminescu 10 has an excellent collection of Neolithic pottery, and even if the thought of pouring over dusty relics does not attract you, give it a chance. These ceramics come mainly from the Cucuteni culture which flourished in what is now northeast Moldavia, and some of the pieces, with their bold, stripey designs and sexy shapes, are beautiful. Groups of miniature clay figurines laid out in circles represent, alternately, males and females, and models of houses from the same period can plunge you into intense speculation about the people who made these things 5000 years ago. These 'gods' and 'goddesses' have been found inside clay vessels in burial sites and in houses. Nobody knows what they were for, but they are almost certainly religious, while the little figures in their circular arrangements look as though they are dancing a *hora*, the round dances that play a vital part in Romania's traditional culture. The Neolithic finds come from sites at Frumuşica, Târpeşti, Izvoare, Poduri and Răuceşti.

Museums can be dead places at the best of times, and although this one is housed in a splendid late-19C building it has a serious funding problem. There isn't any. It does contain one delightful room modelled on a Stone Age home, and if you can see its dingy displays and the didactic notices as a piece of history in themselves, this relic of communism becomes a lot more intriguing than it might otherwise be. There are also interesting things to see from the time of Ştefan cel Mare. Open Tues–Sun 09.00–17.00.

Another point of interest in Piatra Neamţ is the attractive **bungalow** that was home to poet and teacher Calistrat Hogaş (1847–1917) at Str C. Hogaş 1. Well-known around town for his magisterial figure and wide-brimmed straw hat, Hogaş wrote movingly about his travels in the Moldavian mountains. His books include *Amîntiri Dintr-o Călătorie* (*Memoirs of a Journey*, 1882–84) and *Pe Drumuri* (*On the Road*, 1912), and his philosophy can be summed up in the phrase, '*Risul si veselia sunt piperul si sarea vieţii*' ('Laughter and happiness are the salt and pepper of life'). The modest house contains his library, furniture and personal effects; it also shows how the centre of Piatra Neamţ used to look before restructurung took place.

Piatra Neamţ is also very close to the Bicaz Gorges (see p 221). These impressive rock formations rise like cathedrals on either side of the Bicaz pass into Transylvania. Magnificent **wooden houses** still survive in the countryside around Neamţ. It takes a practised eye to tell the stylistic differences between them, but the real beauty of these vernacular buildings lies in their simplicity and their satisfying proportions, irrespective of where they belong. In northern Moldavia village houses evolved from single-room boxes-with-verandahs to more sophisticated three-room farmsteads that, to our eyes, seem impossibly modest.

In time they acquired the handsome, roofed gateways and carved wooden fences that can be seen all over rural Romania.

The shape of Romania's oldest farmhouses is said to have been based on the *mageron*, the living-cum-storage spaces used by farmers in antiquity. It is interesting to compare them with the modern brick-and-wood houses that are springing up all over northern Moldavia (and across Romania as a whole). Some of these new buildings belong to Roma and they resemble Oriental pagodas: they are often three or four storeys high, decorated all over with fancy turrets and domes made of zinc. Although it is usually only rich Gypsies who build with such effervescence, it is not only them: new village houses may be built of clay and straw bricks, but they are often equipped with patterned zinc domes. Their arched gateways and guttering come ornamented with cut-out rosettes and sometimes with animals and birds as well. These glorious decorations are often carried on into well heads and fences.

8km west of Piatra Neamţ, just to the north off the DN15, stands the rugged and beautiful monastery of **Bistriţa**. Head north at the sign to the monastery c 1km after you leave Piatra on the main road west to the Bicaz Gorges and Gheorgheni; the monastery lies within the comuna of Viişoara. Petru I Musat began to develop the site for a masonry church on the foundations of a wooden one in the 14C. It was completed for Alexandru cel Bun sometime before 1407, and seven years after he placed the Moldavian church under the jurisdiction of Constantinople. Medieval chroniclers differ over the details, but they agree that in return the prince received a beautiful icon, either from John II Paleologus or Emperor Emanuel. The icon was the work of Byzantine monks; it was painted in 1350 and depicted the name saint of Alexandru's wife, Sfa Ana. It hangs in the naos, and to this day, Sfa Ana works miracles for believers who are convinced that she can both heal them and bring them luck. Alexandru and Ana are buried in the church.

The church and its museum contain several fine icons from the 15C, 16C and 17C. The monastery **museum** is a monument in itself; it was commissioned by the Craoiveşti brothers and was raised between 1491–94. Open Tues–Sun 09.00–18.00.

Petru Rareş rebuilt the **church** between 1541–46, as did Alexandru Lăpuşneanu in 1554. Its architecture is majestic and sober; some of the stonework has Gothic elements. In Ştefan cel Mare's bell tower (1498) there are fragments of 15C, 16C and 19C frescoes. He also founded a paraclis (chapel or winter church) in the tower in 1494, and Petru Rareş built another nearby. Under Ştefan cel Mare, Bistriţa became an important cultural centre.

It remained open during the communist period, and is now a thriving cenobitic foundation with 50 monks. As in many Romanian monasteries and convents, the monks cultivate and make their own food and drink, including some of the best home-brewed *ţuică* you are likely to find—it is steeped in a special root found only in the mountains. Bistriţa has a tradition of welcoming travellers which dates back to its foundation; if you are offered hospitality here, do not abuse it by taking it for granted. If you come here at the start of post, the Orthodox fast which begins on the first Sunday in June and ends on the last, you will be treated to a deafening concert of bells and *toacă* playing that is far more electrifying than anything you could ever hear in the repertoire of the Western church. It has to be experienced to be believed. Bistriţa is dedicated to Adormirea Maicii Domnului (the Dormition of the Virgin), celebrated on 15 August, and Izvorul Tămăduirii, celebrated on the first Friday after Orthodox Easter.

Almost due east of Piatra Neamţ lies the industrial town of **Roman**. Its main building of historic architectural interest is the **Episcopal Church**, which was begun under Petru Rareş in 1542 and completed during the reign of his son, Iliaş. Inside are some original 16C frescoes.

Bacău

If you take the main E85/DN2 south you will reach Bacău, the county town of Bacău *judeţ*. A local poet, George Bacovia, bemoaned its leaden skies and filthy air. But during the 1990s industrial Bacău has cleaned up its act enough to make it worth putting a foot down here, even if it is only to see **Biserica Precista**, which Ştefan cel Mare's son Alexandru built in 1490. You may also visit the ruins of Ştefan's court, dating from 1481. Bacău is one of the few places in Moldavia which still has a sizeable population of Csángó people. Originally Hungarian-speaking refugees from Transylvania, the Csángó now speak a mixture of Hungarian and Romanian.

Ştefan was born in what is now Bacău county, at **Borzeşti** (1436). He commissioned a church there in memory of his childhood friend Gheorghiţă, who died near the village while fighting the Tartars. Ştefan also founded Runc Monastery at **Buhuşi** in 1457, giving the lie to guide books which tell you that his first monastery was the one at Putna. There is another fine monastery at **Târgu Ocna**, built this time for Radu Racoviţa in 1664.

The 1907 peasant uprising flared up in Bacău and was brutally crushed, and during the First World War Romanian soldiers fought with great heroism at the battles of Caşin, Oituz and Cireşoiaia, all of which lie within the county boundaries. The health spa of **Slanic Moldova** in the mountains to the west is grand and very popular. It boasts 20 separate springs, each of which has a different mineral content. Mihail Sadoveanu sent the heroine of his story, *Baltagul* (*The Hatchet*), on her epic journey from Măgura Tarcăului in Munţii Tarcăului to the northwest.

Bacău has its own specific traditions, and you will be able to learn more about these if you visit the villages of **Brusturoasa**, **Caşin**, **Oituz** and **Sălătruc**. The craftspeople who live here make carpets and rugs, pottery and wooden gates. For more details about these crafts and about Bacău's folk music and dance festivals, contact *Centrul de Creaţie Populară*, Str Caisilor 7, Bacău, ☎ 034 113356, or the **County Ethnographic and Art Museum** at Str Nicolae Tiţulescu 23, which is open Tues–Sun 09.00–17.00.

Practical information

☎ **code**
034

Tourist information

Tourist offices include *Decebal* at Str Bălcescu 12, ☎ 146246; *Inter Tour* at Str Alexandru cel Bun 1, ☎ 170534; and *Sind România* at Str 9 Mai 21, ☎ 112137.

Getting around

By rail The station is on Str Bălcescu, where there also is a *CFR* office at no. 12, ☎ 146340. *TAROM* is at Str Bălcescu 1, ☎ 181749.
By bus The bus station is on Str Unirii. *Trans Europa Bus Tours* is at Str Eroul Ciprian Pintea 2, ☎ 170534.
By plane There is an airport to the south of the city.
By car *ACR* is at Str Bălcescu 12, ☎ 145212. For **car servicing**, try *Turimprest* at Calea Bârladului 133, ☎ 134954.

Where to stay

Among the best hotels are *Hotel Decebal* (✩✩), Str Ioniţa Sandu Sturza 2, ☎ 146211; *Hotel Moldova*, Str Bălcescu 16, ☎ 146322.

Money

Banks include *Banca Agricolă*, Str Iernii 1; *Banca Ion Tiriac*, Str Mihai Viteazul 2; *Banca Naţionala al României*, Str Bacovia 6; *Bancorex*, Str 9 Mai. There is an **exchange desk** at *ACR*, Str Bălcescu 12.

Medical services

Pharmacies include *Elpis Farm*, Str Ştefan cel Mare 7; *Farmarfil*, Str Carpaţi 2; *Medifarm*, Str Mihai Viteazu 1. For the **hospital**, ☎ 134000.

EAST MOLDAVIA

The northern Moldavian Plain rolls east from Bucovina to the Prut River and the Moldovan border. Its main focal point is Iaşi, an ancient city whose brilliant cultural life once brought the world to its gates.

Iaşi

Known in traditional English form as Jassy, Iaşi still holds its own as Moldavia's cultural capital, and this is where you must come if you crave sophisticated urban delights such as theatres, discos and bars.

History

Traces of Stone Age settlement have been found in Iaşi, but the city as it stands today was founded in the Middle Ages. At the end of the 14C it was a modest market place but soon went through a rapid development thanks to the opening of trade routes with Poland. By 1408 Iaşi was advanced enough for Alexandru cel Bun to offer commercial privileges there to the merchants of L'vov. By the 16C it had been transformed into the capital of Moldavia, taking precedence over Suceava and all the other towns where the country's princes had previously established their courts.

Iaşi's academic traditions go back to the 14C, and in 1562 despot Vodă founded the so-called *Schola Latina* (Latin College) in nearby Cotnari. This marked the start of organised humanistic education in this part of Romania.

After Mehmet II took Constantinople in 1453, Moldavian nobles maintained their ancient links with the patriarchate in the Phanar district, but the political situation was very fluid and they also enjoyed friendly relations with the Sultan and the Porte. Princes such as Vasile Lupu (r. 1634–53 and April–

July 1653) and his son Ştefăniţa (r. 1659–61 and February–September 1661) built opulent palaces in Iaşi, and despite their vassalage to the Turks, saw themselves as the new Byzantine emperors. As the Church's power dwindled in Constantinople, Moldavian princes took on a more central role in supporting Orthodox monasteries abroad. One result of this was that several of Iaşi's churches and monasteries, and the lands that went with them, were given up to the control of the patriarchate in Jerusalem and many Greek monks came to settle in the city.

Vasile Lupu encouraged scholarship and thanks to his influence, the Patriarch of Kiev had a printing press installed at Trei Ierarhi. Shortly afterwards Bishop Dosithei of Jerusalem supervised the opening of a Greek printing house at Cetăţuia monastery just outside Iaşi. These presses were mainly used for the production of religious texts for distribution in the Near East, where Christians were under greater pressure from the Ottoman authorities. Vasile Lupu also founded a school in the city called the Vasilian College. Between 1600 and 1750 scholars, merchants and diplomats came here from the Near East and from Russia, Poland and Hungary and from Western Europe.

During the 16C and 17C, Iaşi was the most influential city on the Carpathians' eastern rim. Standing on the main route between Kraków and Constantinople, it formed part of a group of trading states similar to the Hanseatic League. In the 18C, Arabic was taught in Iaşi's Greek Academy, and during the Phanariot period (early 18C–early 19C) Greek priests who had flocked to Moldavia to escape persecution under the Turks used the city's printing presses in an attempt to establish Greek as the main liturgical language.

In the autumn of 1813, the scholar-engineer Gheorghe Asachi established a school for surveyors and building engineers in the precincts of Iaşi's Greek Academy. The *Academia Mihăilena* (Michaelian Academy) opened in the city in 1835, and as a result of radical reforms following the 1859 Union, the Universities of Iaşi and Bucharest were founded within four years of each other. They were founded in 1860 and 1864 respectively, and offered courses in applied sciences and engineering.

Many eminent people have been connected to Iaşi: the chronicler, diplomat and Oriental traveller Nicolae Milescu (1636–1708), who wrote two books about China, the historian and politician Mihail Kogălniceanu (1817–91), the poets Vasile Alecsandri (c 1821–90) and Alecu Russo (1819–59), writers Mihail Sadoveanu (1880–1961), George Topârceanu, both of whom belonged to the brilliant generation of novelists that flourished between the two world wars, Ionel Teodoreanu and the literary critic Titu Maiorescu (1840–1917). Iaşi was also home to the geographer Grigore Cobălcescu, the chemist Petru Poni, the historian A.D. Xenopol (1847–1920), author of the first full-scale analysis of Romanian history, the philosopher Vasile Conta, the founder of Romanian sociology Dimitrie Gusti, the geographer Emil Racoviţă, the philosopher Petru Andrei, the painter Octav Băncilă and many others who were either born and or educated here.

Iaşi remained a haven for artists and scholars until the Second World War. Thanks to restructuring in the 1960s and 70s, much of the old city has disappeared. The tradition of intellectual excellence survives, however, and Iaşi is still a lively and fascinating place to visit, as well as being an important industrial and commercial-banking centre.

Vasile Lupu

One of the most influential personalities to reign in Ottoman-controlled Moldavia was Prince Vasile Lupu (Basil the Wolf, r. 1634–53). Lupu was born in Albania and educated by Greek scholars in Constantinople. Once on the Moldavian throne he set about turning the principality into a latter-day Byzantium, with himself as Emperor. His court impressed English visitor Robert Bargrave so much that he compared Lupu to the Medicis. Fragments of 17C polychrome tiles from Iznik, Transylvania and Lithuania, and from a source that looks like Delft, have come to light in the area around the Culture Palace in Iași, and they give a tantalising insight into Lupu's gilded lair.

But while he lived in luxury, he believed passionately that education was 'more precious than all the earthly treasures put together'. Lupu funded the first high school and the first printing press in Moldavia. At the same time his main political significance lies in the fact that he was Protector of the Orthodox Church and under his rule, the most important religious disputes were settled in Iași rather than Constantinople.

Lupu maintained a precarious balance between submission and rebellion. At the start of his reign he allied himself closely with the Turks, but later he established a *de facto* independence from the Sultan by channelling Moldavia's resources towards the Greek monasteries in Moldavia. In return he received the support of their parent foundations in Antioch and Mount Athos, Constantinople, Jerusalem and Sinai. This symbiotic, and some would say parasitic, arrangement only came to an end in 1862, when A.I. Cuza dismissed the foreign monks from Romania altogether. (It is sometimes forgotten that the Turks were often surprisingly lenient in victory. For a while they maintained a *Pax Turcica* in the Balkans which allowed their subject nations to worship however they liked, provided they did not agitate against the Sultan—and as long as the tribute money kept rolling in.)

Ambition caused Lupu's downfall. Proclaiming himself prince of Moldavia and Wallachia he incurred the anger of Wallachian *voivode* Matei Basarab and was eventually overthrown. Lupu died an exile in Constantinople in 1661.

Practical information

☎ code
032

Tourist information

There is a tourist office in the *Centru Civic* on Str Anastasie Panu, open Mon–Fri 08.00–15.00. You could also try *S.C. Moldova*, at Str Anastasie Panu 29, or the *Unirea* office at Piața Unirii 12, which is a branch of the same company and can organise tours of Moldavia, wine tastings, theatre tickets, car rental and guide-interpreters.

Getting around

By train The train station is on Str Gării to the west of the city centre; the *CFR* office is on Piața Unirii.

By bus Buses serving other cities depart from the *autogara* next to the railway station.

By plane The airport lies to the northeast of the city on Str Aeroportului, and *TAROM* has an office close to Piaţa Unirii at Str Arcu 3.

By car *ACR* is at Str Gării 13–15, ☎ 112345/130177; there are **garages** at Str Baş Ceauş, Calea Chişinaului and Str Păcurari, and B-dul Primăverii. For **petrol stations** try Şos Bucium, Str Cantacuzino, B-dul N. Iorga and Str Sărăriei. **Car hire** can be arranged from the tourist agencies or possibly through the British charity-cum-tour operator, *Link Romania*, ☎ 139915, or in England via its travel section Overthewall, ☎ 01903 529333; fax 529007; email overthewall@linkrom.org; website www.linkrom.org.

By taxi You can hire taxis from the railway station; otherwise take your pick from *Go Taxi*, ☎ 45530, *Taxicom*, ☎ 953 or 146593, *Taxi Lyon Tranz*, ☎ 214214, or *Taxi Romania*, ☎ 215555. Always agree a price beforehand.

Where to stay

There are several decent hotels in the centre of Iaşi, but if you are keen to stay downtown they range from the once super-deluxe *Unirea* (✩✩✩), with beds for over 350 people, located in a high rise block at Piaţa Unirii 5 (or 8), ☎ 142110; the slightly smaller *Moldova* (✩✩✩) at Str A. Panu 29–31, ☎ 142225; the attractively down-at-heel *Traian* (✩✩), which dates from the 19C, at Piaţa Unirii 1, ☎ 143330; the *Orizont* (✩✩) at Str G. Ureche 2, at the back of the *Moldova*, ☎ 112700; and the *Continental* (✩✩), Str Cuza Voda 2–4, ☎ 114320. At the cheapest end of the range come the *Sport* (✩), downhill from the Palace of Culture at Str Sf Lazar 76, ☎ 232800, whose comforts match its prices, and *Conest* (✩) on Aleea Nicolina, ☎ 232816, has rooms for a few dollars a night—but these are both spartan and only an option if all else fails.

Look further afield, and there are several **motels** in or near Iaşi: *Aroma Viilor* on Aleea M. Sadoveanu, ☎ 147715, *Hanul Trei Sarmale*, Şos Bucium 75, ☎ 132832, and *Motel Bucium* (✩✩✩) with 28 beds and three suites, a restaurant and all-night bar, camping site with huts, 12km on the main road from Iaşi to Vaslui, ☎ 140712; fax 211806. These last two and the *Moldova*, *Traian* and *Unirea* hotels are all owned by Turism Moldova.

Eating out

These range from decent fast-food places to the traditional dining rooms of the old Romanian hotels. *Little Texas*, near the cemetery in Str Moara de Vânt (Windmill Street), was established by a Mr Little from Texas and serves Tex-Mex food in an 'authentic' interior decorated with Western saddles and cowboy hats, open Wed–Sun. There are **pizzerias** on Str Moara de Foc (Firemill Street); the *Gelateria Italiana*, which is expensive by Romanian standards and popular with Arab and Greek students; *Mamma Mia* pizza house behind the law courts, another one on the *parter* (first floor) of a building at the corner of Str Arcu and Str Gării, and the *Pizzeria de la Gara*, near the station. There are three **students' cafés** in Str Tudor Vladimirescu, including *East 17*, which is said to make wonderful hot dogs. At the south end of B-dul Copou, *Casa Universitarilor* has a canteen where you can buy good soup and rub shoulders with college students and lecturers. There is a **French café** on Str T. Cucu.

Post offices

There is an international phone centre and post office at Str Lăpuşneanu 21. The main post office is at Str Cuza Vodă 3. It is housed in the former Balş-Sturza residence, a baronial mansion which dates from 1850.

Money

Both the *Centru Civic* and *Unirea* tourist offices have **exchange desks**; there are **banks** on B-dul Ştefan cel Mare, Str Cuza Vodă and Str Independenţei.

Medical care

There are **pharmacies** in the centre at Piaţa Unirii 3; B-dul Ştefan cel Mare, bl A 1–2, *parter*, and at no. 10; and B-dul Independenţei 25. The **hospital** is on Str Berthelot, ☎ 140690.

Shopping

On most days, an open **market** called Sf Spiridon sells fruit and vegetables beside the west end of B-dul Independenţei, and there are several shops for general **groceries** in the immediate neighbourhood.

Entertainment

Iaşi has year-round programmes of festivals and fairs: these include Festum Musicae, a classical music festival in May and a European film festival in July which specialises in documentaries about art and architecture. In September and October the city hosts a huge folk art festival called Trandafir de la Moldova (Rose of Moldavia), and Datini, the traditional winter celebrations are held in December.

The **National Theatre** (incorporating the Opera) and *Teatrul Luceafărul*, the youth theatre on Str Grigore Ureche, have a seasonal repertoire (which means they are usually closed in the summer). Iaşi has a celebrated **orchestra**, the *Moldova Philarmonic*, housed in an early 19C mansion at Cuza Vodă 29, which was also the place where *Voces*, a well-known Romanian quartet, was formed. For more information about entertainment, or tours of the city and surrounding countryside, ask the tourist agencies. Iaşi also has a few commercial **art galleries**: *Cupola* at Str Cuza Vodă 2, and *Anticariat* and *Fondului Plastic* on Str Lăpuşneanu.

Bars and **discos** have sprung up like mushrooms in the city centre; take your pick from the glittering array near hotels *Traian* and *Unirea*.

Maps and books

Being a university town, Iaşi is well supplied with bookshops. One of the best is *Junimea*, on the south side of Piaţa Unirii close to the CFR booking office. There there are several along B-dul Ştefan cel Mare, Str Anastasie Panu, Str Cuza Vodă and Str Sf Lazăr. You can buy secondhand and antiquarian books at Str Lăpuşneanu 24. Copies of a decent **map** of the city, published by Helios, are available from the shop in Palatul Culturii and also from *Junimea*. Written and compiled by two university professors and an architect, it contains brief notes on many historic monuments and listed buildings. The county council also co-publishes a book called *Iaşi*, which has an English-language edition. Contributions are from local historians Ioan Caproşu, Constantin Liviu Rusu, Ioan Holban, Dumitru Vacariu and Lucian Vasiliu. Some American, English and German magazines are on sale from the kiosks in Str Cuza Vodă.

Walking around Iaşi

The attractive neo-Gothic **train station** has a distinguished past: built in 1871, it was once a terminus on the first railway line into Moldavia from Polish Lemberg (now L'vov in Ukraine). Partially destroyed in the Second World War, the building's original shape started to emerge in 1988, when local architect Nicolae Munteanu removed an ugly clock tower. Striped and pinnacled outside, it resembles façades along Venice's Ca' Grande; inside, the halls are cloister-like.

Walking up the hill from the station and right onto Şos Arcu, you pass tiny, tumbledown **cottages** whose handkerchief-sized gardens brim with seasonal flowers and vegetables. Together with the 18C and 19C villas and low-rise apartment buildings that fill the horizon, these little wooden houses show Iaşi as it once was and to some extent still is: a provincial capital that has seen better days. Şos Arcu brings you uphill into Piaţa Unirii, where Prince A.I. Cuza (1820–73), commemorated in a dignified **statue**, declared Moldavia's unification with Wallachia in 1859.

Some of old Iaşi has been preserved in **Piaţa Unirii**: a line of terraced houses and shops on the east side of the square and, on the west side, *Hotel Traian*. The hotel is a traditional-looking neo-Classical four-storey building with two flanking wings and an elegant canopied entrance. It has an iron frame designed by Gustave Eiffel (1832–1923) eight years before he and the Swiss engineer Koechlin created the Eiffel Tower. Eiffel's connections with Iaşi were made through a university friend from the village of Ţibăneşti who introduced him to the city's mayor. The hotel restaurant was once frequented by poet Mihai Eminescu and other sparks who started Junimea, Iaşi's revolutionary literary movement; it opens at 07.00. On the north side of Unirii stands the modern block of *Hotel Unirea*.

In many ways, Piaţa Unirii feels like the town centre, and it is a convenient meeting place. Ahead of you, to the south, B-dul Ştefan cel Mare şi Sfânt makes a beeline for Piaţa Palatului, while Str Cuza Vodă brings you to one of the main halts for trolleybuses and trams. Kiosks beside the road sell copies of English-language news and computer magazines.

B-dul Ştefan cel Mare şi Sfânt

Heading south along this tree-lined road, you pass the colonnaded apse of the **Orthodox Cathedral** on the right. Walk through the pretty gardens surrounding the Baroque building and you come to a west portal as grand as that of any Italian *duomo*. Completed in 1884, the Orthodox Cathedral and its 20C satellites follow a taste for the neo-Classical. To its west is a complex of annexes and residences, together with a set of monumental steps, and fountains in the form of small grottoes. The complex was designed in the 1950s by G.M. Cantacuzino (1899–1960). Cantacuzino was born and grew up in Iaşi; he is best known for some brilliant, functionalist buildings, especially at Eforie Nord and Mamaia (see Dobrogea) and for neo-Classical designs such as the Crissoloveni Bank building in Bucharest.

A vast, Baroque interior reflects the status of this church: it is the seat of the second most important bishop in the country, over whom only the Patriarch of Bucharest takes precedence. Its aisles are flanked with tall marble pillars surmounted by Corinthian capitals, and there are murals by the 19C realist painter Gheorghe Tattarescu (1818–94), and the windows are filled with stained glass. The monumental *iconostas* (icon screen) is a sensational piece of Baroque carving, but in the eyes of the worshippers who flock to her side, it is outshone by the silver casket containing the relics of Moldavia's patron saint, Sfânta Paraschiva cea Nouă. Her feast day is held on 14 October, but the celebrations last for a week.

The Metropolitanate of Moldavia was founded in the reign of Prince Petru I (r. 1375–91), and its patron saint is Sf Gheorghe. You may be asked at the door for

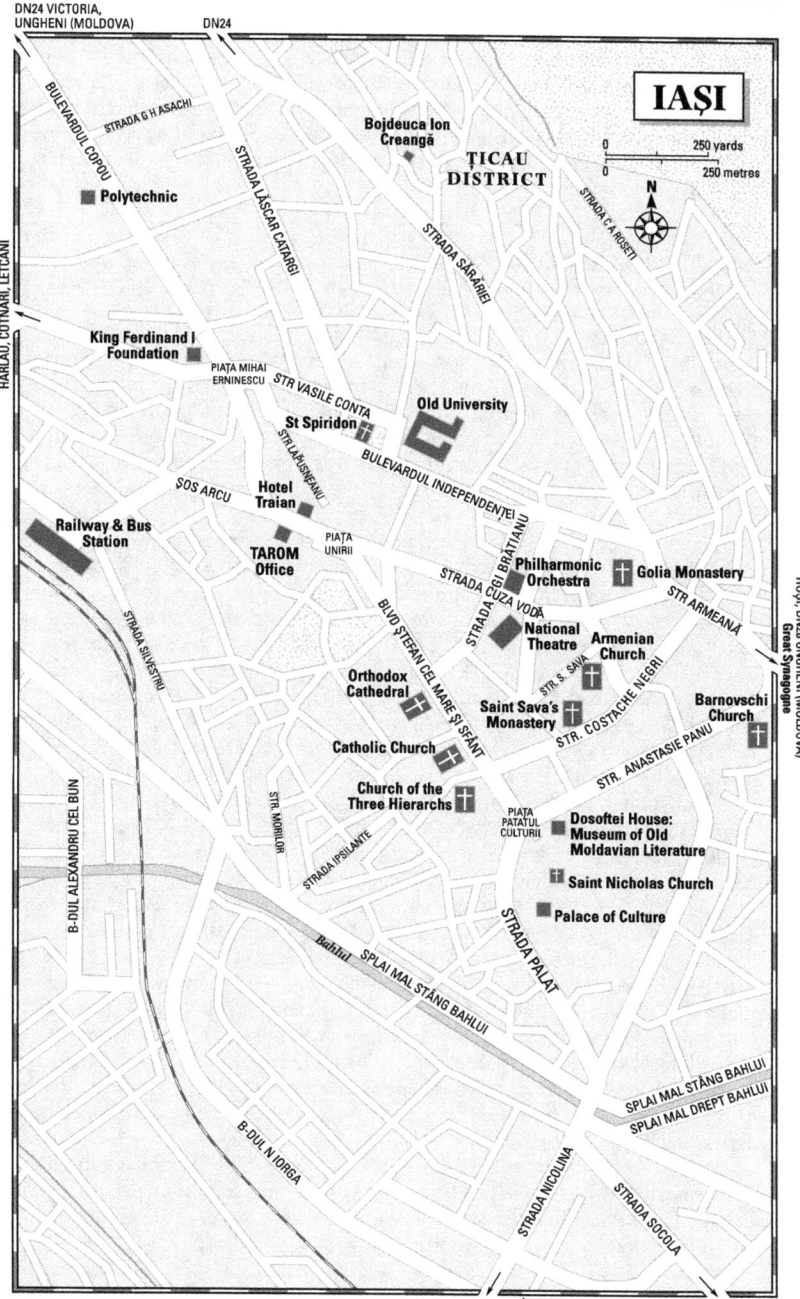

your name and a small donation; if so, the attendant will promise that a priest will say a prayer for you. Many Ieșeni take their religion seriously and although no-one may tell you so, it is considered polite to wear decorous clothing here.

Instead of a spectacular dome envisaged by the architect, the cathedral's ceiling is barrel-vaulted. This was probably wise because Iași lies in a seismic zone, and the engineers were worried that the foundations were not strong enough to carry the dome.

Sfânta Paraschiva cea Nouă

Paraschiva is a popular figure in the Orthodox world, known to Bulgarians, Greeks, Romanians and Russians alike. According to legend, she was born in the 11C at Epivat, a Thracian village beside the Sea of Marmora, now called Boiados and on the Turkish coast. At ten she 'was transfixed by the word of God' and began taking care of the poor. She then went into the desert and spent several carefree years praying on her own before an angel told her to go home and give up 'her earthly body'. After she was buried in Epivat Paraschiva's remains continued to exert a beneficial influence. Their subsequent travels were a result of major political upheavals and classic Byzantine intrigues.

By the late 12C the Byzantine empire had become very weak, and Bulgarian Slavs and Romanians founded their own, independent Orthodox state, with a capital and patriarchate at Trnovo in present-day Bulgaria. Shortly afterwards, 'pilgrims in arms' on the Fourth Crusade attacked Constantinople, venting the Pope's bitter hatred of the Eastern church; the Catholics marvelled at the city's beauty and then mercilessly sacked it. After switching sides from the Byzantines to the crusaders, Tsar Asen of Bulgaria fetched Paraschiva's remains from Epivat to Trnovo via Constantinople. The relics probably stayed there until the Ottoman army captured the Bulgarian citadel in 1393. After the Christians' disastrous defeat by Turks at Nicopolis three years later, Paraschiva was rescued by Serbs and taken to Belgrade.

In 1521, Suleiman the Magnificent turned Serbia into a pashalik. But while his soldiers burned and looted Belgrade, Paraschiva had another miraculous reprieve: the Sultan transported her back to Istanbul and gave her to the Patriarch. A story says that on the way Suleiman displayed the saint's remains to adoring crowds in return for a fee and then threatened to throw them into the sea unless the Patriarch paid him too.

In 1641 the Vasile Lupu had Paraschiva's relics spirited away. According to an official account published by the church, the Patriarch 'would never have sold her under any circumstances' and gave the saint to Lupu in return for his moral support. But Lupu paid the Ottoman authorities handsomely for turning a blind eye to the theft, and Paraschiva was lifted over the wall of St George's Church in the Phanar district at dead of night and shipped across the Black Sea to Galați.

She was brought to the Orthodox Cathedral in 1888. Not to be confused with several other Paraschivas who appear in the Romanian Orthodox Calendar, she was renamed St Good Friday (Vinerea Mare, commemorated on 26 July) and later Paraschiva the New, with a feast day on 14 October.

Continue south along B-dul Ştefan cel Mare, cross Str S. Sava and you come to an arched gateway. Beyond it stands the old **Catholic church**, an 18C structure founded by Polish and Hungarian Catholics who had formed a powerful community in Iaşi since the 15C.

Just further south, across Str Costache Negri, is **Trei Ierarhi** (Three Saints) monastery church. This was commissioned by Vasile Lupu in 1637 and finished in 1639. It is not the most beautiful building in Iaşi, but it is the most extraordinary. Its entire external surface is covered with carvings like a piece of embroidery. The church you see today is a late-19C reconstruction by André Lecomte du Nouÿ of the original Mannerist design created by Ienache Etisi, a Greek architect from Constantinople. And what Etisi left magnificently decadent, Lecomte du Nouÿ wrecked with ruthless precision.

The most remarkable feature of Trei Ierarhi is its ornamentation. Originally it was covered in gold, silver and lapis lazuli, but this glittering surface has long since disappeared, leaving 33 rows of floral and geometrical motifs carved in flat relief. No two rows are alike. To a Western European eye they look distinctly oriental, while in 1659 the Turkish traveller, Evlia Celebi, compared them to European miniature paintings. Art historians are still arguing over the origins of these patterns, but the concensus is that they were probably inspired by Caucasian, Islamic and Russian motifs filtered through Constantinople. The idea of covering the entire surface is a logical development from the richly ornamented cupola at Dragomirna, north of Suceava. It has echoes too of the episcopal church at Curtea de Argeş, whose body and towers are also encrusted with relief work.

Sfa Paraschiva's silver coffin used to reside in this church and may provide a clue to its remarkable decoration. Sorin Iftimi, has suggested that Trei Ierarhi was meant to imitate a giant *chivot* or *kivotos*, a silver and gem-encrusted casket that was placed on the altar and contained holy bread. Adapted from the Jewish kiddush ceremony, the Orthodox *chivot* was shaped like a miniature church. What better way of honouring Moldavia's most precious spiritual treasure than housing it in a church that resembled a jewelled box?

The twisted cord motif, called a *brâu* or *torsadă*, that encircles the church at the top of the walls is a Moldavian speciality, symbolising eternal life.

Vasile Lupu commissioned frescoes from Muscovite artists, but all of the original murals have now gone, although faint outlines showing the prince and his wife can been seen to the left of the arch in the southwest corner of the naos. What you can see on the walls now are copies of the originals, painted by Lecomte du Nouÿ's brother, Jean (1842–1929). A well-known Orientalist and neo-Classical artist, he decorated several other churches in Romania and made portraits of Romanian courtiers and politicians. His work has been described as 'like Ingres in the style of Gérôme', and his frescoes seem fussy and lifeless by comparison with the earlier murals. There are an icon screen of Carrara marble, a bronze candelabra with ostrich-egg decoration, and individual enamelled icons and mosaics.

By the time André Lecomte du Nouÿ saw Trei Ierarhi it was in a sorry state, and he rebuilt it virtually from scratch in a spirit of 'scientific' exactitude. He heightened and Gothicised the twin towers, replacing the original curved drums with polygons and capping the towers with ramrod-straight, flat-sided cones. He also flattened the undulating Byzantine curves in the roof, and at ground level he

> ### Dimitrie Cantemir (1678–1732)
> Buried inside Trei Ierarhi is Dimitrie Cantemir, one of the outstanding Romanian scholars of the early 18C. He was also Prince of Moldavia for just over a year (1710–11). His life epitomises the strong cultural links that the principalities once enjoyed with the Eastern Orthodox world. He was educated in Constantinople, and as well as becoming an expert in Asian languages, he was an authority on Ottoman society and manners. In 1711 he took refuge from the Turks in Russia, where he had time to concentrate on writing. His *Descriptio Moldaviae* (*Description of Moldavia*) is a delightful account of Romanian contemporary life enlivened with astute observations about traditional customs, and he also wrote an excellent history of the Ottoman Empire in Latin. Cantemir died an exile in Russia, but in 1935 his headless skeleton was returned to Iași. One explanation for the missing skull is that Cantemir belonged to the Rosicrucian Society, one of whose members is said to have taken Cantemir's head to Scotland and buried it there. The ruins of Cantemir's residence in the Phanar district of Istanbul are still visible; a plaque marks the entrance.

inserted a stone socle, or plinth, around the whole building, raising it several centimetres from its original height. G.M. Cantacuzino said his alterations were a 'masterpiece of taste'.

The priests like visitors to dress decently and may object if you do not; you can avoid unpleasantness by wearing clothes that cover the thighs and upper arms. Open 09.00–13.00 and 15.00–19.00, and for services Mon–Sat 05.30 and 17.30, Sun 08.00.

On the east side of B-dul Ștefan cel Mare, before reaching the junction with Str Panu and Piața Palatului, you pass a handsome **primăriă** (town hall). It was built in 1831 as a mansion for the Rosetti-Roznovanu family.

Piața Palatului

An imposing, pale grey neo-Gothic building dominates the south end of the long boulevard. Looking like a replica of the Hotel de Ville in Paris, this is **Palatul Culturii** (the Culture Palace). It was completed in 1925 to designs by I.D. Berindei and stands on the foundations of several citadels, the first of which was documented in 1432. Behind the palace to the south stand the remains of an amphitheatre.

A dashing equestrian **statue** of Ștefan cel Mare dominates the entrance to Palatul Culturii. It was sculpted in 1883 by Emmanuel Frémiet, who also created the memorial to Jeanne d'Arc in Paris's Rue de Rivoli. Two Krupp cannons, trophies of Romania's victory over the Turks in 1877, also stand outside, and the clock tower in the centre of the building has an eight-bell carillon that plays the national dance, *Hora Unirii*, on the hour.

Stucco figures bearing the Scales of Justice are to be found on the façade and in the Hall of Honour inside. Berindei's Gothic theme runs right through the palace's interior down to its heavy, dark oak furniture. During the First World War, Queen Marie organised a military hospital in the building, and some of her symbols have been included in the decor, including her *croix gammée* (better

> ### Trei Ierarhi ~ the Three Hierarchs
> The three hierarchs after whom the church is named were Vasile cel Mare (Basil the Great, c 329–79), Grigore Teologul (Gregory the Theologian, also known as Gregory of Nazianus, c 330–89) and Sf Ion Gură de Aur (St John Chrysostom, c 346–407). A hierarch is the Orthodox term for a father of the church, and there were many of them. Most hierarchs lived in the 4C, when a still fluid Christian doctrine was being thrashed out between different factions, each of whom held passionate and often conflicting views. Basil I, the Great of Caesarea to give him his full title, was one of eight so-called Doctors of the Church. Born at Caesarea in Cappadocia, he became famous for reforming the Orthodox liturgy, and his Rule, or *typikon*, governing the daily life of monks, became the basis for eastern monasticism. Basil was also one of the three Cappadocian Fathers who supported the doctrines of Athanasius against those of Arianism. The other two Fathers were his brother Gregory of Nyssa, and Gregory the Theologian.
>
> Gregory the Theologian was born at Nazianus (present-day Bekar in Turkey). He is best known for his definitions of the Trinity and the nature of Christ. In 379 Gregory became leader of the Orthodox community in Constantinople, and he played a decisive role at the Councils of Constantinople and Nicaea. His ideas led eventually to a split within the church which resulted in the dramatic 'Chalcedon condemnation' of 451, when Orthodox bishops expelled the Abyssinian, Armenian and Coptic Christians for refusing to accept the tripartite nature of God. The disenchanted monophysites went off to form their own churches, and when Armenians began settling in Romania they brought their heretical beliefs with them. This is one reason why Armenians appear among the damned in paintings of the Last Judgment on Moldavian monasteries.
>
> John Chrysostom (literally John Golden Mouth) was a patriarch of Constantinople and one of the four eastern Fathers of the Church. After leading a life of extreme self-denial in the mountains of Syria he went home to Antioch, becoming patriarch in 398. His defiant asceticism brought him up against the Emperor Arcadius and the notorious Empress Eudoxia. John Chrysostom's outspoken criticisms of their sybaritic ways angered the imperial couple so much that they had him deposed and sent into exile. He died on the way to Pontus. John Chrysostom earned his name from his skills as a writer whose sermons and homilies were written in a pure, classical Attic-style Greek.

known as the swastika), which you can see in stucco on the frontage. Coloured-glass windows represent scenes from Moldavia's history: Ştefan cel Mare's coronation (1457), and Dimitrie Cantemir's meeting with Peter the Great (1711).

Palatul Culturii used to house the city's law courts and council offices, but now it is used for conferences and official receptions. It also contains four museums, of history, art, ethnography and *politehnică* (science and technology), open Tues–Sun 10.00–17.00.

The old law court, panelled in oak to Berindei's neo-Gothic design, now forms part of the **History Museum**. Although it lacks the money it desperately needs to reorganise, it has some fascinating curiosities: hand-painted Cucuteni pottery, models of Dacian and medieval citadels, a 10C–11C Byzantine ampulla for holy oil, a Turkish relief and a parchment issued by Constantin Movilă in the 17C and written in gold leaf. It also has what is supposed to be Dimitrie Cantemir's funeral tablet, which the Soviet Union graciously sent home with Cantemir's remains in 1935—however, modern Romanian scholars are not convinced the stone is authentic because the emblem it bears is completely different to the one Cantemir used in his lifetime. A good deal of the museum's collection has been filtered off to the National History Museum in Bucharest.

The **Ethnographic Museum** has sturdy wine and oil presses made from whole tree trunks, a collection of beehives and masks, among much else. In the **Art Museum** is an excellent collection of Romanian avant-garde painting from the inter-war period, while the **Science and Technology Museum** contains mechanical musical instruments and early devices for showing moving pictures. All four museums are served by a shop that sells a few traditional crafts and an excellent map of Iași.

Sf Nicolae Domnesc (Royal St Nicholas's) is the oldest documented church in town. It stands on the left of Piața Palatul Culturii as you face the Culture Palace. Founded by Ștefan cel Mare in 1492 to thank the Almighty for helping him repel a Tartar invasion, it later became the first Metropolitan Cathedral in Iași. Many princes were crowned here, including Despot Vodă. Antonie Ruset financed restorations in 1678, when a bell tower, monks' cells and paintings were added, but the church burnt down in the early 19C.

Between 1884–1904 André Lecomte du Nouÿ demolished what remained of the church and rebuilt Sf Nicolae from scratch, adding half a metre to the bottom of the walls. G.M. Cantacuzino, who eulogised Lecomte du Nouÿ's work at Trei Ierarhi, called his solution for Sf Nicolae 'cold and unemotional but perfect'; later commentators have often been ruder. Whatever your verdict, the red-brick shrine certainly catches the eye. The only original parts left are the *pisanie* (inscription) above the entrance and scattered pieces of fresco.

Iași was radically altered during the mid-20C and this area of the city suffered the worst. As a result the old buildings that were left standing look a little forlorn. One of these is a rectangular stone building called **Casa Dosoftei**, which stands between Sf Nicolae and Str Anastasie Panu. Named after an outstanding poet and scholar (1624–93) who became Metropolitan of Moldavia in 1671, it is now a museum housing a collection of early Romanian books and manuscripts. Among these are the most valuable editions of the *Moldavian Chronicles*. Dosoftei was fiercely anti-Ottoman and was imprisoned in Iași for several months before turning his skills to translating and printing religious tracts in Romanian. His most famous publication was *Psaltirea în Versuri* (*The Psaltery in Verse*, 1673). For a long time, historians believed that Casa Dosoftei was originally the bishop's palace and that he kept his press here, but excavations have shown that during his time the site was a cemetery. Open Tues–Sun 10.00–17.00.

Along Str Anastasie Panu

Heading east and passing the Centru Civic and other modern buildings, you come after 300m to the **Barnovschi Church** on the right. This is a hybrid of Austrian Baroque and Byzantine architecture, commissioned by Prince Miron Barnovschi (r. 1626–29) and completed in 1628. Before ascending the throne,

Barnovschi was a *hatman* (a commander in the Moldavian cavalry). Once in power, he galvanised the economy, but when he refused to convert to Islam the Ottoman Sultan had him executed.

Str Ghibănescu to Str Cuza Vodă

A right turn at the north end of Str Ghibănescu brings you to the **Barboi Monastery** whose gate tower and church date from the mid-19C; they replaced a 17C shrine.

Cross to the other side of Str Ghibănescu into Str Costache Negri , and head west until you come to **Sf Sava** on the right. Romania has ancient links with Palestine, and documents show that in 1583 Greek monks from the St Sava monastery in Jerusalem built a church in Iaşi. In 1625 a court official called Ianache Caragia added two wide, squat cupolas placed on drums. Each drum contains 13 windows through which light pours into the interior. The bell tower was added before 1653. Inside is a striking 18C Baroque icon screen containing oil paintings encased in flamboyant oval and circular frames. The church itself has a rectangular plan and fragments of Westernised fresco. It has been used as a school, a printing press for Greek and Romanian books, and a religious library.

From Sf Sava, retrace your steps east along Str Costache Negri, turn left and walk a few metres north along Str Armeana, and you are in all that is left of **Armenimea**, the Armenian quarter. To the left is the ochre-coloured **Biserica Armenească**, a handsome, sand-coloured, early-19C Baroque building that has fallen on hard times and is usually closed. It stands on the site of earlier Armenian shrines which are said to date back to the late 14C. Along the perimeter railings are a row of **tombstones** that have been rescued from the waste land that was once its cemetery. Some of them, inscribed in a beautiful, cursive Armenian script, are older than the church, and several of the slabs are decorated with a pair of small, neatly sculpted hollows in the shape of flower heads, circles and commas, about the size of half a tennis ball. When the slab was lying flat the hollows trapped rainwater, and birds would drink there, dipping their heads as though bowing in deference to the dead person buried underneath.

Head north along Str Armeana, turn right into Str Cuza Vodă, and near the corner with Str Elena Doamna and Str Sarăriei, behind an imposing gate tower, you will find the severely beautiful **Mănăstirea Golia**. *Logofăt* (Chancellor) Ioan

---

Armenians in Iaşi

Armenians are today a shadowy presence in Iaşi, but in the 16C and 17C they monopolised the city's trade. A large community settled in L'vov, which became the spiritual capital for Armenians in eastern Europe as a whole. They put down roots in Moldavia, too, especially in Suceava city (see p 212), while others established thriving industries in Transylvania. On the walls of Sucevita and Voroneţ monasteries Armenians are shown among the pagans being condemned to Hell. Both they and their language have disappeared from Moldavia, although some art historians believe there is an Armenian influence in the carvings on Trei Ierarhi, and on other buildings around Iaşi.

Mănăstira Golia

Golia built a parish church here in 1546. Sixty years later cells were added and the church was placed under the protection of Mount Athos. According to chronicler Miron Costin, Vasile Lupu found the shrine in ruins and commissioned a team of Italian stonemasons, then working in Poland, to heighten the church walls: the result is the satisfying mix of Western and Byzantine styles that you see today.

It has a rectangular plan, and the roof line and cupolas are Byzantine with Baroque inflections. The exterior walls combine Classical and Renaissance elements. Lupu's son Ştefăniţa carried the work forward to 1660, and Prince Gheorghe Duca added the turrets in 1667. Some of the smaller monastery buildings, including the Abbot's house, are from the 18C, and outside, to the left of the gateway, is an attractive rococo fountain installed in 1766.

Inside, the layout is unique: two pillars separate the naos and pronaos, and in front of each one, facing the altar, stands a throne. One is for the prince and the other for his lady. Because the Sultan banned his vassals from wearing crowns, the portraits of Vasile and his wife shown on the pillars have none. To get around this problem, artists inserted a brass Cross of David in the floor to represent the Old Testament king. The Turks, whose Islamic religion was born from the same Jewish sources as Christianity, could not possibly object to this. Above the thrones, a candelabra carried the Cyrillic initials 'BB' for Vasile Voivode (Basil the Prince) and the Moldavian aurochs symbol. The candelabra, which has since disappeared, was moulded in the shape of a crown, another way of subtly asserting the status of the Moldavian monarchy without causing trouble with the Turkish authorities. The painting in Golia dates from its founder's time but was partially redone in the 19C.

When Peter the Great visited Iaşi on a whistle-stop tour of his allies in 1711, he admired Golia and praised its synthesis of Ieşeni, Greek and Muscovite workmanship. Neo-Classicism was fashionable in Russia at the time, and it was from there that the style entered eastern Europe. The church has other Russian connections: *bon viveur* Prince Potemkin lived in what is now the Faculty of Medicine on B-dul Independenţei. He had a chair for his own use in Golia, and it is said that his entrails are buried in a silver box underneath it.

In the early 19C Golia functioned as a hospice. A few decades later, when writer Ion Creangă worked here as a deacon he used to amuse himself by shooting at crows from the gate tower.

Across Str Sărăriei in Str Sinagogelor stands **Sinagoga Mare** (the Great Synagogue), which was founded in 1671, rebuilt in the 18C and restored in the 1970s. It is the oldest Jewish temple in Romania. The first Jewish theatre in eastern Europe is also said to have been founded in Iaşi.

The Jews in Iaşi

Violent anti-Semitism decimated Iaşi's flourishing Jewish community during the first two-thirds of the 20C. Jews replaced the Armenians of Moldavia as the principality's great financial and political 'fixers', but they were also part of the backbone of the city's cultural life. In 1903 the first pogroms began to spread across eastern Europe from nearby Chişinău (now capital of the Republic of Moldova). During this period, hundreds of ancient Moldavian shtetls were destroyed. They included Belz, a village which is lamented by John Jacobs in his *Song of the Ghetto*, composed for Alexander Olshanetsky's play of the same name. Belz later became the town of Bălţi in the Republic of Moldova and lies 60km north of Yaas (the Yiddish name for Iaşi)

During the 1920s and 1930s paranoia gripped Moldavia and Bessarabia, and after the Second World War, Jews were blamed for the loss of the former Romanian province of Bessarabia to the Soviet Union. As in Germany after the First World War, Jews were pioneers of Romania's fledgling communist party. Acting on orders from Moscow they supported self-determination and separation for the newly united provinces of Bucovina, Bessarabia, Dobrogea and Transylvania. Reacting against this perceived threat to a vulnerable Greater Romania, inward-looking politicians encouraged hatred of non-Romanian minorities, the Jews among them.

The influx of Bessarabians into an exhausted and impoverished Romania after 1918 caused further resentment. Once again the large minority of Jews from Bessarabia became scapegoats. Blanket prejudices of this kind fanned the flames of the vicious nationalist movement which came to be known as the Iron Guard. Its original leader, Corneliu Zelea Codreanu (not to be confused with Iaşi-born poet Mihai Codreanu) was educated at Iaşi University, where he was involved with right-wing student organisations. In 1923 several of these organisations merged with the League of National Christian Defence which A.C. Cuza founded in Iaşi. The main preoccupation of the League was anti-Semitism, and the anti-communist Codreanu was Cuza's principal adjutant. Having failed to attract popular support the League split up, and in 1927 Codreanu started another group, called the Legion of the Archangel Michael. This movement was also anti-Semitic and anti-communist (the two were almost synonymous in those days), but also professed conservative ideals. Spawned by a general fear of the effect which external influences might have on Romania's vulnerable identity, these appealed to many Romanians and the Legion attracted many more people than the League.

After Codreanu's assassination in 1938 the Legion was taken over by out-and-out fascists inspired and trained in Nazi Germany. Known to all as the Iron Guard, its members perpetrated horrific atrocities not only on Romania's Jews but on many non-Jewish liberal intellectuals as well.

In 1998 the French Cultural Institute in Iaşi opened the Salle Benjamin Fondane in memory of the Jewish poet. Benjamin Fondane was born in Iaşi in 1898. He studied in Iaşi and Bucharest, where he formed his own experimental theatre company and wrote many film scripts. Later he worked in Paris, where he became a fellow traveller of the Surrealists but was

> murdered by the Nazis at Birkenau. The little theatre is dedicated to bilingual spectacles in French and Romanian, comprising plays, music and dance, and aims to put on a new production every week.

Further west along Str Cuza Vodă, at no. 29 near the junction with Str Brătianu, is the home of the **philharmonic orchestra** and the Enescu Conservatoire. The house was built in 1815 for finance minister Alecu Balş, and Franz Liszt gave a concert here in 1847. At the end of the 19C the Catholic society Notre Dame de Sion bought the building and added the extra wing which is now used by the orchestra.

Opposite stands **Teatrul Naţional V. Alecsandri**, the National Theatre, a poem of neo-Baroque pomposity with a couple of fetching swans on top. It was designed in the 1890s by Fellner and Helmer, who were responsible for the National Theatre in Cluj and others around the Habsburgs' doomed empire, in Cernăuţi, Sofia and Kárlovy Váry. The construction of the building was supervised by an unfortunate architect named Coschitz, who killed himself it was maliciously said, after realising that changes in street layout had transformed, the front entrance to the back. Alecsandri (1821–90) was a famous playwright and poet, and the theatre opened with one of his comic pieces. Inside is a 1000-seat auditorium; it was used as the Parliament House after Romania entered the First World War. The building was restored in 1957, and a new wing was added to it in the 1960s.

Str Cuza Vodă to B-dul Independenţei and Piaţa Eminescu

Several bright-looking shops have sprung up in Str Cuza Vodă and it is a good place to look for groceries. A turn right into Str Brătianu brings you to B-dul Independenţei, where a number of imposing buildings can be found, including **Casa Ruset** at no. 16. This is a mid-18C mansion that became the headquarters of the Physicians' and Naturalists' Society in 1844. Cuza was chosen as Prince of Moldavia here in 1859, and the house is now the **Museum of Natural History**, open Tues, Thurs and Sat 09.00–15.00, Wed, Fri and Sun 09.00–16.00.

A little further to the north on the right, B-dul Independenţei brings you face to face with **Universitatea Veche** (the Old University). A former palace, this was built in the second half of the 18C for the treasurer and finance minister, Matei Cantacuzino. He sold the building to *hatman* Costache Ghica in 1792, and three years later it was turned into a temporary princely residence to replace the court in Piaţa Palatului, which had been burnt down. After passing through private hands, the palace was redeemed for the State in 1860 and began life as a university founded by Cuza. Iaşi is the oldest university in Romania; its origins go back to 1843 when Prince Mihail Sturza founded Academia Mihăilena in a building on Piaţa Unirii. It was later destroyed by the communists.

In front of the entrance stands **Uşa nădejdii** (the Gate of Hope), a double-arched gateway erected by Prince Ion Alecsandru Callimachi in 1796, when the building functioned as a princely court. It earned its name from petitioners hoping for justice who came here as a last resort. Callimachi's blazon and an inscription, 'Io Ale. Ca.' can be seen above the second arch. By the 1890s, the university needed a larger building and moved to B-dul Carol I (now B-dul Copou). The faculty of Medicine and Pharmacology remained here, becoming a self-contained university later on. In the basement is the library where Mihai Eminescu made a living as director. There are no formal visiting arrangements, but if you turn up during working hours, the chances are that you will be allowed to look inside.

Further north along B-dul Independenței you come to an 18C gate tower. This is the entrance to **Sf Spiridon**, a monastery erected between 1747–52. Spiridon devoted himself to healing the sick, and the monks followed suit. The Spiridon Foundation later became very wealthy, thanks to the property it acquired through donations, and it established hospitals and clinics in churches and monasteries throughout Moldavia. The church here has an icon of Spiridon that is said to work miracle cures.

At the northwest end of B-dul Independenței, past the **market** where in season, pyramids of red peppers and purple aubergines splash colour onto a drab street, you reach Piața Eminescu. At the northwest corner of the square stands the elegant, triangular façade of **Fundația Regele Ferdinand I**. Its curved and colonnaded entrance leads into a university library endowed by King Ferdinand after the First World War. Inside, the decor is soberly neo-Classical with an empty niche on the stairs that once held a 4m tall bronze statue of Ferdinand. It was demolished in the communist period. The British Council library occupies part of the southern wing. On the other side of B-dul Copou is a small copse containing Galeria Voievozilor, an unmemorable collection of statues showing princes whom the communists considered historically acceptable. Next to this is the house where Queen Marie lived during the First World War and to the right, on the southeast side, is **Casa Studenților**, students' common rooms containing a bar, disco and billiard room. There is also a small **theatre** used by the Ludic players, a non-professional company that has earned a reputation for fine acting.

On the southwest corner of Piața Eminescu stands **Râpa Galbenă** (the Yellow Esplanade), built to honour Queen Elisabeta in the 1880s. A pair of curved and balustraded stairways drop down each side, connecting Piața Eminescu with a road that leads to the station; a small open-air café does brisk business at the top of the steps.

Northwest along B-dul Copou

The road that brings you into the main university campus is lined with trees. Most of the university buildings that are strung out along the west side of the street were financed by King Ferdinand, but during the communist period his name was removed and replaced with Cuza's. The edifice at no. 11 is the oldest of the campus buildings. It was designed in the 1890s by Louis Le Blanc; other buildings were added in the 1930s by a Romanian architect called I. Pompilian.

Further north on the same side you come to another grand building, which belongs to the **Polytechnic**. Outside are a couple of pretty wrought-iron lamps ornamented with plant motifs. They were used when electric light first came to Iași. Inside, along one side of a long gallery Romanian painter Sabin Bălașa (b. 1932) has created a series of **murals**. His themes weave strands of Romanian and classical mythology into a patriotic allegory of birth, death and rebirth: Eminescu and Ștefan cel Mare are ghostly figures straining towards the heavens—like dematerialising saints from Byzantine art of the Comnene period. Some of the paintings, which date from 1979, are insipid interpretations of communist ideology, but others are striking: his bold *Europa* leaps out at you with tremendous zest, and the procession of monumental students at the south end of the hall is witty and clever. The main **lecture hall**, where the Romanian Senate met between 1916–18, is a grandiose, neo-Baroque affair decked out in solid, varnished wood and plenty of gilt. The lectern is designed to look like a pulpit in an Orthodox church: behind it are two central doors flanked by two large portraits of the Polytechnic's founders, and above them is a small choir gallery.

Still further north along B-dul Copou the houses remain impressive: on the right is the lemon-and-white **French Cultural Centre**, looking like a miniature Petit Trianon, and on the left, not to be outdone, is its German equivalent. After this comes the entrance to the **Copou Gardens**, a pleasant place in which to relax. A few metres inside stands **Obeliscul Leilor** (the Obelisk of Lions). It was erected in 1832 because Ieșeni believed that Iași stood on the site of an ancient Roman camp. The first public memorial in Romania, it contains a rock that symbolises the city's foundation stone, while the lions were thought to be modelled on the escutcheon used by the legions in Dacia. The obelisk also commemorates the 'Organic Rules', a kind of proto-Romanian constitution based on Russian and Austrian models. Further into the gardens you will find **Teiul lui Eminescu**, a venerable lime tree under which, so the fantasy goes, Romania's leading Romantic composed his best verse.

A few hundred yards further north, B-dul Copou brings you to a junction with Str Coșbuc. At the end of this street lies the oldest **Botanical Gardens** in Romania. Naturalist Anastasie Fătu (1816–86) created the gardens in 1856, planting rare specimens of potentilla and mountain orchid, *Rosa mundii*, in his backyard near Piața Eminescu. The garden was moved to its present position in 1962 and now covers over 100ha.

There is an **Eminescu Museum** in the park, which contains photocopies of his manuscripts, photographs of him with Veronica Micle and Ion Creangă, and some pieces from his art collection. Open Tues–Sun 09.00–17.00. The **Museum of Old Moldavian Literature** is in the Casa Dosoftei, aka the Arcades House, see above; there is another **Museum of Romanian Literature** at Str Vasile Pogor 4 (first on the right as you ascend B-dul Copou). It comprises manuscripts, first editions and other interesting objects belonging to Romanian writers from the time of Costache Conachi to 1900, as well as a section devoted to the Viața Românească group. The house belonged to Iași's famous revolutionary literary set called Junimea, and Eminescu once lived here. In the yard there are busts of various writers. They include an interesting portrait of A.D. Xenopol, made of cement and 'rock powder' by the contemporary, Arad-based artist Rudolf Kocsis.

Țicău

One of Iași's attractive old suburbs, Țicău is a former village that lies on the lower slopes of Dealul Țicăului, to the north of the city centre. On Str Simion Barnuțiu stands a small, terraced garden, at the bottom of which perches **Bojdeuca Ion Creangă**, Ion Creangă's cottage, which is hardly bigger than a doll's house. A modern villa next door houses a small literary museum containing photocopies of letters and documents. Creangă (1837–89) was a celebrated storyteller and friend of Mihai Eminescu. He was born in Humulești near Neamț, and spent most of his life in Iași. His best-known book is *Amintiri din Copilărie* (*Childhood Memories*), and he wrote many famous fairy stories. Creangă's work has been translated into many languages, but his humour comes across best when you read it in the original. One of Creangă's legacies is the assertion that Moldavian dogs say 'hum hum'. Open Tues–Sun 10.00–17.00.

Str Kogălniceanu 7A was the home of Mihail Kogălniceanu (1817–91) and is now a **museum** dedicated to his life and work. Kogălniceanu was one of the pioneers of the Romanian national awakening. In 1843 he gave an inaugural lecture on national history at the Mihăileană Academy in Iași which influenced the nationalist movement for decades to come. Kogălniceanu was a man of deep understanding who loved and respected the cultures of other countries as well as his own. Among his many philanthropic actions, he liberated Romania's Gypsies from serfdom and helped painter Nicolae Grigorescu to travel to France. Kogălniceanu was a key activist in the struggle for the union of Moldavia and Wallachia, and he became a reformist prime minister and foreign minister. His preoccupation with history in the context of Romanian nationalism had its downside because it lent itself to manipulative interpretations by the extreme right and the extreme left. Bowdlerised echoes of his pronouncements were heard in the ideology of the Legion of the Archangel Michael and in Romanian communist propaganda. The museum is open Tues–Sun 09.00–17.00.

Two doors along at no. 9 stands the **Museum of Chemistry** in a house which belonged to Petru Poni. Open 09.00–17.00.

Around Iași

A number of impressive monasteries lie outside the city centre. **Galata**, built for the Wallachian-born prince, Petru Șchiopu (Peter the Lame, r. 1574–77 and 1582–91), was completed in 1584 and stands on a hill overlooking the small Nicolina river. From Piața Palatului, drive down the hill to Str Sf Lazăr, turn right over the bridge and continue along Str Nicolina until you cross another river bridge and then come to a junction with Șos Tudor Neculai. Turn right up this road, past the turn down Șos Galata, and the entrance is a few metres further on, to the right.

Galata is a synthesis of Moldavian and Wallachian architecture, and the church became a prototype of the 'classic' Moldavian style for the centuries that followed. It has a traditional trefoil plan, but instead of a single tower over the naos as in preceding Moldavian churches, it has a second one above the pronaos, and both are raised on double-star bases. Another innovation is the endless cord motif around the body of the church—which was also brought here from Wallachia—and a further change was made by replacing the wall between the naos and pronaos with two columns.

From outside, the towers do not look very tall, but from below, where candle grease has blackened everything and pinpoints of light stream in from far above your head, you get the impression of looking into infinite space. For a long time, Galata was run by Greek monks from the Church of the Holy Sepulchre in Jerusalem.

Mănăstirea Frumoasa, the Beautiful Monastery, is a handsome Palladian-style building that has fallen on hard times. It stands in a walled enclosure to the north of B-dul Poitiers and across the railway line from Şos Libertăţii at Str Radu Vodă 1, on the corner with Str Cetăţuia. Frumoasa is said to get its name from one of Ştefan cel Mare's mistresses who was exceptionally beautiful. But the monastery was founded long after Ştefan's death so the story may refer to an earlier building. The monastery, completed in 1733, was commissioned by *voivode* Grigore Ghica II on the site of the 16C Balica monastery. It once stood beside a royal residence, but what you see today is a 19C reconstruction; at the time of writing, it was shrouded in wooden scaffolding. The onion-domed gatetower dates from 1833.

Turn south from Frumoasa, cross B-dul Poitiers and head into the hills for **Cetăţuia** (the Little Fortress) monastery. If you are driving from the the city centre, turn south along Str Palatului beside the Culture Palace, go down the hill and join Str Nicolina at the bottom. Follow Nicolina into the outskirts and turn left into B-dul Poitiers. Turn left at the signs for Cetăţuia. You can see Cetăţuia from the city centre, but it is worth visiting because the fortified buildings, founded by Prince Gheorghe Duca (r. 1665–66 and 1668–72) are impressive and there is a splendid view from the top of the hill across the vineyards to the south and over the city. The complex was finished in 1672, the year of Duca's death, and both the prince and his wife are buried inside the church.

Blackened frescoes of the Last Judgment and other biblical scenes decorate the *pridvor* (porch), and inside, the paintings are so dark that they are hard to make out. The artists were Gheorghe and Mihai Dima, Aromanians from the Turkish lands of Enina, and Nicolae Zugravul cel Bătrân. (Aromanians are Romanian-speaking peoples who live south of the Danube, now mainly in Albania, Bulgaria and Macedonia.) Duca wanted a copy of Trei Ierarhi, and the stone carving is lovely, framing windows and arches with a cord motif that also encircles the external walls. A large bell sits near the gate tower: it was made in the Polish port of Danzig (now Gdansk) in the 17C.

The hilltop gives you a panoramic view of Iaşi and the countryside to the south. It was the monastery's fine position, as well as its name, that gave Nicolae Iorga the idea that there was a citadel here before it was founded. Excavations confirmed his suspicion and it is now known that the city of Iaşi developed from the site. A famous road once ran between Cetăţuia and Galata monasteries. Styled Drumul Ţarigrad, it was used by Moldavian princes on their return from investiture in Constantinople.

Some monasteries south of Iaşi

Driving south out of Iaşi on the DN24 (the main road to Vaslui) brings you close to three monasteries—not to mention **Ceauşescu's former villa**, which has been turned into a five-star hotel. A right turn c 8km from the city brings you to **Bârnova**. In the village is a fortified monastery begun by Miron Barnovschi in the 1620s and finished by Prince Eustraţie Dabija in 1665. It is a grand old tumble-down place within solid perimeter walls. The church has a single cupola and is pleasantly lofty and spacious inside. The interior is painted with white lime wash, but when they have enough money, the monks are planning to cover the walls with murals. Some icons from an older church stand around the walls. Bârnova monastery has a small community of Orthodox brothers, most of whom are under 30 years old. They live a very ascetic life, but this does not mean that they are cut off from the outside world—on the contrary, the monastery runs a primary school and during the summer the courtyard buzzes with activity.

You can return to the DN24 by two roads; once there, turn right and c 12km past the southern road look for another turn-off signposted **Dobrovăţ**, a monastery c 40km from Iaşi. This route brings you through thick woods into a wide, sheltered valley—but take care, because the road alternates between tarmac, cobbles and rutted track, and the further you go towards the village the worse it gets. As you drive into Dobrovăţ, you should be able to see Dobrovăţ monastery standing in green meadows to your right. In fact it is closer to a hamlet called Rusi, and to visit the building you have to take a right turn about halfway along the main street. Follow this to the next junction in c 1km, then turn right again. If in doubt, ask someone in the village.

Dobrovăţ monastery was founded long before Ştefan cel Mare adopted it in 1503, but its true origins have been lost in the mists of time. That there was a monastery here before he and his wife, Maria Voichiţa, endowed the church is beyond doubt.

Ştefan's church was dedicated to the Holy Spirit (Sf Duh in Romanian). Externally it is severely rectangular, with registers of blind arcading and niches running around the top half of the walls. Inside, the east end is shaped as a triconch with the lateral apses inscribed within the walls. As at Neamţ and Bistriţa, Dobrovăţ has three internal, lateral walls, comprising the wooden icon screen and the walls that separate the naos from the tomb chamber and the tomb chamber from the pronaos. The vaults above naos and pronaos are arranged 'on the bias' *à la* Ştefan, each one rising to a hemispherical dome, while the little domed vault in the tomb chamber rises parallel with the walls. The church was finished after Ştefan's death.

In c 1651, the monastery and the use of its land were given to Zogrof monastery on Mount Athos. Zogrof was then a Romanian foundation; it was handed to Bulgarian monks in the 19C. Having survived the boisterous attentions of Jan Sobieski's soldiers, who scratched their names on the frescoes in Cyrillic, Dobrovăţ underwent a far more drastic alteration in 1851. In that year *egumen* Acachie ordered three Byzantine towers with squat helmet domes to be raised on the roof, which was flattened to accommodate them. A far-sighted Historic Monuments Commission rectified this travesty in the early 1970s, recreating Dobrovăţ's handsome profile with faithful copies of the two original steeply ridged roofs. Slender copper slats were used to cover the roof instead of shingles; not everything the communists did was bad.

Inside, the church is frescoed from floor to roof. The now faded paintings were commissioned by Ştefan's son, Petru Rareş, in 1529. The paintings have seldom been retouched sinced they were created, and in the pronaos and tomb chamber many of the frescoes are so pale they are almost impossible to decipher. This is a shame because they are bursting with dramatic incidents. Restoration of the murals was promised to start before the end of the millennium, but at the time of writing there was no sign of it.

One of the most legible scenes in the naos is the votive portrait on the east wall. Ostensibly this shows the donor of the church presenting a model of the building humbly to Christ. This particular painting is full of political overtones. Petru was illegitimate and needed to justify his claims over Moldavia. Coming barely two years after his accession, his decision to embellish his father's church was calculated to win his people's approval. It shows Petru himself beside his father Ştefan and his brother Bogdan III, both of whom had preceded him onto the throne. Having himself presented in this symbolic way as third in line to the throne was an attempt to restore his standing as Ştefan's legitimate heir. Ştefan proffers a model of the church to the seated Christ, who has already accepted a copy of the Gospels, which is lying open on his knees. Models of churches like the one shown here are often useful because they show, as this one does, what the original building was like. The figures of the princes have curiously childlike faces and all of them, including Petru, are shown wearing tall, bejewelled crowns and magnificent robes. Apart from dignifying Petru's recent accession, this is a deliberate reminder that the Moldavian princes were the true inheritors of Byzantium after Constantinople fell to the Turks in 1453.

Unusually, there are no royal women in the painting. This is partly because Petru was a widower when it was carried out, but also because the princess who helped found the monastery was Maria Voichiţa, who was the mother of Bogdan but not of Petru.

Paintings in the naos and side apses show the betrayal of Jesus, his trial, the crowning with thorns and the Crucifixion. These frescoes cover the upper parts of the south, west and north wall above the rows of military saints. In the sanctuary there are scenes from the Last Supper, Jesus washing John the Baptist's feet, two separate scenes showing Christ sharing bread and wine with the Apostles and the figures of Basil the Great and Gregory of Nazianus.

In the tomb chamber or *gropniţa* the frescoes include a **Deësis** (Prayer of All Saints), scenes from the *Sinaxar* including the disembodied heads of marytred saints, and the death of St Anne. Lower down are figures of saints such as Balaam and Joasaph, who are here making their earliest appearance in Moldavian church iconography.

The pronaos contains one of the few known examples of the **Ladder of Virtue**. The theme belongs to the First Judgment of the Soul as conceived by Sf John the Sinaite. Suceviţa has another, more splendid version, but this one can just be made out on the north wall. Other scenes in the pronaos include more episodes from the life and death of Christ and, also on the north wall, a superb series devoted to St George.

The doorway between pronaos and naos was shaped specially so that Ştefan could pass through it without removing his crown, which is why it has a narrower section at the top—he was surprisingly short. Vasile Lupu closed the monastery in 1651, and it only reopened in the mid-19C.

Beside the main church is a paraclis or winter chapel built in the same period as the church. A three-storeyed gatetower from 1743 stands like a sentinel at the main entrance. It contains a chapel, installed in case of siege, and a bell tower. The belfry gives a wonderful view over the valley, but the steps up to it are treacherous.

Six young monks run Dobrovăţ. Bearded like hermits and frighteningly skeletal, they live together in an old school building with flapping casements and echoing corridors. The monks returned here to look after the monastery in 1991 and they are very poor. But their dedication is unquestionable, and if you turn up at a reasonable time one of them will show you around Ştefan's church and the gate tower. At the time of writing none of the brothers spoke English. There is a splendid book about Dobrovăț by Vasile Drăguț in the series *Comori de artă in România*. Called *Dobrovăț*, it has a French summary and is published by Meridiane in Bucharest (1984). If you cannot buy a copy here, look out for it at one of the other Moldavian monasteries or at a good bookshop.

To the border with Moldova

The quickest way to the Romanian/Moldovan border from Iași by car is the road east past the airport and through Holboca. The Prut River marks the frontier, and there is a crossing point at Ungheni. The Moldovan Republic was once named Basarabia (Bessarabia) after a famous Wallachian prince, Matei Basarab (r. 1632–54), whose family ruled the southern part of the country in the 14C. In 1812 Bessarabia was ceded to the Russian tsar, who called it Moldova, and although Romania got it back briefly after the Treaty of Versailles, the Soviet Union annexed the country again after 1944. As a result families and friends were suddenly torn apart, and the stories of Romanians hunting up and down on either side of the Prut for signs of their relations make heartrending reading. The collapse of the USSR allowed the republic to declare its independence in 1991, and a government was formed in the capital, Chishinău. Negotiations for reintegration with Romania have so far been unsuccessful.

SOUTH TO VASLUI

The countryside between Iași and Vaslui does not attract many tourists, but it has a lot to offer. Walk across the rolling hills between the two towns and you can find yourself surveying the world from such splendid vantage points as **Movila lui Burcel**. The hill is named after one of Ștefan's loyal supporters who lost an arm while fighting for his lord. He received an estate here as a reward. Today there is a wooden skete on the hilltop. It was founded in 1994. There is no water supply to the skete, and the monks or nuns who manage the property rely on the kindness of strangers to fetch and carry what they need from a well c 5km away. But there are few places which convey such a pervasive atmosphere of peace.

70km south of Iași lies the town of Vaslui. Its main historic claim to fame is that nearby, Ștefan the Great won a tremendous tactical victory against Mehmet II. An impressive memorial to this fact marks what historians agree must be the place, known only as **Podul Înalt** (High Road or Bridge), 11km south of Vaslui. Ștefan had far fewer men at his disposal than the Ottomans, but he lured them into a trap by the sound of his *buciumi*, the alpenhorns which Romanian shepherds still use to call to each other in the mountains. Confused by the calls and the dense fog that fell on the morning of 10 January 1475, the Turkish army rode into a mire and was cut to pieces.

During Ștefan's reign Vaslui prospered, taking advantage of its position near transcontinental trade routes. When Paul of Aleppo visited the town on his way to Russia in 1650 he was impressed by its 'palaces, public baths, pleasant open spaces and especially its splendid church with its tall and narrow tower... and its beautiful architecture.' He also recalled that it was full of wall paintings, but these have now gone.

Vaslui today is a pleasant provincial town struggling to hold its own in a part of Moldavia which suffered badly under collectivisation. The town centre was totally rebuilt during the communist period, but Ştefan's **church**, founded in 1490 and dedicated to St John the Baptist, is still there, in essence at least, sheltering at the end of a narrow alleyway of trees on the main street. The church was damaged by an earthquake in 1820, and most of its superstructure dates from the following years. The present wall paintings were carried out in oils by a pupil of Gheorghe Tattarescu. Dating from 1893, they are badly in need of restoration. One of the interesting features of this church is that ceramic pots were built into the walls to help its acoustics. In the central town square is an excellent History and Ethnography Museum.

If you want to stay in Vaslui there are several **hotels** including the comfortable *Metro* (✫✫), at Str Bălcescu 2, ☎ 035 361702. Vaslui's main street is lined with bars which are relaxed enough to welcome entire families, and discos. One of the more sophisticated **discos**, designed for people in their late teens and early twenties, is *Splash*. Walk south down the slope from the main street, past *Crama Domnească*, a restaurant serving traditional Moldavian food, and you will find *Splash* in a concrete bunker-style building with an open-air bar and some pool tables outside.

Moreni Monastery

About 27km south of Vaslui, between the villages of Deleni and Costeşti, stands the monastery of Moreni. At the time of writing Moreni consisted of a splendid new quadrangle containing cells, paraclis and workshops, but no *katholikon*. These new buildings have risen Phoenix-like from the remains of a medieval monastery. Founded in 1540 during the reign of Petru Rareş, the first community flourished for a century. Although the church was repaired in 1650, it was again allowed to collapse. After 200 years the church was rebuilt in wood, but in 1883 the last monk died and this spelt the end of the original foundation.

In the 1930s Moreni's pleasant position attracted a small group of monks, but they lacked the funds to make the monastery a success and after ten years it fell again into disuse. In 1958 the communist government officially disestablished most of Romania's monastic institutions, Moreni included. Its present reincarnation is the result of another initiative which has transformed the old monastery into a convent. At the time of writing the *katholikon* is a gleam in the eye of the abbot, but a space has been cleared for the church in the centre of the courtyard.

In the orchard to the side of the courtyard stands the little wooden **church** from 1853. It is a charming building with a traditional verandah-style porch at the west end, where some painting remains. Inside it has a particularly interesting icon screen containing three rows of icons, each one showing the figure of an individual saint.

Moreni was opened in 1991 and blessed in 1997. Today it is home to 50 nuns, who take it in turns to cultivate the fields and gardens, and raise the farm animals. They also operate the sewing and knitting machines in their commercial workshops. The nuns create beautifully embroidered ecclesiastical vestments. Many of them joined the convent in their mid-teens, and their life is very tough. All the same, Moreni gives every appearance of being a happy place, and the fact that it has achieved any of this is extremely impressive. Most of the impetus to get the convent underway came from the abbot and his bishop.

Thinking ahead, the abbot is keen to attract foreign visitors to Moreni. Using the excellent guest accommodation that is already provided, they may stay here for a week or two to enjoy the peaceful atmosphere and the delicious natural produce that is grown and made on the premises. Children are welcome, provided they realise that this is a place of contemplation and retreat. The nuns live quietly and would expect visitors to do the same. With these gentle restrictions, Moreni would make a comfortable and secure base for excursions around eastern Moldavia. Visitors are not obliged or even expected to go to services, but will be welcome if they do. If you want to take advantage of this opportunity, you should contact Stareț Meletie Mercas, Mănăstirea Moreni, județul Vaslui, ☎/fax 035 322376; mobile 094 571763, and negotiate appropriate terms. The abbot speaks some French and German, and there are one or two English-speaking nuns in the convent as well.

SOUTHERN MOLDAVIA

The southern half of Moldavia contains part of eastern Romania's grain basket, the dark-soiled and virtually treeless Lower Siret and Brăila plains which sweep south to the Bărăgan Plain and the Danube. Consequently, travelling around central Moldavia can be bleak: no Romanian experience I know of is more 'Siberian' than the rail journey between Bucharest and Focșani. The industrial cities of Brăila and Galați may look unpromising, but in fact they are interesting cultural centres in their own right and visiting them brings you within easy travelling distance of the Delta. West of the plains lie Munții Vrancei. This little-known section of the east Carpathians is glorious to look at and contains villages so untouched by modern technology that they are hardly credible.

West of the Bărăgan Plain

Vrancea county and the Munții Vrancei
Once famous for the sinister pine forests and eroded mountains that earned it the name Varancha, the region and county of Vrancea stretches south from Adjud to Focșani, and west towards the towns of Onești and Covasna. Two-thirds of Vrancea is covered by forests, about half of which are old woodlands planted in the 19C or earlier.

Vrancea lies on the southeastern edge of the Carpathian curve. At this point the mountains are divided into Subcarpații Vranceii (the foothills) and Munții Vranceii (full-sized mountains, up to 1777m). Once you reach this part of the county, the countryside becomes strikingly beautiful and a welcome relief after the flat plains around Focșani.

Eastern Vrancea is the largest **wine-growing region** in the country. It comprises 35,000ha of vineyards. Its well-known red wines come from the villages of Cotești, Odobești and Nicorești, but the vineyards also produce cognacs, brandies, vermouths and sparkling wines made by the *méthode Champenoise*. If you drive north from Râmnicu Sărat on the E85 you will see plantations stretching to the distant horizon; further west their terraces decorate the hills. Come here in September after the harvest has started, and you can buy clusters of huge, sweet-smelling grapes at the roadside.

> **How Vrancea got its name**
> In the Middle Ages, the region now called Vrancea was famous for its dense and gloomy forests, and there is a theory that its name comes from Varancha, meaning The Black Land or The Black Forest. But another legend says that the land was named after Baba Vrancioia, the mother of seven good-looking girls who joined Ştefan cel Mare's army to fight the Turks. They were so brave that as a reward Ştefan gave each one a mountain in the southeast Carpathians, telling them to call their lands Ţara Vrancei. In Munţii Vrancei, there is a village called Vrancioia, giving credence to this story.

While on the subject of food, one of Moldavia's culinary delights is a maroon-skinned onion shaped like a nine-pin. It has a sweet flavour and is delicious either cooked or in salads.

A number of well-known **writers** were born or lived in Vrancea. They include the 15C chroniclers Miron Costin and Ion Neculce, Grigore Alexandrescu (1814–85), who wrote fables inspired by Romanian folklore, novelist Duiliu Zamfirescu (1858–1922), and Alexandru Vlahuţă (1858–1919), whose memorial houses you can visit, respectively in Focşani and Dragosloveni, and Hortensia Papadat-Bengescu (1876–1955), pioneer of Romania's modern analytical novel and author of the masterpiece *Concert din muzică din Bach* (Concert to the music of Bach, 1927). The little village of Câmpuri, 60km to the west of Focşani, is the birthplace of Moş Ion Roată, one of the extraordinary figures to emerge during the struggle for the union of Moldavia and Wallachia. The largest conurbations in Vrancea are the county town of Focşani, Adjud, Mărăşeşti, Odobeşti and Panciu. But this is predominantly a rural region which has preserved its own set of customs, folklore, vernacular buildings and crafts.

Folklore, customs and rituals
Thanks to their mountainous lands, the Vranceni have traditionally been an independent people. Even when technically subordinate to powerful lords, they were a society of *răzeşi* (yeomen) who cultivated their own fields and were accustomed to making their own laws. *Răzeşi* from Vrancea were staunch supporters of Ştefan cel Mare in his campaigns against the Turks and other enemies, and it was through Vrancea that Ştefan came on his way to claim the Moldavian throne. There is only one vehicular pass from here into Transylvania, but shepherds and their flocks have crossed to and fro between Vrancea and the Bârsa Land for centuries. Vrancea's population has also remained relatively stable, but at the same time its proximity to Transylvania and Wallachia has allowed cultural influences to flow in from both directions. All of these factors, together with the lack of industrial development in the region, have meant that many colourful customs have survived.

Customs belonging to the cycle of life
Vranceni have many symbols to mark important rites of passage through life. These include the tree of life that appears on their costumes, carpets and buildings and types of bread made to be eaten on special occasions.

Valaritul or *Valaretul* is a ritual connected with the period in young people's

The Miorița story

Local historians claim that the attractive little spa town of Soveja in northwest Vrancea is the origin of the folk ballad or poem, *Miorița* (*The Ewe Lamb*). This is one of Romania's most famous songs, so important that it has been taken to symbolise the essence of what it is to be Romanian. *Miorița* is the story of a shepherd who allows himself to be murdered by two rivals who are jealous of his fine sheep. His favourite ewe lamb, a magic beast who can talk, overhears the shepherds plotting and warns her master while refusing to eat and bleating continuously for three days. The good shepherd hears her pleas but does nothing to avoid his fate; instead of running away, he accepts murder with a brave and welcoming heart. His final oration expresses a desire to be married to the sky, the trees and the earth.

No-one knows where or when the *Miorița* legend began, but some historians think that it was invented by the Dacians. The Dacians' moral code included a belief in the immortality of the soul and the immorality of taking revenge. They may have adopted these ideas from the Pythagorean School long before Christians began to preach the same doctrines. The poem was handed down by the Vlachs who were the ancestors of present-day Romanians, and there are many variations on the theme, including those which belong to the Aromâni who live in Macedonia and Bulgaria. The version known best in Romania today was created from folk sources by Alecu Russo and playwright Vasile Alecsandri in the 19C. At the time it was immensely popular with nationalists, who took it as an allegory of the Romanians' non-violent endurance through centuries of occupation and oppression.

---

lives leading up to marriage. On the day after Easter, young men (called *valari*) get together in groups and go from house to house, especially where there are unmarried girls, wishing their hosts *mulți înainte* (many years of life ahead). Part of the ritual demands that they lift the girls up to the beams in their arms. In return, the host must give them money, wine, bread and eggs. The custom ends with a party when the presents are shared out and the boys dance the *hora* (Romanian round dance)—they pay the musicians with the money they have collected.

Surația takes place in parallel with Valarit and allows the girls to dance as well. It usually takes place in the house of one of the participants. Each girl brings red painted eggs, *pașca* (hot cross buns), and *colac* (plaited bread). The *colac* is divided into pieces, one for each participant, and the girls kiss each other on the eyes, saying, 'Let me be kissed until I die and in Heaven too'. The custom ends with a meal which the girls provide for each other, and with a dance.

Laic calendar customs

These customs are not exclusive to Vrancea, but they have been adapted here in specific ways.

Capra (the Goat) begins before Christmas and lasts until Epiphany. A young man wearing a special goat costume parades around the village accompanied by a group of young men in masks. The Goat dances to a specific local folk tune.

Ursul (the Bear) is like *Capra*, except that the costume represents a bear and the man dances to a different tune.

Maștile (the Masks) is one of the most original customs in Moldavia. Anyone male may take part, wearing a mask which he has made or borrowed. The masks may be of wood, leather, fabrics, horns, seeds, or a combination of all the above, and the wearers visit every house in the village, wishing the occupants wealth and good humour. Masks are also worn on certain holy days, but the most popular time is at New Year. The vigil masks of Vrancea, as well as those from other areas in Moldavia, Maramureș and Bihor are famous.

Plugușorul is a traditional procession with a decorated plough that takes place on New Year's Day. Groups of young men scour the village with whips, bells and drums made of small barrels covered with hide at either end. These are played by pulling a tuft of hair which passes through the middle of the cover from end to end, producing a low sound like the roar of a bull. The boys walk from house to house wishing people good luck, health and wealth for the coming year, and singing carols. Vrancea's *Plugușorul* is closely related to the *Tânjaua* celebrations that are still found in Maramureș.

Sorcova is a branch or stick covered with artificial flowers. Children carry these sticks on New Year's Day to wish people health and happiness, touching them lightly with the *sorcova*.

From before Christmas until Epiphany small groups or individuals go from house to house carrying a star symbol to announce the birth of Jesus.

The 'feast of the sheep' in the spring celebrates the moment when the flocks are brought together to go to their summer pastures.

'Winter socials' are when groups of people, young and old but usually women, meet in one another's houses to sew and spin together. While they work they sing and tell each other jokes and stories. Sometimes people come together to help each other build houses, thresh maize or to prepare *cânepă* (hemp) for making rope and sacks. Such gatherings are entirely voluntary and usually very gay.

Vrancea's traditional architecture

Vrancea has enjoyed a great deal of autonomy thanks to its mountainous position. During the feudal period most smallholders had their own flocks of sheep and goats, as well as parcels of land which they used for growing maize, and small gardens and orchards. The Vranceni were skilled carpenters and joiners, but they also made excellent pottery and metal tools. Their buildings reflect the individual needs, occupations and wealth of their owners, just as traditional houses do all over Romania, and they are extremely attractive. In the village museums, everything has been organised according to a standard image of what is typical. If you do not have time to explore Vrancea for yourself, coming here is a good start.

Vernacular houses in Vrancea do not differ radically from traditional buildings in other parts of Romania, and it takes a sensitive and practiced eye to tell the regional differences apart.

In the mountains peasant houses were usually built on stone foundations. The living rooms were raised above animal stalls or stores at the ground level, and wood tiles were often used to cover the walls, as they are further north in Neamț and Bucovina, and in many other parts of the Carpathians.

Lower down houses are less slender, and they change again when you reach the plains, where farm buildings are even more spread out and are often roofed with thatch instead of shingles. The character differences between these houses are as subtle, as indefinable and as undeniable as the differences between the people who live in them. People in the plains still use wattle and daub to make walls, and farmyard barns and sheds can be made of sticks as well as mud. Clay continues to be an important building material. Not just here but all over rural Moldavia you can find houses made of adobe known as *chirpici* (pronunced kirpich). These are bricks the size of brieze blocks. They are made of clay mixed with straw and left in the sun to dry. *Chirpici* are strong and provide a lot of warmth, but do not last long if they get wet.

The oldest houses are built of mud with wooden 'pitchforks' raised directly from the ground, as in the villages of Vulturu and Suraia, or on wooden supports as at Tătăranu and Călimanești, with a low porch. The exterior decoration is usually made of fretworked board. In the plains these old houses often have two main rooms, a hall, a smaller room and a summer kitchen outside.

Cârligele, Colacu, Cotești, Gugești, Paltin and Vulăneasca each have a **Colecția Muzeală Satească**.

Vrancea is not alone in the beauty of its traditions, but if you are particularly drawn to this aspect of Romanian culture it would be an excellent place to start. Museum libraries and, if they have them, shops have learned books on Vrancea as an 'ethnographic zone', but while these are usually full of excellent information they can make dry reading, and of course, most of them are in Romanian. The best way to find out more about Vrancea's traditions is to travel around it, stay with Vranceni families and take part in their celebrations.

Funeral customs
Orthodox Romanians share many complex rituals connected with death and burial. Among these is the wake, which in Vrancea takes place in two phases, one between sunset and midnight, and the other between midnight and dawn. Wakes are carried out as they are in Ireland because of the belief that it is bad for a dead person to be left alone. And also as in Ireland, they are meant to be happy occasions with the whole village taking part. An unwritten law says that there should be no burials on a Monday, a Wednesday or a Friday.

Festivals and crafts fairs in Vrancea
In April there is a folk crafts fair at Vidra. For folk music and dance, try the Comoara Vrancei at Paltin in July. Focșani holds a wine-tasting festival in October and a popular music festival in November. Among the many places where you can meet craftsmen and watch them at work are the villages of Bârsești and Mera, which are well-known for their excellent carpenters, and Irești which has a tradition of pottery making. If you want to find out more, contact *Centrul Județean de Creație Populară*, Str N. Tițulescu 1, Focșani, ☎ 037 626201, or the County Museum in Focșani.

Climate, plants and animals
Ranging from the low-lying plains to the high mountains, Vrancea's climate and natural habitats vary enormously. Generally speaking, the region has warm summers and cold winters. In the foothills and lower ranges of the mountains there are forests of birch, beech, oak and acacia. Higher up, the trees become

more coniferous, and above the timberline the flora is alpine. Vrancea has an abundance of wildlife, and if you are patient and lucky you may see wolf, lynx, fox, bear and deer.

Vrancea also contains 22 **nature reserves**. Among the most interesting are the Lepşa-Zboina forest reservation, the forestry and geological reserve at Tişiţa Quais, and the Cenaru forest.

Lepşa-Zboina, between 600m and 1300m above sea level, can be found near the peak of Zboina Neagra on the left side of the Lepşa brook in an area consisting of peaks and eroded mountain massif. Covering c 600ha, its woods are a combination of pure beech, beech mixed with fir and spruce, and small groups of pine. You can get there through Soveja, on the route to Piepturi.

Tişiţa-Quais reserve lies in a 4.5km long gorge beside the road between Focşani, Tulnici and Lepşa.

The **Cenaru forest** stretches across 380ha between the Cenaru and Milcov valleys. Apart from its mixed woodland it contains a fascinating variety of wildflowers, grasses and animals.

Focşani

The county town of Vrancea, Focşani has a population of 100,000 and lies on the banks of the River Milcov. It was completely redeveloped during the communist period and retains very little of its former self.

History

Archaeological finds made in the town show that in prehistoric times this area was inhabited by Dacians who had contacts with Thracian and Scythian cultures. During the Roman occupation of Dacia few people lived in the region, but Roman coins and other treasures have been found in Focşani.

Dimitrie Cantemir (1628–1723), who published the first known map of Vrancea, tells us that Focşani was founded after a dual between a Moldavian and a Wallachian. The two men fought with wine bowls instead of swords, and the Moldavian won, earning the right to the land. In the 13C when Catholic Cumans lived here, the settlement was called Milcovia, after the river. The Milcov once marked the border between Moldavia and Wallachia. The town gets its present name from the Focşa family who owned large estates here in the 15C. The river was still the frontier in 1859, when Moldavia and Wallachia were united, and Focşani played an important part in the negotiations which led to the creation of the Romanian nation. Monuments commemorating the struggle for union include Str Comisia Centrală 72, where the Central Commission prepared common laws for Romania between 1859–61, and a statue symbolising the union in the pedestrian precinct in the town centre.

Vrancea is prone to earthquakes, and its seismic epicentre has been traced to the mountain commune of Vrancioaia. Focşani took the brunt of the devastating 1977 quake, which is one reason why the town looks so modern. A few neo-Baroque villas survived, their frilly stucco decorations making a striking contrast with the stark 1960s modernism that characterises most buildings here. They were built by 19C businessmen escaping from the hurly-burly of the shipyards at Galaţi. Focşani's tourist appeal is not improved by the lack of signposting: once drawn into its street system it is difficult to find your way out again. Pupils at one enterprising high school have created some excellent web pages about Vrancea, and these include a street map of the county town. Look for Vrancea or Focşani on any other good search engine.

Practical information

☎ code
037

Tourist information
Try *Ernic Tur* at B-dul Unirii 8, bloc A3, ap 1, ☎ 217270, or *Vranceatour* at B-dul Brăilei 9, ☎ 61643; fax 231500.

Getting around
By train The station is on B-dul Gării. The *CFR* office is at B-dul Unirii 59, bloc 1, ☎ 622306, or ☎ 952 for information.

By bus The bus station is on B-dul Gării, next to the railway station; for information ☎ 956.

By car For **car repairs** try *Auto Parc-Service*, ☎ 625512, or *Dacia Service*, ☎ 626760.

Where to stay
Among the better hotels are *Hotel Unirea* (✩✩), Piaţa Unirii 3, ☎ 621100; fax 625146, and *Hotel Vrancea* (✩✩), Str Dimitrie Cantemir 25, ☎ 614700. Alternatively, contact *ANTREC*'s local office, ☎ 673049; fax 616493.

Money
You can exchange money at *Banca Comercială Ion Tiriac*, B-dul Gării 11, and *CEC*, Str Vlahuţă 27.

Police
☎ 955.

Medical care
For the **county hospital**, ☎ 625000.

Entertainment
Focşani has two **theatres**, *Teatrul* and *Ateneul Popular*, and a **folk-dance ensemble** called *Ţara Vrancei*. There is also *Doina Vrancei*, an **orchestra** specialising in folk music.

Focşani has a couple of modest museums housed side by side in attractive 19C villa buildings on B-dul Gării. Although one is named **Muzeul Judeţean**, the County Museum, and the other **Secţia de Istorie şi Arheologie**, the History and Archaeology Section, they are both devoted to history and archaeology and are open Tues–Sun. The county museum at no. 5 admits visitors 08.00–16.00, and the history museum at no. 6 opens and closes one hour later. The curators who work here are very helpful and may be able to organise specialised, guided tours of the region. If you ask for this service, remember that the museums are always in financial difficulties, and if you can provide your own transport and a fee this will help.

On the northern outskirts of Focşani, 7km from the town centre at a place called **Crângul Petreşti**, there is a fascinating village museum. Called **Reservaţia de Arhitectură Vranceană**, it comprises a collection of 40 or so buildings including traditional houses, inns, barns and mills from the whole county. Most of the installations are made of timber with wooden or wattle-and-daub walls. Typical houses have slender verandah posts carved with unobtrusive geometrical designs, and each one has been furnished and decorated in the style of traditional peasant homes. One of the buildings is a handsome 19C *han* (inn) from Odobeşti, in which visitors may stay; ☎ 612130. Open Tues–Sun 09.00–17.00.

The wine-making villages

A few kilometres west and southwest of Focşani, the villages of Coteşti, Faraoane, Jariştea, Odobeşti, Panciu and Nicoreşti are all centres of Vrancea's thriving wine trade. The sandy soil that predominates here posed a problem for vine-growers until they hit on the solution of planting the roots up to 3m below the topsoil. One of the outstanding table wines made in Vrancea is the Băbească de Nicoreşti, a pleasantly acidic red with a strong taste of cloves. At **Coteşti**, c 12km southwest of Focşani, the village has a small ethnographic museum, Colecţia Muzeală Sătească, open Tues–Sun 09.00–17.00.

Faraoane is a little further north on the country road from Coteşti to Odobeşti. Here, Crama Domnească (the princely cellar), founded in 1839, holds one of Romania's largest collection of wines. Faraoane is best known for its gold-coloured whites. Muzeul Viticol (the wine museum) on Str Libertăţii 192, has curiosity value and it is worth checking with the organisers (or with the Village Museum in Bucharest) for dates of some of the music and wine festivals that are held here. Look out for the harvest celebrations in late September and the music festival on the third Sunday in November, when Vrancea's shepherds gather to play their wind instruments.

Driving north from Odobeşti, the next wine-producing village you come to is **Jariştea**, whose wine cellars are at Str Georgescu 52. A few kilometres to the west, four monks look after an 18C **wooden church** that belongs to Schitul Buluc. Ask for directions in Jariştea. There is another historic church at **Secătura**. To find it continue your way north, and turn left in Boloteşti.

To reach Panciu you must turn left after Boloteşti for Tifeşti, and at Satu Nou, head north (right) for 7km. Just before you enter the village from the south, you pass the German First World War **cemetery** of Frunzoiaia. 1.5km southwest of Panciu, **Brazi** skete has a 17C wooden church dedicated to Sf Gheorghe. It was founded by two stonemasons who lived in nearby caves. **Panciu** itself is an ancient village with a monastery set among the vineyards. You can visit the headquarters of the wine company, *Veritas*, at Str Kogălniceanu 24, ☎ 037 635511, fax 635713. *Veritas* produces dessert grapes, red and white wines and champagne made in the traditional way, and boasts a champagne cellar 500 years old and 15km long. *Veritas* welcomes visitors, and wine tastings and tours of the vineyard and ageing cellars are a speciality here. Enticingly, this company also offers a range of 'wine coolers' made from raspberries, bilberries and 'fir buds'.

The war memorials

Romania entered the First World War in 1916 after two years of neutrality. By the summer of 1917 only Moldavia remained free of hostile troops, and the Eastern Front swept right through Vrancea. The county is strewn with old **battlefields** that witnessed Romanian attempts to prevent the Germans from reaching Iaşi: Doaga, Străjescu, Moara Alba, Moara Roşie and the Răzoare forest.

At **Mărăşeşti**, 19km north of Focşani on the E85/DN2 and not far from Panciu, a striking circular mausoleum marks the place where, on 6 August 1917, the Romanians won a great victory—at the cost of over 17,000 Romanian deaths. The odds against them were enormous and the Battle of Mărăşeşti is styled the country's Verdun, a turning point in the country's relationship with the entente cordiale. It is said that the defiant phrase, '*Pe aici nu se trece!*' ('You shall not pass!'), was first coined by Romanian soldiers at Mărăşeşti.

Although austere, the building is remarkably moving. It was initiated by the Romanian Women's Congress. Open Tues–Sun 09.00–17.00.

To the west of Mărăşeşti, you can visit two other First World War memorials, at Mărăşti and Soveja, and the stark, abstract Victory Monument at **Tişiţa** (1934). **Mărăşti** (1928), which commemorates a momentous battle in July 1917, occupies a beautiful setting in the Subcarpathian foothills about 30km northwest of Mărăşeşti. Turn right onto a country road a couple of kilometres after Răcoasa; the site is a further 4.5km and is signposted. Fewer lives were lost here than at Mărăşeşti, but during the struggle the Second Romanian Army liberated 30 occupied villages and forced the enemy to retreat 20km. The building is smaller and less imposing than Mărăşeşti, but two bronze reliefs depict symbolic moments from the battle and the crypts contain the graves of the Austrians and Germans who fought on the opposing side, as well as Russians and Romanians; open Tues–Sun 09.00–17.00. **Soveja** is worth visiting for its own sake (see below), but it has a small war memorial, in the shape of a Greek cross behind a battlemented façade. Completed in 1929, the mausoleum contains the bones of more than 10,000 soldiers who died in the hills around the town. Open Tues–Sun 09.00–17.00. Soveja is also where Alecu Russo 'discovered' the Miorița.

INTO THE VRANCEA MOUNTAINS

The Vrancea mountains form part of the bend in the southeast Carpathians. They stretch over c 60km from Oituz in the north to the Buzău valley in the south, and are highest at Mount Goru (1783m) and Mount Lăcăuţ (1777m). They are irregular and very beautiful. The best mountain walking and climbing is to be had starting from Năruja, c 30km west of Focşani, and heading south for Nereju (c 18km) or west to Herăstrău (c 15km). Experts say that climbing in the Vrancea mountains often looks more tricky than it actually is.

After leaving Mărăşti, rejoin the main road that runs from Panciu to the northwest; in c 2–3km you reach the village of Posculeşa. Immediately after it, there is a turning to the left that crosses the Suşiţa river and brings you shortly to **Vizantea**. In the late 16C Prince Ieremia Movilă (r. 1565–1606) founded a monastery here which is well worth the detour.

Câmpuri (7km from Răcoasa on the road west of Panciu), is a village famous as the birthplace of Ion Roată. Known as Old Man Roată, he was a 19C smallholder whose forceful personality gained him a leading role in negotiations for political union with Wallachia. A champion of farmers' rights, he was also the first peasant to take his seat in the Romanian parliament. **Casa Memorială Moş Ion Roată** is open Tues–Sun 09.00–17.00.

A further 17km west of Câmpuri is **Soveja**, a lovely town 540m above sea level. It was a medieval customs post and now functions as a health resort specialising in helping people who have breathing difficulties.

Further back in Soveja's history, Prince Matei Basarab established a **monastery** here. Its ruins can just be made out beside the *voivode*'s mid-17C church which stands in an orchard at the end of a lane to the left of the main road on your way south through the town. There is a **tourist chalet** in Soveja, named *Zboina*. A summer camp for sculptors is held each year in nearby **Valea Bagului**.

There are two routes from Soveja, both of which are pretty. Turning south brings you in 7km to **Negrileşti**, a fascinating village which is an excellent place to explore if you want to get in touch with 'old, rural Romania'. Modernity in the shape of rows of neat new villas is encroaching on the old part of the village, but if you penetrate this outer shell, there are very attractive traditional farmhouses and cottages, working forges, mills and woodcarvers. Ask for Toma Avram, the local veterinarian who makes traditional cheese moulds, or arrange a guided tour of this and other mountain villages with the County Museum in Focşani (see p267).

At **Dragosloveni** is an historic monastery and Alexandru Vlahuţa's memorial house, open Tues–Sun 09.00–17.00; in 13km turn left for **Lepşa**, an ethnographic zone with a *păstrăvarie* (trout hatchery). A few kilometres further east you come to the **Putna waterfalls**. Although these have the regulation Coca-Cola cabin, they make an attractive place to stop for a picnic. Further to the south of Lepşa, the **Tişiţa forest reserve** is open to the public (times available from the County Museum in Focşani, and listed on a notice board at the entrance). A tarmac road threads its way through narrow gorges beside the Tişiţa river into close range of the impressive Cheilele Tişiţei. Rare species of plants still flourish here.

At **Tulnici** a track leads off to the south for a historic church that is part of the mountain skete of Valea Neagra. Ask for directions from the county museum in Focşani or locally. To the south of Valea Sării (Salt Valley), the village merges with **Prisaca**; both villages claim a wooden church dating from 1770 with oak beams. Continue along this route and you will reach Năruja. Turn left (east) here onto a smaller road for **Reghiu** (c 12km from Valea Sării). A few kilometres southwest is a natural wonder: the gas flares known as *focurile viu* (the living fires). They are located on a promontary c 350m from the road, in a nature reserve near the village of **Andreiaşu de Jos**. The flares cover c 10m and are the result of accumulations of hydrocarbons escaping from fractures in the earth's surface. For more information about this and the other 22 reservations in Vrancea, contact the County Museum in Focşani.

From Reghiu, continue southeast to Sindrilari, Vulcăneasa and eventually **Mera**, whose main claim to fame is that it possesses the only monastery built (1685) in Moldavia by the influential Cantemir family.

Buzău and Râmnicu Sărat

Buzău is an industrial city on the main north–south commercial route, and while most of the heavy traffic takes the lorry route around the city it is easy to get caught up in its wake. Buzău is best avoided unless you have a specific reason for going there. One reason might be to take part in its colourful Midsummer festival, known as Drăgaica. This is held on the last Sunday in June, and is a watered-down version of the once widespread custom of celebrating the moment when the wheat becomes ripe for harvest. Close to the Romanian rituals described by Frazer in *The Golden Bough*, Drăgaica was enacted by young girls who would process singing and dancing through the fields in crowns of straw.

The first known mention of Buzău came in records of the merchants from Braşov with reference to the Buzău Fair of 1431.

Buzău does contain some interesting buildings: the 1649 **Episcopal Cathedral** with its exaggeratedly tall towers, the **Theological College** (1838) and the **Communal Palace** (1899–1903), a turreted confection of Moldavian-style Art Nouveau. The **Dumbravă Cemetery** contains cement copies of Brâncuşi's 'The Prayer' (1907) and next to it, high on a plinth, his bust of Petre Stănescu (1907–10), key pieces in the development of his mature style. Both sculptures were commissioned by Stănescu's widow; you can find the original bronzes in the National Museum of Art, Bucharest.

Practical information

☎ code
038

Tourist information

Offices include *BTT*, Str Unirii, bl B1, ☎ 413850; fax 435051; *Excelent*, Str Bălcescu, ☎/fax 710977; *Hulia Tour*, Str Unirii, bl 4, ☎ 433201; *Intertour*, Str Prelungirea Indenpendenţei, bl 4, ☎/fax 710665; *Pietroasa*, Str Unirii 176, ☎/fax 433333; *Sind România*, B-dul Bălcescu 48, ☎/fax 412358; *Timaiov*, Str Unirii, bl 5A, ☎/fax 710111; *Vacanţă Tur*, Str Unirii 201, bl B1, ☎/fax 710735.

Getting around

By train The *CFR* office is at B-dul Unirii, bl 18B, ☎ 411135.

By car For **car repairs** contact *ACR*, Str Unirii, bl L1, ☎ 411581.

Where to stay

Hotels include *Hotel Bucegi* (✫✫), B-dul Gării 47, ☎ 710113; fax 427699; *Hotel Crâng* (✫✫), Str Spiru Haret 6, ☎ 433366; fax 426223; *Hotel Pietroasa* (✫✫), Piaţa Daciei 1, ☎ 412033; fax 710942. Alternatively, contact the local branch of *ANTREC* on ☎/fax 710851.

Money

CEC is at B-dul Unirii 15A, bl 14 IJK.

Medical care

Spitalul Judeţean (the **county hospital**) is at Str Mareşal Averescu 7, ☎ 421106. **Pharmacies** include *Acropolis*, Str Unirii, bl E1 E2; *Belafarm*, Str Vulcani 48; *EC*, Str Marghiloman bl 17; *Farmacia nr 71*, Complex Unirii.

Entertainment

Buzău's **theatre**, *Teatrul George Ciprian*, is at B-dul Nicolae Bălcescu 50.

Regular events

Contact *Centrul Judeţean de Creaţie Populară*, B-dul Bălcescu 48, ☎ 710383. The village of Gura Teghii holds an ancient festival for New Year; there are excellent woodcarvers at Lopătari, weavers at Bisoca, and Mânzăleşti has a reputation for its makers of musical instruments.

The **County Museum** is at B-dul Bălcescu 50. Items of special interest include a range of Neolithic tools and pottery from the Monteoru culture, Dacian artefacts and finds made at the mountain settlements in the Munţii Buzăului and from various feudal citadels around the county such as Vintilă Vodă, Berca and Bradu. The museum also has a collection of fine and applied art. Open Tues–Fri and Sun 09.00–17.00, Sat 09.00–14.00.

There is an **ethnographic museum** at Str Războieni 8. Open Wed–Mon 09.00–17.00. The villages of **Cotorca** and **Smeeni** have similar collections: look for signs saying Colecţia Muzeală; **Aldeni** also has a small museum, but this one focusses on local archaeology and history rather than ethnography.

Northwest from Buzău

Heading northwest on the DN10 from Buzău, after 20km you reach Cândeşti, where a right turn across the Buzău River brings you to the historic churches of **Berca** and **Răteşti monastery**, and in 9km, to the village of **Scorţoaşa**. In **Dealurile Pâclelor**, the hills to the north of this village, you can find some of the Buzău Subcarpathians' famous 'mud volcanoes', and if you continue heading north to the Slănic Valley, there are 'living fires' near the forests of Lăpătari.

Travelling further west along the DN10, you come to the village of **Măgura** (27km from Buzău) which stands on the edge of the great Dealu Mare vineyard in northern Muntenia. Măgura used to be a centre for stonemasonry, and every summer since 1980, sculptors have gathered here to carve the local stone: you can see the proof standing in the open-air sculpture park. South of Măgura are the old churches of **Niforu** and **Mănăstirea Ciolanu**. Ciolanu was founded in the 16C and stands in the village of Tisău. In the monastery buildings there is a nice little museum which contains traditional handmade utensils connected with housework, farming and pottery-making, and paintings by Gheorghe Tattarescu. Open daily 09.00–17.00. If you continue towards the west you eventually reach Cislău. A few kilometres further north of Măgura, turn right onto a country road to **Cârnu monastery**, c 30km from Buzău, another historic monument.

The **Buzău Mountains** stretch further west, highest at Mount Penteleu (1772m; reached most conveniently from Nereju in Vrancea) and Mount Siriu (1657m). Back on the DN10, going north brings you to Pătârlagele, 37km from Măgura. Turn right (east) here and cross the river for roads and tracks north to the village of **Colţi**, which has a fascinating amber museum. Open Wed–Fri and Sun 09.00–17.00, Sat 09.00–14.00.

There is a **motel** in the town of **Nehoiu**, a further 15km north of Pătârlagele on DN10, and c 10km from there you can reach the narrow fingers of **Lacul Siriu**. The peak of Siriu rises due west of the lake. Easier to get to than the top of Mount Penteleu, the summit allows you to gaze over the surrounding Carpathians for miles. The periglacial lake on the peak is Lacul Vulturilor (Eagles' Lake), also called the Bottomless Lake, for obvious reasons.

16km southwest of Buzău you can sample the mineral waters of **Sărata-Monteoru** and look for the remains of the Roman camp and thermae in **Pietroasele**, 8km southwest. Not far from here, on Dealul Istriţa, two 19C stonebreakers found a marvellous treasure: a gold drinking jar and seven cups representing a mother hen and her chickens. The set now resides in the National History Museum, Bucharest.

Between Buzău and Focşani, the town of **Râmnicu Sărat** sits on the join between the Buzău and Vrancea foothills and the Râmnicu plain. The Râmnicu Sărat River which runs through it means 'salt backwater'; the salt comes into the river water from Dealul Sării (the Salt Hill) up in the mountains. The town is not especially beautiful, but it has a fine Brâncovenesque **monastery complex** that commemorates the Dormition of the Holy Virgin. The buildings were founded by Constantin Brâncoveanu and his uncle, Mihai Cantacuzino. Inside the church are some 17C frescoes. The town museum, **Muzeul Mixt Orăşenesc**, at Str Primăverii 4, is as varied as its name implies. Under its roof are avant-garde paintings and sculpture, traditional dress from Buda and Bişoca, and a collection of exotic flutes from China and the Indo-Malaysian islands. Open Tues–Fri 09.00–16.00, Sat–Sun 09.00–14.00.

To the southeast, the DN22 leads into the featureless landscapes of the Brăila plain and the mud lakes of **Balta Albă** and **Amara** which are famous for their therapeutic qualities. There is a health spa at Balta Albă.

Brăila

The southernmost of the two, Brăila has all the run-down charm of a once-glamorous and flourishing town. Today its ancient port is being redeveloped by the container and shipping industries which have taken advantage of its fine old warehouses. You can still see Anghel Saligny's original concrete silos built in the 1880s, when they were the largest of their kind in the world. But most of the river traffic today is orientated towards the tourist trade.

The city stands on the edge of a group of **islands** which lie at the meeting point between three distinct types of habitat: marsh, forest and steppe. In the tall sandbanks around the marshes there are willow forests and plantations of Euro-American poplar hybrids. The marshes themselves are rich in aquatic plants, many of which are rare species, and the islands are a haven for migratory birds. One of the islands, **Insula Mică a Brăilei** (Brăila's Small Island), has been designated a nature reserve.

Brăila port is an embarcation point for cruises around the island and to other points on the river. Longer trips take place in splendid hotel boats, and you can also book specialist hunting and fishing tours from here. Apart from Little Brăila Island the most common destinations are Fundu Mare, Corotisca, Blasova and Zaton. Contact *Brăila Waterways*, ☎ 039 612372 or any of the many travel agents in the city.

Practical information

☎ code
039

Tourist information

Offices include *BTT*, Str Călăraşi 56, ☎ 633961; fax 611263; *Ducu*, Str Scolilor, bl CPP, *parter*, ☎/fax 611043; *Intertour*, Str Călăraşi 66, ☎/fax 682736; *Liliana*, Str Călăraşilor, bl 3, *parter*, ☎/fax 611226; *Mecon*, B-dul Dorobanţi 54 bis, ☎ 632170; fax 615135; *Nebra Tour*, Str Victoriei 5, ☎/fax 622233; *Panturist*, Str Scolilor 12 *parter*, ☎/fax 636339; *Sind România*, Piaţa Traian 4, ☎/fax 613982.

Getting around

By train This is on Str Victoriei. The *CFR* office is at B-dul Independenţei, bl B1, ☎ 611168.

By car For **car repairs** contact *ACR*, Str D. Bolintineanu, ☎ 611200; *Ceres*, Str Rubinelor 1, ☎ 614302; *Tivoli Trade*, Şos Buzăului 9, ☎ 676000; *Universal Service*, Şos Buzăului 11, ☎ 684670.

By taxi For a *TAXICOM* dispatcher, ☎ 953.

Where to stay

Hotels include *Hotel Belvedere* (✳✳✳), Piaţa Independenţei 1, ☎/fax 635270; *Hotel Tineretului* (✳✳), Str Călăraşi 56, ☎ 611255; fax 611263; *Hotel Traian* (✳✳), Piaţa Traian 1, ☎ 614685; fax 612835.

Post and telephone office

This is on the corner of Piaţa Hristo Botev (named after a 19C Bulgarian poet and revolutionary who lived in Brăila) and Str 1 Dicembrie 1918.

Emergency services

Police ☎ 955 or 611212.
Fire squad ☎ 981 or 611212.

Money

Try *Banc Post*, Piaţa Traian 11; *Banca Agricolă*, Piaţa Traian 15; *Banca Comercială Română*, Calea Călăraşilor 17; *Banca Naţională a României*, Calea Călăraşilor 2; *Banca România de Dezvoltare*, Piaţa Traian 12.

Medical care

There is a **clinic**, *Policlinica nr 3*, at Calea Călăraşilor 123, ☎ 632840. For an **ambulance** ☎ 961 or 611000. **Pharmacies** include *Farmacia 67*, Str Scolilor bl M1; *Iris*, Str Călăraşi, bl 11C, *parter*.

Translations

Birou Public Traduceri, Calea Călăraşilor, Str Frumoasa, ☎ 611818.

Regular events and entertainment

For traditional festivals and crafts fairs, contact *Centrul Judeţean de Creaţie Populară*, Piaţa Traian 1, ☎ 611505. Brăila's main **theatre**, *Teatrul Maria Filotti*, is at Str Eminescu 2; there is also a puppet theatre, *Teatrul de Păpuşei Carabus*, at Str Polona 12.

History

Written records documenting Brăila go back to 1350, when a Spanish geography, Libro de Conoscimento, mentioned it as Wallachia's main port, Drinago. It appears as Brayla 16 years later, and in 1368 Vlaicu Vodă, Prince of Moldavia (r. 1364–77), waived customs duties to the merchants of Braşov who used Brăila as a transit point for their goods. Armenians also thought that the port had a promising future, and in the 16C and 17C they dominated the city's commercial life, helping to establish the carpet-weaving trade that still flourishes here. When the Ottomans gained control of Moldavia's river ports in 1544, Brăila became a Turkish *rayah* (administration centre).

The Ottoman Turks occupied Brăila for nearly 300 years, and in terms of architecture their most influential legacy was the city plan. Based on five concentric rings of fortified walls, bastions and ditches, it made expansion almost impossible. When the Turks abandoned Moldavia after the Treaty of Adrianople (1829), Romanian planners pulled down the fortress walls but adapted to the existing layout by fanning the main roads out from Piaţa Traian (beside the harbour) like wheel spokes. Concentric streets intersect these spokes, following the lines of the old walls. During the mid-19C Brăila's commercial heartbeat quickened and the city attracted settlers from all over Europe. Its cosmopolitan character was reflected in the polyglot cafés and restaurants that sprang up, and a few entrepreneurs made fortunes by shipping cereals from the Bărăgan Plain to Western Europe, showing off their wealth by building extravagant villas. The attractive old façades of these elegant palaces remain. Because of its proximity to the Black Sea, there are plans afoot to make Brăila county a tax-free zone.

Near Anghel Saligny's quay and a stone's throw from Piaţa Traian with its pompous bust of the Emperor Trajan, **Biserica Sfinţi Arhangeli** is an Orthodox church that the Turks built originally as a mosque; it was converted in 1831. Close by, the **clock tower** features Brăila's 'logo', an old ship. The revolutionary poet Panait Istraţi, whose life and work is commemorated all over town, said that life in Brăila was regulated by the dockers' siren, which 'howled at morning, noon and night like an apocalyptic beast'.

Muzeul Brăilei, the County Museum, is at Piaţa Traian 3. Highlights of its collection include ceramics from the Cucuteni II period and Neolithic objects from the Dridu and Babadag cultures. Brăila county has 60 sites of special archaeological interest, including prehistoric settlements, burial sites and isolated tombs from the Stone Age onwards. As well as the indigenous Romanians, ancient Greece and Rome, Byzantium and the Ottoman Turks all played their part in shaping Brăila. The museum contains paintings by well-known Romanian artists from the late 19C and early 20C, photographs of the port, a collection of 78 rpm disks recording oral folklore, and a huge library. It is one of the oldest museums in Romania, having been founded by order of Carol I in 1881; the building was designed as a hotel and dates from 1870. The museum moved here in 1959. Open Tues–Sun 09.00–17.00.

Brăila's **folk art museum** stands in the Public Gardens. It has an interesting display which traces the history of fishing in the area. Open Tues–Sun 09.00–17.00. If you have a taste for natural history, visit the **Secţia Ştiinţele Naturii** in Parcul Monument, which has a splendid array of exotic butterflies and molluscs. Open Tues–Sun 09.00–17.00 in summer, and Mon–Fri 09.00–17.00 in winter.

Casa Colecţiilor de Artă, the Art Museum, at Str Belvedere 1 is exceptionally good. Housed in a fine Early Modern building from 1912, it contains some outstanding examples of modern Romanian painting, sculpture and graphics, and is particularly interesting when it comes to the period between the First and Second World Wars. There are interesting and attractive works by painters

Theodor Aman (1831–91), Grigorescu (1838–1907), Gheorghe Patrașcu (1872–1949), Theodor Pallady (1871–1956), Nicolae Tonitza (1886–1940), Iosif Iser (1881–1958), Ștefan Dimitrescu (1886–1933) and Nicolae Darascu, of whom Brâncuși made a striking bronze portrait in c 1905. There are also some fascinating pieces by Max Herman Maxy (1895–1971), whose wife made the museum a gift of his studio after his death. Open Tues–Sun 09.00–17.00.

There are several **memorial houses** in Brăila. One is dedicated to **Panait Istrați** (see below) and stands in the Public Gardens (there is another Istrați museum in the village of Baldovinești). At Str Cetății 70 a memorial house celebrates the life and work of poet, historian and critic, **Dumitru Perpessicus**. At Str I.L. Caragiale 32 there is a small museum in which you can find information about philosophers **Vasile Bancilă** and **Nae Ionescu**, and the logician **Anton Dumitru**, all of whom were connected with Brăila.

The impressive **Greek Orthodox Church**, a reminder of Brăila's once-large Greek community, stands on Calea Călărașilor. It was completed in 1872 to designs drafted by architect Avram Ioanidis of Bursa; Gheorghe Tattarescu painted the inside.

While **Brăila harbour** may look as though it is drowning in torpor, there are **cruises** to be had along the Danube and into the nearby marshy islands. 5km to the southwest of Brăila on the DN2B, **Lacu Sărat** is one of many isolated lakes formed when the Danube changed its course. Its salty water lies over a thick layer of glutinous, black mud which is used in various therapeutic treatments. The health spa of Lacu Sărat is surrounded by forest and has become very popular.

Panait Istrați
Istrați was the son of a Greek smuggler. He became a communist but never lost the courage to speak out against the Soviet regime. After a suicide attempt in Nice he wrote in despair to Romain Rolland, who was so impressed by his wit that he dubbed Istrați the 'Gorky of the Balkans'. Istrați earned an international reputation, and his books were translated into 23 languages. Among the titles which appeared in English were Kyra *Kyralina*, *Haiducs* and *The Thistles of the Bărăgan*, the latter about the Romany who were deported to the eastern plains. In 1925 he abandoned writing to devote himself to the cause of Russian-speaking Transdniestrians who were suffering under oppressive laws passed by the Romanian government. He was also, briefly, an adherent of the Romanianism Crusade, founded by a former Legionary member of parliament, Mihail Stelescu, who was assassinated in 1936.

Galați

33km north of Brăila lies Galați, a city of 400,000 people, which makes it the second largest in Moldavia after Iași, and the fifth largest in Romania. Dimitrie Cantemir called Galați 'the best known commodity market on the Danube'. Today it is Romania's largest river port, orientated towards shipbuilding and the production of iron and steel, and little of its ancient past is visible 'on the ground'. Under its German name of Galatz, it was the river port from which

Bram Stoker sent his heroes Jonathan Harker and Lord Godalming up river on their way to the vampire's castle in the Bârgău mountains. Stoker mixed geographical fact with fiction in a fascinating way: the Siret River does indeed meet the Danube at Galaţi. So does the Prut, which marks the border between Romania and the Moldovan Republic.

History

Galaţi harbour is very deep, and large ships have anchored here since antiquity. Traces of human settlement have been found in and around the city from as long ago as the 3C BC, but experts are still arguing as to the origins of its name. Some say that it came from a Gallic tribe who built a walled city nearby, while others claim that Galaţi owes its existence to a Christian missionary named Cocceius Gallatos arrived here on orders from Constantine the Great in the 4C. A third theory holds that the city's name comes from a local chief called Gălat who ruled a fishing village long since buried under layers of industrial wasteland. Prince Petru Rareş is said to have gone fishing on Lacul Brates near Galaţi village. By the 11C the town was the most important Danubian port in Moldavia; the first known written mention of Galaţi dates back to 1445. A century later, there was a reference to Schela Galaţi (*schela* being an old word for the place where ships are moored for loading and unloading).

The Turks took Galaţi in the early 16C and remained until 1829. They moored their warships in the harbour, causing a great deal of resentment among the traders and fishermen who relied on the port for their livelihood. The Galaţieni retaliated by stealing down river in their canoes at night and attacking the Ottoman ships. The Turks took vast quantities of wheat, saltpetre and timber and thousands of sheep and horses, and as if that were not enough, Romanian wax went to light the Sultan's seraglio in Istanbul.

In 1837, after the Peace of Adrianople, Galaţi was turned into a free port. It retained this status until 1883. In the 19C the port thrived but this happened to the disadvantage of so many people that Galaţi again became a focus of unrest. Social and economic inequalities drove writers and intellectuals such as Vasile Alecsandri (who aranged the *Miorița* ballad), and Alexandru Ioan Cuza to organise demonstrations that contributed to the 1859 union of Moldavia and Wallachia. Cuza, whose statue stands in the public gardens, was briefly head of state before the new Romanian government chose a German king.

During the Second World War, German troops retreating from the Soviet Union in 1944 devastated the town and reduced the population, then substantially Jewish, to less than half. Most of the city's attractive buildings were destroyed after a bombing raid the same year.

Sidex, the iron and steel works which Gheorghiu-Dej established in Galaţi to defy Comecon, was the largest of its kind in Romania. But the result, on its completion in the 1970s, was a white elephant of staggering proportions. Calls for the closure of such outdated plants have been thwarted by fears of mass unemployment, creating a vicious circle that has been holding Romania's economy back throughout the 1990s. In 1994 Galaţi was declared a free port once again in order to encourage greater foreign investment in the city.

The city is one of the chief access points for Romanian imports and it is the country's leading exporter of timber; Galaţi also has the country's largest shipyard. Apart from iron and steel smelting, its industries include metalworking and the production of chemicals, textiles, building materials, and foodstuffs.

Among the famous people connected with Galaţi are the great American Joyce scholar, Richard Ellmann (1918–88), and his daughter, novelist Lucy Ellmann, whose forebears came from here. There is also a university in Galaţi, called Universitatea Dunare de Jos.

You can catch a **ferry** or a **hydrofoil** from Galaţi to Tulcea: tickets and embarkation are from *Gara Fluvială*, the river harbour station housed in Anghel Saligny's imposing Navigation Palace. Book the day before to avoid hassle, as this is a popular trip.

Practical information

☎ code
036

Tourist information

Offices include *Agatur*, B-dul George Coşbuc 1, ☎/fax 465292; *Pibunni*, Str Domnească 11, ☎ 463885; fax 461166; *Dunărea*, Str Bălcescu 1, ☎ 412227; fax 464312; *Fantastic*, Str Domnească 22, ☎/fax 460893; *Galtour*, Str Domnească 3, ☎ 460700; fax 417014; *Le Vick Vacances*, Str Domnească 70, ☎/fax 460021; *România Impex*, Str Prelungirea Traian, bl K, ☎ 465033; *Sind România*, Str Domnească 58, ☎/fax 413903.

Getting around

By train The station is located east of the city centre. The *CFR* office is at Str Brăilei bl BR2, ☎ 413255.

By car For **car repairs** contact *ACR* at Str Brăilei, bl BR, ☎ 413255.

By taxi Contact *Taxi Gal*, Str Morilor 1, ☎ 467772.

Where to stay

Hotels include *Hotel Dunărea* (✩✩✩), Str Domnească 13–15, ☎ 418041; fax 461050; *Hotel Faleza* (✩✩✩), Str Roşiori 1, ☎ 435237; fax 461388; *Hotel Galaţi* (✩✩), Str Domnească 12–14, ☎ 460521; fax 460144. There are facilities for **camping** and *popas turistic* (little cabins) at Popaşul de la Dunăre, on the Trecere BAC at the bottom of the Danube Cliff (Faleza Dunării); the complex has a restaurant and can organise fishing trips.

Eating out

Upmarket **restaurants** include the *Pescarus Restaurant* and the *Libertatea Hotel-Café* on board the *Libertatea* schooner in the harbour; *Piano* is at Str Brăilei 15. **Pizzerias** include *Dino's* at Str Tecuci 110, *Emporio* at Str Domnească 52A, and *Pizza Nicnic* on the Faleza Dunării.

Money

Banks include *Banc Post*, Str Movilei 2–8; *Banca Agricolă*, Str Brăilei 31; *Banca Comercială Ion Tiriac*, Str Domnească 48; *Banca Internaţională a Religiilor*, Str Domnească 51; *Banca România pentru Dezvoltare*, Str Fraternităţii 1; *Bankcoop*, Str Domnească 24; *CEC*, Str Domnească 24. **Exchange houses** are *ACR*, Str Brăilei, bl BR1C; *Galtour*, Str Domnească 15 and Str Bălcescu 1 bis, *Pibunni*, Str Domnească 11.

Medical care

Pharmacies include *Cristiana Bayer*, Str Bălcescu 26; *Europharm*, Str Brăilei.

bl A5-A6; *Paracelsus*, Str Sfântul Spiridon 1.

Entertainment

For **theatres**, *Teatrul Dramatic* is at Str Domnească 59; *Teatrul Muzical N. Leonard* at St. Mihai Bravu 50; *Teatrul de Păpuți* (puppets) at Str Primăverii 14. A jazz festival is held in Galați during the autumn, and a festival of operetta in October.

Cultural highlights in Galați comprise **Biserica Precistă**, a fortified wooden church dedicated to the Holy Virgin which Ștefan cel Mare founded on a hill overlooking the town. It was reconstructed as a handsome masonry building by *voivode* Vasile Lupu in 1646. There is a small museum containing rare religious books and other cult items in the church buildings. The **Mavromol Church** is interesting although less visually appealing. Gheorghe Duca (r. 1661–65, 1668–72 and 1678–83) founded the church in 1669, and his son made radical alterations to it between 1700–03. The city's first schools were organised in the cells surrounding the church. Other 17C churches include **Sf Dumitru**, which Vasile Lupu endowed in 1649, and **Sf Gheorghe**, dating from 1664–65.

The **City Hall** was designed by Ion Mincu in a style which was inspired by Brâncovenesque buildings and Romanian vernacular architecture. It was completed in 1911.

Muzeul de Arte Vizuale, the art museum at Str Domnească 141, is the former home of Alexandru Ioan Cuza, who was a magistrate of Galați district before he became the first prince of the newly-united Romania in 1859. This is one of the finest art galleries in Romania. It has a collection of over 3500 paintings, sculptures, prints and decorative art, mainly by Romanian artists. Open Tues–Sun 09.00–17.00.

Muzeul Județean de Istorie, the County History museum, stands in a shroud of chestnut trees on Str Cuza 80, and features some of the riches excavated from Paleolithic and Neolithic Criș culture sites which flourished around this part of Moldavia. It also has a collection of rare books and letters from Balzac, Jules Verne and Zola. Open Tues–Sun 09.00–17.00.

Complexul Muzeal de Științele Naturii is Galați's Natural History Museum with a zoo and botanic garden attached. Full of attractive and interesting exhibits such as gymnosperms and electric eels, it is at Str Domnească 91. Open Wed–Sun 09.00–15.00.

At Str Mihai Bravu 46 there is a **museum** illustrating the careers of various famous personalities such as Cuza, Costache Negri and Mihail Kogălniceanu.

Făleza Dunării is a 4km length of promenade along the top of a cliff on Galați's waterfront. Once every three years it becomes the site of the Galați Festival of Metal Sculpture which attracts artists from Romania and abroad.

Around Galați

You can see the remains of a **Roman camp** called Tirighina at **Barboși** on the outskirts of Galați. It was built as a frontier station during Trajan's reign (113–117) and survived until the 4C. When Hadrian became emperor in 117, he decided to abandon Trajan's conquests in Asia and concentrate on reorganising his territories around the Lower Danube. He withdrew his troops from the territories that he held to the east of the Carpathians and the Olt. This river became the new border line and the former Dacia became Dacia Superior. The territories lying to the north of the Danube—formerly in Moesia Inferior—

became a new province, Dacia Inferior. As a result, the Romans had to find new ways of keeping political and military control over the area by the Danube. Their solution was to create military bridgeheads on the northern shore of the river in at least in two places: at Tirighina (Barboşi) and Aliobrix (Cartal-Orlovka in present-day Ukraine). Aliobrix was a *castrum* where an auxiliary unit of the army of Moesia Inferior established its civil settlement. Some fascinating objects have been found at Barboşi, including the marble figures known as the Thracian Knight and the Danube Knight. Experts have noticed a remarkable likeness between the Thracian Knight and the mounted warrior found at Sutton Hoo in England. As yet no-one has established if this is pure coincidence or proof of some hitherto unsuspected cultural link.

An earthen lamp found near Barboşi-Galaţi shows signs which may have come from the Dacian calendar, in which a year of 360 days alternated with one of 365 days. The suggestion is that the lamp came from the reign of Decenius, who evolved the calendar and succeeded Burebista as Dacian king in 44 BC.

2km from Galaţi to the northeast lies **Lacul Brateş**, a popular place for fishing and water sports. **Gârboavele Forest**, about 17km northwest of the city, is an ancient oak forest popular with Galaţieni who like to stroll and picnic here. Other local excursions could include the fishing village of **Crapina** (Little Carp), near the lake of the same name 15km southeast across the ferry to 23 August, and its near neighbour Ghimia. **Gârvan-Dinogeţia**, close to Crapina, is an archaeological site where traces of Daco-Roman and Byzantine settlements have been found. Beyond this, in 10km you reach the sand dunes of **Hanu Conachi nature reserve**. From here the road continues to Isaccea and other interesting stopping-off points on the way to Tulcea city and the Danube Delta, see Dobrogea.

Some 50km northwest of Galaţi lies the village of **Costache Negri**. It is named after a well-known 19C politician who was involved in the Unionist movement. His family home stands in the village and has been turned into a museum memorial house, open Tues–Sun 09.00–17.00.

A Geto-Dacian settlement called Piroboridava has been discovered at **Poiana**. It flourished as an economic and strategic centre from the 4C to the 1C BC. The site of another Dacian community can be seen at **Brăhăşeşti**.

During June there is *Serbătoarea bujorului sălbatic*, a special festival to celebrate the wild peonies in **Pădurea Breana**. Ask a local travel agent for details.

Last but not least, the vineyards at **Târgu Bujor** and **Nicoreşti** produce some of the finest wines in Romania.

Maramureş

The Maramureş is a place of almost unbelievable beauty. Its extraordinary loveliness comes from the fact that it has escaped large-scale industrialisation and collectivisation. It is also set apart from the rest of Romania, enclosed by mountains to east, south and west and by the lazily serpentine bends of the River Tisa to the north. Within this huge bowl lie valleys where alpine pasture descends into dense woodland and brooks tumble over beds of rounded river stones so smooth that you can walk on them barefoot without pain. There are mineral springs and deep gorges, and orchards of gnarled fruit trees and meadows peopled by wonderfully humanoid haystacks. The lower hill slopes are sometimes ridged with low banks of raised earth, defining field boundaries. The ridges follow the rolling contours of the hills and from a distance they are easily mistaken for terracing. These are the only man-made enclosures Maramureş has ever known.

Within its natural boundaries, the landscapes of Maramureş vary dramatically. At the western end of the region, the pass across the Huta mountains rises in gentle stages that you can take at your leisure, but at the eastern end, beyond Borşa where the road to Bucovina crosses the Prislop Pass, the mountains tower above you from awesome heights, plunging almost vertically to the rivers that snake beneath.

None of this on its own makes Maramureş any different from other secluded stretches of the Carpathians. But when you add its compactness and the transcendental peace which you can achieve here—most of the heavy container traffic passes far away to the south—it begins to feel like somewhere in a class of its own.

Although some mining continues here, Maramureş is predominantly an agricultural and pastoral region of small farms and mountain grazing. It covers an area of just over 3,300 sq km. The Ţibles, Guţâi and Rodna ranges have protected it so effectively that during much of the Middle Ages Maramureş was isolated from the outside world. It is a cliché that 'mountain people' are rugged, independent and indomitable, but to an extent the Moroşeni have developed separately from their fellow Romanians. There are reasons for believing that they are the purest living descendants of the Dacians, those 'fair-minded and most courageous of men' who inspired such admiration in Herodotus. Thracian names for rivers, villages and mountains, and for the mines that have been exploited here since antiquity and give us modern Baia Mare and its Hungarian equivalent of Nagybánya, are a faint echo of a long-vanished civilisation that once flourished in the Carpathians.

When the Romans conquered Romania they thought better of tackling the Moroşeni—or at least their mountain passes. The cussedness of the people who refused to be downtrodden by successive Magyar, Habsburg and Horthyist regimes lives on in the determination of local artists and ethnographers to save what is left of their culture.

They are dying out apace, but traditional customs have survived here longer and in a more concentrated form than anywhere else in Romania. Moroşeni men still wear homespun suits for everyday work. For celebrations and feast days, they change into embroidered and sequinned finery of a kind that is nowadays usually found only in museums. In the more remote villages people are often embarrassed by their lack of modern plumbing and cooking facilities, calling themselves '*primitivi*' ('primitives'). But while they are desperately poor by Western standards, these

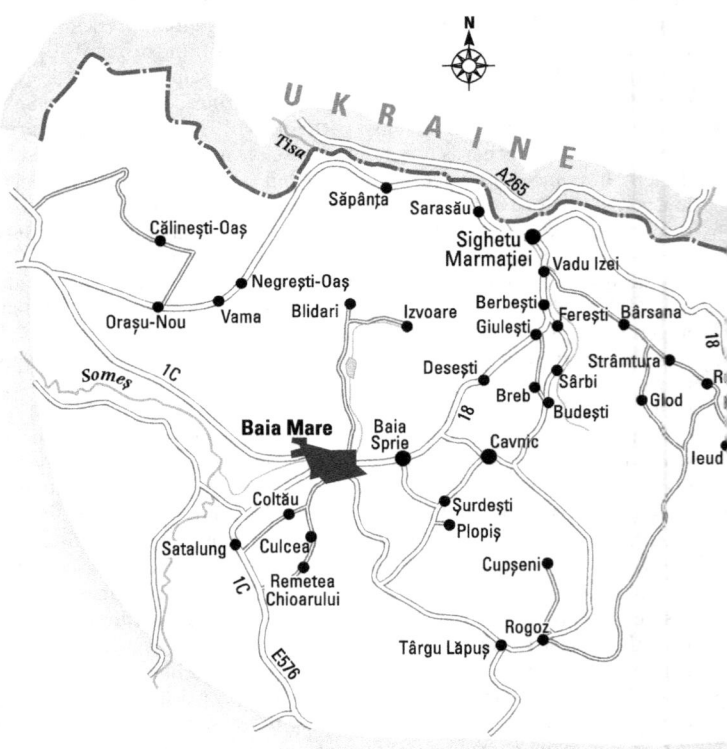

communities are still close-knit: neighbour helps neighbour without thinking twice. Set against this is the fact that most families are in dire need of cash, especially foreign currency. The urge to earn a few dollars by selling irreplaceable costumes and other heirlooms has often been too strong to resist. It may be arrogant to try to stop them. American anthropologist Gail Kligman spent two years in the village of Ieud. She reflects that the Moroșeni may be happier to wave goodbye to their picturesque traditions than sentimental outsiders. One of this region's strengths is its ability to commemorate death and move on.

Traditional rituals such as those mentioned below are not unique to Maramureș or even Romania, but against the backdrop of snow-covered mountains and among hills which are open save for the ridges of ancient field boundaries, they are very appealing.

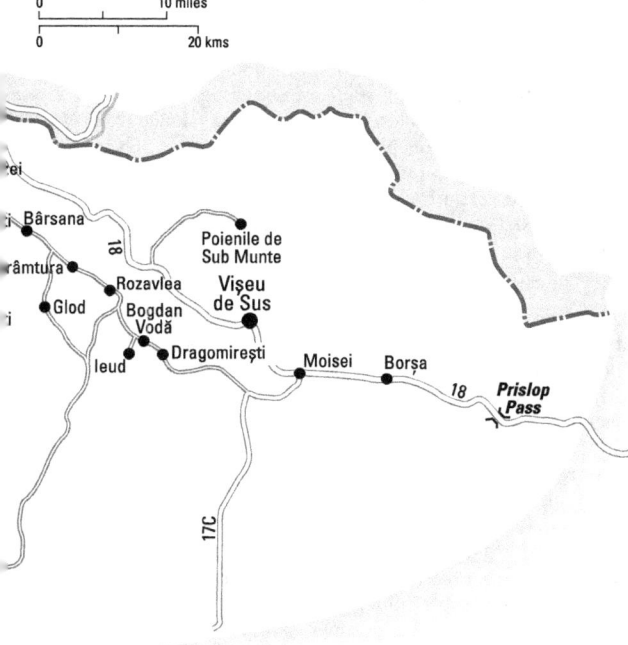

MARAMUREȘ

Blessing the plough

In 1995 a young school teacher in Hârnicești revived the ancient custom of *tânjaua*. *Tânjaua* is a fertility rite which is meant to ensure a good harvest for the year to come. It is held on St George's Day, which in southeastern Europe heralds the start of spring.

Tânjaua begins when the men and boys of the village construct a makeshift plough from tree branches and decorate it with ribbons. The plough can be up to 10m long, and is sometimes longer. Once ready it is carried ceremonially to the house of a man who has been chosen to host the celebrations. He receives the procession by placing his axe symbolically on the ground in his courtyard. This gesture is meant to protect the village

> against storms. The men eat a feast after which their host scatters cinders over the axe to purify it. His fellows then lift him over the cinders so that he too will be cleansed, and he tries to escape. Once the host has been caught, a cornbread bun called *azimă* and water are placed on the ground beside the axe to ensure a fertile harvest. The procession heads off for the river with the plough.
>
> Up to this point women have been excluded from the proceedings (apart from providing the feast). But now everyone wades into the water for a ritual cleansing. This is the signal for all the participants to let their hair down. Finally the party starts.
>
> In Romania ceremonies which involve blessing the plough have been documented as far back as the 14C. During the communist period they were frowned on because gatherings of this kind gave people the chance to meet on their own terms and exchange independent ideas. The same reasoning was behind the closure of mills and public washing places. But villagers at nearby Hoteni kept a muted version of *tânjaua* alive, and today Hoteni still holds the celebrations on St. George's Day, while in the meantime Hârnicești has lost the teacher who organised its festival and no-one has taken his place.

Maramureș is a place of fascinating contradictions: if life continues here much as it did a hundred years ago, it is far from being a rural backwater. The Roman occupation of Dacia did not penetrate as far north as this, but the Moroșeni supplied the legions with salt and precious metals. Right up until the modern period the Maramureș was regarded as a region of free peasants where serfdom was largely unknown. In the 16C, it saw the first miners' strike in Europe. From the 16C its monasteries were famed as centres of learning, and the Moroșeni's reputation for independence and intellectual excellence lasts to this day.

Even Ceaușescu was touched by the magic of Maramureș, or at least he could see its potential as a rallying point for Romanian nationalism. In 1974, he admonished an audience here to 'preserve the customs of your forefathers, and make them your keepsake'. Ceaușescu's influence was almost always malign, but sometimes his self-aggrandisement had a positive spin-off. Spurred on by the singing and dancing competitions that started in the 1970s with *Cânterea al României* (Song to Romania), Moroșeni teachers encouraged their pupils to learn the words of traditional songs and the steps of the round dances. They drilled their teams to perfection, won prizes at national competitions and travelled abroad. The villages of Maramureș now have some of the finest children's folk dance troupes in the country.

History

The origins of the ethnic Romanian population in the Maramureș are clear. The great migrations that swept through eastern Europe from the 4C to the 10C passed it by, and it is likely that settled communities of free Dacians continued to live here after the Romans retreated. Free Dacians left their traces at Oncești, Călinești, Mesteacăn and Oarșa de Sus. Remains found at Mesteacăn, Vălenii Șomcutei, Prislop, Baia Mare and Sarasăn show that proto-Romanian village communities existed in the 4C. The discovery of a hoard of early 10C dirhams on the Upper Tisa Plain has led historians to think that this lay on one of the main routes which the Magyars took into Pannonia (modern

> ### *Rupta sterpelor*
> A custom which continued during the communist period is *Rupta sterpelor*, the annual measuring of sheep's and goat's milk. This ritual may also have originated in the Middle Ages. It is held after St George's Day and before the shepherds take the flocks of sheep and goats to their mountain pastures. Its purpose is to decide how much cheese the shepherds owe to the owners of their flocks. As in the Oaș country, where it is called *Sâmbra oilor*, *Rupta sterpelor* takes place at a *stână* (sheepfold) in the hills near the village. Elsewhere the custom is known as *stană* or *măsuriș*.
>
> In Ieud where most people have their own flocks of sheep and goats, the *stână* lies c 20km from the village. The shepherds decorate their fold before the measuring starts. They place a fir tree in the centre and fix a circular loaf of *colac* to one of its branches. One of the shepherds thrusts an axe into the ground and sprinkles salt around it to symbolise the purity and riches of the earth. *Rupta sterpelor* is an excuse for a party, and the whole village gathers at the *stână* to watch the milking, which is always done by men. Each animal has a special nick in its ear to show who it belongs to, and the shepherds have their own marks which they cut into a stick to record the amount of milk that is yielded. Ewes and goats without milk (*sterpe*) are separated from the rest. After the count, a red ribbon is tied around the top knot of the most beautiful ram, and a goat or sheep is killed and roasted to feed the gathering. Bottles of home-made *țuica* are broached, and the singing and dancing last long into the evening.

Hungary) from southern Poland because Arabic coins of the same origins have been found in Hungary as well. The earliest known Slav settlement in the area was found at Crăciunești.

Medieval Maramureș covered a much larger area than it does today. To the north, it spread across the Tisa to the main Carpathian spine, while to the west it stretched as far as Hust and Tur on the Tisa Plain.

During the 10C and 11C, Hungary's borders had reached the confluence of the Tisa and the Someș, leaving a large area of uncharted forest beyond. The Magyar kings probably regarded this woodland as theirs and used it as a buffer between their territory and Poland. Maramureș appears by name in a Hungarian diploma of 1199, when King Emeric awarded a gift of land to a loyal subject who saved his life during an accident that happened there. Every so often, the Hungarian sovereign would lead an expedition into Maramureș, to hunt and, more importantly, to claim new tracts of land. After the Tartar massacres of 1241–42, the Magyar king Béla IV invited 'Saxon' colonists to settle in Ugocea and Bereg, to the west of the Tisa, and gave them land and privileges in return for protecting the Hungarian border. By the 14C there were German and Hungarian villages as far east as Teceu and Câmpulung la Tisa, and a small number of Ruthenians lived here as well. In 1303 the Magyar king Wenceszlász (Venceslav in Romanian) established a new district in Maramureș itself.

There were Romanians in Maramureș before 1308, when Károly Róbert I of Anjou acceded to the Hungarian throne. In fact, the majority of 14C villages in Maramureș were controlled by ethnic Romanians and were organised into chiefdoms called *cnezaţi*, and *voivodaţi*, duchies or principates. These semi-autonomous communities controlled the valleys under the *ius wolachorum* or Vlachs' law. The existence of these societies gives even more substance to the theory that an autocthonous population evolved here over a long period.

The Magyars tried to convert the Romanians of Maramureş to Catholicism. But while some accepted the change of faith in return for privileges and status, others resented the interference and accused the Hungarians of destroying their ancient rights. In the winter of 1342–43, Bogdan of Cuhea, a *voivode* of Hungarian-controlled Satu Mare, grew so frustrated that he went on the rampage with an army of like-minded Moroşeni, burning local Magyar estates. When he heard the news, King Lajos I immediately outlawed Bogdan and sent troops to put down the rebellion. But Bogdan, 'our disloyal infidel', escaped arrest, and in 1359, while Lajos was otherwise engaged, he crossed the Prislop Pass with a large band of followers and set himself up as the first independent prince of Moldavia. Lajos had Bogdan's lands confiscated and burnt his fortress, which stood near Cuhea (or Bogdan Vodă, as it is now known). Bogdan's family was Orthodox, and sometime between 1330–40 they built a stone church in Cuhea itself. This was one of the few known masonry churches from this period.

In 1381 an Orthodox monastery was established at Peri in prewent-day Ukraine, just across the Tisa from Sighetu Marmaţiei. Ten years later, two Moroşeni nobles rode to Constantinople to ask the Patriarch Anthony to raise the monastery's status to a bishopric. He refused on the grounds that the Magyar king had not given his permission, but the Patriarch agreed instead to turn Peri into an exarchate under his own protection. He also gave the priest in charge the right to train his own monks. The monastery now had authority over all the Orthodox in Maramureş and some of northern Transylvania as well. As a result of this, Peri became an important centre of learning: in the 16C some of the first books in Romanian were printed here.

The Angevin dynasty which ruled Hungary from the 14C–17C caused massive unrest. Thwarted in their efforts to control Moldavia and Wallachia, the Magyar kings concentrated on keeping a tight hold of the lands they owned. After the abortive rebellion at Bobâlna in 1437, feudal lords made ever-increasing demands on the smallholders who lived on their estates. By the 16C most peasants had become little more than serfs.

In 1514 Pope Leo X called for a crusade against the Ottoman Turks, promising freedom to peasants who would join the campaign. When the nobility objected, the Pope withdrew his offer. Transylvania erupted into open warfare as a result. A minor Székely noble named Gheorghe Doja (Dózsa György in Hungarian) led a peasants' revolt, demanding the abolition of feudal obligations. Doja's army consisted of ethnic Hungarian and Romanian farmers, miners, a number of poor and wealthy townspeople, and some yeomen. At first things went well: the protesters defeated Transylvanian Governor Stephen Báthory and succeeded in capturing several important towns. Doja's luck ran out at Timişoara. He was taken outside the walls by Ioan Zápolya, the *voivode* of Transylvania, tortured and killed along with many of his supporters.

The boyars who met at the Diet of Rakoş at the end of 1514 decided that the heads of 32 landowning families should lose their estates for their part in the rebellion. Even harsher restrictions were imposed on the peasantry: the boyars raised the *robota* (the peasants' work obligations) to 52 days a year, forbade smallholders to leave their estates, prevented their children from working for other peasants and made it impossible for the son of any smallholder to reach the rank of bishop if he entered the Church. Laws like these were common in eastern Europe at the time, but in Hungary peasants were freed from their tied status in 1530 whereas in Transylvania, serfs remained shackled to one estate until the end of the 18C.

After the Turkish conquest of Hungary, Maramureş was left in limbo until Ioan Zápolya, the Ottoman candidate for the Magyar crown, beat Ferdinand I of Habsburg and captured fortresses on the Tisa plain. Zápolya annexed Maramureş to the principality in 1538, leaving the Hungarian plain and the Banat to be turned into *pashaliks*. During the same period, Calvinist and Hussite missionaries came to the region, and Protestant schools were set up in Sighet.

The Habsburgs' 'liberation' of Transylvania and the Banat also affected Maramureş. As in Transylvania, the Viennese court imposed heavy taxes here and tried to bring its new subjects to heel by forcing them, once again, to accept Catholicism. Rebellious smallholders and *nemeşi* (Moroşeni nobles who lived on their own land) joined a rebellion led by Ferenc Rákóczi II. For eight years, from 1703–11, the Transylvanian prince fought to break the Habsburgs' grip on this outpost of their empire. But the smallholders found their position unchanged, and support for the struggle evaporated. Peri monastery was destroyed during the Rákóczi uprising.

In 1717 the Austrian emperor removed a Turkish vassal prince from the Moldavian throne. Retaliating, the Sultan summoned Kazaks and Tartars from the Crimea to help restore Ottoman rule. The mission failed. Instead the Tartars crossed the border into Transylvania. They looted and burned and captured thousands of Christians. Having ridden north to Cavnic, the Tartars turned west as far as Satu Mare and set out for home along the Tisa Valley over the Ignis Pass into Maramureş. They were said to number at least 10,000 men and were encumbered with an equal number of prisoners. Hearing of their imminent arrival, the Moroşeni hoped that the Tartars would join them in their fight against the Habsburgs. Their hopes were rudely dashed when they saw their villages and precious churches going up in smoke. Many people fled to the mountains. Not to be beaten on their home ground, Romanian bandits attacked the invaders as they rode through the forests near Sighet. A little further on, between Bârsana and Strâmtura, soldiers from Baia Mare fell upon the Tartars again, supported by miners from Coştiui and peasants from the Iza Valley.

By now hungry, exhausted and furious, the Tartars set fire to the churches of Dragomireşti. On their way to the Prislop Pass they fell into a trap laid by a priest from Borşa, who lured them into a narrow valley from which all the trees had been felled. According to legend, all the invaders were slaughtered except their chieftain, who escaped never to return. This was the last time a Tartar invasion troubled Maramureş.

In 1733 Maramureş was annexed to Hungary. By now the Austrians had come up with a religious compromise. While still refusing to accept the eastern church, they encouraged Moroșeni to become Uniates, or Greek-Catholics. This hybrid creed allowed Romanians to retain their Orthodox theology and their church buildings while recognising the Pope as their supreme temporal head. Many Moroșeni accepted the proposal, and Greek Catholicism became the most popular religion in Maramureș. And even though they were forced to convert to Orthodoxy during the Communist period, the Uniate church is still this region's strongest faith. But the compromise was hotly resisted by Orthodox priests; monks at Moisei monastery tried to stem the flood and in 1759, Egumen Calistrat of Putna in neighbouring Moldavia begged the Moroșeni not to tie their churches up with Rome.

The first quarter of the 18C witnessed a flowering in the visual arts. In rural villages painters were commissioned to decorate churches which had been restored or built from scratch after the Tartar attacks. New stone churches appeared as well. The churches were often decorated by Moroșeni painters who learnt their skills in the traditional centres of Moldavia and Wallachia, where they could absorb the developing Brâncovenești style at its source. Neo-Byzantine painting from Moldavia had been an important source of inspiration here in the previous century, when students from the painting school at Moisei were in demand to create murals in churches in nearby valleys and around Năsăud in northern Transylvania. But as the century wore on, the hieratic style of Byzantine art began to give way, little by little, in Greek Catholic churches, to the naturalism and fuller volumes of Austrian Baroque. One book on the subject calls this development a 'contamination'.

When the Hungarians rose against Austrian hegemony in 1848, they carried many Moroșeni with them. But a spirit of nationalism was growing among ethnic Romanians too. The initiative was taken by Avram Iancu, who demanded recogniton of Romanians' national rights. Iancu's doubts about Magyar promises to establish democracy in Transylvania caused many Romanians to think again about joining the struggle on the Hungarian side. Some of those who rejected the Hungarian rallying cry were Moroșeni, and they were persecuted along with the other Romanian Transylvanians who refused to support the Magyars. In the autumn of 1848, Maramureș and Transylvania formally refused to accept union with Hungary, trusting the Habsburgs to ratify their claims for independence. In the end both revolutionary factions were let down when the Russian Tsarist army marched into Transylvania and destroyed them. Leaders on both sides were condemned to death. They included four Moroșeni. In 1861, Maramureș was again unwillingly annexed to Hungary.

At the 1918 Declaration of Independence, Maramureș was claimed by Romania along with Transylvania. Its demands were sanctioned by the Treaty of Trianon two years later. But in 1920 the Maramureș lost nearly two-thirds of its total area when its northern section, across the Tisa, was given to Podkarpatska Rus, the Ruthenian region of Czechoslovakia. In 1991 this part of former Maramureș was absorbed into the Ukraine. Southern Maramureș underwent yet another change of status in 1940, when Hitler's Vienna *Diktat* awarded it and part of northern Transylvania to Horthy's fascist regime in Budapest. By the time it was restored to Romania in 1944, c 90 per cent of southern Maramureș's Jewish population had been deported to death camps.

In the 1960s efforts were made enforce the collectivisation of Moroşeni villages. These moves were often abandoned because of difficulties in farming the mountainous terrain and the innate independence of the villagers themselves. To give one example, Ieud, which was collectivised in 1950 and 1962, had been more or less left to its own devices by the early 1970s.

Tractors were in relative abundance during the Communist regime, but after the Revolution they suddenly disappeared. They were sold to the highest bidders on the black market. This left most smallholders with no choice but to resort to their 'traditional' methods. Horses and oxen still do much of the heavy work here, although farming is gradually becoming more mechanised. Agriculture and mining remain staple industries. Before the Second World War, the mines of Maramureş produced a significant amount of the nation's income from gold, silver, lead, copper and salt, and although this level has never been achieved since, Cavnic is still a centre of silver and gold mining. In the nearby valleys you can often see people selling chunks of sparkling crystals at the roadside.

In 1991 Ukrainian Romanians came south to join the New Year celebrations in Sighet. It was the first time that these two closely-related communities had been in contact for over 40 years, and the event was an emotional one. Even now, *peste Tisa* (across the Tisa) as Moroşeni say, Romanian-speaking communities preserve their traditional costumes, and a handful of typically Moroşeni churches have survived there.

The land of wood

During the Middle Ages Maramureş was densely forested, and it still has large areas of woodland. The trees provided shelter, fuel for burning and cooking and, last but not least, building materials. The wooden houses, farmsteads and churches that you can still see here are among the most attractive features of this region. Graceful and sturdy, they hug the land as though they had grown where they stand, unobtrusive as the trees they came from.

Traces of permanent wooden structures have been found dating back to the 2C, and there is evidence to show that log cabins were in common use by 400 AD. It was on these simple constructions that the first timber churches were modelled. In 1271, the Hungarian authorities forbade the Moroşeni to build in stone. This may have been because there was a shortage of stone for fortifications, but the law was seen as an attempt by Catholics to discourage the Orthodox Church. Whatever the reasons for the prohibition, there was no shortage of wood for building, and whole villages of oak and pine houses became the norm. Local nobles such as *voivode* Bogdan of Cuhea constructed their residences using the same methods as peasant farmers: hewn wood laid horizontally in the *blockbau* technique and caulked with clay, with the walls buried a few centimetres in the ground for extra stability.

Wooden churches

The earliest extant timber churches date from the 14C, although the majority were built after the Tartar invasion in the early 18C or later. The builders were local craftsmen who faithfully copied the style and decoration of the older churches. But they also introduced new elements such as shingles and double-skirted roofs. Their subtle improvements made the buildings ever more elegant.

Legend has it that the carpenters were inspired by fir trees. Today, the finest of these churches float self-contained as galleons over the fluid landscape.

There are 93 wooden churches in Maramureș, all of them listed buildings and many still in use. Eight of them comprising the churches at Bârsana, Budești, Desești, Ieud (Biserica din Deal), Plopiș, Poienile Izei, Rogoz and Șurdești, have been adopted by by UNESCO as being in need of urgent restoration. The wooden churches and houses of Maramureș belong to a family of timber buildings which evolved right across the forested areas of Europe, from Scandinavia to Croatia and Serbia. Regional styles blended with each other when teams of carpenters and joiners travelled from Maramureș to Galicia and Slovakia and immigrant builders came to work here.

In the four valleys which comprise Maramureș proper, most churches have a five-sided apse that is smaller in diameter than the main body of the building. Another striking feature is the wide, open porch, or *prispă*, at the west end. This is like a verandah with an arcade supporting the roof and was almost certainly modelled on domestic houses. Door and window frames may be decorated with symbolic geometrical and phytomorphic carvings.

In the naos or nave a barrel-vaulted ceiling springs from a ledge that is stepped in from the walls. The sanctuary and narthex ceilings are generally lower than the nave and are usually flat. The narthex usually supports the full weight of the tower, which is held together with cross beams. But the most unusual feature of Moroșeni churches is the double roof. Covered in shingles that fit like sealskin, they comprise a steeply-ridged main roof that rises high above the barrel vault, while a secondary roof fans out like an underskirt below, concealing the step in the nave walls. They have a practical purpose in a climate where rain, hail and snow are common for many months of the year, but with their sheer, swooping lines, they are a thrilling sight.

The spires contain watchtowers and belfries, and in some cases they soar to great heights. Șurdești church, for example, has a tower that measures 54m from ground to tip. For centuries it was hailed as the tallest wooden spire in Europe, but in 1995 the nuns of Bârsana commissioned a higher one for their convent church. It tops Șurdești by 2m. Most of the spires do not have the corner turrets that you see in Saxon areas of Transylvania, but the Gothic influence is unmistakable.

An ornamental gate often stands at the entrance to church yards. The patterns on the gates are identical to those on local *nemeți* gateways, with raised ropework that probably originated in the Stone Age.

Wall paintings in Maramureș churches

Most of the churches in Maramureș contain wall paintings. These were created as a way of bringing the liturgy to life, helping those who could not read or understand Church Slavonic by illustrating the Bible in vivid pictures. But they were also there to lift the hearts and minds of the congregation at large, so that everyone could see as well as hear the Church's heavenly purpose. In the low-ceilinged, barrel-vaulted and usually very dark interiors of the wooden churches, they make a startling and wonderful difference, flickering mysteriously in and out of focus in the candlelight.

The paintings usually cover every visible surface except the floor: walls, ceilings and vaults, and sometimes the protecting balcony or gallery. Rain and smoke damage have destroyed many of these painting cycles, but in a few cases they have been saved and something of their original vitality remains. While they are cruder than the frescoes in the painted churches of Bucovina, the murals were designed to appeal to an audience of down-to-earth peasant farmers, and this is reflected in their frankness and zest.

The style of painting is neo-Byzantine, with an emphasis on hieratic symbolism rather than naturalistic description. But here and there a Western note creeps in. Most of the surviving murals date from the 18C or later, after the Maramureş adopted the Greek Catholic Church. Greek Catholic priests introduced a range of iconographic subjects that were influenced by the Counter-Reformation. They also brought an awareness of Western painting styles, notably the Austrian Baroque. As the Uniates gained ground the Orthodox Church came under increasing pressure and fought back. As a result artists were inspired with a new sense of urgency which is clearly visible in their paintings.

Moroşeni artists were often self-taught or trained in local monasteries such as Moisei. In the 18C, two painters in particular came to the fore. One of these was Radu Munteanu, who came from Ungureni in the Lăpuş Valley, outside historic Maramureş. Active between 1767–1800, in 1771, he illustrated a *Book of Gospels* for the villagers of Botiza and painted a group of icons for the church at Glod. Two years later Munteanu decorated the interior of the church at Săliştea de Sus, and later moved on to Deseşti in the Mara Valley, where he collaborated with Gheorghe Vişovan in 1780 to create the marvellous fresco cycle that you can still see in the old church. Munteanu was also employed at Budeşti and created a number of icons for Sârbi as well. His style is very like that of traditional icons on glass. The other painter was his contemporary, Alexandru Ponehalschi, a Moroşeni of Polish descent who was born in Berbeşti. Ponehalschi led an itinerant workshop and his narrative style shaped Maramureş mural painting. He and his team created icons and wall paintings in most of the churches in the Mara, Cosău, Iza and Vişeu valleys. His last known scheme dates from 1782. He created the fresco cycles in the lower church at Budeşti and worked at Călineşti, executing wall paintings and a series of icons for the icon screen. The sprightly scenes in the Church on the Hill at Ieud have also been attributed to him. One way to identify their work is that both of these artists outlined their figures in black.

The artists who painted Maramureş churches had to work on rough, irregular surfaces. They overcame this difficulty by glueing strips of cloth to the gaps in the timbers lining the walls. They then applied a thin layer of plaster to make a smooth surface (in many cases you can still see the grain of the wood). Colours were generally inexpensive pigments ground or crushed from local plants such as madder and indigo, but some artists also used minerals, including minium, iron oxide and malachite. Vegetable colours fade rapidly in contact with lime, so the ground must have been made of another agent. To bind their colours, the painters used egg or animal size.

Old versus new

Inside the churches you can often find old icons and furniture, although the most valuable paintings have often been removed to museums. Sometimes the walls and floors are covered with beautiful flatweave rugs in colours which range from the most subtle, faded vegetable hues to roaring pinks, reds and oranges that are psychedelic in their intensity. As Rebecca West noticed while visiting village churches in Serbia during the 1930s, these buildings have a very special atmosphere. It is not just the smell of incense and candle smoke, damp wood and sweat, although these all play their part. It comes from the people who love and cherish them. It is usually the village women who weave the brightly embroidered towels which adorn the icons and candelabra, who bring flowers and light candles for the living and the dead, and devotedly place fronds of pine around their family graves on saints' days.

There are a lot of new, concrete churches in Maramureş, but not everyone wants to abandon their old timber shrine or see it turned into a museum piece. This is not always a sentimental choice. Owing to the revival of Greek Catholicism, there are not enough churches to go round. In previous centuries, when a village grew too large for its church, instead of leaving it to rot, the people would give it to a smaller community, who would drag it away on logs. But this no longer happens and a problem of preservation has arisen in its stead. Services are often held every day, and the wear and tear caused by decades of human exhalation and candle smoke are destroying the paintings and the ancient fabric of these buildings as well. Teams of conservators have spent years analysing the problem and money has been found to restore some of the worst affected churches. But the problem remains: if you shut the congregation out, the churches may be saved from falling down, but they will never be the same again.

Traditional Moroşeni dress

For special occasions Moroşeni women wear a daintily embroidered blouse of snowy white cotton with puffed sleeves under a dazzling waistcoat of embroidered leather. Their skirts consist of a two-piece woollen apron called a *zadie* worn over a cotton underskirt. The *zadie* is patterned with broad horizontal stripes of black and red, and is very striking. Sometimes the stripes are black and yellow or orange, or more rarely black and white. If they are going to dance, the women wear black leather calf-length boots.

Clad in their 'Sunday best', the men have loose-fitting cotton shirts and calf-length trousers with very wide legs, like exaggerated bell bottoms or a pair of culottes. The shirts vary in colour from white to black with many shades of grey in between. They also very in length, and these differences give a clue to which valley and even from which village they come from. Men also wear richly-embroidered leather or sheepskin waistcoats, and to complete their ensemble, they have a jaunty straw hat called a *clop*. This is fastened under the chin and looks like an upturned flower pot. The shallow crown is decorated with a patterned band of multicoloured beads. The *clop* is traditionally a shepherd's hat and used to be made of felt. To make it waterproof, the shepherd would soak it in lamb's blood with a mixture of butter, beeswax and rosin.

Baia Mare

Baia Mare (Nagybánya in Hungarian; the English translation is, more prosaically, Big Mine) is the administrative centre of Maramureş county. It is an industrial city of around 150,000 people which lies on a plateau near the foothills of the Guţâi mountains, outside Maramureş proper but close enough to make it a comfortable base. Baia Mare has some of the highest toxic gas emissions in Romania. But its worst offender, a tower emitting sulphur and lead fumes in the industrial sector to the east of the city, has been raised so that the pollution now gets carried over a wider area in a less concentrated form. To set against this off-putting introduction, Baia Mare has a number of fine old buildings, good communications and a smart modern centre. It also has a better range of hotels than Sighet, the region's other large town, but is less convenient for journeys into the valleys of historic Maramureş.

In 1329 Baia Mare was mentioned as Rivulus Dominarum, 'the Ladies' River'. The name comes from a legend about the young women of Baia Mare who are said to have charmed the Hungarian army into forgetting that it was supposed to destroy the town. During the period of Hungarian rule, a royal mint was established here. Its remains can be seen on Str Monetăriei (Coiners' Street), where the county museum stands today. But Baia Mare is known best as a mining city specialising in non-ferrous metals such as gold and silver. Today the city is a surreal mix of urban and pastoral: goats wander across patches of unkempt grassland overlooked by the smart marble façades of banks and offices.

Practical information

☎ code
062

Tourist information
Baia Mare has several tourist offices and agencies. These include *SC Mara SA*, ☎ 211995; *Mara Holidays* at B-dul Unirii 11, ☎ 26660/ 221100; *Nord Nord West*, Str Minerva 16, ☎ 214812; *Sind România*, Str Culturii 1, ☎ 411043; *International Triumph* at Str Şcolii 9, ☎ 224784; *Roxtur* at B-dul Bucureşti 23, ☎ 433248; *Vacanţa* at Str Şincai 34, ☎ 217028/417573.

Getting around
By train The station is in Strada Gării, southwest of the town centre. ☎ 952 for information or 433424. Long-distance tickets should be booked in advance at *CFR*, Str Victoriei 57, ☎ 42161/432364.

By bus Baia Mare's national bus terminus is next to the railway station at Strada Gării 2. Local transport is provided by *URBIS SA*; contact its head office at Str 8 Martie 3, ☎/fax 213825.

By plane Baia Mare airport is west of the city on the road towards Seini (take B-dul Independenţei from the *Hotel Carpaţi*), ☎ 222245, 222246, ☎/fax 223394. *TAROM*'s local office can be found at B-dul Bucureşti 5, ☎ 221624.

By car *ACR* at Str 8 Martie 1, ☎ 412345, should be able to arrange car hire and recommend service garages. Garages offering **repair services** include *Iatsa*, Str Independenţei 32, ☎ 424586; *Merit Grup*, B-dul Bucureşti 57, ☎ 223298, and *Siromex Dinks* at Str Băii 3, ☎ 417515. There are **petrol stations** on Str Victoriei, B-dul Bucureşti, Str Minerilor, Str Lucaciu and B-dul Independenţei.

Where to stay

Baia Mare's smartest hotels are the *Minion* (✯✯✯), Str Mălinului, ☎ 417056; fax 414545; the **Maramureş** (✯✯), Str Gheorghe Şincai 37A, ☎ 416555; and the *Mara* (✯✯), Str Unirii 11, ☎ 462219, fax 460718 (18 places). The dour *Hotel Carpaţi* (✯✯✯) at Str Minerva 16, where Dervla Murphy stayed while researching *Transylvania and Beyond*, has improved considerably; ☎ 214812. *Hotel Minerul* (✯) at Piaţa Libertăţii 7 is a handsome Secessionist building with 48 rooms; ☎ 216056; fax 215940. Alternatively, there are one or two smaller hotels such as *Vila Minion* (✯✯✯), which has seven rooms. It is located near the northern edge of the city at Str Mălinului 22, ☎ 276056.

A few kilometres north in Baia Sprie is a pleasant motel called *Montana-Giesswein* (✯✯) at Str Igniş 2C, ☎ 460718, which has several twin-bedded rooms and charges reasonable prices. With help from the German company that is a part owner, the motel has built a suite of crafts workshops to help promote local industries. Also in Baia Sprie, *Mogoşa Chalet* (✯) in Str Mogoşa, ☎ 460800, has 32 rooms and a restaurant. The *Şuior Tourist Resort* near Baia Sprie has 2-star accommodation; ☎ 460842.

At Firiza, a few kilometres to the northeast of Baia Mare, there is the *Căprioara Guest House* (✯✯) with seven rooms and a campsite. ☎ 222099/222049; mobile 018 626945.

If you want to stay in a private household, contact the local branch of *ANTREC*, ☎ 415046, or *Centrul Judeţean de Creaţie Populară* at Piaţa Libertăţii 13, ☎/fax 211560 or write to Str Culturii 7A, PO Box 24.

Money

Most of Baia Mare's **banks** have congregated on B-dul Unirii; among them are *Banc Post* at no. 16, *Banca Agricola* at no. 18, *Banca Comerciala Română* at no. 15, and *Bancorex* at no. 9. There is a *Cambio* **exchange house** at B-dul Traian 6, and *Platinum Exchange* is located at B-dul Unirii 14.

Post office and telephones

You can make national and international calls at PTTR at Str Şincai 36. The main post office is housed in the same building.

Medical care

If you need a **pharmacy**, try *Farmacia Alga* at Piaţa Libertăţii 9, *Balsam* at B-dul Republicii 30, or *Helena* at B-dul Republicii 1. The county **hospital** is at Str Coşbuc 31, and there is a **polyclinic** at B-dul Bucureşti 22.

Food and shopping

The open-air market on Piaţa Izvoarelor beside the rotund Butchers' Bastion is the most picturesque place to buy food, but keep a wary eye on your belongings.

Maps and books

Ask at the tourist agencies, hotels or the county museum to give you an up-to-date map of the town and the region. Failing more recent publications, the old maps produced during the communist period were excellent—if you can get hold of one.

Traditional crafts and folklore festivals

The place to start is *Centrul Judeţean de Creaţie Populară* at Piaţa Libertăţii 13, ☎/fax 211560. Here you should be able to get hold of the latest information on traditional festivals throughout the region. The centre can also help you to find accommodation in rural villages and organise guided tours of the ethnographic zones which comprise Maramureş county, including historic Maramureş and the old 'countries' of

Chioar and Lăpuş. Ask here for a leaflet listing the names and addresses of local 'masters', craftspeople who specialise in textiles, pottery, woodcarving, embroidery and other traditional skills.

> ### Maramureş: gateway to the heart of Old Europe
>
> The *Folklore Centre* is managed by poet and former dissident Dumitru Iuga. A descendant of Bogdan I and a flamboyant Eminescu lookalike, Dumitru has dedicated his life to promoting knowledge and understanding of the Maramureş, not just in Romania but also abroad. He believes that Maramureş is the cradle of European civilisation, pointing to the fact that the geographical centre of Europe lies only 25km north of Sighet. Under his direction, the Centre has compiled an impressive video archive of life in Moroşeni villages. This includes films about traditional festivals such as *Tânjaua* and *Rupta sterpelor* and the colourful celebrations which accompany traditional Maramureş weddings.
>
> Dumitru Iuga's wife Georgeta is an archaeologist, ethnographer and painter of icons on glass. In 1998 she founded *Fundaţia Social-Culturală pentru Democraţie 'Identitate. Unitate. Generozitate. Acţiune'* (The Social and Cultural Foundation for Democracy IUGA), which aims to encourage students of Moroşeni culture and to help visitors appreciate its unique qualities. The traditional timber house which she has built in the village of Şurdeşti functions as a study centre and a base for tours around the region. Contact Fundaţia IUGA by e-mail at iuga@mail.alphanet.ro or ☎/fax 226739. An excellent CD-Rom about Maramureş is available from the Folklore Centre or from CDIMM, B-dul Unirii 13, ap 201, ☎/fax 224870/ 222409; e-mail cdimm@mail.alphanet.ro.

Muzeul Judeţean Maramureş at Str Monetăriei 3 houses some of the many exciting Stone, Bronze and Iron Age discoveries made around the county. At Str 1 Mai 8, the **art museum** contains an excellent collection of paintings from the Baia Mare School. Known also as the Nagybánya School because many of its adherents were ethnic Hungarians, it was founded by Simon Hollósy (1875–1918) in 1896. The School flourished until c 1930 and became an outpost of Post-Impressionism and early Modernism. Its standards were very high. Many of the artists involved studied abroad in Paris, Munich and Vienna, and highlights of the collection include some small but intense canvases by the Expressionist painter Dávid Jándi (1893–1944) and János Krizsán (1886–1984). Krizsan and Iandi were close friends, and Krizsan made valiant attempts to save the Jewish Jándi from Fascist squads during the Second World War. The museum also has a small but select group of icons on glass and wood. Created by artists working in the Iza, Lăpuş, Cosău and Mara valleys, they show some of their stylistic differences, which range from strong linearity to a more volumetric approach. One of the liveliest pieces is a double-sided icon from 1671 which was made for a church across the Ukrainian border in Munkacevo (Muncaci) in what was once northern Maramureş. Open Tues–Sun 09.00–16.00.

Icons on glass ~ Icoane pe sticlă

Icons on glass have a special place in Romanian folk art. They express the symbiotic relationship between Christian and superstitious belief that shaped religious faith in many country areas. Glass icons are two-dimensional and both more colourful and cruder than icons on wood. By and large, they were made for peasants who could not afford the wood variety, which took longer to make and were consequently much more expensive. Glass icons are very decorative, but they were not made to be ornamental: their purpose was to protect their owners from harm, to bring them luck and provide them with objects of veneration in their homes.

The technique involves painting a reverse image on the back of a piece of glass so that the glass acts both as a support and a medium through which to view the scene. Glass painting is thought to have originated in Byzantium and it is also known in the former Yugoslav peninsula. By the 14C glass painting was known in Italy, from where it spread to Austria, Bohemia, Moravia and Galicia. The practice arrived in Romania sometime in the 17C, its popularity enhanced by a gigantic leap late in the century when the monks of Nicula needed to mass-produce images of the miraculous weeping Virgin. Armenians in nearby Gherla were able to supply them with cheap glass, and an industry was born.

During the 17C and 18C separate schools sprang up. Pupils from the studios at Nicula set up workshops in Făgăraş which passed on the skills in turn to other craftsmen-priests in Braşov and Sibiu. Each school has its own distinctive features: Maramureş icons have more subdued colours than the other schools, and black and red predominate.

As in conventional Orthodox icons, the themes shown on glass icons comprise the saints and religious subjects such as Adam and Eve, the Annunciation, the Entry of Jesus into Jerusalem, the Last Supper and the Crucifixion. Before they were taught to think differently, peasant farmers, shepherds and craftsmen believed that some saints had magical powers. They would collect paintings showing these particular saints, hoping that the icons would protect them against disease, keep an eye on their animals and crops, and help them to prosper. The custom was not confined to villages and isolated sheepfolds, but spread to towns as well. Today it is still common for a private household to have its own shrine, usually set up in a corner of the living room.

St George was one of the most popular saints in Maramureş. According to traditional belief, he was a herald of spring who ensured that the trees would grow green and the crops ripen. He kept wolves at bay and warded off evil spirits who wanted to ruin the grain and destroy the cattle. He looked after the flocks, helping sheep to drop their lambs 'at a sweet and beautiful time'. St Nicholas was another favourite because it was thought that he brought good luck and protected against smallpox and accidents.

St Haralambie kept the plague in chains; St Elijah kept control of the rain and protected crops against hail. Sts Michael and Gabriel looked after the souls of the dead. St Dumitru guarded against wolves, as did St Peter, who also held the keys to Heaven and prevented hail from battering the crops. St Paraschiva was also proof against hail and was believed to cure

> headaches as well. John the Baptist guarded the household against fire, wild beasts and fevers. The Virgin Mary was also credited with healing powers: women would wash her icon with holy water and give it to people suffering from the evil eye.
>
> The market for icons on glass owed its existence to the Miracle of Nicula in 1694. After the rush on images of the Virgin who wept real tears, demand for protective icons of all kinds increased out of all recognition. Icon sellers would tout glass and xylograph images of saints around villages as though they were holy objects made in a monastery. Women would cluster round, making sure they had a full set to protect their homes. Sometimes the icons had another function: images of the Virgin were prized as fertility symbols, and they were often an important part of a girl's dowry. The scene showing Christ squeezing grapes grown inside his body has connections with Bacchus.
>
> Glass painting continued to be practised for its original religious and superstitious purposes until the mid-20C. It has since been revived by a number of priests and lay people. In Maramureş the best exponents are Georgeta Iuga, Anamaria Iuga and Maria Timiş. The finest public collections of icons on glass can be found in Muzeul Țaranului Român in Bucharest and the little village museum in Sibiel, near Sibiu. A book about glass icons in Maramureş, *Icoane pe sticlă*, was published by Editura Cybela, Baia Mare, in 1995. It contains reproductions of icons by Georgeta Iuga and a text by her husband Dumitru.

Muzeul de Mineralogie (the Mineralogy Museum) at B-dul Traian 8 is small but well worth a visit. Plans and 3-D models on the ground floor explain the geological and mineral constituents of the mountains which encircle Maramureş. On the first floor is a dazzling display of crystal 'flowers'. Open Tues–Sun 10.00–17.00.

Muzeul de Etnografie şi Artă Populară on Str Dealul Florilor is worth a visit if you have time, but it has few open-air installations and is generally less exciting than the open-air museum in Sighetu Marmaţiei. Open Tues–Sun 10.00–17.00.

The old centre

At the heart of Baia Mare, on the main through road to Sighet, stands Piaţa Libertăţii. Stop and walk around: several of the buildings which line the square are worth looking at. The oldest is **Casa Elisabeta**, near the northeast corner, which was built between 1446–90. Only the ground floor, basement and foundations remain. The house was designed for Iancu de Hunedoara and his son Matei Corvin. Between Str 1 Mai and Str Crişan are the remnants of a school called Schola Rivulina. The school was founded in a 15C building and ran from the mid-16C until 1755. **Piaţa Libertăţii 13** is a medieval building whose walls are over a metre thick. On the first floor you will find *Centrul Judeţean de Creaţie Populară* (the county Crafts and Folklore Centre),

Radiating outwards from Piaţa Libertăţii are several old streets where you can find other fragments of Baia Mare's past. Walk north on Stra Dacia towards the river and you come to **Str Monetăriei**, a narrow lane which was part of the medieval town. To the right stands the County Museum and beside it Monetăria Veche, the Old Mint. This is actually an early 20C building, but it incorporates a bastion and part of the original mint which was installed here for Sigismund of Luxemburg in 1411 when he was both King of Hungary and Holy Roman Emperor.

To the south of Piața Libertății lies Piața Cetății. Dominating the square is the impressive hulk of **Turnul Ștefan**, Stephen's Tower, which Iancu de Hunedoara commissioned in the 1440s. On the south wall of the tower you can see a bas relief showing Roland the Knight, while the west façade bears the city's arms and a window with a Gothic-style frame. On the south side of the square is a collection of **Baroque buildings** including Biserica Sfânta Treime (Holy Trinity Church, 1717–20) and a former gymnasium, now a primary school.

Head south along Str Crișan for Str Cloșca, turn right, and you reach Piața Izvoarelor. This is the main *piața* (open–air food market) in Baia Mare. Beside it stands **Bastionul Măcelarilor**, the Butchers' Bastion, sometimes called the Ammunition Tower because it was used as an arsenal. The bastion was built in the 15C as part of the medieval fortifications; today it is often used to house crafts fairs and folk festivals. The famous outlaw, Pintea Viteazul, met his end here in August 1703 after taking part in Prince Rákóczi's anti-Habsburg rebellion.

Sighetu Marmației

Lying a couple of kilometres from the Ukrainian border where the Iza flows into the Tisa River, Sighetu Marmației (population 44,500) is the main centre of historic Maramureș. Most people know the town by its shortened name of Sighet. It makes a good focal point for exploring the region and is an attractive place in its own right.

Traces of late Bronze Age settlement and a 10C fortress have been found both in and near Sighet. The first known mention of the town came in 1328. From 1383–1402 it was the seat of a local prince, Dragoș Vodă, and in the 16C it was a centre of Calvinism. During the communist period, Sighet had the unpleasant distinction of being home to a notorious political prison.

At the end of December, Sighet hosts a two-day pageant, *Festivalul datinilor de iarnă* (the festival of winter customs). During these two days the central square brims with colour. Everyone wears their best clothes, and the parade gives men a chance to show off their outrageous New Year costumes, so that the jostling crowds are full of Ruritanian princes and chain-bedecked generals in uniforms of puce and sky blue and canary yellow. This is one of the most exuberant events in the calendar, and it attracts singing and dancing groups from all over Romania. During the first Christmas after the Revolution, the 1990 festival gave Moroșeni the chance to meet relations from across the Tisa in Ukraine—in many cases, it was the first time they had seen each other for 40 years.

Practical information

☎ **code**
062

Tourist information

Marmaţia at Piaţa Libertăţii 21, ☎ 213815. Sighet has a new tourist information service, the *Renaşterea Sigheteana Foundation*. This has a large data base giving details of tourist facilities around Maramureş, and has for sale a range of CDs, books and catalogues about the area. Contact Ion Maris or his colleagues at Str Constructorului 2/1, ☎/fax 317071; mobile 094 513050; e-mail cdl@mail.alphanet.ro.

Getting around

By rail The station is at Str Iuliu Maniu 1.
By bus The bus station is opposite the railway station.
By car **Petrol stations** can be found at Str Bogdan Vodă 59, Str Dragoş Vodă, and Str Tepliţei.

Where to stay

Some smart new hotels have recently opened in Sighet. Highly recommended is the villa and restaurant, *Perla Sigheteana* (✩✩✩), which opened with Swiss funding in July 1999 at Str Avram Iancu 65A, ☎ 310268. *Motel Buti* (✩✩), established in January 1999, is at Str Bărnuţiu 6, ☎ 310783. There are also *Ardealul* (✩), Str Iuliu Maniu 91, ☎ 5121 72; *Marmaţia* (✩), Str Parcul Mihai Eminescu 1, ☎ 512241; *Tisa* (✩), Piaţa Libertăţii 8, ☎ 312645; *Motel Tepliţa*, Str Tepliţei 56, ☎ 313174. *Boarding House Flamingo* (✩), Str Gheorge Coşbuc 36, v 317265, is both cheap and pleasant.

Alternatively, *ANTREC* has a regional office in Maramureş and can help you to find accommodation in local farmhouses. ☎ 415046.

Money

Banks include *Banca Agricolă*, Str Andrei Mureşanu 6; *Banca Comercială*, Str Iuliu Maniu 32; *Banca Română de Dezvoltare*, Str Bogdan Vodă 4; *Bancoop*, Str Basarabiei 7; *Banc Post*, Str Bogdan Vodă 1A.

Town hall

The *primăria* is at Str Bogdan Vodă 14, ☎ 312396.

Medical care

The town **hospital** is at Str Avram Iancu 27, ☎ 311541. **Pharmacies** include *Manna*, Str Libertăţii 12, ☎ 315633; *Minerva*, Str Libertăţii 23, ☎ 311977; *Mirana*, Str 1 Mai 10, ☎ 319152; *Soranda*, Str Avram Iancu 22, ☎ 317677; *Tedana*, Str 9 Mai 61, ☎ 315462; *Farmacia No. 17*, Piaţa 1 Decembrie 1918, ☎ 311909.

Sighet has reasons to be both ashamed and proud of its history. During the Second World War the town jail functioned as a deportation centre for the 38,000 Jews who were sent from Maramureş to Nazi death camps. A memorial to the deported Jews stands in the centre of town. There is a **Jewish Cultural Centre** at Str Vişeului 8. Sighet was the birthplace of Elie Wiesel (b 1928). A survivor of Auschwitz and Buchenwald Wiesel is a tireless campaigner for human rights and a prolific writer about Jewish and notably Hasidic culture. His books include *Night* (1960), *A Beggar in Jerusalem* (1970) and *From the Kingdom of Memory* (1990). He won the Nobel Peace Prize in 1986. In his own words, Elie Wiesel tries to 'unite the language of humanity with the silence of the dead'. The house in which he was born, at Str Tudor Vladimirescu 1, has been turned into a commemorative museum, open Tues–Sun 10.00–18.00.

The **jail** stands on the corner of Str Bărnuțiu and Str Șincai. An elegant Eclectic design dating from 1897, it was built as part of a larger complex which also contained the Palace of Justice and the Law Courts. Prison and courts ran along the whole length of Str Bărnuțiu turning a smooth and forbidding face to the street. The architect was Gyula Wagner, a Hungarian who devoted his life to building penitentiaries. Ironically in view of what Sighet prison was to become, Wagner's designs were considered to be among the most enlightened of their time.

During the Second World War, Jews, Gypsies and anti-Fascists were held in the jail before being deported to death camps. In 1948 it was turned into a detention centre for opponents of the communist regime. It was here that the country's political and religious élite were tortured and eliminated. They usually died of starvation, without mercy and in secret.

The building reverted to its former function as a criminal penitentiary in 1964, and 13 years later it closed. After that it was used as a storage depot until the 1990s, when the town council decided to transform Sighet jail into a museum and a centre for the study of totalitarianism.

On the stretch of prison wall which runs beside Str Bărnuțiu, a series of marble slabs once bore the names of poets, academics, politicians and religious leaders who were condemned to death here during the Stalinist purges of the 1950s. They included Iuliu Maniu, the leader of Romania's liberal Peasant's Party who died here in 1953, and politician and historian Gheorghe Brătianu, whose life was brought to a brutal close the following year. The plain slabs also recorded the names of the Greek Catholic bishops who were persecuted by the communists in the campaign to wipe out the Uniate Church. Among the brave priests tortured here was Monsignor Suciu, famous in 1940 as the youngest Catholic bishop in the world. The 81-year-old grandson of the last reigning prince of Moldavia was also murdered at Sighet.

To the sorrow of many people who found these simple memorials both dignified and moving, they have been taken away in an attempt to sanitise the prison's murky past. At the same time the prison building was restored and the museum and study centre were opened. After four years in limbo, the plaques have been cleaned and are due to be put back in their original positions along the outside wall. The cells where so many fine people ended their lives have been arranged in a way that tries to recreate the coldness, darkness and suffering they experienced. The prisoners' drab clothes, their chains and some of the things they made in secret, such as little crosses carved from bone, are displayed here, and some of the cells belonging to famous detainees such as Gheorghe Brătianu contain their personal possessions and documents relating to their lives. In one of the prison courtyards is an underground room called 'A space to collect one's thoughts in'. The museum, of which these new arrangements form a part, goes by the curious title of the Museum of Arrested Thought. Its entrance is at Str Corneliu Coposu 6, open Tues–Sun 10.00–18.00, ☎ 319424/319848

The **Monument to the Deported Jews** stands in the central square, c 300m from the jail.

Sighet has an excellent **ethnographic museum**. Its open-air section, at Str Dobaieș 40, contains many examples of vernacular architecture rescued from

Moroşeni villages. Among the timber buildings are ten houses from Călineşti and a wooden church. The museum's indoor installations, comprising an array of agricultural and domestic tools as well as regional textiles, costumes and pottery, can be found in a fine 18C house at Str Libertăţii 15. Open Tues–Sun 10.00–18.00.

Simon Hollósy (1857–1918), another famous son of Sighet, was the founder of the Baia Mare painting colony. His birthplace at Str Ion Mihalyi de Apsa 43 has been turned into a **memorial museum**, open Tues–Sun 10.00–18.00. Hollósy established the Baia Mare School in 1896 after studying art in Western Europe. The work of these artists was inspired by Post-Impressionism and Expressionism, and was often exceptional. Examples can be seen in the Baia Mare art museum.

To the west of Sighet lies **Sărăsău** with its fine wooden church, and beyond it the rapidly growing tourist mecca of Săpânţa. **Săpânţa** is known throughout Romania for its 'Happy Cemetery'. This is a churchyard where every tomb is adorned with a wooden cross painted a cheerful blue. Each cross carries a verse inscription and a picture in shallow relief, making gentle fun of the person buried beneath. Local carpenter Ioan Stan Pătraş began the custom, which is now being carried on by his pupil Dumitru Pop.

Săpânţa has a flourishing cottage industry which specialises in dyeing and weaving textiles. Walk along the streets to the left (south) of the Happy Cemetery, and among the imitation Persian rugs you can see traditional flat-weave carpets and *cergi* hung out for sale. *Cergi* (the singular is *cergă*) are thick, hairy woollen blankets patterned with stripes of white with red, orange, grey, brown or black. These attractive coverings were once used to keep livestock warm in winter, but now are more often kept for domestic use.

In summer, women sit outside their houses making skeins on beautifully ornamented wooden spindles or sitting at their spinning wheels. They are hoping to attract customers who will buy their textiles. Ask if you want to see the dyeing and weaving rooms. If you get the chance, have a look at a 'clean room'. This is the room in a family home which is reserved for guests and traditionally contains the daughter of the house's dowry. Some of these are crammed with gorgeous rugs and towels and huge embroidered pillows.

If you travel north of the border, look out for the old **Moroşeni churches** at Aleksandrovka and Sokirnitsa along the Ukrainian side of the Tisa Valley near Khust. There are others at Danilovo, Sleblevka, Krainikovo and Serednee Vodyanoye (Apşa de Mijloc, near Sighet). All these churches have little corner turrets around their spires. Architectural historian David Buxton includes a brief description of them in his book, *The Wooden Churches of Eastern Europe* (1986). According to Dr Buxton, the ones listed above are 'pure', Romanian churches while other wooden churches nearby show a Lemk influence.

HISTORIC MARAMUREŞ

The region known as Maramureş proper consists of four main valleys: Cosău, Iza, Mara and Vişeu. They lie within the ring of mountains to the north of Baia Mare. The best way to explore the villages and mountains would be on foot or horseback. Contact *Centrul Judeţean de Creaţie Populară* in Baia Mare at Piaţa

Libertății 13, ☎ 062 211560, to ask about local guides, or join one of the package tours arranged by *Over the Wall* and other tour companies (see pp 13–15). Otherwise, most of the villages are accessible by 4WD.

The Cosău Valley

Starting from Sighet, take the road south through Vadu Izei to Berbești. Before entering Giulești turn left for **Ferești**, which has an early 18C wooden church containing fine icons and rugs. The following village of **Cornești** has an 18C church which was decorated in the late 18C by Toader Hodor. Further south at **Călinești**, where Biserica Susani (the Upper Church) dates from 1784 and is the only example of a trefoil plan in Maramureș. Built on the ashes of a medieval church which the Tartars destroyed in 1717, it was the inspiration of the village priest, Filip Opriș, who had studied in the Moldavian city of Iași. The church has a polygonal pronaos and was clearly influenced by the lovely north Moldavian churches of the 16C and 17C; inside, its frescoes show a Moldavian influence too. Remains of a Dacian settlement and a hoard of Roman coins have been found near Călinești.

Detail of a gateway, Sârbi

Follow a smaller road south-west out of Călinești and you come to **Sârbi**. This village has one of the few remaining *vâltori* in Maramureș. A *vâltoare* is a whirlpool for washing and fulling woollen textiles. It is made of wooden slats that fan out from a central base. Water from a nearby stream is fed into it from above through a system of narrow sluices. The sluices force the current to flow fast so that it hits the clothes with tremendous force. Villagers use their communal washing machine once a week (in Sârbi washday is Friday). A couple of households in Sârbi contain tailoring workshops which make thick felt coats for men, a local speciality.

Two appealing little **timber churches**, Sârbi Josani and Susani, stand above the village. They can be found a few hundred metres apart, on the hillside beside the left bank of the Cosău stream. They were built respectively in 1532 and 1700. Inside both churches there are wooden icons by local masters, and the door frames and entrances are decorated with attractive carvings. These are rough, handmade designs in which you can see the toolmarks left by the craftsmen who cut them with chisel, adze and axe.

Budești is the home of one of the finest children's folk-dance groups in Maramureș. If you are lucky you may be allowed to watch them rehearse in one of the local schools. To find them, just follow the sound of thundering feet! Budești also has two **wooden churches**. Biserica Josani (1628) is protected by

UNESCO and has recently been restored. It was built for the *nemeși*, the ancient Romanian nobility, and is one of the largest timber churches in Maramureș. The church has an unusual, central watchtower and belfry placed above the porch. The spire is one of the few in this region to have four corner turrets. Budești Josani stands on the site of a 14C church, and was frescoed in 1762 by Alexandru Ponehalschi of Berbești. It also contains a fine collection of icons on wood and glass, some of which date from the 1550s. The chain-mail jacket of a famous outlaw called Pintea Viteazul (Pintea the Brave) is also kept here. Pintea took part in the Rákóczi revolt of 1703–11, and his grave lies beside one of the hairpin bends on the Guțâi Pass. The building has tiny windows which are designed to let in just enough light to illuminate the murals. The windows are glazed with circular pieces of hand-blown glass which is several inches thick.

The entrance to the churchyard is decorated with thick, raised rope patterns forming anthropomorphic symbols. Archaeologists believe the designs originated in the Stone Age because they are identical with patterns found on nearby Neolithic grave goods. A rare *masă moților* (elders' table) stands in the cemetery and comprises a row of stone slabs lying on the ground. These tables were traditionally used to carry food prepared for the old people of the parish on feast days. The custom has all but disappeared.

Budești Susani (1760) has a pair of splendid Royal Doors. They were made in 1628 and came from the previous church on this site. Beside the stream which runs through the village is another old-fashioned *vâltoare*.

From Budești, take the road west to Ocna Șugatag and you pass a left turn down a hillside to the village of **Breb**. Ask in the village for directions to the old wooden church, and you will come to a lovely building dating from 1531. The frescoes, which are partially ruined, are later in date, and the interior also contains 17C icons. In the hills above the village lives a craftsman named Ioan Pop a Niții who specialises in **traditional wooden handicrafts**, such as ritual cups and hand crosses for use in church. To find him, ask for a guide from the village; alternatively, ask *Centrul Județean de Creație Populară* in Baia Mare (see p 294) to help you see examples of his work.

From Breb you can travel west to **Hoteni**. This is the home of Ion and Georgeta 'Anuța' Pop, stars of Iza, the famous Romanian folksinging group. It is also the village where English violinist Lucy Castle celebrated her three-day wedding to a local musician in 1996. Lucy sings with Ion Pop in the band Popeluc and the event made national TV. Beyond Hoteni lies Hârnicești, which brings you into the Mara Valley, or you can continue north to **Ocna Șugatag**. On market days this old salt-mining centre comes alive with people from outlying villages who come to buy and sell livestock, food and household goods.

Head north to Berbești, and beside the road on the northern edge of the village is an 18C ***troița***. This is a very rare wayside cross combining a group of carved figures showing St John, Mary Magdalene and the Virgin and Child, and pagan symbols of the sun and moon. The cross was designed to dissuade evil spirits from entering the village.

Villages in the Cosău Valley have recently launched a pilot scheme which is designed to promote culture and tourism in the valley on a mutually cooperative basis. This means that certain households are willing to make rooms available for visiting tourists and arrange a programme of events. To find out more, contact *Centrul Județean de Creație Populară* in Baia Mare (see p 294), or *Fundația IUGA*, under whose auspices the scheme was established in 1998 (see p 295). You can write to *Fundația IUGA* at BP 710, 4800 Baia Mare 7.

The Mara Valley

The main road south to Baia Mare takes you to **Giulești**. This village was once the centre of a 14C *cnezate*, a self-governing community presided over by a lord or *cnez*. The *cnez* was elected by village elders and had the right to judge and allot land according to the *jus valachichum* (Wallachian Law). According to some historians, the *cnezates* were either part of or identical to the ancient Romanian 'countries' (*țări*) ruled further south by such leaders as Glad and Menumorut. During the medieval period when Hungary ruled Transylvania, some of these communities, including Țara Maramureșului, survived. The Árpád kings recognised the independent Romanian lands which they called Terra Blacorum (the Vlachs' Country), and invited their leaders to their Diets (Congregations). But after the Angevin dynasty gained control of Hungary in the 14C, Romanian autonomy gradually disappeared. Starting with Károly Róbert I (reigned 1308–42), Magyar rulers made a concerted attempt to suppress Orthodoxy in favour of Catholicism.

Giulești contains the remains of a parish **church** from the same period. It was probably commissioned between 1350–60 by the family who gave their name to the village. Excavations carried out in the 1960s showed that the church was Late Romanesque in style, consisting of a small nave with a bell tower. Unusually, it was built of stone. It may have been built like the masonry church at Cuhea by masons from nearby German or Hungarian settlements who were familiar with the Western, Catholic architecture. However, this does not necessarily mean that it was used for the Catholic rite. There is also a wooden church in Giulești.

Before reaching the next village to the south, ask directions for **Mănăstirea**, a hamlet which lies secluded in woods to the east. Here you can find a church built in 1653 containing icons by local artists.

Sat Șugatag is one of the poorer villages of Maramureș, and its wooden church is in a critical state. In the cemetery, Celtic-style crosses mark some of the graves. No-one knows whether or not this denotes a former Celtic presence here. Beside the stream you can find two water mills (*mori de apa*) and an old-fashioned distillery for *țuica*.

Some 3km further south lies **Desești**. The 18C wooden church in this village contains one of the finest mural cycles in the entire region. Turn right at the *Poliția* sign in the centre of the village and walk up the lane. After c 500m you reach the church, standing in an attractive orchard cemetery on the other side of the former narrow-gauge railway line between Desești and Sighet. The church has a handsome double roof. If the church is locked you will have to ask the priest or his wife to let you in. They live next door to the church: follow the path around the north side and go through the wooden gates to the house on the left. It is worth the effort because the paintings, originally carried out by Radu Munteanu and Gheorghe Visovat, have been beautifully restored. They are truly stunning. One of the most striking images is the Creation of Eve, which shows Eve sitting tremulously in God's right hand.

In the early 1990s the Romanian Ministry of Culture consulted teams of international conservators for additional advice on restoring some of the most valuable churches in Maramureş. Working with the British Museum, a buildings-preservation firm from England installed over 200 micro-sensers in the interior of Deseşti church, hoping to monitor changes in the atmosphere and fabric that would help prevent further damage. The sensers were linked to computers at the company's headquarters in Basingstoke, but problems with the telephone connections have made it difficult to collect the information.

Follow the Baia Mare road a few kilometres south and you reach **Mara**. At house no. 88, on the right-hand side as you leave the village, is one of the oldest surviving **nemeşi gates** in Maramureş. It dates from 1936 and is covered with symbolic carvings including little figures of axes, suns and moons. The gate has been adopted by the county museum in Sighet.

> ### Rites of passage
> The Moroşeni celebrate important rites of passage in special ways. When a young person dies before being married, a symbolic wedding is held at the funeral. Weddings of the dead were once held all over Europe, and in the Maramureş people still believe that it is dangerous to bury someone before they have had the chance to marry. According to their folklore, sexual frustration will drive the young person to rise from the grave and look for a mate. This is one origin of the Romanian *strigoi*, the living dead. In Transylvanian legends, *strigoi* are closely related to vampires. If the dead person is a young man, his sweetheart or another girl plays the part of his bride at the funeral. A young woman who dies while single is married to a crown, symbolising her wedding to Christ. To find out more about these folk beliefs, read Gail Kligman's *The Wedding of the Dead* (1986), a fascinating account of the two years she spent in Ieud during the mid-1980s.

The Iza Valley

Most of the upper part of the valley, from Rozavlea to Săcel, lies in a national park and the countryside here is exceptionally pretty. In **Vadu Izei** is the tourist office and information centre established in Maramureş by Opérations Villages Roumains. It goes under the name of *Fondation Touristique Agro-Tur OSR* and is located Izei beside the main road from Sighet at 161 Vadu, ☎/fax 062 330171.

From Vadu Izei head southeast towards Nănești, then follow the road and river to **Bârsana**. Here you can find a Baroque masonry church which was once part of a monastery founded in the 18C, and two wooden churches, one medieval and the other modern. The modern timber church is a magnificent piece of craftsmanship. It stands in the new convent of Bârsana, at the top of a steep hill beside the main through road. The church is embellished with fine neo-Baroque carvings and its spire stands 56m high. Together with the convent's other fine wooden buildings it was built by local craftsmen on the initiative of the dynamic abbess. The older timber church is also very handsome. It dates from 1390 but has 18C additions. Bârsana convent can accommodate visitors. Contact Abbess Filotea Olteanu or her colleagues on ☎ 331101.

In c 6km you reach the gorges where a small army from Baia Mare attacked the marauding Tartars in 1717. A right turn here across the bridge follows the Slătioara stream by road and track to Slătioara village, c 7km, and then **Glod**, another 7km. Glod's early-18C wooden church has a beautiful icon screen which was completed in 1823. From Glod, there is a track over the hills to Poienile Izei and Botiza but it's too rough for cars. Take a local guide or make sure you have good directions, because this route is not easy to follow.

Back on the main road turn southeast for **Strâmtura** (which means 'narrow place'). The wooden church here was donated by the villagers of Rozavlea in 1661. **Rozavlea** itself has an elegant pine church from 1720, built on the site of one that the Tartars burnt down on their rampage through Maramureş three years earlier. Further south, **Şieu** has a timber church, this time from 1760, which contains a well-preserved fresco cycle. From Şieu you can head southwest for Botiza: take the left-hand fork c 4km past Şieu.

Botiza has a superb wooden church which was brought here from Vişeul de Jos, where it was built in 1699. It has carving around doors and windows, and in the cemetery some of the tomb posts carry anthropomorphic motifs and solar symbols. In the early 1990s, a new concrete church was built beside the old one. Although it was needed by Botiza's growing Orthodox congregation, the new church spoils the view of the older building, which has far more beautiful lines.

Botiza is the centre of a **textile-weaving cooperative** founded after the 1989 revolution by wife of the parish priest. Under her direction, women from the village make kilims whose designs are modelled on traditional Moroşeni patterns. Her house serves as an exhibition centre for the textiles and can accommodate up to ten adults. The village also has a network of householders offering bed and breakfast. Visitors can learn to weave and dye wool in Botiza, and the village is a good base for exploring the hills. For the latest information about courses on offer and where to stay in the village, contact Victoria Berbecăru in Botiza, ☎ 062 334207, or *Centrul Judeţean de Creaţie Populară* in Baia Mare (see p 294).

The right fork past Şieu leads to **Poienile Izei**, which has a fine timber church from 1604. Unusually for this region, it has a square apse. Ask in the village for the *parohia* or the keyholder so that someone can show you inside. There are some 18C murals in the pronaos. On the left-hand side as you face the altar are a number of scenes from an individualistic version of the Last Judgment. Among them are a number of refreshingly direct paintings showing devils tormenting a prostitute and someone who has slept through a church service; another of their victims is a greedy landowner. The paintings on the right-hand side show Christ and the Woman of Samaria and Christ with three women who kept faith with him during his persecution. Drive southeast from Şieu on the main through road to reach the commune of **Ieud**. Ieud is known as the intellectual village of the Iza Valley because it has produced generals, lawyers and priests, but it has also been immortalised by Gail Kligman in her book, *The Wedding of the Dead*. In her introduction she gives some of the theories as to how the village got its name. One of these says that 'ieud' is a corruption of the Romanian word for 'I hear', recording a time before the village was founded when two men heard the sound of a spring and decided to stay. As Kligman discovered, this is a village with many old traditions. Most of Ieud's smallholders keep a flock of sheep, and every spring, after St George's Day, the villagers gather at a *stână* in the mountains to witness *Rupta sterpelor*, the annual measuring of sheep and goats' milk (see p 285).

Ieud still has many handsome vernacular buildings, although some of its oldest houses, dating from the 17C and 18C have been moved to the Village Museums in Bucharest and Sighet.

Turn right from the main road, and before reaching the centre of Ieud you pass the hamlet of Gura Ieudului, the Mouth of the Ieud Stream. Modern brick houses are springing up among the old timber buildings, but the asphalt road comes to an abrupt end when you reach the next junction. As in most Maramureș villages, all the other streets are paved with dirt. When you reach the end of the made up road, turn left and follow the brook for a few metres. Cross the bridge and above you, hidden among trees on a steep hillside, stands **Biserica din Deal**.

This charming little church was built in 1364 and is one of the few to have escaped destruction by the Tartars. It is often said to be the oldest church in Maramureș, but there is an earlier timber church across the Tisa in the Ukrainian part of Maramureș. Inside Biserica din Deal are a group of frescoes painted by Alexandru Ponehalschi in the second half of the 18C. They include a remarkable Passion of Christ. In the narthex, the ladder leading to the belfry is made from a single tree trunk. The church was closed for many years during the communist period. When it reopened it was found to contain several valuable books in Romanian. These included *Zbornicul de la Ieud* ('The Manuscript of Ieud'), printed by Deacon Coresi in Brașov in 1534. A reprint was published by Editura Academiei, Bucharest, in 1977.

Ieud's Lower Church, **Biserica din Șes**, belongs to the Greek Catholic faith. It is a larger and much grander building, known locally as the Cathedral. It is considerably younger than Biserica din Deal, dating from 1717. Biserica din Șes has the typical Maramureș double roof, the upper one rising almost vertically to the ridge, capped by a slender Gothic-style tower. Inside it contains some glass icons from the Nicula school as well as attractive traditional rugs and furniture.

Return to the main road and the next commune you come to is **Bogdan Vodă**, the sometime fief of Prince Bogdan I of Moldavia one of Maramureș's most famous *nemeși*. During his lifetime it was known as Cuhea. The ruins of a 13C fortress which belonged to the prince and his descendants can be seen near the village. In the centre of Bogdan Vodă stands a large concrete church which overshadows its wooden predecessor. The old wooden church was built in c 1718. It has a triangular roof, and a square tower with a wide balcony supported by 13 columns. A *funie* (a skuamorphic 'rope' belt carved in wood) around the body of the church gives the illusion of holding it together. Further along the main through road on the right-hand side is another church. Next to this, sheltered in a wooden hut which is normally locked, lie the foundations of the 14C stone church which Bogdan's family built before his escape to Moldavia. Stone churches were rare in Maramureş not only because wood was in greater supply, but because Magyar authorities forbade the Moroşeni to construct masonry buildings.

Continuing to **Săliştea de Sus**, the wooden church in the village is known as Biserica a Balenilor because of the whales which Radu Munteanu included in the murals he painted here. Its foundation inscription dates it to 1752. Biserica Nistoreştilor has some icons by Alexandru Ponehalschi as well as fragments of murals. At Săcel you can turn northeast along the DN17C and cross the ridge into Moisei and the Vişeu Valley.

The Vişeu Valley

This route brings you along the main road east into Moldavia. The Vişeu Valley was the birthplace of Toador Hodor, another of the artists who worked extensively in this region. Between 1806–09 he decorated churches at Corneşti, Bârsana, Văleni and Năneşti. There are fewer wooden churches in this valley, but it is well worth visiting because from here you can explore the mountains between Maramureş and the Ukraine.

From Sighet the road follows the Rona Valley past the ancient mining town of Coştiui and crosses the Maramureş Hills before dropping into the Vişeu Valley near Petrova. The railway from Sighet passes to the north of this road. At Leordina you could take a road into the hills, turning left along the Ruscova Valley. This eventually brings you to **Poienile de Sub Munte** (the Meadows under the Mountain). This village was once inhabited by Huţuls, a Slavonic-speaking people who are descendants of the Celts. There are small communities of Huţuls in the Vişeu and Ruscova valleys and others also survive further east, in Bucovina. So isolated were they during the communist period that photographer Kosei Miya recalls meeting a Huţul man on his way on foot from Poienile to Baia Mare wearing a suit made entirely of leaves. Huţuls speak a dialect of Ukrainian and have their own literature and customs which distinguish them from their fellow Romanians. But the name Huţul is better known in connection with the sturdy little horses which are bred in Romania and prized as draught animals (see pp 219–220).

If you have the chance, take the **narrow-gauge railway** from Vişeu de Sus which follows the Vaser River almost to its source on the Ukrainian border. The 45km-long Vişeu line is the most famous forestry railway in Romania. It is the only one of its kind and remains indispensable because it serves several villages which have no roads. Besides heavy, steam-hauled timber trains, it carries a variety of traffic from busy passenger and freight services. Vişeu operates a variety of eccentric carriages which have been rebuilt from cars, buses and lorries. One of the locomotives is a Resiţa 0-8-0T steam engine dating from the 1950s. Access to the narrow-gauge station in Vişeu is through the timber yard. Trains leave every morning at 07.00 and begin the return journey from Coman at 15.00. You can book tickets from *Ocolul Silvic Vişeu de Sus*, Str 1 Mai 21, ☎ 353941, 352787.

Moisei and its near neighbour Borşa once belonged to Prince Bogdan. Today **Moisei** is a nondescript little town c 12km west of Vişeu. It has a **monument** to the 29 Romanians who were massacred here by Horthyist soldiers as they retreated in 1944.

Moisei monastery lies on the edge of the town at the foot of Pietrosul Rodnei. Take the road to the south towards Săcel, and after c 1km fork left. First mentioned in 1637, the monastery was one of the few places in early 17C Maramureş where local boys could train as artists. Even though the monastery was a bastion of Orthodoxy, students from Moisei learnt to synthesise the traditional forms of Byzantine art with Western influences introduced by the Habsburgs. After being ordained they went on to decorate churches in Poienile Izei, Vişeul de Mijloc, at Giuleşti monastery and in Năsăud, across the Rodna Mountains to the south. Moisei formed close ties with the eastern church in each of the other Romanian principalities. It contains three icons which were painted in the school. On 14 and 15 August Moisei monastery holds a magnificent procession and feast to celebrate the Assumption of the Virgin. All the neighbouring villages take part, and the full *Akathistos* hymn is chanted at a service which lasts throughout the night.

Borşa

Moisei merges with Borşa, a resort town of 30,000 inhabitants which lies c 90km from Sighet. Mountains tower over it from a height of over 2000m, and nearby are several beauty spots such as Cascada Cailor (the Horses' Cascade), the highest waterfall in the country with a 100m drop. Borşa also has the longest natural ski jump in Romania at 90m, a large number of mineral springs and facilities for fishing and hunting.

Practical information

☎ code

062

Tourist information

The *Tourist Information Centre* is at Str Decebal 2, ☎ 344512/344310. But the driving force behind Borşa's fledgling tourist industry is the director of the town hospital, **Dr Bărcan**. Contact him or his office if you want to organise horse-trekking or hiking tours at Str Floare de Colţ 1, 4990 Borşa, PO Box 14, ☎ 343577; fax 343169.

Where to stay

Hotels include *Iezerul*, Str Decebal 2, ☎ 344310; *Cascada*, Str Fântana 25, ☎ 344512; *Stibina*, Str Fântana 27, ☎ 343466; *Brădet*, Str Fântana 23, ☎ 342252. *Perla Maramureşului*, a motel and restaurant at Str Victoriei 37, ☎ 342539, is strongly recommended.

Money

Banks in Borşa are *Banca Comercială*, Str Decebal 4, and *Banca Română de Dezvoltare*, Str Libertăţii 51.

Town hall

The *primăria* is at Str Libertății 175, ☎ 342322/342553.

Medical care

The **Recovering Hospital** is at Str Floare de Colț 1, ☎ 343272.

Pharmacies include *Elixir*, Str Vișeului 15, and *Davilla*, Str Victoriei 16, ☎ 342994.

Borșa has a handsome **church** made of pine logs. Dating from 1718, it has a verandah-style porch and the door and window frames are embellished with attractive carvings. The church stands a few hundred metres to the north of the main through road; as you head east through the town, turn left up a narrow lane beside the army building before you reach the left turn to Băile Borșa. The paintings inside were done by Zaharia Zugrav in 1765; they are deteriorating but the interior is very attractive.

Immediately to the south of Borșa the nature reserve of **Pietrosul Mare** perches 2303m above sea level. Quaternary glaciations have gouged the terrain into great circuses, morraines, waterfalls and gorges. Its alpine and subalpine zones support a wonderful variety of wild and sometimes rare plants, such as punctate gentian, pulsatilla, Alpine campanula, Moldavian aconite and mountain geum. Saxifrage and sempervivum cling to the cliff sides, but there is also a wide range of wetland plants and glacial relics. And in the forest belt that surrounds the reserve there are brown bear, lynx and marten, chamois, marmot and adder. The marmots were introduced from the French Alps and the chamois from Transylvania. Eagles sometimes wheel overhead and there are woodcock in the forests. In all, Pietrosul Mare covers around 33 sq km. You must get a pass from *Ocolul Silvic Borșa*, Str Victoriei 56, in Borșa ☎ 342137, or from Reservația Pietrosul Rodrei, Str Zorilor 2, ☎ 342227. When visitng the reserve, keep to the marked paths.

On the climb to the Prislop Pass, you come to Preluca Tătărilor where the Borșa priest Ștefan Lupu put paid to the invading Tartars in 1717.

North-east of Baia Mare but south of the Guțâi and Lăpuș Mountains lies the **Lăpuș Valley**. This is a lovely region which, while closely related to historic Maramureș, has its own ethnographic and architectural character. Wooden churches here are more varied in plan than they are in historic Maramureș; some have sanctuaries which are narrower than the naos, others have seven-faceted apses, as at Coșteni, and there are Gothic style spires, with and without corner turrets. But in the Lăpuș Valley two-tier roofs are unknown.

To get there from Baia Mare drive to Baia Sprie and turn right in the town centre for Șișești and Cavnic. Between the two towns, at **Șurdești** in the Cavnic Valley, stands a superb oaken church which confounds all the rules: its plan follows the Maramureș type, even to the double roof. Turn right off the main road and follow the tarmac down the hill to the cul de sac by the churchyard. The *parohia* stands next to the church gates, and you will need to ask the priest if you can borrow the key.

Burned by the Tartars in 1717 and rebuilt either in 1724 and 1738, Șurdești Church of the Holy Archangels stands in a beautiful orchard. Its spire, allegedly the highest wooden tower in Europe until Bârsana capped the record, rises 54m from its base. Its roof has one of the finest profiles of any Moroșeni church, being pitched almost vertically to get rid of snow more easily. Its design marks a high point in Romania's vernacular architecture, and from a distance the shingles resemble a soft cloak. At the west end is an elegant, arcaded porch echoed in a gallery above the lower roof, and inside the walls are decorated throughout with some of the most interesting murals in the Maramureș.

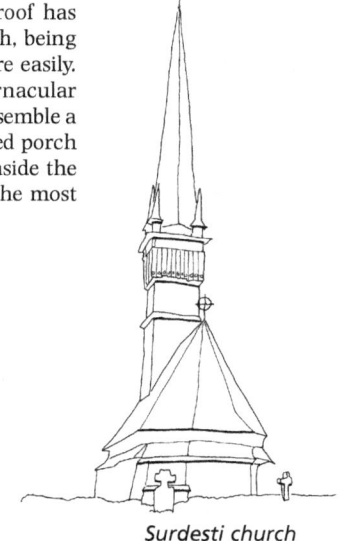

Șurdești church

Șurdești's murals

According to conservator Fran Weatherhead who studied the paintings in 1992, the murals are by an unknown hand. They were probably carried out in the late 18C or early 19C. The best scenes are on the high barrel-vaulted ceiling of the naos and are exceptional even for Maramureș. Here you can see a centrepiece containing a painting of the Trinity with roundels containing the Lamb of God and the Virgin Mary above and below it. In the four corners are the Evangelists, but the most remarkable are four scenes showing the Apocalypse, St John sleeping, the Prophet Elijah ascending to heaven, and Jacob's Ladder. Angels and stars fill the gaps between the more important figures; one of the angels carries a human soul. The clouds surrounding the scenes are a Baroque rather than a Byzantine feature.

Murals on the upper side walls depict the Stations of the Cross, while *trompe l'oeil* columns and pediments articulate the west wall and the apse. On the lower side walls there are saints, martyrs and scenes from the Old and New Testaments, and the west wall also contains four roundels showing Adam and Eve and their expulsion from Paradise.

On the pronaos ceiling is a design which represents a pre-Copernican universe, with the planets and the Sun orbiting the Earth. Surrounding this are two circular borders which may signify the limits of God's cosmos; the inner one with its green scales could be the serpent Ouroboros, while the outer band may represent flames. On either side of these rings are a Sun and a Moon, each one with a human face, and another spangling of stars fills much of the remaining space. You can find the Sun and Moon motifs in other Moroșeni churches and on wayside crosses, but the cosmos in the centre is probably unique.

The pronaos walls contain pictures of the Wise and Foolish Virgins, the Last Judgment, the Weighing of Souls (with soldiers wearing contemporary dress and foreign costumes, perhaps indicating that they are Turks or Tartars), as well as scenes showing Doubting Thomas, and Jesus and the Woman of Samaria.

An analysis of the paints shows that they were from cheap local sources: the blues are from indigo, the reds come from minimum, the greens are

> probably malachite and the yellow may be iron oxide. Luckily the murals on the naos ceiling have not deteriorated so badly as other areas of the church, but the cosmos in the pronaos is in much greater danger from candle smoke and rain. Şurdeşti is one of seven Moroşeni churches whose fabric and murals are to be restored with the help of money from the Getty Foundation.

The road north leads past Creasta Cocojului, one of the impressively jagged peaks which characterise the Maramureş skyline. Shortly afterwards you reach the old mining town of **Cavnic**, where the metals are still sifted in flotation tanks beside the road. Moroşeni surprised the Tartars here in a famous battle of 1717, and there is an obelisk commemorating those who gave their lives in the revolution of 1848. There is a road, or rather a track, between Cavnic and Budeşti, but it is only worth trying to find your way along it in the summer.

South of Şurdeşti at **Plopiş**, the timber church was modelled on Şurdeşti's and dates from 1796–1811. Further on at Lăschia, you can contrast these two elegant buildings with a quite different style: the sturdy 19C church which stands beside the main through road has an odd but commanding Baroque onion dome on a solid, square tower. Turn east in Copălnic Mănăstur and head for Târgu Lăpuş. Taking the star role in this wide and pretty valley is the little elm church of **Sfânţi Arhangeli** in Rogoz. Rogoz village stands halfway between Târgu Lăpuş and Lăpuş. Ask for the *parohia*, and the priest (who now presides over a Neo-Baroque concrete temple) will probably be happy to show you round.

The two **wooden churches** in this village share the same cemetery. Both churches are still in use. Sfânti Arhangeli is the earlier Orthodox church, built in 1661, and is unmistakeable because of its jutting roof consoles. The consoles support the wide overhangs of the roof. Projecting in graduated tiers from interlocking corner joints, they are shaped in the form of stylised horses' heads. You can find motifs like this on old wooden buildings all over Romania. They are apotropeic symbols, meant to ward off evil spirits. Similar carvings of animals' heads have been found at the entrances to houses found at Dacian sites, and you can see them in some of the village museums, on half-buried dwellings from Wallachia which were still being built in the 18C. The outer and inner doors at Rogoz are particularly small, forcing worshippers to show a proper humility by bowing their heads on entry to the sacred space. Radu Munteanu painted the interior in 1785 with a local artist called Nicolae Man. The other timber church at Rogoz is an 18C building belonging to the Greek Catholics. It contains a fresco cycle illustrating the life of Paraschiva, one of Romania's most popular saints (see p 244).

Crişana and the northwest borderlands

Crişana is the area of northwest Romania that lies between the Apuseni massif and the Hungarian border. Its southern edge is defined by the Mureş River, while to the north it meets the River Tisa, and the frontiers of the Ukraine. In the west, its western horizons merge with the Great Hungarian Plain. Oradea and Satu Mare are its largest cities, occupying the western flats, but as you drive east and north the landscape quickly becomes prettier and more interesting. (Straddling the Mureş, Arad has one foot in Crişana, but because it is closer to Timişoara than Oradea, this town is covered in the next chapter—see pp 344–350.)

Crişana is a multicultural region that has known many different masters. As a result, German, Hungarian and sometimes Slovak are still spoken here, as well as Romanian. Strictly speaking, Crişana is the name of a smaller, ethnographic zone between Arad and Oradea, where three rivers converge. These are Crişul Alb, Crişul Negru and Crişul Repede (the White, Black and Swift-runnig Criş), and they have the equally poetic name of Ţara Crişurilor. Criş also denotes an early Neolithic culture that flourished here from c 5500–4000 BC. One of its legacies was the strong sense of design that survives in the region's folk art. While it is often seen as a staging post on the way to more scenic places, Crişana has a lot to offer. Scattered all over the region are castles and lovely churches, traditional villages and other signs of its fascinating, multicultural history. And at Căciulata in Sălaj county archaeologists discovered some of the oldest cave paintings in Europe, dating from the Upper Paleolithic era (c 28,000–10,000 BC).

Oradea

Surrounded by industrial wasteland, Oradea is not obviously appealing. But this is Crişana's main cultural centre and once past its grimy environs, you will find streets full of lively Secessionist architecture, a few fine civic and ecclesiastical buildings and several absorbing museums. Comprising some 225,000 people, the city is the county town of Bihor. It sprawls across Crişul Repede, c 14km east of the Borş crossing into Hungary, on one of the main arteries connecting east and west.

If you are driving between Oradea and Borş on the E65, keep an eye out for thieves in fast cars. Do not stop beside the road to talk to strangers, especially not if they ask you to change money for them. If they say they are police officers, they should be wearing uniforms and have ID. This stretch of road and the Borş frontier crossing have become notorious for highway robbery.

Stone Age, Bronze Age and Dacian peoples have lived here, and in the Middle Ages Oradea flourished as *citas Varadiens*. Oradea was once a fortified town, and the ruins of its early 12C citadel can be seen near the centre. If you need to take stock before deciding where to go next, stay overnight here or in Băile Felix, and spend a few hours looking around.

314 • CRIȘANA AND THE NORTHWEST BORDERLANDS

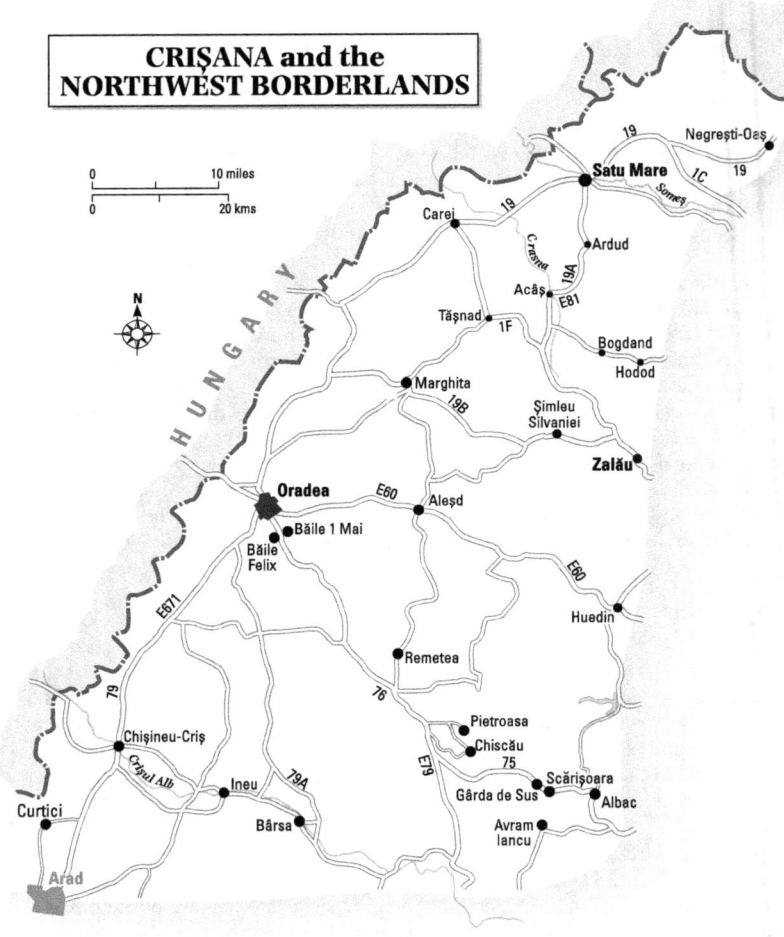

Practical information

☎ code
059

Tourist information
This can be found at *Lucon* at Str General Traian Moșoiu 1, ☎ 436613; *BTT* at Str Jules Cazaban 49, ☎ 454156; *Chiro Tour* at Str Libertății 2–4, ☎ 435389; *Sind România* at Parcul 1 Decembrie 1918 nr. 10, ☎ 136652; and *Gigolo Inter Tour* at Str Independenței 1.

Getting around
By train Oradea is on the main international railway line connecting Romania with Budapest, Prague and Kraków, and the central train station is on Piața București, a short walk north of the city centre and close to the county museums. For booking tickets in advance you will need the *CFR* office at B-dul Republicii 2, ☎ 130578/414970.

By bus The *Trans-Europa* international bus agency is on Str Traian Mosoiu, ☎ 436613. Terminals for buses to other western Romanian towns and to Hungary can be found southeast of the centre at Str Războieni 81 and near Oradea Est train station. Buses and trams also serve the city centre.

By car Romania's national automobile association, *ACR*, has a branch at Piața Independenței 12, ☎ 130725. If you need a **taxi**, try *City*, ☎ 131111, *Confort*, ☎ 444444, or *Marco Taxi*, ☎ 444055.

By plane This lies southwest of the city on șos Aradului; tickets and flight information can be obtained from *TAROM* at Piața Regele Ferdinand 2, ☎ 131918.

Where to stay
Oradea is not especially well provided with hotels, and the health spa of Băile Felix (the Happy Baths), c 9km to the southwest, has a far greater choice. Oradea's best hotel is the ***Dacia*** (☆☆) at Aleea Strandului 1, ☎ 418656; fax 411280. You could also try the *Astoria* (☆) at Str Teatrului 1, ☎ 136094, *Crișul Repede* (☆) at Str Libertății 8, ☎ 132509, or *Parc* (☆) at Str Republicii 5, ☎ 411699. Other options include the *Tineretului* (☆) at Str Cazaban 49A, ☎ 444600, *Transilvania* (☆) at Str Teatrului 2, ☎ 130508, and the hikers' bolthole, the old palace of *Vulturul Negru* (☆) at Str Independenței 1, ☎ 135417.

Eating out
Restaurants *de luxe* include the *Atlantic* at Str Iosif Vulcan 9, and *Mignon Caly* at Str Roman Ciorogariu 1, while Oradea's very own *McDonald's* is at Str Republicii 30. There is also a pizzeria at Piața Cetății 28. If you need general supplies try the *Crișul Supermarket* next to *McDonald's*.

Post office
The main post office is on Str Roman Ciorogariu.

Money
Exchange houses include *Alicante Office* at Str Republicii 29, and *Dacia* at Piața Unirii 2–4. There are **banks** at Str T. Vladimirescu 1, Piața Muncii 1, Piața Cetății 18, Str D. Cantemir 2B, and Str Independenței 51, bl A1.

Police
There is a police station at Parcul Traian 18, ☎ 412472, and the town hall is at Piața Unirii 1.

Medical care
Pharmacies can be found at *Europharm*, Str Ady Endre 2, and *Farmexym*, Str Avram Iancu 2.

Entertainment

Theatres in town include *Teatrul de Stat* at 6 Piaţa Regele Ferdinand 1, and the puppet theatre at Str V. Alecsandri 8. There are **discos** at Str Strandului 2 and the confidently styled *No Problem* in Parcul Magnolia. Hotels *Dacia* and *International* have **casinos**, and you can try your hand at **billiards** at the *Monaco* at Str N. Grigorescu 2.

Maps

The Crişana Museum can supply an excellent map of the city showing both old and new street names. The town hall may also be able to provide books on Bihor county, which covers this part of the region; otherwise try the tourist agencies.

Muzeul Ţării Crişurilor is the Crişana Museum, housed in a splendid U-shaped Baroque building at B-dul Dacia 1–3. Modelled on the Belvedere Palace in Vienna and completed in 1770, it was created for Oradea's Roman Catholic bishops and forms part of a Baroque ensemble that includes the Roman Catholic cathedral and the arcaded Şirul Canonicilor, the Canons' corridor, both on Str Stadionului. The palace and cathedral were designed by Austrian architect Franz Anton Hillenbrandt (1719–97) in collaboration with Giovanni Battista Ricca. (Ricca's façade for the Gesù in Rome is the natural father of the cathedral's magnificent west end.)

Sober but sumptuous, the palace is arranged on three floors, with a grand staircase connecting the first two. On the first and most ornate storey is a splendid Hall of Festivities frescoed by Francesco Storno in 1879, and a chapel. A phalanx of Baroque doorways along the corridors increases the impression of grandeur. If you have time, visit the **museums** on the mezzanine and second floor. The paintings by Surrealist Victor Brauner, Hans Mattis Teutsch and Max Hermann Maxy from the period leading up to the Second World War recall a time when Romania's intellectual circles were a ferment of new ideas. A great deal of exciting work was done by artists who later fled from fascism and the communist system. There are also fine works by Iosif Iser, Pallady, Toniţa and Ştefan Dimitrescu, but the collection has a much wider remit, holding examples of European art from the 16C onwards.

Highlights of the **History Museum** include a Bronze Age megaron temple from Sălacea, Celtic and Greek pottery and Dacian silver, while the **Ethnographic Museum** offers an appealing journey through the colourful crafts of Bihor county. Wonderful dinosaur fossils and information on local nature reserves such as Cetăţile Ponorului, Izbucul de la Călugări (near Vaşcău) and the wildflower meadows near Goroneşti can be found in the **Natural History** section. All four museums are open Tues, Thurs and Sat 10.00–15.00, Wed, Fri and Sun 10.00–18.00 in summer, and Tues–Sun 10.00–16.00 in winter.

Around Oradea

Băile Felix, 7km south of Oradea on the E79, has been a health spa since the Romans were here in the 2C and 3C. Some of its central buildings are old and atmospheric, but its skyline today is dominated by the profiles of smart, modern hotels.

The phone code is 059. The town's 3-star hotels include *Termal*, ☎ 261214; fax 470037, and *Internaţional*, ☎ 261055; fax 470002. The 2-star hotels include *Felix*, ☎ 261421; *Mureş*, ☎ 261450; *Lotus*, ☎ 134355; *Poieniţa*,

☎ 261172; *Unirea*, ☎ 261124; *Someş*, ☎ 261248; and *Nufărul*, ☎ 261143. All the above-mentioned hotels are managed by *Turism Felix*, and there is a map of all the hotels and treatment spas at the entrance to the hotel complex. You can get a bus here from Oradea train station. Some of the more exotic treatments on offer include applications of invigorating hot black mud mixed with paraffin (*namol şi parafina*), which is supposed to purify your skin and help alleviate rheumatism. There is also a wide selection of saunas and thermal swimming pools, massage parlours and gyms.

About 13km north of Oradea on the DN19 lie the remnants of an **earthen fortress** called Biharea, built by the 10C leader Menumorut. On your way south on the E79, take a look at the 18C church at Beiuş and its gallant wooden counterpart at Rieni.

Travelling east of Chişineu-Criş, a town almost halfway between Oradea and Arad, the DN79A brings you through pretty landscapes of open farmland and pastures. As you drive into **Ineu**, 30km east, on the left of the road and before you cross the river bridge in the town centre, stands an 18C castle that now functions as a school for handicapped children. Next to it, but barely visible from the road, are the stumpy remains of a Turkish fortress dating from the time when a *beglerbey* made the town his headquarters.

Bârsa, 17km east of Ineu, is typical of this region. It was founded in the mountains during the 1430s, but under Maria Theresa the whole community was resettled here in the plains near the Crişul Alb River, where it was re-organised according to the current Habsburgic canons. So if you venture beyond the main tarmac road you will find that the village has **stone-lined streets** that were laid out at a certain width to allow horse-drawn traffic to flow throughout the year, even when one side of the road was under repair. Such a large expanse between the neat rows of houses, facing gable-end-on as they do in all the former Habsburg colonies, also helped to prevent fires from destroying the entire village.

Snaking through Bârsa in a most un-canal-like way is the **Criş canal**. It runs parallel to the river and in places is narrow and very deep; it is no place for a barge, so the boats must have been slender and short. The canal was cut in 1852–53 to support the magnificent flour mills that once patrolled almost every kilometre of its 75km length. Today, only a few of these superb Baroque warehouses remain; one in Bârsa, near the semi-derelict barns of the collective farm, has been turned into a café.

To the southwest of the village, where one of its track-streets drops into pastures and a meandering stream, stands a **rugă**, a tall, simple cross with a semicircular hat. Imposing in its stark simplicity, it is used once a year when the village Orthodox priest comes here to celebrate prayers (*rugăciuni*) on St Peter and St Paul's Day, 29 June.

Bârsa is the home of the dynamic anthropologist Ioan Godea and his wife, Anna, who are determinedly transforming the village into a centre for tourism. Their mini *complex d'agrement* comprises traditional houses and wooden lakeside cabins with places for up to 40 people and a commercial pottery. The Godeas do not have a phone, and the best way to contact them is to ask for them by name when you arrive.

A 20-minute drive east of Bârsa brings you to villages such as **Botfei**, on the edge of the Codru Moma range. From here tracks penetrate deep into the unspoilt forest, and in Botfei a pretty watermill is named after John F. Kennedy for the good reason that the owner used to look like the late American President. Take a guide if you want to trek into the mountains; beyond Botfei to the east there are no houses for 100km.

Break your journey at the unpretentious country town of **Sebiş**, a further 5km east off the main through road, and you will find an open-air theatre (summer season only), a modest café and six churches, five of them catering for different faiths.

If you are looking for a place to stay overnight, the health spa of **Moneasa**, c 20km further north into the Codru-Moma mountains, has several adequate hotels. The *Moneasa* (✶) is one of the best: without being strikingly glamorous, it is a pleasant, spacious modern building with twin-bedded and three-bedded rooms in Str Principală, ☎ 057 439292. You could also try *Club Castel Moneasa* (✶✶✶), ☎ 057 439162; fax 191548. Since 1989 many of the pretty pavilions and villas in Moneasa have been neglected, and the resort is a ghost of what it once was. But you can hike into the mountains from here and although the paths are strewn with litter, the walks are beautiful. One of the pathways brings you to a 13C citadel called Dezna. Moneasa has facilities for winter skiing. Trains between Sântana and Brad stop at Sebiş whence a bus can ferry you to Moneasa; alternatively you can come here by bus direct from Arad.

Caves
Between the E60 and the E79, forming great holes in the rock sponges of Pădurea Craiului and the Bihor Mountains, are some extraordinary caves. **Peştera Meziad**, 16km northeast of Beiuş and c 10km east of Remetea in the Munţii Pădurea Craiului Reserve, is one of the largest in the country. It measures over 4km long and has many different levels. Most exciting of all the caves in the Bihor Mountains is Piatra Altarului (Altar Rock). These amazing underground halls can be found in Valea Ponorului, c 35km southeast of Beiuş, in the reserve that lies north of the road from Lunca to Câmpeni. Experienced potholers will need a pass and a guide to visit Piatra Altarului; it is not open to non-caving tourists.

Piatra Altarului contains a series of galleries known as the Palace, the Geode, Paradise and the Bear's Altar. It can be found close to Izbucul Alunului, under a limestone cliff which is hemmed in by peat marsh and shallow ponds and woods of birch and pine.

Discovering the caves
Potholers from Cluj Polytechnic explored the caverns for the first time in 1984. This led to a momentous discovery. After forcing their way through an entrance 'small enough to shelter a racoon', they were about to give up when they felt a draught of air coming through a narrow window. They tell us, 'with ears pressed against the stone... [we]... deciphered... the call of a great cave.'

As the explorers walked, crouched and crawled their way from cavern to cavern they found themselves in a fantastic, crystalline world. Giant arches and columns soared above their heads like pieces of crenellated Baroque architecture, silvery needles like modernistic fountains rose beside them, and diaphanous waterlilies floated tantalisingly in pools of water. At the further end the potholers found themselves in a horizontal passage with vaulted ceilings and tubular stalactites. Then came the greatest surprise of all. Here on the ground they saw a small skull, covered with strange growths like popcorn. Then they found two more, each one having a long bone in front of the snout. Farther away, half hidden in a dip of the floor, was a skull measuring almost a half a metre wide. More remains of jaws, skulls and vertebrae lay in a niche and skulls lay all around the cavers. All the bones had belonged to bears. They had come from young and adults alike, but were hardly recognisable under a thick layer of calcite—the 'popcorn'. Strangest of all, four of the skulls were arranged in tight formation, like a cross, with the occipital bone facing toward the centre.

This cave is known as Peștera Ursilor, 'the Bears' Cemetery', and the bones had been used in the Palaeolithic cult of the bear. Fragments of the crust which covers some of the skulls were found to be at least 75,000 years old. This makes them tens of thousands of years older than the Magdalenian wall paintings in caves such as Altamira and Lascaux. The strange cross-formation may represent a link in the chain that connects us with the awakening of human spiritual consciousness.

Following the discovery of Piatra Altarului, strenuous efforts have been made to protect the caves from vandals. As a result, the Romanian Speleological Foundation has mounted a campaign to promote a new Cave and Karst Protection law. A book of 57 photographs by Dr Cristian Lascu, called *Piatra Altarului: the Album*, has been published to support the campaign. If you want to know more about it, or if you want to get permission to visit the cave or buy the book, contact Mihai Gligan, Calea Florești 81, ap 261, 3400 Cluj-Napoca, ☎ 064 178629, or Mihai Botez, Piața 14 Iulie 4, 3400 Cluj-Napoca, ☎/fax 064 187657, or send a message by e-mail to speo@mail.soroscj.ro. If you have access to the internet, you can find all these details on the Romanian Speleology Home Page. Alternatively, write to the Romanian Speleological Institute at Str Clinicilor 5, PO Box 58, 3400 Cluj-Napoca, or ☎/fax 064 195954.

Piatra Alartului is close to several other cave complexes, including Măgura, Focul Viu and Scărișoara (see p 410).

Satu Mare

Tucked away in the northwest corner of Romania, the border crossing from Hungary at Petea is usually calmer than the international frontiers further south. It lies a few kilometres northwest of Satu Mare, a town of c 130,000 people that provides a useful starting point for detours into some of Crișana's fascinating ethnographic zones such as Țara Oașului, Codru and Sălaj. And Maramureș is also close at hand. There are spas in Satu Mare itself, Tășnad, Acâș and Mădăraș (ask at the tourist office for more information).

Little is left of Castrum Zotmar, the citadel from which the town originally took its name. According to legend, this was the headquarters of Duke Menumorut, who thwarted the Hungarian advance into Transylvania.

History

Satu Mare is mentioned in documents as far back as 1181. In the Middle Ages it was an important trading post on routes between Transylvania and central Europe, and huge quantities of salt were sent here down the Someş River on their way abroad. Separated from Hungary after the Battle of Mohács in 1526, the town flourished as a border crossing. It was coveted by successive Transylvanian princes who were allowed to govern Transylvania as long as they paid tribute money to the Ottoman Sultan. But in 1657, following provocation by the Transylvanian prince Gheorghe Rákóczi II, Polish troops occupied Satu Mare and the surrounding countryside. After several skirmishes a peace was signed between the Transylvanians and Jan Sobieski.

Some 30 years later Sobieski reappeared as the exotic king of Poland whose turbanned soldiers routed the Turks from Vienna. The Habsburgs took advantage of the Ottomans' retreat, sweeping eastwards on a campaign to regain their 'hereditary' lands in central and eastern Europe. But the Turks clung to Transylvania and in the 1660s, during the reign of Mehmet IV, they ravaged Satu Mare. Eventually they were forced out, and in the early 18C both Transylvania and Hungary were absorbed within the Habsburg Empire. Crişana came under the leadership of Austrian military governors called

Duchies and cnezaţi

History books published both during and after the Ceauşescu regime often make much of Romania's prior claims to Transylvania. Their chief argument was that present-day Romanians are direct descendants of the Daco-Romans who continued to live in the country after the Roman withdrawal in 207 AD. 9C and 10C 'dukes' owned large estates in western Romania before King Árpád staked his claim to the 'empty land' of Transylvania. No-one has identified the real ethnic origins of these dukes, but at the time of the Hungarian incursions the population of Transylvania was probably a mix of Cumans, Pecenegs, Slavs and ethnic Romanians, none of whom had formed a polity powerful enough to resist the warlike Magyars. But Menomorut was a historical figure. Besides Zotmar he owned a citadel at Biharea, near Oradea, and according to a Hungarian chronicler he held out against King Árpád at each one for several days.

Apart from the duchies of Menumorut, Glad and Gylas (or Gyula), which may or may not have predated the first Hungarian incursions, the Romanian lands had *cnezaţi*, village communities ruled by a *cnez* and formed sometime before feudalism was introduced. Again, no-one knows their real origins, but *cnezaţi* also existed elsewhere in the Slavic world. After the introduction of feudalism, some *cnezi* were given privileges by their respective princes. In Moldavia and Wallachia some became boyars, while in Transylvania the kings of Hungary gave them titles and land. Others became freeholders, with a status somewhere between feudal lords and tied peasants.

verwalter. To many, the Habsburgs' regime was as oppressive as the Turks', but it allowed Satu Mare a period of unfamiliar stability.

Formerly part of the Hungarian county of Szabolcs-Szatmár, Satu Mare means 'Big Village'. In Hungarian its name was Szatmárnémeti, indicating that there was a German presence here too: *német* is the Hungarian for German. After their conquest of Transylvania, the Habsburgs pursued a policy of Germanisation in Crișana and the Banat further south, repopulating the towns and villages left empty by the Ottomans with colonists from western Europe. The majority of these newcomers were from towns such as Ravensburg and Biberach in Swabia. They were invited by agents from the Viennese court, who set up special offices to recruit them.

Around Satu Mare, the immigrants were called Sathmar-Swabians, and they established farms on land that had once belonged to the Károlyi family near Carei. This colonisation was seen by the Magyars as deliberately anti-Hungarian, but the hard-working Germans flourished and their culture came to dominate the western borderlands. Both Banat and Crișana have produced excellent ethnic German writers. During the Second World War the Nazis treated the Swabians as though they were Romanian, and many were dispossessed. In the 1980s the German population dwindled further because of Ceaușescu's repatriation deals with the old German Federal Republic (West Germany). Now, with rare exceptions, only the older generations remain. After 1989 the Swabians created their own political forum, but they are not represented in parliament so their attempts at self-determination carry little weight.

In 1920 the Treaty of Trianon somewhat arbitrarily cut the old county in two, and Satu Mare began a long decline. But since the 1989 revolution it has improved out of all recognition.

Practical information

☎ code
061

Tourist information
The main tourist office can be found in the *Aurora Hotel* at Piața Libertății 11, but if you are looking for budget prices, try *BTT* at B-dul Traian 7.

Getting around
By rail his lies to the west of the town centre, on Str Griviței.
By bus he main bus station is next to the railway station.
By car For **car repairs** try *Euromobil Satu Mare* at Str Fabricii 6 or the *ACR* at Str Mareșal Ion Antonescu, bl 3, ☎ 716749/712345. There are plenty of **petrol stations** in Satu Mare: these include the old *PECO benzinaria* on Drumul Botizului, and others at Str Cuza 16, Piața Viitorului, Piața George Baitor, Str Lucian Blaga and Piața Țitulescu.
By plane Romania's airline, *TAROM*, has an office at Piața 25 Octombrie 9 that can organise internal flights.

Where to stay
If you have to stop over in Satu Mare choose the *Hotel Dacia* (✫✫) on B-dul Traian, ☎ 714276, for aesthetic rea-

sons if nothing else. Built to a prize-winning design by Ödön Lechner in 1902, it stands beside the central park on the site of a former city hall. Lechner had the town's coat of arms embedded prominently into the cornice from where it dominates the façade. But the impression of civic pomp evaporates into pure fantasy in its pink-and-blue colour scheme, and the bold curves that dominate the frontage. After such a wonderful start the interior is disappointing, but at least the *Dacia* is large; it has 107 rooms. It also has a casino, fax bureau, travel agency, and an exchange and VISA service.

Hotel Aurora (✫✫) on Piaţa Libertăţii, ☎ 714199, is a stark modern building, but is otherwise comparable to the *Dacia*. Other hotels include the *Sport* (✫) at Str Mileniului 25, north of Piaţa Libertăţii and near the food market on Str Wolfenbuttel. For accommodation out of town, you could try the *Amelia* (✫) motel, ☎ 732398, with its thermal complex in Mădăraş, 14km to the south on the E81. There are few campsites in Satu Mare, but you can find cheap bed and breakfast accommodation in advance through *ANTREC* (see p 114).

 Eating out

Because of its architecture, its German traditions and its proximity to Hungary, Satu Mare has a distinctly Middle-European atmosphere. Something of this unpretentious *gemütlichkeit* also comes from the fact that the town has a variety of bright restaurants, pizza houses and cafes— and that it is so near the border. Take your pick among general restaurants from the *Dacia* at Piaţa Libertăţii 8, *Mioriţa* at Str Viteazul 5, *Lotus* at Str Pod Golescu bl C1, *Orizont* in Str Octavian Goga. *Aurora* at Piaţa Libertăţii 11, *Dorna* at Str Avintului 17 and *Tei* at Str Lucian Blaga UU34 specialise in local cuisine. There are **pizzerias** at *Ninette*, Piaţa Octombrie 1, *Raphaello* at Str Cuza Vodă 1 and *Sam Gelato* at Calea Traian 3. The town's greatest claim to bacchanalian fame is its **beer**. This is famously brewed by descendants of the German colonists and is available from cellars at Str Coşbuc 9, Calea Traian 3 and Str Pumnul 9.

Post office

The main post office and telephone bureau are on B-dul Traian, between *Hotel Dacia* and the Ethnography Museum.

Money

The *Coop* **bank** has a branch at Str Decebal 2, while there are **exchange desks** in and around Piaţa Libertăţii and in the hotels.

 Medical care

There are **pharmacies** at *EuroRegal*, Str Ravensburg 2; *Farmacia 83*, B-dul 25 Octombrie 9; *Hyperion*, Str Pauleşti 1–3. The county **polyclinic** and **hospital** are at Str Ravensburg 1, ☎ 742050.

Crafts and traditions

Some of the county's finest traditional **crafts** can be found in the Oaş region which lies to the north of Satu Mare on the way to Maramureş. There are villages in Oaş which have become known for specific cottage industries or for distinctive architectural features. **Halmeu**, at the northern end of the E81/DN1C, has fine timber gateways; **Cărmăzana**, 23km northwest of Negreşti-Oaş, and **Certeze**, 5km north of Negreşti-Oaş on the DN19, are worth seeing for their attractive farmhouses and wood carvings, and **Tur**, 5km to the west of Negreşti, is a centre of glass icons and pottery.

Ţara Oaşilor has preserved some of

the oldest **folk rites** in the country: if you are here in May find out about *Sâmbra oilor* (collecting the sheep's milk), which takes place near Huta Certeze, a village 10km north of Negreşti on the DN19. *Sâmbra oilor* is an ancient custom which marks the start of the summer grazing. The shepherds who look after the village flocks gauge how much milk and cheese they must give to each individual owner during the coming months. They do this by measuring the yield from each flock on one day, marking the amount with special signs on a wooden crook. The event is usually a cause for a holiday with a feast and dancing in the hills above the village. If you are interested in local folklore festivals and crafts fairs, contact *Centrul Judeţean de Creaţiei Populară* at Str Republicii 24, ☎ 732347.

Events and festivals

In October Satu Mare hosts two music festivals: *Festivalul internaţional muzical*, an international festival of classical music held at the beginning of the month, and *Ceteră, lemnuţ de dor*, celebrating popular violin music.

Satu Mare's **theatre**, *Teatrul de Nord*, is at Str Horea 3, and the *Filarmonica Dinu Lipati*, its **orchestra**, has its headquarters at Piaţa Libertăţii 8.

The **Art Museum**, opposite the *Dacia* at Piaţa Libertăţii 21, is notable mainly for its collection of paintings by Aurel Popp (1879–1960). The building was raised on the site of a house in which the leader of Transylvania's rebel army, Ferenc Rákóczi II, signed the Peace of Satu Mare, which re-established Habsburg rule in Transylvania in 1711. Today it comprises a Baroque wing commissioned by the Vécsey family at the end of the 18C, but its main façade is Neo-Gothic and was constructed in 1842. Open Tues–Fri and Sun 10.00–16.00, Sat 10.00–14.00.

The **history and ethnographic sections** of Muzeul Judeţean Satu Mare (the Satu Mare County Museum) can be found at Str Lucaciu 21. Established by social reformer Ferenc Kölcsey and his circle in 1891, the museum charts the history of northwest Romania. It has a shop which sells an information sheet about Satu Mare county with French and German translations. The sheet also gives phone numbers for some local services and is translated into French and German. Open Tues–Fri and Sun 10.00–16.00, Sat 10.00–14.00.

Around Satu Mare

Carei, 34km southwest of Satu Mare on the DN19, is named after the Károlyi family who once owned large estates here. Their former home is the Neo-Gothic castle that now houses the local history museum, at Str 25 Octombrie 1, open Tues–Fri and Sun 10.00–16.00, Sat 10.00–14.00. There is a rare **Ruthenian Orthodox church** dating from 1738 at Str Doina 24.

A further 11km southwest of Carei at **Petreşti**, there is an interesting little museum devoted to the history of the Swabians in Crişana. It is called Muzeul Stăbesc and stands on the main through road; open Tues–Sun 10.00–17.00.

The Dacians flourished at Medieşu-Aurit, c 20km to the east of Satu Mare. Several years ago, archaeologists unearthed the remains of 13 kilns here. They have also found signs of late 9C and early 10C **settlements** belonging to the duchy of Menumorut.

THE OAŞ COUNTRY

To the northeast of Satu Mare, spread across the 'V' of the Munţii Oaşului, lies the Oaş region. This is a distinct ethnographic zone. Its focal point is the town of **Negreşti-Oaş** which lies 50km east of Satu Mare. You can visit Muzeul Orăşenesc to get a picture of the region's vernacular buildings, pottery, furniture and textiles. It has a wooden church which was brought here from the village of Lechinţa-Oaş; open Tues–Sun 10.00–18.00. Better still, explore the villages themselves, such as Remetea-Oaş, Boineşti and Călineşti-Oaş and the ones mentioned above.

Ancient inheritance laws that granted land equally to all the children of a family mean that most properties are now too small to farm. Living in a border region where land is limited anyway, the men of Oaş solve their unemployment problem by working abroad. This is not unusual in poor areas, but here labourers often invest their earnings in bricks and mortar. When you travel around Oaş you will see their houses, broad as palaces and several storeys high, standing in rows. They are designed to accommodate several generations at once, and some of these homes are so big that they have lifts as well as stairs.

About 23km on the way to Negreşti-Oaş from Satu Mare lies the village of **Livada**. Here, on the corner between the roads to Sighetu Marmaţiei and Baia Mare, you can see a fine manor house that once belonged to the Vécsey family. The Vécsey were Hungarian nobles who owned property all around Satu Mare before the communist purges. The manor still has its own spacious, wooded grounds, although these, like the house, are neglected. Today the house functions as a holiday home for orphans from Satu Mare. Fragments of its former feudal status are still visible in the sculpted coats of arms. On the façade by the front entrance are two drainage spouts that have been fashioned into fierce dragons' heads. A wrought-iron staircase and some well-proportioned rooms and windows are all that is left of its grandeur. When the communists arrived the last members of the Vécsey family fled or were forcibly removed, but they have not been entirely forgotten.

SOUTH OF SATU MARE

Leaving Satu Mare and the plains behind, head south along the E81. Rough tracks run off from the road at right angles on either side, disappearing like windblown ribbons into the hills. Beyond the cultivated fields, the countryside is hauntingly wild, sheltering villages remote from any sign of 20C progress. To explore these you will need a 4WD vehicle.

To the left of the approach to Ardud, 19km south of Satu Mare, is a **ruined castle** that looks like a folly. Hungary's most popular Romantic poet, Sándor Petőfi (born 1823), stayed here before he disappeared while fighting Russian troops in the revolution of 1849. Next to the castle is a mound with a curious landscaping of chimneys. This is the roof of an old *pivniţa*, a wine and beer cellar. You can see two of the entrances leading into it at the bottom of the slope. Legend has it that several tunnels lead from the cellar to neighbouring villages.

About 8km south of Ardud, just past the turn to Socond, make a detour to the left and follow the rutted track for c 8km until you reach **Stâna** (Sheepfold), passing the hamlet of Șandra on the way. Alternatively, you can get there via Bolda, which has a tiny, late-13C wooden church and its own collection of wonderful farmsteads; a third option is the road that connects Stâna with Beltiug.

Stâna's 17C **church** is a gem, even though the roof is a mess of rusting zinc and the painted plaster is falling off in lumps. It stands next to the new Orthodox church on a hill at the southern edge of the village. The main attraction of the old church is its porch, which is embellished with a tiny veranda and an entrance covered in ancient decorative motifs. The door itself has an arched lintel, rare in itself—most lintels are square—and the woodwork is studded and bolted with timber pegs.

> ### The porch
> Wooden churches in Romania often took their inspiration from the rectangular plan and pitched roofs of domestic dwellings, and in the earliest Romanian farmhouses the porch represents a need both to communicate with the outside world and to retreat from it. Symbolically and literally, the porch is a halfway station between two states of being, the place where people most like to rest and from where they can keep a watch over their surroundings in relative safety.

Turn right on the bend in Acâș village, 19km south of Ardud, and in c 250m this brings you to an impressive **twin-towered brick church**. It was founded in the 12C as a Benedictine monastery but is now used by the Hungarian Reformed Church. It has a lovely cool interior that contrasts attractively with the painted pews and ceiling. A bricked-up doorway behind the choir stalls is said to conceal a tunnel that allowed local people to escape underground to Hodod when they were under attack.

Make a detour to the east from Supur, 8km further south, and you pass more derelict remains of former Hungarian manors. Beside the main road through **Bogdand** is a small museum dedicated to the history of Magyar culture in this area; open Tues–Sun 10.00–18.00. Turn right (south) off the main road in Bogdand towards Ser, and in c 1km you come to an odd, T-shaped church that dates from the 15C. Inside is a pulpit by Dávid Sípos, a celebrated Transylvanian sculptor who combined local motifs with Renaissance innovations. The church has a gorgeous coffered ceiling. It is one of a cluster of Hungarian churches raised in this part of Crișana: there is another one further down the road at Nadișu-Hododului.

Further along the road east from Supur to Benesat, the Wesselényi manor in **Hodod** stands in a courtyard to the right of the main through road before it reaches the bottom of the hill in the village centre. Before the communist period, the Wesselényi family were important landowners in this area and built several magnificent residences, including the palace at Jibou. The house in Hodod was constructed between 1736–76, but is now a decayed hulk of broken statuary and dingy interiors that barely function as an administrative centre and local library. Further on, 200m below the road as it rises up the hill on the other side, stands the former Degenfeld residence, another Baroque building used as a *Scoală Generală* (secondary school).

Before leaving the village, have a look at the 15C **Hungarian Reformed church** that stands on the hill at Hodod's eastern edge. Inside is a coffered ceiling picked out with the Wesselényi emblem of a mermaid and swan, and another stone pulpit by Dávid Sípos. Ask for the key from the priest, who lives in the house beside the church on the right-hand side of the road. The wooden lych gate is decorated with pre-Christian motifs symbolising the sun. Thought to have been introduced by the Persians, the ancient solar symbol is one of the most popular decorative motifs in Romanian and Hungarian folk art. It looks more like a rosette (its Romanian name is *rozeta*) and appears in thousands of different permutations, on buildings, gates and household objects.

The church is a handsome building with a shingled roof and Gothic windows. But although concrete piles have been sunk into the ground to support the foundations, it needs underpinning: a large vertical crack has appeared right down one corner of the nave. The church stands on a fine positon, commanding lovely views over Dealurile Silvaniei. Follow the road to the east, and an even more satisfying panorama opens out as you climb towards the ridge on the way to Cehu Silvaniei.

SILVANIA

The Silvania region lies to either side of the E81, the main road from Satu Mare to Cluj. Bordered to the east by the Meseş and Şes mountains, little is left of the forests that gave this region its name, but if you have time, visit the museum of traditional Sylvanian architecture in **Valea Vinului**, c 22km southeast of Satu Mare on a minor road to Baia Mare. The towns of Cehu Silvaniei, Sighetu Silvaniei and Şimleu Silvaniei are almost the only topographical indications that Silvania exists in its own right; those and its **vineyard**, Podgoria Silvania, whose vines produce excellent sparkling wines in the Meseş foothills.

A 14C fortress once stood on a hill in the northeastern outskirts of **Cehu Silvaniei**, c 80km southwest of Satu Mare: today all that is left of the citadel is a 16C circular fountain near Str Crişan 17. Inside the fountain are two tunnels that were designed as hiding places. The earliest known mention of Cehu citadel comes in a document of 1319, when it belonged to Károly Róbert, the first Angevin king of Hungary. At first the citadel was made of wood and earth, but later it was rebuilt in stone and became part of the extensive defence system that protected the border area between the principality of Transylvania and the Banat. After playing an important role in the anti-Habsburg rebellion led by Ferenc Rákóczi, Cehu castle was abandoned. By the 18C only a few rooms were left standing. The town was once famous for an annual market that specialised in foreign goods. It also has a handsome Reformed church, presented to the townspeople by the Drágffy family in the 15C.

You can find interesting out-of-the-way churches in the Crasna Valley. Although poor even by Romanian standards, this area is indeed pretty, and lies to the south of the E81. Its main focus is the medieval town of Şimleu Silvaniei.

2000 years ago, Dacians populated the Crasna valley. Hoards of coins and other treasure were discovered at Șimleu at the end of the 18C and early 19C: these are now in the Kunsthistorisches Museum in Vienna.

On your way to Șimleu, the Hungarian Reformed church at **Uileacu Șimleului** is a fine masonry building with a white polygonal tower. It was once part of a 13C Benedictine monastery founded by descendants of the Hungarian king, Árpád. Another interesting church, Sfinți Apostoli, dating from 1765, can be found at nearby **Cehei**. A carved rope band with a 'wolf's teeth' border above and below it girdles the walls. These patterns, found in religious and secular buildings all over the country, may be Neolithic in origin. The continuous band symbolises eternal life and the continuity of life. Some historians believe that it is a skuamorphic motif inspired by real ropes that used to hold early medieval timber churches together.

West of the E81, visit **Șimleu Silvaniei** to see the ruined castle that once belonged to the Báthory family.

> ### The Báthorys
> Descended from the Hungarian tribe of Gutkeled, the Báthorys rose to prominence in the 13C. It was then that they adopted their surname, which means 'brave'. Owning large estates in Transylvania, they generated one king and a succession of princes, cardinals, bishops and judges before dying out altogether in the mid-17C. Under Turkish suzerainty, Báthory princes harassed Transylvania almost continuously for 40 years. Inbreeding drove some of them mad: the vain and vampirish Erzsébet Báthory lured young virgins to her castle in western Hungary and killed them so as to bathe in their blood, believing that this would improve her looks. István (Ștefan) Báthory (1533–86) was elected king of Poland and was especially popular in Șimleu because he gave the town important tax concessions that allowed it to grow very rich.

An earlier citadel was built here sometime between the 12C and the 13C. It stood on a hill called Măgură Șimleului, on the northern edge of the present town. The lower castle was in Báthory hands by 1351. It was surrounded by a deep ditch armoured with sharp stakes, and four cylindrical bastions protected the walls. The Báthorys built a new castle here in the mid-16C. Altered in the mid-17C and again in the early 18C, its perimeter walls and towers are now in ruins but its focal point is a beautifully proportioned carriage entrance set into a section of the (now gutted) living quarters. The Sălaj county museum wants to turn the building into a small exhibition centre; meanwhile children play football and tag in the courtyard, and steel poles prop up the sagging masonry. In the valley floor below the citadel, the town comes alive in a colourful fruit and vegetable market.

Tourist agencies in the town are *Ardelean-Zoo Tour* at Str Partizanilor bl 1, ☎ 060 674502, and *Măgura Comtour* at Str 1 Decembrie 1918 no. 24, ☎/fax 060 674503.

History

Şimleu citadel represents a microcosm of Transylvania's troubled history. Ottomans smashed it in 1520 and returned to the attack in 1551, when the Habsburgs invaded the principality. This time the Turks occupied Şimleu on their way into the Transylvanian plateau from the west. A few decades later, in 1594, Tartars riding east from Debrecen razed Şimleu and Zalău. Mihai Viteazul tried unsuccessfully to take the citadel from General Basta's Habsburg troops. (In 1600, Mihai Viteazul united Moldavia, Transylvania and Wallachia for the first time.)

Local historians tell us that in the 17C Şimleu became 'an enclave of Austrians in a sea of Turks', but the town and fortress still technically belonged to the Báthorys. Gabriel Báthory asked the Ottomans to help him oust the Habsburgs from his family home but, realising that this might be a long-term political error, he changed his mind and attacked the Turks instead. This also turned out to be a mistake. Thoroughly beaten by the Ottoman army, Gabriel retreated west to lick his wounds at home in Şimleu, but on 14 May 1660 Mehmet Pasha's soldiers wreaked another vengeance, setting fire both to the town and the citadel. After this the fortress fell into a decline from which it is only now being rescued.

Drive to the ruins of **Valcău citadel** southwest of Şimleu for a similar story. The fortress stands near the village of Subcetate (Under the Citadel) above the Barcău river. To reach it from Şimleu the road west passes **Nuşfalău**, where you can buy commercially distilled *ţuica* and *palinka*. Hungarians built the citadel in the 13C after Batu Khan's Mongol troops devastated Transylvania, and it formed a link in a long chain of fortifications that circumscribed the Meseş range to the west.

Valcău also played an important role in the struggles between Magyar feudal lords. But in the late 14C the property came into Bánffy hands, not as a war prize but by marriage. Its possessions comprised 22 villages, most of them inhabited by Romanian-speaking peasants. In 1665, the Turkish army destroyed the citadel during its offensive in central Transylvania. The same year, Prince Mihály Apaffi sent his own soldiers to repair the building, which he hoped to take for himself. But Hamza Pasha, an Ottoman general who commanded a garrison in nearby Oradea, got wind of Apaffi's plans and attacked the citadel once more. Several other attempts to rebuild Valcău met with failure, and the old fortress was more or less abandoned from the 17C. Little is known about the castle's original shape except that it was probably trapezoid. Archaeologists have identified its perimeter walls, which lie c 300m below the top of the hill. To the northeast and west of the citadel are the ruins of two more massive walls, each about 2.25m thick.

Zalău

Resist the temptation to turn tail when you approach Zalău: from the north on the E81 you see its worst face, but the centre is better. Apart from its usefulness as a place to stock up with basic supplies, its history museum is worth checking out for information on local sights.

Practical information

☎ code
060

Tourist information
Agencies include *BTT* at B-dul M. Viteazul, ☎/fax 633110; *Porolissum Tour*, Piața Iuliu Maniu 3–4, ☎ 633251; fax 631575; *Silvania Comtour*, Piața Unirii 1, ☎ 613313; fax 611862; *Sind România*, Str 9 Mai 4, ☎ 613280; fax 621037; *Trans Sălaj*, Str Fabricii 30, ☎ 612701; fax 612704, or Str T. Vladimirescu, ☎ 617510.

Getting around
By train *CFR* Zalău Nord is at B-dul Mihai Viteazul 101, ☎ 620313/620706; fax 620700. The *CFR* office is at Str T. Vladimirescu 2, ☎ 612885.
By car For **car servicing** and repairs try *ACR*, Str Mihai Viteazul 28, ☎ 613839. **Petrol stations** are at Str Depozitelor 4 and B-dul Mihai Viteazul 85. For **taxis** contact *J&J Service*, Piața Iuliu Maniu 3–5, ☎ 633433.

Where to stay
Hotels in town include *Porolissum* (✮✮) at Piața Unirii 1, ☎/fax 611862; *Meseş* (✮✮) at Piata 1 Decembrie 1918, no. 11, ☎ 614720; fax 616431; *Stadion* (✮✮) at Str Stadionului 5, ☎ 632010.
Popasul Romanilor (✮✮), 11 km to the south of Zalău on the E61 to Cluj, is a very pleasant motel. It is modelled on a log cabin and has twin-bedded rooms and a restaurant; ☎ 613453.
Alternatively, for information about where to stay in this area, contact *ANTREC* (see above).

Eating out
Restaurants and bars include *Dacia*, Str Gheorghe Doja 55; *Tip Top*, Str 22 Decembrie 1989, nr. 12; *Fast Food*, B-dul Mihai Viteazul bl D; *Marsel-Selaru*, Str 9 Mai bl U, *parter*; *Silvania*, Piața Iuliu Maniu 25. There are bread **shops** and general grocers along Str Unirii.

Post office
This is at Str Parcului 2.

Money
Banks include *Banc Post*, Str Simion Barnuțiu 10A; *Banca Agricola*, Str Unirii 20; *Banca Comercială Română*, Piața Iuliu Maniu 2; *Banca Română de Dezvoltare*, Piața Unirii 1; *Banca Trasilvania*, Piața Unirii 1–3; *Bancorex*, Str. Republicii 1; *CEC*, B-dul Mihai Viteazul 1.

Town hall
Contact Piața Iuliu Maniu 3, ☎ 632177.

Medical care
Pharmacies include *Farmacia 85*, Str Torentului bl T6; *Gallenus*, B-dul Mihai Viteazul bl C1, *parter*; *Neofarm*, Str Crișan bl U2, *parter*.

Traditional festivals and crafts
Annual events include *Măsurișul de la Pria*, a folklore festival at Pria during May; an international festival of

women's dance, held near *Motel Popașul Românilor* outside Zalău at the end of August; and a national folklore festival, held in Zalău during October. Although it is a comparatively poor county, Sălaj is rich in traditional **cottage industries**. The villages of Fildu de Jos, Creaga and Buciumi to the south are known for their excellent **joiners** and carpenters; Fildu de Mijloc has some beautiful monumental **gates**; Cristur-Crișeni, Var and Tihău specialise in making **domestic goods** from wicker and straw, and Buciumi has some excellent **potters**. If you are looking for embroidered blouses and waistcoats, woven skirts and other examples of **traditional dress**, visit Agrij, Meseșenii de Jos and Moigrad. Find out more from *Centrul Județean de Creație Populară*, Piața Iuliu Maniu 4, ☎ 631433. Curators at the county history museum should also be able to advise you where to find what you are looking for.

The County Museum of History and Art, **Muzeul Județean de Istorie și Artă**, is at Str Unirii 9, ☎ 612223. Its holdings include Bronze Age pottery and Dacian ceramics, but it is also useful as a place to find leaflets about local historic monuments. Contact the museum for details about guided tours around the county of Sălaj and accommodation at the Roman camp of Porolissum. Open Tues–Sun 10.00–18.00.

Secția de Artă, the Art Section of the County Museum at Str Gheorghe Doja 6, is a small gallery which, apart from a fascinating collection of beetles and butterflies, is devoted almost entirely to the delightfully breezy post-Impressionist paintings of local artist Ioan Sima, who studied in Paris at the end of the 19C. Only a small fraction of the 1200 portraits, still lifes and landscapes that he left to the museum is on view, but these paintings alsone are well worth half an hour of your time. Open Tues–Sun 10.00–18.00.

Zalău lies just inside the Roman Limes Porolissensis, a continuous barrier of earth *vallum*, or rampart, and stone wall that once protected the northwest edge of Roman Dacia. Archaeological teams from Zalău have uncovered several sections of the Roman *vallum* as well as some of the camps that were established along the barrier. The most impressive of these is **Porolissum**, which gets its name from a nearby Dacian citadel. Porolissum lies on a hilltop above the village of Moigrad, c 10km east of Zalău. To get right to the top, you will need a 4WD vehicle or a pair of stout boots.

From Zalău centre, follow the main road to Satu Mare and in c 1km, turn right for **Ortelec** village. Before you enter Ortelec, there is a small hill to the left where the foundations of a 9C **citadel** have been found. The citadel had a customs post which extracted payments for goods that passed along the road. Ortelec lay on one of the old trade routes that connected Dej in Transylvania with Sălacea near Oradea. The passes through the mountains of Sylvania are lower than those to either side, allowing pack horses into, and more importantly out of, the gold- and salt-bearing mountains further east.

Just past Ortelec the valley narrows to a point called **Strâmtura** (Romanian for 'a narrow place') where the first fortifications in Roman Dacia were built. The wall was constructed during Hadrian's or Trajan's reign and stretched for about 4km to the north and south of the existing road. You can see its remains in a few half-buried slabs, and the foundations of a small castrum have been found at its northern edge.

Passing through Moigrad village, a steep road leads to the Roman camp, becoming a grassy track as it nears the top. Dominating the hilltop you can see a copy of the original Imperial gateway. Walk around the site, and you find sheep-grazed meadows scattered with the remains of temples dedicated to Pater Liber and Bel, an early Christian basilica, and a chunk of authentic Roman road. To the southwest is a beautiful oval **amphitheatre**, perched vertiginously on the edge of a sheer drop to the valley below. The view is wonderful; from here, Transylvania's mountain ranges stretch far into the distance like an immovable sea. In a valley to the west of the camp, archaeologists have discovered fragments of an aqueduct.

With a garrison of some 4000–5000, the total inhabitants of Porolissium must have numbered c 20,000. Excavations are still in progress here, and it is hoped that they will uncover more of the civilian town. There are information boards in English at the entrance to the site, but conducted tours are also available if you ask at the County Museum in Zalău (see p 330). Parties of up to five people can stay on site; again, contact the County Museum for details.

Wooden churches

Northwest Romania has a wonderful range of wooden churches, some of which date back to the 17C. A register of historic monuments for Crişana and the Someş valley (between Jibou and Dej) lists 140 of them. There are some 70 in Sălaj alone, notably at **Baica**, **Chieşd**, **Dragu** and **Voivodeni**, and others are described here. Sălaj churches often have a tower with four miniature spires at each corner of the base. This embellishment was inspired by the Gothic stone churches built by Saxons in Transylvania. Together with the lovely churches you can still find in Maramureş, they form part of an unbroken chain of timber architecture that crosses the entire continent from Scandinavia south through Russia, Poland and Ukraine to Wallachia, Bosnia and western Serbia. The County Museum in Zalău sells a booklet giving details of some of the finest churches in Sălaj.

A country road to Baia Mare

If you decide to visit the Maramureş from here, take the road along the Agrij Valley, starting from Romănaşi, south of Zalău, or Creaca. A charming wooden church stands in the centre of **Creaca**, while a few kilometres away another perches on a hill beyond a smallholding south of the road through **Borza**. Heading north, in the centre of **Jibou** restorations are under way at another former Hungarian manor, the Wesselényi Palace. This is a magnificent Baroque building with outbuildings and stables arranged around three sides of a huge courtyard. Located in the same complex as the botanical gardens, it is open daily 07.00–19.00. At Benesat, 15km north, you can see an unusual, stone-built church from 1741.

The Agrij Valley between Zalău and Ciucea

Leave the E81 by turning right on the crest of the pass south of Zalău. This road brings you into the heart of the Meseş mountains. Far from the main tourist routes, this is lovely, unspoilt country. At **Treznea**, 5km past the turning, a notice commemorates the date in 1944 when General Horthy's Hungarian troops massacred the village's entire (Romanian) population. Turn left in Agrij and head north again for **Pauşa**. Standing in a little orchard below the through road, the church contains wooden icons from the Blaj school. There are frescoes both inside and out by Ion Pop, the artist who decorated the church at Sânmihaiu Almaşului (see below), but the frescoes are suffering terribly from rain damage.

Alternatively, continue across country through the Meseş foothills to the southwest. It is an attractive route and the road is in good condition, meeting the E60 at Ciucea, on the northern edge of the Apuseni mountains.

From Zalău the E81 south brings you to Cluj via **Ciumârna**, where the *biserică* has a beautifully carved door, **Poarta Sălajului**, whose church has marvellous, wing-like consoles, and **Sânmihaiu Almaşului**, where the church has late-18C frescoes by a local master, Ion Pop. Pop was taught by the celebrated Master David, who learnt his skills in the Wallachian monastery at Curtea de Argeş and spread the distinctive Brâncovenesque style across Orthodox churches in Transylvania, notably in the Crişul Negru and Crişul Repede valleys east of Oradea, where he painted icons and fresco cycles. Ion Pop did not always sign his paintings, but paintings by his hand have been identified at wooden churches in Stână (see p 325) and Păuşa (see above).

The Banat

Lying on the edge of the Great Hungarian Plain, the Banat has been especially vulnerable to the fickle winds of history. Once known as the 'land between the three rivers', it occupied the flatlands between the Danube, the Tisa and the Mureș, with its beautiful eastern borders rising into the Carpathians through the Almaj hills. But today the historic Banat is shared by Hungary, Romania and Serbia, and its indigenous population is a mixture of Romanians, Magyars, Slavs and Germans, some of whose ancestors fled from or were settled here during one or other of its many changes of occupation.

History

Dacians flourished in the Banat before the Roman invasions into Transylvania, which began across the region in 98 AD. After 150 years of occupation the legions withdrew in 270, leaving the way clear for waves of migrations from central Asia; the immigrants included Avars, Bulgars, Slavs and Magyars. There is some documentary and physical evidence to show that Daco-Romans continued to live in the Banat in the early Middle Ages.

During this period the Magyars settled in what we now call Hungary, and by the 10C they began to expand their control across the Tisa into the Banat and Transylvania. They were resisted by indigenous leaders such as Glad, and further north, by Menumorut. A century later Szent István Király founded the Christian state of Hungary and consolidated the Banat into his Catholic kingdom. The Tartar invasion of 1241–42 devastated the region, along with much of eastern Europe. While many towns were quickly rebuilt, King Endre II of Hungary invited the Knights of St John to colonise the Banat's southern borders, and for a while they occupied part of Oltenia as well.

It was the Habsburgs who introduced the region's present name. Although some people think that it comes from the Turkish word for a governor, *ban*, its source has never been identified. Some experts believe it was an old term for a landowning noble, equivalent to a shire reeve in England. Before the Ottoman occupation, the area between Caransebeș and the Danube and part of present-day Oltenia was known as 'the Banat of Szörény' or Severin (Zeurino in Latin documents) by the Hungarians, who gave it to the Knights of St John.

In the early 14C Angevin King Károly Róbert defeated his rival Otto of Bohemia and took the Hungarian crown, and in 1316 he installed his court in Timișoara. After only eight years, during which his entourage was ravaged by pestilence from the surrounding marshes, Károly Róbert moved his capital to Visegrád, north of present-day Budapest. Timișoara and the southern Banat formed the Christian frontier with the Muslim Turks. Apart from the great armies that passed through, refugees from the crumbling Vlacho-Bulgarian tsarate and the kingdom of Serbia fled north and settled in the southern Banat.

In 1396, King Sigismund of Hungary organised a crusade to rout the Turks from their fortress at Nicopolis (present-day Nikopol) on the Danube's Bulgarian shore. His Transylvanian and Wallachian supporters rallied at Timișoara, including a Wallachian army under Mircea cel Bătrân (r. c 1386–95 and 1397–1418). It was the first time that Romanian troops had

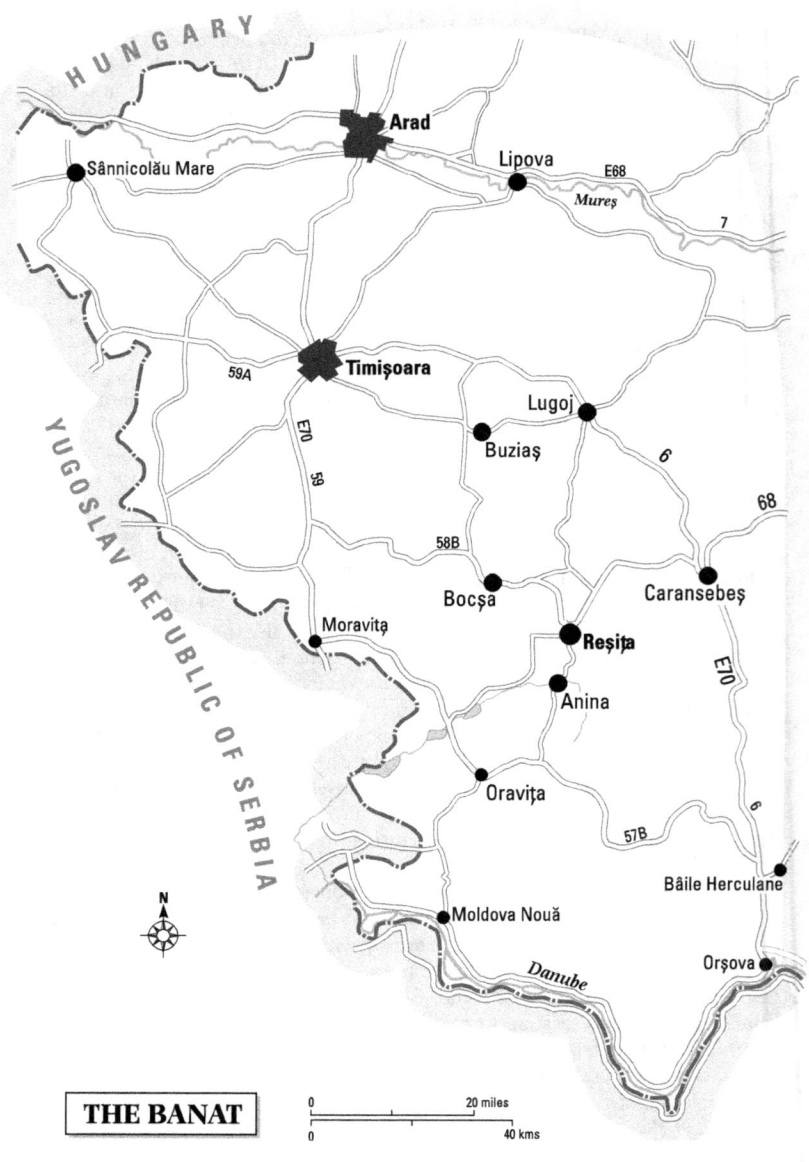

joined a crusade, and as 'schismatics' they were treated with some disdain. The ensuing battle was a disaster for the Christians. Thanks to the arrogance of the French leader, Jean de Nevers, the Europeans found themselves at the mercy of Sultan Bajazet the Thunderbolt, and hundreds, if not thousands, of prisoners were slain. An Islamic conquest of the Balkans was assured, and the European disaster at Nicopolis also paved the way for Bajazet's greatgrandson Mehmet II, to attack and take Constantinople in 1453.

For the next 150 years, Hungary and her neighbours Moldavia and Wallachia were left holding the fort. The independence-seeking principalities vacillated from outright defiance to pragmatic acceptance of the Ottoman yoke according to the prevailing interests and abilities of their princes. During this period the Banat became a frontier that was fought over by Magyars and Turks, and the boundary between Catholicism and Islam was pushed to and fro, depending on which army had the upper hand.

The Muslims took control of the Banat and part of Crișana in 1552. This was 30 years after the fall of Hungary at Mohács, and in the interim the Ottomans were content to let their vassal Romanian and Transylvanian princes take charge. Under the *pashalik* of Timișoara, the Turks allowed the Serbs and Vlachs to found Orthodox churches and sanctioned trade with the outside world. In 1658, Romanian princes started another anti-Ottoman campaign at which the Sultanate promptly extended its holdings in the Timișoara *pashalik* to include the fortresses at Lugoj, Caransebeș and Ineu, together with the mountainous lands in the eastern Banat and Hălmagiu.

But if the Magyars were temporarily in abeyance, throughout the 17C the region was coveted by the Habsburgs, and in 1716, after numerous attempts, imperial troops captured Timișoara under the dashing Prince Eugene of Savoy (widespread use of the name 'the Banat' for the region dates from this time). To ensure their control of the Banat, the Habsburgs brought in settlers from western Europe, most of them German-speaking farmers and miners from Swabia, the Palatinate and the Rhineland. The policy encouraged the regeneration of agriculture in devastated areas and brought much-needed prosperity to the region, but it also effectively prevented the Magyars from recolonising their ancient estates. Most of the new colonists had arrived by the 1740s; they were moved into areas vacated by existing communities or into new towns built specially for them. The Habsburg organisational machine drained the plague-ridden marshes and turned the fertile flatlands into prolific grain production. Driven by economic need and a love of progress, the Empress Maria Teresa encouraged scientific studies into the viability of new cash crops.

The Venetian agronomist and historian, Francesco Griselini, visited the Banat between 1774–77. He was much attracted by this 'little-known part of Europe' and its reputed mineral wealth. While he was there, Griselini was asked for his opinion on the wisdom of cultivating rice, and of growing mulberry trees for silkworms. The Banat fascinated him and he sent a series of letters about his experiences there to the governor and other officials. These missives not only contained his views on practical matters but also his enthusiastic observations on the region's customs and natural history. And Griselini's letters contain his qualified admiration for the Romanians themselves; he thought they were 'singularly industrious but quick to lose heart and thus fall prey to their natural sluggishness'. He also noted that Romanians derived their chief pleasure from dancing. Published collectively as *Lettere Odeporiche* ('Letters from a Journey'), Griselini's observations remain one of the most detailed and engaging accounts of late-18C life in the Banat. A Romanian version was published in 1984.

Between the late 18C and 1867 the administration of the Banat remained in a state of flux. Control passed from the regional Austrian *verwalter*, to the Hungarians, to the Viennese court and back to Hungary while the region also enjoyed a certain amount of local autonomy. Throughout the 19C ethnic Romanians and Serbs claimed the Banat as their own, and in 1919 the northern part of the region became part of Romania while the southern sector passed into Serb-held Vojvodina. Hungary retained only a small slice of the Banat, between the Romanian border and the Tisa.

During the Second World War, many of the non-Magyar minorities were deported from the Banat as Hungary sought to re-establish its hold over this area. Shortly afterwards, in the most oppressive years of the Stalinist regime, many ethnic Germans were sent to Soviet labour camps.

Timişoara

Although Timişoara sits in the middle of a plain, it has occupied a strategic position on the fault line between Christianity and Islam for a thousand years. It has been a focal point of conflict, and each occupying power has established its administrative mark, leaving few physical remains of the Dacian, Roman or Turkish buildings that once stood here.

History

Excavations have revealed pre-Roman fortifications, and some sources suggest that these were in place as early as 1000 BC. There was definitely a Dacian settlement here prior to the Roman occupation, and their citadel was used by the Romans as the foundation of their *castrum*, Zambara. After the legions left, small rural communities established settlements here, using the marshes for protection. A Romanian Orthodox church is said to have been founded in a medieval fortress known as Themes or Thymes and named after the Timiş River, which flows to the south of the city. A fortified Magyar town called Temesvár is known to have existed by 1212, but the town was demolished by the Tartars in the mid-13C. Charles Robert of Anjou came here while maneouvring himself onto the Hungarian throne, and he employed Italian masons to construct a palace within the citadel walls. As Károly Róbert, he proclaimed Timişoara the new Hungarian capital in 1316.

Iancu de Hunedoara, a Romanian noble who became governor of Timişoara in 1438, and later of Hungary as a whole, rebuilt the old palace in the 1440s. Iancu (known as János Hunyadi in Hungarian) pursued energetic campaigns against the Turks, and Pope Pius IV dubbed him an 'athlete of Christ' for thwarting the Ottoman advance into Europe. In the 1430s and 1440s Iancu stationed his troops outside the city while trying to unite the Romanian principalities in the anti-Muslim struggle. In 1443 he defeated the Sultan at Nis in Bulgaria. The following year he took part in the Varna crusade, which proved a crushing defeat for the Christians, and in 1448 he led a Hungarian and Romanian army against the Turks in Kosovo. After being imprisoned briefly by the Serbs, Iancu went on successfully to defend Belgrade against Mehmet II. After his death in 1456 his widow threw herself and her family on the mercy of the new king, Ladislas (László), who repaid her trust by executing her eldest son and deporting the second to prison in Prague. Iancu's third son, Matei, later took vengeance for his brothers' death, and as Matei Corvin (Mátyás Corvinus) became king of Hungary.

In the early 16C the nobles' increasingly arrogant demands on their resources pushed Transylvania's smallholders into violent retaliation. In 1514 Gheorghe Doja led a peasants' revolt, successfully defeating Stephen Báthory, Timișoara's governor, before marching on the city itself. Doja was himself a minor noble, rewarded with a title and land in return for his courage in fighting the Turks. But when Pope Leo X initiated an anti-Ottoman crusade in which all serfs who fought were promised freedom from bondage, the nobles objected and the campaign was cancelled. Doja and his co-agitators presented a plan of reforms to the Hungarian Diet, and when these were rejected he set out to capture Timișoara.

After trouncing Stephen Báthory's attempt to become *voivode* of Transylvania, John (Ioan) Zápolya hunted down the peasant army and assassinated its leaders. Doja was executed with great brutality. He was forced to sit on an incandescent iron throne where he was literally cooked to death, his flesh being torn off with pincers and fed to his fellow rebels. Legend has it that the burning took place on the corner of Piața Maria, in the Iosefin district. A statue of the Virgin Mary stands in a chapel on the square. It replaced the original memorial, an icon of the Virgin in a glass case. Jesuit monks placed the icon here after seeing Mary's face in a vision which came to them while they intoned religious chants beside the tortured Doja.

When the Muslims gained Timișoara after a nine-month siege in 1551–52, they transformed the town, building a mosque, a barracks for the Janissaries, schools and even a university. Baths and a bazaar were also constructed within a new, pentagonal fortress, and a gunpowder mill was built outside the walls. Provided they paid for the privilege, non-Islamic citizens were allowed to worship as they pleased, and several Orthodox and Catholic churches held services within the Turkish city. However, nothing of the Muslim town remains, save for an Arabic inscription on the Old Town Hall in Piața Libertătii, which commemorates the former bathhouse. The Ottoman traveller Evlia Celebi recorded in 1660 that Timișoara was a flourishing place, with many new buildings both inside and outside the walls. He also tells us that small industries sprang up to supply the needs of the Pasha, the Beglerbey and the Turkish army. In the early 1680s Timișoara had to provide victuals for the Ottoman troops on their campaign to conquer Vienna.

Two hundred years of Austrian hegemony began in 1716, when General Mercy, the first Habsburg governor, began reorganising the city. By the 1760s it was unrecognisable, being equipped with a spanking new citadel of the Vauban type, with seven star-shaped bastions and majestic gate towers, and new squares and streets in concentric rings. This led people to call Timișoara, 'Little Vienna'. Baroque mansions and officers' residences, barracks and warehouses, churches for different confessions and hospitals sprang up.

Many of these are still standing, although the fortress was pulled down in 1902 to make way for housing developments and a modern sewerage system. The Habsburgs laid the foundations for modern Timişoara, introducing systematised quarters outside the walls which were modelled on a typical Banat village: the centre of town is still known as Cetate (Citadel), while the sector Maierele, to the south, was begun (the zone is now called Elizabetin), and in 1720 General Mercy commissioned the city's first industrial buildings in a district known as Fabric. Iosefin, across the Şaisprezece Bridge, was begun in 1744, and soon afterwards Mehala, traditionally a Serbian quarter, appeared to the northwest. Piaţa Unirii, which had been the citadel's economic and social centrepiece, gave way to Piaţa Victoriei after the walls came down.

The revolution in Timişoara

In 1989 the world woke up to the existence of Timişoara when its streets erupted in anti-government demonstrations. The uprising was triggered by the house arrest of László Tőkés, a young priest of the Hungarian Reformed church who had spoken out against injustices and corruption in both church and state since 1983. Having already been jailed for his outspoken attitudes, in November 1989 Tőkés was intimidated and beaten by Securitate men. A few weeks later he was confined to his house, and he and his family survived for three weeks on clandestine food parcels brought to him by his parishioners.

Word got out that he was due to be forcibly evicted on 15 December. On that morning a crowd of his parishioners began to gather outside his house in Str Cipariu in the Iosefin district, and the Securitate officers disappeared. By the afternoon there were 1500 people protecting his door, and on the following day the numbers increased. A delegation to the city hall demanded that Tőkés should be released, but their request was rejected. That evening c 5000 people gathered by the priest's house, most of them Romanians, and Tőkés recalls hearing *Hora Unirii*, the old Romanian national anthem, being sung outside his door. During the night police broke into his church, which is attached to his house, and kidnapped him as he was standing by the altar. They drove him to the little village of Mineu, where he was interrogated and asked to confess to being a traitor; on the way he saw demonstrators being attacked by militiamen.

Street battles raged in Timişoara for the next five days. They were filmed by foreign TV crews who had been alerted by yet another dramatic sign of the collapse of communism in eastern Europe. Hundreds of people were wounded and many died, shot by the army or the police, but by the end of the week the army had joined sides with the people, and the revolution was now focussed on Bucharest. What began as a localised revolt in Timişoara marked the end of the Ceauşescus' reign of terror.

Memorials to the dead lie scattered all around the city, but you can visit the special monument to the revolutionaries in the cemetery in Calea Aradului. You will find the Tőkés house and former church in Str Cipariu, its graffiti fading along with memories of those historic events. László Tőkés was later appointed Bishop of Oradea.

Timişoara is an elegant and vibrant city, with a tradition of radical journalism and art. Newspapers began to be published here in different languages during the 18C and 19C and continued, although in muted form, under the communists. When Ceauşescu clamped down on freedom of expression in the 1980s, Timişoara was one of the places where a few artists refused to give in. A recent census recorded 330,000 people in the city: 80 per cent of these are Romanians, while Magyars account for some 9 per cent, Germans for 4 per cent and Serbs for 2.5 per cent. Smaller minorities include Roma, Bulgarians, Ukrainians and Jews, and there are some Slovaks, Czechs, Poles and Greeks.

Practical information

☎ **code**
056

Tourist information

The city is used to catering for visitors and has a plethora of tourist agencies. Try *Atlantic* at Str Hector 2, ☎ 130512; *BTT* at B-dul Revoluţiei 26, ☎ 198888; *Unitours Fuhry & Sipos* at B-dul Republicii 3–5, ☎ 220770; and *Venerable Tour* at Str Prahovei 8. *Eco Tours*, at Piaţa Sf Gheorghe 1. ☎ 193617, may be able to help you find accommodation in private farmhouses, but do not expect information on wildlife or conservation holidays, as Romanian ecotourism usually means bed and breakfast in a traditional household.

Getting around

By train The main railway station is **Gara de Nord** (also called **Domniţa Elena**) on Str Gării, west of the city centre. The booking office for train tickets, *CFR*, is at Piaţa Victoriei 2, ☎ 191889.
By bus The main national and international bus terminus is at Str Iuliu Maniu 54. ☎ 193471. Other companies offering information on tours in and out of Romania include *Global Travel* at B-dul Eminescu 20, *Lar Tours* at Str Goethe 2, *Nelta Bus Tours* at Str Nedelcu 1, and *Oz Murat Transcom* at St Iuliu Maniu 54. **Trams** and **trolley-buses** serve the city centre; the trams were introduced in 1899.
By plane Timişoara airport, serving national and international destinations, is at Giarmata, c 6km northeast of the centre; tickets and information are available from *TAROM*, B-dul Revoluţiei 3–5, ☎ 190150.
By car For repairs and **garage services**, contact *Central Auto Iatsa 2* at Calea Sagului 201, ☎ 200215, or *Timnovdac* at Str Intrarea Doinei 2, ☎ 134730. Alternatively, you could try *ACR* at the same address, ☎ 133863. Timişoara has plenty of **petrol stations**. *Intercity*, ☎ 208686, *Rock-sy*, ☎ 166881 and *Scart Taxio Fans*, ☎ 185555, are **taxi** companies.

Where to stay

If you want a deluxe hotel, try the *Company Grand Tomy* (✯✯✯) at Str Demetriade 4, ☎ 200266, or the *International* (✯✯✯) at B-dul Loga 48, ☎ 190193. A little lower down the scale are the *Continental* (✯✯) at B-dul Revoluţiei 3, ☎ 130481, the *Euro* (✯) at Str Mehadia 5, ☎ 201253; the *Sydney* at Str Horia 110, ☎ 199806. Budget hotels include the *Central* (✯) at Str Lenau 6, ☎ 190091, the *Cina* (✯) at B-dul Republicii 5, ☎ 190130; and *Casa Tineretului* (✯) at Str Aries 19, v 162419. There is a **campsite** at Aleea Padurea Verde 6, tel 208925, and a motel called *Ana Lugojana* on the Lugoj road, ☎ 313060.

Eating out

Timişoara has a clutch of reasonable restaurants, among which are *Faleza* at Parcul Justiţiei 1, *Gil Hercules* at B-dul Pârvan 7, and *Myth 777* at Str Ciprian Porumbescu 87. There are also *Central* at Str Lenau 6, *Cina* at B-dul Republicii 5, *Marele Zid Chinezesc* (the Great Wall of China) at Str Vasile Alecsandri 2, and *La Dama Biana* (the White Lady) at Str Horia 110. The city boasts several **fast-food** restaurants: *Haya Plaza* at 71 B-dul 16 Decembrie 1989, *Munart* at Str Aurelianus 19, *Universa* at Str Alba Iulia 7, and **pizzerie** at Str Neculuţa 3, *Pizza & Go*, ☎ 201019, and *Pizzeria 3+1* at Str 16 Decembrie 5.

Shopping

The centre is becoming almost chic: there are smart **boutiques** and shoe shops in the old centre and in the Iosefin district, but students always recommend the clothes and flea **market** on the outskirts; ask for its whereabouts at the tourist agencies. There is a pleasant open-air food market along Str 1 Mai, north of the centre.

Post office

The central post office is housed in a splendid building at 2 B-dul Revoluţiei 1989, and you can make international phone and fax calls here. There is another international phone and fax bureau in a side street to the east of Piaţa Victoriei.

Money

Banks include *Banc Post* at 2 B-dul Revoluţiei 1989, *Banca Agricola* at B-dul Loga 40, *Banca Ion Tiriac* at Piaţa Unirii 3, and *Bancorex* at Piaţa Sf Gheorghe 1; you can also **exchange** currencies at the *TAROM* office or at *Cardinal's Exchange* at Str Piatra Craiului 3, and *Royal* at Str Alba Iulia 2.

Police

The main police station is at B-dul Take Ionescu 44–46, while the town hall can be found at B-dul Loga 1.

Medical care

Timişoara has **hospitals** at Str Lucian Blaga 4, Str Buftea 5 and Str Diana 7. The county **clinic** is at B-dul Liviu Rebreanu 156. **Pharmacies** can be found at Piaţa Libertăţii 1, Str Maciesilor 1 and Str Mercy 9, and there is a **dentist's surgery** at Str Irlanda 39.

Entertainment

As befits a multicultural city, Timişoara has a lot to offer. German, Hungarian and Romanian **theatre** companies share the elegant National Theatre building at the north end of Piaţa Victoriei. There is a puppet theatre on B-dul Tineretii 3, and a **jazz club** at Colţ Şaisprezece (Corner 16) on the Şaisprezece Bridge (named after the first day of the revolution on 16 December 1989) across the Bega.

Maps and books

Bookshops in the city centre should sell decent maps of the town; failing this, ask at the hotels and tourist agencies. Timişoara has a new university (it lies southeast of the centre across the canal), and this has encouraged stallholders to sell erudite volumes of philosophy and history on the street. If you need a **translation service**, try *Quicktrad* at Str Olimpiadei 14, ☎ 134058.

Folk art and traditions

For up-to-date information on folk music festivals, and where to buy crafts specific to the Banat, contact *Centrul Judeţean de Creaţie Populară* at Str Ungureanu 1, fax 130533.

Walking around Timişoara

If you do not have time to see anything else, do not miss **Piaţa Unirii**. This is a grand square in the Viennese style flanked by colourful 18C and 19C buildings. In the middle of the formal garden with its worn stone benches stands a tall Baroque monument, commemorating people who died in the 18C plagues. Most of the square has been pedestrianised, and at one end a **fountain** dispenses free supplies of alkaline water. This is a popular focal point for evening gossip, and you will often see people filling plastic bottles here. Part of Piaţa Unirii's charm comes from the contrast between its grand architecture and the relaxed atmosphere created by the children who use it as a playground. In the 18C it was known as Piaţa Principală because it lay at the heart of the city's social and commercial life. On the east side stands the twin-towered **Roman Catholic Cathedral**. Rated as one of the finest Baroque churches in the Banat, it was designed by Fischer von Erlach Junior and completed in 1774. The Bishops' Palace is of like splendour and can be found to the south of Piaţa Unirii at Str Rodnei 4.

Piaţa Unirii

At the opposite, west end of Piaţa Unirii is a complex of buildings that make up the **Serbian metropolitanate**. The confection of pistachio and white is the metropolitan's residence, while the church is a Baroque edifice in bright yellow. This has been the centre of Serbian Orthodoxy in Romania since a split with the Romanian branch in 1864. There are c 10,000 Serbs in Timişoara. Walk to the southeast corner of Piaţa Unirii and you come to the former Prefecture, which was begun in 1754. It also served as the Austrian governors' residence, and has been beautifully restored to house the city's **Art Museum**. The collection comprises some fine paintings from 15C–17C Italy and prints by leading European artists. Open Tues–Sun 10.00–17.00.

Walk east from Piaţa Unirii along Str Palanca, and you will reach the last fragment of the Austrian citadel, at Str Popa Sapcă 4. Known as the **Teresa Bastion**, it was constructed between 1730–33 and was used primarily as a store for food. Today it contains bookshops and commercial art galleries, as well as the ethnographic section of the Banat Museum. Head back along Str Ceahlău to the south and you pass the **Dicasterial Palace**, an Eclectic administration building inspired by the early Renaissance and completed in 1860. It was designed as a local administrative centre.

Turn south into Str Eminescu to find two fine **18C buildings**. At no. 5 Casa Deschan is a neo-Classical palace embellished with a loggia, built in c 1735 by a city councillor and altered several times since then. No. 7 is Casa Mercy, another neo-Classical residence named after Timişoara's first Habsburg governor, General Mercy, who had the marshes drained. It was restored in c 1800.

Continue west through Piaţa Sf Gheorghe into **Piaţa Libertăţii**. During the 18C this was the city's military and administrative centre, created by the

342 • THE BANAT

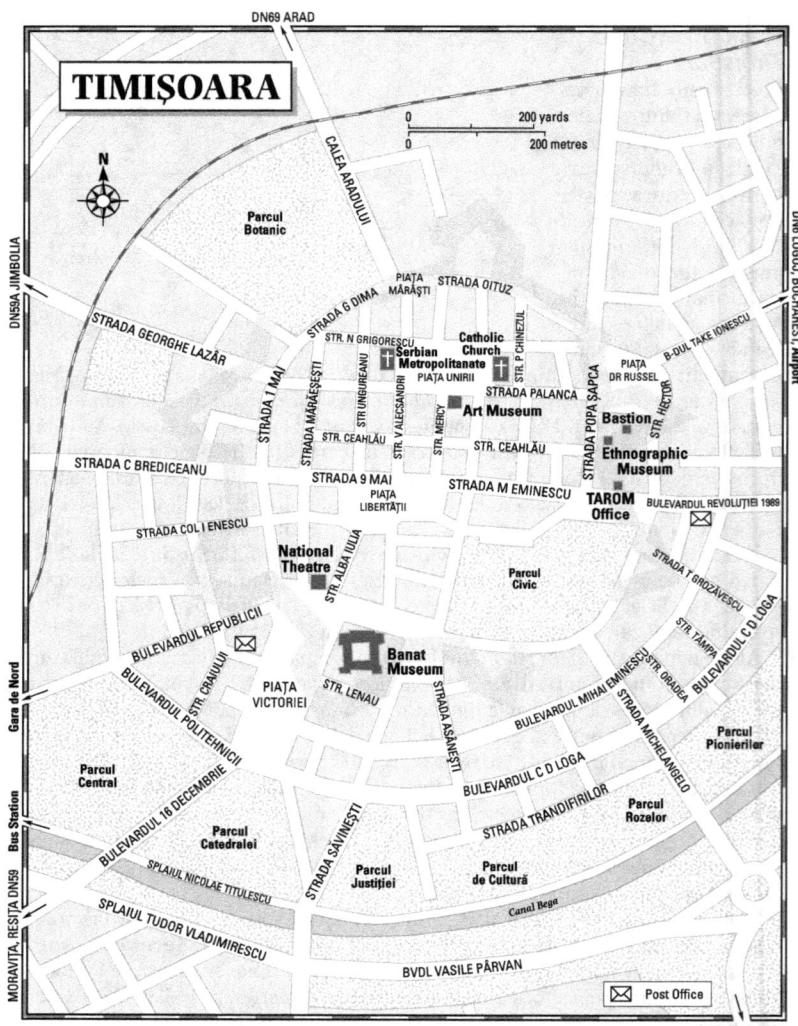

Austrians on the site of the Turkish bazaar. Three Baroque edifices survive: the Old Town Hall at no. 1, with its Arabic inscription showing that this was once the site of the Turkish baths, the military barracks at no. 7, and the 1756 statue of the Virgin and St John Nepomuk that stands in the square's garden. Walk 200m south into Piaţa Victoriei and you reach the **National Theatre**. This is a building of clean and simple lines with an eye-catching neo-Byzantine arch. It was designed in the 1920s by the Romanian architect Duiliu Marcu (1886–1966) and replaced the frothier Eclectic theatre by Fellner and Helmer, which was destroyed by fire.

Piaţa Victoriei is the modern centre of Timişoara. Ceauşescu liked to harangue the populace from the National Theatre; no-one took the dictator's bombast and interminable speeches seriously but his appearances meant that everyone got a holiday. In 1989 the theatre became a focal point of the December revolution.

Secessionist architecture

Timișoara's rapid modernisation attracted many go-ahead designers. Many of them took their ideas from Ödön Lechner (1845–1914), the pioneer of Jugendstil in Hungary, and his pupils Marcel Komor (1868–1944) and Dezső Jakob (1864–1932). The leading architectural historian Ileana Pintilie says that Secessionism developed in Timișoara in two distinct phases. The first phase, lasting from c 1900–08, provided buildings that were curvilinear and floral in style, while the second, from 1909–14, concentrated more on geometrical designs with massive, simplified volumes and restrained decoration. Timișoara's outstanding Secessionists were Martin Gemeinhardt, who created the Peacock house in Piața Plevnei, and László Székely (1877–1934). Romania's Secession provided an important link between the country's post-Byzantine traditions (such as the Brâncoveanu style) and modern art.

In Timișoara architectural innovations went hand in hand with technological progress: the city had gas lights in 1857, and you can see plaques proudly proclaiming its acquisition in 1884, the first European city to have this luxury. The first and only regional railway line was built here and, with the Bega canal and the converging roads, Timișoara became the region's most important communications centre. Today, trams still trundle round the city as they have done since 1899, and it is sometimes hard to remember that this dreamy 'Little Vienna' lies to the east of Belgrade, Sarajevo and Zagreb.

When Timișoara began to industrialise, the city planners created a completely new quarter between the Citadel and the Iosefin district to the southeast. This gave architects a free rein, and the most imaginative of them came up with houses like the ones that border Piața Plevnei, built between 1900–08: festoons of vine leaves, magnolias and animal motifs cover their façades, along with peacocks, swans and other graceful and exotic birds. Gemeinhardt's Casa cu Pavni (the Peacock House, 1905) stands here too. Other fine houses from Timișoara's first Secessionist period include those on Splaiul Tudor Vladimirescu and Str 13 Dicembrie, by Gemeinhardt and his father. Komor and Jakob created the striking Banca de Scont (1906–08), and to get the full flavour of Timișoara's exuberant past, it is worth having a look at Str Mercy 7 and 9 and Str August, which was built all of a piece to link the Citadel and the industrial centre of Fabric to the east.

Timișoara's second Secessionist phase produced the impressive buildings in Piața Victoriei, which used to be called Corso and the Vienna Gate. Among these is the elegantly elephantine building known as Palatul (the Palace). Székely designed it in 1911–12, after he became the city's official architect; next to it stand Palatul Löffler and Palatul Széchényi. The dark grey cement used on these buildings was meant to look like a mineral, and ceramic pieces were embedded in the façades. Székely also designed Podul Decebal and the domed mansion that stands opposite, at Str Galați 1 (also

> called Palatul Neptun). If you are lucky enough to enter it, you will see one of the few authentically Jugendstil interiors still left in Timişoara. Hungary's pottery workshop, Zsolnay, provided the ceramic decoration.

At the opposite end of Piaţa Victoriei towers the badly-proportioned Orthodox Cathedral. Completed in 1946, it combines the influences of Byzantine and North Moldavian architecture. Walk back towards the theatre and turn right into Str Lenau. To your left is the imposing **Castel Huniazilor**, Iancu de Hunedoara's castle, now the history section of the Banat Museum. Erected between 1443–47, it is the city's oldest surviving monument. The castle stands on the site of Károly Róbert's 14C palace, and originally had a rectangular courtyard with a raised ground floor and two upper floors. It was badly damaged during the bombardments of 1552, 1716 and 1849, and in 1856 it was rebuilt incorporating Neo-Gothic and Romanesque elements. All that remains of Iancu's original building are the stone vaults. In the 18C the castle was used as an arsenal and a barracks.

The Banat Museum has a collection of around 220 portraits, many of them from the 18C and 19C, when the Habsburgs' administrators set up homes in the city and in the outlying towns, villages and estates. They brought with them a ready-made culture and cultural attitudes, and constituted the region's wealthy 'bourgeoisie'. The History Museum has lively displays describing the struggle for power in the Banat. It also traces the development from the Paleolithic and Neolithic settlements found at Băile Herculane, Parţa and Hodeni (two million years BC to the 4th and 3rd millennia BC), through the Thraco-Dacian period to the Ottoman-Habsburg wars. Open Tues–Sun 10.00–17.00.

In the outskirts, 2km northeast of the city at Aleea CFR 1, is the open-air section of the **Ethnographic Museum**, located in a park called Pădurea Verde. The village museum itself comprises a wooden church, dwelling houses, farmsteads, barns and mills from all over the Banat, including German as well as Romanian *gospodărie* (farmhouses). In the 18C the Venetian historian Francesco Griselini noted that typical village houses in the region had only two or three rooms, one of which served as the main living space for the whole family. Some of these dwellings have been preserved in the museum. Although timber churches are more usually associated with northern Transylvania, a few have survived in the Banat. They are similar in design to the wooden hill churches of Serbia and have faceted or semi-circular apses. The museum is open Tues–Sun 10.00–17.00.

Arad

Lying with one foot in the Banat and one in Crişana, Arad is only an hour's drive from Timişoara. It is smaller than Timişoara (its population is reckoned at 190,000) and its outskirts are as unappetising as those of most Romanian towns. But the centre contains some very attractive buildings that provide an insight into the Banat's development under the Habsburgs.

History

Arad is one of the oldest towns on Romania's western borders; it had a fortress by the mid-11C. Tartars burnt the town in 1241, but it recovered well enough to be upgraded to a civitas in the following century. During the Turkish invasions of Serbia in the 15C, Serb refugees fled here and settled in the southern sector. In 1552 Arad fell under Ottoman rule and the Hungarian citadel was destroyed. The Ottomans set the town on fire and massacred most of its inhabitants. They left after the Treaty of Karlowitz which heralded the start of a new, Habsburg hegemony in 1699. The Serbs rose against the Habsburgs in 1736, and together with the plagues that devastated the Banat at the time, their exodus caused a dramatic fall in Arad's population.

The Habsburgs began building a massive fortress on the eastern bank of the Mureş in 1763. It was modelled on the star-shaped defences developed earlier in the century by Vauban. But by the time it was finished, the citadel was largely redundant because the Turks had gone long ago. But it came into its own as a prison. Tantalisingly forbidding, it now functions as an army barracks and visitors are not allowed in; you can get a reasonable view of the citadel from the city's river bridges.

Frequent floods and epidemics threatened to destroy Arad altogether. Throughout the first half of the 18C, the townspeople were thrown into limbo when the emperor announced that they must move further from the river. No firm decision was taken, but in the meanwhile new building was halted and Arad stagnated. In 1783, Joseph II agreed that Arad could stay where it was, provided that effort was put into regenerating the city's economy. Among its new businesses was the metalworking foundry which produced some of the beautiful wrought-iron balconies and balustrades still visible in the centre. Joseph commissioned architects and engineers to draw up systematic plans for Arad's future development, but little new construction took place here until the flood barriers were installed in the early 19C.

Joseph's plans to abolish serfdom, though enlightened, were not far-reaching enough to allay the growing fears of his poorer subjects, and they came too late to prevent the peasants' revolt of 1784. Many people from Arad joined its leaders, Horia, Cloşca and Crişan, but the rebels were rounded up by the Austrian army and left to the cruel mercy of one Colonel Kray. Similar retribution followed the 1848–49 revolution, when Hungarians rose against Habsburg despotism. On 6 October 1849, the Austrians executed 13 rebel generals from the Hungarian army near the walls of Arad fortress. The killings were carried out beside the fortress; a monument marks the place today, and the executions are commemorated annually; 'Aradi Vértanúk', an affecting painting of the executions by János Thorma (1870–1937), hangs in the Hungarian National Gallery in Budapest. But the most important date from the Romanians' point of view is 1918, when Ştefan Ciceo Pop organised the first meeting of the Romanian National Council in Arad to discuss Transylvania's unification with Transylvania.

Practical information

☎ code
057

Tourist information

There is no shortage of tourist agencies in Arad. These include *Artexin-Atic* at Unirii 5–7, *Sirius* at B-dul Revoluţiei 55, and *Zarandul* at B-dul Revoluţiei 76.

Getting around

By train The train station can be found north of the centre, to the side of Calea Aurel Vlaicu in Piaţa Gării, and the *CFR* booking office is at Str Unirii 1, ☎ 212177.
By bus The main bus depot is next to the train station; Arad has a **tram** service through the centre.
By plane This is on Calea Bodrogului, ☎ 252564, and *TAROM*'s office is at Str Unirii 1.
By car If you need information on **car hire** or **repairs**, ask *ACR* at 2 Str 1 Decembrie 1918, ☎ 281445, or contact *Auto Bila* at Str Ştefan cel Mare 1, ☎ 286014, *Auto Schunn* (a Mercedes-Benz specialist) next door at Str Ştefan cel Mare 2–4, ☎ 281474, or *Station Car Service* at Str Ştefan cel Mare 26, ☎ 287666. There is a *Peco* **petrol station** at Str Cometei 1.

Where to stay

Arad's top-class hotels include the *Astoria* (✯✯) at B-dul Revoluţiei 78–81, ☎ 281700, and the *Paradis* (✯✯) at Str Molidului 2/5, ☎ 287377. You could also try the *Central* (✯) at Str Horia 8, ☎ 256543; or contact *ANTREC*, ☎ 254046, for information on bed and breakfast accommodation in the area.

Food and shopping

B-dul Revoluţiei is Arad's 'main drag' for eating out (if you are desperate, it has a *McDonald's* too) and shopping, but you could also try the *Bulevard* at Str Horia 1, *Corona* at no. 44, and the appetisingly named *Big Belly* burger bar at no. 8. Italian pasta and pizzas have become very popular in Romania; in Arad there are **pizzerias** at B-dul Revoluţiei 84–86 (*Casata Vernieri*) and at no. 63 (*Ciao Italia*). B-dul Revoluţiei also boasts two **bars**, the *Coco Jolly Rocker* at no. 91, and *Paperone* at no. 9. *Perla* is a **fish restaurant** on the strand at Str Splaiul Mureş 31B.

While not wildly exciting as a shopping centre, Arad does have a number of picturesque **markets**. The central ones are in Piaţa Mihai Viteazu and Piaţa Catedralei.

Post office

Arad's main post office is on the west side of B-dul Revoluţiei near the corner with Str Crişan.

Money

Banks include *Banc Post* at B-dul Revoluţiei 9 bloc 1, *Banca Naţională a României* at B-dul Revoluţiei 72, *Banca Româna de Dezvoltare* at B-dul Revoluţiei 5–7, and *Banca Agricola* at Str Vasile Goldis 1–3. There is also a *Bancorex* at Str Lucian Blaga 11, and you can **change money** at *IDM*, B-dul Revoluţiei 55.

Police station

This is at Str Vârful cu Dor 17-21, ☎ 281633, and the City Hall can be found at B-dul Revoluţiei 75.

Medical care

There are **pharmacies** at Str Nicolae Bălcescu 1 and B-dul Revoluţiei 80.

Traditional arts and crafts

Arad county stretches east into the Apuseni and covers several distinct ethnographic zones. These include Țara Zarandului, Ineu-Sicula and Birchiș-Capâlnaș, as well as the Mureș Valley and the Crișul Alb plains. If you want to find out more about these specific areas and their products, such as the fine handmade sheepskin coats and red-and-black embroideries from Buteni, contact *Centrul Județean de Creație Populară* at B-dul Revoluției 85, ☎ 281805. This organisation should be able to provide the latest details on where to buy good-quality crafts and give you the dates of traditional folk festivals, such as those at Hălmagiu, Talasele and Miniș.

Walking around Arad

Arad's skyline is dominated by the Austrian **fortress** on the east bank of the river, but this is a military base which is closed to tourists. The closest you can get is the memorial to the 13 generals who were executed in 1849.

The oldest part of the city was built on the west bank of the Mureș River, in the southern section of modern Arad. It contained German, Hungarian and Jewish quarters, and there was a substantial Serbian population here too. After the Serbs' anti-Habsburg uprising in 1736, many of them fled; those who remained pooled their energies with the Germans and developed manufacturing businesses. Few Romanians lived in the city centre before the beginning of the 19C; previously they were mainly confined to the outlying villages.

Walk south from the north end of B-dul Revoluției and you pass in clearly graduated stages from 20C opulence to 18C simplicity, past neo-Gothic, Secession and Judendstil buildings into neo-Classical and Baroque.

B-dul Revoluției is a real boulevard: long and wide and treelined, with trams running along the centre. It contains many 19C and early 20C buildings that sprang up after the flood barriers were put in place. These include fine edifices by local architects Lajos Szántay (1872–1953) and Emil Tabakovits (1860–c 1927). Szántay's **Red Church**, on the left side of B-dul Revoluției as you continue to walk south, is a Lutheran foundation erected in 1905–06, named after the pink granite used in its construction. The combination of neo-Gothic with Secessionist elements was an unusual choice for Szántay, but the church is refreshingly simple and light inside. Organ concerts are often held in the church.

Continue south, and you pass imposing 19C apartment blocks. Some of them have fine wrought-iron balustrades and tantalisingly hidden internal courtyards. One of the buildings, no. 87, is Palatul Lloyd, another of Szántay's projects. A little further on you reach Arad's **City Hall**, an opulent affair completed in 1876. Ödön Lechner, who is best known for his marvellous Decorative Arts Museum in Budapest, devised the original, prize-winning plan. But lack of funds drove the city fathers to ask the Arad architect Ferenc Pekár to come up with something more modest. With Lechner's approval, Pekár reduced the surface area and height. During the revolution of December 1989, 18 people were shot in Arad; you can find their names on a remembrance plaque in front of the Hall.

Walk behind the City Hall into Piața Enescu, and to the right is Szántay's magnificent **Culture Palace**. This was finished in 1913 and is a hybrid of several different styles. Each side of the palace follows an individual mode, be it Romanesque, Gothic and neo-Classical, but inside the building was designed to be all of a piece, so that decorations and furnishings contribute to a grand Secessionist effect. Its main showpiece is a grand theatre and concert hall, exuberantly ornamented with floral glass windows. The building houses the **County**

History Museum, open Tues–Sun 10.00–18.00, and guided tours of the Palace are available.

Cross to the other side of B-dul Revoluției and turn left onto Str Horia. This brings you to Str Gheorghe Popa (or Stejarului) on the right. At nos. 2–4 stands the **Art Museum**, an elegant early 20C building that houses a range of Neo-Classical and Biedermeyer furniture and a modest collection of canvases by minor European masters from the 17C onwards. It also possesses one of the few permanent displays of contemporary Romanian art. One room has been dedicated to the work of the Arad-born artist Ione Munteanu (born 1944), who took the chance of the brief liberalisation of the 1960s to give vent to his emotions in his work. He committed suicide in 1968. Open Tues–Sun 10.00-18.00. There is a market near the Art Museum, on Piața Viteazu.

Return to B-dul Revoluției, turn right and walk south on the right-hand side, and at no. 98 is the *Hotel Mureșul* (originally the *White Cross Hotel*). This was once the city's most glamorous hostelry. Built in 1841, it has an attractive Neo-Classical interior and a concert hall (now a cinema) with a special roof that could be raised on hydraulic shafts. Bartók, Brahms, Casals and Liszt all performed here, and during its heyday, several well-known Hungarian and Romanian writers stayed in the hotel, among them George Coșbuc, I.L. Caragiale and Octavian Goga.

Continuing south along B-dul Revoluției, on the same side you come to a majestic **Catholic church** with a Baroque interior, dedicated to St Anthony of Padua. Inside the porch is a bronze statue of the Holy Trinity from the first half of the 18C. This was commissioned as a memorial to Arad's plague victims. It used to stand outside, where it collapsed and was rescued from a scrapyard before being installed in the church; the cherubs' feet have been polished by decades of worshippers seeking contact with the holy figures. The main body of the church is plunged in a stygian gloom, and you can only enter it during services.

Continue walking south beyond the National Theatre at the end of B-dul Revoluției, and you enter Piața Avram Iancu. On the right-hand side as you pass the theatre is a bank with brass railings outside. It occupies part of **Palatul Bohuș**, another Secessionist building by Szántay, which stretches the full length of the square. Some of the flats on the top floor are used as artists' studios.

Piața Avram Iancu is a pretty place surrounded mainly by 19C Eclectic or Secessionist buildings. A Stalinist statue still stands in the central garden, surrounded incongruously by patterned flowerbeds. The figure was put here to replace the monument to the 13 martyred generals. At no. 16 stands the Dománay Palace, which was built on the site of the old town hall. It belonged to a wealthy wine merchant who made his fortune by supplying the Habsburg emperors.

Turn off down the side streets to the right of Piața Avram Iancu to reach more veins of **old Arad**: shops with old-fashioned advertisements still fixed to their walls and sleepy courtyards. But this quarter has not always been so innocent as it seems: Str Metianu, for example, was the centre of Arad's black market during the 1980s. Combining features from Islamic and Byzantine architecture, the type of design here is also known as the Ion Mincu style, after the architect who first developed it. Head west along Str Goldiș and you will find the **Orthodox Cathedral** (1865) and next to it Arad's main market square, where you can buy anything from bolts to bananas. On the corner of Str Ștefan Cicio Pop and Str

Mihai Eminescu stands the **Farmacia Grozăvescu**, formerly the Földes pharmacy, whose Secessionist interior was designed by Emil Tabakovits. It is protected by Romania's Historic Monuments Commission but still functions as a pharmacy. The façade at Str Cicio Pop 3 is another Secessionist design by the same architect. Emil Tabakovits won prizes for his building designs and worked in Austria and Hungary as well as in Transylvania. For Arad, he designed several churches and schools but his grandest projects were **Palatul Neumann**, on B-dul Revoluției beside the City Hall, and the Banca Națională building opposite.

Return to Piața Avram Iancu and cross the square. Turn left down Str Gheorghe Lazăr, and on the left at no. 2 you come to the **Hirschl Theatre**. Constructed by a local businessman, Jakob Hirschl, on the site of his house in 1817, it was one of the first theatres on Romanian territory. During the course of its lively career, many famous actors came to work here, and the poet Mihail Eminescu was employed as a 'breather' or prompt before turning his talents to more polemical activities. In the early 20C, the Hirschl was converted into a cinema and was later abandoned, but the building has recently been restored with the aim of reopening it as a theatre.

Str Lazăr was near Arad's Jewish quarter, and it contains several atmospheric old buildings. One of Arad's two **synagogues** can be found hidden in the recesses of Tribunal Dobra 10, near the north side of Piața Veche (the other is in Str Cozia). Tribunal Dobra also has **Casa cu Lacăt**, the House with the Padlock. It gets its name from an early 19C sign showing a tree and a padlock which used to mark a crossroads. At this period Arad attracted many metalworkers, and apprentices would hammer a nail into the tree which stood beside this building to show they had passed by.

Walk south into **Piața Veche**, Old Square, and appropriately, rural Romania comes vividly to life. This is the heart of Arad's oldest district. It was once known as Hal Tér, Fish Square, because of the fish markets that were held here regularly in the 18C and 19C. Walk to the right along Tribunal Axente, and you will find graceful single-storey **18C houses**. They were once a common feature of the city before Joseph II began transforming it into a metropolis fit for his progressive ideas. Many of the houses have small gardens in front and courtyards behind, but the majority are semi-derelict, having been abandoned or requisitioned by Roma, who could not care less about their upkeep. The earliest building is no. 15, unbelievably narrow for its height, and no. 21 is thought to have once functioned as a town hall.

At the southern end of Arad's old town lies the **Serb district**, whose principal streets radiate from Piața Serbească. Str Sava Tekelia is named after the 18C Serbian benefactor who commissioned the pretty Baroque tower on the **Orthodox church** near the square. Built in 1702 by Tekelia's grandfather, it originally had a Byzantine tower. The ceiling barrel was painted in 1865, but the frescoes inside are so blackened with smoke and exhalations that you can hardly see them. This is the oldest church in Arad, and there are plans to restore both building paintings. At the intersection between Str Desseanu and Str Episcopiei streets you can see Arad's oldest *ronde bosse* public **statue**, an unloved but charming figure of St John Nepomuk dating from the 18C.

Serbs began migrating north into what was then part of Hungary, to escape the Turks. The largest influx came in 1690. In 1951–52, many Serbs were deported from the Banat to the inhospitable Bărăgan Plain, along with others who were considered too rich, or too critical of the Stalinist regime. The Serbian monastery of **Bezdin** lies 7km to the west of Arad. Take the road through Zădăreni, Bodrogu Nou and Felnac, and at Sânpetru German turn on to the village road to the north and follow the signs for the monastery, which stands on the other side of a forest. On religious holidays a priest comes out from Satu Mare to celebrate services.

Around Arad

In the suburbs to the northwest of the city centre stands the pretty monastery of **Gai**. You can reach it by taking tram no. 6 to the terminus and walking for another 1km, or drive along Str Aurel Vlaicu (which leads to Nădlac) and follow signs to the monastery. Gai was opened in c 1760. It has an extra wooden church, which was dragged there from a neighbouring village. Now managed by nuns, the Baroque complex contains a museum with rare books and a superb collection of icons in glass and wood; open daily 08.00–18.00. One of them shows St Nicholas with a particularly zany face, painted by the 18C artist Nedelcu Popovici.

Southeast Banat

Oravița is an ancient town, c 115km southeast of Timișoara, on the edge of the Banat's loveliest landscapes. The Romans mined here for gold, silver and iron. In c 1642, it was settled by the Bufeni, Romanians from Oltenia, who were absorbed into the existing Romanian population. After the Habsburgs 'liberated' the town from the Turks, they gave parcels of land around the town to Swabians, Serbs and Croats. Oravița became a cultural centre for Romanians in the Banat and had its own theatre.

Now Oravița is a quiet backwater. Its long central street is bordered by 18C and 19C houses; the chemist's shop has a plaque stating with simple pride that when it was opened it was the only one in these mountains. The road between Oravița and Anina brings you into some of the loveliest countryside in this region. It is also one of the most attractive routes to Băile Herculane and the Danube. Every so often you may come across abandoned mining or quarrying plants standing by the roadside. Covered with a patina of rust, some of these structures are impressive and even beautiful in their dilapidated state. They have already inspired a number of contemporary French installation artists.

Between Arad and Deva

The E68 highway between Arad and Deva is on the international trucking route and is an excellent road. 36km east of Arad, it passes through Lipova, a small town surrounded by oak woods. **Lipova** has a spa, a fine 14C Orthodox church and a very attractive museum which contains 18C and 19C icons and rare books. Called Colecția de Carte Veche și Icoane 'Ștefan Crișan', the museum can be found at Str B. P. Hașdeu 22; open Tues–Sun 09.00–17.00.

Lipova's mineral springs have been in use since the 16C. The spa complex lies 1km to the south of the town. Some 3km northeast of Lipova stand the remains of the medieval Castelul Șoimoș. If you are travelling by train, the nearest station is at Radna on the western edge of the town. Radna stands at the junction of the Arad–Bucharest and Timișoara–Radna lines.

Dobrogea

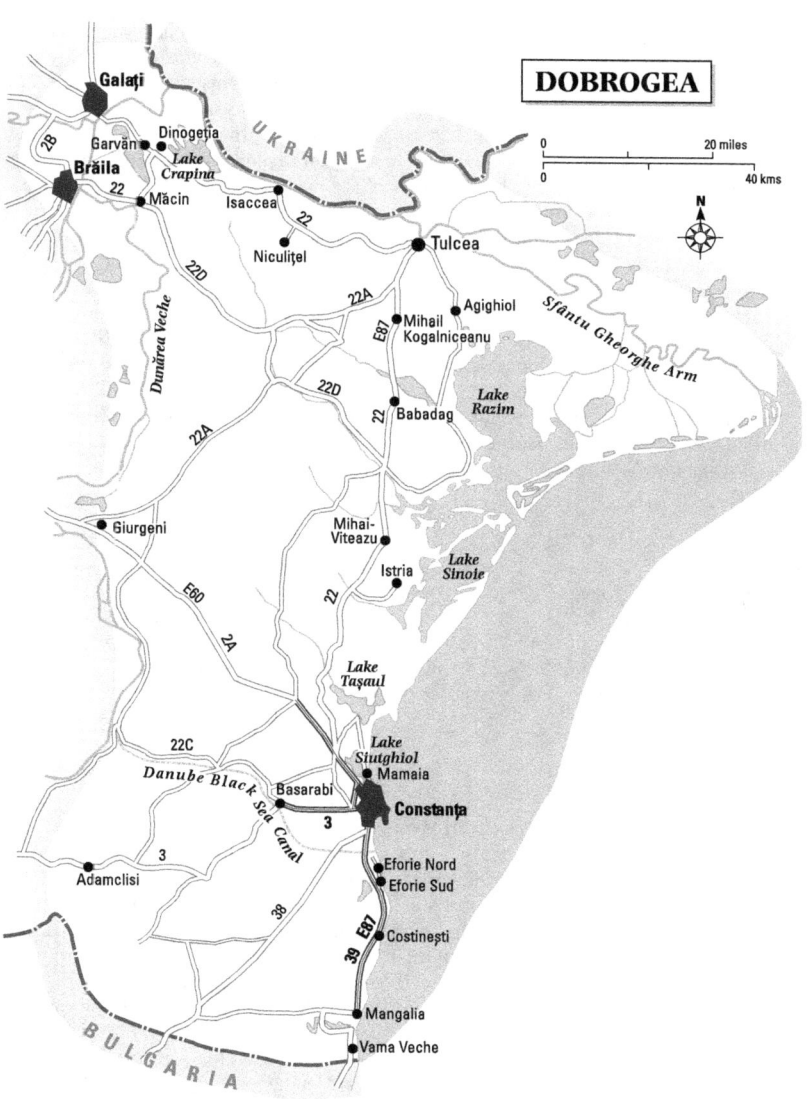

Lying between the Danube and the Black Sea coast, Dobrogea is physically and psychologically separate from the rest of Romania. As you turn east from the river, the Bărăgan Plain gives way to the bleak, rolling steppe of Podişul Dobrogei. It is hard to avoid the conclusion that this is a forgotten region. Driving northeast from Giurgeni or Hirşova towards Tulcea, the roads become smaller, rougher and emptier, the fields are strewn with stones, and horses give way to donkeys. But while these may be marks of Dobrogea's poverty, they signal its unspoilt wildness as well. The skies are huge here and Romanian Impressionist painters loved the Dobrogean coastline because of its light.

An hour's drive east from the Danube brings you to places colonised by ancient Greeks six centuries before Christ. This is where Jason is supposed to have landed with the Argonauts. At the northern edge of the plateau are Munţii Măcinului, a range of rounded, chalk hills whose profile resembles the worn spine of a stegosaur. They are the oldest mountains in Romania, created c 400 million years ago. Today they provide the main ingredient for traditional distemper. Further south, near the vineyards of Murfatlar, steppe and marshland have yielded Getic and Thracian treasures of incomparable beauty. And there are places where the landscape is peppered with hillocks which seem to promise yet more tombs. The museums of Constanţa and Mangalia are foci of Dobrogea's richly cultured past. And in a landscape dominated by high-rise hotels, there are still a few stretches of coastline that have not been completely commercialised. If you do not have time to go anywhere else, head for the Delta.

The name Dobrogea

During the Ottoman occupation Dobrogea, sometimes spelt Dobrudja or Dobruja, was ruled as a Turkish vassal state while Moldavia and Wallachia were left to rule themselves. Opinions differ as to the origins of its name, but some say it comes from a Bulgarian *despot* called Dobrotic who owned the land here in the Middle Ages, while others think it derives from the Turkish word for the province, Dobruca.

History

Set apart geographically from the rest of Romania, Dobrogea has had a separate history as well. Greeks from Miletos colonised Dobrogea's coastline in the 7C BC, establishing the cities of Tomis, Histria and Callatis, whose inhabitants conducted a flourishing trade with the indigenous Thracian peoples. In 514 BC King Darius of the Persians led an army across the province on his way to Poland. After the Roman invasion Dobrogea became part of Scythia. Following the division of the empire into two halves in the 4C AD, it fell under the jurisdiction of Eastern Rome, with its capital in Constantinople. Dobrogea remained part of the Christian Byzantine Empire that emerged from Rome's dying embers.

Between the 7C and the 13C, Dobrogea's borders shifted continually as the Byzantines fought to retain this valuable and fertile territory against invading Slavic and Turkic hordes. Terrible Avars attacked the old Greek cities in the 7C, and in the 9C Pechenegs descended into Dobrogea, followed 200 years later by Uze peoples on their way to Thessalonica in northern Greece. Later in

> ### Ancient Greeks in Dobrogea
> From the 8C to the 6C BC many Greeks left their homeland and founded colonies around the Black Sea's rim. Their reasons for emigrating were a complex combination of economic, social and political factors. At first the emigrants went east from the Bosphorus. They spread to the west coast, including the area that is now Romania's seaboard, after they had founded trading colonies along the north coast of Anatolia. The first known Greeks to arrive in Dobrogea were mainly Dorians from Miletus (or Miletos) on the southwest coast of present-day Turkey. They established communities beside natural harbours where it was easy to trade with the indigenous peoples. These settlements evolved into towns and cities modelled on Greek city-states. Among the most important were Tomis (present-day Constanţa), Callatis (Mangalia), and Histria (an archaeological site) where fascinating traces of their ancient culture remain. According to Neal Ascherson in his book *Black Sea* (Random House, London, 1995), the Greeks' contacts with the indigenous, autochthonous farmers, fishermen and nomads (the so-called 'barbarians') made Athenian intellectuals reflect deeply on the nature of civilisation itself.

the same century, Cumans also passed through Dobrogea before settling in southern Moldavia and northeast Bulgaria. But the most influential group of migratory tribes to settle in Dobrogea were the Tartars or Kipchaks. These descendants of the Golden Horde came in 1241 with the armies of the Mongol emperor Ogedei after conquering the Crimea. During the next century they established colonies in southern Moldavia between the Prut and Dniestr rivers, and south as far as Babadag in Dobrogea.

Dobrogea's increasingly multi-ethnic society included Seljuk settlers from Anatolia. These Turks came with the blessing of Michael VIII Palaeologus (c 1225–82) as he strove to extend the Byzantine empire's shrinking borders; in return for guarding his frontiers they received land around Babadag. Their leaders were Issedin and Sara Saltuq Dede; the latter's tomb became a place of pilgrimage for local Muslims and can still be seen beside Babadag's attractive mosque (see pp 365–366).

For brief periods during the 14C and early 15C, Wallachian prince Mircea cel Bătrân and his fellow Romanian *voivozi* wrested control of Dobrogea from the Turks. But between 1462–84 inexorable pressure from Sultan Mehmet II brought Dobrogea and the Delta into a single province that stretched from the Dniestr in the north to Nicopolis on the southern bank of the Danube.

Ottoman Turkey wanted this part of the Black Sea coast as a military and commercial route to the Crimea, Poland and Russia; it was also a convenient base for keeping watch over Moldavia and Wallachia, the empire's buffer zones which were under Turkish suzerainty but governed themselves. Dobrogea was desirable in its own right as well: rich soil and a temperate climate ensured a constant supply of crops and livestock which was needed to feed an extensive empire.

By the 16C, Dobrogea had become the *vilayet* of Silistra. A *vilayet* was an administrative region within the Ottoman Empire. It was ruled by a governor who was supported by a garrison of Turkish troops. Turkish immigrants were encouraged to settle in the towns along with Crimean Tartars; the population was further enriched by Armenians, Bulgarians, Greeks and Jews. Dobrogea remained technically under Ottoman domination until 1878, when it was united with Romania after the Congress of Berlin.

Although it is an integral part of Dobrogea, the Danube Delta has had a different history. Many of its 30,000 people are Lipoveni. Lipoveni are Russians whose long-bearded ancestors belonged to a religious sect that was persecuted by Catherine the Great. They were led by the monk Philip who renounced the priesthood, marriage and military service and refused to swear allegiance to the Tsar. At first the Lipoveni fled to Bucovina, where the Habsburg Emperor Joseph II appreciated their mild-mannered diligence and exceptional skills; he let them live as they pleased. But Lipoveni are traditionally people of the river and the sea, and many gravitated to the Delta to earn their living from fishing. While the men no longer sport the long beards which infuriated Catherine, their houses are noticeably different from those of ethnic Romanians. Instead of using textiles, they decorate walls and woodwork with flowers and leaves. During the heat of the summer the Lipoveni often cook their food in outdoor ovens and some Lipoveni homes have traditional saunas.

THE DANUBE DELTA

At the far northeast corner of Dobrogea lies the great reed-, poplar- and willow-fringed expanse of the Danube Delta. The Delta is a haven for birds. Many of them are migratory species which come to rest and breed during spring, summer and early autumn, but there are other birds that live here all year round; among both types are birds that are seldom or never seen in western or northern Europe. To the south of the Delta, silt deposits have created two huge salt-water lagoons, Lacul Razim and Lacul Sinoie. These are separated from the sea by long sandbanks which on the map look as fragile as strips of lace.

Man has inhabited the Delta since ancient times, leaving a scattering of ruins and archaeological sites that have yielded information about Neolithic cultures specific to this region. At the other end of the timescale, Ceaușescu changed the Delta's face by draining huge areas of wetland for (as it turned out) useless agriculture. But in spite of this and continuing industrial devastation, pockets of the old landscape have been preserved.

Navigating the Danube: who makes the rules

The first attempts to regulate shipping on the river began in the 1830s, when Austrian, English and Russian interests converged powerfully enough to form the joint Danube Commission. During the 1920s, 12 European nations ratified the Danube's free, international status. But after the Second World War, the USSR tried to limit its use to those countries through which the river ran. A stalemate ensued, but the Commission survived and today the Danube is still an international waterway. Together with the Central Rhine Commission, the Danube Commission coordinates the interests of all the countries through which it flows. In 1992 the Rhine-Main-Danube canal opened. Linking the Black and North Seas, this brought to fruition a plan that had been envisaged in classical times.

Efforts to save what is left of the magnificent wilderness began in earnest in 1990, when UNESCO designated the Delta a 'Biosphere Reservation'. UNESCO also nominated it as the world's third most important wetland, second only to the deltas of the Amazon and the Nile; in Europe only the Volga's mouth covers a larger area. In the early 1990s, Jacques Cousteau helped to set up an education and research foundation at Uzlina, a tiny village on the north bank of the Sf Gheorghe channel. Still, the list of damages is depressing: deforestation, erosion, polluting industries and illegal hunting are all threatening what many ornithologists see as the most important avian breeding grounds in eastern Europe, if not in Europe as a whole.

Worse than this, there are villages in the Delta which have only recently, in 1996–97, received a fresh-water supply. Before that, a few cases of cholera were recorded each year. But there is a greater problem facing fishermen and their families: overfishing and pollution caused by the dumping of raw sewage on the Black Sea's northwest shelf have drastically affected fish supplies.

Tulcea

Most of the ferries and hydrofoils that ply the Delta channels start at the county town of Tulcea. In antiquity, this was the site of Dacian and Roman Aegyssus, a citadel whose origins have been traced to the 8C BC. Its walls were so tough they even impressed the repining Ovid. Today, the highway from Bucharest sweeps you past low, vine-covered hills. Tulcea's social heart is a wide esplanade which curves along the riverside: the town's main streets converge here. Opposite, on the northern shore, you can see the village of **Tudor Vladimirescu**, the birthplace of a 19C champion of Romania's struggle for independence who bore the same name. Vladimirescu (1780–1821) was a leader of the 1821 uprising that helped to end Phanariot rule in Moldavia and Wallachia.

There are few old buildings left in Tulcea and none of the single-storey wooden houses which caught the eye of French paleontologist Boucher de Parthes, when he came here in 1853. Boucher was delighted by the windmills whose sails whirled on the hill tops above the town; he described the weird effect they made above the forest of tall masts and funnels in the harbour below. Today Tulcea is a sprawling industrial city that cranks out aluminium in outdated plants; its windmills have disappeared, and the ships are less than elegant—even so, it has an exhilarating atmosphere. Apart from being a good place to hire boat trips into the Delta, Tulcea is close to the fascinating countryside of northwest Dobrogea.

Practical information

☎ **code**
040

Tourist information

Tulcea has several tourist agencies: *Agenţia de Turism Tulcea* at Str Isaccei 4, bloc G0, ☎/fax 511607; *BTT*, Str Babadag bl 1, ☎ 512496; fax 516842; *Eurodelta*, Str Isaccei 1, ☎ 516604; fax 515032; *Loitsikas Travel* in the *Hotel Egreta*, Str Păcii 3, ☎ 515583; *Lotus Travel*, Str Portului 26, ☎/fax 511245; *Mithos Tur*, Str Gării 34, bl 17P, ☎ 514704; fax 516055; *Nouvelles Frontières*, Str Isaccei 2, ☎/fax 515753; *Satul de Vacanţa Roşu*, Str

Babadag bl 1, ☎ 512496; fax 516842; *Sind România*, Piața Independenței 1, ☎/fax 515091.

Getting around

By train and bus Both the railway and bus station are on Str Portului. The *CFR* building is at Str Babadag 6.

By car For **car repairs** try *ACR* on Str Babadag, southwest of the port, where Babadag joins Str Griviței, or there are **garages** on Str Păcii, just south of Caloniștilor, or Str Elizeului. There are several **petrol stations** in Tulcea, including at least one on Str Babadag near the main road intersection with Str Barajului.

By plane This lies c 15km south on the E87 near the village of Mihai Kogălniceanu (there are at least three villages with this name in eastern Romania; two of these are in Dobrogea, one here and the other 25km north of Constanța). *TAROM* has an office at Str Gării 60.

By boat The national shipping and ferry authority, *Navrom*, has a branch on Str Portului.

Where to stay

Hotels in Tulcea include the **Delta** (✬✬✬) at Str Isaccei 2, ☎ 514720; fax 516260; *Egreta* (✬✬) at Str Păcii 3, ☎ 517103; fax 517105 (it also has a large restaurant, a disco and its own tourist office); *Europolis* at Str Păcii 20, ☎/fax 512443. *Hotel Tineretului* at Str Isaccei 24, ☎/fax 550781, is designed for young people. *ANTREC* has a local office, ☎ 515753.

Eating out

Do not expect too much from restaurants in Tulcea, but you could try the *Danubiu* on Str Portului, the *Union Complex* and the quaintly named *Big Restaurant*, both on Str 23 August, and the *Central* on Str Babadag. Coffee shops advertising 'breakfast' include *Aida* on Piața Civică and *Tosca* on Str Mahmudiei.

Post office and telephones

The post office is at Str Păcii 6. Telephones can be found at any of the four *PTTR* bureaux, at Str Păcii 18, Str Portului 5, Str Isaccei 7 or Aleea Marișor 4.

Money

You can change money in some of the hotels listed below.

Police

The police station is at Str Spitalului 2, and the *primăria* (town hall) at Str Păcii 20.

Medical care

There are **hospitals** on Str 11 Iunie and Str Gloriei.

Regular events

Tulcea holds an international folk festival for the Danube region in August. It also hosts a winter carnival, Lerui Ler, which takes place throughout December when carol singers from different towns and villages parade the streets in traditional costumes. And do not miss the chance to go on wine-tasting tours at Niculițel vineyard. Trips to the vineyard can be arranged from the tourist offices.

Specialist tours

Atbad has offices at Str Babadag 11, ☎ 514114; fax 517625, and runs a fleet of *pontoni* or floating hotels, each with luxury accommodation for up to 20 people; the company offers 10-day trips for birdwatchers and anglers, and its boats can be hired for business conferences as well. There are a number of companies which organise specialised tours for naturalists in the Delta. These include the English-based *Naturetrek*,

Chautura Bighton, nr. Alresford, Hants SO24 9RB, ☎ 01962 733051; email info@naturetrek.co.uk. *Ibis Excursions* runs an annual seven-day birdwatching tour to Dobrogea and the Delta, usually during December. The itinerary includes visiting the freshwater wetlands near Călăraşi, crossing the Danube by the small ferry to see the limestone cliffs at Canaraua Fetei where eagle owls breed, and looking for black-necked grebe on Lake Techirghiol. Other highlights of *Ibis*'s tours are the chance to see the rare red-breasted goose, *Branta ruficollis*, on Lake Sinoe and Lake Razim, and Syrian woodpecker, rough-legged buzzard and Calandra lark near Enisala. Contact *Ibis* at Ganløseparken 46, Ganløse, 3660 Stenløse, Denmark. ☎ (+45) 48195940; fax (+45) 48195945; e-mail: jeffprice@ibis-excursions.dk; websitre http://www.ibis-excursions.dk. Do not confuse this company with a local travel firm called Ibis. *Wexas International* organises tours of the Delta from 45 Brompton Road, London SW3 1DE, ☎ 0171 581 4130.

Maps and books

Try the tourist agencies. In 1992, *Harta Turistica Dunării* appeared. This was a tourist map of the Delta with parallel texts in French, English and German as well as Romanian. It does not show every village and the English translations are quaint, but it does give an interesting overview of the Delta's geography. Otherwise you may be able to find maps in the leaflets published by the Natural History Museum (see below). An English-language guide to Tulcea was published in 1990; failing all else, ask for it at the Archaeology and History Museum (see below).

While Tulcea does not pretend to be a great cultural centre, it has several museums that are surprisingly good. For a start, a few minutes' walk from Piaţa Republicii along the esplanade at Str Alexandru Sahia 2 brings you to **Secţia de Artă** (the Art Section of Tulcea's Delta museum complex). Despite its dingy interior it has fine Impressionist and Post-Impressionist paintings by many of the best-known Romanian artists of their day. Names include the usual pantheon: Grigorescu, Tăttărescu, Ţuculescu and Pallady, but there are striking figurative scenes by less well-known painters, including Iosif Iser (1881–1958) and Francisc Şirato (1877–1953). There are also a few early paintings by the internationally known Surrealist Victor Brauner (1903–66) which give an insight into his progression through Cubism, and some canvases by the leading Dadaist and architect, Marcel Iancu (1895–1979). Many of the landscapes show Dobrogea, especially the coast. There is also a collection of Oriental decorative art, including textiles, carpets and furniture, dating from the time when the Turks ruled the province. Open Tues–Sun 09.00–17.00.

It is worth the short hike up the hill to see the view from the Independence Monument on Str Gloriei. Beside it stands the History and Archaeology Museum, **Secţia de Istorie şi Arheologie**. This has been built on the site of a Geto-Dacian camp whose ruins are strewn beguilingly around its little garden. Inside are gorgeous examples of Cucuteni pottery and Getic funerary tablets, their surfaces alive with horsemen. These images may be a source for the traditional Christian image of St George. There are also wonderfully detailed ornaments and apotropeic symbols recovered from pre-Christian burials and Roman settlements; some of these are made from gold, silver and bronze, Greek and Roman statuary and ceramics, Byzantine pieces found at Dinogeţia and Thraco-Getic figures from Enisala make this a fascinating excursion into Dobrogea's past. Guided tours in English may be available. Open Tues–Sun 09.00–17.00.

Delta wildlife

Huge areas of the Delta are covered by reed beds, and it is an important migratory hub that attracts hundreds of thousands of breeding birds every year. Species such as egrets and herons flourish along the waterways—the Delta is home to every European breeding variety of heron—while black-necked and red-necked grebes and ducks breed here too. In the woods you can often hear golden orioles and thrush nightingales; penduline tits frequent the willow trees by the water's edge. Hobbys are common, and there have been sightings of other birds of prey such as white-tailed eagles, red-footed falcons and even sakers. White and black storks can be seen here too. Further south, near Enisala, and in Babadag and the Măcin hills there are other excellent bird-watching sites.

In summer, flocks of white pelican congregate around Lacul Nuntaşi, Vadu Bay, Lacul Băclaneşti Mare and Lacul Lunga. Sometimes you can see them sharing piles of fishing nets with cormorants; there is a pelican reserve near Mila 23. Pygmy cormorant and glossy ibis feed in the channels. Grey Dalmatian pelican are much rarer; they sometimes nest on Sahalin Island and Lacul Nuntaşi. In 1992, German ornithologists noted that 5 per cent of the world's pelican population brought up its young here.

Because of the danger to breeding species, the Romanian government has tried to restrict entry into some parts of the Delta. The area has been divided into 16 official 'no-go' areas plus so-called buffer zones, and land has been set aside for ecological restoration. There are also zones that have been designated for use in 'traditional economic activities' (mainly fishing). But if this sounds as though the Delta is rigidly controlled and supervised, you will not notice anything! However, if you want to visit the nature reserves, you must ask a tourist agency or contact the Delta Administration Office, ARBDD, at its Tulcea office (see below).

Fish used to be plentiful in the Delta, but catfish is now the staple diet. Stocks of other species have declined dramatically since the 1960s, when beluga were common and sturgeon used to swarm up the Danube in their millions during the breeding season. Black Sea herring and mackerel have dwindled too. Nearly half of the Delta's fish live in fresh water, but there are also clams and other forms of shellfish. Carp, pike, zander, sheat fish and perch are still common. Among the causes of their demise are the heavy pollution from the Danube and Dniestr Rivers, and the raw sewage that is dumped around the river deltas. Another has been the arrival of a rapacious jellyfish from the east coast of the USA, which has no natural predators here. In *Black Sea* (see above), Neal Ascherson starts his fascinating history of the sea with a description of the great shoals of anchovies which used to circulate the coastal areas in antiquity. Now there are barely enough to garnish a decent-sized pizza.

But the picture is not all black. The Delta still has plenty of wildlife, and you may see wild boar, wild cat, black bellied fox and hare. Recent intruders include the Central Asian enot dog (*Nyctereutes procynoldes*), which resembles the badger and is hunted for its fur.

Fishing and hunting restrictions are decided on a yearly basis. The Romanian Tourist Office's leaflet on the Delta contains brief information about them, and if you are interested, it is advisable to contact the ARBDD (the Delta Biosphere Administration) in Tulcea at Str Păcii 20.

Secția de Științele Naturii (the Natural History Museum), at Str Progesului 32, is an old-fashioned institution bravely trying to face the 21C. Examples of typical Delta habitats are reproduced in old-fashioned dioramas and glass cases, complete with stuffed versions of some of the birds and animals you may see on your visit. Ask for a guided tour because the museum staff can provide an excellent introduction to the Delta's nature reserves. Open Tues–Sun 09.00–17.00.

Tulcea has one of the region's few remaining mosques, the 19C **Azizia Cami** (*geamia* in Romanian), which was restored in 1924. The mosque houses part of the art gallery's holdings of Oriental art. Dobrogea's first **secondary school**, which you pass on your way to the Archaeological Museum, is dedicated to a philanthropist called Spiru Haret. It opened in 1883 and has a splendid neo-Byzantine façade.

INTO THE DELTA

The Delta is young by global standards: c 6500 million years ago, it was nothing more than a shallow indentation in the Black Sea coastline. It grew because of the enormous quantities of silt which the river deposited there—scientists reckon that 80 million tons were dumped on the coast every year, and the Danube still carries an afterbirth of quartz and other solid grains. Today the shoals are forcing their way outwards into the sea at the rate of between 80 and 100 feet a year.

According to Herodotus, the Danube split into five branches while it ran through the Delta; Pliny and Ptolemy gave it six channels, and Strabo seven. Today most of the river traffic uses the three main channels. The first two begin a few kilometres north of Tulcea, which lies on the southern branch; c 17km east of the city, that arm of the river divides again, the new southern arm winding away to the coast at Sf Gheorghe. Brațul Sulina (the Sulina Arm), so-named because it meets the sea at Sulina, is the central and shortest one. It reaches the coast c 80km after leaving Tulcea and is the one most used by international shipping. There are roads of a kind in the Delta, but the best way to get around is by boat.

River transport

NAVROM in Tulcea runs hydrofoils and ferries along all three channels to the sea, as well as from Tulcea to Galați. Times of departure will vary, but in summer there is generally one service a day to and from Tulcea's esplanade; both hydrofoils and ferries call at villages en route. Journey times for hydrofoils are approximately as follows: Tulcea–Sulina: 1hr 30mins; Tulcea–Periprava: 2hrs 30mins; Tulcea–Sf Gheorghe: 2hrs; Tulcea–Galați: 1hr 30mins. Ferries: Tulcea–Sulina: 4hrs; Tulcea–Periprava: 5hrs 30mins; Tulcea–Sf Gheorghe: 5hrs; Tulcea–Galați: 3hrs 15mins. By Western European standards, fares are minimal.

The Sulina Channel

During the 1830s and 1840s, Anglo-Austrian and Austro-Russian conventions legalised free navigation along the full length of the Danube. In 1856, the Paris Treaty set up the first Danube Commission, which maintained the river as an international waterway. Having decided that the Sulina arm was the one best suited for sea-going ships, the commission had it straightened and dredged, so that between 1862–1902 its overall length was reduced by c 30km. But because of silting at the eastern end, deep-draughted ships could not get past Sulina. To solve the problem, the English engineer Charles Hartley installed pitch-pine dykes along a 6km extension into the Black Sea. The dykes worked well until 1894, when dredgers were brought in to clear the channel's mouth. In 1915, the First World War put a stop to further work for some time. The average width of the Sulina arm is 120–200m while the depth, maintained by draglines, is 7–18m.

Maliuc, c 22km east of Tulcea and 20 sea miles from the coast, is a good stopping-off point for exploring the meandering channels and lakes that surround it. A lot of birds frequent this area, but Maliuc itself is not attractive. It developed into a small industrial centre after a research station was established here to study the Delta's wildlife. It can offer accommodation in the modest *Salcia Hotel*, ☎ 040 511515, and there is at least one inn here.

About two-thirds of the way from Tulcea to Sulina, the traditional fishing village of **Crişan** consists of one row of houses c 3km long. It lies along the river's southern edge. A small camping site near the landing stage has tiny wooden cabins and a bar. It is also possible to find lodgings in private houses; for more information, contact ANTREC or one of the other 'eco-tourist' agencies for more details (see p 116).

Across the river from Crişan's ferry landing stage is the *Hotel Lebăda* (☆☆☆) (the Swan Hotel), ☎ 040 543778. This is a pseudo-traditional building with a thatched roof, modern, carpeted rooms, a bar, restaurant and disco.

> ### Delta food
> Fish figures prominently in the local diet, and one Delta speciality is the soup called *bortsch de peşte pescuit* (literally 'soup of freshly-caught fish'). Served with freshly baked bread, this is a delicious meal in itself, containing three or more different types of fish steamed and simmered in fresh chives together with other herbs, onions and garlic. Traditionally it is cooked in an iron cauldron over an open fire.

You can book boat trips and rowing dinghies from the *Hotel Lebăda*. If you have no personal contacts here and want to be sure of a measure of conventional hygiene, then this is probably your place. Close to the hotel on the south bank of the Danube is a long building which features a wide, sloping roof thatched in reed and walls plastered in snowy white distemper: called a *cherhana*, it is one of a few remaining fish-trading posts which date from the Turkish occupation. The roof and thick walls conceal a refrigeration room kept cold with blocks of ice. Between the *cherhana* and *Hotel Lebăda* stands an obelisk. Its French inscription commemorates the date in 1894 when King Carol I opened the new channel cutting.

While staying in Crişan you can visit another village, **Mila 23** (literally the 23rd Mile, because it lies 23 sea miles from the coast). Mila 23 lies on a side channel further west up Braţul Sulina. Life here is even more rural than in Crişan. Cross the Danube in a timber dugout or hire a boat from the *Lebăda Hotel*. A small, abandoned Orthodox church is slowly collapsing beside a pathway leading away from the river. It was modelled on Russian churches and has a wide, octagonal dome. Only the altar has been protected, but the exposed timber framework of this little church has an extraordinary beauty. Houses in Mila 23 have reed thatch roofs, and some of their fences are made of the same material painstakingly built into neat, thick walls. Floral and 'tree of life' motifs decorate green or blue gable ends which face the street in the traditional way; some households have home-made saunas.

You can walk from Crişan to the end of the channel at **Sulina**, but it is quicker to go by boat. Lying only 3.5m above sea level, Sulina still has the wooden, clapboard houses of the type that used to grace Tulcea, but today they are swamped by factories. Historians have traced the history of Sulina to 950 AD and Constantine Porphyrogenitus mentions it as Solina. Since then the little port's fortunes have risen and fallen dramatically. Its most recent heyday came after the Crimean War, when the English engineer Charles Hartley extended the port and dykes. English and French traders settled here in large numbers, and until the outbreak of the First World War, Sulina was a thriving freeport. There are some handsome 19C buildings in the town centre, including the former Danube Commission's headquarters and the 1802 lighthouse. But the remarkable thing about Sulina is its cemeteries. A legacy of the international effort that went into developing Sulina as a port, there are burial grounds for Orthodox and Catholics, Protestants and Anglicans. The town has one hotel, the *Sulina*, ☎ 040 543017. Ferry services connect Sulina to Odessa, Sevastopol and Constanţa.

The Chilia Channel

The northernmost branch of the Danube, Braţul Chilia is the longest of the three at 117km; it is also the fastest running, taking well over half the water run off from the parent river. This can make navigation difficult but also more exciting. It is the deepest of the three arms, with recorded depths of up to 36m. The channel gets its name from Kilija, a town on the northern, Ukrainian, bank, about halfway along its length. Kilija used to be part of Bessarabia, one of Moldavia's medieval provinces; Chilia Veche, on the southern shore, is its Romanian opposite number. Breaking up into side channels and winding its way past islets of varying sizes, the stream merges with the sea in the Ukrainian flood plains and the eyots of Kuban and Limba (the border with Ukraine turns south of the river a few kilometres before it reaches the sea).

Periprava was notorious for a prison in which the communists treated political prisoners with horrifying brutality. Here Braţul Chilia touches the northernmost tip of an ancient landscape that originates in pre-Delta times. In the middle of this triangular piece of land is **Grindul Letea**, one of the most interesting nature reserves in the Delta. Together with the reserve at Caraorman, which lies just to the north of the eastern end of Braţul Sfântu Gheorghe, oak and liana forests flourish here amid sand dunes. A *grind* is a rectangular strip of land that was the Delta's equivalent of a field; it was the basic agricultural division, without fences or physical borders, similar to strip farming in medieval England. Both conservation areas harbour many animal and plant species including the only poisonous snake in the Delta (*Vipera renardi*). You can also reach Letea forest from Sulina; the tracks go through the villages of Letea and C. A. Rosetti. You will need official permission to visit the Letea Reserve on your own but the tourist agencies in Tulcea should be able to arrange group tours (see pp 355–356).

The Sfântu Gheorghe Channel

This is the prettiest and most tortuous of the Danube's three arms. Historians argue that it is the oldest, too, because the channel is mentioned by Strabo, who called it Hieron Stoma (the Holy Mouth). It also appears on Ptolemy's atlas of the ancient world. A Romanian tourist magazine recommends spending the six-hour journey from Tulcea to Sf Gheorghe 'in a revery in which the water and the sky are blending with the willow forests and the birds'. It should make a picturesque cruise.

From Tulcea, Brațul Sf Gheorghe takes you past several old settlements which are also accessible by road. First, 7km east of Tulcea on the south bank, comes **Nufaru**, where the Romans built a citadel called Talamorium. Between the 10C and 14C this became the castle of Perislava. The road south from Nufaru reaches **Victoria**, a village set back from the channel where archaeologists have found traces of a prehistoric settlement.

A further 20km from Nufaru along the Channel to the west of Mahmudia, which has the *Plaur* inn and a name adapted from Turkish, a 4C BC Getic fortress was discovered on the Beștepe hills. Near Mahmudia stood the fortress of **Salsovia** where Constantine had the pagan Emperor Licinius killed in 325. Licinius was one of Constantine's rivals. Appointed Emperor Augustus of the Western Empire in 308, he became ruler of Illyria. With Constantine's help he gained control of the Eastern Empire in 313. But Licinius soon quarrelled with Constantine and lost his all his European lands except Thrace. He started persecuting the Christians, and in 324 Constantine defeated Licinius's troops at Adrianople and Chrysopolis. In the confusing political climate of the day, contemporaries saw the conflict as nothing less than a crusade against the pagans. Constantine banished Licinius and ordered his execution when Licinius tried to regain control.

A further 3km along the road to the southeast, at **Murighiol** you can see traces of a Romano-Byzantine fortress dating from the 4C–6C AD. Known in the communist period as Independența, it now has the *Pelican* hotel and a camping site with cabins. Beside Murighiol is Lacul Săraturii, now a bird sanctuary. The channel skirts Murighiol in one of its spectacular meanders, flows past the *cherhana* at Dunavăț and Ivancea, then splinters into three more arms at Sfântu Gheorghe. Travelling here on an overcrowded ferry just after the 1989 revolution, the American journalist Robert Kaplan found the town and its surroundings unremittingly bleak. **Sf Gheorghe** is still little-known as a tourist destination, but much of its attraction lies in its isolation; a fishing village-cum-port with a lighthouse but no hotels, it perches on the coast amid huge sand dunes of wild and spectacular beauty.

NORTH AND NORTHWEST DOBROGEA

From Galați the road to the southeast heads towards Garvăn; shortly before reaching it you come close to the site of a Getic citadel known as **Dinogeția**. Ptolemy marked the fortress on his atlas; it was destroyed in 375 AD, after which Byzantine emperors Anastasius (r. 491–518) and Justinian (r. 527–65) rebuilt the citadel. The Slavs demolished Dinogeţia in the 6C, and in the 10C it became a link in the chain of garrison fortresses protecting Paradunavon province.

The remains of an unusual and lovely **church** were found here. A modest chapel standing in the middle of a feudal citadel, it was rediscovered in 1950. It stands over the remnants of older buildings from the Romano-Byzantine period, and was probably used by the Byzantine garrison stationed here. The surviving walls are between 30–80cm tall, almost square, forming a Greek cross with short arms, and a semicircular apse with a polygonal exterior profile. Some of the building material was taken from the ruins it replaced: you can see a Roman socle and a row of neat Roman brickwork. In the apse a characteristic Byzantine pattern, one row of stones alternating with three of bricks, gives a clue to its early date: this particular element must have been here between the 4C–6C.

Fragments of plaster found in the debris, on the west walls and in the northwest niche give more insights into what the church was like when it was intact. Floral and geometric motifs survive in faded red, dark blue and yellow tempera colours. Among them are crosses within circles, similar to the oldest known art forms in medieval Romania. If these fragments are anything to go by, the whole church must have been glorious.

Răzvan Theodorescu gives a date for the entire building of no earlier than the second half of the 11C and no later than the mid-12C, during the Byzantine conquest of the Balkans. Like some paleo-Christian churches and antique tombs found in Asia Minor, it had an entrance on the north side. A small, square tower has survived as well.

During the 11C and 12C, Dinogetia had a quasi-urban community that benefited from the money, goods, art and culture that poured in from the nearby trade routes. The remains of jewellers' workshops have been found among the excavations.

Close to the town of Garvăn is a late-19C **monument** which was raised to commemorate Romanians who gave their lives during the 1877 War of Independence when Dobrogea was reunited with Romanian lands.

Follow the DN22 to the south from Garvăn, and in c 12km you reach **Măcin**. Because of its strategic position on important routes to and from Dobrogea, the town has a rich history. This is illustrated best by the ruins of the walled Geto-Dacian city of Arrubium to the northwest. This name has Celtic origins, but although Celts invaded Dobrogea in the early 3C BC, there is no evidence that they settled here. Instead, archaeologists have found Getic coins and pottery from that time. Traces of the Roman auxiliaries who fortified Arrubium during the reigns of Vespasian and Trajan have also emerged; after this, in the 2C AD, the camp was attacked by the Goths. Between the 5C, when the citadel was reconstructed, and the 10C, when Romanians moved here, Arrubium's story has been lost. During the medieval period, the town of Măcin developed to one side of the original citadel and played a major role in Dobrogea's economic life. There is a hotel, the *Turist* (✫), and a campsite here, and if you take the road west to Brăila, after 13km there is another *han* (inn) at the riverside village of Smârdan, where you can see another **monument** honouring Romanians who fought in the 1877 War of Independence.

From Garvăn, the DN22 rolls east 28km to **Isaccea** on the way to Tulcea. This town sits on the south bank of the Danube at a place where the Persian king

Darius is supposed to have crossed the river in 514 BC. Isaccea was known in antiquity as Noviodunum and, like Arrubium, its name has Celtic origins. The Romans were here too and used the town as a base for their fleet, Classis Flavia Moesica, from the 1C BC. Fragments of buildings, sculptures and funerary carvings show that Roman Noviodunum flourished. From the 4C–7C the Emperor Justinian lavished attention on the town and established a bishopric here.

Archaeologists have identified hundreds of coins and seals from Noviodunum; dating from the 7C–10C, they show how important the town was in the Byzantine period. The Archaeological Museum in Tulcea holds even more coins found in Isaccea from the 10C–12C, when Byzantine emperors ordered a reorganisation of Dobrogea and strengthened the town's walls. The 14C geographer Abulfeda recorded that Isakgi (from which Isaccea gets its name) belonged to Alualak, the country of the Vlachs (or Wallachians) ruled by Basarab I. In 1484 the Ottoman Turks conquered Dobrogea, and they too recognised Isaccea's strategic importance. Sultans frequently crossed the Danube here on their way north to fight the Christians. One of them was Osman II, who came to Isaccea in 1620 while leading an expeditionary force to Poland. He ordered new fortifications to replace the antique citadel walls, but they were destroyed in the 18C.

One of Romania's best vineyards is located at **Niculiţel**. To reach the village, continue east on the DN22 from Isaccea for 8km, then turn right (south) for 2km. Wine tastings are available, but the village also has the ruins of a late 4C/early 5C Byzantine **basilica**. It was discovered in the 1970s. The church has a trefoil plan, and in the apse was a martyirium that mentions the names of four Christian martyrs who died during the reign of Diocletian (r. 303–304) or Licinius (r. 319–20).

There are two other interesting **churches** here. One is an 11C–12C Byzantine building dedicated to Sf Anastasie; this is contemporary with the church at Dinogetia-Garvăn, and the site is still clearly related to the monastic tradition. This church is modelled on a simple trefoil plan and is not very sturdy; the northern apse is gone. The other is a 13C church with a Greek cross plan and a tower over the nave.

Turning off the main road in the village and driving northwest brings you to the monastery of **Cocoş**. This too has its origins between the 4C and the 6C (the early Christian period), and the monastery probably had links with the basilica in Niculiţel. Byzantine remains from the 12C and the 14C have been found nearby, and in the late 17C the site functioned as an Anchorite hermitage, but this was either abandoned or destroyed in the Russo-Turkish wars of the late 18C and early 19C.

The present monastery was founded in the early 19C by a shepherd called Poenaru and some of his friends. Poenaru used to bring his flocks to winter in Dobrogea after their summer grazing in the high pastures of the Carpathians, a practice called transhumance, which in Romania can be traced back to the 14C. A verandah and balcony adorn Cocoş's attractive western pavilion. Other parts of the monastery were designed by architect Toma Dobrescu and reached completion in 1914. The frescoes in the church are by an Italian artist, while a local painter called Cardaş decorated the eastern part of the chapel. There is a museum of religious art here, open Tues–Sun 10.00–18.00.

North of Niculiţel, beside a track that skirts the marshes, lies **Mânăstirea Saun**. Further east towards Tulcea, to the south of the DN22 in the village of Teliţa is a **museum** housing archaeological finds made nearby, open Tues–Sun 10.00–18.00. A little further south this minor road passes close to **Celic-Dere monastery**, a working convent founded in the 19C. Its Orthodox church stands on top of a hill surrounded by countryside as rolling and meadows as lush as any in Ireland; an impression enhanced by the presence of soft-eyed donkeys; you will see them practically everywhere in northern Dobrogea, where farmers and small holders often cannot afford horses, let alone tractors. Dobrescu designed this monastery too, creating a complex of buildings that represent various different aspects of traditional Romanian architecture. There is a museum of religious and decorative art and rare books here; it is officially open Tues–Sun 10.00–18.00, but do not be surprised if you cannot get in during those times.

In a field below the monastery church stands one of Dobrogea's few remaining **windmills**. A handsome relic of a bygone age, it is now maintained by the Village Museum in Bucharest. Further east, beyond Frecăţei the country road joins the E87; turn north here, and brings you to Tulcea in c 14km.

FROM TULCEA TO CONSTANŢA

The E87 south of Tulcea passes through **Mihai Kogălniceanu**, named after the liberal statesman who played a leading role in the 1848 revolution. Kogălniceanu (1817–91) was an enlightened liberal who, among many fine political actions, spoke out against Romany slavery. His statue stands in the middle of Piaţa Kogălniceanu in downtown Bucharest. (Confusingly, there is another village with this name near Constanţa.) A left turn along a track at the north end of Mihai Kogălniceanu brings you in c 13km to **Agighiol**, where traces of an important Iron Age burial have been found. The discoveries here include fine silver armour decorated with hunting scenes, pieces of bridles, cups and some imported Greek red figure pottery that dates the grave to c 350 BC. Many of these exceptional finds are held by the National Museum of History, Bucharest.

You can drive the 37km from Agighiol east through the villages of Iazurile, Colina, Sarinasuf and Plopul to Murighiol, which stands on the edge of the Sf Gheorghe channel.

Babadag is the next town, 16km on the route south from Mihai Kogălniceanu: run-down but charming, it is a historic place where a beautiful early 17C mosque still stands. Traces of Thracian Hallstatt culture (11C–13C BC) have been found here.

History

One legend says that Babadag takes its name from the leader of a group of Seljuk Turks, called Baba Saltuq Dede, who was given land here by Byzantine Emperor Michael VIII Paleologus; another says its name means 'Turkish mountain' (*Baba* means Turkish and *dag* is a mountain). Arab traveller Ibn Battuta mentioned Babadag in 1333. He noted that 'Baba Saltuq... was an ecstatic mystic, though stories are told about him which are condemned by law'. Ibn Battuta also says that Babadag was the last town in the area to be ruled by Tartars. Judging by the fact that a huge Tartar-Byzantine treasure was found on Uzumbair hill, c 15km to the north, he could well have been right. In 1484 Dobrogea became part of the Ottoman Empire and Babadag flourished as a military and commercial centre. Two hundred years later, the Pasha of Silistra moved his residence to the town, which became the Turkish army's regional headquarters. Babadag's decline began as a result of devastation caused by the Russo-Turkish war of 1771.

Ali-Gazi-Pasga's mosque

Ali-Gazi-Pasha's mosque stands in the town centre, its lovely proportions making up for a gutted interior and general air of neglect. This is the oldest Muslim monument in Romania, with a minaret that rises to 23m. Nearby are the **tombs** of Ali-Gazi-Pasha and Baba Saltuq Dede, typically Turkish in style and with attractive circular flower motifs carved in relief. Next to the mosque stands Casa Panaghia, which was originally built as a prayer house. You can see a lingering Turkish influence in the colourful *shalwar* (baggy trousers) still worn by Muslim women here. There are a *han* (inn), a petrol station and a garage in Babadag, as well as a bus station and a small hotel.

About 5km to the north of Babadag, where the road crosses the tip of a small lake, archaeologists have found a **Roman fortress** from c 370 AD. It was probably built during the reign of the Emperor Valens, but Huns destroyed it in the mid-5C. A few architectural remains are visible at the site. And at the foot of **Denis Tepe** hill, a little north of Babadag, is a bay where the Argonauts are supposed to have dropped anchor on their way back from Colchis.

Ask for directions in Babadag for the rough road c 7km east to **Enisala**. There are few signposts in the town and it is hard to find. Enisala is a small village containing a traditional peasant house that is now a museum. The house dates from the early 20C; you can find it in the village centre on the main through road. Restored in 1971, the household buildings comprise a granary and a stable. Its dwelling quarters are decorated attractively with woollen, cotton and silk hangings. Open Tues–Sun 10.00–18.00.

Enisala **citadel** crowns a rocky hill c 5km from the village which lies to the southwest. The ruins command a superb view of the encircling marshes the plains. They stand at the end of a narrow track—do not take your car here unless you're sure of being able to turn it: there is no layby. On one side of the hill, reedbeds stretch away to the shores of Lake Razim and on the other are the flatlands of the Babadag Plateau. The design of the gateway into the citadel suggests that it was founded between the late 13C and the early 14C. The architecture is similar to the style introduced by Genoese merchants who were active here at the time. The Wallachian prince Mircea cel Bătrân installed a garrison at Enisala at the end of the 14C. He defended Dobrogea's borders until 1417, when Ottomans captured Enisala and part of the territory around it. Items have been found here dating from the 13C–16C; among them are weapons, glazed pottery, tools and coins of Byzantine, Romanian, Serbian and Tartar origins. At the bottom of the hill archaeologists uncovered the remains of a small, 4C Roman camp that protected the ancient bridge over Lacul Babadag. Nearby are two huge **necropolises**, one Getic dating from the 4C BC, and the other 15C Romanian.

Near Enisala is a **wetland habitat** that attracts a wonderful variety of waterbirds. Among them are terns and waders, collared pratincoles and white and Dalmatian pelicans. Histria, too, is close to a bird reserve where you can see—or hear—stone curlews, calandra larks, rollers and shrikes. To the south, **Hagieni forest** is a place where Levant sparrowhawks and long-legged buzzards make their summer homes.

The road from Enisala continues southeast and then south, reaching the quiet resort of **Jurilovca** in 17km. In its more recent history, the town was known as a place where communist party bosses would bring their secretaries for discreet weekends. Jurilovca stands close to the ruins of Argamum, a walled city built by Greeks in the 6C BC. Contemporary with Histria, the first important Greek city in Dobrogea, it was conquered by Romans in the 1C BC. Excavations began in 1926, revealing basilicas, secular buildings and citadel walls. There is a small hotel here called *Albatros* (✫).

Return west to the E87 via the village of Ceamurlia de Jos. As you travel south the countryside changes, becoming a surreal mix of dense woodland and completely treeless steppe. A few kilometres north of Mihai Viteazu village, a track heads east for Sinoie and then south, passing Istria, the impressive ruins of ancient **Histria**, 'the Romanian Pompeii'. Named after the river Istros (the Greek name for the Danube), beside which it once stood, this 7C Greek citadel flourished for 1200 years. For the Greeks it was Dobrogea's most important port and political centre until the river and the sea swept so much mud and silt into its harbour that it became completely unnavigable. Istros may have Thraco-Getic origins, but the name also occurs in ancient Egyptian legends as a river encountered by the god Osiris. It was the Romans who gave the Danube its present name, which comes from a Celtic word meaning 'bringer of rivers'. The Romanian historian Vasile Pârvan identified Histria's ruins in 1914. Today you can see walls between 3–8m high, 3C Roman towers and bastions, temples to Aphrodite and Zeus, baths and a Roman forum. There is also a **museum** here, open Tues–Sun 09.00–20.00 in summer, and 09.00–17.00 in winter.

Back on the E87, Constanța lies 53km south of Mihai Viteazu, although you can reach the city by following country roads through Săcele, Corbu, the industrial enclave of Navodari and Mamaia-Sat.

Mamaia

Mamaia resort and beach lie immediately to the south of this village, an extension of Constanţa proper. Legend has it that Mamaia got its name from the piteous cries of a young girl yelling for her mother while she was being abducted by a Turk. The beach here is wide and sandy; at its northern end, there is a camping site that has bungalows and cabins. During the summer, the campsite's bathhouses attract tiny emerald-green frogs. Only a couple of centimetres long, they cling to waterpipes and ledges with their long prehensile toes.

Practical information

☎ code
041

Tourist information
Litoral in the *Hotel Bucureşti*, ☎ 831152; fax 831276; *Talaz Turism* in the *Hotel Caraiman*, ☎/fax 831300.

Getting around
By car Mamaia has two car-hire firms: *Rent Auto Service* on B-dul Mamaia, ☎ 831696, and *Touring ACR*, ☎ 831171.

Where to stay
Mamaia has over 50 modern hotels. They include the *Albatros* (✩✩✩), ☎ 831381; fax 831346; *Majestic* (✩✩✩), ☎ 831005; fax 831981; *Ambasador* (✩✩✩), ☎ 831185; *Hotel Bucureşti* (✩✩✩), ☎ 831360; fax 831169; *Hotel Orfeu* (✩✩✩), ☎ 831048; *Hotel Bicaz* (✩✩), ☎ 831535; *Comandor* (✩✩), ☎/fax 831138; *Hotel Dacia Nord* (✩✩), ☎ 831669. All these hotels stand in line beside the sea; you have to cruise along the coast road looking for the one you want. Most of them have restaurants.

Motoring to Constanţa from the northwest: Giurgeni and the E60
The dual carriageway from Bucharest to Cernavodă, and the old DN3A which runs parallel to it for two-thirds of the way, are the most direct routes to Constanţa by road. But there is an interesting alternative: the DN2. This leaves Bucharest further to the north and crosses the Danube over a striking modern bridge at Giurgeni. You have to pay a nominal tariff at the bridge, but coming this way allows you to explore some places that are not generally visited by tourists.

One of these is **Muzeul de Artă 'Dinu şi Sevasta Vintilă'**, a private art gallery in the village of Topalu, which stands beside the Danube's eastern bank, c 37km southeast of Giurgeni. It is definitely worth the half-hour detour south from the E60/DN2A via Hârşova. The Vintilă collection comprises over 200 pieces, and highlights some of the most important phases in Romanian art, from the Impressionist period until the mid-20C. Artists represented include the heavyweights of Romanian avant-garde art: Andreescu, Bancilă, Grigorescu, Ştefan Luchian, Gheorghe Petraşcu and Nicolae Tonitza. There are sculptures by Paciunea and Medrea, and prints by Theodor Aman, Tonitza, Corneliu Baba and Nicolae Dărăscu. Open Tues–Sun 09.00–17.00.

From Hârşova the DN22A heads northeast for Tulcea; the road is terrible, but the landscape becomes more appealing as you approach the city.

> **The Black Sea**
> Black Sea coastal resorts once attracted millions of visitors every year, but not any more. Thanks to pollution from raw sewage, dead fish and rotting algae, beaches along the littoral are often closed. While some dumping of waste has been stopped, the polluted waters have caused outbreaks of cholera in towns along the coastline. Meanwhile fields of vital *Phyllophora algae*, which once carpeted the sea's northwest shelf, have been destroyed, depriving many fish of their main source of food and shelter. Consequently, many fishermen have lost their livelihoods as well. A branch of the UN has tried to coordinate a salvage operation among national environmental conservation groups, but the Black Sea remains an unsalubrious place to bathe.

South from Topalu, a country road follows the Danube south as far as Cernavodă, 25km away. On the way, after c 20km, this road passes the ruins of **Capidava**, the most important Dacian citadel yet excavated outside Sarmizegetusa (see Transylvania). A rectangular site contains stone walls and foundations, outlining the character of the citadel and the Roman camp that was built over it. A museum is attached, open Tues–Sun 09.00–17.00.

The E60 runs into Constanţa past the city's airport. This lies to the west of another of the villages named Mihai Kogălniceanu. There is a Romany quarter here which was attacked when resentment against Gypsies boiled over in 1992.

FROM CERNAVODĂ TO CONSTANŢA

Cernavodă is not a pretty place, but it has a distinguished past. For a start, it stands on the site of a cemetery containing c 400 graves belonging to a Neolithic culture dating from 5000–4000 years BC. One of the graves yielded two astonishing **figurines**. The most remarkable was the 'Hamangia Thinker', a tiny, angular model of a naked man, less than 20mm high, who sits on a low stool with his chin in his hands. His face is recognisably human, and he is only presumed to be male because he does not have any sexual organs. His counterpart is a female with overlarge breasts who lies with one leg outstretched and the other knee bent upwards with her arms around it. She too has identifiable features. Both figures are in the National Museum of History in Bucharest (see p 139).

Too few other statuettes have been found to tell if they were made by an especially sensitive artist or were part of an often-repeated repertoire. Most of the known statuettes found at Hamangia have small heads on long necks and exaggerated sexual organs. They are unusual for Balkan art of the period. Hamangia gets its name from an archaeological site in northern Dobrogea. No-one knows exactly what kind of community it was, but the polished black pots that accompanied burials are quite different from the ceramics made for everyday use. Hamangia graves also contained beads of stone and oyster shell.

An ancient **Greek citadel** named Axiopolis was founded here. This fortress was later commandeered by ancient Romans and Byzantines lived here as well.

Romania's first railway linked Cernavodă to Constanţa. It was built by English engineers in the late 19C. During the 1930s, a plan was mooted to link

Bucharest to the sea by **canal**. While this project has not yet been realised, work on a shorter cut, from the Danube at Cernavodă to the Black Sea, had begun a century earlier but was abandoned. Resumed in 1949, it became notorious as *canalul morții* (the canal of death), where 100,000 labourers died. The following year, the communist government legalised forced labour and sent political prisoners to work on the canal without trial. Typically these men belonged to the hated 'bourgeois élite'; they were landowners, intellectuals and priests, but smallholders were also sent to work there. Valued only for their muscle power, these men were forced to hack through the 80m tall Canara Hills. Many died in accidents or through sickness and exhaustion. By 1953 the canal authorities realised that their chosen route to Navodări, north of Constanța, was impracticable, so they halted the project once more. Cutting began again in 1973, this time towards Agigea, south of Constanța. The channel was open for traffic by 1984, having reduced the distance between Cernavodă and the sea from 400 km to 60km. Ceaușescu dubbed the project the Blue 'Magistrală'.

Cernavodă is also the site of Romania's first **nuclear power station**. Ceaușescu had it built on a shoestring budget, rendering four-fifths of the reactor useless. However, in 1996 plans to reopen the power station came to fruition with the commissioning of a new 700 MW reactor. It is expected to produce 900 million Kwh per year.

The village of **Saligny**, 8km to the southeast, is named after engineer Anghel Saligny (1854–1925), who in c 1887 designed the world's first prefabricated concrete silos for the cities of Brăila and Galați. He also masterminded the iron Podul Cernavodă (the Cernavodă Bridge) over the Danube, which was the longest in Europe when it opened in 1895.

At Medgidia, 17km further east, factories have swamped the 19C town. It was named after Sultan Abdul Mejid and founded in c. 1840. A mosque and some Islamic-style buildings are virtually all that is left of its oriental origins. From here the road drops into the coastal plain, and in c 30km it reaches **Basarabi**. Turn right in the centre of the village, follow the DN3 across the canal bridge, and immediately to your left are a group of early-Christian **rock churches**. Little more than tiny caves hollowed out of the limestone and chalk, they are concealed behind an unprepossessing entrance and when I last saw them, they were still covered in tarpaulins. Consisting of churches, chapels, tomb chambers and galleries, this complex dates from the late 10C and was probably Romania's first monastery. The churches follow the basic plan of a Byzantine shrine, containing a naos framed by rough-hewn arches and a sanctuary.

Archaeologists began studying the churches at Basarabi in 1957. Since then they have deciphered ancient **inscriptions** and drawings on the walls of apse and naos, and in the cells. Although the marks are very faint and extremely crude in design, they show that the artists who made them were in touch with far-ranging cultures. The words include Greek and palaeo-Slavonic terms such as kirica, and words in Cyrillic, Runic and Glagolithic characters. The drawings are a mixture of the sacred and the profane: they include anthropomorphic figures, Maltese crosses like the ones found in Cappadocia, fishes, stars and dragons which could have a Celtic, Scythian or Scandinavian influence. There are images of the Virgin and Child, saints and bishops and a scene that looks very like the

Birth of Jesus. Other scratches on the walls show hunters, horses, birds and plants, and symbols such as trees of life and labyrinths. You can only see these images if you look very carefully with a torch. Some of the inscriptions are much shallower than others, showing that they were made in at least two distinct phases. Traces have been found of a brick-red pigment that was used to draw the images. Two of the written inscriptions show the name of a priest who served at Basarabi in 1042.

When these rock churches were first in use, priests around the edges of Byzantium were withdrawing from lay society en masse. Concealed shrines of a similar type and period have been found in the Crimea, Georgia and southern Italy. Art historian Răzvan Theodorescu believes that the Basarabi monks may have been Pecheneg nomads who had recently converted to Christianity. He speculates that the images they put on their walls show that they were in touch with Vikings. In the 10C, Viking ships still travelled along the rivers between the Baltic, Russia and the Black Sea. Pechenegs traded on the Dniepr River in the second half of the 10C, and merchants and soldiers came to Byzantium (or Micklegarth as the Vikings called it) during this period, sometimes using the Siret River which flows through Moldavia to get into Dobrogea.

One of the chambers in the cave complex has no floor. It was probably designed as a trap to catch intruders. In another room is a small stone coffin sarcophagus. The cave churches are managed by the History and Archaeology Museum in Constanța.

For Constanța, return to the village centre and turn right. Some 5km further east, the DN3 reaches **Valu lui Traian**, Trajan's valley. In May the village celebrates the Kures folk festival, in which actors dressed as Tatars re-enact ancient battles.

Constanța

The city is the capital of Constanța *judeţ* (county), southeastern Romania, on the Black Sea. Situated about 200km east of Bucharest, it is the country's principal seaport. Since 1960 Constanța has administered the huge coastal conurbation which stretches from Navodari to Mangalia, including the largest Black Sea resort, Mamaia, 8km to the north. Constanța has a population of c 400,000. 75 per cent of the county's inhabitants live in towns and cities, and it is one of the most densely populated in the whole of Romania. This contrasts strikingly with Tulcea county to the north, which has only 230,000 people.

History

Constanța's origins go back to the 6C BC. It was then that Greeks from Miletos on the west coast of Turkey arrived here and founded the port of Tomis (sometimes called Tomi). Today, identical apartment blocks line the long, straight boulevards into Constanța, but the remnants of its old centre contain a handful of buildings that by contrast seem outrageously ornate. At first Tomis was built as an outpost of the ancient town of Histria (see p 367). But after Histria's seaway silted up, Tomis became the foremost Greek city in Dobrogea. During the 1C AD, the Romans conquered the town and brought it within their empire. They renamed it Pontus Sinister and made it capital of the province of Scythia. Archaeologists have located most of the ancient city's walls under the sea, but you can see some of its Roman and Byzantine remains as you walk around the old quarter.

Between the 4C and the 5C there was an Orthodox bishopric here that was answerable to the Patriarchate of Constantinople. In the 6C, Byzantines changed the city's name to Constantiana in memory of Constantine the Great, the Roman emperor who converted to Christianity and founded the eastern Roman church. Invaders came in waves, the most destructive being the Avars in the 7C. They spelt decline for Constanța, and by the 9C it was little more than a fishing village. But in the 12C, after regaining Constantinople from the Latin crusaders, the eastern Byzantine emperors granted trading concessions to Genoese merchant venturers, allowing them to revitalise the Black Sea ports, including Constanța.

Ottoman Turks conquered Dobrogea in the early 15C and turned Constanța into Küstendje. From this period Constanța went gradually downhill. It suffered very badly during the Russo-Turkish war of 1877. Its renaissance came in the late 19C, when King Carol I made it popular as a tourist resort. Like any high-spirited sea port Constanța has its raffish side, and it was here that the future mistress and wife of Carol II, Elena 'Magda' Lupescu kept house with a disreputable sea captain.

Excavations carried out in the 1950s and 1960s revealed a fantastic archaeological record. While 19C Eclectic buildings were demolished to make way for 'restructuring', the foundations of ancient Greek, Roman and early Christian buildings were found. They included churches and temples, houses, street networks, cemeteries, workshops and warehouses. Many of these extraordinary discoveries, comprising intact columns and finely carved architraves, beautiful statues and silverware, are on show in the Archaeology and History Museum (see below). Digs carried out during the 1960s also revealed vestiges of the port dating from the 4C AD.

Although it caters for thousands of tourists, Constanța is primarily a city of heavy industry. Next to the expanding container port, there are oil, LPG and cereal terminals, and the shipyards build oil tankers, wrack carriers and ore carriers. There are firms specialising in **oil and gas extraction**, and others which produce chemicals, plastics and paper. The company Petromar has seven offshore rigs, extracting 700,000 tons of crude oil and 400 million mc of gas a year from the Black Sea shelf. Electric and thermal energy is turned out by the power stations at Constanța, Ovidiu and Navodari. Navodari also manufactures phosphatic and sulphuric acid fertilisers.

In spite of recent discoveries of natural gas, Romania is not producing enough gas for its own needs. At the moment Romania imports half its gas from the Russian federation. The government is placing its hopes on the LPG terminal which the privately owned Black Sea LPG has built in Constanța. The terminal currently holds 100,000 tonnes. Plans to extend its capacity to 600,000 tonnes by 2002 should be enough to keep Romania supplied without relying on the Russian federation. Another source of income should be the proposed **pipeline** that Constanța's oil terminal wants to build from the Black Sea to Trieste. Petromar, due to be privatised shortly, has signed a contract with Kazakhstan to transport and refine oil from the Caspian Sea. If Romania can capitalise on this opening and succeeds in building the pipeline across Europe, the future of its oil industryif not its environment looks bright.

Through the Danube-Black Sea Canal, industrial barges can travel from the Black Sea to Ostrov-Cernavodă and Hârşova and through the Danube-Main-Rhine waterways to the North Sea.

Practical information

☎ **code**

041

Tourist information

There are at about 15 tourist agencies in Constanţa. These include *Danubius*, which has branches at B-dul Ferdinand 36 and Piaţa Ovidiu 11, ☎ 615836; fax 618010. *Danubius* is one of the largest agencies in the city. It can organise individual and group tours around the whole country and find accommodation in private houses. Alternatives include *Angels Turism* at B-dul Ferdinand 7, ☎/fax 672827; *BTT*, B-dul Tomis 20–26, ☎ 615262; fax 616524; *Christian Travel*, St Iorga 34, ☎ 639705; *Dianthus*, Str Caiuţi 18, ☎/fax 696551; *Filiala Birta Tours*, B-dul 1 Decembrie 1918 nr. 12, ☎/fax 691949; *Nouvelles Frontières-Sipaturism*, Str Răscoalei 9, ☎ 660468; fax 664403; *Liotsikas Travel*, B-dul Ferdinand 53, ☎ 614783; *Marshall*, Str Brătescu 26, ☎/fax 665696; *Scorpion Turism*, B-dul Ferdinand 51C, ☎/fax 614233; *Sind România*, B-dul Alexandru Lăpuşneanu 1, ☎/fax 632208; *Sarmis*, B-dul Tomis 235, ☎ 655797; fax 640674.

Getting around

By train There is an excellent rail link between Bucharest and Constanţa, and if you are looking for a seaside break you may prefer to take the train instead of driving over seemingly endless miles of plain and steppe. The train station is in the southwest of the city, close to the southwest end of B-dul Republicii.

By bus The southern bus station (*autogara sud*, which serves places to the south of Constanţa, Varna and Istanbul) is next to the train station, while the northern bus station (*autogara nord*, serving northern Dobrogea) stands near the corner of B-dul Tomis and Str Soveja. For booking train tickets in advance, the **CFR** office is at Aleea Vasile Canarache, open Mon–Fri 07.00–19.00, Sat 07.00–13.00.

By plane The nearest airport is 25km away, to the northwest of Constanţa at Mihai Kogălniceanu, and the Romanian airline, *TAROM*, based at Str Ştefan cel Mare 15, provides buses to and from the airport.

By car There are **petrol stations** on B-dul Aurel Vlaicu, B-dul Tomis and Str Brătianu, and at Str Eminescu 9, Str Stefan Mihăileanu 9 and Şos Mangaliei 96. The Constanţa branch of *ACR* is at Str Tomis 141. The office should be able to help with queries about **car repairs**, **car hire** and **taxi services**.

Where to stay

While the resorts to the north and south are well off for hotels, Constanţa itself has relatively few. These include *Intim* (✮✮✮), Str. Titulescu 9, where Romania's national poet, Eminescu, stayed in the 1880s, ☎ 617814; fax 615194; *Tineretului* (✮✮), B-dul Tomis 20–26, ☎ 613590; fax 611290; *Astoria* (✮✮) at Str Mircea cel Bătrân 102, ☎ 616064; fax 615194; and *Eurosantis* (✮✮) at B-dul Brătianu

24, ☎ 665693. The *Danubius* tourist agency (see above) may be able to find accommodation in private houses.

Eating out

Among Constanța's restaurants are *Au Coq Simpa* at Str Ştefan cel Mare 19; *Club Italia* at Str Bucureşti 15; *Pelican* at Str Sulmona 9; *Hotel Tineretului* at B-dul Tomis 20–26; *Tirbuşon* at Str Duca 21A; and *Club Royal* at Str Mircea cel Bătrân 5. *Casa Olt* in Sat de Vacanța specialises in Oltenian cooking, and the *Restaurantul Arabesc* at Str Atelierelor 21 in Middle Eastern cuisine. *Club Amadeus* at Str Ştefan cel Mare 86 and *Show Burgers* at Str Ştefan cel Mare 46 are fast-food restaurants.

Post office

The original general post office, housed in a building dating from 1838 that mixes Islamic and Romanian styles, is on B-dul Tomis.

Money

There are several **exchange houses**, including *Litoral* at Str Remus Opreanu 5–7, *Romania Exchange House* at B-dul Republicii 94, *Super Yldiz* at Str Petre Romulus 19, and *Tomitana* at Str Ştefan cel Mare 23, otherwise try one of the hotels.

Medical care

There is a **hospital** on B-dul Tomis.

There are at least five **pharmacies** in Constanța: *Eurosantis-Farmacris* at B-dul Lăpuşneanu 107; *Farmacia 6* at Str Ştefan cel Mare 23; *Farmacia 2* at B-dul Tomis 80; *Proxi-Farm* at B-dul Ferdinand 11; and *Santis* at B-dul Tomis 309.

Shopping

Constanța's main shopping streets include Str Ştefan cel Mare, Str Brătianu, Str Cuza Vodă and B-dul Tomis.

Entertainment

The city has a number of **theatres**: *Teatrul de Dramă şi Comedie* at B-dul Mircea cel Bătrân 97; *Teatrul de Balet* (ballet) at Str Răscoalei din 1907 nr. 5, ticket office Str Ştefan cel Mare 34; *Teatrul de Revistă Fantasio* (revue) at B-dul Ferdinand 11, and *Teatrul de Papuşi* (puppets) at Str Karatzali 16. The *Filarmonica Marea Neagră* is based at Str Mircea cel Bătrân 97, and the *Opera House* is in the same building. There are several **cinemas**, a **sports palace** on B-dul Tomis, and an Olympic-size **swimming pool** close to the northeast edge of Lacul Tăbăriei, not to mention *Parcul de distracţii* (the park of distractions), on the north side of town. The **planetarium and dolphinarium** that can be found to the north of the city near B-dul Mamaia are disappointing.

Walking around Constanța

Constanța is not well served by bookshops and if you need a map the best places to try are the tourist agencies, the hotels or even the museums. Apart from the museum complex, which includes the dolphinarium, planetarium and the small **Museul Mării** (Museum of Sea Life) beside B-dul Mamaia in the northern sector of the city (open Tues–Sun 09.00–20.00 in summer, and 09.00–17.00 in winter), most of Constanța's cultural attractions are clustered around the southeast sector, where a spit of land juts into the sea, adjoining the shipyards.

In 9 AD, the Emperor Augustus condemned the poet Ovid to exile in Tomis, probably as a punishment for writing erotic verses that implicated Augustus's daughter. Tomis was then considered quite literally the end of the world, and in his *Tristia* and *Pontica*, Ovid lamented the freezing winters, the barbarity and lack

CONSTANŢA • 375

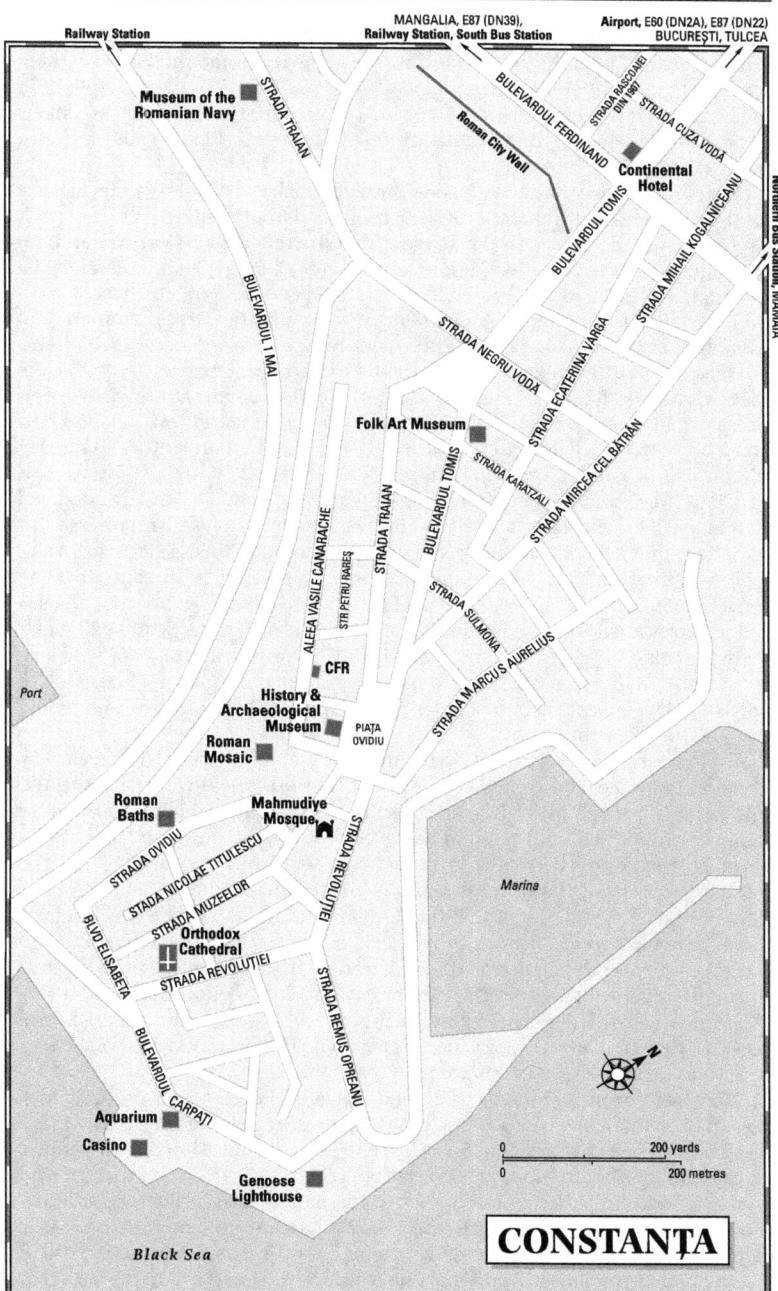

of wine that he encountered here. But reading between the lines of his sorrow, it is clear that he found the 'barbarians' warm and friendly and that actually there was plenty to drink. A **statue** of the poet stares soulfully down from its plinth in Piața Ovidiu. It was created in 1887 by the Italian sculptor, Ettore Ferrari, and is entirely imaginary. Right in the centre of the old town, Piața Ovidiu makes a good starting point for a tour.

Jason and the Argonauts are said to have disembarked at Tomis while looking for the Golden Fleece. Whether this is true or not, fascinating traces of the city's Greek origins can be seen in the **Muzeul de Istorie Națională și Arheologie** (Museum of National History and Archaeology) at Piața Ovidiu 12. This is a splendid, neo-Brâncovanesque building which opened in 1878. It has a collection of objects ranging from prehistory through the Greek, Roman and Byzantine periods to the present. But its ancient history section on the lower floors is the most engaging. Among the items on display here is a copy of the Glykon, a stone figure of a coiled serpent standing about 1m high. It has a sheep's muzzle (some experts say it is an antelope), human eyes, ears and hair and a lion's tail. The Glykon was unearthed in 1962 from under the old railway station. The original is Greek and has been dated to the 2C BC, when statues such as these were worshipped from Paphlagonia to Rome as incarnations of Aesculapius. Glykon means 'one who brings blessings by his own powers'. But there are many other enchanting statues in the museum, their delicate faces and tender expressions revealing a shy eroticism that might have comforted the unfortunate Ovid: there are the deities Fortuna and Pontos (or Pontus), the sea god who protected Tomis, a bust of Isis and a statue of Hecate. Scattered among them are coins, jewellery and pottery and alluring amphorae that once held aromatic wines and expensive, scented oils. The upper rooms are worth a look, if only to enjoy the architecture. Open Tues–Sun 09.00–20.00 in summer, and 09.00–17.00 in winter.

Head towards the waterfront by turning left and left again from the History Museum entrance, and you will come to the **Roman mosaic** and the **4C port**. The mosaic, covered by a glass and steel pavilion, is a partially reconstructed pavement decorated with a severe floral and geometric design in faded polychrome. It measures over 600 sq m and was created in the early 4C AD. The mosaic was probably three times as large as the restored fragment, and may once have been part of the Forum that the Romans built on top of the Greek Agora. Both are now concealed beneath Piața Ovidiu. Roman anchors, amphorae and statuettes surround the pavement, and if you go through the museum towards the seafront you will see the sealed arches of Roman **thermal baths** (also visible from Aleea Canarache), open Tues–Sun 09.00–20.00 in summer, and 09.00–17.00 in winter. Exit on the other side of the pavilion to see the arcades with their vaulted chambers that once flanked the port.

A few metres south of the mosaic stands **Casa cu Lei** (the House with Lions), named after the lions' heads that glower imperiously down from the building's façade. Just beyond this, on Str Muzeelor stands Ion Mincu's **Orthodox Cathedral**. This is an early work, erected between 1884–95 by an architect who famously went on to design many 'Neo-Romanian' houses in Bucharest, drawing on influences from Western Europe and Romanian vernacular architecture. At the other end of the street, at Str Muzeelor 26, is **Colecția 'Ion Jalea'**, worth visiting only if you like conventional public art, open Tues–Sun 09.00–20.00 in summer and 09.00–17.00 in winter.

A short walk east from here brings you down to the seafront. On your left stands the sparsely-stocked **Aquarium**, which contains species from the Black Sea, the Delta and the lakes, open Tues–Sun 09.00–16.00. Beside the Aquarium is an elegant promenade bordered by iron railings; from here you can return to Piaţa Ovidiu past the 1860 'Genoese' **lighthouse**, believed to stand on the site of a 14C lighthouse built by Genoese merchants. Opposite the Aquarium stands the magnificent Secessionist **Cazino**, now a restaurant and bar. King Carol I liked Constanţa and made the town fashionable as a health and tourist resort. With his encouragement, spas and tourist villages sprang up along along the coastline. The Cazino is as fanciful as a wedding cake. It was completed in 1909 for Carol's wife, Queen Elisabeta. Five years later, the Romanian and Russian royal families met here briefly in an attempt to forge a political alliance between the two countries. Queen Marie and King Ferdinand hoped that Prince Carol would fall in love with the Tsar's oldest daughter. Had it gone better, this meeting might have saved her from assassination.

A few seconds' walk south from Piaţa Ovidiu brings you to the unobtrusive entrance to the pretty **Mahmudiye mosque**, built in 1910 on the site of an older mosque. Its minaret soars 50m high and offers a wonderful, panoramic view of Constanţa. There is lovely stonework in the prayer hall. The carpet comes from the famous workshops at Hereke, Turkey, where it was made on the orders of Sultan Abdul Hamid. The Sultan gave it to the island of Ada Kaleh (see Wallachia), and it was rescued before the island and all its Ottoman buildings disappeared under the Danube following the damming of the Iron Gates in the 1960s. The Mahmudiye is a working mosque but is open to visitors Tues–Sun 09.00–18.00.

Walking northwest from Piaţa Ovidiu along B-dul Tomis brings you to **Muzeul de Artă Populară** (the Folk Art Museum) at B-dul Tomis 32. This has an excellent collection of traditional folk arts from all over Romania, notably carpets and embroisered clothes. The museum itself is a superbly proportioned Islamic-style building that was originally designed as a town hall. If you are bemused by the intricacies of Romanian national dress and have the time, this is the place to study it at your leisure. Here you can see the three main types of skirt which women from different regions wear for special occasions: the *catrânţă*, and *fotă*, the *vâlnic* and *zadie*. The *catrânţă* has two narrow, embroidered pieces, one hanging in front and the other behind; these are joined by a double belt called a *béte* and worn over a long shirt. The *fotă* is a wraparound worn on the hips and held together by the *béte*, while the *vâlnic* is a pleated skirt with a tight waist. There is an English-language guide to the museum, which is open Tues–Sun 09.00–20.00 in summer, and 09.00–17.00 in winter. Another **mosque**, Geamia Hunchiar (1869), stands opposite the Folk Art Museum.

A few blocks to the northeast of the Folk Art Museum towards the beach, at Str Mircea cel Bătrân 36, stands the **Church of the Transfiguration** (1865), which was built for the Greek community in Constanţa.

Retrace your steps along B-dul Tomis, turn right into B-dul Republicii and, skirting the southern edge of Victoria Park, walk into Str Traian for **Muzeul Marinei Române** (the Museum of the Romanian Navy) at no. 53. A curious collection, it understates the ignominious role played by Romania's navy in the Second World War, and looks back to a time before the nation existed, housing models of ancient Greek triremes. Photographs show mutineers from the battleship *Potemkin*, which moored in Constanța harbour during Russia's 1905 revolution. Open Tues–Sun 09.00–20.00 in summer and 09.00–17.00 in winter.

If you return to Victoria Park, you can see fragments of the Roman defense wall, columns and amphorae, and the Byzantine **Turnul Măcelarului** (Butchers' Tower) on its northern side, along B-dul Republicii. From here, cross B-dul Tomis for the **Muzeul de Artă** (the Art Museum), housed at no. 84, which houses the work of many important Romanian artists, starting with the Impressionists. Open Tues–Sun 09.00–20.00 in summer, and 09.00–17.00 in winter.

SOUTHERN DOBROGEA: CONSTANȚA TO MANGALIA

From Constanța to the Bulgarian border the E87 follows the coastline, sandwiching a clutch of resorts between the road and the sea. Known collectively, together with Mamaia, as **Litoralul** (the Littoral) and named after planets such as Jupiter, Neptune and Venus, these resorts were once the preserve of the rich and powerful. Some of them are more upmarket than others, especially Neptun and Olimp, which boast smart shopping precincts and sports centres. But from the air their box-like hotels and villas look identical. Even if you do not want to stay here, these self-contained mini-towns are worth visiting, if only because the boxes reveal some pleasant architectural surprises. In the early 1930s, G.M. Cantacuzino created two lovely, purist buildings in Eforie Nord. One was the beautiful **Villa Aviana**, which curves forwards to face the sea like an abstract bird in flight, and the other was the extraordinary ***Bellona Hotel***, whose outline resembles an ocean liner. Further down the coast in Aurora is a later group of hotels designed to resemble pyramids. Maps of the coastal resorts are available from tourist agencies in Constanța and in the resorts themselves.

While Littoral resorts cater for holidaymakers in summer, from October to May Eforie Nord, Neptun, Saturn, Mangalia and Mamaia function as **health spas**. Featuring the famous *nămol*, a black, medicinal mud that comes in this case from Lake Techirghiol, the treatments they offer are designed to alleviate a kaleidoscopic range of illnesses, including rheumatism and nervous and gynaecological disorders. Three of the spas date from the reign of Carol I: Carmen Sylva, founded in 1898 in honour of Queen Elisabeta; Mamaia, founded in 1906, and Eforie Nord, which opened in 1910. There are excellent rail and bus links from Constanța to and from these resorts; Eforie Nord and Sud (Carmen Sylva) have their own railway stations.

East of the E87 a side road leads to **Techirghiol** (18km from Constanța) and its eponymous lake which provides the mud and saline waters used in medical treatments. Techirghiol is a Turkish name, tekir meaning 'salty', or 'bitter'; ghiol is a body of water or a channel. The lake used to be a gulf of the Black Sea; now it lies several metres below sea level.

Some 4km south of Eforie Nord stands the oldest resort on the coast, **Carmen Sylva**. During the communist period it was known more prosaically as Eforie

Sud. Carmen Sylva is a quiet place with a high beach; there are currently 38 hotels and villas for hire here as well as cabins. **Costineşti**, where a former fishing village has been transformed into an international youth camp, is the next port of call as you go south; 6km from Eforie Sud, accommodation here is now open to anyone, and there are hotels as well as villas and small cabins for rent. The phone code is 041. You can book villas at *Coral* (☆), *Staţiunea Costineşti*, ☎/fax 734278; *Amiral* (☆☆), ☎/fax 734154; and *Belvedere* (☆), ☎ 734016. For information about wood cabins ☎ 734202. Hotels include the *Forum* (☆☆), ☎ 734000. Costineşti hosts a jazz festival in late August or early September.

Neptun, where Nicolae Ceauşescu had a holiday villa, exudes an exclusive air: hotels, private houses and artificial lakes are scattered discreetly among tall trees and shrubbery. There are nearly 40 hotels to choose from. The phone code is 041. The *Neptun* (☆☆☆), ☎ 711020; fax 731447, has always had the best reputation, and the following is a random selection from the rest. *Hotel Belvedere* (☆☆☆), ☎ 731952; fax 731447, can arrange car hire; *Amfitreatru* (☆☆☆), ☎ 731456; fax 731447; *Doina* (☆☆☆), ☎ 731816; fax 731447; *Mioriţa*, ☎ 731918; fax 731447; *Hotel Transilvania* (☆☆), ☎ 731123; fax 731447; *Panoramic* (☆☆☆), ☎ 731356; fax 731447; *Callatis* (☆☆), ☎ 731619; fax 731447; *Clabucet* (☆☆), ☎ 731716; fax 731447; *Dacia* (☆☆), ☎ 731719; fax 731943; *Istria* (☆☆), ☎ 731819; fax 731447.

Olimp resort to the north is an annexe of Neptun; together they are the most glamorous locations on Romania's seaboard. From here you can follow the resort roads through four cheaper centres that rub shoulders with each other until you reach Mangalia. **Jupiter-Cap Aurora** has two huge campsites and an attractive beach; it is is the newest resort on the Littoral, notable for three vast complexes in the shape of stepped pyramids that confront the sea. The phone code is 041. Inside are two hotels: *Onix* (☆☆), ☎ 711358; fax 731762, and *Opal* (☆☆), ☎/fax 731374. **Venus** has several private hotels including *Vila Caltun* (☆☆☆), ☎/fax 731701; *Claudia* (☆☆), ☎ 731603; *Lidia* (☆☆), ☎ 731609; *Raluca* (☆☆), ☎ 731502; and *Nora* (☆☆), ☎/fax 731389. The complex also has a campsite, riding stables and artificial beaches.

Saturn caters for general family holidays and has several hotels, an unattractive campsite and two holiday villages. The phone code is 041. Among the 2-star hotels are *Aida*, ☎ 752966; fax 755559; *Balada*, ☎ 751367; fax 755559; *Cleopatra*, ☎/fax 751168, *Semiramis*, ☎ 751399; fax 755559; *Siret*, ☎ 751071; fax 755559. For the *Vile Dunărea* campsite and cabins ☎/fax 731373; for renting cabins you could also try *Casuţe Delta*, ☎ 751315; fax 755559; for cabins and bungalows, try *Dunărea*, ☎ 751319; fax 755559.

Saturn, Venus, Cap Aurora, Jupiter, Neptun and Olimp are all administered by the town of Mangalia. Bus and minibuses travel regularly between the town and the summer resorts.

By the coast 3km to the north of Mangalia stands the attractive **Herghelia Mangalia**, an Arabian horse stud that opened in 1928. Its original breeding stock came from a nucleus of Shagya Arabians and thoroughbreds whose ancestors were imported into Romania by the Habsburgs in 1789. Apart from watching dressage displays, visitors may be able to ride here. There are plans to open the trotting and race tracks to the public. Meanwhile, the stud is very short of funds. Unless it receives sponsorhip soon it may have to close.

Mangalia

Far smaller than Constanţa, this is a seaside town of around 45,000 people. It has a pleasant beach, a health resort and a thriving port. In 1997 Daewoo agreed to start building ships in the port. But Mangalia's main claim to cultural fame is its history. It stands on ancient Callatis, a Greek citadel founded in the 6C BC. Luckily, because it is so small, modern buildings have not destroyed the ancient ones, and large areas of the citadel have survived. Six main precincts have been excavated in Mangalia itself, and there are several other archaeological digs in progress nearby. A local team is also carrying out excavations under the sea. A large proportion of Callatis was submerged when the coastline moved west. It is possible to arrange **guided tours** to all these sites from the Archaeology Museum, but you will have to provide your own diving equipment if you want to see the marine digs. To contact the Director ☎ 041 753580/752872. On land the excavations show the remains of street systems, public and private buildings, schools, basilicas, water channels and burial grounds from the Greek, Roman and Byzantine periods. Callatis's workshops produced exceptionally fine carvings, statuettes and jewellery, and some of these can be seen in the Archaeology Museum (see below).

History

Callatis was founded by Dorians from Pontic Heraclea, in Asia Minor. Its name is thought to have come from the River Calles near Heraclea, but Pliny the Elder tells us that the town was originally called Cerbatis or Acervatis. Getae already occupied the site, and the Greeks who settled here played an intermediary role between the Getae and the Greeks' principal base at Histria. Ptolemy, Strabo, Memnon and Ovid all mentioned Callatis, but knowledge of its early history is limited.

At the start of the 4C BC it became a manufacturing centre in its own right, producing fine pottery and other artefacts for exchange with indigenous peoples. In the same century Callatis came under the protection of the Thracian Odrysii, whose capital was at Tylis. Shortly afterwards Philip II of Macedonia (382–336 BC) and Alexander the Great (356–323 BC) forced the Pontic cities to accept their rule, Callatis included. The Macedonians pushed their empire as far north as the Danube. In c 260 BC Callatis and Histria were at loggerheads with Byzantium over who should control Tomis. Byzantium won the argument, and after that Callatis never regained its former importance in the Greek-speaking world.

In 148 BC Macedonia fell into Roman hands. Resistance in the Black Sea ports came mainly from Mithridates IV Eupator, who organised a large union which he commanded from his kingdom. After three battles the Romans defeated Mithridates and took control of the Black Sea's western coast. Callatis accepted Roman domination at the start of the 1C AD; an inscription shows that its citizens were given tax concessions.

The Costoboces tribe invaded Callatis in c 170 AD. They attacked so savagely that its defence walls had to be rebuilt. Goths and Carpae attacked in the 3C. But under the Roman emperors Diocletian and Constantine (r. 306–37) Dobrogea prospered as the empire shifted eastwards and Byzantium became the capital of East Rome. In the 5C Huns attacked Dobrogean cities and were repulsed by Anastasius and Justinian. But from the late 6C the era of Greek and Roman civilisation in Dobrogea came to an end. Avars destroyed the town, and little is known about what happened here until the 10C, by which time Callatis had been forgotten.

A 12C map published in Pisa shows that a fishing village called Pangalia or Panguala existed on this site in the 13C. The name comes from Byzantine Greek and means 'the most beautiful'. And, as in Constanţa, between the 12C–14C Genoese merchants brought new life to the town. The Turkish traveller Evlia Celebi left a vivid description when he came here in 1652. He says Mangalia was both beautiful and rich, adding that it boasted seven schools, 300 shops ('a small number for such a large town'), a modest bazaar, a Turkish bath, several mosques and many solid merchants' houses. The port, too, was thriving. Celebi tells us that the population consisted mainly of Lazi from northeast Anatolia, but that many Greeks and Jews lived here as well. Fragments of the dyke that the Genoese built to protect Mangalia's harbour were still visible in the 17C. Ships coming into port often foundered on them.

By the 18C Mangalia had become a rural backwater, and in 1829 Cossacks destroyed it. This was the first of several devastating attacks that occurred during the Russo-Turkish wars. When Xavier Hommaire de Hell visited the town in 1846, it was in ruins. But among the modern rubble he noticed scattered fragments of ancient Callatis: walls, columns, pedestals, marble statues and grave goods thrown up by the conflict. In 1877 retreating Turks burnt down Mangalia three times before the Russians gained control of Dobrogea. In November 1878 the province was united with Romania after the war of independence with the Turks. Today the port accounts for most of Mangalia's business: a new sea port was dredged in 1985, and now vast container ships are built here.

Practical information

☎ **code**

041

Getting around

By train The station is on Str Constanţei, to the north of the town centre, ☎ 751026. The *CFR* office is at Str Ştefan cel Mare 16, ☎ 752818.

By bus There are a number of private bus and transport companies: *Age Trans*, Str Portului 1, ☎ 755289; *Negrila Gigel*, B-dul 1 Decembrie 1918, bl B2, ap 9, ☎ 752577; *Soder*, Str 1 Mai 3, ☎ 750188.

By car For **car repairs** and servicing contact *Atelier Reparaţii Auto*, Str 9 Mai 18, ☎ 752585; *Atlas*, Şos Constanţei, ☎ 018 611195; *Auto Service*, Şos Constanţei, ☎ 751737; *Service Automobile Dacia*, Str Saturn, ☎ 751715. *Atlas and Elastoman* is a **car wash** on Şos Constanţei.

Vulcanizare specialise in **tyre repairs** and replacements, ☎ 831200. **Petrol stations** include *Dan Oil* and *Atlas* on

Șos Constanței.
By taxi Try *Danus*, Str Sirenei 5, ☎ 754953; *Grigoras Petre*, Str Rozelor 21, ☎ 755721; *Purcar Vasile*, Str Rozelor 9, ☎ 754206.

Where to stay
Hotel President (✶✶✶) (formerly *Hotel Scala*) at Str Teilor 6, ☎ 755861; fax 755695, must be the first choice if you can afford it. Its dining area overlooks foundations of Greek and Roman streets that are still being excavated. Incorporating a 'business centre', it has international phone and fax facilities and you can also hire interpreters here. Alternatives include *Hotel Mangalia* (✶✶✶) at Str Rozelor 35, ☎ 752052; fax 632650; *Astra* (✶✶) at Str Teilor 9, ☎ 751673; fax 632650; *Orion* (✶✶) at Str Teilor 11, ☎ 751156; fax 632650; *Zenit* (✶✶), Str Teilor 7, ☎ 751645; *Național* (✶✶), ☎/fax 831895.

Eating out
Crama Olimpus in Piața Centrală offers a range of Dogrogean specialities. *Eliante*, at Str Mihai Viteazul 9, and *Hotel President* have luxury restaurants. Pizza houses include *Callatis* at Str 1 Decembrie 1918 bl M4, *Exotic* at Str M. Viteazul 4, and *Tineretului* at Șos Constanței 4. There are fast-food restaurants at *Amicii*, Str Teilor 3 and *Olivia*, Str Ion Creangă, bl A1, parter. The hotels have their own restaurants. **Bars** include *Café Bar Sens*, Șos Constanței; *Ciociia Star*, Șos Constanței; *Complex Delta*, Str Vasile Alecsandri 8; *Impex Cameleon*, Str Cetății 1; and *Ritz Electronic*, Str Vasile Alecsandri 5.

Post office
This is on the corner of Str Ștefan cel Mare and Str Oituz, the main road to Albești.

Money
Banks include *Banca Agricolă*, Str Teilor 7; *Banca Comercială Română*, Șos Constanței 25; *Banca Română pentru Dezvoltare*, Str Matei Basarab, bl MG12; *CEC*, Str 30 Decembrie, bl M5. **Exchange houses**: *Nasty Change*, Șos Constanței 15; *Centrul Financiar OK*, Str Rozelor 17; *EDF Asro*, Șos Constanței; *Goldmar*, Șos Constanței bl M; *Trans Danubius*, Șos Constanței.

Police
The police station is at Șos Constanței 1 bis, ☎751305/751306. The *primăria* (town hall) is at Șos Constanței 13, ☎ 751060.

Medical care
Mangalia has a **polyclinic** at Str Mircea cel Bătrân 3, ☎ 751368; the town **hospital** is at Str Rozelor 2, ☎ 752260. **Pharmacies** include *Farmacia 47* at Șos Constanței 27; *Iris*, Șos Constanței 3; *RH*, Str Oituz 36; *Santa Farm*, B-dul 1 Decembrie 1918, bl X2.

Shopping
Gift shops include *Cezar Mixt*, Șos Constanței bl 9, parter; *Eclatant*, Șos Constanței 4; *Flores*, Str Muncitorului 2, bl M5, parter. There are **luxury stores** at *Bia Parfume*, Șos Constanței, bl F, parter; *Conftex*, Str Constanței 10, bl M, parter; *Mar Conftrico*, Șos Constanței, bl 8, parter. *Levent* is a **department store** at Str Ștefan cel Mare 4.

Entertainment
Hotel President has a **disco**; there is a **sports centre** called *Stadionul Callatis* on Șos Constanței. *Club Fonzi* at Str Oituz 51 and *Complex Delta* at Str Alecsandri 8 have **games rooms**. *Complex Cazino* on Str Teilor has a disco, restaurant and coffee bar.

Muzeul de Arheologie 'Callatis' (the Callatis Archaeology Museum) at Şos Constanţei 23 is small but full of delightful pieces. They range from the prosaic, such as terracotta drainage pipes, wool carding tools, building blocks, coins and imported Greek amphorae, to lovely Tanagra figures, stone reliefs, and ravishing gold and silver jewels. There are also clay moulds for figures of gods, actors' masks and animals. Callatis was known for its beautiful ceramics, and some of the modelling in the statuettes is exceptional. Here too is a 4C BC cyst tomb, conserved *in situ*, and the only known grave in Romania to contain papyrus, although the papyrus itself has perished. Guided tours are available in several European languages. Open Tues–Sun 09.00–20.00 in summer, 09.00–17.00 in winter.

Evlia Celebi mentions several mosques in his 17C description, but all of them have disappeared except the **Esmahan Sultan mosque**. Located in a pretty garden on Str Cituz, 600m south of the Archaeology Museum, it dates from 1525, although the present building was constructed in 1753. It is an elegant mosque with a single minaret and is still in use. Open to non-Muslim visitors during the summer, Tues–Sun 09.00–18.00. Women visitors are asked to cover their heads with scarves. Mangalia and Constanţa once had a sizeable Tartar population; they came in the 10C and 11C, and there are still some Tartar villages around Mangalia.

Archaeological sites in Mangalia

Open excavations are scattered all over the centre of Mangalia. They represent a small fraction of the remains which still lie underneath the town. Archaeologists have uncovered six main sites within Mangalia's present-day limits. The most central ones are a **Sarmatian burial ground** and a **Hellenistic necropolis**. These two sites overlap each other along the present-day line of Str Constanţei between Str Pârvan and Str Matei Basarab.

There is another **Sarmatian graveyard** to the north. It lies between the road to Saturn and Str Constanţei. Even further north, on the outskirts of Mangalia, and to the west of Şos Constanţei, is a group of **tumuli**. A Romano-Byzantine necropolis has been discovered to the west of the town centre, with the road to Albeşti running through it. Between 1990–92, a network of **Hellenistic streets**, courtyards and wells from the 4C and 3C BC were also found here.

Another element in this intriguing archaeological jigsaw is the Roman and Romano-Byzantine **citadel wall**. Forming three sides of an irregular rectangle, it runs westwards from the sea with the *Hotel President* to its north, turns north just past Str Mihai Eminescu, and heads east again in Aleea Cetăţii. Visible traces of the wall remain along its north and south sides.

The walls were built during the reign of the Emperor Galienus (253–268). They follow the line of an earlier curtain wall dating from the 2C. The 3C walls were probably designed by Cleodamus and Athenaios, two Byzantine architects sent by Galienus to repair fortifications along the entire Dobrogean coast. Mangalia's Roman walls contain several square towers, similar to the ones Cleodamus and Athenaios construsted at Histria and Argamum. The curtain wall in Mangalia is c 2m thick and made of cut stone; in some places it incorporates the 2C wall. There were two gateways into the citadel: one in the west side and the other in the south. The south entrance was the larger and probably served as the main town gate.

Along the northeast corner of the wall are the remains of a 5C **Syrian basilica**, an atrium and a palace. You can walk into the site from Str Izvor, opposite the *Mangalia Hotel*. With its north–south axis and rectangular plan, the basilica is unique in Dobrogea. It was probably built by a Syrian architect and served as the episcopal seat. The complex is divided into three sections containing the basilica itself, an atrium and a palace. It was begun during the 5C, but the buildings underwent two alterations before the 6C. You can still see how fine the masonry was: crisply cut limestone blocks line the interior walls, and in some places stone alternates with brick in the classic Byzantine style. At the north end of the church there are three naves or aisles separated by rows of columns, culminating with the altar and two sacristies. A superb, carved capital decorated with acanthus motifs, rams' heads and striking anthropomorphic creatures was found here. It can be seen in the Archaeology Museum. The floor is paved with limestone flags.

Some of the most exciting **Romano-Byzantine remains** can be found inside the *Hotel President*. They emerged while the hotel was being repaired and are now a special feature of the restaurant. During 1993–94, archaeologists uncovered more than 1000 square metres of Romano-Byzantine Callatis, including a 6m wide street paved with limestone slabs and a network of conduits. Coins were found from the reigns of Justin I (518–527) and Justin II and Sofia (565–578). Other streets from different periods cross the site. At the east end of the main street, excavators uncovered the walls of a 6C building. Underneath this they identified the foundations of a 4C house; searches among its paving stones revealed a coin with a polychrome glass rim from the reign of the Emperor Theodosius (379–395).

To the southwest of the town centre, a few hundred metres to the south of the mosque lies a Hellenistic '**Sacred Zone**'. It occupies an area of 50m x 60m and contained a temple and several altars. One of the altars was made of ashlar blocks, measuring 6m long by 4.70m wide. Nearby, further excavations revealed the foundations of a temple measuring 6m x 6.8m, identical with the Megara temple at Delphi. About 35m to the northeast of the temple a fragment of another altar was found, semicircular this time. Pottery and coins were also discovered at this site. The coins date from the 4C BC and they, together with the style of the buildings and the pottery, show that the area was the Sacred Zone of Callatis.

Callatis's **port** now lies under the sea, some 80m from the beach. It stretches south to the students' resort at Doi Mai. If you bring your own diving equipment, you may be given permission to explore the site, but contact the Archaeology Museum beforehand for confirmation of this.

Around Mangalia

At **Limanu**, c 4km southwest of Mangalia on the country road that skirts Lake Mangalia to the south, is a cave with over 3000 galleries. Legend has it that this was the site where the Romans buried a Dacian chief and his men alive.

Some 3.5km away, close to the northeast boundaries of Mangalia, lies **Movile cave**. Sometimes called Movilă, this is the place where in 1986 Romanian speleologist Cristian Lascu discovered an **ecosystem** of animals and plants which live entirely on chemical energy. Known technically as 'chemosynthesis', the system depends on sulphur and water to produce organic molecules. The discovery of the cave attracted international attention, not only from biologists but also from journalists. It was a period when environmental issues had become highly sensitive. No trace of the radioactive isotopes from Chernobyl's reactor were found in the cave's sediment, even though after the 1986 explosion they were common in Romanian soil. In the words of its custodians, 'Movile is an extremely small and fragile environment which deserves our protection'. More than 30 new species were found in the cave, all of them endemic. Because of this, Movile can serve as a valuable model for understanding how life can thrive even in the absence of light and under extreme conditions. It may even give scientists clues as to how to produce food to meet growing human consumption. A similar ecosystem has been found in Italy and biologists believe there are others elsewhere, but Movile was the first one discovered recently by man.

You can find out more about Movile Cave by contacting the **Mangalia Field Centre**. The Centre was built with help from the Soros Foundation, AIDROM, Shell Romania and many other corporate sponsors. Located 2km from the entrance of the cave, it is the main research facility for the cave project and consists of underground laboratories where Movile's physico-chemical conditions are reproduced, a conference room, a diving centre with scuba-diving equipment available both for diving and for exploring the Black Sea. Researchers, students and others with the appropriate qualifications may visit the Centre. Write to Mangalia Field Centre, PO Box 57, Mangalia 8727, Romania, or send an email to movile@yahoo.com. Alternatively, you can visit the project's website on www.geocities.com/rainforest/vines/5771.

Discovering the ecosystem

Engineers who were excavating for a major construction project found the entrance to the cave in 1986. Realising that they had come across something extraordinary, they contacted Dr Lascu at the Speleology Institute in Bucharest. He began exploring Movile in 1990 with a team of biologists. Until its discovery, the cave's 12,000 square metres had been completely sealed. Although it is only 300m long, the cave is riddled with narrow passages covered in clay. Its orientation is mainly horizontal, and some of the pits are less than 3m deep. At its lowest part there is a small lake which connects the cave with the water table. The passages continue underwater, forming air 'bells' in three places. In these bells, the atmosphere is rich in carbon dioxide (up to ten times more than outside) and poor in oxygen (one third of the amount outside). Movile also has high quantities of hydrogen sulphide and methane.

Some 45 separate small species flourish here in total darkness. They are all invertebrates. When the Earth's climate changed 5.5 million years ago, this region went from being tropical to temperate. The only animals that survived were those living in warm underground caves. Movile's fauna have adapted to their incarceration through a process called troglomorphy. In other words, they have lost pigmentation, learnt to navigate without seeing, and survive on bacteria and fungi that feed on hot sulphur springs below the cave. This process is known as chemoautotrophy, as opposed to the phototropism used by organisms that need light to survive. The predatory leeches, rare water scorpions, and other inhabitants of Movile are similar to species found in deep sea vent communities.

You will need a special pass to visit Movile; apply in writing to the Centre, or the Institute of Speleology in Bucharest at Str Frumoasă 11, 78114 București 12, Romania. ☎/fax 01 2113874.

In Romanian, *movilă* means a hillock, and there are many of them around Mangalia, some probably tumuli. At **Movilă Documaci**, not far from the lightless cave, archaeologists have found a **tomb** that belonged to a Thracian prince. Still three-quarters buried, it stands in unmarked fields c 5km west of Mangalia on the road to Albești. You can reach it by driving along a farm track to the left of the road from Mangalia to Negru Vodă, but clear directions are difficult to give because it is not marked. You must ask for permission to visit the site and ask for a guide the Archaeology Museum in Mangalia.

A strikingly elegant and simple piece of architecture, the building consists of a low, narrow entrance hall leading into a rectangular crypt that rises to 3.6m high. Faint traces of polychrome fresco are just visible in the crypt, and the original entrance had a marble frame decorated with geometrical motifs. Building took place in two phases, the first consisting of the tomb chamber and about half the tunnel leading to it, the second an extension to the tunnel. Surprisingly, the earliest phase is the most sophisticated. A fine barrel vault bound with mortar covers the entrance tunnel at the west end while the extension is roofed crudely in large stone blocks.

It was ransacked twice in antiquity, once in the 2C AD, and later in the 6C, when intruders used the tomb as a hideout and scratched graffiti symbols and figures in the hallway. Archaeologists have deciphered a single Christian chrismatory (votive vessel) among the stick figures of men and animals. When excavations started in 1993, all that was left of the prince's eathly treasure was a gold ring with a turtle motif and two bronze arrowheads. Further discoveries have shown that nearby walls of mortared, limestone blocks played a double role in protecting the first burial and enclosing a second one, erected during the Romano-Byzantine period.

SOUTHWEST DOBROGEA: MANGALIA TO CĂLĂRAȘI

A few kilometres further west from this tomb and 15km from Mangalia, the road reaches the village of **Albești**. In a fold of hills to the south lie the gridlines of an ancient **Getic citadel**, laid bare for ponderous tortoises to explore among the wild flowers. Details of the excavations here can be obtained from curators at the Archaeology Museum in Mangalia; they can also arrange guided tours of this and other sites around the town.

Follow the country road west through Albești for Negru Vodă, where it crosses the DN38 for Constanța, and keep heading west. This route goes through Cerchezi village and passes to the north of Dumbrăveni before coming to Șipotele. A few kilometres further north the road joins the DN3. If you turn west here, in another 3km you arrive at Adamclisi, but these roads are not well marked and it may be simpler to return to Constanța and take the DN3 to Adamclisi from Basarabi.

At the end of a long, tree-lined avenue stands **Tropeium Traiani**. This is literally a giant trophy celebrating the supremacy of ancient Rome and Emperor Trajan's conquest of Dacia, Moesia and Scythia Minor. The monument you see today is a 1977 copy of the 2C original—the only authentic part is the cylindrical base. On top stands a fearsome, faceless centurion. It is not a beautiful structure, but around the side are metopes, rectangular spaces between the triglyphs that show not only scenes of military might but glimpses of the indigenous population's everyday life: shepherds and domestic scenes appear alongside the soldiers. 19C archaeologists found the remains of a street system, houses and basilica nearby, and later the ruins of Byzantine buildings and a necropolis were also discovered, but you cannot see anything of them now. In the cemetery was the tomb of a local prefect who had been slaughtered by the Dacian king, Decebal, during the Roman invasion, and, excitingly for Daco-Roman continuity enthusiasts, an inscription proving that Dacians were beginning to call their children by Roman names. The *tropeium* is open to the public all year round from 08.00–20.00.

A further 53km west, on the roadside to the right of the DN3, you come to the 20C buildings of **Mănăstirea Dervent**. Built on the site of an earlier shrine destroyed by the Turks in 1830, the church was completed in 1942. Legend has it that Sf Andrei (St Andrew) was martyred here in the 2C while baptising the Vlachs (Romanians). The story also says that after his death, four stone crosses 'grew' from the ground. Copies survived into the early 19C, when two were destroyed by the Ottoman army along with the previous monastery. The remaining two crosses are nothing more than stumps. One is housed in a side room of the church and is believed to cure sick people.

To stay within Romania's borders, you have to cross the Danube where the frontier meets Bulgaria just beyond the vineyards of Ostrov, c 12km west of Dervent. The car **ferry** to the northern shore is a platform with a small steamer attached, and until the Romanian and Bulgarian governments give the go-ahead for the long-awaited bridge, this is the only way across. Do not miss it if you have the chance: this is probably one of the last ferries of its kind in Europe and makes for a highly romantic experience. The river is about a mile broad at this point. The ferry runs throughout the day up to midnight, but crossings tend to be at the whim of the captain, especially late at night.

The ferry's destination, **Călăraşi**, is named after the horsemen who used to take letters between Prince Constantin Brâncoveanu (r. 1688–1714) and Constantinople. In the first days of the new year, the people of Călăraşi celebrate a **horse festival**. Together with neighbouring Borcea and Independenţa, they christen their horses to coincide with the Baptism of Christ, which is traditionally observed on 6 January, hoping that the animals will remain healthy over the next 12 months.

Opposite, on the Bulgarian bank, stands Silistra. This was once a Roman settlement, and between 1919–40 it belonged to Romania. 9km downstream from Călăraşi, the island of **Păcuiul lui Soare** contains vestiges of a Byzantine town. From Călăraşi, the DN21 heads north for Slobozia (43km), while the DN3 continues its way to the capital (120km).

Transylvania

Transylvania lies right in the centre of Romania on a plateau surrounded to the north, east and south by the Carpathians and the Apuseni mountains to the west. It has great natural beauty: majestic forests cloak the mountain slopes, and in spring the open meadows are full of wildflowers. Lower down there are vineyards, and some of the hills are scored with lines of ancient terracing said to date from Dacian times. Highlights include Sighișoara, Sibiu and the Saxon villages, the Székely country to the east and the Apuseni.

Isolated physically from the rest of the country, some would say Transylvania has a separate identity as well. The Hungarians who colonised it from the 10C called Transylvania *Erdély*, 'the forest land', a place full of promise that they thought was theirs for the taking. Germans still know it as *Siebenbürgen* ('the Seven Towns'). For Romanians, taught to see themselves as descendants of the Daco-Romans who preceded the Magyars, Transylvania was *their* ancient land. Today they call it *Transilvania* or *Ardeal*.

History

For almost a millennium, the region was part of Hungary, the Habsburg Empire or Austro-Hungary. Between 1526–1689 it became a virtually independent principality under Turkish suzerainty, and for a few months of 1600–01, Mihai Viteazul (Michael the Brave) brought it into union with Moldavia and Wallachia. But since the Middle Ages, Western Europe has had a dominating influence on Transylvania's culture—an important element in this orientation came with the 'Saxons' who settled in the territory from the 12C. Self-reliant and clannish, these newcomers made a huge impact on Transylvania. Their presence was felt most powerfully in the south, around Brașov, Sighișoara, Mediaș and Sibiu. The Germans' influence was only weakened in the 1980s, when Ceaușescu persuaded the then West German government to pay for their release. Religion too was a western affair: Transylvania has seen the bloody consequences of intolerance in Reformation and Counter-Reformation alike. Usually, the Orthodox church was cold-shouldered, and its churches were periodically burnt to the ground.

Such a rich land was bound to be fought over. One of the worst raids was carried out by Mongol soldiers of the Emperor Ogedei, successor to Genghis Khan. Known as the 'Devil's horsemen', they pillaged, burnt and murdered their way through the principality in 1241–42. This was not their last attack: Tartar invasions continued periodically until 1717. The Turks invaded Transylvania as well, hitting the Saxon townships hard in the 15C and 16C. And when the Saxons withdrew their support for his terrible regime, Vlad Dracula took his revenge on them too.

The Habsburgs intervened in Transylvanian politics long before they finally 'liberated' the unwilling citizens of Brașov and Sibiu. The long-suffering serfs exploded into violence several times from the 15C, when Gheorghe Doja led a peasants' revolt that was viciously suppressed. Wretched conditions made serfs rebel again in 1784, this time after months of fruitless petitioning; castles were burnt and landowners were killed. The Habsburg Emperor Joseph II ordered the three ringleaders, Horea, Cloșca and Crișan, to be punished as an example to the masses. They were captured and brought to Alba Iulia. Crișan committed suicide, but Horea and Cloşca were broken on the wheel. Some churches in the Apuseni and southwest Transylvania, where the uprising occurred, contain frescoes illustrating the death of Christ on a wheel. But even more impact was made by the revolution of 1848–49. Part of a snowball effect that ran right across Europe from west to east, it was started by Hungarians as a protest against the Habsburgs' rule. Romanians saw it as their chance for independence from Hungary, and famously declaring 'Nothing about us without us', they began their own struggle for self-determination. The revolution was crushed with help from Russia, and neither Hungarians nor Romanians succeeded in their demands.

Amid all this unrest there were rare periods of stability, such as the reign of Gabriel Bethlen (1613–29), a prince who encouraged humanistic values, founded colleges and commissioned some fine Renaissance palaces. The Habsburgs too had a calming effect, although this was due more to their policy of enlightened despotism than because they were loved for themselves. They were also great builders: their citadels, palaces, and churches introduced the Baroque into Transylvania, and it was still developing in the 18C, alongside vernacular styles.

Romania's independence movement was largely forged in Transylvania, even though the principality, which was then part of Austria-Hungary, only joined Romania after the First World War.

But Transylvania has a fame which surpasses mere history. In the collective imagination, it has become a place of fantasy. The mythical Transylvania is inhabited by clichés, of which the most prominent is the figure of a grey-haired vampire. Bram Stoker created his 1897 Dracula from a composite of fact and fiction, and never went to Transylvania at all. In his 1925 travelogue, *Raggle Taggle*, Walter Starkie wanders through Transylvania like a Roma, weaving together the factual and the supernatural. A sense that this is the edge of the civilised world persists in the minds of western journalists, thanks to the Balkans' apparently chronic instability.

Transylvania's folklore is a fecund mix of pagan and Christian beliefs, nourished by a society that has only recently left the land. Historically folk have endured here by hiding in the forests which once enclosed Transylvania on all sides. '*Codrul primul prieten omului*' goes a well-known saying: 'The forest is man's best friend'.

SOUTHWEST TRANSYLVANIA

Transylvania's southwest corner is small enough to explore in a few days and is a good place to get your bearings. Besides being relatively compact, it has a lot to offer: Iron Age observatories, Roman towns, medieval castles and idiosyncratic stone churches lie sprinkled over a landscape that can be extremely pretty.

If you are travelling south from Oradea or east from Arad, spend a little time looking at **churches** near the Mureş River. Beyond this lie the zone's largest cities, **Deva** and **Hunedoara**, with the **fortresses** of ancient Dacia in the nearby Orăştie hills. Further south, the **Haţeg country** is an appealing mix of cultivated fields and open grazing land, undulating hills and little, secluded val-

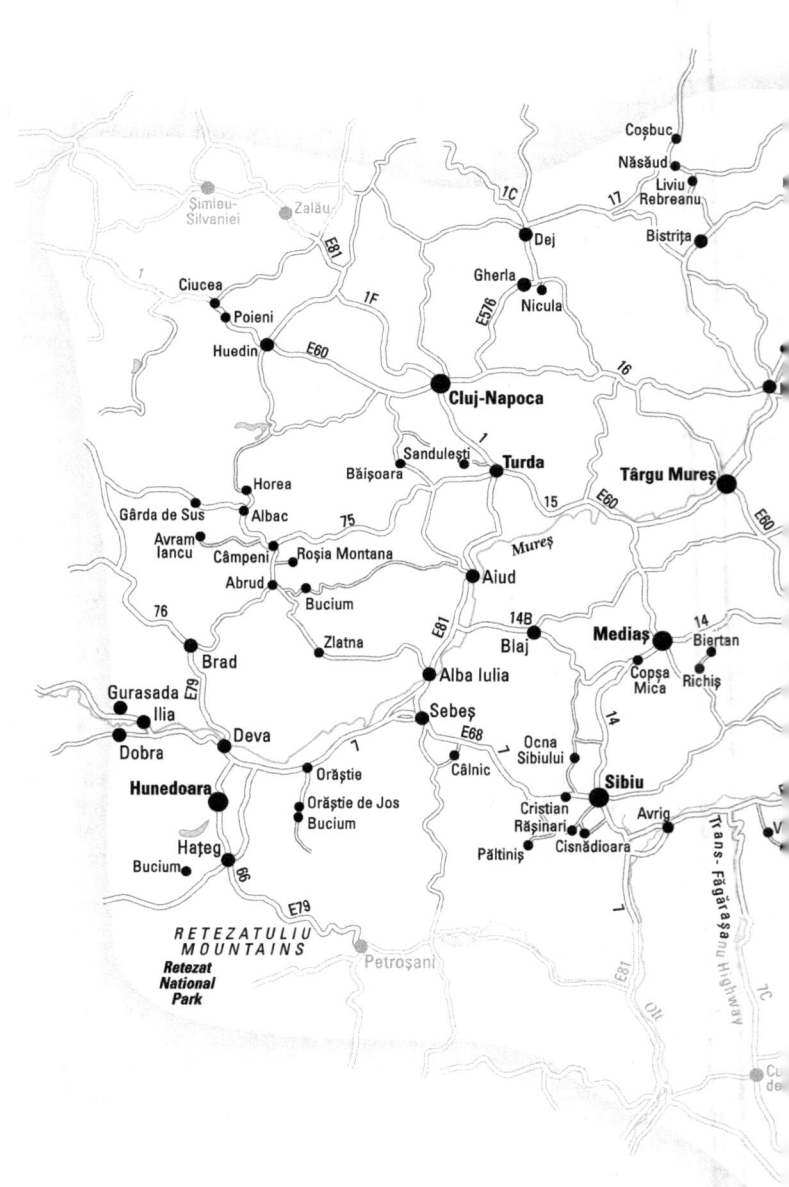

TRANSYLVANIA • 391

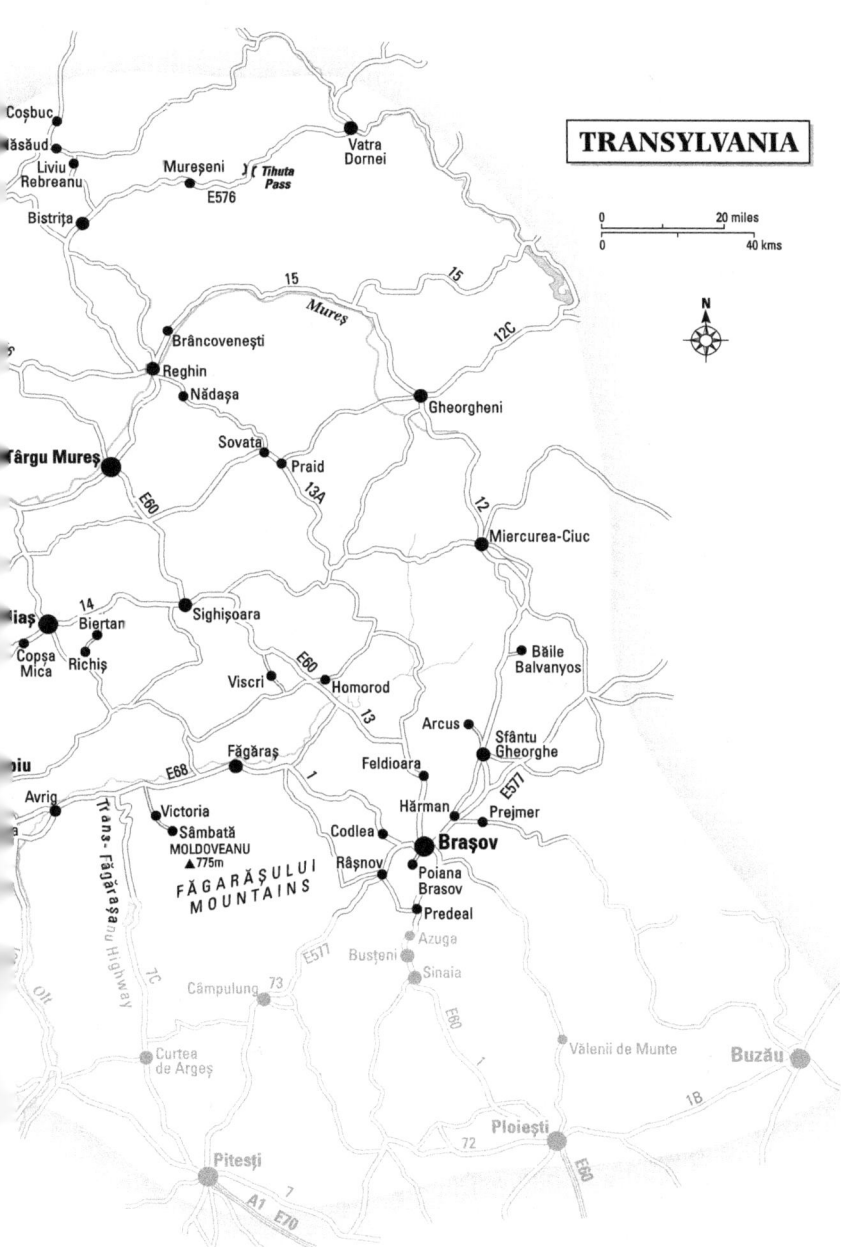

leys. Here you can find ancient stone **churches**, historic **monasteries** and the **ruins** of **Sarmizegetusa Ulpia Traiana**, Trajan's power base during the Roman occupation. At the southern edge of this zone you come to the wild and beautiful **Retezat Mountains**, where the Hungarian kingdom once shared a frontier with Wallachia.

Orthodox churches

North of Deva, turn west towards Arad at the junction of the E79 and the E68. This brings you past Veţel and the Roman *castrum* of **Micia** whose ruins contain a temple to Jupiter, a small amphitheatre, and a necropolis. Fork right and cross the river, and in 2km you reach **Ilia**, birthplace of the Transylvanian prince Gabriel Bethlen (r. 1613–29). The village also contains a castle built for Ştefan Báthory, who became king of Poland.

Some 6km beyond Ilia the road rounds a bend past **Gurasada**'s extraordinary Orthodox church; you may have to ask for the keyholder because the church is normally locked. Orthodox churches of this age are a rarity in Transylvania, and this is a particularly spirited building. Combining Byzantine and Gothic elements, it was begun as a four-lobed cross with the west end slightly longer than the apse; this was extended sometime in the 15C to include a new, square apse beyond the first one, which now opens into it. Square side apses were also added. Both sections of the church slot together so that it looks like a space capsule docking with its maternal rocket. It was probably founded when the village was a Romanian *cnezat* in the late 12C/early 13C, and the earlier section has Balkan origins. It has 15C Byzantine frescoes, but it is the impression of ruggedness and intimacy that remain with you long afterwards. Its fortress-like towers are also unusual: the central and western ones are made from masonry walls capped by wooden roofs.

Gurasada's Orthodox church

OVER THE MUREŞ

Across the river to the south there are a number of other fascinating communities. Go back to the turning with the DN68A and head southwest for Lugoj. The road passes **Brâznic**, a village that was once a port for the salt trade. It has a 16C wooden Orthodox church made out of massive logs and decorated with fine carvings. Inside there are naive frescoes. At Lăpuşnic, you can turn south (left) along a rough track which brings you into rural Romania at its most picturesque, past traditional houses and footbridges made out of single logs. In c 3km you come to **Răduleşti**, which has another embattled wooden church standing in an attractive meadow.

Further west along the Lugoj road, you come to **Dobra**, the site of a medieval citadel. In 1721, local smallholders made a stand at Dobra and forced the

Poarta Mureşului

The Mureş River, called the Maros by Hungarians, was once an economic and social lifeline between the Transylvanian highlands and the outside world. Between Deva and Zam, the valley is known as Poarta Mureşului (the Mureş Gate) and has been inhabited by man for thousands of years. In the caves at Godineşti and on the terraces of Almaş Sălişte, Boholt, and Veţel, archaeologists have found evidence of a Neolithic culture called Cuţufeni. At Piatra Coziei there are signs of a Bronze Age settlement, and Iron Age tools have been discovered at Gherghes, Lesnic and Vetel.

Many more settlers arrived during the Dacian period, and in the 2C AD the Romans found the area just as attractive. Castrum Micia, beside Veţel, was a *pagus*, an important customs post and social gathering place with a public baths and amphitheatre. The countryside around the river is peppered with Roman camps that guarded the valley roads. Further east, between Cigmău and Geoagiu de Jos, was another *pagus*, called Germisara, which the Romans founded on a Dacian citadel. The resident garrison was an auxiliary unit called Numerus Singularium Britannicorum, manned by British soldiers. 5km to the north, the thermal spa of Geoagiu Băi was built over a set of Roman baths. Excavations here have revealed a special chamber, dedicated to the worship of gods of healing and containing altars and votive statues to Aesculapius, Hercules, Diana and Hygia. Coins were found here too, but, more excitingly, the digs uncovered eight plaques of wafer-thin gold. A few centimetres long, these tokens are shaped like fleurs-de-lys and decorated with primitive *repoussé* work. Some of them carry images of the gods, and some have inscriptions bearing the givers' names. You can see the plaques in Deva's Archaeology Museum.

The Middle Ages saw a great upsurge in building around Poarta Mureşului. There were Magyar castles at Ilia, Deva and Dobra in the 13C. Memories of Austrian and Hungarian repression remained strong in this region, which is why some Orthodox churches show crucifixions on a wheel and not a cross: the martyrs of the 1784 rebellion were tortured in this way. War returned to Poarta Mureşului in 1848–49 when Hungary rose against the Habsburg Empire, a struggle that in Transylvania became tangled with the Romanians' desire for unification with Moldavia and Wallachia—so that Romanians turned against Magyars as well as Austrians.

Habsburg army to retreat. Turn south at this point to see the wooden churches at **Mihăeşti** and **Roşcani**, 8km off the DN68A. A 4WD vehicle would be preferable if you want to see these villages. **Lăpugiu de Jos**, 8km west of Dobra, has a 17C church and frescoes, and **Lăpugiu de Sus** lies south of the DN68A beside one of the Mureş's feeder streams. In Lăpugiu de Jos the 17C church has some frescoes showing the martyrdom of Cloşca, a leader of the peasants' revolt against the Habsburgs in 1784–85. To the west, **Crivina de Sus**, **Poieni**, **Curtea**, **Româneşti**, **Tisa** and **Zolt** all have fine Orthodox churches. Tisa's 18C church was dragged from a nearby village in 1815; it has a rectangular plan with a polygonal apse, and its decoration is a mixture of Gothic and Baroque elements, showing a marked western influence. Murals were added in 1828, and there are crucifixion scenes inspired by the 1784 peasants' revolt.

Deva

Southwest Transylvania's principal town and the county town of Hunedoara, Deva is a centre for the mining, engineering and power-generating industries. Its only charm for the history-loving visitor is the castle, whose ruins overlook the town from the dome of an extinct volcano, and a small enclave of Baroque buildings that huddle close to the castle mound. Deva has been a victim of radical urban planning, and the few old civic buildings left unscathed include a couple of museums, the law courts, the town hall and some churches. But for all it lacks in beauty, it is a convenient base that is far preferable to Hunedoara, the other nearby town to the south.

Practical information

☎ code
054

Tourist information

Deva has several travel agencies, including *BTT* at B-dul Decebal, bl I, *Atlassib* at Str Libertăţii bl B1, and *Sarmis* at Piaţa Victoriei 3. For other local information and services, you could try the *prefectura* on B-dul 1 Decembrie 28.

Getting around

By train and bus The main train and bus stations occupy Piaţa Gării, and the *CFR* booking office for train tickets is at Str 1 Decembrie 1918, bl A.

By car *ACR* at Str G. Cosbuc 21, can give information on **car repairs** and **car hire**, and there are **petrol stations** on the main roads leading into the city centre.

By taxi Taxis are available from *City Taxi* at Str Oituz 6, ☎ 211111, *Eurotaxi* at Str Eminescu 1, ☎ 223344, and *Fulger*, ☎ 969.

Where to stay

Deva has some grand hotels, such as the *Decebal* (✫✫✫) at Str Lucian Blaga 7, ☎ 217499; fax 219245, and *Venus* (✫✫✫) at Str Eminescu 16, ☎ 217106. Further down the scale are the *Deva* (✫✫) at Piaţa Victoriei 3, ☎ 211290; fax 215873, *Sarmis* (✫✫) also at Piaţa Victoriei 3, ☎ 214730; fax 215873, and the *Bulevard* (✫) at Str 1 Decembrie, ☎ 211976.

Eating out

Apart from the hotel restaurants, you could try the *Transylvania* on Piaţa Victoriei; otherwise the area around B-dul Decembrie, Libertăţii and Decebal has a modest range of food shops.

There is also a 'non-stop' **food market** at Str Aurel Vlaicu 25.

Money

There are **banks** at Str Decebal, bl P, B-dul Decebal 2, and Str 1 Decembrie 10, and an **exchange house** at B-dul Decebal, bl 8.

Medical care

There are pharmacies at B-dul Decebal bl 24, and B-dul 22 Decembrie bl 7.

Entertainment

If you cannot bear to leave Deva without experiencing its nightlife, you could try the *Bratu & Tabacu* **disco** at Str Victoriei 4, *Max's*, or the *Nova Perla Restaurant* on Str Octavian Iosif. Otherwise, the hotels and travel agencies should be able to make helpful suggestions.

Maps and books

Hotels and travel agencies should also be able to supply you with maps of the town and surrounding areas, and failing these options, the town hall at B-dul 1 Decembrie 28 may have maps and books about the county. You could also ask for information on the region at the history museum. The county **library** is at Str 1 Decembrie 28, and there are **bookshops** at Piața Unirii 10 and B-dul 1 Decembrie 28.

Traditional festivals, crafts and folk art

Contact *Centrul Județean de Creație Populară*, the regional centre for folk arts, crafts and music and dance festivals, at Str Timișoara 28, ☎ 213966, internat 155.

Literally, **Muzeul Civilizației Dacice și Romane** is the Museum of Dacian and Roman Civilisation, but it is also known less pompously as the county history museum. It can be found at B-dul 1 Decembrie 39, backing onto the castle mound at the end of an attractive *cul de sac*. Its collection of Dacian and Roman objects is superb, and comprises pictorial funeral tablets and altars from Sarmizegetusa Ulpia Traiana and Micia, and the gold plaques found at Germisana, near Geoagiu Băi. The museum also contains a model of the Dacian citadel complex in the nearby Orăștie hills—especially helpful after you have spent hours trying to locate them in the woods. But loveliest of all is the house itself: called Castelul Magna Curia, it is a 16C Renaissance building with Baroque additions, and was once the home of the Bethlen family. Open Tues–Sun 09.00–17.00.

You need plenty of energy to climb the 184m to the top of the castle mound, but the view over the Mureș Valley makes up for the agony of getting there. Access is easiest from Str Octavian Iosif behind the county museum. This Magyar **citadel** was founded in the 13C on the cone of an extinct volcano. It later became one of the most powerful fortresses in Transylvania. In the 19C it was used as an arsenal, but in 1849, during the anti-Habsburg revolution, it exploded. Besides a tangle of rubble and ivy, all that is left are a few blasted walls and door frames.

The Dacian citadels

From Deva, the easiest way to the Dacian strongholds is via **Orăștie**, a town 29km east that you may hardly notice as you drive through on the E68/DN7. Although there is little to see here now besides a modest square lined with Baroque and Renaissance houses, this was one of the first northern European plantations in Transylvania.

The Romanian historian Gustav Kisch believed that Orăștie's Saxon name, Broos, came from a Wallonian immigrant, Anselm de Braz. Anselm emigrated to Hungary with his children in 1103 and may have been promised an estate here after taking part in the First Crusade to Jerusalem (1096–99). He was one of many minor nobles who abandoned an increasingly difficult existence in the Carolingian empire for a new life in the Land beyond the Forest. Tartars destroyed the town in the 1240s, but by the 15C it had become a centre of Romanian culture. The humanist Nicolae Olahus (1493–1568) was born here, and Mihai Turdas, a Calvinist bishop of Romanian origins, established a printing press in Orăștie in 1582. But the town is better known as a gateway to the country's most extensive Dacian strongholds.

These sites are not easy to find first time round, even with a county map and the leaflets that are available. It would be wise to hire a guide from one of the travel agencies or the history museum in Deva, otherwise you might persuade someone local to show you the way when you arrive at Costeşti. To get there, follow the minor road south from Orăştie over the river bridge to Beriu and continue for c 20km. There is a combined *cabana* and campsite at Costeşti that offers accommodation at very reasonable rates. To contact the manager, ☎ 103 through the Orăştioara exchange. A notice board at the entrance to the reserve shows the rough layout of the hill forts and temples that make up the whole complex, but it gives a general idea of their whereabouts. It would take at least three days to do justice to all the sites, and if you are short of time, **Sarmizegetusa**, **Blidaru** and **Costeşti** are the most rewarding.

The two hill forts of Costeşti and Blidaru are easy to reach from the road south of Orăştie, and you should be able to see both of them on the same day. **Cetăţuia Costeşti** stands on a mound to the south of Costeşti village, on the left bank of the Apa Grădiştii. Take the road which hurdles the bridge and follows the river course for a few hundred metres, then turn left and climb the winding path to Cetăţuia Hill. There is also a shortcut that brings you onto the hill via a square embankment. This is all that is left of a Roman citadel used by Trajan's soldiers while they attacked the Dacians. On the right, surmounting a hillock called Ciocuţa, stands a stone tower that once guarded the entrance to the main fort. Founded in the 1C BC, Costeşti was Burebista's first capital, and he is said to have created the first Dacian 'state' from here.

Costeşti citadel was constructed in several stages, and at each one the builders added a new perimeter wall. Parts of three of these walls are visible today: the outermost ring was an earthen ditch, followed by a 3m thick stone wall strengthened by three bastions, while the inner defense was a double palisade. Remains of the 3m wall can be found on the south side of the citadel. In the middle, on the highest part of the mound, are the remains of two stone-and-brick towers used for living quarters, and an observation point. There are other watchtowers scattered around the site, and you can also see four rectangular sanctuaries or temples, delineated by stumps of pillars. The most impressive sanctuary can be found beyond the northern edge of the ditch. The others lie on the east side of the citadel, one inside the ditch and the other two together, near the citadel's southeast corner.

As its name suggests, **Blidaru citadel** stands on Blidaru Hill, to the south of Costeşti. It consists of two adjoining forts and a superb view. Getting there on foot takes about an hour.

Sarmizegetusa Regia, sometimes called Sarmizegetusa Basileion, is quite different from the Roman camp at Sarmizegetusa Ulpia Traiana. It is also the most interesting Dacian citadel yet found. It stands at Grădiştea de Munte, c 20km south of Costeşti. Sarmizegetusa was Dacia's most important spiritual and military centre. Its most striking features are two stone calendars which use a unique system that evolved over hundreds of years. Leave a whole day for your visit and, if possible, take a 4WD vehicle.

Sarmizegetusa was the capital of Dacia under Decebal (r. 87–106 AD). It comprises a series of terraces destroyed by the Romans, which were then reconstructed and enlarged in the 2C. The complex is surrounded by sturdy walls of dressed ashlar masonry filled with rubble and held together with wooden ties. This is a method known as *murus dacicus*, and the Dacians may have learnt it from the Dobrogean Greeks. Scattered around the site you can see the remains of

Dacia

Together with their close cousins, the Getae, the Dacians were members of a large group of Thracians who inhabited southeast Europe and the Balkan peninsula in the Classical period. Like the Iron Age Celts with whom they came into contact, the Dacians developed a sophisticated culture which continued to flourish outside the Roman sphere of influence, even after the legions conquered Wallachia and Transylvania. Contact with the Hellenistic Greeks who settled in Dobrogea from the 7C BC was an important factor in their development. The Greeks traded oils, wines, ceramics, jewellery and coins in return for agricultural products and slaves, but they also passed on useful skills, such as how to conduct water through pipes and build walls of dressed masonry. In the 5C BC, Herodotus wrote that the Dacians were the 'most noble and just of the Thracian people', and while their slaves might have disagreed, he was not the only Classical author to find them admirable or enviable. The Dacians possessed enormous mineral wealth, and after Trajan's conquest, Rome is said to have extracted huge amounts of gold and silver from the Apuseni.

The kingdom came into existence during Burebista's reign (c 80–44 BC), when the focus of Dacian power moved from Wallachia to Transylvania. Burebista created some stability and expanded his territory far outside Romania's present-day borders. According to Julius Caesar, who was on the point of mounting a campaign against the Dacians when he died, Burebista's empire extended west across the Hungarian plain into Austria and north into parts of Moravia, in the present-day Czech Republic, and Slovakia; an assassin killed him in the same year that Caesar was murdered. Dacians also settled in the Ukraine and northern Bulgaria, where they caused some consternation within the Roman leadership. The Emperor Domitian paid them to stay away, and Trajan was stung into retaliation.

The Romans attacked Dacia in 101–102 AD and again in 105–106. The Dacian king, Decebal, withdrew to his mountain fastness, committing suicide rather than be taken captive. Trajan's Column in Rome is a celebration of the two Dacian wars that destroyed Decebal's kingdom. Apart from battles, it also shows what the Dacians looked like: they wore long beards and tall hats, and dressed in leather.

Classical authors say the Dacians were a peaceable, cultivated and sedentary people. They lived by hunting and agriculture, and had a rudimentary written language. But they believed in an afterlife and were interested in astronomy, botany and medicine. They were also expert craftsmen and made sophisticated tools from iron, silver and bronze. They were fine builders, too. Dacian culture survives in many of the place names of present-day Romania, and the word 'Carpathian' itself is a throwback to that period. But there is a mystery about the Dacians: given that their mountains were so rich in gold, why have archaeologists found so few items of worked gold from their period? One possible answer is that the Romans took it all away; another is that the Dacians hid their hoards so well that most have never been found.

secular houses and workshops, but the nerve-centre is a group of temples dedicated to sun worship.

In the southeast section of the fortress, an ancient paved road brings you into a clearing which contains a sacred zone, consisting of two large rectangular temples. These are marked as in a ground plan by the stumps of pillars, and close by are two circular sanctuaries. Archaeologist John Nandriş has described how a series of pegs was moved twice around the larger sanctuary's circle of 180 andesite blocks to make up a year of 360 days. Each half-year was shown on an inner circle of 68 posts. The innermost, D-shaped ring marked the total Dacian cycle of 34 years. This system was unique in the ancient world and worked to an accuracy of one and a quarter hours over the whole 34-year period.

Standing a few metres to the west of the larger sanctuary is a round stone slab scored with lines making ten equal divisions. This is known as the sun disk, and may date from a later period. Dotted around these shrines are the ruins of towers, walls and water channels. The Romans looted much of what they found here, but during excavations that began in the 1950s, a huge iron shield decorated with the image of an aurochs, and some bronze armour were found.

Feţele Albe (whose name means the White Girls) is the closest of the smaller Dacian settlements to Sarmizegetusa, lying almost directly 12km south of Costeşti, off the main track to Sarmizegetusa. It was a compact settlement, built on terraces supported by limestone blocks of *murus dacicus*. As well as a number of dwelling houses, there is a ruined circular sanctuary here. The Romans burned the houses and sanctuary during the second Dacian war.

Piatra Roşie (Red Rock) is a fort lying c 8km to the southwest of Grădişta de Munte. By car it can be reached by a road that runs from Călan through Streisîngeorgiu and Boşorod towards Cioclovina in the mountains. From Călan the journey will take about an hour and a half, depending on the state of the road. Piatra Roşie was part of a defence wall that protected Sarmizegetusa from the east. It comprises four bastions enclosing a barracks for the garrison and a cistern. Outside there were two large buildings, a sanctuary and four towers. At a later stage, a rough stone wall replaced two towers on the west slope, making the enclosure much larger.

Hunedoara

About 19km south of Deva lies **Hunedoara**, a city that has been destroyed by the iron-ore industry. Traces of Bronze and Iron Age settlements have been found here, but mining is the town's main *raison d'être* today. It is also home to one of Romania's spectacular medieval castles. Standing on a rocky promontory next to smoking chimneys, this gaunt building has a chilling atmosphere that is increased by its unimaginative museum.

Hunedoara **castle** was mentioned in the second half of the 13C, but this was an earlier building of which almost nothing remains. In 1409 King Sigismund of Luxembourg gave it to Voicu, the leader or *cnez* of a local group of self-governing Romanians. Voicu's son, Iancu de Hunedoara, commissioned a magnificent new building that was designed as a princely court as well as a fortress.

Following construction of an outer ring and a moat cut out of the rock, the inner castle was built between 1430–50 and consists of a rectangular block around a sloping courtyard. To the right of the main entrance, Iancu installed a **Knights' Hall** containing a two-storey chamber linked by a narrow spiral staircase. Each level has two aisles roofed with rib vaults on either side of a row of octagonal pillars. In the doorway to the upper storey are the Hunyadi arms, showing a raven holding a ring in its beak. To the west of this hall is a vaulted passage with lovely bay windows that look very impressive from the outside. There is a fine **chapel** in the east side of the building; it has a vault boss showing the Hunyadi blazon, and in the gallery parapet you can see another coat of arms, this time from the Szilágyi family into which Iancu married. On the south side of the complex is an enclosed and fortified **passage** called the Nebojsa, meaning 'Have no fear' in Slavonic. It was the castle's ultimate place of refuge.

Iancu's son, King Matei Corvin of Hungary, inherited the castle. In the late 15C he extended it to the north, building the brick apartments known as the **Golden House**. This has a two-storey arcade opening onto the courtyard. The upper level is decorated with wall paintings thought to represent Iancu's legendary genealogy.

In the 17C Hunedoara castle came into the hands of Prince Gabriel Bethlen. He added new extensions and divided the Knights' Hall into three rooms. Years of neglect and a devastating fire left the castle virtually in ruins. Restorations began in the late 19C, and in the early 20C István Möller, pieced together its original plan from history books. In the 1960s the chapel and upper Knights' Hall were returned to their original state.

The ramparts give you a stunning view of the industrial chimneys.

ȚARA HAȚEGULUI

South of Hunedoara the landscape fans out into lush valleys in which you can breathe again. Medieval chronicles refer to this region as Terra Hertszog or Harsoc, the Duke's Country, while in Romanian it is styled Țara Hațegului. In the 12C it belonged to the Romanian *voivode* Litovoi and spanned part of northern Oltenia. Today Țara Hațegului centres around the country town of Hațeg.

Follow the road south to Teliucu from Hunedoara, and this brings you to a local beauty spot called **Lacul Cinciș**. Alternatively, take the eastern route from Hunedoara towards Călan, and then head south. This brings you to **Strei**, which has a rare 13C stone Orthodox church. This has been extensively restored, but you can still see a faint Romanesque influence in its tower. Ask in the village for the priest to show you the Byzantine frescoes around the door and in the apse and nave. Outside, you can see where the builders found their material: there are Roman inscriptions in some of the wall slabs.

Hațeg, called Wallenthal in German, was settled by Walloons in the 13C. They were 'guests' of the Hungarian king, who granted them privileges in return for their services in war. Hațeg would make a pleasant base for excursions into the Retezat national park. It boasts one motel, the *Pascom* (✩✩) at Str Viilor 42, ☎ 054 777480, but if you prefer traditional bed and breakfast accommodation, contact *ANTREC* in Bucharest first (see p 116).

Head west from Hațeg for **Densuș**. This village has an 11C/12C Orthodox church which is even more eccentric and wonderful than the one at Strei. It is the oldest masonry church in Romania and, as at Strei, it has elements of late Romanesque design—but here the interpretation is more dashing. Its extraordinary pyramid shape is easily visible from a distance. Pieces of Roman stonework have been incorporated in the body and roof of the church, and the asymmetrical tower crowns a square nave that is exactly 6m square. Four thick pillars, decorated with stone reliefs, hold up the roof. The church was designed as a court chapel for some Romanian boyars and stands on the site of an even earlier building, dating from the 4C. Alterations were carried out in the 13C, and the apse was added in the 14C when it was taken over by the Hungarians. In the mid-15C the walls were decorated with Byzantine frescoes. These have have survived, but only in blackened fragments. Restorations were carried out in the early 1960s, and Densuș is still a working Orthodox church. Its cemetery is a haven for butterflies and wildflowers.

Sarmizegetusa Ulpia Traiana

Emperor Trajan left another sign of his presence further down the road at Sarmizegetusa Ulpia Traiana. Its Roman name was even longer, but this was the capital of Roman Dacia between 107–271 AD, and it is the best-preserved Roman town in Romania. This is no small archaeological dig but a site of European importance. Opposite the site car park is a small archaeological museum that is open Tues–Sun 10.00–17.00 in summer, but most of the interesting material has been sent to the National History Museum in Bucharest (see p 145). Excavations are still going on here, coordinated by the history museum in Deva. Among the most spectacular ruins is the oval **amphitheatre**, which lies a little to the west of the car park. Estimates say that it could have held up to 5000 people, and it is made of brick and stones, some of which were quarried and some taken from the river bed. Next to the amphitheatre on the southeast side is a shrine to Nemesis, the goddess of luck and destiny, while beside it to the north is the Scuola Gladiatorum.

To the east of the car park stands a four-sided precinct enclosing more **temples**. Nearest to the park are the remains of a shrine to Liber Pater. With his consort, Libera, he was popular in central Italy as a protector of vineyards and agriculture. A couple of truncated gritstone pillars flank the entrance, and at the west end is the base of an altar dedicated to Silvanus, the forest god. Another temple to Silvanus stands beside the Great Temple directly south of this point, just outside the precinct walls. Close by are a group of walls belonging to a hospital, and near the road is a basilica.

Follow a track south beyond the temple to **Silvanus**. After meandering through some orchards past the baths and the procurator's office, this brings you to a grand finale: the Augustan Palace with the forum behind it. Both are scattered with the remains of fine antique sculpture. Sarmizegetusa Upia Traiana lies beside the DN68 between Hațeg and Oțelu Roșu.

Continue west along the DN68 for Poarta de Fier a Transilvaniei, the Gates of Iron pass into the Banat region.

The Retezat Mountains

Due south of Hațeg, in the wooded hills between Râu de Mori and Mălăiești stand the stark ruins of a castle and a church called **Colț**. They were the inspiration for Jules Verne's Gothic sci-fi mystery, *Le Château dans les Carpathes*. This novel draws on many of the superstitious clichés associated with Transylvania while exposing them to a supposedly rational light. 'It was impossible to distinguish the indefinite outlines of this structure.... It did not stand out in relief from the mountainous background. What might have been taken for a donjon might be only a stony mound.... The whole was vague, floating, uncertain... [and it was protected by] an infectious terror...'

Behind the castle, rising in sharp crags, are the **peaks of the Retezat**. The highest is Mount Peleaga at 2509m, but the really impressive thing about this range is the glacial action that has scooped out great circles in the rock. The mountains are a national park with a rich (and protected) wildlife; black goat, deer, bear and wild boar live and breed here, along with rare plants such as mountain orchid and wild walnut. The Retezat are popular with climbers. There are cabins at **Pietrele**, 15km south of Mălăiești, at **Gura Zlata** near the country road south of Clopotiva and Râu de Mori, and at **Buta**, on the southern edge of the range. For more information about staying in the mountains, contact *Cabana Rotunda Retezat*, ☎ 054 214296, or fax 219245. Marked paths show the most popular routes into the mountains but hire a guide first by getting in touch with one of the travel agencies in Deva. Tim Burford's *Hiking Guide to Romania* (Bradt, 1992) contains excellent information about this area.

To the southeast of Petroșani, itself 49km southeast of Hațeg on the E79/DN66, are another impressive group of mountains, the **Parâng range**. The tallest peak is Mount Parângul Mare at 2519m. A cable car from Rusu brings you to within 1000m of the summit and a cabin. For the latest information, contact *Cabana Start '93*, ☎ 054 542833, or write to the manager at Masiv Parâng, 2675 Petroșani.

The Apuseni

In Romanian, *apus* means the place where the sun rests—in other words the west. True to their name, the Apuseni form a mountainous barrier at the western edge of the Transylvanian Plateau. This collection of ranges and karstic massifs includes the **Șes** and **Meseș** mountains, which enclose the region of Sylvania to the north of the E60/DN15, and a central area which comprises **Pădurea Craiului** and the **Vlădeasa range**, the lovely **Padeș plateau** and **Mounts Gilau, Mare** and **Bihorului**. Further south, intersected by the E79, lies the gold-bearing arc of **Munții Metaliferi**, with **Munții Trăscău** to their east. West of the E79/DN76 you can find the **Zarand** and **Codru-Moma** mountains. The Mureș River separates the Apuseni from the more southerly ranges associated with the Carpathians.

This is a landscape of dramatic contrasts: hidden gorges, caves and waterfalls lie close to undulating expanses of open grassland, and sheltering in remote valleys are villages where life appears to have continued unchanged for thousands of years. Farming methods are also archaic, giving the countryside its tiny orchards, tumbledown houses and attractive hayricks. However misleading this appearance of contentment may be, the hardiness and independence of the Apuseni people is legendary. This region was always resistant to invasion and produced several of Romania's best known rebel leaders.

If you only have time for one visit, head for the Arieș Valley. The DN75 runs alongside the river from Turda west to Lunca, stopping at Lupșa for its ethnographic museum, and making detours to Roșia Montana and Munte Găina for the annual Girl Fair. Here too you can find the extraordinary caverns of Scărișoara.

Valea Arieşului ~ The Arieş Valley

One of the loveliest routes you can take into the Apuseni region meanders along the Arieş Valley. The 30km-long river valley slices its way to Câmpeni and Nucet between the Apuseni massif and the Trăscău, Metaliferi (literally, metal-bearing) and Bihor ranges to the south.

A **narrow-gauge railway** line built in the 1890s runs 86km parallel to the road along the river valley from Turda to Câmpeni, where it turns south to Abrud. The train, called the *Mocăniţa* (literally, the Little Mountain Shepherdess), trundles at a snail's pace but the engine drivers claim that this gives them the chance to see the wild animals that roam the mountains, including, sometimes, the rare lynx. If you take the road from Turda, after 7km you pass an unsignposted right turning to the **Cheile Turzii**—the magnificent Turda Gorges where 300m-high cliffs used to shelter outlaws—c 2km after Mihai Viteazu village. The path to the gorges is marked by red and blue crosses and is a 5km hike from this turning.

Another route goes via Tureni village, 10km north of Turda on the DN1, from where a path identified by blue triangles brings you south to the gorges in about an hour and a half. There are two mountain cabins in the area: the *Cabana Turzii*, with a campsite near the gorges, and the *Cabana Băiţoara*, which you can reach via Petreşti de Jos, Iara and Băişoara village in about 12–13 hours from Turda. Tucked into the triangle of roads between Turda, the gorges and Tureni is another village called **Săndulești** (turn left just after leaving Turda for Cluj), where there is a 14C Orthodox church built in stone, one of the rare exceptions to the rule that Romanians in Transylvania were only allowed to construct their places of worship in wood. For more information about footpaths to the cabins and the gorges, ask at the *Hotel Arieşul*, Str Drumul Ceanului 1, in Băile Sărate near Turda, ☎ 064 316844, or in Turda at the *Potaissa Hotel*, Str Republicii 6, ☎ 064 311691. Alternatively, try the travel agent *Tudor Turism* at Str Republicii 34, ☎ 064 432120.

At the village of Buru, c 20km west of Turda on the DN75, turn right for Băişoara. A few kilometres west of the village is the **Băişoara mountain resort**, which offers skiing in winter and walking in summer. The resort is also a well-known health spa where treatments include special teas made from local plants, and the air of Munţele Băişoara is recommended for those suffering from nervous and pulmonary illnesses. There is skiing for babies, beginners and experienced downhill skiers, teleski and sledge tracks. When the snow has melted the resort is a good starting point for trips to Mounts Buscat (1677m) and Mare (1825m) and the Scăriţa-Belioara reserve, which has rare animals and plants and a beautiful limestone landscape.

If you want to stay near Băişoara, try the *Tourmont pension*, a lovely *cabana* set in the midst of fir woods at 1350m which has accommodation for nine people. Fully equipped for Western tourists (inside lavatories and hot water), it is run by a husband-and-wife team who can arrange guided tours of the area. For more information contact Maria Ciugudean at B-dul 22 Decembrie 23–31, bl B, Scara II, Ap 24, 3400 Cluj-Napoca, ☎ 064 191350.

Between the villages of Lunca Largă, c 11km north of Ocoliş, and Sălcuia de Jos, 57km to the west of Turda on the DN75, are three further gorges that should not be missed. The 1200m-long **Cheile Runcului** offer pleasant, meandering walks and 450m cliffs for mountain climbing close to the road from Luncă Larga and Runc. A little further south, **Cheile Pociovaliştei** stretch for c 2km. The landscape on either side is strikingly different and these gorges are famous for two vertical peaks called the Gates of Pociovalişte. The shorter **Cheile Poşăgii** and **Poşaga Gorge**, at c 1km long, are near Poşaga village. They have magnificent limestone ridges and two intermittent springs. The Poşaga Orthodox **monastery**, whose church is decorated with wood carvings, lies near the entrance. The monastery celebrates its *hram* (saint's day) on 15 August. Poşaga village is a Moţi community where the inhabitants have preserved their traditional ways of life, including ancient styles of dress.

Back on the DN75 a little to the south of Poşaga, the village of Sălcuia de Jos makes a good starting point for trips to the **Huda lui Papară cave** and the Şipote waterfall. Much of the cave's 2022m is open to the public; it is a beautiful, eerie place with lakes and waterfalls that were created by the river that flows through it.

About 65km southwest of Turda on the DN75, the village of **Lupşa** has a 15C wooden church and a superb ethnographic museum, open Tues–Sun 10.00–17.00. One of the highlights of the Arieş region, the museum was founded in 1939 by a local teacher, Pamfilie Albu, who spent much of his life (and his small salary) begging, borrowing and buying household and agricultural objects from the surrounding country. The collection is a wonderful ragbag of objects, organised by category and housed in an early 19C farmhouse. The museum needs restoration, but it gives a unique insight into the local wood and mining industries and especially the Moţi people. Ask here (or at the Ethnographic Museum in Cluj) for guided tours of Moţi communities.

The Romans invaded Transylvania because Emperor Trajan was irritated by the Dacians' impertinence. But he also needed to fill the imperial coffers. He had his eye on the mineral wealth in the mountains. The Romans found great seams of **gold** in the Arieş Valley, which they appropriately called Aurarum and proceeded to milk as hard as they could: legend has it that the legions took so much of the precious metal from here that the waggon trains stretched in an unbroken line from the valley to Rome itself.

The greatest concentration of **mines** was, as you would expect, in the Munţii Metaliferi, to the south of the valley. Follow the signs for Galeriile Romane after you leave Abrud and you will reach **Roşia Montana**, a village east of the DN74A going south between Câmpeni and Abrud. Hidden under a place known as the Cetate is the Roman town of Alburnus Maior, a fortress and cemeteries which have never been properly excavated. Plans to start open-cast mining here, and at three other sites which belong to a whole chain of Roman towns and mines may mean they never will be. Roşia also has a small but fascinating Muzeul Minier (gold mining museum), which shows how the industry developed in the region from its earliest known beginnings in the late Neolithic period (c 2800–2500 BC) until the 19C. It gives you the chance to visit a long chamber that has changed little since it was first exploited by the Romans. The museum is surrounded by active mine workings, and has an open-air section containing reconstructions of Roman turbines and original wooden technology from the 18C, as well as examples of miners' houses. Open Tues–Sun 08.00–16.00. To get to the museum from the Arieş Valley, turn left off the DN75 just after Bistra and in about 8km go left again onto the mountain road that leads to the village (6km). Walk around what is left of Roşia to see picturesque traces of its Habsburg mining heritage, and follow the mountain road upwards to the ancient accumulation lakes. If it survives the latest attempts to exploit gold and silver reserves, you may still find that the countryside is spectacularly beautiful.

About 4km south of the turn-off for Roşia Montana, **Abrud** was the area's main cultural focus during the gold-mining boom early in the 20C. Today this unusual and lovely town looks desolate. Neo-Baroque façades clad in caryatids and floral stucco, and generous Italianate balconies stand cracked and grime-covered, and the magnificent church that towers over the street has a great gash in its roof and will soon come crashing to the ground. Given one or two facelifts, Abrud is fascinating in a decrepit sort of way—along Str XX is a late-18C **pharmacy**, *Farmacia Romaniţa*, complete with its original furniture and Latin labels—and, in spite of its downtrodden appearance, it stands in a lovely position and has tremendous potential.

Abrud became a focus of battles between Romanians and Hungarians during the 1848 revolution. Many buildings were burned in 1849, when the Romanians went on the rampage because the Hungarians reneged on an agreement and hanged three Romanians.

The collapsing church in the centre was once a Unitarian (Protestant) one. During the 18C and 19C many different nationalities were attracted to the area by the flourishing mines: the newcomers included Slovaks who were renowned for their mining skills. A sign of the town's heterogeneity is the fact that it has several **churches** from different denominations: today, there are two Protestant churches, one Catholic, one Orthodox and one Greek Catholic. Of these, the (Hungarian) Catholic church was originally 13C Saxon in the Gothic style; it was occupied by Protestants in the 16C and taken by the Catholics in the 18C. A Roman tombstone was found in the fabric of its tower. The church in the town centre sprouts shops around its walls, an arrangement that dates from the Middle Ages.

At **Câmpeni** you reach into the heart of the Moţi Land, **Ţara Moţilor**. The Moţi traditionally live by their carpentry skills. Their villages are scattered over the mountains to the north and south of the Arieş Valley, but the highest concentration is around this area. While young people are leaving the villages because they see no future here, those that are left continue to live much as they have done for centuries: if you visit the region on a Sunday you may find yourself hemmed in by a throng of promenaders showing off their best clothes and exchanging news.

BRAD TO POARTA MUREŞULUI

Brad is a small town 36km north of Deva, in the foothills of the Munţii Metaliferi, the Metal-bearing Mountains that are its *raison d'être*. It was settled in the Stone Age, and although its name has no connection with minerals—it means 'pine tree'—Brad became the main gold mining centre of western Transylvania. Today it is known for its **gold-mining museum** which traces Transylvania's gold rush from pre-Roman times. Housed at Str Moților 14 and run by the mining industry, the museum also features the history of the famous Jiu Valley mines of Oltenia (although these are nowhere near Brad) and an alluring gallery devoted to rock crystals; open Tues–Sun 09.00–17.00. If you have time, you could visit Brad's ethnographic museum, **Muzeul de Istorie Locală și Etnografie**, at Str Cloșca 2, open Tues–Sun, 09.00–17.00. Brad is the spiritual and cultural centre of an ethnic zone called the Zarand country, and the museum focusses on this as well as showing fine examples of Dacian pottery, ironwork and tools and Roman carvings.

Brad and its surrounding villages were involved in the anti-Habsburg rebellions of 1784 and 1848–49. A few kilometres further north, the E79/DN76 brings you through Țebea where, every summer, people gather to commemorate the men and women who died in the struggle for Romanian unity. In the roadside churchyard, beside some of the revolutionaries' graves, is a vast, shattered **oak**, half-encased in concrete. It marks the place where the smallholders' leader, Avram Iancu, made some of his rallying speeches against the Hungarian nobility. Moving further north, the village of **Baia de Criș** is the site of another ancient mine exploited by Dacians and Romans; it is also where Iancu died in 1872. Apart from his plaque, there is a 16C Reformed church with Gothic windows and no tower; there was also a Franciscan monastery here, but nothing is left of it except the grave stones. From Baia de Criș, you can drive to Mount Găina on a scenic, but possibly treacherous, country road that weaves through Rișculița and Bulzeștii de Sus. If you are in any doubt about your vehicle's capacity to cope with it, get local advice before setting out.

On the way back to Brad, a minor road to the left brings you to **Ribița**, which has an archaic stone church with a square apse. The paintings inside are thought to be the oldest surviving Byzantine-style frescoes in Romania. This is a very old village, said to have been a *cnezat*, one of the autonomous localities comprising the Romanian duchy of Menomorut in the 11C.

From Brad, you can turn east into the hills on the DN74. Some 6km along the road, past the sprawling mine works, lies **Crișcior**, an ancient seat of Romanian princes from the Zarand country. One of them, *voivode* Ștefan Balea, founded an Orthodox church here in the 13C. Such masonry churches are few and far between because the Hungarian kings were reluctant to let Romanians build in stone. This one has a rectangular plan with a tower and polygonal choir, and inside there are fragments of Byzantine paintings showing the founder's family, and Cyrillic inscriptions.

The northern Apuseni

At **Ciucea**, halfway between Oradea and Cluj-Napoca on the E60/DN1, the country villa of the writer Octavian Goga is open to the public (its opening times are available from the History Museum or tourist offices in Cluj). A little further east, beyond Poieni, the *Pensiunea Romanța* at No. 13, **Bologa** village offers accommodation to tourists. The *Romanța* is an important centre for agrotourism in the northern Apuseni and can supply addresses of other bed and breakfast farmhouses in the area. It also offers cycling and caving tours, and guided tours of historic monuments. Contact the manager on ☎/fax 064 251585, or ask for *Pensiunea Romanţa* (check the phone number through *ANTREC*, see p 116).

Valea Almaşului ~ The Almaş Valley

Heading northwest from Cluj on the E81/DN1F to Zălau, turn right at Zimbor, 18km southeast of Românaşi, and head south from there. This gives you the chance to see the **medieval citadel** at **Almaş**, 12km further on.

The earliest known documents relating to Almaş (1239) speak of a Benedictine monastery. This would have been one of the fortified monasteries that the Magyars supported in their efforts to bring Catholicism into Transylvania. But the Tartars destroyed the buildings three years later on their way into Hungary, and they were never replaced. In 1249 King Béla IV gave the Almaş estate to his magistrate Pál as a reward for his help in fighting the Mongol Tartar hordes. Pál built a stone fortress on the hill, and during the next 400 years his citadel played a crucial role in defending the Almaş plain and providing refuge in war time. The fortress consisted of a *donjon* with living quarters on top of the hill, surrounded by a horseshoe-shaped earth *vallum*. Today a massive bastion on the west side (its base is some 3.5–4m thick), a tower, some broken walls and its striking position are all that remain.

History

In 1278 the Hungarian sovereign Endre II reclaimed Almaş castle together with its estates and appointed an administrator, Dezső, to manage both of them. Dezső wielded enormous power: he collected revenues, raised armies from local villages and judged all the legal cases that came within his jurisdiction. But if he was a tyrant he evidently had more contact with the local population than Pál, because after his time documents refer to the castle as Dezsőfalva (Dezső's citadel).

Almaş was close to the citadel and to a road that linked Cluj with the surrounding estates; the road was one of the main salt-trading routes, and there was a customs post here. The village profited from its strategic location and its inhabitants grew rich as shopkeepers, craftsmen, farmers and fruitgrowers (Almaş comes from the Hungarian word for 'apple'). In 1470 the village became an *oppidum*, an official market town.

In the early 16C King László II sold Almaş to Matei Corvin's son, Ioan. A few decades and several proprietors later, another Transylvanian prince, Emeric Balassa, became lord of the Almaş estates. After the Battle of Mohács, Balassa took up arms with Ioan Sigismund against the Habsburg prince, Ferdinand (1503–64), in a struggle for the crown of Hungary. The king of Hungary, Ioan Zápolya, was a Transylvanian supported by the Ottomans. He was therefore Sigismund's enemy and attacked and took Almaş castle in 1540. The story becomes ever more complicated with the arrival of the Moldavian *voivode*, Petru Rareş, who was courted by both Ferdinand and Ioan Zápolya. Petru Rareş had lost large estates in Transylvania and came back to reclaim his former property. He took Almaş—which had never been his—in 1545, but relinquished it again the following year.

After distractions which kept him busy in other parts of his hereditary lands, Ferdinand turned his attention to Transylvania again in the early 1550s. He succeeded in capturing Almaș, but by the end of the 16C little of the castle was left to defend. In 1594 Prince Sigismund Báthori, who ruled Transylvania under Turkish suzerainty, gave the land and some villages in the estate to the Csáki family, and the Csákis rebuilt the citadel. Successive burnings, first by Austrians and then by Turks, rendered it to the ground and the old fortress was finally abandoned. In the early 17C the Turks obliterated Almaș and several other villages in the valley. A few inhabitants escaped to the mountains, and they returned to rebuild Almaș village near its former location. Regional archives show that hundreds of serfs from Almaș (and from Sălaj as a whole) fled across the Carpathians during the second half of the 17C for fear of the Turks stationed in Oradea. The citadel was partially salvaged in 1806, when Count Csáki converted it into stabling for his horses.

A few kilometres southwest of Almașu the road reaches Fildu de Jos (Lower Fildu). From here there is a stony track west to the villages of Fildu de Mijloc (Middle Fildu) and immediately afterwards, **Fildu de Sus** (Upper Fildu), where the spire of a beautiful wooden church pierces the sky. This is one of the most impressive churches outside the Maramureș, and the three villages closest to it are full of architecture specific to the region: tiny cottages and barns half-smothered by tall thatched roofs, and great wooden gates decorated with pre-Christian motifs. Foreigners are still a curiosity here, so do not be surprised if the villagers treat you as though you were exotic (a nice role reversal!).

The 18C church stands, like a sentinel on its mound, to the south of the village, reached through a private farmstead. The wooden lock and key that fasten the door are ingeniously designed to baffle intruders. The priest is the church custodian and keeps the key; if you want to see inside, ask in the village for directions to his house. The church interior is especially attractive because of its frescoes; the scenes depict men and women in traditional dress which is not in fact local—its origins are unknown. If you climb into the belfry, you can see the entire structure of the steeple right up to its apex. The lookout platform gives you a superb, close-up view of the shingles that cover the swooping roof like a skin, and the vicarious thrill of being able to see into people's private backyards.

From a tourist's perspective Fildu de Sus is the embodiment of a rural idyll: its farmhouses have magnificent wooden gates, and horses and buffalo are used to bring in the hay and cereals from the fields. As recently as 1995 there was only one telephone in the whole village, and the buildings represented a catalogue of Romanian folk architecture. As in villages throughout Romania, religion and spiritual beliefs play a vital role in its community life. In Fildu this is not a new phenomenon: during the 18C it was one of several communities in the Sălaj county region that helped to spread the teachings of the Orthodox church across Transylvania. Part of a widespread drive to re-energise Romanian political consciousness, these efforts consisted mainly in laboriously copying out religious texts by hand.

NORTH FROM THE ARIEŞ VALLEY: MUNŢELE MARE, MĂGURA CĂLĂŢELE

Back on the DN75 and about 18km northwest of Câmpeni, you come to the attractive village of **Albac**. The earliest known documents referring to Albac date from 1688. In 1700 a large number of Romanians from Beiuş came and built houses, and by 1782 there were two villages and four churches on the settlement's present site. Thirty years later the number of churches had doubled, and today Albac (which Hungarians call *Fehérvölgy* or White Valley) is a flourishing manufacturing centre for traditional crafts, including stone- and woodcarving. But the village is most famous for its connections with Horea, the leader of the 1784 rebellion.

Accommodation in traditional farmhouses is available in and around Albac; contact *ANTREC* for more details (see p 116) or ask locally. Turn north in the middle of the village for a picturesque mountain road that veers off on a 75km ramble over the mountains to either Gilău or Huedin (both on the E60/DN1 northwest of Cluj; the road forks just before Lake Fântenele). The asphalt ends at Horea and becomes cobbles, dirt track and occasionally cement blocks dating from the 1950s, but the road (perhaps because of its romantic surroundings) feels much older. This route brings you, between Horea and Beliş, through forests of gigantic pines and past some of the earliest 'scattered' settlements in Romania. Ethnographically these are the oldest known village types, predating the more common nucleic and ribbon settlements.

At **Horea**, c 10km north of Albac, Romanians have commemorated the birthplace of another national hero. Horea's house was destroyed during the First World War and its massive entrance tower is now in the ethnographic museum in Sibiu, but a monument records its position. Horea was a master builder, responsible for the lovely wooden church from Cizer in Cluj's village museum. However, it was his struggles on behalf of his fellow peasants that made his name a household word, to Romanians at least. After unsuccessfully lobbying Maria Teresa and Joseph II at the Viennese court four times between 1779–84, he led a series of uprisings that triggered a knee-jerk reaction. The Habsburgs were terrified by similar events unfolding in France, and Horea and his lieutenant, Cloşca, were tortured to death in 1785, while the third member of the rebel leadership, Crişan, committed suicide.

Taking the northern route through Munţele Mare, instead of heading west for Ocoale, the road becomes ever more lovely. It climbs over the Ursoaia Pass (1320m) and runs beside a stretch of the Someşul Cald river before reaching Lake Fântenele (where the surface begins to improve again). Further to the west, the villages spread out over the karst of the **Padiş Plateau**. This is wonderful walking country and there are opportunities for serious potholing, as well as skiing at Stâna de Vale; turn left at Poiana Horea for a mountain road that crosses the Padiş in a spectacular serpentine to arrive eventually in Pietroasa.

Beside Lake Fântenele the road splits again. One branch, to the right, does a southern loop climbing high into the mountains, from where it heads northeast for Mărişel, Lake Târnica and Someşu Cald, Someşu Rece and Gilău, on the E60/DN1, 17km west of Cluj. (There are plenty of other roads and tracks to explore in this area, but it would be wise to take a local guide.) The alternative is to go through **Beliş**, a village which was moved from its original position lower down the valley when Lake Fântenele was flooded to make a reservoir. At the lakeside before you reach Beliş is a small tourist resort which makes a good place to stay overnight. If you have time, take a boat trip on the lake; the scenery is wonderful. Beliş's fascinating wooden church was moved along with the village houses, which now sit on a hilltop where they are protected as national monuments.

Once past the brow of the hill, things become more mundane and the road drops in stages through three villages to the town of **Huedin**. Known in Hungarian as Bánffyhunyad, Huedin was the former heart of the Bánffy domain. It is notable today for its Gothic Reformed church, which contains a marvellous split-level coffered and tiled ceiling. The section above the choir is the best; it dates from 1483 and each tile depicts an emblem, a fantastic figure, a plant or a piece of text; only half of the original 200 tiles have survived. Artists Johann and Lorenz Umling created the ceiling in 1780, while the master mason Dávid Sípos carved the stone pulpit. Sípos was a particular favourite of the Bánffy family, and his work can be seen in several churches founded by Magyar nobles in northwest Transylvania as well. The *Hotel Montana*, on the E60 towards Cluj, is a recommended place to stay; ☎ 064 253090.

Into the Bihor mountains

From the DN75 on the turning west beyond Câmpeni towards Avram Iancu, the road climbs into the Munţii Bihorului, and in about 11km you come to **Vidra** (formerly Vidra de Jos). This village is one of the oldest settlements in the Moţi territory. It has a 13C church with a 16C bell tower and internal paintings from the late 17C. From here you can make detours to **Ponoarele**, a village with an interesting watermill, and **Gojeieşti**, which has a wooden church typical of the Arieş valley and wooden houses from the early and late 18C. Nearby, on **Dealul cu Melci** (Snails' Hill) is a site where paleontologists have found thousands of fossils from the mussel *Actaeonella gigantea*.

The village of **Avram Iancu** is named after the man who led a revolt against the Habsburgs and the Hungarians in 1848. You can see his birthplace and memorial house in the village. Iancu was a carpenter, and the community here is still famous for its woodcarvers, many of whom specialise in making musical instruments.

Southwest from Avram Iancu you can reach Munţele Găina, where the famous **Girl Fair** (*Târgul de fete*) takes place every year on the feast day of Sf Elie (St Elijah) or the nearest Sunday (the Sunday before 20 July). The fair started in 1816, when its main purpose was to allow isolated Moţi shepherds to find wives, but now it is more of an excuse for the region's largest folk music and dance festival. The best music groups perform here and people come to share in the festival from all over the country. The event traditionally opens with a fanfare of alphorns (*buciumi*) played by musicians from the mountain settlement of Târsa. There is a special bus service from Avram Iancu to the festival site, but the best way to see the Girl Fair is to camp on top of the hill the previous night. (Another Girl Fair takes place near here on 26 October, and similar traditions linger on at Mount Călineasa and near Lupşa.)

Apart from Târsa, where archaeologists have found remains of a Roman camp, there are 38 small **Moţi villages** scattered in the mountains around

Avram Iancu; these include Cocești (1200m), Ticera, Valea Uțului, Verdești, Călugărești and Bădăi (1360m).

West of Albac, the DN75 passes one of Romania's most celebrated natural spectacles, the *peșterul ghețarul* (ice cave) called **Scărișoara**, open daily 09.00–17.00. Confusingly, the cave is not in Scărișoara village, and the best way to get there is by driving or walking from **Gârda de Sus**, 4km to the west. This village has some attractive, old wooden houses and a semi-wooden church built in 1781 with some attractively naive paintings inside. Gârda de Sus also holds five or six markets a year for its thriving woodcrafts industry. Ask at the village post office and telephone exchange about where to stay.

Walking to Scărișoara entails a 2–4hr hike, depending on which path you choose, and it is best to get local advice. A path marked by blue stripes from near the campsite takes you through the gorges of **Ordâncușa** (3–4hrs). Inside the chambers there is a series of galleries in which the ice is as thick as a small house. At the far end of the main chamber the glacier has created a series of pillars known as 'the church', and at the bottom of a 48m hollow, there is a block of ice 4000 years old; a guide is needed for exploration.

From the cave there are two paths leading northwest to the Padiș *cabana* in the southeast corner of the Padiș zone, where there are many more caves and great opportunities for climbing, trekking and walking.

Between Arieșeni and Nucet the DN75 winds up and over the Vârtop pass (1160m) and joins the E79/DN76 after Câmpani.

Alba Iulia

Built on the site of a Roman fort called Apulum, Alba Iulia became the most important Renaissance city in Transylvania. Two distinct archaeological levels have been discovered, one dating from the 8C–9C, and the other from the late 10C–early 11C, when a number of Hungarian warriors were buried here. Today it is a small, industrial town with a new university and a compact medieval centre, which sits on a plateau overlooking the Mureș River. Alba's vivid history is condensed into a few buildings within its citadel, and if you are driving through, make time to look at its Roman Catholic cathedral, the Batthyaneum Library and the Baroque fortress. Alba is well placed for journeys into the interior of Transylvania, and you can get trains from here direct to Budapest and Bucharest.

There is a difference between 'town' and 'gown' in Alba Iulia; up in the citadel, strolling around the green quadrangle, marvelling at the cathedral's soaring naves and crunching the gravel in the hushed tranquillity of the Bishop's Palace,

Naming Alba Iulia
At the time of the Hungarian invasion in the 10C, the rulers of Transylvania were said to be Romanian lords, known as *voivozi* or *cnezi*. The most powerful of them was Gelu, Gyula or Iulius, from whom the town gets its name. Hungarians call Alba Iulia Gyulafehérvár or Gyula's White City, while the Slavs knew it as Bălgrad.

you get a whiff of dreaming spires and hallowed cloisters. But the reasons for Alba's sense of exclusivity are more military than ecclesiastical. Its citadel is encircled by a huge brick curtain wall, laid out in a star pattern following an 18C plan made famous by the French architect Vauban. It was built for the Habsburgs after they gained control of the principality in 1689.

Practical information

☎ code
058

Tourist information

Tourist agencies include *Albena BTT* at Str Parcului 2, ☎ 812140; fax 810385; *Cetatea Apuseni*, Str Unirii 3, ☎ 815152; fax 831501; *Transilvania Turism*, Str Iuliu Maniu 22, ☎ 812547; fax 811195; and *Sind România*, Str Primăverii 12 ☎/fax 811099.

Getting around

By train and bus The *autogară* (bus) and train stations are about 2km south of the citadel on Str Republicii. The railway ticket agency *CFR* is at Str Moților 1. If you need a **taxi**, try the *Taxicom* dispatcher, ☎ 953; there is a network of *Maxitaxis* connecting the railway station with the main streets of Alba.
By car Garages that do **repairs** include *Divers Auto* at Str Republicii 34, and a *Dacia* service point at Str Gării 2 bis. The *ACR* office, which should be able to give advice on garages and **car hire**, is at Str Ardealului 5. **Petrol stations** in Alba Iulia include one on the northeast exit road towards Cluj, one at the western exit towards Zlatna and the Apuseni, and two in town.

Where to stay

There are several 2-star hotels here, including *Parc* at Str Primăverii 4, ☎ 811723, *Cetate* at Str Unirii 3, ☎ 811780, and *Transilvania* at Piața Iuliu Maniu 22, ☎ 812 547, which also has a tourist office. *ANTREC* has a base in the town hall, ☎ 991/149, and can help you to find bed and breakfast accommodation in private farmhouses. When dealing with *ANTREC*, it is always better to contact the head office in Bucharest first because the company's regional agencies frequently change hands and the numbers given here may not be reliable.

Eating out

The lower town has several general **food stores**, and there are others in the modern quarter to the north of the citadel, in B-duls 6 Martie, Transilvaniei and Victoriei. Apart from the restaurants in the hotels, Alba is not well supplied with places to eat. There is one restaurant *de luxe* called the *Flamingo*, at Str M. Viteazul 4, and there are a few **fast-food cafés**, including the imaginatively named *Fast Food Nr 1* at B-dul Transilvaniei 23, and *Prometeu* at Str Parcului 4. B-dul Victoriei has a number of modest eating houses alsong it; the *Roberta* **pizzeria** is bright, clean, pleasant and by Western standards, extremely cheap.

Post office

The main post office and telephones are at Piața Eroilor 2.

Money

Exchange houses are located at Piața Iuliu Maniu 16, Str 1 Decembrie, and Calea Moților bl S1F, while there are banks at Calea Moților 5A and at Str Iuliu Maniu 13 and 14.

Police

Both town and county police have stations at Str Brătianu 1, and the **town hall** occupies the same building.

Medical care

Pharmacies are at Str Iuliu Maniu 4, B-dul Transilvaniei 11, B-dul 1 Decembrie, or Str Clujului bl A4. For an **ambulance**, ☎ 961.

Maps and books

The street names in Alba Iulia have recently been changed, and new maps of the town are available from the *Eminescu* bookshop on B-dul Horea, opposite *Hotel Cetate*.

Walking around Alba Iulia

While it is now something of a backwater, historically Alba Iulia was one of the most important towns in Transylvania. It has been a capital, the site of a great Habsburg citadel, a religious centre and the place where Transylvania's unification with the rest of Romania was celebrated in 1918, although its change in status was not internationally recognised until 1920, after the Treaty of Trianon.

Alba Iulia's **fortress** stands to the west of the main through road, the E81/DN1/DN7. Under Roman leadership there were two camps here, the first on the right bank of the Mureș and the second more or less where the present citadel stands today. Nothing is left of these above ground, however, except the stone tombs, inscriptions and tools, which are kept in the history museum (see below).

The well-preserved Austrian *cetate* was built between 1715–38 by an Italian military architect, Giovanni Morando Visconti. Visconti copied Vauban's seven-pointed star, a shape that gave its defenders maximum visibility as well as protection. Taken as a whole, this fortress is the largest and most complete Baroque monument in Transylvania.

Most of the walls and two of the original six triumphal arches have survived on the east side. This is also where the wall is at its most impressive. It forms a virtual cliff face beside the cobbled road that connects citadel and town. One arch stands at the bottom of this road, adorned with statues of Greek deities and emblazoned with the Habsburgs' coat of arms. At the top end is *poarta a treia a cetății* (the third citadel gate), which also bristles with animal and plant motifs as well as trophies, emblems and all the symbolic paraphernalia of an invading conqueror. Its main panels show, on the outside, Prince Eugen's investiture as commander of the army, the Goddess of Victory presenting him with a model of the fortress, and inside, the Habsburgs' excuse for occupying Transylvania: Austrian infantry and cavalry attacking the Turks. Emperior Charles VI rides above this assemblage with perfect confidence.

Two portholes in the mansard roof are the windows to a tiny cell where Horea, a martyr of the 1784 rebellion, was forced to endure two months of freezing captivity before his execution the following year. He and his comrades in arms, Cloșca and Crișan, were pursued by the vengeful soldiers of Emperor Joseph II. Joseph was the very man whose promises gave them the courage to rebel against oppressive Magyar landowners. The Habsburg Emperor's career had begun so promisingly in the footsteps of Maria Teresa's liberalising genius, but he was terrified by the rising power of the proletariat in France and suddenly lost his nerve. The prison contains a modest display showing facsimile prints and documents relating to Horea's political activities, and smudged illustrations of his death, which like Cloşca's, took place on the wheel, although Horea was granted the doubtful benefit of being run through twice with a sabre beforehand. Pieces of the rebels' bodies were then displayed prominently around the streets as a warning to others. The army, which is sensitive about its installations, has a barracks overlooking the gate, so be careful where you point your lens.

Walking up Str Mihai Viteazul into the citadel from the third citadel gate, you come to the university campus and a small square surrounded by trees. If you keep straight ahead, to the west, the road brings you past Oscar Han's 1968 equestrian statue of Viteazul, with the Renaissance **princely court** behind it— you cannot visit the building, because this too is currently occupied by the army. If the authorities should relax their rules when you are there, see it in case something remains of its former splendour. It was once very striking indeed. The 16C traveller Evlia Celebi wrote that when he visited the palace, the walls and doors were ornamented with coloured stone and all the columns were faced with green granite and marble. His fascinated list went further, stating that bronze frames encased the windows while the panes were of crystal from Murano and Indian mosaic covered the floors. There had been palaces on the site before, but it was Gabriel Bethlen, Prince of Transylvania from 1613–29, who introduced its Renaissance innovations, inviting two Italian architects, Giacomo Reti and Giovanni Landi, to supervise the construction. Gheorghe Rákóczi I (r. 1630–48) introduced other alterations, including a second storey and a ridged roof. He also commissioned Giovanni Fontanici to create fountains in the citadel, but the Italian fled from Transylvania in 1652, complaining that he had been paid too little for his works, 'which were good'. But nothing of them remains for us to judge for ourselves.

Further west stands the Roman Catholic Cathedral of St Michael's, with the Orthodox Cathedral to its right. Beyond St Michael's is the **Bishops' Palace**, which has an intriguing armoured wooden gate, and to the west of this is an open space leading to a shopping precinct, *Hotel Cetate* and the suburbs.

Catedrala Arhiepiscopală Sf Mihail (St Michael's Cathedral) is a building in which Romanesque, Gothic and Renaissance elements coalesce in harmony, despite its lopsided west front. Its beauty is worth a look even if you don't care tuppence for its history. Inside the cool, dark entrance, the overall effect is breathtaking because your eyes are immediately drawn to the main altar, whose Baroque form is dissolved by a pool of light that pours in on three sides of the apse through tall, double-arched Gothic windows. Slim piers separating the window bays meet at the top in an arched canopy. Above the choir stalls are busts of the Apostles, Jesus and the Virgin Mary, and virtually every capital and plinth is an individual piece of carving.

There has been a Roman Catholic cathedral in Alba Iulia since 1009, when the Hungarian king Stephen I (Szent István Király, 997–1038) founded a bishopric here. But the building was an earlier one, and excavations have shown that it was modelled on the style of a typical palaeo-Christian basilica, with a nave and two side aisles, and a semi-circular apse. It also had a circular chapel attached to the south side of the nave; carvings from this, in the form of heads, fragments of cornices and pilasters and a sculpted boss, have been found on its site. Historians think the chapel was a baptistery modelled on one which Stephen founded earlier at Esztergom in Hungary.

After the first cathedral was abandoned, it was succeeded by the present one, which was founded during the reign of King László I (1077–95) and finished in the following century. This building has a much wider ground plan, based on Romanesque churches in Burgundy and Alsace. What you see today is a mutation of the original idea, created by successive repairers, rebuilders and innovators who had to salvage what they could from the disasters which continually struck the church. Like its predecessor, it had a nave and two side aisles, but a transept and a tower over the crossing were added as well. The twin towers above the west portal were originally only two storeys high and were raised later (the north tower was blown up in 1603 and never replaced). Other subsequent additions included the sacristy, eastern nave, northern narthex and main entrance, but they were probably in place before the Tartar invasions of 1241–42. On their terrible march westwards the soldiers of Emperor Ogedei came through Kiev and Poland. One branch of the army then turned south across the Carpathians and attacked Transylvania. According to contemporary accounts two commanders, Kadan and Buri, led the attacks, leaving a ghastly trail wherever they went. One witness to the atrocities was a monk called Rogerius, whom the Tartars captured in Oradea. In his *Carmen Miserabile* Rogerius tells us that Alba cathedral was burnt to ruins and its broken walls were covered in bloody corpses.

Restorations to the building began quickly but in 1277 an angry mob of Saxons from Ocna Sibiului destroyed the cathedral again. This time King László IV (r. 1272–90) came to the rescue by donating his income from the salt mines at Turda. St Michael's also came under attack in 1439, when Turks under Murad II plundered southern Transylvania. Its benefactors then included Iancu de Hunedoara, who gave the feudal income from three villages and in return claimed the right to be buried in the cathedral with his brother.

On the south side is a lovely early 16C chapel commissioned by Canon Lászai. The interior is a mix of Gothic and Renaissance features: diamond-shaped vaulting makes a striking effect above plain walls which suddenly spring to life around the stone altar and door. Three vault bosses carry the Canon's personal coat of arms. Lászai dedicated the altar to the Souls of the Faithful, but the carving represents mythological as well as Biblical figures and saints (Hercules and a Centaur join Judith, Moses, St Sebastian and several kings). Lászai himself kneels before the Virgin Mary. The door complements the altar with a magnificent jutting Classical cornice, and this too is ornamented with animals, plants and human figures.

Iancu de Hunedoara paid for the great, decorated west portal. Based on a Gothic, ogival arch, it was originally meant to have a balcony above it, but an 18C bishop obliterated this feature with the present triangular façade.

After Mihai Viteazul's brief success in uniting the three principalities in 1599–1600, the cathedral was besieged for two years by Austrian troops and then used as a barracks. Iancu de Hunedoara's sarcophagus was damaged, and other marble tombs suffered during the 1658 campaigns against the Turks. It is said that one bishop took some of the stone to make new altars in the cathedral.

Beside St Michael's and commanding the view from the northern suburbs stands **Catedrala Reîntegirii Neamului**, the Cathedral of the Reunion. This is a neo-

Brâncovenesque building, based on a Byzantine cross-in-square church, that was completed in 1922, in time for the coronation of King Ferdinand and Queen Marie. The cathedral is a monument to Romania's 'reunification', which was recognised in Transylvania in 1918 although technically it was not ratified until two years later, after the Treaty of Trianon. At their coronation the royal couple wore gorgeous embroidered robes copied from Byzantine frescoes in Romanian churches.

Standing back to back with the Orthodox Cathedral (to its east) is Str Muzeului, which contains two museums. **Muzeul Naţional al Unirii Alba Iulia** (the National Unification Museum) is a history and ethnographic museum which was founded in 1887. There has recently been a change of management, and the drab decor and uninspiring displays are beginning to be replaced by exciting innovations: the new ethnographic section positively glows with colours. It is located in a section that was once dedicated to eulogies of Ceauşescu. This museum has some wonderful items, bearing witness to the region's 600,000 years of settlement. There are ornaments and carvings from the Dacian citadel of Apoulon as well as the Roman citadels, and ancient gold and silver jewellery. It is housed in an impressive mid-19C edifice with a symmetrical and regimented façade that give a clue to its origins: before becoming a museum, it was an army headquarters. Open Tues–Sun 10.00–17.00.

Opposite is an equally grand hall, **Sala Unirii**, which celebrates the day in December 1918 when Romanians gathered in Alba Iulia to declare their independence from Hungary and their union with Romania. Originally this building was the central section of the military casino, but after unification it was transformed so that the interior resembles a medieval gallery with a barrel-vaulted ceiling. Documents, photographs and marble inscriptions tell the story, together with lunettes containing portraits of some of the leading personalities in Romania's struggle for independence.

Head north from here along Str Şaguna and turn west into Str Bethlen for **Biblioteca Batthyaneum**, the Batthyaneum Library. It stands at the corner of Bethlen and Str Cristea and when you first see it, you could mistake it for a warehouse, so restrained is the façade. In fact it is a very graceful building, based on an early 18C Trinitarian monastery. In 1784 the Habsburg Emperor Joseph II dissolved the order, and eight years later he gave the premises to Ignaz Batthyány (1714–98), who had recently become Bishop of Alba Iulia.

Batthyány was a true man of the Enlightenment, and his wide-ranging interests are reflected in his collection of rare books, which forms the nucleus of the library today. He was born in the former Hungarian town of Németújvár (now Güssing in eastern Austria), and studied theology in Slovakia, Graz and Rome. He started buying books and manuscripts in Rome, and brought them with him to Alba Iulia, where, as well as becoming bishop, he set up learned societies and founded the first large-scale astronomical observatory in Transylvania. Highlights in his collection include about half the complete folios of a 9C Carolingian gospel, and the 18C *Codex Aureus*, written on parchment. It also contains valuable documents relating to the history of Transylvania. The main reading room brings the 18C brilliantly to life, and the library is open to visitors and readers Mon–Thurs 07.00–15.00, Fri 07.00–13.30.

If you retrace your steps east along Str Bethlen, you come to **Palatul Apor** (the

Apor Palace), which once belonged to one of Transylvania's most powerful feudal lords. Turn right into Str Şaguna and left into Str Iorga, pass the university buildings, and at the eastern end next to the barracks is **Colegiul Academic**, a college founded by Gabriel Bethlen. This was the principality's first university-style college. It is built around two quadrangles, on much the same Renaissance lines as the princely court, which was also commissioned by Bethlen.

FROM ALBA IULIA NORTH TO THE APUSENI BORDERS

Some of the country's oldest **vineyards**, known as the Ţara Vinului (literally the Wine Country) and mentioned by Strabo, run southwest along the Mureş Valley from Aiud to **Vinţu de Jos**. Herodotus described Vinţu as one of the largest settlements on the banks of the ancient Maris, and it has yielded a fascinating collection of objects from the Neolithic, Bronze and Iron Ages. Vinţu became a feudal domain under Radu de la Afumaţi (r. 1522–29). Today you can the ruins of a splendid Renaissance **palace** which was built in 1550 for Gheorghe Martinuzzi, Bishop of Oradea and Governor of Transylvania. The palace has a ghoulish reputation: Martinuzzi was assassinated here a year later on the orders of General Castaldo, and the Lord of Moldavia, Aron Tiranul (r. 1595–97) also met a sudden end inside its forbidding walls. The Habsburg Empress Maria Teresa is said to have lured handsome young soldiers to Vinţu Palace, where, after she had done with them, she disposed of them in a particularly horrible way. According to an old lady who looked after the premises until the 1990s, their piteous shrieks could still be heard at certain times of the night.

Nearby, in the village of **Vurpăr**, you can see traces of a 13C peasants' fortress. There are two **vineyards** in this vicinity: *podgoria* Alba Iulia-Turda, which is located between Aiud, Şard and Ighiu, and *podgoria* Târnavelor, which lies between Jidvei and Blaj.

You can also reach the Arieş Valley and the Apuseni region by taking the DN74 west from Alba to the heavily polluted town of Zlatna (c 40km) and then on to Abrud and Câmpeni. **Zlatna** is a centre of the copper-mining industry and the plants here are so toxic that they have reduced the life expectancy of their workforce to ten years less than the national average. There is an interesting 15C church in the town containing paintings from the 15C–17C. Taking the train from Alba to Zlatna gives you a chance to get an unusual view of **Piatra Craivii**, where the citadel of Apoulon has been excavated (there is little to see here on the ground because the digs have been covered over for protection but the Unification Museum in Alba Iulia has a special section devoted to the site.

About 26km northwest of Zlatna, a side turning to the right leads to the village of **Bucium** (named after the local alpenhorn), the focal point of the region's mining villages. The traditional costumes worn by the highlanders have incorporated elements from a kind of uniform that the miners keep for special occasions. Bucium is another village which may be destroyed by a planned open-cast gold mine. The Romans tunnelled for gold here in the 2C AD.

Some 16km north of Alba on the E81/DN1, **Teiuş** boasts several fine old churches, especially the Gothic Catholic church signposted off the road west to

Stremţ, and at Râmeţ. Both these villages also have beautiful churches: the Orthodox church in **Stremţ** (4km) is an interesting mix of Saxon Gothic and Baroque, with a square tower and lookout platform. It was built on the orders of Iancu de Hunedoara in 1449. The 14C monastery at **Râmeţ**, 12km west of Aiud, has a Byzantine triconch church overshadowed by the rocks of the Râmeţ gorge. There is also a *cabana* here, and at the other end of the gorge you can visit the **Huda lui Papară cave**. There is a railway junction in Teiuş from where trains run to and from Sighişoara.

Turn right in Teiuş for **Blaj** (24km, with a petrol station) and an alternative route to Mediaş. Blaj has little to offer except as a landmark of Romanian nationalism, although it is also the site of a 15C mansion built by the Bethlen family, which now houses a history museum at Str Armata Roşie 2, open Tues–Sun 10.00–17.00. Romania's great Romantic poet, Mihail Eminescu, called the town 'Little Rome' because it was here that Avram Iancu organised a demonstration of solidarity with the Romanian-speaking population of Transylvania during the 1848 revolution. When the Magyars demanded that the Habsburgs return the 'lost lands' of Transylvania to the Hungarian crown, they goaded the Romanians into making a stand of their own. Forty thousand protesters turned up when Iancu summoned his followers to Blaj, and their chant, '*Nimic despre noi fără noi*' ('No decision about us without us'), rang out from the Câmpul Libertăţii (Field of Liberty) south of the town. A semicircle of busts depicting Romania's revolutionary heroes commemorates the event. There is more information about the history of Romanian nationalism in the history museum.

Blaj also has the distinction of being the headquarters of the Uniate Church. Adherents of this sect, which was established in Transylvania in 1699 under pressure from the Calvinists, follow most of the Orthodox rites but accept the authority of the Pope. The Uniates (also known as Greco-Catholics) represented a minority of the total Romanian population in Transylvania. But under the leadership of Bishop Inochentie Micu Clain, who lobbied for their rights at the Viennese court in the early 18C, they formed Transylvania's proto-nationalist movement. This is why Iancu made his rallying cry from Blaj. The communists forced the Uniates to convert to Orthodoxy, but since 1989 there has been a great revival of interest in the church, especially in the Maramureş.

About 10km from Blaj on the DJ107 heading northeast towards Târnăveni, you reach the village of **Sona**. Turn north here towards Sânmiclăuş, a distance of 4km, and you will find a fine late-Renaissance **castle** built by the Bethlen family between 1668–83. Many traditional festivals are held in Sona. Ask for specific details at Centrul Judeţean de Creaţie Populară in Alba Iulia, Str Brătianu 2, ☎ 058 813076/ 813380.

Continue northeast on the DJ107 from Sona, and in c 13km you reach **Cetatea de Baltă**. An ancient fortress was built near here, on Dealul Sântămăriei, during the 1C BC, but both this and the 11C *cetatea de baltă* (marsh fortress) on the banks of the Târnavă Mica have disappeared. Matei Corvin modernised the medieval palace and it was later given to Ştefan cel Mare, who bequeathed it to his son Petru Rareş. But the most impressive monument here is the **castle**. This is another splendid Renaissance building commissioned in 1624 by the Bethlen-Haller family; it is open to the public. The village lies much closer to Mediaş than to Alba Iulia and is right on the edge of the cluster of Saxon churches between Mediaş, Sibiu and Sighişoara.

Celtic weapons from the 2C BC have been found at the pretty town of **Aiud** (Strassburg in German), 11km north of Teuiș on the E81/DN1, but its main focal point is the forbidding 14C **fortress** that stands out from the elegant 18C houses which surround it on all sides. Between the 15C–18C Aiud became an important cultural centre; the mathematician and co-founder of Cluj University, Farkas Bólyai (1775–1856), went to school here. The rugged citadel now contains the History Museum, open Tues–Sun 09.00–17.00. There are **train** and **bus** stations here, and **accommodation** is available at the *Mureșul* hotel at Str Transilvania 3. The Căprioara **campsite** is 5km to the south of the town on the main road to Alba Iulia, and there are two **petrol stations** in town on the main through road.

On the way north to Turda, the E81/DN1 passes through **Mirăslău**, where Mihai Viteazul fought a battle on his way to achieving the brief unification of Romania in 1600. Once past Decea (where archaeologists have discovered Neolithic tools) and Unirea, the road starts dropping down into the Arieș Valley. Alternatively, leave the main road by turning left in Aiud and cut a corner here by joining the Arieș Valley road (the DN75). This route goes through the attractive **Cheile Vălișoarei**, the Vălișoara gorges. Take another short detour from Aiud for Râmeț Monastery, which stands at the head of the Râmeț Gorges; follow either road and you will eventually join the DN75, one of the prettiest roads in the Apuseni, with Turda to your east.

For anyone interested in **potholing** there are local clubs that organise expeditions to Peștera Mare and Peștera Piatra Ponorului, but the first base is the Speleological Institute in Cluj.

FROM TURDA TO CLUJ

The ancient town of **Turda** lies incarcerated within a belt of dirty factories. There was a Dacian settlement here called Potaissa, and the ancient Romans kept the name when they built a *castrum* on the same site. The Romans also established salt mines here, and these are still visible on the outskirts c 2km to the northeast at the spa of Turda-Băi. When Patrick Leigh-Fermor came here in the 1930s he found 'echoing chambers which reached deep into the mountain sides', and the miners were convicts. Archaeologists have identified 5C Christian tombs among the Roman remains.

Patrician stone **houses** dating from the 15C and 16C mark the town's importance as a Hungarian stronghold. Str Hașdeu 2 was a royal mansion, and the Transylvanian Diet used to hold meetings here until 1759. In 1568 the Diet made a famous proclamation by which the Orthodox church was dispossessed in favour of Calvinism, Lutheranism and Unitarianism. The building now houses **Muzeul de Istorie** (the History Museum), open Tues–Sun 10.00–17.00; other interesting structures include the severe **Reformed Church** on Str Avram Iancu—this has a portico dating from 1400, but the rest of the building is later— and the **Roman Catholic church** on Piața Republicii, which was completed in c 1500 and has a Baroque interior.

Turda's main **hotel**, the *Potaissa* (✩✩), is at Piața Republicii 6, ☎ 064 311691. The nearest **train** service runs at Câmpia Turzii, and a **narrow-gauge steam railway** runs between Turda and Abrud. Do not set out unless you have plenty of time: it takes five hours to reach Abrud, and there are only two services per day. **Buses** to and from Cluj leave from Str Gheorghe Lazăr to the east of Piaţa Republicii.

Taking the E81/DN1 north from Turda brings you through the village of **Feleac**, where the 15C Moldavian prince, Ştefan cel Mare, commissioned a church while visiting Transylvania in 1488. The west door bears a Slavonic inscription dating from 1516. Feleac also offers a panoramic view of Cluj, which lies about 10km away in the valley below.

Further down the hill is the **Făget campsite**, about 7km out of Cluj. To get there, turn left off the E81/DN1 up a long, signposted drive. The site is located among beautiful trees on a meadow overlooking the town. It offers cheap accommodation in wooden A-frame cabins, and there is overnight parking for camper vans. The sanitation is just bearable if you are not too fussy, and the view of the city lights at night compensates for many shortcomings.

Cluj-Napoca

The discovery of polished stone tools from the Someş Mic river valley suggests that the region was settled in prehistoric times. In the 2C BC, Dacians inhabited the site on which Cluj-Napoca stands today. They styled their citadel Napoca, a name that the Romans also used when they turned the fortress into the capital of Dacia Parulissensis (or Porolissum) in 124 AD. A tight cluster of hills rises steeply to the north and south of the Someş river, cradling the old city between them. To the east lies the Transylvanian Heath, while the wild ranges of the Apuseni stretch away to the west. During its more recent history Cluj became the cultural capital of Erdély (the Hungarian name for Transylvania). It was the centre of the royal administrative region of Kolozs (hence its Hungarian name, Kolozsvár), and its Magyar connections are still strong. The German name for Cluj, Klausenburg, is thought to come from '*clus*' or '*clusus*', vernacular Latin for an 'enclosed space'. Local German dialect turned this into Cluj.

History

No one knows exactly what happened in Cluj after the Romans left, and the subject has been the cause of some heated debate. Excavations still under way have found no proof that anyone lived on the site of Cluj itself between the Roman period and the arrival of King Árpád in 1001. However, signs of 9C Romanian *cenezi* or *cnezi* (local leaders) have been found in the outskirts, on the site of the Romanian Orthodox church at Cluj-Mănăştur, and at Dăbâca, where the remains of a citadel belonging to *cneazul* Gelu have also been identified. Magyar cemeteries dating from the 10C are known to have existed near Cluj.

In the early Middle Ages, Germans settled here. They were among the thousands of 'Saxons' who came to Transylvania at the invitation of the Hungarian kings. In reality they were northern Europeans from as far afield as present-day France and Belgium, but by far the greatest majority came from German-speaking lands, and they were called 'Saxons' for convenience. These colonists were invited by Hungary's kings who wanted men to protect the country's borders with the east and to develop a thriving economy. Most of the indigenous population were forced to retreat to the mountains and forests. In Cluj the Germans built their village in what is now the northwest corner of the medieval town. This nub of streets was known as the Altenburg (the Old Town) after Saxon Klausenburg developed around it. Before 1325, the Altenburg was extended by a large German quarter, which had a rectangular market place amid a regular network of streets.

Hungarians moved into Cluj in the mid-15C. They built houses of wood and stone in a Late Gothic or Renaissance style, which usually had a cellar and two main storeys. Most of the late-Medieval houses in Cluj have been altered beyond recognition; only the Late Gothic parish house, opposite the northeast corner of Piața Unirii, remains intact.

Structural details and inscriptions from the 16C have survived well. After Alba Iulia declined, Cluj became the most important Renaissance centre in Transylvania. Architecture and stone carving flourished here, and in 1530 a stonemasons' workshop was established in the town. Its craftsmen specialised in a style known as the 'Flower Renaissance' because luxuriant plant motifs figured prominently in their work. Dávid Sípos was a leading exponent, and this kind of carving survived well into the 18C and even appears in some forms of 20C vernacular art. It has some close parallels with the Brâncovenesque style that developed in Wallachia during the 17C.

In 1556, Ferenc Dávid (1520–79) founded the Unitarian sect in Cluj. Unitarianism is an ultra-rational—and exceptionally tolerant—faith which originally had close ties with the Anabaptists. Its most important tenets include a rejection of the idea of the Trinity and of the doctrine of Christ's divinity. A branch of the Unitarian sect, known as Socinians, flourished in the nearby town of Turda. Its followers took their name from Claudio (or Fausto) Sozzini, a wandering preacher from Siena. Sozzini eventually turned up in Cluj where he stayed for two years before moving to Kraków in 1580. There are around 250,000 Unitarians in Romania today, mostly Hungarian-speaking and not to be confused with the Uniates, who are primarily Romanian—not for nothing do Transylvanians compare their religious history to the Tower of Babel.

Cluj has some superb Baroque buildings, dating mainly from the 18C, when the Habsburgs invaded Transylvania. Most of the architects and sculptors who introduced the style came from the German-speaking lands, but by the late 18C some excellent Transylvanian masters had emerged as well.

In the 19C neo-Classical, Romantic and Eclectic buildings appeared, contributing to the melange of architectural styles that makes Cluj so attractive. Those that survive include the twin-towered Calvinist church, a Neo-Classical building from 1829–50, while the Catholic parish church has an impressive neo-Gothic tower on its north side.

Apart from its architectural attractions, Cluj is a lively and sophisticated university town. It has around 24,000 students, second only to Bucharest. In 1974 Ceaușescu added Napoca to the city's medieval name in recognition of its Dacian origins.

Practical information

☎ code
064

Tourist information
Cluj's main tourist office, *Turism Feleacul*, is at Str Șincai 2, west of the Ethnographic Museum on Str Memorandumului; open Mon–Fri 08.00–16.00.

Getting around
By train The train station lies on Piața Gării to the north of the old centre, about 20 minutes' walk from Piața Unirii along B-dul Horea. Tickets for international journeys can be booked at the *CFR* on Piața Unirii 9, while internal tickets are sold from Piața Mihai Viteazu 20.
By bus *Autogara 1* is on Str Aurel Vlaicu, to the east of Piața Marasti, while *Autogara 2*, which serves the north of Cluj as well as Budapest, is just under 1km to the northeast of the train station on Str Locomoviței; Cluj also has **trolleybuses** and **trams**.
By car The *ACR* garage at B-dul 21 Dicembrie 131, ☎ 198680, will do **car repairs**. Alternatives are *Auto Moto* on Aleea Moghioroș and *Gabism* on Str Alvernaw 24. There are plenty of **petrol stations** around the city.
By plane The airport, running internal flights for *TAROM*, is on Str Traian Vuia 149, ☎ 192238, beside the road to Dej and Apahida to the northeast of the city. The *TAROM* office is at Piața Mihai Viteazu 11.

Where to stay
Until very recently, many of Cluj's hotels were dire, but during the last five years things have radically changed and you may be spoilt for choice. Right in the centre of town, overlooking Piața Unirii at Str Napoca 1, there is the splendid *Continental* (★★) with its Neo-Baroque dining room, ☎ 191441; fax 193977. Then there is the sumptuous *Vila Continental* (★★★★), under the same management, at Str Șincai 2–4, ☎ 195582. *Vila Casa Alba* is another 4-star hotel, at Str Emil Racoviță 22, ☎/fax 432277. *Hotel Victoria* (★★★) is at B-dul 22 Dicembrie 54–56, ☎ 197963; fax 197573. *Hotel Transilvania* (★★★) stands on top of the old Hapsburg citadel at Str Călărășilor 1–3, ☎ 432071; fax 432076. You can climb up to it from Aleea Scărilor off Str Drăgălina. Contact *ANTREC* (see p 116) if you prefer to stay in a private household.

Eating out
If you need to buy basics there are lots of groceries, fruiterers and delicatessens around the city centre and department stores such as Central on Str Doja: try Str Memorandumului and the streets between Piața Unirii, Str Gheorghe Barițiu to the northwest, and Piața Avram Iancu to the east. Alternatively, you could visit the food market on Piața Mărăști on the way to the main bus station. In terms of food and decor, the **Continental Hotel** in Piața Unirii has one of the best **restaurants** in Cluj: it has a Baroque-style dining hall redolent of 1930s hedonism. Cluj also has an Arabian restaurant, called *Fahid*, at Str Napoca 6–8. *Restaurant Matei Corvin* is at Str Matei Corvin 3, tel 197496, while the *Maestro* is at Str Dobrogeanu Gherea 25, ☎ 118056. If you want to look outside Cluj, the *Tamás Bistro*, 26km from the city at Săvădisla, specialises in Transylvanian dishes. It is on a road signposted for Baișoara which turns south from the main Cluj–Oradea road (the E60) between Florești and Gilău.

There are a number of **pizzerias** and **fast-food** outlets, including *Ares*

Pizzeria, Str Brâncoveanu 32, ☎ 414025; *Gente*, Str Brâncuşi 3, ☎ 414820; *McDonald's*, Piaţa Mihai Viteazul; *New Croco*, Str Victor Babeş 12; *Summer Time*, Str Tomis 3; *Shining Time*, Str Louis Pasteur 77, ☎ 438738; *Vlădeasa*, Str Gheorghe Doja 20.

Post office and telephones

The telephone bureau is on Parcul Caragiale. This is behind the post office at Str Gheorghe Doja 33 opposite Str Saguna, unusually open Mon–Fri 07.00–20.00, Sat 07.00–13.00; there is another on the south side of Piaţa Unirii, open every day 07.00–22.00.

Money

Exchange houses have burgeoned everywhere, and some of them accept *Visa* and *Mastercard*. Otherwise there are **banks** on and around Piaţa Unirii, on Str Memorandumului and at B-dul Eroilor 36. Avoid the black-market money dealers on Piaţa Unirii.

Police

The two main police stations are at Str Traian 27 (county) and Str Decebal 28 (municipal). *Primăria* (the town hall), which can sometimes help with local information, is housed under the clock tower at Calea Moţilor 1–3.

Medical care

A list of late-night **pharmacies** is displayed in the pharmacy on the southeast corner of Piaţa Unirii, and there is a **polyclinic** for the treatment of injuries on Str Micuş 3 (but it is usually packed); for urgent help or advice, try *Farmacia Karl Linné* at Str Braşov 12 or *Ditafarm* at B-dul Eroilor 18, both of which are large concerns.

Entertainment

When Patrick Leigh-Fermor visited Cluj in the summer of 1934 he found a city dreaming in *fin-de-siècle* Viennese culture. His companions told him that everything came alive in winter with 'parties and theatres and the opera in full blast'. Today, Cluj still has its **opera** and internationally recognised **theatres**, but the frivolity has gone. Instead, you can take a course of **Tae Kwan Do** (in the Liceul Agricol Gheorgheni, Aleea Tineretului 57) or join the Romanian **Numismatic Society** (at Str Ion Vidu 11). The university runs excellent summer courses in **Romanian language and literature**: ask for details from the Romanian Cultural Foundation in Bucharest (see p 32).

Teatrul Naţional şi Opera Româna (the Romanian National Theatre and Opera House) is housed in Hellmer and Fellner's early 20C factory-cum-Baroque masterpiece on Piaţa Ştefan cel Mare, opposite the Orthodox Cathedral. *Teatrul Maghiar de Stat şi Opera Maghiar* (the Hungarian State Theatre and Opera) is an early 19C building near the river, to the west of Parcul Caragiale and between Splaiul Independenţei and Str Băriţiu at Str Emil Isac 26–28. It opened in 1821. The **opera** season starts in October and ends in July.

The *Filarmonica de Stat* (State Philharmonia) is on Str E. Martonne (named after the French geographer and Transylvanophile), and *Casa Studentească de Cultură* (Student of Culture House), which has its own theatre and concert halls, is at Piaţa Lucian Blaga 1–3, to the right of Str Republicii which climbs steeply towards the Botanic Gardens. *Teatrul de Papuşi Puck*, the **puppet theatre**, can be found on Str Brătianu near the junction with Str Tomis. Cluj has several **cinemas** including the *Arta* on Str Universitatii, opposite the Piarist Church, and the *Bingo* on Str Memorandumului.

Bars and clubs include the *Diesel Club* at Piața Unirii 17, ☎ 198441; *Club Harley Davidson*, adjoining the *Diesel*; *Flash Bar* at Piața Unirii 10.

Apart from the academic nucleus of the Babeș-Bolyai University itself, the city teems with a seemingly endless supply of learned and cultural institutions, research laboratories, specialist hospitals, clinics and religious centres and libraries. Try a visit to the **observatories**, one on the northwest outskirts near Calea Baciului, and the other in the Botanic Gardens.

Cluj lies on the edge of the Apuseni mountains, an area rich in underground water courses and caves. If you are interested in **potholing**, contact *Institutul de Speologie Emil Racoviță* (the Speleological Institute) at Str Clinicilor 5, which has up-to-date information and the names and addresses of local and national caving clubs. Racoviță (1868–1947) fathered the science of caving when he published an essay on 'biospelaeology' in 1907. He founded the institute, the first of its kind in the world, in 1920.

Bookshops, maps, libraries and newspapers

Cluj has a good supply of bookshops where you can buy decent maps of the city and the whole of Transylvania. The *Erdély* sheet map, published in Budapest, is worth looking out for here as well as in Hungary because it shows many villages and mountain routes neglected by others. There are several bookshops on and near Piața Unirii, and Cluj is the place to find a series of informative booklets about Transylvania's Hungarian churches. For Romanian and Hungarian literature, try *Humanitas* on Str Brătianu 22. The city has libraries specialising in a number of foreign languages, including English (*Biblioteca Britanică* at Str Avram Iancu 11), German (*Biblioteca Germană*, at the southern end of Str Universității, and *Biblioteca Austriacă* at Str Horea 31), and Italian and Spanish (*Biblioteca Italiană* and *Biblioteca Spaniolă*, both at Str Horea 31). There is a French **cultural institute** at Str Kogălniceanu 12–14, while its German counterpart is on the same street at nos. 7–9.

Cluj has always attracted people of independent and often courageous views: one of Ceaușescu's most outspoken critics was Doina Cornea, a university lecturer who first told the outside world about Ceaușescu's plan to destroy nearly half the country's traditional villages. The Romanian and Hungarian writers' unions publish **journals** such as *Steaua*, *Korunk*, named after a famous modernist review of the 1920s, and *Helikon*, whose title was inspired by a celebrated 19C Hungarian literary movement; *Echinox* and *Thalia* are highbrow students' rags—all these journals are published in Hungarian. Romania's pop and rock **radio** station, *Radio Contact* (founded in 1996), has a base here at Str Beethoven 25.

Muzeul Național de Istorie a Transilvaniei

The National Transylvanian History Museum, Str Daicoviciu 2, ☎ 191718. Open Tues–Sun 09.00–17.00 in summer, 09.00–16.00 in winter. Standing in a quiet precinct on the edge of Piața Muzeului, to the northwest of Piața Unirii, the museum is one of the oldest in Romania, having opened in 1859. On the first floor the displays introduce prehistoric animals found in Transylvania and lead you through the Neolithic and Bronze Ages. The museum has an impressive collection of Bronze Age tools; some of the most rewarding Bronze Age settlements have been found half-an-hour's drive to the northeast of Cluj. The Roman period is illustrated by lovely, simple stone carvings, mostly from tombs. Later periods are represented by pieces of furniture, glassware and ceramics. On the ground level across the courtyard from the entrance is a *lapidarium* containing Roman funerary monuments, votive reliefs and inscriptions from camps and settlements all over Transylvania. There are medieval and Renaissance stone carvings as well. Most of these come from in or around Cluj and show how local craftsmen adapted ancient Roman, Tuscan and northern Italian styles to their own skills.

The museum's entrance is on Str Daicoviciu, named after a Romanian archaeologist who was responsible in the early 20C for investigating the extraordinary Dacian citadels in the Orăştie mountains (see pp 395–398). On Piaţa Muzeului, a few metres to the northeast on the corner of Str Deleu and Parcul Caragiale, is an **area of excavation** showing paved streets, walls and hypocausts of Roman Napoca.

Muzeul Naţional de Arta

The National Art Museum, Piaţa Unirii 30, ☎ 116952. Open Wed–Sun 10.00–17.00. Formerly this was the Bánffy Palace, a late Baroque mansion that the Sibian architect Johann Eberhardt Blaumann (1724–85) created for György Bánffy, the Habsburg Governor of Transylvania. Figures of gods and goddesses, vases and garlands decorate the façade, and behind the elegant carriage entrance is a symmetrical courtyard in which a sense of imperial pride hits you smartly between the eyes. But Blaumann balanced pomp with graceful restraint as he did in Sibiu's Brukenthal residence. Palatul Bánffy was one of the most important commissions of its day and had an enormous influence on other Transylvanian architects.

Inside, the collection ranges from the 16C to the modern period. It contains 18C glass icons, a marvellous 16C altar from Jimbav, silverware, furniture and weaponry, and paintings, sculptures and prints by progressive 19C and 20C Romanian artists. Notable among these last are the Romantic painter, Theodore Aman (1831–91), Impressionists Nicolae Grigorescu (1815–1907) and Ion Andreescu (1850–82), both of whom joined the French Barbizon painters, and the early modernists, Ion Ţuculescu (1910–62), Nicolae Tonitza (1886–1940), Gheorghe Petraşcu (1872–1949) and Nicolae Dărăscu (1883–1959). There is also a collection of prints by the Dadaist and architect, Marcel Iancu (1895–1983). Among Romanian sculptors represented here are Ion Jalea (1887–1983), Dimitrie Paciurea (1873–1932), Cornel Medrea (1889–1964), Frederik Storck (1872–1942) and Gheza Vida (1913–80). The gallery also has paintings by 16C and 17C Dutch and Flemish masters, and there are 19C canvases from Austria, France, Germany, Hungary and Russia. Other notable non-Romanian works in the collection are sculptures by the Expressionists Ernst Barlach (1870–1937), and George Kolbe (1877–1947), and there are prints by Daumier, Degas, Kollwitz and Piranesi.

Muzeul Etnografic al Transilvaniei

The Transylvanian Ethnographic Museum, Str Memorandumului 41, ☎ 192344. Open Tues–Sun 09.00–17.00. Guided tours available. A vaulted carriageway and elegant wrought-iron gates divide the blue façade of this building neatly in two. And beyond, the courtyard allows you to appreciate the original spirit of this 16C building. During the 18C it was known as Calul Bălan (Bălan's Horse) and had a reputation as Cluj's best inn. From 1790–1865 it housed meet-

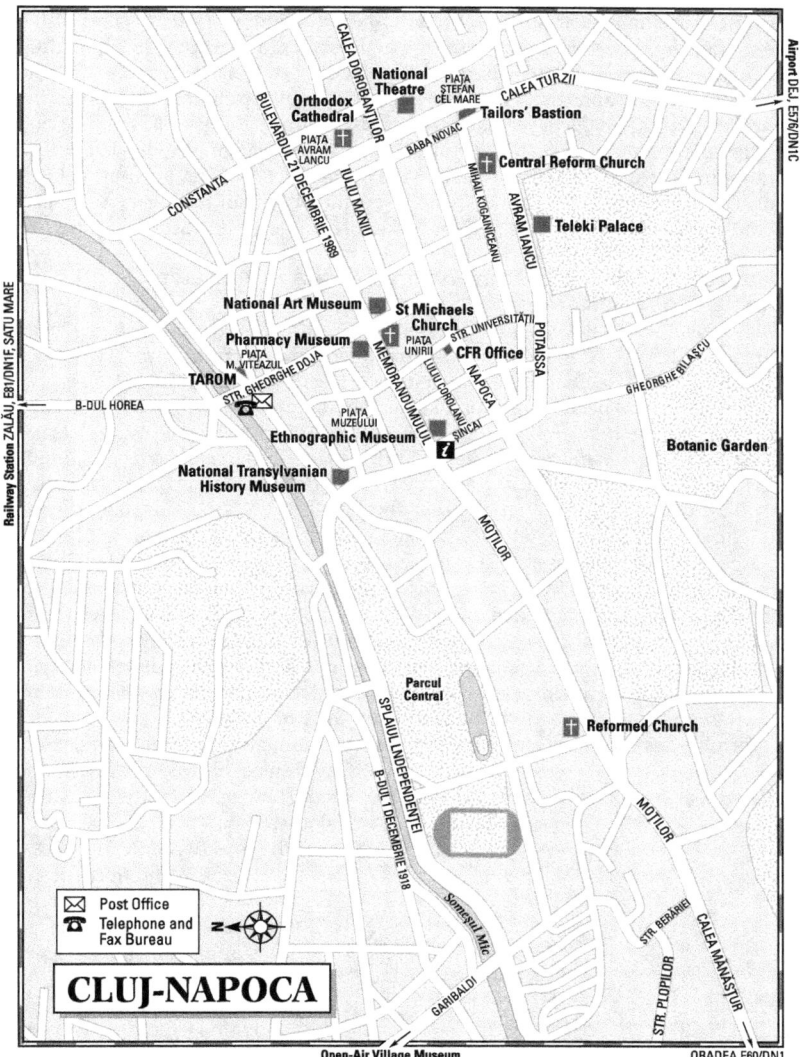

ings of the Transylvanian Diet, and in 1894 the executive committee of the Romanian National Party went on trial here. They were arrested for publishing the 'Memorandum' (from which the street gets its name), a protest against the Hungarian government's treatment of Transylvania's Romanians. Most of the committee went to prison, but the Memorandum Movement helped pave the way for unification with Romania in 1918.

The museum, which opened in 1922, is an appealing place, not least because of the way it responds to Transylvania's complex ethnography. Displays are arranged in small, informative sections devoted to an individual technology (fishing, hunting, sheep-rearing, weaving and textiles and pottery). Highlights include a superb collection of embroidered clothes, headgear and masks—do not miss the goat costume, with its snapping jaws and multi-coloured tassels, used in the New Year's Eve *Capra* festival. There is also a superb display of regional flat-weave carpets. Concerts and lectures are held here regularly. In 1929 the museum's original director, Romulus Vuia, established the first open-air village museum in Romania (see below), where you can check out his theory that illiterate Transylvanian builders made intuitive use of the Golden Section.

Muzeul Etnografic al Transilvaniei, Secţia in Aer Liber ~ *Parcul Etnografic 'Romulus Vuia'*

The Open-Air Village Museum/Romulus Vuia Park, Str Tăietura Turcului. Open Tues–Sun 09.00–16.00, 1 May–1 Nov. Check the opening times with the Ethnographic Museum first, as it is a long way to go for nothing. Guided tours are available, but you need permission to take photographs. If you do not have a car, bus 27 from the railway station or 30 from Piaţa Unirii will take you to Cartier Grigoreşti, from where you can walk. The museum sits in a park on top of a hill between the Someşul Mic River and the railway line, c 5km northwest of Piaţa Unirii. If you go by car from the centre, take Str Dacia and Drăgălina after crossing the river on Str Voineşti and then head west along Str Grigorescu.

Modelled on the Skansen village museum in Norway, the traditional buildings in the museum are divided into three sections: smallholders' households, churches, and technical and agricultural buildings. Included in these are presses, mills, hydraulic saws and mining equipment, most made of wood or with wooden frames. A house from the Moţi village of Vidra was the only exhibit left unscathed after retreating German and Hungarian troops burnt the museum down in 1944. After this, collecting started again from scratch.

Farmhouses now in place include Romanian, Hungarian, Székely and Saxon buildings made of wattle as well as wood. There are monumental gates dating from the 17C–20C. One of the three wooden churches, from Cizer in the northwest, was built by Horea, the revolutionary leader. It has a polygonal entrance and chancel with a three-sided porch, and inside there are charming paintings and carvings.

Thatched farm-houses in the Open Air Village Museum

Grădina Botanică 'Alexandru Borza'

The Botanic Garden, Str Republicii 42, ☎ 197604. Open Mon–Sat 09.00–14.00. Guided tours are available. This is the largest and one of the loveliest gardens of its kind in Romania. It is spread out over 14ha of banks and hollows which contain c 10,000 plant species. Getting here on foot involves a strenuous climb up Str Republicii, south of the town centre. University professor

Alexandru Borza founded the garden in 1920, and it still functions as part of the university's Botanic Institute. As well as the herbarium for medicinal and commercial plants, it has sections devoted to ornamental, Sino-Japanese and Roman varieties. There is also a Roman garden. The greenhouses contain tropical, subtropical and desert species, including prized rare orchids. The species grown here come from all over the world including the Americas, Australasia and Africa, as well as the Pyrenees, the Alps and the Balkans. From Romania, there are plants from the Transylvanian Plateau, the Carpathians, the Banat, Oltenia and the Danube region.

Monumental gate in the Open Air Village Museum

Colecţia de Istorie a Farmaciei

The Pharmacy Museum, on the corner of Piaţa Unirii 28 and Str Doja 1. Open Mon–Sat 09.00–16.00. Housed in the 15C Hintz-Mauksch house, the home of Transylvania's longest-running apothecary shop (1573–1948), this is a collection of ancient instruments, bottles and medical recipes dating from the 16C–18C.

Walking around Cluj

In the centre, most of the old street façades have survived intact, and apart from the village museum, most of the worthwhile sights are in the downtown area and can be visited within a couple of hours. If you are short of time, do not miss Piaţa Unirii and its surrounding streets, especially those to the northwest, and the old university precinct.

Piaţa Unirii stands on the former Altenburg marketplace and is a logical place to start a tour of the city. At the north end of the square the Roman Catholic church of **Sf Mihai** (St Michael) dominates the scene. This Late-Gothic building is one of the largest of its kind in Transylvania. Its spare, dark interior gives the impression of soaring up to a high ceiling, the vertical thrust being emphasised by rows of slender supporting pillars that line the nave walls. Surmounting the wall shafts are densely carved capitals, some of them depicting men at work, such as shepherds and masons. Fragments of Early Gothic

---

Hall churches

Wilhelm Lübke invented the term *hallenkirche* in his 1853 book on medieval Westphalian art. It denotes a church in which the aisles are the same or nearly the same height as the nave. A hall church has no clerestory, but light floods into the nave from the side aisles. The effect is more spacious than a basilica, where the side aisles are generally much lower than the nave. Hall churches were cheaper and easier to build than Gothic basilicas because they did not need flying buttresses. They are a mainly German phenomenon and are known to have existed from the 11C, although there are a few in southwest France. Southern and central Transylvania have some splendid examples too.

stonework have been found in its walls, showing that an earlier church once stood on the site. This earlier shrine was probably built on the orders of Petrus, the Bishop of Transylvania (r. 1270–1307). The present building dates from 1349, when the Pope in Avignon sent indulgences to its founders; his parchment is still preserved in the sacristy. Its polygonal rib-vaulted choir was installed in the second half of the 14C. The original three-aisled basilica was converted into a five-bay hall church in the 15C.

What started life as a Catholic church was at various periods also used by Protestants, the Reformed Church and the Uniates. During the Austrian invasion of 1698 a fire destroyed much of the interior; this was restored with a Baroque altarpiece and pulpit that were the first examples of this style to arrive in Cluj. They were made by Johannes Nachtigall and Anton Schuchbauer (born c 1720) and date from the 1740s. The altarpiece painting of the Adoration of the Magi (1748–50) is by Franz Anton Maulbertsch, and the trace vaulting over the nave dates from the same period. The church has four magnificent portals decorated with carved stonework; over the main entrance is a bas relief that contains the arms of the Magyar King Sigismund of Luxembourg. Inside, the sacristy door is a fine example of the Transylvanian Renaissance style; it was made in 1528. Inscriptions in the nave show how important the building has been to the Hungarian community of Transylvania. Its neo-Gothic bell tower on the north side was a 19C afterthought.

Another striking feature of Piața Unirii is the **statue** of Matei Corvin on his horse. The bronze, by sculptor János Fadrusz, was erected in 1902. It stands on an ugly castellated plinth and is flanked by four dignitaries.

The communists left the **old centre** of Cluj intact, and while its one-way system gives the impression that this is a thrusting metropolis, it is easy to slip away from the traffic into meandering alleys where time seems to pass more slowly. At Str Matei Corvin 6, at the end of a side street to the northwest of Piața Unirii, stands an attractive **medieval house**. Now part of the university's art school, it is famous as the place where Matei Corvin was born in 1440. It was built as a hanjust inside the citadel's first perimeter walls, fragments of which are still visible nearby, and started life as a Gothic building. Its shape changed radically with

---

Matei Corvin (1440–90)

Corvin (Mátyás Corvinus in Hungarian) was born in Cluj and came from a noble Romanian family. He was the son of Iancu de Hunedoara (János Hunyadi), who built an impressive castle at Hunedoara in southwest Transylvania that is still standing. Corvin, who reigned 1458–90, was one of the most admired Magyar kings, famous not only for defeating the Turks but also for his love of culture. After his marriage to Princess Beatrix of Naples in 1476, the impact of Italian humanism on the Hungarian court increased and Matei is known to have commissioned paintings from Mantegna, Filippino Lippi and Botticelli. He also created a wonderful library, the Bibliotheca Corviniana, which was filled with illuminated manuscripts and reflected almost the entire scope of contemporary learning. Although Matei reigned over a kingdom that stretched from eastern Austria in the west to Bohemia in the north, the effects were also felt in Transylvania, where Italianate palaces and castles can still be seen to this day.

the addition of Renaissance window and door frames and, later, a Baroque courtyard. When Secessionism was all the rage, the house acquired yet another, radically different face. In 1944, Transylvanian architect Károly Kós began removing some of the fussier, outer layers, and the restoration process was completed during the 1950s.

Head north, turn left and right and you arrive in Piața Muzeului. To the east is the **History Museum**. On the other side of the square, at the corner of Str V. Deleu and Str Zola, is a Baroque Franciscan **church and friary**, complete with Franciscan emblem. The church was founded by Matei Corvin in 1486 and built by the same master who created the Dominican friary in Str Tomis (see below). Opposite the northeast corner of Piața Unirii, on the eastern corner of Str Memorandumului and Str Gheorghe Doja, stands the *parohia* (parish house) of 1477.

Follow Str Universității to the south from the southwest corner of Piața Unirii beside the *Continental Hotel*. This takes you into the heart of the university district and another part of the Altenburg. At Str Universității 5 is an 18C **Piarist Church** whose interior is curiously at odds with itself: a confection of delicate pink and grey culminates in an altarpiece which makes such a dynamic statement that it threatens to break out of the apse altogether. In fact the church was the first Baroque church in Cluj, built by Jesuits between 1718–24. Completed at the height of the Habsburgs' counter-reformatory campaign (which helps to explain the overpowering altar), it was turned over to the Ordo Scolarum Piarum later in the century. The Piarists, who were dedicated to the education of the poor, were one of several Catholic orders who established foundations in Transylvania after the Austrian invasion.

Turning left just before the end of Str Universității brings you into **Str Kogălniceanu**, an attractively secluded road that contains several pretty buildings. Facing the junction with Str Universității is **Biblioteca Germană** (the German Library), with the pretty 18C Piarist School to its left. The Library is housed in a building commissioned by Governor Bánffy. On the left at no. 1 are the main buildings of the **Babeș-Bolyai University**, comprising the rectorat (administrative offices), several faculties and a mineralogical and paleontological museum. Some of the lecture neo-Baroque lecture halls are magnificent. To the right of the entrance is a sculpture from 1973 depicting three Enlightenment philosophers, Petru Maior, Samuil Micu-Klein and Gheorghe Șincai. They were leading nationalists who formed the Scoala Ardeleana, the 18C 'Transylvanian School' that nourished the idea of a separate Romanian identity a century before the nation came into existence. Babeș-Bolyai University was founded in 1872; its illustrious graduates include Edmund Bordeaux Székely, who translated the Dead Sea Scrolls.

In 1918, just after Transylvania's unification with Romania, the new authorities forbade schools and universities to hold classes in Hungarian, taking revenge on the Magyars for what they regarded as the systematic anihilation of their language and culture in the preceding century. When the Germans placed northern and eastern Transylvania under Hungarian rule in 1940, the law was promptly reversed. Despite the provisions that have been made for Hungarian-language teaching in schools since 1990, the issue is still a contentious one.

East beyond the University and across the road on the left is a 20C building that is home to the Philharmonic orchestra and Casa Universitărilor. The left-hand part of this complex was once a **Dominican friary**, designed in the late 15C by the workshop of Frater Johannes. It is the only example of its kind from medieval Hungary to have survived in its original form. Johannes was also in charge of building the Franciscan friary (see above).

A few metres further east on Str Kogălniceanu is the delicate Baroque entrance to the former **Teleki Palace**. Created by the architect Josef Luder, the mansion was completed in 1795. It is now the county library. Across Str Tomis is the Emil Racoviţa **high school**. On its north flank stands another beautiful Magyar **mansion**, built for the Toldalagi-Korda family by Carlo Justi between 1801–07. Almost directly opposite are the State Archives, while further down on the right is the Radiological Institute. Beyond this is a small square containing a delightful equestrian **statue** of St George killing the dragon. It is a replica of the 1373 St George that stands in the courtyard next to St Vitus's Cathedral in Prague. The sculptors, two brothers, Gheorghe and Martin, were born in Cluj.

Immediately behind the statue is the solid but elegant Gothic bulk of the **Central Reformed Church** (also known as the Hungarian Reformed Church). Founded by Matei Corvin in 1490, it is a hall church with a handsome, polygonal choir that still preserves the original 15C vaulting. The ceiling tracery in the nave dates from 1603. Around the choir windows is some superb stonework. During the reign of Gheorghe Rákóczi (1638–47) the church was extensively restored. It has a fine organ, and concerts here are worth catching; check the notices on the door.

Past the church and a few metres to the right along Str Baba Novac stands the impressive pentagonal ruin of **Bastionul Croiţorilor**, the Tailors' Bastion. Beside it is a chunk of 15C wall from the citadel's southeast corner and the attenuated figure of Baba Novac by the 20C sculptor Virgil Fulicia. General Novac was aide to Mihai Viteazul, the leader who first united Romania's three main principalities in 1600–01. Novac was betrayed during the scramble for Transylvania that ensued, and mercenaries working for the Austrian General Basta killed him on this spot.

Most of the surviving features of the **Citadel** date from the second half of the 15C. It was a Saxon fortress, consisting of two perimeter walls and 12 bastions. The first ring was erected in around 1316, while the second was completed in the early 16C. Apart from the Tailors' Bastion, only odd pieces of the second wall are visible elsewhere: Bastionul Postăvarilor, the Drapers' Bastion, at Str Potaissa 1, Bastionul Cizmarilor, the Cobblers' Bastion, at Str Potaissa 15, and Turnul Pompierilor, the Firemen's Tower, at Str Tipografiei 17. From the first curtain wall there only remains a tower, at Piaţa Unirii 25 bis.

Turn north again, and on the other side of the wall along Calea Turzii you come to the southwest corner of a long, narrow square. In fact, this is two squares in one: Piaţa Ştefan cel Mare and Piaţa Avram Iancu. The combined **National Theatre and Opera House** is on Piaţa Ştefan cel Mare. It was built between 1904–06 on the site of some of Cluj's oldest wooden houses. The design is by the Habsburg architects Hellmer and Fellner, specialists in theatre buildings. To the north, the top-heavy **Orthodox Cathedral** in Piaţa Avram Iancu was constructed between 1923–33 as a triumphal celebration of Transylvania's independence. The building has a concrete core and inside, the cathedral is frescoed throughout with depressingly formalised versions of 1950s socialist realism, the result of instructions from the Kremlin via Romania's then Minister of Culture, Leonte Rautu.

If you walk west along the north side of B-dul 21 Dicembrie on your way back to Piaţa Unirii you pass two late-Baroque **churches**, one Reformed and the other Lutheran, both of which have pretty interiors.

The continuation of Str Memorandumului is Calea Moţilor, in which, at nos. 1–3, you can see an early 20C confection consisting of the *prefectura* and *primăria* (the county and city councils).

Around 800m further to the west, on the corner of Calea Moţilor and Str Coşbuc, stands the clean-lined and beautifully proportioned **Reformed Church**, which architect Károly Kós designed around the theme of Peter's betrayal of Christ. It is better known as the 'Cock' Church because of the cock motif that occurs throughout in the interior, symbolising Peter's triple denial. But the overall shape is modelled on the vernacular architecture that inspired Kós's most innovative work. He adapted the belfry and spire from Transylvanian wooden churches, while the ideas for its mass and volume come from traditional Finnish designs. Kós saw the building to completion in 1913.

Even further west, in the Mănăştur district is a 15C Gothic Roman Catholic **Calvary church**, notable for its fine statue of the Virgin and Child on an exterior wall. The building stands in a park to the north of Calea Mănăştur beside a spaghetti junction. To reach it, turn off onto a small road, Str Berariei, to the right just after you leave the Calea for Str Plopilor, which heads north from this intersection. There is also a **19C church** in this district, built on the site of a Romanian Orthodox church founded by Gelu in the 9C.

Károly Kós (1883–1977)

A Magyar by parentage, Kós studied in Budapest, where he joined a widespread Hungarian movement that favoured vernacular and 'organic architecture' over the more exotic and sinuous forms of Art Nouveau. Like many of his contemporaries, he drew inspiration from the British Arts and Crafts Movement, and especially from John Ruskin, William Morris and Walter Crane. A large retrospective show of Crane's work was held in Budapest in 1900, but other influences included the Finnish architects, Eliel Saarinen and Lars Sonck, who studied traditional, wooden buildings in Karelia. Encouraged by their example, Kós and his friends did the same thing in Transylvania, recording variations in regional styles. Kós later synthesised these with designs based on Finnish architecture. After 1920, he became involved in politics and designed few buildings, but he wrote and illustrated several books on architecture, some of which were inspired by Morris's Kelmscott Press. His delightful *Erdély* (Transylvania), published in Budapest in 1929, contains his linocuts of the vernacular buildings he recorded earlier (an English-language edition appeared in 1989). Many of his early 20C buildings can be seen in Sfântu Gheorghe (see p 454).

CLUJ TO NICULA

Even though the countryside on either side is less spectacular than the Apuseni, the E576/DN1C to the northeast of Cluj brings you past several interesting places. **Bonțida**, a village across the river to the east of the road, c 30km from Cluj, is the site of a Bánffy family residence. Built in the 17C and decorated with magnificent Baroque architecture, it is now used as a stud farm. At **Iclod**, a few kilometres further north on the E576/DN1C, is a modest but enterprising archaeology and history museum. A further 15km north lies the small town of **Gherla**, once an Armenian stronghold, which has some superb 18C houses; one has been converted into a local history museum, open Tues–Sun 10.00–17.00.

Take a side road to the east of Gherla, and turn right over the river bridge. In 1km you reach the small village of **Nicula**, an old Romanian settlement dating back to at least 1326. Its name is said to come from the man who first owned property here. Later it was acquired by the Bánffy family, who in 1467 rose up against the Hungarian king, Matei Corvin. Having suppressed the revolt, Matei gave the village to the Bishop of Oradea. In the late 17C Romanian-speaking *nemeși* (local nobles) regained much of the land here.

Tall wooden crosses stand in the gardens beside the road; the Niculeni are proud of having had a church as early as 1552, whereas nearby Gherla's Orthodox community had none until the 18C. But the villagers are also conscious of their 'miracle': when an icon of the Virgin Mary wept real tears. The painting in question was painted on wood by Luca of Iclod. It originally hung in the parish church, of which the present building is a 19C replacement. Now the icon is the centrepiece of the icon screen in the new monastery church. The 17C was a time of great insecurity for Transylvania. Raided by Tartars and fought over by Austrians and Turks, it was no wonder that the principality's inhabitants should cling to any sign that seemed to come from a greater and more universal power. On the evening of 15 February 1694 a group of Austrian army officers came to Nicula, curious to see an Orthodox church. Attracted by Luca's painting, they were amazed to see tears pouring from the Virgin's eyes. Eventually, 27 eyewitnesses swore in court that they had seen the icon crying without cease, day and night, for 26 days.

Follow the crosses through Nicula villages to the Mănăstirea. The road becomes a track which bends to the left and rises steeply. At the end of it, sitting on a ledge with a wooded hill behind and a spectacular view of the valley in front, is Nicula **monastery**.

The monastery was founded in the early 17C and, thanks to the Virgin's tears, it was home to a celebrated school for *icoane pe sticla* (icons painted on glass). Today, it has a small but delightful museum devoted to these objects, open daily 08.00–16.00. In the centre of the monastery buildings is a tiny church made from trunks of oak. The roof and octagonal spire are covered with shingles. Constructed in the Maramureș, it replaced another wooden shrine which burnt down in 1973. Luckily, the miraculous icon of the Virgin and Child had already been moved to the 'new' late 19C/early 20C church beside it. Inside, the walls are decorated with Moroșeni wood icons as well as icons on glass. You can visit both churches and the icon museum if you ask one of the monks. The monastery and the icon school are still flourishing under the directorship of Stareț (Abbot) Ilarion.

Nicula's glass icons

As news of the miraculous icon spread, thousands of pilgrims came to Nicula to see it. Demand for replicas quickly outstripped supply, and the monks turned to glass, which was in plentiful supply thanks to the Armenians of Gherla, and also because it was cheaper and quicker to work with than wood. Nicula monastery ran its own painting school for the sons of local children, and soon they and their parents were pressed into service; some of the students later left to set up their own workshops elsewhere in Transylvania. Painting on glass is not exclusive to this part of the world; the technique has been known since the 3C BC. It is possible that Romanian monks learnt the method in Bohemia, Moravia or Slovakia, or perhaps artists from these regions visited Transylvania. Nicula was the first Romanian school.

To create an icon the painter lays the colour down in reverse, so that the resulting image gains depth by being seen through a transparent surface. As for colours, the early painters prepared their own, using powdered charcoal of lime or pinewood for the blacks while other shades were procured from local plants and minerals. They used linseed oil as a binding agent. Each family worked from a sketch drawn on paper, so multiple versions of the same icon could be produced at a sitting. Traditionally, it was the women's job to apply the colours while the men made the wooden frames and backs. Themes and iconography were standard; not suprisingly one of the most popular subjects was the Virgin and Child. Others comprised the Birth of Christ, the Last Supper, the Resurrection and the Baptism. The early saints, Gheorghe, Dumitru, Ilie (Elijah), Nicolae, Paraschiva, Mihail and Gavril (Gabriel), were also in great demand, for apart from their religious attributes they were believed to ward off evil spirits. Some of Niicula's oldest icons can be seen in the monastery museum. Abbot Ilarion who runs Nicula monastery today, has an international reputation for his paintings.

The villages at the western end of the Transylvanian Heath are famous for their traditional **folk music**. Some of the best can be found in the village of Sic. You can get there by continuing south from Nicula, through Bonț and Săcălaia. Each household has its own instruments, and bands gather informally every weekend to play Magyar, Romanian and Romany tunes.

TÂRGU MUREȘ AND THE SZÉKELY COUNTRY

Târgu Mureș is a cultural centre and has an atmosphere that is quite different from other nearby towns. The whole city seems to revolve around a single square, Piața Trandafirilor (Roses' Square), which is flanked by buildings of amazing grandeur.

Practical information

☎ code
065

Tourist information
There is a travel agency at Piaţa Trandafirilor 31 that can change travellers' cheques.

Getting around
By train Tickets for trains, including a narrow-gauge service to Sovata, can be booked at *CFR* on Piaţa Teatrului. The main station is on Str Griviţa Roşie.

By bus Buses can be more convenient for travelling in the area; the bus station is at Str Gheorghe Doja 52. *TAROM* has an office at Piaţa Trandafirilor 6. **Taxis** can be hired from *Cornisa*, ☎ 132222, *Relaxa* on Str Baneasa, ☎ 126555, and *Taximur* at Str Bega 2A, ☎ 133056/133883.

By car Ask *ACR* on Piaţa Teatrului if you want information on **car hire**. If you need a **garage**, try *Iatsa* at Str Livezeni 2, or *Metalul* at Str Gheorghe Doja 292. For **cycle repairs** there is a bicycle shop at Str Arany János 1.

Where to stay
Târgu Mureş has several hotels, ranging from the cheap *Transilvania* (✩✩) at Str Trandafirilor 46, ☎ 165616, to the more elegant *Grand* (✩✩) at Piaţa Victoriei 28–30, ☎ 160711; fax 160288; the *Ambasador* (✩✩✩) at Str Garofiţei 2–4, ☎ 130909; fax 125742; and the *Continental* (✩✩✩) at Piaţa Teatrului 5–6, ☎/fax 160999. Outside town, near the 7km marker on the road to Sighişoara there is the *Stejeriş* motel (✩✩), ☎ 133509. For *ANTREC*'s local office ☎ 160286.

Eating out
Most of the food shops are clustered around Piaţa Trandafirilor. But the outskirts of Târgu Mureş are showing signs of an uplift; try the *Gemini Vendéglő* **restaurant** in Sângiorgiu de Mureş at Str Principala 1058. Other places to eat out include *Mureşul* at Piaţa Trandafirilor 44, *Rosen Garden* at 163A B-dul 1 Decembrie 1918, and *Ristorante Italiano* at Piaţa Teatrului 5. **Pizzerias** include *Itala* at Str Petőfi 2, *Pizzeria Italia 1* at Piaţa Trandafirilor 1, and *Pizzeria Italia 2* at 219 B-dul 1 Decembrie. There are a couple of **minimarkets**: *Barcomex* at Str Voinicenilor 54A, and *ABC Non Stop* at Str Crinului 4. *Romarta Lux* is a **general store** at 2 B-dul 1 Decembrie.

Post office
The main post office is at Str Revoluţiei 2A.

Money
Banks include *Bank Post* at 93 B-dul Decembrie 1918, *Banca Agricola* at Str Bolyai 2, *Banca Comerciala Româna* at Str Gheorghe Doja 1–3, and *Banca Naţională a României* at Piaţa Trandafirilor 50. **Exchange offices** include *Alicante Office* and *Romanian Exchange*, both at Piaţa Trandafirilor 43.

Police
The county police station can be found at Borsos Tamás 16, and the **city hall** is at Piaţa Victoriei 3.

Health care
Pharmacies include *Atlas* at Piaţa Trandafirilor 55, *Salvia* at Piaţa Trandafirilor 16–17, and *Novoform* at Str Infratirii 4.

Entertainment
Târgu Mureş boasts a few **bars**: *Bob Marley* at Str Verii 47, *Club Joe* at Str Livezii 6, and *Cornisa* at Str Victor Babeş 2. The city also has its own

orchestra, *Filarminica de Stat*, based at Str Enescu 2. There are two **theatres** in town: the *Children's Theatre* at Str Postei 2 and *Teatrul Naţional* (the National Theatre) at Piaţa Teatrului 1, ☎ 164848.

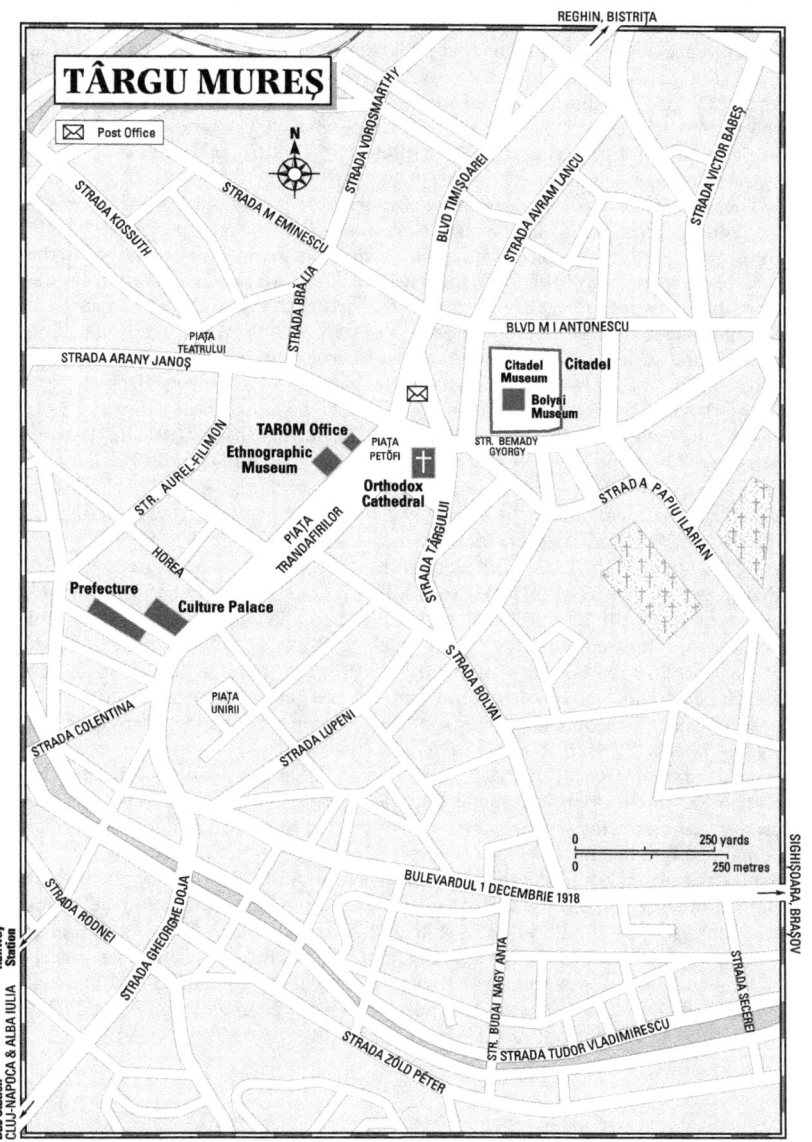

Walking around Târgu Mureş

Known as Marosvásárhely in Hungarian, Târgu Mureş grew up as a garrison town that formed part of Hungary's eastern defences. It is still a predominantly Magyar in character, but from the 18C its reputation became more highbrow than military. As well as a small university, a citadel and a few museums, the city is home to one of Romania's great libraries. **Piaţa Trandafirilor** is bordered by elegant Secessionist and Jugendstil buildings that resemble the façades found in towns and cities much further west, in Arad, Oradea and Timişoara, for example, and across the Hungarian border in Budapest and Kecskemét. In Târgu Mureş the architecture comes to a climax at the west end of Piaţa Trandafirilor with the *prefectură* and **Palatul Culturii** (the Palace of Culture). Completed in 1913, both buildings are immensely grand.

The Culture Palace houses a couple of museums. On the first floor the decor is very dark, with lots of ebony furniture and gilt. Daylight percolates dimly through 12 densely-peopled stained-glass windows depicting Hungarian myths in a style inspired by the English artists William Morris and Walter Crane. Opposite these are ranks of tall, gilt-framed mirrors that give the hall its name of Sala de Oglinzi (Hall of Mirrors). **Secţia de Artă** (the Art Gallery) contains fine and decorative art by ethnic Germans, Hungarians and Romanians, including artists from the Baia Mare school and a portrait of Gheorghe Doja (Dózsa György), a local peasant who led an abortive revolt against the nobility in 1514. Open Tues–Fri 09.00–16.00, Sat 09.00–14.00, Sun 09.00–13.00. The **History Museum** has some rare treasures from the 12C BC as well as proto-Dacian pottery. The Culture Palace is huge and comprises several other monumental halls, a library, concert hall and the galleries of the Artists' Union. It was restored in the late 1970s; open Tues–Fri 09.00–16.00, Sat–Sun 09.00–13.00.

North along Piaţa Trandafirilor from the Palace of Culture, at no. 11 is the **Ethnographic and Folk Art Museum**. This is housed in an 18C Baroque mansion that was built for the Toldology family. The collection comprises colourful objects such as traditional clothes, carpets and icons, as well as tools. Open Tues–Fri 09.00–16.00, Sat–Sun 09.00–13.00. Just to the south, at Str Horea 24, the **Natural History Museum** features indigenous and exotic butterflies and boasts the second largest Carpathian stag in the world. Open Tues–Fri 09.00–16.00, Sat–Sun 09.00–13.00.

At the northeast end of Piaţa Trandafirilor the skyline is dominated by the **Orthodox Cathedral**, which was built between 1925–34. Its frescoes include scenes tracing the lives of two martyrs who died in the cause of Romanian independence. Further north, Piaţa Bernády György contains the **citadel**, a 15C Protestant **church** and the technical **university**. At Str Bolyai 17 you can visit the **Teleki library** and the **Bolyai museum**. Comprising some 120,000 books and manuscripts, the library was started by Count Sámuel Teleki, a dynamic Transylvanian chancellor who opened it to the public in 1802. The museum celebrates the lives of mathematicians, Farkas Bolyai (1775–1856) and his son, János (1802–60), who invented non-Euclidean geometry; open Tues–Fri 09.00–16.00, Sat–Sun 09.00–13.00.

Palatul Culturii and the Tulip style

Like many of their Hungarian contemporaries, Palatul Culturii's architects Marcell Komor (1868–1944) and Dezső Jakab (1864–1932) were inspired by the British Arts and Crafts Movement. But their main role model was the Hungarian architect Ödön Lechner (1845–1914), whose Secessionist buildings can be seen in Budapest (especially the Museum of Applied Arts, 1893–97), Kecskemét (the 1890 Town Hall), and in Satu Mare's splendid *Hotel Dacia*. Interest in vernacular and 'organic' architecture was also sparked by the Magyar Millenial Celebrations of 1896, when Hungarians celebrated their 1000-year-old conquest of the Carpathian basin. In a mood of enthusiastic nationalism, many artists, including musicians such as Kodály and Bartók, turned to folk art as a way of identifying more closely with their roots.

Lechner set out to create a Hungarian national style. His work emphasised Hungary's ancient links with Asia, and were based on his studies of eastern ceramics and Anglo-Indian colonial architecture in London's South Kensington Museum (now the Victoria & Albert Museum). But while his work had 'exotic' origins, he preferred natural forms to the flamboyant motifs of the most exuberant Art Nouveau artists. Komor and Jakab belonged to Lechner's circle and, like him, they liked simple shapes. In the Palace of Culture they designed everything down to its stained glass and furnishings, and used a recurrent image based on the tulip to bring the decor together. Tulips were an obvious choice, with their clean, sinuous lines, but they gained a political significance in 1906, when Hungarians wore red cloth tulips to protest against the economic dominance of Habsburg Austria.

NORTHERN TRANSYLVANIA

Some 60km north of Cluj-Napoca, **Dej**, which lies on one of Transylvania's medieval salt routes, is a pleasant place to break your journey. It is an unpretentious town with a superb and beautifully restored Saxon church in the centre. Turning east from Dej, the DN17 heads towards the county town of Bistriţa. At Beclean, named after the Bethlen family who ruled Transylvania in the 17C, a country road goes north across the foothills of the Năsăud range and into the Maramureş. Among the region's attractions are the **Tihuţa Pass** into Moldavia with its modern, all-singing, all-dancing *Dracula Hotel*, as well as deep-snow skiing and trekking on horseback. Other sights include the nature reserve at **Pietrosul**, the vineyards in the **Bârgău valley** and **Rodna**'s medieval citadel. To the southeast, the Carpathian chain grows wilder still in the volcanic **Căliman range**, which contains some of the wildest scenery in Romania. It stretches from around Vatava and Tiha Bărgăului (close to Bistriţa) in the west and rises to a height of 2102m, running slightly northeast as it crosses the border into Suceava county in Moldavia.

Bistriţa

Archaeological finds in the area have revealed the existence of some prehistoric dwellings, but the first known mention of Bistriţa is found in a document dating back to 1244. It was officially mentioned as a city 20 years later. During the 12C and 13C, Hungarian kings attracted northern European settlers to the area with promises of tax concessions and land in return for exploiting Rodna's silver mines.

History

> From the end of the 13C Bistriţa's economy flourished in spite of the troubles which beset Transylvania as a whole. In 1241–42, the Tartars devastated the town and its surroundings on their way to Central Europe. From 1353, Bistriţa gained the right to hold an annual 15-day fair and to have its own seal (a crowned ostrich head holding a lucky gold horseshoe in its beak). By 1465 the Saxon guilds which controlled the town had flung up a massive fortification of 18 towers and bastions, against repeated attacks from Turks, Tartars and sometimes from their fellow Transylvanians as well. During this time, Bistriţa became one of the most important cities in Transylvania, along with Sighişoara and Sibiu. Some of its fine medieval buildings can still be seen today, including the Gothic Cathedral, the 13C Church, Şugalete, the commercial archway store, Casa Argintarului, the 16C Silversmith's House, the old fortress walls and the Cooper's Tower.

An important mining centre in the Middle Ages, today Bistriţa is a curious but not unattractive mix of old and new. Its traffic congestion comes as a shock after driving dreamily west from the Tihuţa Pass. Bistriţa's older quarters were all but removed during the modernisation programmes of the 1960s and 1970s. Even so, there are a few attractive streets in the centre, and it is a pleasant place to stop for an hour or two. There are orchards in the surrounding countryside, and to the north and east the landscape is spectacularly beautiful. In its German identity of Bistritz, the town appears in Bram Stoker's *Dracula*, but he portrayed it entirely from his imagination. A map from the communist period boasts that Ceauşescu created ten new industries here—it doesn't take a Gothic novelist to visualise the effect. However, Bistriţa does have a flourishing cultural scene.

Bistriţa-Năsăud county was the birthplace of several famous Romanian writers, including Liviu Rebreanu and poet George Coşbuc (1866–1918).

Walking around Bistriţa

The oldest monument in town is the **Orthodox Church** on Piaţa Unirii, which was formerly Uniate (or Greco-Catholic). Elements of the original, late 13C Franciscan monastery survive in the choir, but a series of alterations has meant that the church has Baroque as well as Gothic features. The Gothic Evangelical church or **Cathedral**, in Piaţa Centrală, was constructed in several phases on the site an earlier parish church. Building started in 1470 and lasted until 1564. Its steeple is 75m tall. In the 16C the former basilica was converted into a hall church. An Italian master, Petrus Italus of Lugano, had a workshop in Bistriţa between 1559–63, and he made the fine Renaissance portals which adorn the church today. The 18C altar and organ, the choir stalls and the sacristy door are also lovely.

Practical information

☎ code
063

Tourist information
Tourist agencies include *Coroana*, Piaţa Petru Rareş 7A, ☎/fax 212060; *Coroana de Aur*, Piaţa Petru Rareş 4, ☎ 232470; fax 232667; *Sind România*, Str Alexandru Odobescu 3, ☎ 223569; fax 222325; *Ştefan*, B-dul Independenţei 11; *Hebe*, Str Izvoarelor 94, ☎ 370228; fax 370035. The Tourist Information Centre, *CIT Bistriţa*, is recommended as a first stop if you are looking for hotels, tours or general advice about the region. Contact CIT at Str Florilor 1, Ap 86, ☎ 231780, e-mail: cit@elcom.ro.

Getting around
By train The station is on Str Rodnei. The *CFR* office is at Piaţa Petru Rareş bl 7A, ☎ 213938.
By bus This is next to the train station.
By car For **car servicing** and rental, try *ACR*, Str Decebal 1–3, ☎ 231608; for **car hire**, contact *Moişan Trans*, Str Libertăţii 81, ☎ 231528.
By taxi Contact *TAXICOM* dispatcher, ☎ 953; *City Taxi BN*, Piaţa Petru Rareş 5, ☎ 2217600.

Where to stay
Bistriţa has several central hotels: *Hotel Bistriţa* (✮✮✮), Piaţa Petru Rareş 2, ☎ 231205; fax 231626; *Hotel Codrişor* (✮✮✮), Str Codrişor 28, ☎ 231207; fax 232260; *Hotel Ştefan* (✮✮✮), B-dul Independenţei 11, ☎ 221255; fax 232667; *Hoel Coroana de Aur*, Piaţa Petru Rareş 4, ☎ 212627; fax 232667; *Hotel Decebal*, Str Cuza Vodă 9, ☎ 212568. For staying in private homes, the local *ANTREC* office is ☎ 231803; fax 216260, but start with the Bucharest central office before trying the local agencies.

Food and shopping
There are small grocers, bakers and other **food shops** around the central square. **Restaurants** include *ACR* at Str Dornei 43, *Corida* at Piaţa Centrală 32, *Coroana de Aur*, Piaţa Petru Rareş, and *Transilvania* at Str Şincai 2. *Pastruga* is at Str Dornei 23, while *Ramond* is a **pizzeria** at Str Şincai 19.

Post office
The main post office is at B-dul Independenţei 69.

Money
Banks include *Banc Post*, Str Eminescu 2; *Banca Agricolă*, Str Odobescu 11; *Banca Comercială Română*, Piaţa Petru Rareş 1A; *Banca Naţională a României*, Str Odobescu 11; *Banca Română de Dezvoltare*, Str Titulescu 50A; *Bancorex*, Ansamblul Mihai Eminescu 13; *CEC*, Str Eminescu 2.

Town hall
The *primăria* is at Piaţa Centrală 6, ☎ 213638.

Medical care
For an **ambulance** ☎ 961. The county **hospital** is at Str General Bălan 43, ☎ 214390. A doctor's **surgery** is at Str 1 Decembrie bl 9A, ☎ 231397.
Pharmacies include *Hygeia*, B-dul Independenţei 1; *Multivita*, Str Teodoroiu 17; *Remedia*, Piaţa Centrală 7.

Festivals and crafts
In May, Bistriţa county holds an international pop music **festival** in Năsăud. During June, the village of Silivaşul de Câmpie hosts a song, dance and traditional dress festival representing the northern part of the county. An international folklore festival called Nunta Zamfiriei (the Wedding of the Pipes) is held between 8–13 August in

Bistriţa itself, and there are Zilele Liviu Rebreanu at the end of September. In December you may catch another celebration of Romanian folk traditions called Rădăcinile Eternităţii. If you want to buy traditional flat-weave **carpets** and **pottery**, visit Bârgău village; Bistriţa Bârgăului is a centre for weaving as well. Ilva Mare is the place to find examples of the beautiful traditional **costumes** which are still made in this region, and in **Şanţ**, northeast of Bistriţa, c 20km beyond Sângeorz Bai along the DJ171, you will come across houses with fascinating stone doors and an interesting folk art museum. For more information contact *Centrul de Creaţie Populară* at Piaţa Petru Rareş 1, ☎ 212023.

Maps and books

The old communist-period county map, Judeţul Bistriţa-Năsăud, is actually still excellent if only as a fallback, and you may be able to find copies in European languages other than Romanian. It shows minor as well as major roads, highlights the relief, and tells you how individual mountain paths are marked.

Museums

Muzeul Judeţean Bistriţa-Năsăud, the county museum, is housed in a former armoury at Str Bălan 19. It has another section in the handsome 16C **Casa Argintarului** (the Silversmith's House) at Str Dornei 5. Neolithic pottery, Dacian, Celtic and Roman artefacts, *flori de mină* (naturally formed crystal flowers from the local mines), traditional dress and tools are just some of the objects laid out in a characteristically didactic display. Open Tues–Sun 09.00–18.00.

The most atmospheric part of old Bistriţa survives in and around **Piaţa Centrală**, where the architecture reflects an unusual openness to Western European styles, including Gothic, Renaissance and Baroque. Some of these lovely buildings have been taken over by Romany families who have no interest in their upkeep, and little is being done to save them. Nearby is a group of late-15C Gothic houses known collectively as **Şirul Sugălete**. They were the first two-storey dwellings in town. Within the row is an attractive carriage entrance to *casa parohială* (the priest's house) from 1480. **Casa Ion Zidarul** initially had a Gothic façade, but this was later changed to incorporate Renaissance features. **Casa Argintarului** (the Silversmith's House) at Str Dornei 5 is 16C and houses part of the county history museum's collection. The main seat of the **county museum** is at Str General Grigore Balăn 19. Another 16C building and a former barracks, it is a good place to go for tourist information as well as boning up on Bistriţa's past. Open Tues–Sun 10.00–18.00.

Around the perimeter of the old town, vestiges of medieval **curtain wall** are also visible together with **Turnul Dogarilor** (the Coopers' Bastion).

Names and culture

Villages in this part of Transylvania often have multiple names revealing a multicultural society: Viişoara was Heidendorf in German and Besenyő in Hungarian (the Magyar term for the Pecenegs who lived here); Unirea was known as Walldorf, 'Walloon village'; Crainamătul was the German Bayersdorf, while in Hungarian it was Királynémeti because Magyar kings gave land in and around this village to German settlers.

Liviu Rebreanu (1885–1944)
Rebreanu was the author of *Ion* (1920) and *Pădurea Spânzuraţilor* (The Forest of the Hanged, c 1924) and many other novels and short stories which explored issues of Romanian identity and peasant life. He was born 3km south of Năsăud in the village of Târlisiua, the son of educated smallholders and the oldest of 13 children. Rebreanu joined the Austro-Hungarian army in 1903 but resigned five years later because he wanted to write. He settled in Bucharest, but in 1910 the Hungarian authorities demanded that he should be imprisoned at Văcăreşti prison. He was later extradited to Gyula, where he remained until August the same year.

During the First World War, Liviu's brother Emil served in the Austro-Hungarian army and was hanged after trying to cross over to the Romanian lines. Rebreanu used the tragedy as the basis for *Pădurea Spânzuraţilor*. In the novel, the hero, Apostol Bologa, is the son of a Romanian lawyer from Transylvania. He is educated in a Hungarian school and becomes a conscientious Austrian officer. The novel begins during the court martial of an ethnic Czech officer who has deserted. Apostol Bologa votes along with other members of the tribunal that the Czech should be condemned to death. But later, under the influence of a Czech officer called Klapka, he experiences a change of heart. Apostol is sent to serve in the Eastern Carpathians where, after being forced to condemn a Romanian peasant for spying, he too tries to join the Romanian side. He is caught and hung.

In *Ion*, the action takes place in Pripaş village and in the little town of Amaradia. It is a tale of jealousy and tragedy.

Rebreanu's successful writing career began with a collection of short stories called *Frământari* (1912) while he was working as literary secretary at the National Theatre in Craiova. He followed this debut with *Golanii* (1916), *Marturiţire* (1916) and *Răfuiala* (1919). *Ion* won him recognition by the Romanian Academy, and after this he published several other novels.

Around Bistriţa
The village of **Târlisiua** has been renamed Liviu Rebreanu in the writer's honour. It lies on the DN17C which runs north from Bistriţa, and at Str Principală 126 you will find Liviu Rebreanu's **memorial house**, open Wed–Sun 10.00–18.00.

Continue north through Năsăud and Salva and you will reach **Coşbuc**, where George Coşbuc's birthplace houses a small museum commemorating his life and career. The building was designed by his father, who was a priest. Open Wed–Sun 10.00–18.00.

Travel east from Bistriţa along the DN17, and after c 10km you arrive at the old Saxon village of **Livezile** (the Orchards). **Casa Saşească**, no. 153 Livezile, belongs to the Bistriţa-Năsăud county museum. It has been arranged as though it were a functioning farmhouse, and contains a fascinating variety of domestic and agricultural objects specific to the ancient Saxon communities which flourished in this area from the 13C. Opening times are relaxed and you can visit the museum on any day of the week provided it is still light. All you have to do is turn up at house no. 152, home of the Pavel family, and ask to be let in; alternatively you can phone the Pavels on Livezile 83. Across the street at no. 82 is another attractive collection of Saxon furniture and implements which complements Casa Sașească. Called **Colecția Ion Rus**, it has the same opening arrangements.

Surrounded by beech forests and volcanic hills, the health spa of **Sângeorz Băi** dates back to the 1770s, when its mineral springs were exploited commercially for the first time. The spa offers electro- and hydro-therapies and black mud baths. You can get here by **train** on the Rodna Veche–Ilva Mică line and on the DJ 171 from Năsăud. There are a couple of **hotels**: *Hotel Someș* (☆☆) at Str Trandafirilor 15, ☎ 370079; fax 370774, and *Hotel Hebe* (☆) (named after the locally produced mineral water) at Str Izvoarelor 94, ☎ 370228.

Located in the Bârgău range, the pretty village of **Lunca Ilvei** (the banks of the Ilva) makes a good base for exploring the mountains. From Bistrița go to Năsăud, take the DJ171 northeast through Sângeorz Băi and turn south at Rodna. Follow the stream east from Măgura Ilvei through Ilva Mare. The total distance is c 70km, but allow extra time for bad roads and getting lost. Lunca Ilvei has a **railway station** and plenty of private **accommodation** (it belongs to the local *Rețea Turistică*). It also lies at the hub of a network of nature trails. There are facilities for skiing and horse-riding. You can also reach Lunca Ilvei from the east: turn right along a country road or track in the village of Dorna Candrenilor, c 10km west of Vatra Dornei, and drive through Teșna. Lunca Ilvei lies c 25km west of Dorna Candrenilor, but check before you set out to find out whether the road is passable.

You can also **ski** from **Piatra Fântenele**, 1100m up in the mountains near the Tihuța Pass, and home of the splendid *Castel Dracula Hotel* (☆☆☆) at Str Principală 4, ☎ 063 266841; fax 266119.

Some 18km south of Bistrița, the parish of **Herina**, near the village of Galații Bistriței, contains a massive mid-13C Evangelical church. Unusually, its 'twin' towers are in two different styles, one Gothic and the other Romanesque.

Reghin

About 60km south of Bistrița, on the eastern edge of the Câmpia Transilvaniei, this is a country town with a strong agricultural flavour about it. It has a long and handsome central square with two-storey **Baroque houses** decked out in jaunty colours such as lemon, saffron and dusty pink. The finest of these is the Town Hall, but there are several others decorated with attractive stucco, stonework and wrought iron. The town is first mentioned in a document of 1228, when it was settled by Saxons.

The little wooden **Orthodox church** in the Orthodox cemetery is known as the Petru Maior church because the 18C humanist came to services here. The church was built in 1744 and was left derelict for a long time during the communist period. Reopened by the parish priest in 1985, it is the oldest Romanian monument in Reghin (if not the zone) and is protected—in theory anyway—by being listed. It has a polygonal apse and a crucifix form that is very unusual for this region. Lots of geometrical rosettes decorate the wood around the doors and windows. It also has the *balaur* (dragon) device which is also inscribed in the rock churches in Basarabi (see Dobrogea). The church is very like the old wooden church at Putna in Suceava county. Visits can be made by appointment with the priest, or at the Ethnographic Museum.

The **Ethnographic Museum** itself is housed in a pretty Baroque pavilion built by local Hungarian landowners who were dispossessed by the communists. Open Wed–Sun 09.00–16.00, it stands at Str Vânătorilor 51 in a small park behind a new, monumental wooden gateway. It has a modest collection of agricultural tools and houses, but is worth visiting if only because its enthusiastic director is a fount of knowledge about the architecture, culture and geography in this part of Transylvania. She may also be able to help you find accommodation in town, and can offer a few beds for guests in the museum itself. For more information contact Maria Borzan on ☎ 065 421448.

A few hundred metres outside the town to the northeast, at Str Duzilor 25 stands the smart premises of lutier Vasile Gliga. Self-taught during the communist period, Gliga opened for business shortly after 1989 and now has an international clientèle. Like Stradivarius and Guanerius before him he uses well-seasoned maple and spruce from the nearby Carpathian forests.

From Reghin you can explore three separate ethnographic zones: **Valea Gurghiului** (the Gurghiu Valley), the **eastern Transylvanian plateau** and the **Upper Mureş Valley**. Valea Gurghiului is specially interesting because its inhabitants live remote from the modern world and have kept many ancient customs alive. According to a Romanian version of history, many ethnic Romanians were forced to retreat here from the west to evade persecution by the Magyars, Székelys and Saxons who colonised Transylvania from the 10C onwards. Known by several different names, including *vechile scaune ale Mureşuluior Giugeului*, the territory was defended by the Moldavian princes Ştefan cel Mare and his son, Petru Rareş. This region has always had close links with Moldavia.

Valea Superioara a Mureşului ~ The Upper Mureş Valley

The DN15 runs northeast through striking alpine country along a defile of the Mureş valley. Beside it rise the **Călimani Mountains**, which are among the wildest peaks in Romania. Experienced **potholers** can explore the cave system if they contact the Reghin caving club, either through the Ethnographic Museum in Reghin (see above) or the Speleological Institute in Cluj-Napoca. Winter **skiing** is available here too. Footpaths kept open by generations of shepherds cross the range into Moldavia, but it is possible to walk here for several days without seeing another soul.

At **Brâncoveneşti**, c 10km northeast of Reghin, an impressive 14C Hungarian castle has been turned into a home for disabled children run by a Norwegian charity. The castle was the home of Sava Armaşul, who fought alongside Mihai Viteazul, the 17C prince who unified Transylvania, Moldavia and Wallachia for the first time. It also belonged to János Kemény (1607–62), who is remembered for the philosophical autobiography, *Önéletírás*, which he wrote while being held prisoner by Tartars at Bakhchisarai. In 1661 he became prince of Transylvania but was killed the following year.

Further along the DN15, **Brad** is a thermal spa near Topliţa. The Sf Ilie monastery, which lies beside the main through road in **Topliţa** itself, has a fine wooden church from 1847 and a museum containing icons and old manuscripts; open daily 08.00–18.00.

Valea Gurghiului ~ The Gurghiu Valley

This lies due east of Reghin. Its highlights include the wooden church at **Lăpușna** and the tree park and hunting museum in **Gurghiu**, while several villages have **workshops** that specialise in making traditional clothes. There are pipe and flute *ateliers* in **Hodac** and **Ibăneşti**. At New Year, Hodac holds a festival of traditional customs called *Udatul nevestelor*. If you want to explore this region in more detail, contact the Ethnographic Museum in Reghin.

Valea Beicii ~ The Beicii Valley

In this valley, which runs northeast to the east of the DN15, there are painted 18C wooden churches at **Urişiul de Sus** and **Jos**. The valley is also noted for its traditional farmhouses and cottages.

Going southeast from Reghin, the most direct road to Sovata brings you through some beautiful countryside. Take the DN15 south out of Reghin, and turn left (east) for Sovata after c 3km. About 10km along the Sovata road you will go through Beica de Jos, and in another 5km, if you stay on the main road, you will reach the linear village of **Nădaşa**.

Set back from the through road to the left just after you enter the village is a little wooden church that has been converted into a museum. Ask the parish priest to let you inside, and you will find an attractive array of 17C, 18C and 19C icons on wood and glass, statuettes and carvings, many of them painted in an appealing peasant style, and several valuable manuscripts. In its modest way, this little museum is a microcosm of a particular period in Transylvania's history.

Nădaşa church as it now stands was built in 1852 and restored between 1978–80 after floods had reduced it to little more than a shell. However, according to the wooden inscription outside the apse, the original church was dragged here in 1719, when it was a possession of the old monasteries of Chiherul de Jos and Chiherul de Sus, the next villages on this road to the east. After Ferenc Rákóczi II and his followers devastated the Upper Mureş Valley in 1708, Transylvania became a 'hereditary principality' of the Habsburg Empire. Many Orthodox monasteries were destroyed as a result, thanks to the Jesuits who wanted to convert the Orthodox to Catholicism. Defying the Habsburgs, a local priest called Pătru Todoran built a number of new Orthodox churches in this area. Nădaşa's little church was one of them, and it was constructed using wood and carvings recovered from monasteries which had been burnt down, and from other ruined churches in the village.

The monastery of Chiherul de Sus survived until 1761, a year when the future of Transylvania's Orthodox Church hung in the balance thanks to continuing pressure from Vienna. Chiherul de Jos disappeared later, and Nădaşa church inherited some of its treasures, including a copy of *Cazania lui Varlaam* from 1643, a New Testament from Belgrade (1648), an *Antologhion* from Iaşi (1726), and a pair of royal doors from 1775. Meanwhile, Nădaşa church had become Greco-Catholic rather than Orthodox, because so many girls 'of the old faith' had married Uniates from neighbouring villages.

Sovata

The spa of Sovata lies in a superb position at the feet of Munţii Giurghiului. Its clapboarded and balconied villas evoke an air of genteelly decaying exoticism, but its history goes back much further than its buildings: people have came here for cures since 1578, and salt extraction began here in prehistory.

An entrepreneur called József Veress started developing Sovata as a spa in the 19C, and the town became so popular that the Romanian Royal Family used to come here between the two world wars. Wide, slatted wooden esplanades and spartan treatment parlours surround Lacul Ursu (Bear Lake), a salt lake which is said to be full of healthy minerals. You can also opt for one of the four smaller lakes such as Lacul Aluniş or Lacul Negru, which lie nearby. Marked footpaths bring you into wild mountain and moorland country.

Practical information

☎ code
065

Tourist information
Contact *Iomar Turist* at Str Vulturului 68, ☎ 570311; ☎/fax 570149.

Getting around

By train The station is to the northwest of the town centre, as is the **narrow-gauge line**, *Gara Sovata-Băi*.
By bus The bus station is at the west end of Str Trandafirilor, near the open-air market. A regular bus service run by *Impex Eurotour* connects Sovata with Budapest; coaches leave Sovata at 13.00 every Wednesday and Saturday; ☎ 165341 for details.
By car For **car servicing** and repairs, contact *Auto Service Rapide* at Str Principală 192, ☎ 570323.

Where to stay

Hotel Tivoli (✩✩✩), at the northeast end of town between Lacul Ursu and Lacul Tineretului, has 18 rooms; *Hotel Brădet* (✩✩), Str Vulturului 68, ☎ 578651; fax 578505; the large *Hotel Faget* (✩✩), Str Vulturului 18, ☎ 578651; fax 578505; *Hotel Sovata* (✩✩), Str Trandafirilor 82, ☎ 578151; fax 578335.

Sovata has nearly 80 **tourist villas**. Some, like the *Ciocârlia* and the *Victoria* at Str Trandafirilor 19 and 20, have delightful oriental-looking towers and balconies, and they offer the services of a general store, a bar and a solarium. For more details ask at the tourist agency. There are also pensions, bed and breakfasts, camping sites and a handsome chalet-style **motel**, the *Ursu Negru*, at Str Principală 150, ☎ 578987; fax 578808.

Eating out

There are butchers, grocers, fruiterers and general stores along Str Principală and Str Trandafirilor. Most of the hotels have decent **restaurants**, but you could look out for *Stâna de Vale Doi Brăzi*, which offers Transylvanian specialities at Str Trandafirilor 153, and the *Transilvania* at Str Trandafirilor 65. **Bars** include *Dodex* at Str Stejerişului 8, which has billiard tables and a terrace. There is also a pub here called the *Betyár*. Most of the hotels have their own bars.

Post office
This is halfway along Str Trandafirilor, opposite Complexul Cooperaţiei Meşteşugăreşti (the Craftsmen's Cooperative).

Money
Banks include *Banca Agricolă* at Str Trandafirilor 79 and *Banca Comercială Română* at Str Trandafirilor 125.

Police
The police station is at Str Vulturului 1, ☎ 570204.

Other activities
Ask at the tourist office for information about taking the waters. You can ski from Sovata in the winter and play tennis in summer.

Praid
A few kilometres south of Sovata on the DN13A lies the village and salt mines of Praid. Salt-extraction in Romania has a fascinating history, and Praid is one of the earliest sites still in active use. Its story begins with the Romans, but the first subterranean gallery dates from 1762 and looked like a vast bell. In its heyday, Praid had one of the largest salt reserves in Europe. In the 1960s, following discoveries made in Germany during the First World War, a treatment centre was opened here for asthmatics. Together with the mines themselves, speleoterapia or 'cave therapy' attracts some 2500 visitors a year. The **treatment caves** lie 120m below the surface and comprise a gym, a chapel, a buffet and games rooms to help patients pass the recommended four hours' inhalation a day. Visits to the mines and treatment caves can be arranged daily between 09.00–12.00. Praid is historically a Székely community (see below).

Around the Transylvanian Heath
On the eastern edge of the Transylvania Heath there are several interesting villages. At **Zau de Câmpie**, for example, there is a nature reserve famous for its peonies, and **Băita** has a museum of 'Romanian spirituality'. For more information about the history and ethnography of this region, contact the Reghin Ethnographic Museum or the county museum in Târgu Mureş at Str Enescu 2, ☎ 065 432179.

The Székely lands
East and southeast of Târgu Mureş lie the counties of Covasna and Harghita. Traditionally these are Székely, or Szekler, areas, settled by the Hungarian-speaking people who arrived in the 10C or 11C to protect Hungary's borders. While the Székely (pronounced 'Saykay') speak Hungarian and are thought to be closely related to the Magyars, no-one really knows where they came from. They were in Transylvania before the Saxons, and like them were employed by the Hungarian kings to police Transylvania's borders. As the Saxons flooded into western and southern Transylvania, the Székely moved east, and they have remained here ever since. They have a unique, rune-like alphabet, and you can see these characters carved as inscriptions on their gateposts. These splendid wooden entrances are similar to the ones you can find in other rural areas, but they have their own characteristics, one of which is the choice of floral rather than geometrical motifs, and another the use of slender vertical shafts, like a palissade. In English the Székely are often called 'Szeklers', while in Romanian they are known as 'Secui'.

EASTERN TRANSYLVANIA

In this area, the landscape can be intensely beautiful. Miles of open grassland rise to the east into great, subalpine forests roamed by bear and wolf, lynx, marten and deer. Giant fir trees tower above you like the piers of a huge cathedral and on a hot summer's afternoon their gravity wraps you in a healing silence. Above and to the east lies the Carpathian curve, where the highest peaks of **Munţii Vrancei** reach nearly 1800m. Further north, needle-like pinnacles form the skyline of **Cheilele Bicazului** (the Keys of Bicaz) and tower over a spectacular pass into Moldavia. Away from the dung-spattered roads and the scattered villages, the most common means of transport is a horse and cart.

This is an area rich in mineral springs: **Borsec** to the north produces a well-known brand of mineral water, but there are many other sources, for example at **Bodoc**, **Băile Tuşnad**, **Sâncrăieni** and **Jigodin Băi**; the mineral-rich waters and lakes have attracted health spas and sanatoriums. However, this tranquil landscape has seen plenty of trouble: 13C Tartar invasions were followed a few centuries later by General Basta's troops who looted and pillaged for the Habsburgs, while Ottomans invaded in the late 17C and a plague killed thousands shortly afterwards. In 1991 Târgu Mureş was the scene of conflict between Hungarians and Romanians in which at least three people died.

The enormous variety of rocks in this region has created an intricate system of karstic **grottoes** and **caves**. Among them are the **Şugău Cave** near Voşlăbeni (8km south of Gheorgheni), the **Bears' Grotto and Ice Cave** near Borsec Spa, and **Peştera Mereşti** in Valea Vârghişului to the west of Tuşnad. Mereşti is the longest cave in the Eastern Carpathians.

In spring and summer, wild herbs and flowers carpet the pastures and woodlands. If you are keen to see **wild flowers and plants**, there are several special reserves which contain rare species. Most of these occur on marshland (*mlaştina*) near mineral springs. **Mlaştina de la Valea Mijlocie** is a reserve beside the Olt River to the south of Tuşnad Nou. Here you can find Siberian birch growing at

---

Mineral springs and spas

Stretching from the mountains north of Borsec and Topliţa down to the towns of Cristuru Secuiesc, Vlăhiţa and Băile Tusnad in the south, Harghita county has a geological structure and climate that has made it ideal as a location for health spas. This used to be a volcanic area, and the residue of volcanic activity still shows in the great number of carbo-gaseous table waters (known as *borvíz* in Hungarian) and mofettes (gaseous emanations of carbon dioxide and hydrogen sulphide). There are over 2000 springs in this area, and people have been coming here to take the waters since Borsec Spa became popular with the Romans. Băile Tuşnad in the glorious Tuşnad Pass is another attractive and popular spa, and there are others at Lacu Roşu, Homorod, Bradul Topliţa, Mădicea, Băile Harghita, Băile Jigodin, Valea Intunecoasa, Băile Chirui, Praid with its thermal waters and aerosols from the old salt mine, and Izvorul Mureşului, which is designed for young people and children. These spas have developed over a long period of time, and many of them offer excellent accommodation, restaurants, therapeutic baths, sports facilities, boating and fishing.

its southern extreme. **Mlaştina de la Sâncrăieni**, 7km southwest of Miercurea, is permanently warmed by hot springs, and there are other marshland reserves at **Beneş-Tuşnad** and **Voşlăbeni**.

Driving south from Praid on the DN13A brings you into the ribbon-like village of **Corund** with its splendid Székely gates, but the village's chief claim to fame is its **pottery**. Practically every household has a kiosk outside, selling ceramics as well as knitwear, basketwork and long-handled wooden spoons. Corund pottery typically has a white ground decorated with robust, deep blue scrollwork, or is a plain green or ochre. You will see it on sale in most decent crafts shops around the country. One of the best-known potters here is János Józsa. He has a shop on the main street. A ceramics fair is held in Corund every year on or around 25 August. The village has a small museum, featuring traditional dress from the region, domestic and agricultural utensils, and of course, pottery.

Following the pretty road to the south brings you into **Odorheiu Secuiesc** (Székelyudvarhely in Hungarian), where you can see the ruins of a **Roman camp** and a formidable 16C medieval **citadel**. The latter lies at the end of Str Cetăţii. Nearby in Piaţa Libertăţii and Piaţa Aron there are three interesting 18C **churches**, while at Str Kossuth 29 there is a fascinating **ethnographic museum** that contains the narrow, carved wooden funerary posts used by the Protestant Székely (see above). Open Tues–Fri 09.00–16.00, Sat–Sun 09.00–13.00.

Almost 10km southwest of Odorheiu Secuiesc lies the village of **Mugeni**, whose 14C church has a lovely coffered ceiling and interesting frescoes. 14km further west, at **Cristuru Secuiesc** is another **church** worth seeing, this time from the 15C, which now belongs to the Unitarians. The town also has an excellent **museum** dedicated to the pottery industry; ask at Muzeul Orăşenesc, the wide-ranging town museum at Str Libertăţii 45, open Tues–Sun 10.00–18.00. Further off the beaten track, in the hills due south of Mugeni and c 15km from Odorheiu lies **Dârjiu**, another village with a fine Unitarian church. Its murals from 1419 are worth seeing.

If you head c 50km northeast from Praid the road runs along the Târnava Mica valley to **Gheorgheni**, which has a fortress dating back to the 14C. A few kilometres to the northwest of Gheorgheni on the DN12 stands **Lăzarea castle**, an impressive, half-restored ruin that originated in the late Middle Ages. A museum devoted to the history and ethnography of this area now occupies the former Knights' Hall. The castle gets its name from the Lazar family, who were closely related to the Bethlen dynasty, under whom Transylvania enjoyed rare moments of peace and prosperity in the 17C. Close to the castle are a Catholic monastery and a fortified church. If you need to stay in Gheorgheni, the *Hotel Mureşul* at Str Cartierul Florilor 1 is acceptable, ☎ 066 161904.

Miercurea Ciuc

Driving c 57km south from Gheorgheni on the DN12 brings you into the Olt flood plain and the county town of Miercurea Ciuc. Called Csíkszereda in Hungarian and Szeklerburg in German, it lies at the centre of a group of fascinating Székely villages in Bazinul Ciucului (the Ciuc Basin).

Miercurea Ciuc is an industrial town with a population of c 50,000. It was named after the Wednesday (*miercuri* in Romanian, *szerda* in Hungarian) markets that used to be held here. People have lived on this site since the Neolithic period, but although the town centre has some fine architecture, most of its ancient buildings have gone, leaving the Mikó citadel and a few old churches and chapels from the 16C to the 18C as the main focus of its historic past. But Miercurea is a handsome place, although much of its appeal comes from the woodlands of spruce and mixed beech, birch and fir which surround it and cover nearby Mount Şumuleu as well.

History

Miercurea Ciuc was founded in the 16C, close to the existing 13C and 14C villages of Şumuleu, Topliţa-Ciuc and Jigodin, with which it eventually merged. The first known document about Miercurea is a letter written in 1558 by Queen Izabella, mother of János II Zsigmond, Prince of Eastern Hungary (Transylvania, 1540–51 and 1556–71), which certified Miercurea as 'a plain town' whose inhabitants were exempted from taxes, but not from the tributes due to the Ottoman Empire.

Miercurea was attacked by Tartars, Turks, and Habsburg troops, and its rare periods of peace came at the hands of local tyrants who kept Transylvania in an iron grip. In 1717–19, two-thirds of the townspeople died in an epidemic of bubonic plague.

Miercurea's spectacular development came about thanks to the fortress which Ferenc Mikó of Hidvég (1585–1635) raised between 1620–35. From 1764–1884, the first Székely Infantry Regiment was stationed in the castle, and in 1849 it became the headquarters of Sándor Gál, commander-in-chief of the Székely revolutionary troops. It was in that year, shortly before he was killed, that the revolutionary poet Sándor Petőfi stayed in the castle. Petőfi wrote to his wife, telling her how wonderful Miercurea was.

During the Second World War the USSR annexed Bessarabia, and in retaliation Hitler announced the Vienna Diktat, which allowed Hungary control of northern and eastern Transylvania from August 1940. After the Axis defeat, the Allied Powers ordered a return to the borders set 25 years earlier at the Treaty of Trianon, restoring the whole of Transylvania to Romania.

Practical information

☎ code
066

Many streets here are **signposted** in Romanian and Hungarian; you should be able to get a street map that gives the street names in both languages from tourist offices or hotels. The Romanian names are used here.

Tourist information

Tourist offices include **Bradul**, Str Timişoarei 10, ☎ 112124/111493; fax 113181; **Sind România**, Str Kőrösi Csoma Sándor 2, ☎ 171280; fax 171096; **Univers Tourist**, Piaţa Majláth 6, ☎/fax 171178, or the agency at Str Florilor 32, ☎ 112951.

Getting around

By train The station is at the southwest end of Str Florilor. The **CFR** office is on the east side of Str Petőfi and Str George Cosbuc, opposite the junction

with Str Majláth and Piaţa G. Károly.
By bus The main bus station can be found beside the railway station.
By car There are several **garages**; try *ACR* or *Dacia* on Str Harghita (the DN13A) northwest of the centre and just south of the crossing with Str Poenii, or *Prestarea Autoservice*, a little further south, just past Str Vultur. From its office on the southeast side of Piaţa Cetăţii, *ACR* should be able to advise on car hire; ☎ 111446. **Petrol stations** can be found on the main routes in and out of town. If you want a **taxi**, ☎ 114444/115555.

Where to stay

Miercurea Ciuc has several hotels, including the *Harghita* (✯✯✯), a modern block with 300 places at Piaţa Libertăţii 1, ☎ 116119; fax 113181, and the smaller *Bradul* (✯✯) at Str Bălcescu 11, ☎ 111493; fax 172181. Other possibilities include *Hotel Floare de Colţ* (✯) at Str Fraţiei 7, ☎ 172068; fax 172068, and the cabins at *Popas Turistic Univers*, ☎ 116319; fax 153447. If you prefer bed and breakfast with a Romanian family, *ANTREC* has a base in Miercurea Ciuc, ☎ 570484; fax 570484, or try the head office in Bucharest (see p 116).

Eating out

Alimentară shops selling food can be found on Str Majláth and B-dul Fraţiei, and further out on Str Harghita; the tourist office will be able to tell you where the best open-air markets are. There is a large *Magazin Universale* called the *Central* at Str Petőfi Sándor 18. **Restaurants** include the attractively named *Mistic Pizza Grill Bar* at B-dul Fraţiei 93, and the *Alzo* at Str Petőfi 16.

Post office

Phones and the main post office can be found on Str Majláth near its intersection with B-dul Timişoara.

Money

There are plenty of banks around the town centre, including *Banca Naţională Trezorera* in Str Kőrösi and *Dacia Felix* on Str Zöld-Péter; or you could try the **exchange desk**, *Casa de Schimb Valutar*, at Str Gál Sándor 2–4.

Police

The police station can be found on B-dul Fraţiei, and the **Town Hall** stands on the east side of Piaţa Cetăţii.

Health care

There are **pharmacies** at Piaţa Majláth 4, Str Florilor 12 and Str Harghita 2, while the **polyclinic** and county **hospital** (Spitalul judeţean Harghita) are close to the south end of Str Tudor Vladimirescu.

Traditional crafts and folk art

If you are looking for local craftspeople or want information on folk festivals, contact *Centrul Judeţean de Creaţie Populară* at Str Florilor 30, ☎ 112904. Typical products include beautifully embroidered traditional costumes, ceramics, textiles and stone carvings. Apart from at Corund, a special black **pottery** is made at **Dăneşti**, while the women of **Sâncrăieni** and **Corbu** are famous for beautiful flat-weave **carpets**. **Tuşnad-Sat**, a few kilometres to the north of Tuşnad spa, has a community of **stonecarvers**.

Walking in Miercurea Ciuc

The **Mikó Citadel** is an Italian Renaissance-style castle on the west side of Piaţa Cetăţii. Mikó was a relation and confidant of Gábor Bethlen, and Chief Captain of Csík, Gyergyó and Kászon Szék (Magyar names for the Székely counties). He gave the castle four corner bastions and a rectangular ground plan and some fine

Italian detailing which was much admired. The fortress was burnt down by the Tartars in 1661, then fortified by an Austrian garrison in 1714. The Habsburg troops added an outer defence wall consisting mainly of ramparts.

Today it houses part of the **county museum** and **Muzeul Secuiesc al Ciucului** (the Ciuc Székely Museum) at Piața Cetății 2, open Tues–Sun 10.00–18.00. It has a good collection of paintings by Imre Nagy and Sándor Szopos.

Complexul Baroc Șumuleu (the Șumuleu Baroque Complex) is a group of Baroque-style buildings erected in 1804 on the site of a mid-15C Franciscan monastery founded by Iancu de Hunedoara. In 1676 a Franciscan monk called Johannes Kájoni opened a printing press here. Șumuleu is the Romanian name for the medieval village of Somlyó which was long since absorbed by Miercurea; it is now a district in the northeast quarter of the town.

Among the oldest religious buildings in town are Capela Passio from the 15C and the 17C Capela Sf Anton and Capela Salvator. All three **chapels** can be found northeast of the centre, in a district called Kis-Somlyó. To get there from the town centre, take Str Székand turn right (south) at the end where it meets Str Șumuleu Mic. Look for the chapels to the east of the point where this road does a dog-leg on its way south.

Harghita county has a fine collection of **village museums** specialising in local history and ethnography. These museums can be fascinating even though they are often very small. Many of them were begun by local enthusiasts and are less stuffy than the main county museums. They are usually under-funded and because of this, they often follow their own individual timetables—some only open on request. You should be able to find them in the following villages under the name of **Colecția Sătească**: Atid, Bisericani, Cârța, Ciumani, Dănești, Joseni, Lăzarea, Lunca de Jos, Lunca de Sus, Merești, Ocland, Plăieșii de Jos, Praid, Remetea, Rugănești, Sărmaș, Sândominic, Sâncrăieni, Subcetate, Suseni, Tulgheș, Volăbeni and Zetea.

AROUND MIERCUREA CIUC: THE SZÉKELY VILLAGES OF BAZINUL CIUCULUI

A string of 14 picturesque villages runs to the north and south of Miercurea Ciuc. Dating from the early 14C, they were founded as Roman Catholic parishes by Székely communities who came to Bazinul Ciucului in the late 12C and early 13C. Most of them are named after a patron saint, such as **Sâncrăieni**, **Sânmartin**, **Sângeorgiu**, **Sândominic** and **Sânsimion**. Others include **Armășeni**, **Nicolești**, **Racu** and **Ciuboteni**. Originally, their stone-built **churches** had identical features, including a square or semicircular apse, no tower, and a triumphal arch separating the sanctuary from the nave. Some of them preserve fragments of fine, Romanesque carving, especially around the door frames, while others, such as the chapel of Sf Margareta at **Sântimbru** (Csíkszentimre in Hungarian), c 20km southwest of Miercurea, contain fascinating frescoes from the second half of the 14C.

In the mid-15C many of these **churches** were rebuilt in a Gothic style and fortified with massive towers to protect them against Turkish and Tartar attacks. All the towers consisted of either three or four storeys, with large ogival windows surrounding the bell chamber. These windows were later remodelled to follow the Baroque style. According to art historian Géza Entz, the stonemasons who worked here copied the towers from the old Franciscan church in Şumuleu, which was itself based on the Franciscan church in Târgu Mureş (now the Reformed Church). Some of the Székely churches were protected by an oval perimeter wall instead of a tower, and you can see one of these at the parish church at **Cârţa**, c 20km north of Mercurae Ciuc, where the wall reaches c 8m high.

Among the striking Gothic innovations seen in these churches were the ceiling vaults. These were usually groined, and both they and supporting consoles were often decorated with floral motifs or coats of arms belonging to the founding families. There is only one known star vault in the Ciuc region; this is in the apse of **Leliceni** church, about 5km southeast of Miercurea, on the country road to Misentea and Bancu, while **Armaşeni**, lying c 25km east of Miercurea, boasts a unique fan vault. Most of the carving around the doors and windows is simple in style, one exception being the south entrance to Sf Ioan (St John) in **Delniţa**, which lies about 10km to the north of Miercurea, just off the DN 12A to Frumoasă, Lunca de Sus and Gheorghe Gheorghiu-Dej. Here you can also see a lovely late-Renaissance altar and a painted cassette ceiling, both from the 1670s.

> ### Sf Ioan, Delniţa
> Saint John's Church in Delniţa (Csíkdelne) was recorded for the first time as the parish church of three villages: Ciceu (Csíkcsicsó), Delniţa and Păuleni-Ciuc (Csíkpálfalva), in the 14C. The building consisted of a tower, nave, choir and a sacristy connected to the northern façade of the choir. Its present form dates from the 15C, when masons built the Gothic door frames and choir vaulting and artists painted frescoes on the outside of the south walls. A stone wall surrounds the courtyard of the church and its cemetery. The building was badly damaged in 1661 and renewed between 1673–75, and it was during those restorations that the painted panel ceiling was installed. The Renaissance altar in the choir is dedicated to Saint John. The church was damaged again at the beginning of the 18C, and after this the tower was heightened and a gallery was added. The porch which used to stand in front of the southern entry was demolished in 1934.

At **Nicoleşti** and **Ciucsângeorgiu** polygonal perimeter walls were built around the churches in the 17C, when the threat of an Ottoman invasion increased. Here, villagers built and then manned a defence tower in the curtain walls. There are few examples of Renaissance architecture around Ciuc, and most of the finest carvings, including some beautiful polyptychs, are held by the Hungarian National Gallery in Budapest. When Baroque-style architecture arrived in the mid-18C, Ciuc churches acquired wider naves, side chapels and plenty of gilt and stucco, along with onion-domed towers.

Heading further south, the DN12 from Miercurea Ciuc brings you into Covasna county via **Băile Tuşnad** (c 35km). This is an old health spa where hotels and villas nestle discreetly among majestic conifers at the foot of Ciomatul Mare massif. From here a strenuous one-and-a-half-hour climb up a marked path brings

> **Narcissus meadows**
> In late May and early June, a dense carpet of narcissi comes into flower in the meadows around Vlăhița, c 18km west of Miercurea Ciuc. They are very splendid and statistics say that, at their best, the blooms cover a surface of 30ha and have a density of 180–200 flowers per square metre—but don't let that prosaic information spoil your enjoyment!

you through the ancient forest to the volcanic bowl of **Sfânta Ana** lake. This is a popular place for campers and is the scene of an annual pilgrimage and a festival of performance art.

If you have the chance, make a detour to the 17C **Daniel's Castle**, which lies almost due west of Băile Tușnad at **Vârghiș** (Vargyas in Hungarian), about 9km north of Baraolt. It was built to a Renaissance design, although it also has Baroque elements. Its superb stone carvings make this one of the finest Székely palaces in eastern Transylvania.

Sfântu Gheorghe

This ancient town lies beside the Baraolt Mountains. It is not spectacularly beautiful, but is interesting enough to stop in for an hour or two; it would also make a good base for exploring the Székely villages of Covasna county.

Practical information

☎ code
067

Tourist information

There are several travel agencies here that may be able to help with local information. Try *BTT* at B-dul Gen Grigore Balan 18, *SCTA Oltul* at B-dul Balan 1, or *TREFF* at Str 1 Decembrie no. 5.

Getting around
By train and bus The railway and bus stations lie to the west of the centre on Str Gării.

Where to stay
There are a couple of reasonable hotels in town: *Park* (✶✶) at Str Gábor Áron 14, ☎/fax 311307, and *Oltul* (✶✶) at Str 1 Decembrie 18, ☎ 311292; fax 153787. Cheaper options are *Consic* (✶) at B-dul Balan 21, ☎ 326984, and *Korona* (✶) by the station at Str Gării 1, ☎ 325164. For bed and breakfast accommodation around the town, contact *ANTREC* in Bucharest (see p 16).

Post office
The main post office is on the corner of Str 1 Decembrie 1918 and Str Oltului.

Money

Banks include *Banc Post* at 18 B-dul 1 Decembrie, *Banca Agricolă* at Str Gábor Áron 1, and *Banca Națională al României* at Str Kossuth Lajos 10. You can also **change money** at *TREFF* (see above) and *Romania Exchange* at Str 1 Decembrie 18.

Known as Sepsiszentgyörgy in Hungarian, Sf Gheorghe has a group of buildings by the ethnic Hungarian architect, Károly Kós, who also designed the Cock Church in Cluj-Napoca. Some 20 of the buildings he planned for Sf Gheorghe are still standing. One of the most attractive is **Muzeul Naţional Secuiesc** (the National Székely Museum) at Str Kós Károly 10, open Tues–Sun 10.00–18.00. This dates from 1912–13, and shows Kós's interest in Finnish as well as Transylvanian traditional building. Its collection covers archaeology, ethnography, natural history and art, with a special section dedicated to the Székely. In the museum garden is a fascinating collection of carved Székely gates and funeral posts. A guide to Sf Gheorghe's other historic buildings, including Kós's other projects, is available from the museum.

AnnArt

Sf Gheorghe is home to a group of artists who made a stand against Ceauşescu's manipulative anti-Hungarian policies. In the early 1980s, Imre Baász and Gusztáv Ütő invited ethnic Romanian and Hungarian artists to take part in a joint exhibition which took place every three years. After the 1989 revolution, Baász and Ütő continued to hold the shows and started a performance art festival as well; this is held every year on the shores of Lacul Sfânta Ana, a volcanic lake in the mountains above the town. Artists come from all over the world. Contact Ütő at the Baász Art Foundation, Str Kőrösi Csoma 24, 4000 Sf Gheorghe.

Around Sf Gheorghe

With its rolling pastures and maize fields, its forests and mountains, this is a beautiful part of the country that would be ideal for walking or cycling holidays.

Some 50km northeast of Sf Gheorghe, the town of **Târgu Secuiesc** (Székely Town) has preserved its medieval centre of narrow alleys and inner courtyards. A town museum at Str Curtea 10, open Tues–Sun 10.00–18.00, charts the history of local guilds and the Csángó or Csenger Hungarians who fled to Moldavia to escape religious persecution in the 15C. In one of several interpretations, Csángó is a Székely word for 'wanderer'. Today their community has shrunk to a few villages in an area of Moldavia between Adjud and Bacău, and the upper Trotuş valley between Oneşti and Mount Sălămaş, near where the river rises.

On the way along the E574/DN11, you could make detours to **Reci**, with its 259ha nature reserve, and **Cernat**, where ornamental Székely gates are made. Cernat also has several 18C and 19C manor houses, one of which contains an ethnographic museum. 2km to the north stands the ruined 15C **Ika** citadel.

About 5km north of Târgu Secuiesc, **Sânzieni** has a 12C chapel and the ruins of Tarnóczy castle. Nearby **Perkő hill** is a habitat for rare plants, such as stipa and pulsatilla, and it contains the remains of a Bronze Age settlement. **Estelnic** has a 14C fortress church with Romanesque elements, and a wooden house from 1702. At **Breţcu**, 16km northwest of Târgu Secuiesc, there is an 18C Orthodox church built in the Byzantine style.

To the south of Târgu Secuiesc, the road to Covasna has a turn-off to **Ghelinţa**, whose church was built before the Tartar invasions of 1241. Reconstructed in the 14C, it contains a series of ancient murals showing the legends of Sf Ladislău. The paintings are based on an early 13C Latin text which set out to extol the chivalric virtues of Szent László Király, Hungary's King László I (r. 1095–1116). It also has some attractive Baroque furniture. Further south, **Zăbala** is home to the late-17C Mikes castle with its vaulted halls and pretty gardens; it also has a 14C church worth seeing for its beautiful Gothic and Renaissance carvings.

Covasna is a spa town with plenty of **hotels**, such as the *Căprioara* (✯✯✯) at Str 1 Decembrie 1918 no. 2, ☎ 067 340401; fax 191545, and the *Cerbul* (✯✯) and the *Covasna* (✯✯), both of which share the same address, phone and fax numbers as the *Căprioara*. But there is little else to keep you here. However, 3km to the southeast lies **Valea Zinelor** (the Fairies' Valley), where 19C engineers constructed an inclined plane that covered a 300m drop and allowed foresters to lower tree trunks safely down to a logging train. Both the plane and the **mountain railway** are still there.

About 5km northwest of Sf Gheorghe, on a country road that leads to Valea Crişului, lies the village of **Arcuş**. This is the site of the late-19C Szentkereszti Castle, which stands in its own landscaped park. To the south, the Evangelical (Protestant) citadel church at **Ilieni** was once the largest of its kind in this district. It has an impressive bell tower and the ruins of a double inner wall built in the 16C and 17C.

To the southeast of Sf Gheorghe, c 15km if you go across country, and 20km if you take the bigger roads, lies **Bicfalău**, where you can see well-preserved peasant houses and the remains of a few once-elegant Baroque mansions. To get there from Sf Gheorghe, take the main road south to Chichiş where it joins the E574 (DN11), turn left (north), and in 4km take the first right at Ozun. Further east, at **Dobolii de Sus**, is another attractive church interior that was installed after the 14C Gothic church was rebuilt in 1773. It has fine wooden furniture and a painted coffered ceiling.

SOUTHERN TRANSYLVANIA

Sibiu, Sighişoara and Braşov were among the earliest Saxon settlements in Transylvania. The area east of Sibiu is known as the Altland, the Old Land, because it contained the highest concentration of Saxon villages before the devastating Tartar invasions of 1241–42. The new colonists started coming here in the 12C, and their descendants survived for 800 years. The first came from the over-crowded and war-torn countries of northwest Europe, not only Saxony but also the Low Countries and France. They were invited to Transylvania by the Hungarian king, Géza II (r. 1141–62), who granted them extensive privileges in return for their help in stabilising his eastern borders. Mostly minor nobles and farmers, the newcomers were known collectively as Saxons because the majority of them spoke German. Germans still call Transylvania the *Siebenbürgen*, after the seven most important towns in the region. The Saxons were extremely clannish and evolved an exclusive, disciplined and wealthy society. Now that most of them have gone, all that remains are their fortified towns and cities and the memory of their strong determination to survive.

Sibiu

This is the most solidly German of all the 'Saxon' towns in Transylvania. It has rugged houses with thick walls and steep red-tiled roofs. The walls are painted in a wonderful variety of bold colours and their dormer windows are shaped like eye slits, making them look surreal or quaintly medieval, according to your inclination.

In *Danube* (1986), Claudio Magris noticed a lingering melancholy in this part of Transylvania. This was a symptom of the German exodus that began in the 1980s, leaving many houses and farms abandoned. Today many of their fine town houses and farmsteads have been taken over by Romany families. But Sibiu is showing signs of economic regeneration, and there are those who say that it should be the capital, lying as it does almost exactly in the centre of Romania.

The city occupies a shallow river valley below the Făgăraş, Cibin and Cindrel mountains and lies near the Turnu Roşu pass, on a trade route between the Balkans and western Europe. It developed from a single row of houses built by Flemish, Franconian and Saxon settlers in the mid-12C. This street still exists, having become part of Str 9 Mai, which curves west from the railway station in the Lower Town. The village spread out towards the river, and you can follow Sibiu's oldest streets as they sweep in an arc around the base of the hill. The Lower Town was eventually enclosed by the last of the town's four defence walls. Massive gate towers, long since demolished, were constructed at four strategic points. Access to the Upper Town (the citadel) was provided by stairways as well as roads. For the Habsburgs, Sibiu was the most important garrison east of Vienna.

Naming Sibiu

Sibiu's Romanian name comes from the Cibin River, which flows sluggishly through the Lower Town from the nearby Cibin mountains. One of the earliest known references to Sibiu comes in a papal bull dated 1191, in which Pope Celestin III gave the Saxons permission to organise their own ecclesiastical affairs. He called their domain Praepositum Cibinensis, 'the German church beyond the forest'. But the Saxon settlers named their colony Villa Hermanni, supposedly after the *greav* Hermann, one of their early leaders. In the 14C the town became Hermannstadt, and Germans still use this name for Sibiu.

Practical information

☎ **code**

069

 Tourist information

The main tourist information office is at Piaţa Unirii 1. Tourist offices include *Atlassib*, Str Tractorului 14, ☎ 224101; fax 224296; *BTT*, Str Şcoala de Înot 1-3, ☎/fax 423559; *Continental*, Calea Dumbrăvii 2–4, ☎/fax 210125; *Fan Tours*, Aleea Eminescu 1, ☎ 442748; fax 421685; *Paltiniş*, Str Tribunei 3, ☎ 215223; fax 218319; *Prima Ardeleană*, Piaţa Unirii 1, ☎ 211788; fax 2179233; *Sind România*, B-dul Victoriei 10, ☎ 215141; fax 218339.

Getting around

By train The station lies on a main east-west route; it stands in Piaţa 1 Decembrie, a few minutes walk to the west of the Lower Town. You can book train tickets and get information about the service from *CFR* at Str Nicolae Bălcescu 6; open Mon–Fri 07.00–19.30.

By bus The bus station stands with the railway station in Piaţa 1 Decembrie.

By tram Sibiu has a limited tram service which stops at the ASTRA Open-air Museum and runs between the southern end of Calea Dumbrăvii and the village of Răşinari (9km to the south). It opened in 1929, and the company that built the line was given permission to extend the tracks to Răşinari on condition that it provided the town with a zoo. After the 1989 revolution Romania was in dire need of rolling stock, and Geneva gave Sibiu some of its discarded trams, which is why they fly the Swiss flag.

By car Sibiu has many **service garages**. The *Concordia* at Str Câmpului 13, ☎ 222909, is a registered Bosch agent; alternatives are *ACR* at Bloc 13, Str V. Milea, and *Autoservice* on Şos Alba Iulia, opposite the town's bus station, *Autogara 2*. **Petrol stations** can be found at B-dul V. Milea, Calea Mediaşului, Şos Alba Iulia and further along Şos Alba Iulia near the airport. **Parking** in the centre of Sibiu is relatively easy, but avoid the pedestrian areas on Str Bălcescu and Piaţa Mare, which are not well marked. There are pay parking lots outside the *Hotel Bulevard*, beside the Turnul Gros on B-dul Spitatelor and just inside the ramparts near the three defence towers on Str Cetăţii. Sibiu has several **taxi** firms; among the largest are *Negoiu*, ☎ 444444, *Nicsan*, ☎ 439941, *Parc*, ☎ 436666 and *Star*, ☎ 953.

By plane The airport can be found beside the E68 on the way to Sebeş. Tickets for flights within Romania are obtainable from *TAROM* at Str Bălcescu 10; open Mon–Fri 07.00–18.00, Sat 08.00–14.00.

Where to stay

There are enough hotels in Sibiu to suit a wide range of budgets. The finest and most expensive is the *Casa Moraru* (☆☆☆☆) at Str A. Vlahuţă 11A, ☎ 216291; fax 215490, with a swimming pool, terrace bar and an excellent restaurant. *Împăratul Romanilor* (☆☆) at Str Bălcescu 2–4, ☎216500; fax 213278, 'the Emperor of the Romans', is a hotel with a history. It used to be the *Blue Flag Hotel* but changed its name after the future Emperor Joseph II visited Sibiu in 1773 and stayed there for a few days. Liszt, Strauss and Romania's leading Romantic poet, Eminescu, all stayed here. Fitted with modern furnishings, it is renowned for its traditional Romanian cooking and the sliding ceiling in its dining room. *Hotel Continental* (☆☆☆) is a high-rise block to your right before you turn onto Calea Dumbrăvii on the way out of town, ☎ 416910. *Hotel Bulevardul* (☆☆) is the huge, dour-faced building with an equally uninspiring foyer that faces Piaţa Unirii from the west at Piaţa Unirii 10, ☎ 412140.

The *Parc* (☆☆) at Str Scoala de Înot 21 (near the Hunting Museum), ☎/fax 423559, and *Silva* (☆☆) on Aleea Eminescu, ☎ 442141, are both moderately priced hotels slightly further out from the centre at the edge of Valea Aurie, a long, narrow stretch of woodland and water meadow. Valea Aurie has been a public park since the 18C, and you can walk along it as far as the zoo at Dumbrava. If you prefer somewhere more secluded, a bright, comfortable and surprisingly cheap option is the *Hanul Dumbravă* (☆) at Pădurea Dumbrăvei 14, ☎ 422920/214022; fax 228777. This motel lies about 4km from Piaţa Unirii on the country road to Răşinari; turn right at the intersection with Calea Dumbrăvii towards the Muzeul in Aer Liber and pass the Orthodox cemetery on the left. Trolleybuses 1 and 14 go there from the train station.

Eating out

If all you need is a snack, along Str Bălcescu and around Piața Mare there are some dimly-lit **cafés**, **kiosks** and **restaurants** where you can buy expresso coffee or Ness (the Romanian version of Nescafé), sweet cakes and pizzas, *ciorbe* (traditional soups) and *plăcinte* (flaky pastries with cheese or fruit inside). Most Sibieni eat in hotels when they go out, but there are interesting alternatives. *Crama Sibiul Vechi* at Str Papiu Ilarian 3, ☎ 431971, and the *Crama Național* (behind the *Casa Artelor* on Piața Mica) are both pleasant restaurants offering traditional Romanian cuisine in picturesque cellars; be prepared for live and exuberant folk music. *Bufnița* on Str Bălcescu also specialises in Romanian dishes, ☎ 214133; the *Transilvania* at Str GoRăslău 1 is more expensive and more adventurous. You could also try *Sub Arini* at Str Eminescu 4 and *Regency Pizzeria* at Piața Unirii 1–3. If you are prepared to travel out of Sibiu, try the *Cabana Curmătura Stezii* at km 14 on the road between Sibiu and Paltiniș, ☎ 557310, *Cabana Mai* at km 12, ☎ 557269, or *Hanul din Bătrâni* on the road from Sibiu to Rășinari, ☎ 420215, *internat* 18. *Hanul Dumbrava* (see above) also serves excellent food.

There are a few small **food shops** and supermarkets in Str Bălcescu and at the north end of Str Mitropoliei, but for vegetables and fruit try the main **open-air market** in Piața Cibin beside the river in the Lower Town. Alternatively, there is a smaller open-air food market on the south side of B-dul Spitalelor. Two kiosks on the opposite side of B-dul Spitalelor sell a good range of bread and fruit.

Post office

The main post office, which has a *poste restante* service, is at Str Mitropoliei 14, while the international telephone bureau at Str Bălcescu 17 also has a *cabana fax* (fax office); open Mon–Fri 06.30–22.00, Sat–Sun 07.00–22.00. For local directory enquiries ☎ 931.

Money

Sibiu has several **banks** where you can cash travellers' cheques—but only in the morning. These include *Bancorex*, housed in a handsomely restored mansion on Str Tribunei, *Banca Comercială* (which has a *Visa* cash machine) at Str Bălcescu 11, and *Banca Dacia Felix* on Str Ion Rațiu. Most of the banks accept *Visa* cards. There are several independent **exchange counters** in the town centre, including *Cambio* at Piața Unirii 4; *Platinum* at Piața Unirii 1, and *România Exchange*, which has branches at Str Vasile Milea, bl 11A, and Piața Mare 16.

Police

The Inspectoratul de Poliție is at Str Revoluției 4–6.

Health care

There are two 24-hour **pharmacies**, one at Str Bălcescu 53 and the other at Str N. Iorga 50 in a modern residential quarter on the south side of town.

Entertainment

Sibiu's **theatre** is located on B-dul Spitalelor near Piața Unirii. Across the road from its uninspired modern building is the massive roundel of Turnul Gros, where Sibiu's first professional theatre opened in 1788. The tower, originally part of the town's 16C fortifications, is slowly being transformed into an **opera house**. In 1993 a group of students organised the first annual youth theatre festival in Sibiu (see page 467). There is a **puppet theatre** at Str Alexandru Odobescu 4, and two **cinemas**: the *Pacea* on Str Bălcescu, ☎ 432335, and the *Tineretului* on Str Odobescu, ☎ 411420. Night life in Sibiu is limited, but the *Bulevard* and *Continental* hotels have **casinos**, and there are a couple of **discos**. For up-to-date information contact the tourist office or one of the hotels.

Maps and books

For maps and books about Transylvania in general try *Librăria Eminescu* or *Humanitas* in Str Bălcescu. There is also a bookshop in Piața Mare, while the Austrian-owned *Thausib* in Piața Mica sells German guides to Transylvania and English novels. The town's main public **library**, *Biblioteca 'Astra'*, open Mon–Fri 08.00–20.00, is worth looking at even if you cannot manage any Romanian. The university *rectorat* at B-dul Victoriei 10 holds books in several European languages, and the *Casa de Cultura Studentească* specialises in French literature.

Traditional crafts

The open-air market on Piața Cibin is an enjoyable place to look for traditional wooden utensils made and sold by Calderaș gypsies. During the summer there is a stall here specialising in ceramics from Corund, a Székely village in eastern Transylvania famous for its potters. At the time of printing there are three **crafts shops** in the centre of Sibiu: *Art Antic* in Piața Grivița, one in Str Avram Iancu and another in Str Bălcescu. *Art Antic* has links with the ASTRA Museum (see below) and can help you to find local craftspeople specialising in traditional ironwork and costumes. The ASTRA Museum also has specialists available to give advice on craftspeople and crafts fairs, both locally and nationally.

At Piața Mare 4–5, the **Brukenthal Museum and Library** is one of the most charming art galleries in Romania, and deserves to be much better known. It opened officially in 1817, seven years earlier than the National Gallery in London, although Brukenthal made his own art collection available to the public in 1790. Today the collections comprise European paintings, prints and sculptures from the 15C–20C.

The holdings include Brukenthal's own collection of pre-19C European paintings and modernist works from the ASTRA Museum. Only a small proportion of the paintings and sculptures are on show at any one time. The museum also has a substantial collection of prints from many periods. Unforgivably for such an important and delightful gallery, it has no up-to-date catalogue although one is in the pipeline. But you can buy brochures about the building in English, French and German and the museum has a website: *http://www.brukenthal.verena.ro*. You may also contact it by e-mail: *brukenthal@verena.ro*.

Brukenthal's own collection, displayed on the second floor, comprises European paintings from the 15C–18C. It is particularly strong in Dutch and Flemish paintings and scenes by Caravaggisti. Among many beguiling canvases are *Mary Magdalene Reading her Bible in Prison* by Caracciolo (1578–1635) and some of the small personal altarpieces kept in secret by Catholics during the Protestant Reformation. Open Tues–Sun 10.00–20.00 1 May–31 Oct, otherwise 09.00–17.00 1 Nov–30 Apr. Guided tours in English are available. ☎ 417691/411545.

Brukenthal prized scholarship so much that he made it a condition of employment that his librarians should have at least three doctorates. One of his librarians

> ### *Brukenthal and the Brukenthal Palace*
> Samuel Brukenthal (1721–1803) was one of the most able men of his generation. He was born in Nocrich, a village c 34km east of Sibiu. While studying abroad he became fascinated by the German Enlightenment and developed a passion for painting, music and literature. He had an astute and cultivated mind and this, together with his knowledge of Transylvania, brought him to the notice of the Empress Maria Teresa (1717–80). They were rumoured to have been lovers, but whether the story is true or not, the Empress encouraged his interest in art and appointed him as her representative in Transylvania in 1777. She also gave him paintings.
>
> Brukenthal married Sophie Klockner, the daughter a mayor of Sibiu. As part of her dowry, Sophie brought the parcel of land at the corner of Piața Mare where the Museum stands today. Brukenthal began collecting paintings long before he became governor, and the walls of his house at Avrig were reputedly covered with canvases from floor to ceiling. After his only child died, Brukenthal stipulated that his palace, his collections and his library should remain intact and be opened to the public.
>
> Brukenthal commissioned the handsome late-Baroque palace as his official residence in 1779. He took a great interest in the plans, and consulted a Viennese architect, Martinelli, before asking a local builder, Johann Blaumann, to carry out the work. Blaumann had just completed the Bánffy Palace in Cluj, but this house has a much less formidable design and, on its peripheral site, it does not command the same presence. Together with the Jesuit Church that stands nearby, the Palace transformed this corner of Piața Mare. Most of the interior decoration was the work of Simon Hoffmeyer, another Transylvanian, whose light and humorous touch makes a brilliant complement to Brukenthal's sensuous paintings. Hoffmeyer was also responsible for the figures of Atlas that flank one of the entrances into the inner courtyard, but he was best known for his splendid altars at Dumbrăveni, Odorheiu Secuiesc and Gherla, as well as the lovely altar and pulpit that he made for the Roman Catholic Cathedral in Alba Iulia. Three first-floor reception rooms that face Piața Mare have been preserved as they were in the Governor's day; they are sometimes used for concerts as well.

was the inventor of homeopathy, Samuel Hahnemann. Brukenthal collected around 14,000 books, and the **Brukenthal Library** has grown to around 280,000 volumes (counted in 1996). Used mainly for research, it compares in scope with the two other great personal libraries created in Transylvania, the Batthiányeum in Alba Iulia and the Teleki Library in Târgu Mureș. Highlights include the early 16C *Brukenthal Breviary*, a lovely parchment manuscript illustrated with miniature paintings by Simon Bening (1483–1561) and Geeraert Hornebaut (1465–1540), and a 1518 copy of Thomas More's *Utopia* illustrated by Hans Holbein the Younger (1497–1543). The library also has nearly 400 incunabulae and several important early Romanian Orthodox texts. Visits can be made by appointment at the Brukenthal Museum.

The **ASTRA Museum** occupies two sites, one at Padurea Dumbrăvii beside the

SIBIU • 461

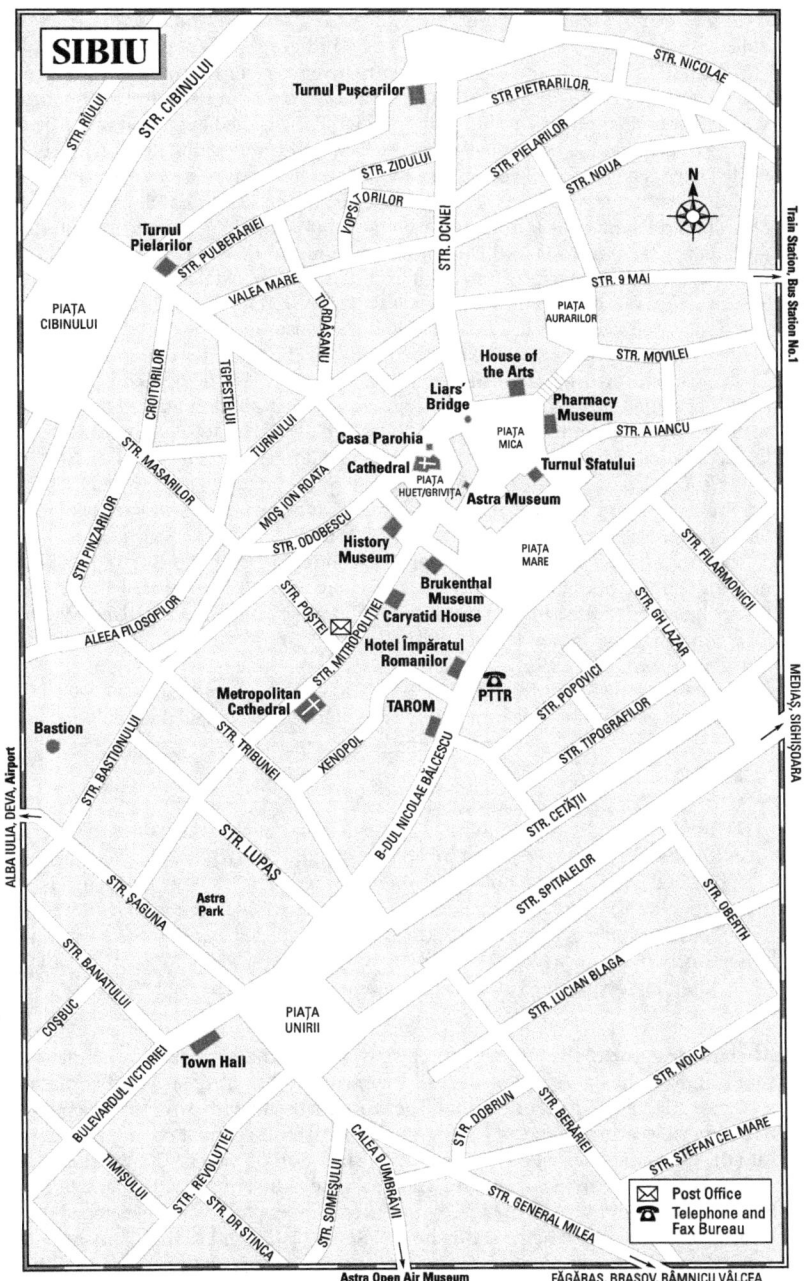

road to Rășinari and the other at Piața Mica 11–12, where you can visit a small collection from the Far East, the excellent ethnographic film studio and small temporary shows. This site is the most attractive open-air museum in the country. It contains c 340 buildings, including watermills and windmills, gigantic wine, fruit and oil presses, fulling mills and forges arranged in graded walks over 100ha of parkland so that you can choose how much you want to see on any one visit. There is a wonderful collection of wooden farmhouses, a *cherhana* (a traditional collecting and storage point for fish) and sheep folds, as well as a wooden church. Trolleybuses T1 from the railway station and T4 barred from B-dul Spitatelor both run to Hanul Dumbravă; take buses 17 (to Rășinari) or 15 (to Paltiniș). Trams run past the museum from B-dul Dumbrăvii and from Rășinari. The museum has its own minibus which will ferry you from the Piața Mica site if you book in advance. ☎ 420215, or ask at the museum.

The museum publishes an illustrated guide in English Romanian Millenary Civilizastion in "Astra" Museum-Sibin. Don't be put off by the pompous title; the book is excellent and contains details about each installation as well as a short history of the museum itself. Guided tours are available, too. A programme of lectures is held here throughout the summer, and the museum organises several crafts festivals as well. It has a café and a traditional *han* that can be hired for parties. You can also visit the museum by horse-drawn cart, but if you are walking, allow at least an hour and a half for the full tour.

The driving force behind the museum is its director, Corneliu Bucur. In 1992 he founded a National Academy for the Promotion of Traditional Crafts. Dr Bucur has turned the Museum into such a dynamic cultural centre that Sibieni joke that Astra is better known than the city. Dr Bucur was elected to the Romanian Senate in 1996.

Open 1 May–15 October, Tues–Fri 10.00–18.00, Sat–Sun 10.00–12.00. Groups can visit out of season and English guided tours are available.

ASTRA
Astra is an acronym for Asociația Transilvenene de Artă și Literatură, a society that encouraged Romanians in Transylvania to value their own culture and political identity. Founded in 1861, many of Transylvania's most distinguished writers and scholars became members. The society held its meetings in a house near the Metropolitan Cathedral. ASTRA also gave its name to Sibiu's first history museum, founded in the late 19C, and to the elegant neo-Rococo library which stands in Str Barițiu, to one side of Parcul Astra. The building opened in 1905 and still houses Sibiu's main public library.

Muzeul de Istorie, the History Museum, is housed in a very attractive building that stands in the courtyard of the Old Town Hall at Str Mitropoliei 2. It contains sections on local and national history. The museum began with a nucleus of objects and curiosities acquired in the 18C by Samuel Brukenthal, and it provides insights into the German colonisation of Sibiu. Open Tues–Sun 09.00–17.00, ☎ 412500.

Expoziția de Istoria Farmaciei, the Pharmacy Museum, is at Piața Mica 26. Samuel Hahnemann (1755–1843) invented homeopathy and developed his treatments in the basement of this house. Some of his phials and plans are on display. The museum occupies a former apothecary's shop, *La Ursul Negru* (At the

Black Bear), which opened at the start of the 17C. It contains over 6000 ancient medical instruments and dispensing tools from the time when Sibiu had more chemists' than anywhere else in Transylvania. At the front, a reconstructed *oficina* (shop) is decked out with wooden counters and stacks of glass jars creating the atmosphere of an 18C apotek. In fact, the furniture is Viennese and it came from another pharmacy, *La Vulturul Negru* (At the Black Vulture), which had to be dismantled to make way for the Jesuit Church in the 1720s. Open Tues–Sun 10.00–18.00.

Muzeul de Istorie Naturală, the Natural History Museum at Str Cetății 1, contains over 1 million exhibits concerned with zoology, botany, mineralogy and petrology, all housed in a neo-Renaissance building dating from 1894, which stands on top of the 16C Haller Bastion. Open Tues–Sun 09.00–17.00.

Walking around Sibiu

Much of Sibiu's old centre is semi-pedestrianised, which makes walking around it a pleasure. A great deal of its charm lies in the hidden courtyards, narrow passageways and tiny squares which you will only find if you have time to wander on your own. The town is lucky to have survived as well as it has: in fact, it escaped the depredations of Ceaușescu's rule only because his son, Nicu, was the town mayor. But in 1983–84 the dictator raised the base of the statue depicting Gheorghe Lăzar and demolished the gardens that had flourished in Piața Mare since 1848 to make room for the large, adoring audiences he expected to attract.

Piața Mare was begun in the 14C as an extension to the existing citadel; it was designed especially for open-air ceremonies, including processions and public executions. The houses ringing the square are mainly sturdy two- and three-storey buildings painted in a range of pretty colours and overhung by large tiled roofs that sweep outwards at the bottom. Much of their attraction lies in their rugged individuality and the secure, womb-like effect of the square itself. Some of them, such as **Casa Haller** (no. 10), have the original owners' coats of arms emblazoned on the gates. This was the home of the 16C mayor, Petrus Haller, who was a staunch supporter of the Habsburg Emperor Ferdinand I during the Austrians' attempts to wrest Transylvania from the Hungarians. The **watchtowers**, as at Casa Haller, were used for living in as well as defence. No. 8 belonged to Mayor Georg Hecht, who defeated the Turks at Turnu Roșu in 1493.

The **Jesuit Church** was completed in 1733 and replaced a row of medieval, porticoed houses. It was imposed on the town by the Habsburgs after their successful invasion of 1689, and is more attractive outside than in. Immediately to the left, underneath the church tower and its onion dome, is a **medieval passageway** into Piața Mica. To the right of the church is another entrance to Piața Mica through the 16C **Turnul Sfatului** (the Old Town Hall Tower), which stands on the site of a 13C gatetower. If you want to see the dungeon and a small exhibition featuring the town, ask at the History Museum first to avoid disappointment.

As Sibiu became ever more prosperous, Piața Mare and its satellite streets were taken over by the elite, and the houses here became grander as their owners rose up the social scale. Leaving Piața Mare with Turnul Sfatului on your left, you come to **Str Avram Ianc**, an attractive side street that contains some of the grandest. **Saxon houses** flank it on either side, many of them with carriage entrances leading to inner courtyards. No. 9 has an arcaded court based on an Italian Renaissance design, and at the back of the yard you can still see the ruin of a defence tower, marking part of the citadel wall that ran parallel to the street. The remains of other towers are embedded into the fabric of nos 13, 21 and 29. No. 21 was the home of composer, Gheorghe Dima (1847–1925), who wrote choral music inspired by Romanian folklore. About halfway down Str Avram Iancu, turn left into a steep passageway, **Pasajul Şcolii**, which joins two schools, one at the top and one at the bottom. This brings you below the city walls into the rutted cobbles of Str Movilei.

Walk into **Piaţa Aurarilor**, Goldsmiths' Square, to the left, and you will find a square of proportions so small that they are almost absurd. Its original German name was *Fingerlin* (a finger ring), for obvious reasons.

Turn right here and you face two alleys that lead into **Str 9 Mai**, the place where Sibiu began. Here and in the parallel **Str Nouă** (New Street), the houses still show the social development that took place between the 13C–14C, when agricultural farmsteads gave way to smaller craftsmen's dwellings. Walking away from the citadel along **Str Ocnei**, the signs of old Sibiu continue here and in **Str Zidului** (Wall Street). At the further end of this street stands the circular **Turnul Puşcarilor** (the Gunpowder Tower). Follow Str Zidului west into Str Pulberăriei, and at the next junction stands an octagonal tower built by the Tanners' Guild, **Turnul Pielarilor**. This has suffered more than its fair share of misfortunes, having been blown up twice before it was burnt down in 1638.

Retrace your steps to the south along Str Zidului and you come to Str Ocnei named after the salt mines that lay to the north of Sibiu. To the right before you climb up to Piaţa Mica is a little, winding side street called Azilului (Asylum Street). This still contains the **hospital** (now an old people's home) which was founded by the Order of the Holy Cross in the late 13C. Next to it, set back in a small courtyard, is the apparently neglected carcase of a **Baroque church**, which stands on the remains of a choir belonging to the Gothic church built at the same time as the hospital. Archaeologists from the Brukenthal Museum are excavating the pre-Christian graves below the church. Walk through the dark barrel-vaulted tunnel that disappears off to the right of the courtyard, and you come to another courtyard containing **traditional houses** that have been converted into old people's flats and a short-stay children's home.

Return to Str Ocnei and turn right up the hill into **Piaţa Mica**. Mentioned in the earliest known documents by its Latin name, Circulus Parvus, this is a lovely, crescent-shaped space that was added to the first oval citadel where Piaţa Huet/Griviţa stands today. Of the three original gate towers defending the square, only one, **Turnul Sfatului**, remains intact.

As you enter Piaţa Mica from Str Ocnei the road is flanked by a set of **steps** on either side. The road itself passes through the remains of a mid-15C tunnel which used to emerge close to Turnul Sfatului. The tunnel was opened up in 1851, having been condemned by Sibiu's doctors as a murky hole that caused people severe palpitations. For good measure, they added that it was a breeding ground 'for every kind of pestilence'.

Crossing the road is the wrought-iron footbridge, **Podul Minciunilor**, the Liars' Bridge, installed some ten years later. Some say its name comes from a legend that anyone who tells a lie while standing on the bridge will cause it to collapse. Others believe that it is named after Băncuţele Minciunilor, benches that stood between the tunnel and Casa Artelor in the 16C. Apparently, shoppers would rest here and spin fantastic yarns to each other when they ran out of more factual gossip.

Piața Mica became Sibiu's principal market place and remained its commercial centre even after Piața Mare was built. Many of the **arcaded houses** that surround it were once shops with open-air premises. They were owned by craftsmen such as cobblers, furriers and goldsmiths, who formed some of Sibiu's most powerful guilds.

> ### Sibiu's fortifications
> Sibiu's defence system began with the 13C wall around Piața Huet/Grivița and developed into a mighty complex that was the envy of Transylvania. At the height of its strength, there were four tiers of curtain wall and five bastions designed to withstand artillery fire. The Turks who besieged Sibiu three times in the 14C called it 'the Red City', partly because of the blood that was shed here, but also because all they ever saw were its massive red-brick defences. The heart-shaped bastions (two of which remain as ruins) were constructed on the orders of the Habsburgs in the 16C and 17C. A series of lakes and fish ponds was dug around the perimeter walls to prevent enemies from getting too close.

On the north side of Piața Mica, the free-standing **Casa Artelor** (House of the Arts), is the square's earliest building. It was originally a market hall, constructed from river stones in 1370. Its steep gable ends were copied from Franconian homesteads introduced to Sibiu by German immigrants. Also known as Hala Măcelarilor, the Butchers' Hall, it was used by butchers and furriers before becoming by turns a town hall and a theatre. Beautifully restored in the 1970s, it now houses temporary exhibitions organised by the Brukenthal Museum.

Continue clockwise around the square, and you come to a row of 16C **arcaded houses** and the remains of one of the original gate towers. Through this is a set of steep steps leading back into Piața Aurarilor. Adjoining the tower on the other side is a row containing the Pharmacy Museum.

With your back to Turnul Sfatului, walk across Podul Minciunilor into the intimate space of **Piața Huet/Grivița**. This was the site of Sibiu's first, oval-shaped, citadel. The Gothic **cathedral** that now dominates the square stands on the site of a Romanesque basilica which stood inside the fortress. Before the Protestant revolution, the cathedral was a Catholic church. After the Reformation it became the flagship of Lutheranism throughout southern Transylvania. It is a fine example of central European masonry by craftsmen trained in the famous Parlerian schools of Prague and Schwabisch-Gmünd. The design, too, is typically central European, with a tower over the fourth and fifth bays of the nave rather than at the west end. Construction began in 1322, but a series of political and economic hitches meant that work could only continue sporadically. The present building, modelled on German hall churches, was completed in 1520.

The exterior is plain save for slender buttresses, a few exuberant stone carvings and a magnificent square portal at the south entrance. Inside, the grey stone walls create an austere atmosphere that is slightly mitigated by exuberant carving in the vaulting and in the stone **epitaphs** that are fixed to a wall on the north side of the nave. One of them commemorates the unlucky Mihnea cel Rău

(Mihnea the Bad), who was stabbed to death by a hired assassin after he attended a mass here in 1510. Mihnea was the son of Vlad Țepeș, the Impaler, and he was *voivode* (prince) of Wallachia for just one year.

A gigantic **fresco** (over 9m high) covers much of the chancel's north wall. The mural shows the Crucifixion and marks a transition in Transylvanian painting from the coldly ethereal late Gothic to the more human concerns of the renaissance. The painter, Johannes of Rosenau, created a sense of great dramatic tension by crowding the base of his composition with a host of biblical and historical figures. At the top of the fresco he added the royal Hungarian insignia with the apostolic cross of Silesia, the Bohemian vulture and a lion rampant. To the sides are an *Ecce Homo* and a scene showing the Vision of St John of Patmos. Below the fresco, Rosenau depicted Hungary's two first Christian kings, Stephen (István), shown with a sceptre, and Ludovic Lajos with an axe, and there are 'niches' containing the portraits of various donors. The mural is framed by a *trompe l'oeil* pattern of architectonic motifs. The artist's signature appears in minute Gothic script on the border together with the date: 1445.

To the north of the crossing is a **polyptych** painted in the style of Dürer, completed in the first quarter of the 16C. The cathedral has a choir loft on the south side with a beautiful fan-vaulted ceiling. There is also an immense **Baroque organ** designed by a German master in 1671. Six thousand pipes were installed in 1914, making it the largest of its kind in Transylvania. Evening concerts are held here on Wednesdays during the summer, starting at 18.00.

Opposite the cathedral's south entrance is the German-language **school** established in the 18C by Samuel Brukenthal for the children of his employees. The building replaced Sibiu's first school, founded on the same site in 1380, and is still functioning today.

Facing the north side of the cathedral at no. 1 is the *parohia* (the parochial offices). This has a lovely Gothic entrance of interlaced stone, carved in 1502 by Andreas Lapicida. He was one of the great Transylvanian sculptors of his day, and was much in demand. He is known to have converted several basilicas into hall churches, among them the churches at Cârta, Cristian, Moșna and Richiș. Above the lintel is a plaque inscribed in Latin with Gothic lettering which tells you that the work was commissioned by a priest called Johannes of Olczna (Alțina, a village near Mediaș). Surrounding the plaque are four portraits depicting Johannes himself (top right), St John (top left), Pope Alexander VI (bottom right) and Johannes's patron, the Emperor Frederick III (bottom left). The portraits show an awakening interest in individual character, a sign that Lapicida was beginning to be excited by the wave of humanism that was spreading across Europe from Italy.

Beside the parohia stands a 15C **tower and archway** through which you can descend once more into the Lower Town. Before walking down, have a look to the right-hand side of the stairway. This is one of the hidden places that makes Sibiu so satisfying to explore: through another archway is a 17C **courtyard** of private houses that seems to be dreaming in its own time warp, completely untouched by the 20C. Turn left at the bottom of the steps, and you can come up again via another appealing **passageway** built into the wall around Piața Huet. These steps bring you to a road leading downhill from Piața Grivița, from where you can get a superb view of Sibiu's haphazard medieval roofscape.

Cross the road and walk a few metres left to the History Museum. Inside is a spacious courtyard that contains several interesting buildings, notably the Gothic **tower** (c 1470) at the further end and **Casa Altemberger** (15C) to its right. Lapicida designed a *loggia* here; note the two amusing cornices depicting the busts of a stonemason and a carpenter, who are shown wearing contemporary 15C dress. A third, larger male bust probably represents Lapicida himself, shown for some reason clutching his sides. In the mid-16C the town council bought the house and turned it and the Gothic tower into Sibiu's new town hall. The tower has been extensively renovated since it collapsed during the 19C and is now used as the museum's administration offices.

Walk southwest along Str Mitropoliei, and on the left at no. 13 is **Casa cu Cariatide** (the Caryatid House). Its striking Baroque portal was created by a pupil of Simon Hoffmeyer. The house itself dates from c 1786. It stands on the site where Sibiu's master goldsmith, Sebastian Hann, had his workshop. Hann came from Levoča in present-day Slovakia, one of many Protestants who fled here in the 17C to avoid persecution by the Catholics.

Further along Str Mitropoliei is the **Metropolitan Cathedral**, looking very smart in its Byzantine stripes. It was completed in 1906, and the glittering interior was modelled on the old Orthodox church of Hagia Sofia in Istanbul. The frescoes are in coloured cement; one of the artists who carried them out was Johann Köber from Târgu Jiu, whose main claim to fame lies in the fact that he once taught Constantin Brâncuși.

Walk further along Str Mitropoliei and turn right into Str Lupas before Casa de Cultură Studentească. At the next junction turn left along Str Bastionului. At the end of this street on the right are the ivy-covered remains of one of Sibiu's great **bastions**, finished in 1629. You can get a better view if you walk a few metres down Șos Alba Iulia.

Go back to the end of Str Mitropoliei and turn right into Astra Park opposite the grey Jugendstil house. Turn left into Str Bălcescu, a semi-pedestrianised shopping street bordered by **Saxon houses**. It is named after Nicolae Bălcescu, a leading light in Transylvania's independence movement, and is a pleasant place to linger in. At the other end, it joins Piața Mare. Parallel with Str Bălcescu is Str Cetății (Citadel Street), which contains an evocative array of **fortifications**: three towers, a roundel and a bastion, some of them virtually intact, have survived, as well as a long brick rampart that borders B-dul Spitalelor. The roundel is **Turnul Gros**, a 16C tower that was converted into Sibiu's first professional theatre in 1788 and is currently being restored as an opera house.

Around Sibiu

Sibiu is surrounded by five distinct ethnographic areas, each of which has its own subtly different forms of traditional customs and dress. To the east lies a region known to Germans as the **Altland**, the Old Land, which contains many of the first villages settled by Saxons in Transylvania. Ethnic Romanians have lived here for centuries too. They have their own name, Țara Oltului, the Olt Country, for an almost identical area that is bordered on one side by the Olt River. One of the conundrums which continues to fascinate historians is who came first, and how the Olt River got its name: was it Dacian or German in origin?

The Altland lies between Sibiu and the villages of Nocrich and Cincu, which can be found north of the main Sibiu-Făgăraș road, the DN1. Getting to Nocrich involves a drive along Valea Hârtibăciului (the Hârtibăciu Valley), an ancient cattle-raising and fruit-growing area. From Sibiu, the valley road heads for Agnita and can be used as a cross-country route to Sighișoara. Places to look out for here include **Vurpăr**, **Marpod**, **Alțina**, **Agnita** and **Chirpăr**, and, closer to **Sighișoara**, **Apold** and **Șaeș**. Two cultures have merged in the valley so that instead of geometrical designs, Romanian costumes are embroidered with flowers in the German fashion. Each spring the people of the valley hold a dance and music festival at Agnita. Details are available from the local museum, Muzeul 'Valea Hârtibaciului', Str Spitalelort no. 29, or contact *Centrul Creației Populare* in Sibiu.

A **narrow-gauge railway** connects Sibiu with Agnita. If the service is still running this is an appealing way to see the countryside, but the one-way trip takes two hours and there is no return service to Sibiu on the same day. Embark at Sibiu station.

You can reach the eastern Altland more easily from Făgăraș, but if you take the E68/DN1 from Sibiu, stop in **Avrig** (c 27km) to see the manor that Samuel Brukenthal built before becoming Governor of Transylvania. It stands to the left of the road in the town centre, just past the church. The grounds are open to the public although the building itself is now used as a hospital.

About 18km further east on the E68/DN1, a road to the left brings you **Cârta**. The village contains the ruins of Transylvania's first Gothic church. Founded in 1202 by monks from Pontigny in France, it has groin vaults with ogees and bosses typical of Cistercian buildings. It was destroyed by the Turks during a 15C raid, and King Matei Corvin closed the monastery in 1474, giving its lands to Sibiu. Restoration began in 1961.

The fortified churches of Cisnădie and Cisnădioară

Cisnădie and Cisnădioară are a ten-minute drive south from Sibiu. Styled Michelsburg by its German settlers, **Cisnădioară** has a handsome Romanesque church which perches on a crag (the Michelsberg) 70m above the village. The citadel hill is fenced in at the bottom, and there is a small entrance charge (the key-holder lives in a house to the right of the entrance gates).

A legend says that in the Middle Ages, young Saxon men from Cisnădioară who wanted to marry had to prove their worthiness by heaving a large boulder from the river bed to the top of the Michelsberg. At the top you can see the western end of the Făgăraș range almost as far as Turnu Roșu, the nearest pass into Oltenia.

Documents show that the Michelsberg was given to the Cistercian monastery of Cârta in 1223 by a Wallonian immigrant, Master Gocelinus (or Gosselin). This was before the village came into existence. Gocelinus held a high position at the Hungarian court of King Endre II (r. 1205–35) and played an important part in organising the Transylvanian colonies.

The perimeter wall that encloses the **church** has been restored, and a thick band of mortar shows where the new stones were laid. Villagers brought their livestock with them when they sheltered here, and there are signs of storerooms and stabling both outside and inside the walls.

The church dates from between 1162–1223. Cistercians from northern France introduced Gothic elements into the Romanesque building when it was still unfinished. Here, the Gothic influence shows most clearly in the stone carvings around the west door. For unknown reasons, the church was abandoned before it was finished, and the two towers planned for the west end never materialised. Faded patches of fresco are all that remain of the painting that once covered the interior walls.

In the centre of Cisnădioară stands an old **Baroque church** that has been recently restored by village craftsmen. Its woodwork and altarpiece are very smart. The **village museum** contains an attractive collection of artefacts and tools from Saxon households; opening times are available from the Brukenthal Museum in Sibiu. Cisnădioară lies in a very attractive position and several foreign families have bought properties here, giving it a flourishing air. Tourist accommodation is available in the village if you ask at the houses showing '*han*' signs. There are footpaths leading across the hills to Rășinari (ask at the post office for directions).

During the Middle Ages Saxon immigrants introduced new technology into Transylvania, including wooden looms, and **Cisnădie** became an important centre for the wool trade. The **Expoziția Muzeală 'Istoricul Industrial Textile 1974'** (the textile museum) at Str Apărării 4 illustrates the local development of the industry in an old and pretty building. Open Mon–Sat 08.00–16.00. But the most important monument in Cisnădie is its **Saxon church**, which stands in the centre of this small town. Beautifully restored, the church is surrounded by a double ring wall. A medieval shopping arcade that was built into the perimeter wall still contains shops.

The church was originally a Romanesque building from the 12C. In 1400 it was transformed into its present Gothic form, although some of the Romanesque windows were left intact. Its perimeter walls date from 1500, a time when the Turks intensified their attacks on Transylvania. The original altarpiece was broken up before 1904 and only the predella, with scenes from the life of St Michael, and the top, showing St Sever, have survived intact. An inscription on the predella states that the original scenes were painted in 1525. The new central panel represents the Baptism of Christ, and there are scenes from the life of St John on either side.

Rășinari and Paltiniș

Driving southwest into the Cindrel mountains from Sibiu takes under an hour. On the way the road passes through **Rășinari**, another former textile centre. It is named after *rășină*, a resin that the villagers used to collect from the woods nearby in order to polish the heddles of their looms. Rășinari is the birthplace of two famous Romanian personalities, writer Emil Cioran (1911–96) and the ill-fated prime minister, Octavian Goga (1881–1938). Goga's association with the anti-Semitic National Christian Party led to his political downfall. But Goga was also a poet, and his house has been turned into a memorial museum. When the Saxons began leaving, many of their houses were taken over by Roma, mainly in the southern part of the village. There is a folklore festival here on the third Sunday of April. Trams from Dumbravă in Sibiu run to Rășinari and back.

During the climb to **Paltiniș** to the southwest, the road opens out into a superb panorama, giving views over the Transylvanian plateau. New **hotels** and cabins have been constructed in Paltiniș; the *Hotel Cindrel* is one of the most well-established, ☎ 069 213237. However, the village is orientated more towards **skiing** than summer holidays. *Paltin* means 'aspen' in Romanian, and the ski resort was Romania's first; it opened in the 1890s. At the entrance to the village is a nuns' skete which has a new wooden church. There are many marked footpaths into the forests, but it is easy to get lost unless you have a guide or a good local map. To the west of Sibiu is an area known as the **Marginimea Sibiuliu** (the margin of Sibiu). This is one of the five ethnographic zones that surround the city, and its traditional costumes are very sober, using black embroidery on a white ground. But the choice of black may have been pragmatic: a story says that the villagers used to embroider their clothes in red but changed when local textile merchants offered them a cheaper consignment of black cotton instead. Technically Marginimea runs from Tălmaciu to the village of Vinţu de Jos near Sebeş, excluding Cisnădie and Cisnădioară.

Cristian, c 10km west of Sibiu, has a Gothic citadel hall church that was converted from a 13C basilica by Andrei Lapicida between 1472–86. In 1969 a small ethnographic museum was opened here in an 18C farmhouse; visiting is by request.

Nestling in the Cindrel foothills lies the picturesque village of **Sibiel**; you can walk into the mountains from here, but do not miss **Muzeul Sticlelor**, the glass icon museum; again, you may visit it on request.

Sheep have been grazed in the Cindrel mountains for centuries, and the region is famous for its traditional shepherds' villages. One of them, **Sălişte**, is home to a well-known folk choir that performs all over the country. Every year, dance groups from Transylvanian and Oltenian villages gather here for a New Year festival. Other nearby villages to look out for near here include Galeş, Tilişca, Poiana Sibiului and Jina. **Galeş** and **Poiana Sibiului** have ethnographic collections and the museum in Galeş boasts a traditional house from Sălişte complete with furniture, and a *stână* (sheepfold).

A few kilometres south of the E81 between Sebeş and Miercurea Sibiului, c 9km east of Sebeş, stands the magnificent fortress of **Câlnic**. This is a Saxon citadel which has been turned into an international conference and cultural centre. Begun in the mid-13C by a nobleman called Chyl de Kelling, it had a huge rectangular *donjon* surrounded by an oval-shaped curtain wall which were completed by towers and a moat completed the original fortifications. They have all been beautifully restored. Câlnic remained in Saxon hands until 1430, after which time it was extended several times. During one of these alterations, it gained a chapel in which you can still see fragments of early 16C fresco and panels from 1733 painted in the Renaissance floral style that was popular at the time. The citadel is protected by UNESCO, and in 1995 the Institute of Archaeology and Art History of the Romanian Academy in Cluj and an organisation called Ars Transilvaniae founded the cultural centre which offers a year-round programme of concerts, exhibitions, scientific conferences and symposiums.

Sebeş, sometimes called Sebeş Alba, is 55km west of Sibiu. It lies on the E68/E81/DN1/DN7. Archaeologists have found traces of Neolithic, Bronze Age and Dacian settlements in and around Sebeş, and there was a Roman camp near here too. During the Middle Ages it was an important cultural centre, and although it is a modest place today, some of its old buildings are very fine.

The main road through the town has some attractive old houses, but its main focal point is the Gothic choir, which has some of the finest **medieval carving** in Transylvania. During the relatively stable reign of Lajos I (1342–82), the towns of Sebeş, Mediaş and Sighişoara competed with each other for status by upgrading their religious buildings. Sebeş leapt ahead of the rest with its new choir, completed in 1382. Standing in the centre of town, the choir looks oddly truncated because it rises so abruptly from the main body of the church. Masons who trained under Hans Parler Junior in Nuremburg provided expressive carvings both outside and in. There is a particularly fine group showing the Magi Worshipping the Infant Jesus. Some of the sculptures, including a figure of John the Baptist, are thought to be from c 1420 or later. The altar at Sebeș is of decorated polychromed wood, with a sculpted central panel showing the Virgin and Child. On the outside are Late-Gothic carvings showing scenes from Christ's life by Transylvanian craftsmen. Full of emotional energy, they were inspired by the celebrated Nuremberg sculptor, Veit Stoss (c 1450–1533), and the Slovakian master carver, Pavel of Levoča.

Turnul Studențului (the Student's Tower) is virtually all that remains of the Saxon town razed by the Turks in the 15C. It gets its name from the *studentul din Romos* (the student from Romos) who, together with a group of other townspeople, refused to give himself up to Vlad Țepeș when the Wallachian prince made a joint attack on Sebeș with the Turks in 1438. After 20 years' captivity in Istanbul, the student escaped and made his way to Rome, where he published an extremely unflattering account of Ottoman life and manners. It was entitled *De Ritu et Moribus Turcorum* ('Of the Religion and Customs of the Turks'). Republished for a more sensational market in 1530, the book became a bestseller. Martin Luther became one of its greatest fans.

If you have time, visit the **town museum** at Piața Primăriei 4. This 16C house once belonged to Ioan Zápolya, whose treachery led to Hungary's defeat by the Ottomans at Mohács in 1526. Zápolya was prince of Transylvania between 1526–40. Open Tues–Fri 08.00–16.00, Sat 09.00–13.00.

A little to the north of Sebeș, on the north bank of the Secaș River, is the **Râpa Roșie**, an astonishing red sandstone cliff.

On the way from Sibiu watch out for churches and fortresses in **Șura Mare**, **Slimnic**, **Seica Mare** and **Agârbiciu**. At **Axente Sever**, you enter the Târnavă Valley, a region that is famous for its white wines. Axente Sever is named after a leader of the 1848 revolution who was born in the village. The citadel church stands beside the main through road. It has a very short lateral axis compared to its watchtower and looks hunched like a crow.

Just down the road is **Copșa Mica**. The Hungarian name of this town is Kiskapus, Little Gate, dating from the time when it lay on Hungary's eastern borders. Székely settlers were living here by the 10C. Today Copșa Mica contains a graveyard of rusting industrial plants. During the communist period, carbon-blacking and lead smelting factories were established in the town centre. They caused irreparable damage, and Copșa Mica became an international scandal. The carbon-blacking factory closed down in 1993, but lead-smelting continues here, although on a much reduced scale.

Take a country road to the south for **Valea Viilor** to see the superb hall church. It has two defence towers of equal height, one raised above the choir and one at the west end. The towers were added in the late 15C, when the nave was also raised.

Mediaș

Mediaș gets its name from *meggy*, the Hungarian word for a sour cherry, but this is an ancient settlement that dates back to the second millennium BC. Graves found in the town show that the Székely were here before the Saxons. However, during the 12C they moved further east, and the Germans transformed the village into an influential political and commercial centre that grew to rival Sighişoara and Sebeş. Today the medieval **centre** of Mediaş is small and charming. There are industries here, including one of the only firms in Romania that makes harnesses and saddlery for horses. There is a **tourist agency** called *Velimed* at Str Turnului 2, ☎ 069 815131.

Two **gate towers** on Str Cloşca are virtually all that remains of the citadel walls. While it is far smaller than Sibiu, Mediaş has a picturesque central square, Piaţa Republicii. Have a look at the Gothic Evangelical **church** on the north side of the square; it stands within a fortress wall. Inside the church are a fascinating fresco cycle from 1415–25 and a collection of Islamic carpets acquired for similar reasons to those in the Black Church at Braşov. Vlad Ţepeş attacked Mediaş in 1476 because the town refused to support him against the Hungarians. He was caught and locked up in the church tower.

Muzeul Orăşenesc (the Town Museum) is housed in a former Franciscan monastery at Str Mihai Viteazul 46, open Tues–Sun 09.00–17.00. It covers history and natural sciences and has examples of Neolithic and Dacian pottery and metalwork.

Like Sibiu, Mediaş is surrounded by a cluster of lovely old Saxon villages with marvellous churches. **Cetatea de Balţă**, **Băgaciu** and **Dumbrăveni** to the north, and **Moşna** and **Aţel** to the south of the Mediaş-Sighişoara road, the DN14, are all worth seeing if you have time.

The fortified churches of Biertan and Richiş

Make time to see **Biertan church**. To get to Biertan, turn right (south) off the Sighişoara road at Şaroş and head along the narrow valley lined with terraced hills. After a few kilometres the hills give way to Biertan village. The church rises out of it, soaring and compact like a miniature rocket cathedral waiting to be launched into space.

Encompassed by four rings of curtain wall and seven towers, it is technically a late-15C hall church that became the seat of the Lutheran bishops of Transylvania between 1562–1867. The details are beautiful: the **west portal** is decorated with curved and cross motifs in three registers and bears the arms of the Hungarian kings Lajos II and Ioan Zápolya, and the 16C door into the sacristy is ornamented with intarsia designs of extraordinary delicacy. Biertan's **altar** is a polyptych of polychromed wood comprising 28 separate scenes; they are painted in tempera and date from between 1483–1525. In the centre is a sculpted Crucifixion, restored in 1979. Here, as at Mediaş and Braşov, Islamic **carpets** decorate the walls, a mark of Transylvania's thriving trade with the Balkans. The pews are made of inlaid limewood. The **pulpit** (also inlaid) is covered by a *baldacchino* with reliefs depicting plant motifs, while at the back there are 20 panels decorated with more geometrical intarsia work. The inlays at Biertan were probably created by a local *atelier*, because they closely resemble woodwork at Aţel, Băgaciu, Dupuş and Richiş, all of which are known to have come from a single workshop.

The **fortifications** at Biertan were established at the same time as the church although, judging by its crude frescoes, the tower on the south side is probably earlier. The entrance lobby to the citadel at Biertan often contains helpful information about local accommodation, as well as maps highlighting other Saxon churches in the area.

An inscription found at Biertan shows that Christianity arrived here long before the Saxons. Dated to the 4C, it is a bronze votive plaque of local workmanship saying '*Ego Zenovius votum posui*'.

Continue southwest along the valley for 6km and you reach the village of **Richiş**. The church here is also very attractive, not least because of its sculpture. The **portal** at the west end depicts scenes from the Crucifixion which are almost identical to those found in the west door at Freiburg Cathedral. The figures are barely discernible, but an inscription dates them to shortly after 1400. Inside are bosses representing human, animal and plant motifs, and human masks peer out from capitals and consoles. The **door** into the sacristy was probably inlaid in the early 16C by members of the same *atelier* who worked at Biertan. If the church is locked, ask for the key from the custodian, who lives in a farmhouse just above the church as you walk up the hill past the apse.

Sighişoara

This is a place that you must not miss. Perched on a rock encircled by the silver coils of the Târnava Mare, and surrounded by forested hills, it is a wonderful place in the most literal sense of the word. The citadel is the most complete of its kind in Transylvania. From a distance it looks unbelievably romantic, but once you climb into the Saxon fortress you find that it is no fantasy but as solid as the colonising Germans could make it—the houses of Schässburg, as they call it, have walls several metres thick.

Sighişoara citadel stands on a network of tunnels and catacombs, and according to one version of the myth, this is where the Pied Piper brought the children of Hamelin after their ungrateful parents refused to pay him his due (another story says the Piper emerged in the centre of Braşov a few kilometres down the road).

History

The prehistory of this site dates back to the Bronze Age, and remains of a Dacian fortress and a Roman camp have also been found here. There were German-speaking colonists in Sighişoara by 1190. They started building beside the Saes Brook, which flowed through the town near where the market stands today. The stream was moved during the mid-19C. The Saxons' earliest buildings were made of wood, but few of these survived the Tartar invasion of 1241–42, when Khan Ogedei's horsemen devastated the entire principality. Later settlement developed from the southern end of the crag and extended north to include a second plateau. At the height of its power, Sighişoara had three curtain walls and 14 towers. In 1298, Dominican monks established a monastery on the citadel they knew as Schespurch, and later a Franciscan church was founded here as well.

Sighişoara enjoyed its greatest prosperity during the 15C and 16C. Its merchants and craftsmen formed close commercial ties with other Saxon towns in Transylvania and with Wallachia, but it was also well-placed to take advantage of Braşov's position on the trade route that ran between the Low

Countries and Persia. The 35 Oriental carpets hanging in the Dominican monastery church are a proof of this.

Education also rose to great heights: between 1402–1520, 95 Sighişoreni became students at the universities of Vienna and Kraków. The oldest school in the town was founded in 1522. And Sighişoara was also proud of its artists and craftsmen: during the 16C painters, sculptors, cabinetmakers, masons and organ-builders came here from Salzburg, Bohemia and the Tyrol as well as from nearby Braşov.

The most dramatic event in Sighişoara's history remains the great fire of 1676. The flames tore through the wooden houses on the Citadel and spread into the Lower Town and the outskirts—the reason why most of the houses in the Citadel date from the end of the 17C and later. In 1704, revolutionaries laid siege to Sighişoara. They blew up the Goldsmiths' Tower and the Castaldo bastion, and you can still see the results of their attack on the Tinsmiths' Tower. On 31 July 1849, the Russian army defeated revolutionary Hungarian troops at Albeşti, near Sighişoara.

Practical information

☎ code
065

Tourist information
There is a tourist agency on Str 1 Decembrie 10.

Getting around
By train Sighişoara's train station lies in a modern precinct to the northwest at Str Libertăţii 51; the *CFR* office is at Str 1 Decembrie 2.

By bus National buses can be found near the rail station, at Str Libertăţii 46.

Where to stay
Try the *Steaua* (✫) at Str 1 Decembrie 12, ☎ 771930; fax 771932, and *Pensiune Chic* (✫) near the station at Str Libertăţii 44, ☎ 775901; fax 164149. There is also a **campsite** near Sighişoara called *Villa Franka*, ☎ 771046; fax 164149. If you are looking for bed and breakfast and the more 'authentic' experience of staying with a Romanian family, contact *ANTREC* in Târgu Mureş or Bucharest (see p 116).

Hotel Rex (✫✫) on Str Dumbrăvei, c 1km from the town centre, is not recommended.

Post office
The post office and telephone bureau occupy the same building on Piaţa Oberth.

Money
The main **bank** in town is *CEC* at Str 1 Decembrie 8–10.

Police
The police station is on Str Justiţiei.

Health care
There is a **pharmacy** at the northeast end of Str 1 Decembrie, and the **hospital** is on Str Zaharia Boiu.

Regular events
In 1993 two young musicians from Bucharest started a medieval music and theatre **festival** in Sighişoara. Larger and more ambitious each year, it is usually held in the first or second week of July.

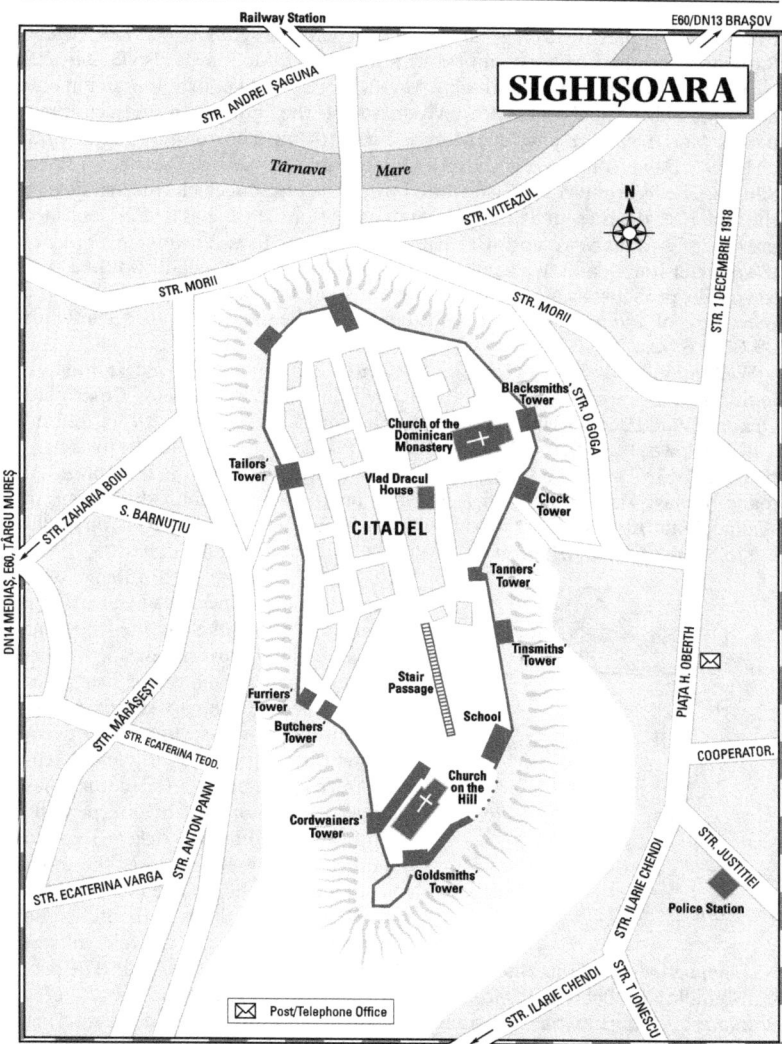

Walking around Sighişoara

There are several ways into the citadel, but the most impressive entry takes you through the 14C **Turnul cu Ceas**, the massive Clock Tower that stands in the eastern walls. Fortified with machicolations and standing 64m high, it is connected to the lower town by a steep ramp that makes it seem even more forbidding. Until 1556 it was the seat of the town council, but now it houses a small history and science museum. Climb to the top to see the clock mechanism and the seven **oak figures** that spin out when the hour strikes. Symbolising the days of the week, these statuettes were inspired by a mixture of ancient German,

Greek and Roman mythology and carry alchemical symbols on their heads. Sunday is a woman with a sunburst around her face; Monday is also female and carries a moon on her head; Tuesday, Mars's Day, is a soldier in a Roman kilt balancing a male symbol on his head; Wednesday is the figure of Hermes, counterpart of Mercury; Thursday, Jove's Day, is a god hurling a bolt of lightning; Friday or Freya's Day is a woman with the female symbol on her head and Saturday is Saturn. The figures were probably fitted when the original clock was installed in the mid-17C; the present Swiss movement dates from 1906. Beside the clock face are other figurines representing Peace, Justice and the Law. A drum player marks the quarter hours, and two small angels symbolise Day and Night. On the lower town side, probably as a warning to unwanted intruders, is an Executioner. The Baroque roof and pinnacles were added in 1677. The museum is open Tues–Sun 09.00–16.00.

Walking to the west from the Clock Tower brings you past the oldest building in the citadel—most of the houses here date from the 17C and 18C—**Casa Vlad Dracul** (Vlad Dracul's House), now a restaurant. Vlad Dracul (r. 1436–42 and 1443–47) was the father of Vlad the Impaler (Vlad III Dracula), and he lived here between 1431–35. It is possible that Dracula himself was born in the house. He made his last visit to Sighişoara in 1476 on his way to claim the throne of Wallachia for his last, short-lived reign. The house is the oldest surviving building in Sighişoara citadel; most of the others date from the 17C and 18C.

Str Şcolii

Go past the 'House with a Deer', turn left into Str Şcolii, and ahead you will see the mid-17C **Pasajul Scărilor** (the Stair Passage), a long, covered wooden stairway. Climb this to reach the highest point of the citadel. To the east stands an old German **school** whose interior is decorated with Baroque frescoes and a splendid staircase. The janitor sometimes indulges in a bit of private enterprise by letting visitors climb the rickety steps to the attic, which looks out over the town and surrounding hills. On a nice day, this is worth the effort. Sharing the hill is the magnificent fortified church of Sf Nicolae, better known as **Biserica din Deal** (the Church on the Hill). The present building probably dates from the early 15C, but it stands on the site of a Romanesque chapel which is much older. In 1704 a fire damaged the interior, but in the 1990s many of its flamboyant carvings and frescoes were restored by students from the Fine Arts Academy in Bucharest, and you can almost imagine what it must have looked like when new.

Substantial fragments of the late-15C **frescoes** survive. They include an almost complete painting of the Last Judgment (at the east end of the north nave wall) and, in the nave vaults, a group of devils plaguing the Archangel Michael while he tries to save souls.

On the ceiling of the west tower you can still see paintings of St Francis of Assisi (on the north wall) as well as scenes from the Passion. Here, the rich colouring and vigorous handling suggest that the artist was of Tyrolean origins.

In 1777 the murals were covered over with lime; this was cleaned off in the 1930s. The church has some fine **carvings** as well; most of these are central European in character and date from the second half of the 14C. Elias Nicolai also created pieces for Biserica din Deal, including the tabernacle, pulpit, font and several tombstones. Elias Nicolai was one of the most skilful Baroque sculptors in Transylvania and he also worked at the Dominican monastery church. The **altarpiece** is a polyptych made by Johannes Stoss. He was the son of the celebrated Nuremburg sculptor, Veit Stoss (c 1450–1533), and he had a workshop in Sighişoara for nearly 20 years.

Around the citadel walls are the ruins of towers and bastions which the guilds erected during the 15C to protect the town from Turkish raids. Each of the 14 towers was built by one of the guilds, and nine of them remain. They are delightfully individual. Near the west end of Biserica din Deal you can see **Turnul Aurarilor**, the Goldsmiths' Tower, which, together with the Castaldo Bastion, forms the key to the citadel's defence system. Further north between the old school and the Clock Tower are **Turnul Tăbăcarilor**, the Tanners' Tower, and **Turnul Cositorarilor**, the Tinsmiths' Tower. The Tanners' Tower is one of the oldest in the citadel and the Tinsmiths' is especially handsome, rising to 25m high. There are also **Turnul Frânghierilor** (Cordwainers'), **Măcelarilor** (Butchers') and **Cojocarilor** (Furriers'), and a simple, massive **Turnul Croitorilor** (Tailors' Tower). **Turnul Cizmarilor**, the Cobblers' Tower, dates from a later period and is more elegant, with several turrets for keeping watch. The most modern of all the towers is the 1631 **Turnul Fierarilor**, the Blacksmiths' Tower.

The **church** of the Dominican monastery faces Piaţa Muzeului to the north of the Clock Tower. Inside the Dominican church is a fine Baroque altarpiece from 1680; the rest of the building evolved between the late 15C and the late 17C. It also has a bronze font from 1440, and a collection of antique Islamic carpets.

Around Sighişoara

The landscape around Sighişoara is still relatively unspoilt. It gets even better when you drive into the hills around **Criş**, 19km to the southwest. In this village you can visit the ruins of a castle that was completed in 1589. It belonged to the Bethlen family, who helped to introduce Renaissance styles into Transylvanian building. At **Mălâncrav** the Evangelical church has the most spectacular medieval frescoes in Transylvania. Take the DN14 west towards Mediaş and turn south in c 10km at the sign for Laslea. Ask here which fork of the road you should take to Mălâncrav; it may not be clearly marked, but heads south on a separate track from the one to Floreşti. The distance from Laslea is c 14km. The paintings in the church at Mălâncrav were carried out in the mid-14C and represent a last flowering of the International Gothic style. They are also well preserved, and you can still see the meticulous detail used in the portrayal of dress. Most unusually, the murals also combine Byzantine and Western painting styles. The altarpice was made by a Transylvanian *atelier* in 1450.

Braşov

From the railway station, Braşov hides its secrets well. Faceless, grey apartment blocks confront you as you emerge, giving no warning of the spectacular medieval city that exists a short bus ride away. Wooded hills rise in graceful curves on either side of the old town, separating it physically and, it seems, historically from the outside world. Today, Braşov is one of Romania's most popular holiday destinations. It lies on an edge of the Carpathian bend, where the mountains from east and south meet in a head-on collision, forcing them to their greatest heights of over 2000m. A great swathe of peaks separated by deep, forested valleys stretches to the south, while the city's modern suburbs spew out on to the Olt River plain to the north.

Braşov is the main focal point of Ţara Bârsei, an area that lies historically between the ancient citadel of Hălmeag, just north of Şercaia village to the west, the River Olt, the Prejmer stream in the east and the Carpathians. Its name means the Land of the Bârsa, the river that forms one of its borders, and it is known to have been inhabited by Cumans and Vlachs (prototype Romanians) when the Hungarians arrived. In the early 13C a Hungarian king gave the Bârsa Land to the Teutonic Knights, who brought in settlers from Thuringia and Flanders, as well as 'Saxons' from nearby Sibiu. This was the origin of Braşov's predominantly German character, which only declined when Ceauşescu allowed West Germany to 'buy' back its people in the 1980s.

Neighbouring the Bârsa Land to the west is **Ţara Făgăraşului**, another historic region which was inhabited by ethnic Romanians before the Hungarian invasion. And while Braşov was mainly colonised by Germans under Hungarian sovereignty, until the early 16C Făgăraş was ruled for much of the time by Wallachian princes from over the mountains. A magnificent castle from the late medieval period still stands in **Făgăraş** town, and nearby at **Sâmbătă de Sus** is the superb 20C copy of an Orthodox monastery which *voivode* Constantin Brâncoveanu (r. 1688–1714) commissioned in the late 17C.

Its German name of Kronstadt (Crown City) shows how important Braşov once was. Now more of a mecca for skiers and tourists, it was founded on a major trade route between Central Europe and the Balkans. The Germans who colonised Braşov from the 13C turned it into one of the powerful *Siebenbürgen*, the seven towns or seats that controlled Transylvania during the late Middle Ages. By the 15C Braşov was the largest town in the principality and had commercial links with the Middle East. But if it was founded for prosaic reasons, Braşov has an extraordinary beauty. Something remains of the 'melancholy poetry of orderliness and repetition' that Claudio Magris appreciated on his excursion here while researching his book, *Danube*. Its proud German roots are shrivelling with every year that passes, but Braşov's medieval centre survived the drastic replanning that gutted so many Romanian cities, and its steep, rust-coloured roofs make a wonderful contrast with the forested hills that rise directly behind them to the south. If you have time for nothing else, stroll around Piaţa Sfatului (Town Hall Square) and visit the Black Church and the Weavers' Bastion.

Practical information

☎ code
068

Tourist information

Braşov has a number of new, privately-owned tourist agencies that should be able to help you find your way around: *Postavarul Turism*, in the *Hotel Aro Palace*, B-dul Eroilor 8, ☎ 141648; fax 150427; *BTT Braşov*, Str Republicii, ☎ 150624; fax 144009; *Cristianul Braşov*, Str Toamnei 2, ☎ 187002; *Kron-Tour*, Str Bariţiu 12, ☎ 151070; *Happy-Hollyday*, Str Sadoveanu 1, ☎ 151504; *Divers-Turism*, Str Neptun, ☎ 134581; *N.C. Travel*, Str 15 Noiembrie 50, ☎ 150635; *Dim-Travel*, Str Iuliu Maniu, ☎ 151084; *Big-LM*, Str15 Noiembrie 43, ☎ 152224; *Bizant Tour*, Str Unirii 46, ☎ 154461; *Micomis*, Str Iuliu Maniu 43, ☎ 413707; *ANTREC* and *Bran-Impex* in Bran village, ☎ 236642.

Getting around

The main train station lies north of the centre on B-dul Gării.
By bus The main *autogara* where you can catch national buses is next door to the railway station on B-dul Gării, with a second bus station at Str Avram Iancu 114 and a third on Şos Hărman. For information about train times and tickets, the *CFR* office is at Str Republicii 53.
By car For **car repairs** there are garages at Str Nucului 28, ☎ 182985, and Str A. Iancu 87, ☎ 420858; **petrol stations** lie on the main routes in and out of town. *AVIS* **car rental** has an office in the *Aro Palace Hotel* on B-dul Eroilor, ☎ 142840; fax 150427, or you could ask for information about other firms from *ACR* at Calea Bucureşti 68. If you need a **taxi** try *Eurotax* at Str Independenţei 11, ☎ 181413, or *Rey Taxi*, ☎ 154060.

Where to stay

Braşov's smartest hotels are the *Aro Palace* (✫✫✫) at B-dul Eroilor 27, ☎ 142840; fax 150427, which promises fine Romanian and Italian cooking, and *Capitol* (✫✫✫) at B-dul Eroilor 19, run by the same company, ☎ 142840; fax 150427. Coming down the scale are *Coroana* (✫✫) at Str Politehnicii 2, ☎ 144330, and the intriguingly named *Petroflux* (✫✫) at Calea Bucureşti 242, ☎ 314183; fax 314194. *Aro Sport* (✫) in the centre at Str Sf Ioan 3, ☎ 142840, is cheaper still, but there are also unstarred hotels, such as *Stadion* at Str Cocorului 12, ☎ 187435; fax 132511, and *Tâmpa* at Str Matei Basarab 68, ☎ 115180. *Dârste Camping* is a **campsite** southeast of the centre on Calea Bucureşti, ☎ 259080; and there are similar facilities at the *Complex Turistic* on Dealul Cetăţii, tel 417614. *ANTREC*'s local office, ☎ 152598, can help you to find rooms in private houses, but it might be wise to contact the head office in Bucharest first (see p 116).

Some 12km away in **Poiana Braşov** there are several luxurious hotels and villas which offer saunas, swimming pools, massage and the like. Try *Hotel Alpin* (✫✫✫,129 rooms), ☎ 262343; fax 262211; *Hotel Ciucaş* (✫✫, 227 rooms), ☎ 262181; *Hotel Piatra Mare* (✫✫, 160 rooms), ☎ 262226; fax 150504. Nearby Pârâul Rece and Predeal also have plenty of hotels, but try *Manci's Motel*, a restored Saxon farmhouse at **Codlea**, 14km west of Braşov, at Str Lungă 169, 2252 Codlea, jud. Braşov, ☎ 185200; ☎/fax 252983. The manageress, Margareta (Manci) Pusztai, speaks excellent English and can arrange guided tours of the region; her cooking is good too.

Eating out

Braşov town centre has several open-air fruit and vegetable **markets**; one of the largest is on Str Bălcescu near Piaţa Teatrului. Otherwise there are bakeries, butchers', delicatessens and minimarkets on Str Republicii and other streets in the old centre. Braşov's best-known **restaurant** for Romanian food is *Crama Cerbul Carpatin* (the Cellar of the Carpathian Stag), housed in part of a splendid 16C merchants' hall at Piaţa Sfatului 14; otherwise you could try the national cuisine at *Cetate*, *Salon Medieval* or the *Transilvanean*, all on Dealul Cetăţii. *Stradivari* on Piaţa Sfatului is a **pizzeria** with an attractive terrace; *Pizza Iulia* is at Str Aleco Russo 6. There are plenty of other restaurants in the centre. In **Poiana Braşov** restaurants include *Capra Neagra*, *Coliba Haiducilor*, *Sura Dacilor*, *Miorița* and *Vânătorilor*.

 ## Post office and telephones

The central **post office** is housed in a fine 19C building at Str Iorga 1, while Braşov's main international **phone bureau** is halfway along B-dul Eroilor.

 ## Money

Central **banks** and **exchange houses** include *Banc Post* at Str Iorga 1, *Banca Agricolă* at Piaţa Sfatului 26B, *Banca Naţionala a Romaniei* at Piaţa Sfatului 26, *Banca Comercială Româna* at Str Republicii 45, *Bachide Exchange* at Str Mureşenilor 26, and *Bridge* at Str 15 Noiembrie 20.

Police

The *primăria*, the town hall, is at B-dul Eroilor 8.

Health care

There are **pharmacies** at Str 13 Decembrie 113 and B-dul Victoriei 10, and a doctor's **surgery** is at Str M. Eminescu 12, ☎ 414991.

Wildlife tours

The countryside around Braşov is laced with footpaths that go deep into climax forest. Every year there are stories of someone being attacked or killed by bears or wolves (not always near Braşov), but it is more often the other way round: hunting represents a lucrative business in Romania. Still, not everyone wants to destroy these animals, and for those who get a thrill out of simply watching them and studying their habitats, companies such as *Avian Adventures* of Stourbridge, *Wildwings* of Bristol, and *Waymark Holidays* of Slough, all in the UK, offer bird watching and wildlife tracking tours near Braşov (see pp 13–14).

Traditional crafts and folk art

For the latest information on folk-art festivals, contact *Centrul Judeţean de Creaţie Populare* (the County Folk Arts and Crafts Centre) at B-dul Eroilor 33, ☎ 141733. Alternatively, try the *Ethnographic Museum* a few doors away at Eroilor 21A, open Tues–Sun 09.00–17.00. Both institutions will be able to provide names and addresses of local craftspeople and can tell you where to buy good-quality products.

 ## Entertainment

On the first Sunday in May, the young men of Braşov assemble at Piaţa Unirii in traditional dress and ride through the old town to celebrate the coming of spring. The parade is called *Sărbătoarea junilor* (the Pageant of the Juni; *juni* comes from a Latin word for 'youth'), and afterwards the participants retreat to Pietrele lui Solomon to the west of the Schei district, and dance furious *hore*. In July, Braşov hosts an international pop **festival** called Cerbul de Aur (the Golden Stag), which is held in Piaţa Sfatului; there is also an annual theatre festival in Aug–Sept and a jazz festival in early December. On some weekday evenings between 18.00–18.30 there are **organ concerts** at the Black Church; the town also has a **theatre**, the *Liric* at Str Operetie 51. There are two **casinos**, the *Cristoleţi* in the nightclub at Piaţa Teatrului 1, and the *Salto Grand Casino* in the *Aro Palace Hotel*. The *Violeta* is a **disco** in Poiana Braşov.

Some of the big hotels in Poiana Braşov have decent restaurants, swimming pools and other sports and health facilities that are available all year round, and there are **cablecars** from here into the spectacular Postăvarul massif. Mountain cabins are available for rent as well. Like Predeal and Buşteni further south, it is a popular centre for **mountain climbing**, and you can get information on organised climbs and hiring guides from the hotels and tourist agencies here. But Poiana Braşov is mainly a **ski** resort which enjoys four to five months of snow a year.

Maps and books

For the latest maps, ask in one of the tourist agencies or the hotels; alternatively you could ask for books about Braşov at the Press Office in the Town Hall, ☎ 114172; fax 152628. There is a British Council **library** on B-dul Noiembrie.

Cetaţea Braşov şi Fortificaţiile din Ţara Bârsei, the Museum of Braşov Citadel and Bârsa Land Fortifications, is in **Bastionul Ţesătorilor** (the Weavers' Bastion or *Weberbastei*) at Str George Coşbuc 9, one of the extraordinary remnants to have survived from 16C Braşov. Built to withstand the Turks, the original hexagonal structure has been restored to show an extraordinary inner network of galleries, cells and stairways used by the weavers and their families during sieges. A small history museum contains a model of the medieval citadel and charts the history of Braşov's guilds. Braşov's textile industry has a fascinating past: established in the 14C, its products were said to rival those of western Europe and were exported to Egypt, Turkey and Bulgaria. Open-air concerts and folk-music displays are often held here. Open Tues–Sun 09.00–17.00.

Muzeul de Etnografie, the Ethnography Museum, is at B-dul Eroilor 21A. As well as its permanent collection of painted eggs, glass icons and gorgeous traditional dress, this museum often has excellent temporary shows focussing on the folk arts and ethnography of Ţara Bârsei. Open Tues–Sun 09.00–17.00.

Muzeul Judeţean de Istorie, the County History Museum at Piaţa Sfatului 30, is divided into sections covering archaeology, feudal, modern and contemporary history; it contains pottery and tools from Hallstatt and La Tène graves as well as items from the ruined citadel in nearby Râşnov. Another famous treasure is the first known document in Romanian, a letter written to a Braşov magistrate in 1521. The present building stands on the site of a medieval watchtower and dates from the 16C, when it was used as the town hall. It was rebuilt in the 18C. Open Tues–Sun 09.00–17.00.

Muzeul Scheii Braşovului, the Museum of the Schei Quarter, is at Piaţa Unirii 1. Housed in the first recorded Romanian school, which opened in 1495, this modest but appealing museum traces the cultural history of Braşov's Romanian quarter. It contains a valuable collection of early religious texts printed in Romanian, Greek and Slavonic, as well as examples of medieval church art. Open Tues–Sun 10.00–18.00.

Walking around Braşov

Because of its history Braşov is a city with very distinct areas: the old Saxon town, enclosed by vestiges of curtain wall with a hilltop citadel to the north, the rural Schei district, outside the city walls to the southwest, and the modern town, which was added after the Second World War and sprawls to the north and east. **Biserica Neagră** (the Black Church), or Sf Maria to give its correct name, was a nerve-centre of Transylvanian Protestantism. Here Johannes Honterus (1498–1549) preached Luther's message, and from here he pioneered the spread of the puritanical religion throughout Transylvania. Sf Maria was altered from a Romanesque to a Gothic church between 1385–1477. A fire caused by the Habsburgs' invasion in 1689 left it a charred ruin (hence its nickname) and the interior had to be virtually rebuilt from scratch. After the Reformation it became an Evangelical Church.

This is the largest medieval shrine in Romania, and from a distance it has a tremendous bear-like presence. But its crouching, downward thrust is balanced by long, narrow windows and a series of slender, stepped buttresses that sweep upwards into carved finials, so that from closer to, the effect becomes ascetic and elegant. Midway up each buttress is a canopied **niche** containing the figure of a saint. As in the magnificent Gothic choir at Sebeş, these statuettes follow two main sculptural styles. One, exemplified by John the Baptist, Jesus *Salvator Mundi* and the Virgin and Child, shows the sinuous, elongated bodies and individualised faces made by Parlerian masons who travelled here from Kosice in Slovakia between 1430–40. The other, seen in the statues of the saints Hieronymous, Nicholas and Luke, is far stiffer, but surprisingly dates from a decade later. One of the figures shows Toma, the donor, carrying a model of the church. Several of the portals are framed with fine carvings and deeply recessed arches.

The Saxon town

Between the two extremes of industrial suburbs and village lies the old German centre, with Piaţa Sfatului and the Black Church at its heart. A cluster of **medieval streets** surrounds them, notably Str Băriţiu and its extension into Str Mureşenilor, Str Republicii, Str Postăvarului, Str Bălcescu and Str Castelului, which are all more or less parallel to each other and which once stood inside the defence walls. This inner-city area was the last to be colonised by the early settlers and was known as Krone (hence Kronstadt). Small manufacturing businesses and workshops sprang up here from 1235. At the height of its power in the 15C, Saxon Braşov was protected by a three-tier wall punctuated by 30 towers and bastions. Along with a section of adjoining wall, each bastion or tower was built, maintained and defended by an individual guild.

Braşov became an important trading centre not only for German goods but for Greek and Romanian products as well, while in the 16C its energetic scholars conducted Transylvania's Protestant Reformation from here. In 1689, on the pretext of defending the city from the Ottomans, Habsburg armies burst into Braşov and burnt much of it down, including the Black Church and the Town Hall. This marked the end of the Saxon golden age, and at the eastern end of Str Republicii and Str Mureşenilor, and in the Sf Ioan church in Str Sf Ioan, you can see the influence of Austrian Baroque and Jugendstil superseding the medieval and Renaissance architecture.

BRAŞOV • 483

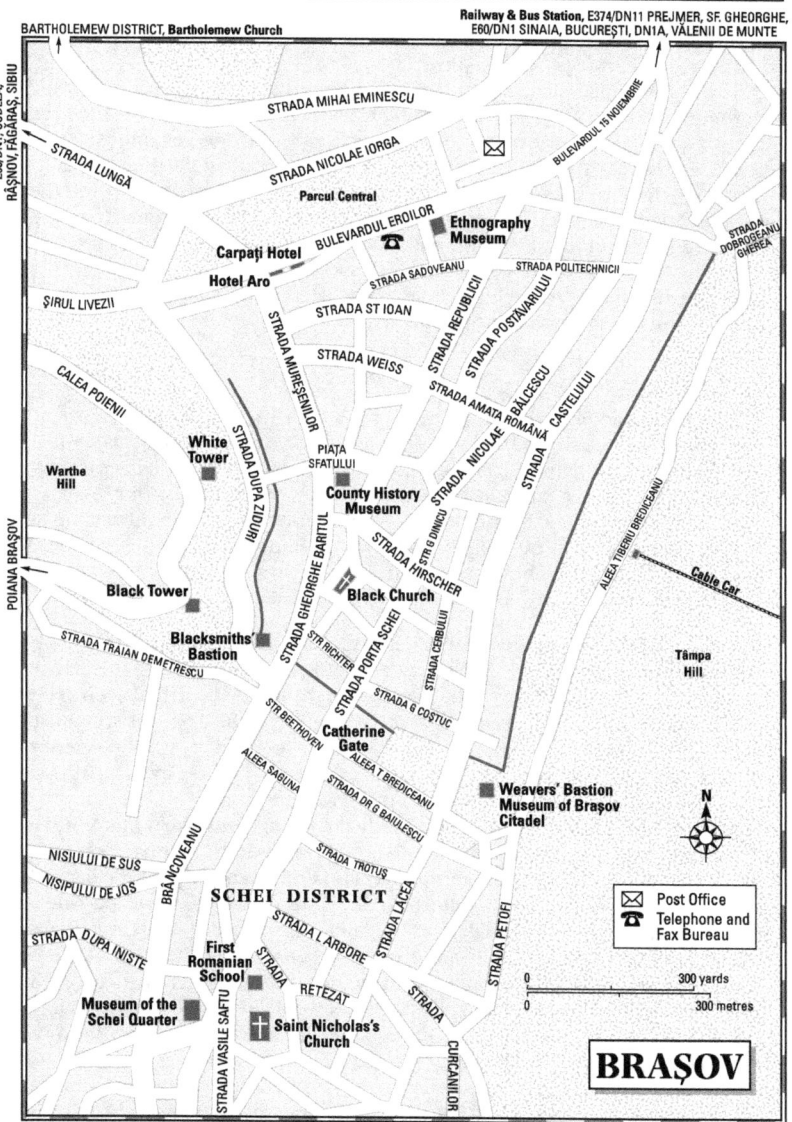

Inside, it is a hall church (see p 427), with naves of almost equal height. Together with the tall windows and white walls, these make it refreshingly light and help to show off the painted emblems on the wooden furniture and the gorgeous Islamic **carpets** that hang from the galleries. From the second half of the 15C, carpets like these were taken in lieu of taxes from Balkan merchants travelling through the city on their way north. These particular examples are from the

17C and 18C; you can see similar collections in Sibiu and Mediaş, towns that also stood on major east-west trade routes.

Still, the iron will of its Germanic protectors makes itself felt in the **tombs**: according to Claudio Magris, one inscription reads 'I know and believe', and the figure 'of a warrior in full armour, helmet, gorget and all and great moustaches' recalls Dürer's Knight in his unswerving determination along the path of life. In the sacristy there is a Renaissance-style **screen** made of carved stone, and the high altar is from Vienna. The **organ**, built by Buchholz in 1839, is said to be the largest in southeast Europe. It has over 4000 pipes and certainly makes a splendid noise.

Opposite the south entrance is a statue to Honterus, whose birthplace is halfway along the south side of Str Bălcescu, at no. 40.

> ### Brassaï
> The avant-garde photographer Brassaï (1899–1984) was born in Braşov. His real name was Gyula Halász, and as an ethnic Hungarian he called the city by its Magyar name, Brassó—Brassai means someone who comes from Braşov. Working as a journalist in France, he discovered a talent for taking photographs and made his name as a chronicler of the more bizarre characteristics of Parisian nightlife in the style of Toulouse-Lautrec. His style had a lasting effect on photojournalism.

Piaţa Sfatului is a marvellous, theatrical space which, not surprisingly, is often used for concerts and festivals. Opposite the old town hall on the east side of the square, down a short alleyway, is the entrance to the late-19C Orthodox **church** of Sf Adormire, and on the south side of the square is the 16C market house called **Cerbul Carpatin**, the Carpathian Stag. At no. 23 is a small **museum** dedicated to the Mureşeanu family, who helped to found newspapers in Braşov and supported the Romanian nationalist movement.

To the west, across Str Băriţiu at no. 12 is a charming **courtyard** that used to be the Greek trading centre. It contains a Baroque-style Greek Orthodox **church** from 1787 behind which lies an appealingly run-down cemetery. At the back of the cemetery, parallel with Str Băriţiu and Str Mureşenilor, lies Str Dupá Ziduri (Behind the Walls Street). Beside this a small stream called the Graft flows between two of the old city walls and then disappears under the Graft bastion. Opposite this, on Calea Poenii to the north, stands the isolated **White Tower**, a circular, medieval ruin erected as a watchtower by the Tinsmiths' Guild, and further southwest along Calea Poenii is the square **Black Tower**, another lookout point which earned its name by being severely burnt in 1559.

If you walk west along Str Dupá Ziduri to the corner of Str Băriţiu you come to the **Blacksmiths' Bastion**, which contains the city archives. Gheorghe Băriţiu (1812–93) was a well-known historian and publisher who had a house on Str Republicii. Turning southwest again, this time down Str Beethoven, you come to the Renaissance-style **Poarta Ecaterinei** (the Catherine Gate), which dates from 1559. The city walls were once tripled at this point. Keep going southwest along Str Brădiceanu, passing schools and tennis courts, and eventually you reach the great **Weavers' or Linenweavers' Bastion**, mentioned in the museums section. Said to be unique in Romania, it was built in stages

The Teutonic Knights

In 1211 King Endre II of Hungary (r. 1205–35) gave the Bârsa Land to the Teutonic Knights. He was following the precedent set by Géza II (r. 1141–62) who began colonising Transylvania with 'guests' from northern Europe, in return for their developing the land and protecting Hungary's borders. The newcomers were granted virtual autonomy, with the freedom to collect taxes, and take salt, wood and even gold for their own use. But with the Knights Endre had another aim: as well as bringing in peasants to work the land, he wanted them to convert the Orthodox population to Catholicism. Catholic 'pilgrim soldiers' on the Fourth Crusade had just sacked Constantinople and installed a Flemish emperor on the hated Byzantine throne. Fired with success, an aggressive proselytism swept the Catholic world, which included the Hungarian kingdom. But Endre also had a temporal agenda: he very much wanted to extend his lands to the east.

The Teutonic Knights were initially a charitable Catholic brotherhood. They were formed by German merchants during the Third Crusade (1189–92) and in 1198 they became a military-monastic order on the lines of the Knights of St John and the Templars. Several of their members, including their Grand Master, came from the Thuringian aristocracy, into which Endre married in 1203. Unable to gain the land they wanted in Palestine, the Knights found themselves in a precarious position, and Endre's invitation could not have arrived at a better time for them.

Only a few of the Knights came to live in Transylvania; most, including their Grand Master Hermann von Salza, went to northern Germany, where they pursued the *Drang nach Osten* (thrust to the east) and founded the Prussian state. Their activities in eastern Transylvania began well enough. But after a few years, in some confusion over whether they owed allegiance to the Hungarian sovereign, the pontiff in Rome or their own Grand Master, they abandoned all pretence of obeying the king. In 1224 they arrogantly ceded Țara Bârsei to the Pope. An act of such bare-faced arrogance demanded a sharp put-down. It came the following year, when an exasperated Endre threw the Teutons out by force and placed the country under his own direct protection. Many of the farmers who had come to Țara Bârsei with the Knights were equally disenchanted with their German lords and stayed behind in Transylvania.

But the Knights did achieve one of Endre's goals by pushing the Cumans out of southeast Romania. Documents also show that by 1231 the knights had constructed at least five stone fortresses. These have been tentatively identified as being one of the citadels in Brașov (either on Tâmpa, on Dealul Sprenghi or an unknown fortress on Dealul Cetății); a lost citadel near the church in Feldioara; Râșnov citadel; Cetatea Neagra, the Black Citadel, near Codlea; and Cetatea Crucii at Teliu, near Prejmer.

between 1421–36 and 1570–73. From here you can walk along the pleasantly wooded lane behind the city walls to the circular **Tuchmacherbastei** (the Clothiers' Bastion), or explore the boschy attractions of Tâmpa Hill.

Brașov's guilds were very proud of their ancient rights and stood up for themselves. In 1688 the shoemakers declared war against the German Emperor and they stood firm against the Dual Monarchy in the 19C. But sometimes they went to ridiculous extremes: in 1848 the Saxons of Transylvania were unsure whether or not to accept union with Hungary. Feelings became so polarised that the people of Sibiu refused while the citizens of Braşov were in favour. Militants in each city tried to prevent anyone of opposite views from entering their gates.

The top of **Tâmpa Hill** provides a spectacular view of the mountains to the south, and the hill is also a thickly wooded nature reserve. Walking to the top takes about an hour, but there is also a cable car whose lower access point is halfway along the straight section of Str Brădiceanu. Legend has it that the Teutonic Knights built a citadel called Braşovia just below the peak; there are still some vestiges of walls here, but whatever their provenance, the buildings were destroyed in 1445. It is possible that they were part of a monastic foundation because a chapel dedicated to St Leonard was found among the ruins.

Cetatea ~ The Citadel
At the top of Dealul Cetăţii, to the north of the old town, stand the picturesque ruins of a 16C citadel. Access to Dealul Cetăţii is from the north side of Str Nicolae Iorga and Str Eminescu, or from a number of points further east, where Str Iorga meets Str Maniu, and from the west side of Str Ioan Cuza. Four corner bastions were added in 1630, and curently the building houses the *Cetatea* restaurant.

Bartolomeu
This district was colonised by German settlers in the 12C before the Krone district came to represent the heart of Saxon Braşov. It lies to the north of the old centre, near Dealul Sprenghi. Stone Age remains have also been found here. It was named after **Sf Bartolomeu**, the oldest church in Braşov, a lovely, simple building that stands under two great west towers at the northern end of Str Lungă and Str Andreescu. It was started in the second half of the 13C and may have been part of a Premonstratensian convent. Later Transylvanian Early Gothic overlaid the original Benedictine Romanesque, and the apse windows show the influence of Cistercian architecture, most probably from Cârta. The choir has one square and one polygonal bay, and there are two pairs of side chapels containing frescoes and stone carvings. It also has a transept and three aisles. In its early days, a curtain wall protected the church (only one of the planned watchtowers was built), and it was overlooked by a timber or stone fortress on Dealul Sprenghi.

Schei Braşovului ~ The Schei District
Said to be the oldest part of Braşov, even predating Bartolomeu, the Schei district is very different in character from the Saxon town. Between the 13C–17C, the Germans forbade anyone else from owning property in the city and the Romanians settled here, outside the walls to the southwest. Today their ghetto still has a sleepy, rural atmosphere, characterised by multicoloured houses standing with their gable ends to the narrow streets and a village green grazed by hobbled cows and goats. Technically the quarter stretches from the fine, triumphal arch of Poarta Schei, at the crossing of Str Schei with Str Brădiceanu, to Cheile Pietrele lui Solomon (the Stones of Solomon gorge), which begins where narrow Str Invăţătorilor merges into a stony track and disappears into hills cloaked with fir and deciduous trees. From here there are footpaths that lead to Poiana Braşov.

Romanians may have been excluded from the citadel, but they were not helpless or dependent. Encouraged by Wallachian princes such as Neagoe Basarab I (r. 1512–21) and Constantin Brâncoveanu, they traded with their neighbours in the Romanian-speaking principalities, and when the Habsburg army arrived in the late 17C they profited from the ensuing chaos and used the proceeds to build some fine town houses. Relations between Germans and Romanians were by no means all bad: the first books to be published in Romanian were printed by German Protestant humanists, and Romanian nationalism took its lead from the Saxons' determined self-preservation.

In a pretty garden on the southern corner of Piața Unirii stands the Orthodox **church** of Sf Nicolae and the first Romanian **school**. A Romanian church was mentioned in Schei during the late 13C, but the present building dates from the mid-15C/early 16C and has been altered many times. Both church and school received financial help from neighbouring Wallachia. At the end of the 16C Sf Nicolae was extended to the west with a three-aisled narthex, and in c 1740 the single bay of the apse was replaced by a trefoil plan. The west door is very attractive with a frame of Brâncoveanu-style scrollwork.

The school was built in 1495 and is now a museum dedicated to the history of Schei and Romanian culture in Brașov.

Around Brașov
Included in this section are descriptions of the northern **Prahova Valley** and the roads to Buzău and Vălenii de Munte which, strictly speaking, belong to Wallachia. If you are short of time for trips around Brașov, do not miss the citadels in Hărman and Prejmer, or a cablecar ride into the **Bucegi massif** from Predeal.

SOUTH FROM SIGHIȘOARA

Driving southeast from Sighișoara on the E60/DN13, you pass striking citadel churches at **Viscri** (on a country road to the southwest of Bunești) and at **Homorod**, where the church has a lovely frescoed choir. To the east of the main road between them the ruins of **Rupea citadel** dominate the landscape. A stiff climb up a narrow path from the centre of the village brings you into the castle precinct, where orchards of plum and apple now fill the space between the curtain walls and the *donjon*. The citadel, properly called Cetatea Cohalului, was built in the 12C. Even now, in its dilapidated state, you can see how it could have survived the Tartar invasions of 1241, when the 'devil's horsemen' swept murderously across Transylvania, burning everything in sight. Nearby is the Racoș **geological reserve**, where you can see strange formations of basalt rock. Some 8km further southwest, at Hoghiz, lie the remains of a **Roman camp** called Pons Vetus, and a 16C castle. Between Hoghiz and Maieruș, the road crosses the Perșani mountains through **Pădurea Bogății**, the Forest of Riches, which is a hunting reserve.

At **Feldioara**, 11km south of Maieruș, is a mid-15C *cetatea țărăneasca* (peasants' citadel) built by parishioners to withstand the Turks. Nearby, built on the skeleton of a 12C Romanesque shrine, stands a 15C Lutheran **citadel church** of great splendour. The Teutonic Knights may have built one of their stone fortresses near the church, but historians are unsure of its exact location and some think it lies beneath the peasants' citadel.

Northeast to Sf Gheorghe

To the north and northeast of Braşov lie two **citadel churches** of exceptional size and strength, even for Transylvania. One of them stands in **Hărman**, c 12km northeast of the city and just off the E574/DN11. In the 15C, parishioners began constructing thick walls and colossal bastions around their Romanesque church to protect themselves from marauding armies. Inside, the 13C funerary **chapel** contains some delightful frescoes in the Late Gothic International style. On the west wall is a Last Judgment surrounded by associated themes. Opposite, on the east wall is a Crucifixion flanked by groups of apostles, while the evangelists look down from vaulted ceilings. Another set of **paintings** on the south wall show the Exaltation of the Virgin, and around her are four ancient, animalistic symbols of Christ's life. These comprise 'The Virgin with a unicorn', representing the Virgin birth, 'The Pelican feeding its young on its own blood', for Jesus's sacrifice, 'The Lion waking its cubs on the third day', symbolising the Resurrection, and 'The Phoenix', representing the Ascension. There are also a couple of paintings symbolising purity of Mary. Vigorous floral and vegetal patterns and geometric devices frame the paintings. Several artists were probably involved, and, judging by the energetic style of some of the scenes, these may have included Tyrolean painters.

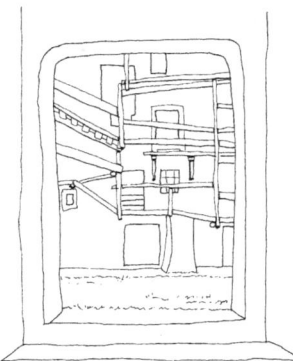

View of the medieval citadel through a doorway

About 18km northeast of Braşov lies **Mlaştina de la Hărman**, a nature reserve that contains rare animals, carnivorous plants and glacial relics.

East of the DN11 at Hărman and 5km along the DN10, the citadel church at **Prejmer** is if anything more forbidding than Hărman's fortress. It stands to the left of a road leading to the station. To enter the citadel, you have to pass through the 18C Bakers' Courtyard, the 16C 'town hall courtyard' and a low entrance tunnel into a final, central court containing a church. This inner sanctum is protected by a thick, circular wall 12m high. Probably constructed in the 1400s, it is an integral part of the city wall. Its inner face contains several tiers of cells connected by wooden stairs and balconies. Prejmer had a particularly troubled history and needed protection: the chronicles mention at least ten uprisings here as well as many attacks by foreign armies, so the citadel was no *folie de grandeur*. The 13C Gothic **church** is austere but charmingly so: like Sf Bartolomeu in Braşov, it is said to contain Cistercian elements. Inside are some appealing painted wood furniture, bearing German Gothic inscriptions, and a mid-15C triptych painted in tempera, thought to come from a Transylvanian workshop. The central panel of the altarpiece shows a Calvary accompanied by two smaller panels of Jesus weeping, and an Ascension on the left, and on the right, a Deposition. On the back are four more scenes from the New Testament. The church is still in use.

To the east of Prejmer, the DN10 rises over the Buzău pass and follows the Buzău River as it pours from the Carpathians into Moldavia, past Cârnu monastery and eventually into Buzău city itself.

To the Bratocea Pass and Vălenii de Munte

Leaving Braşov southeast on the DN1 brings you to a bridge over the Prahova River. If you turn left here you come immediately into **Săcele**. Spoilt by lorry traffic that thunders through on its way to Bucharest, the village seems little more than an extension of Braşov. But it does have a separate identity. An **ethnographic museum** at B-dul Braşovului 153 highlights distinguishing features of local dress, especially of the Mocăn and Csengő peoples. The museum is housed in the early 19C Casa Dijmelor (Tithes' House), open Tues–Sun 10.00–14.00. In June, young men in Săcele celebrate an ancient rite marking their passage from youth to adulthood; as in Schei Braşovului, this is not taken too seriously and is an excuse for parading the streets in traditional dress.

Trucks apart, crossing the mountains into Wallachia via Săcele and the DN1A through the Teleajen Valley can be a lovely experience, and the road is often less congested than the more popular Prahova Valley. About 30km southeast of Săcele, it brings you to the edge of the **Ciucaş mountains**, where the peaks form weird shapes like ruined castles. Part of the range is a nature reserve, and you can ski here in winter.

On the way southeast, you could stop at the old monasteries of **Cheia** and **Suzană**, both of which stand in magnificent scenery. Accommodation may be available here for women travellers. Further south, you come to **Vălenii de Munte**, from where you can sample the delights of **Slănic** saltwater spa.

INTO WALLACHIA: VALEA PRAHOVEI ~ THE PRAHOVA VALLEY

There are two main routes to Bucharest from Braşov. Both are attractive, but the road through Vălenii de Munte is often less congested. On the route through Valea Prahovei, the terrible road that once made this journey such a frustrating experience has been widened and improved, but you may prefer to take a train, which lets you enjoy the wonderful views and stops at several interesting places. Short of hiking there from Poiana Braşov, this is the most direct way into the Bucegi massif, the tallest range in the Carpathians.

In the mountain resort of **Predeal**, 24km south of Braşov on the DN1, where the local code is 068, dilapidated **villa/hotels** that have seen glamorous days line the road and railway line. These include the *Predeal* (✩✩✩) and *Carmen* (✩✩), both at Str Muncii 6, ☎ 456517, *Carmen Ana II* (✩✩) at Str Mihail Săulescu 104, ☎ 456517, *Porumbita* (✩✩) at Str Eroilor 71, ☎ 456364, *Bulevard* (✩) at Str Mihail Săulescu 129, ☎ 456022, and *Cirus* (✩) at Str Avram Iancu 3, ☎ 456035. Most of these hotels can give you information on how to find cablecars, ski lifts and can recommend mountain guides. There are also scores of villas and cabins for rent; contact *Ingrio Tourism* at Str Gării 1, ☎ 456972, for more details.

Southwest from Braşov to Bran

Southwest of Braşov centre, the DN73 brings you to two lovely Saxon villages lying in the shadow of the mountains. **Cristian** (10km) has a fine Gothic church that was completely rebuilt in the 19C, and **Râşnov**, 5km further, is the site of a hilltop citadel built by the Teutonic Knights and taken over by villagers in the 14C when they needed a place of refuge. Getting up to the citadel involves a stiff half-hour climb on foot because there is no road. The path brings you into the castle's outer ward; the main bailey has vestiges of bastions and gives a marvellous view over the neighbouring mountains and the Bârsa plain. Since its foundation, it was rebuilt several times and remains impressive; a modest museum explains its history, but only in Romanian.

Towering above the road from a crag c 12km further southwest stands 14C **Bran Castle**. Bran is famous for its association with the Dracula legend, but today it functions as a very attractive **museum of medieval furniture**, open Tues–Sun 09.00–17.00. Bran was mentioned in 1377, when it was used as a defence and customs post on the pass between Transylvania and Wallachia. Between 1395–1427 it belonged to Mircea the Wise, grandfather of Vlad Ţepeş (Dracula). In 1441 the Hungarians defeated the Turks here and shortly afterwards Vlad Ţepeş briefly captured the castle. In the 1920s it became a favourite home of Queen Marie, and under her influence the medieval building was transformed into something resembling a modern Spanish villa. She also planted a pretty chrysanthemum garden.

Bran Castle

Part of Bran's medieval outline is still intact, notably a large 15C cylindrical **tower** that dominates the north end. A taller tower on the east side and the main entrance were added by Prince Gabriel Bethlen in the 17C. Inside the museum, exhibits are arranged without much sense of atmosphere, but the objects themselves are often strikingly beautiful. In the former 18C customs post on the south side of the castle is a modest but excellent **history museum**, open Tues–Sun 10.00–18.00. To the north of the castle precinct there is an open-air **village museum**, open as above, and the area is surrounded by wooded hills and open pastures. Bran thrives on tourism, and there should be no problem in finding **accommodation**; *ANTREC* also has a base here. Contact *Bran Imex* in the castle car park, ☎ 068 236642.

From here to Câmpulung the road passes through the beautiful, alpine country of **Munţii Piatra Craiului** and, further south, **Culoarul Rucăr-Bran** (the Rucăr-Bran corridor). Both areas are sprinkled with villages where you can still see vernacular buildings of considerable charm. Some of these settlements are of the scattered type, showing that they are among the oldest villages in Romania.

Munţii Făgăraşului ~ The Făgăraş Mountains

The serrated peaks of Munţii Făgăraşului run from east to west along the southern edge of the ancient lands of Bârsa, Făgăraş (or Olt) and Sibiu to Ţara Haţegului, a constant reminder of the cultural as well as the physical barriers that once separated Catholic and later Protestant Transylvania from Orthodox Wallachia. Information about the paths, cabins and roads that you can find in different sections of the range is available from tourist offices. A useful guide to the mountains of this and other regions is a series of Romanian books called *Munţii Nostri*, published during the communist period, and if there is any sense in this world, this will be translated into other European languages; Tim Burford's *Hiking Guide to Romania* (1992) is also informative—and has the added advantage of being published in English.

INTO ŢARA FĂGĂRAŞULUI

From Braşov the DN1 crosses a low pass over the Perşani mountains and heads west along the northern edge of the Făgăraş range. Before you get to the pass, the road goes through **Codlea**. By the 15C the town's guilds were competing with Braşov for the position of regional capital, and lost by a whisker. In 1432, after the first Turkish invasion of Ţara Bârsei, a fortified church was built here, possibly on the site of the Schwartzburg, the Black Citadel that the Teutonic Knights erected in the first quarter of the 13C to defend the roads over the Perşani pass. Each of the five guilds added a **tower** to the curtain walls around the church, now in ruins. From Codlea you can explore more old German settlements by travelling south on the country road to Vulcan.

At Şercaia you cross the border between Ţara Bârsei and Ţara Făgăraşului. A few kilometres north of this village is the site of the old **citadel** of Hălmeag, which was mentioned in King Endre's invitation of 1211 to the Teutonic Knights. South of Şercaia is **Poienile cu Narcise de la Dumbravă Vadului**, a meadow famous for its May-flowering narcissi.

Făgăraş lies 66km west of Braşov. A small medieval island has survived in the middle of town, and its centrepoint is a superb 15C **castle** which has been beautifully restored. Converted into a history and ethnographic museum in 1954, the building has housed many famous Romanian princes, notably Mihai Viteazul (Michael the Brave, r. 1593–1601) and his family. The **museum** contains extraordinary items such as Roman festival costumes from the 2C and 3C, coins minted by Romanian *voivodes* and rare books and maps. Open Tues–Fri 09.00–16.00; Sat–Sun 09.00–15.00.

The Land of Făgăraş had a special status within Hungarian Transylvania. Until the 14C it counted as part of Wallachia, and was ruled by Orthodox boyars rather than Catholic noblemen. It remained intact till the 16C, when the area became a royal estate reserved for Transylvanian princesses. But even after that, the Wallachian influence persisted. In the hills to the south of **Sâmbăta de Sus**, c 25km west of Făgăraş, stands a monastery founded by the Wallachian prince Constantin Brâncoveanu. At the time, the Sâmbăta estate belonged to his family but his decision to build the monastery owed more to Brâncoveanu's fears for the survival of Orthodoxy in Transylvania. In the 1680s the Habsburgs invaded Transylvania and 'liberated' the principality from the Turks. At the same time they tried to eradicate the Orthodox church.

Sâmbăta **monastery** was completed in 1698, and at first the Austrians' demolition squads left it alone. Brâncoveanu himself and his four sons were executed by the Turks in 1714. But 60 years later the Habsburgs flattened the monks' cells and left the church a smouldering ruin. Even then the Brâncoveanu family held onto the land, only losing it during the agrarian reforms of 1922, when it passed to the Metropolitanate of Sibiu. The present building is a 20C copy of the original monastery. It follows the celebrated Brâncoveanu style that flourished in Wallachia between the late 17C/mid-18C. Its 16C **Healing Spring** is the oldest surviving structure in the foundation. Restoration continued into the 1980s, when the Metropolitan of Transylvania rebuilt the precincts and had some of the capitals and paintings repaired in the church. It is a fine achievement, showing off the characteristic double arcades of Brâncoveanu architecture in dazzling white, and the plain walls make an attractive contrast with decorated balustrades, doors and windows. Sâmbăta monastery finally reopened in 1993. It is also a centre for glass icons from the Făgăraș school. There is a Lippizaner Stud in the village of Sâmbăta de Sus. You may be able to ride the horses, but please remember that national stud farms such as this one are very short of funds and are not geared to catering for tourists.

In the valleys between Făgăraș and Sibiu are more secluded Saxon villages. To reach them, turn right in the village of Voila, 11km after you leave Făgăraș. At **Cincu** the citadel church has a beautiful altarpiece of sculpted and polychromed wood. Its tempera **paintings**, created by a workshop in Sibiu, feature Doubting Thomas (in the central panel) with St Christopher and the baby Jesus. A small intermediate panel depicts various saints, and the predella represents the '*Vir dolorum*'. An inscription on the central panel dates the paintings to 1521.

Cincu was also the home of the painter **Nicolae Suciu** (d. 1997). Suciu was a former dissident who earned himself an international reputation for his glass icons. He trained at the Bucharest Academy of Fine Arts but had to abandon his teaching career after being harassed by the Securitate for his anti-communist views. A man of enormous charm and modesty, he later had numerous exhibitions abroad; you can find out more about his work through the Ethnographic Museum in Brașov.

From Cincu, head north for **Dealul Frumos** (Beautiful Hill). Here, the original 13C Romanesque **basilica** was fortified during the 14C so that it became more important as a fortress than a church. It has a massive, rectangular defence wall and several towers.

During the summer you can drive over the spectacularly beautiful **Transfăgărașanu Highway**. From the northern side, this climbs in a series of dramatic hairpin bends past the Bâlea cascade and lake and then drops in a series of graceful loops into the county of Argeș on the other side. Turn onto the Transfăgărașanu from the E68/DN1, c 22km west of Voila; it is signposted to the highway and to Cârțișoara. There are spectacular views and a network of footpaths on both sides of the pass; if you want to stay overnight, you could use one of the mountain **cabins**. For further details, contact *Săliște-Bâlea Turism* in Sibiu.

INDEX

A
Abrud 404
Agapia 227
Agnita 468
Aiud 418
Alba Iulia 410
  Batthyaneum Library 415
  Biblioteca Batthyaneum 415
  Bishop's Palace 413
  Catedrala Arhiepiscopală Sf Mihail 413
  Catedrala Reîntegirii Neamului 414
  Colegiul Academic 416
  Fortress 412
  Muzeul Naţional al Unirii Alba Iulia (National Unification Museum) 415
  Palatul Apor (Apor Palace) 415
  Sala Unirii 415
  Str Bethlen 415
Albac 408
Alexandria 187
Almaş Valley 406
Alţina 468
Andreiaşu de Jos 270
Apuseni 401
Arad 324
  Art Museum 328
  B-dul Revoluţiei 327
  Casa cu Lacăt 329
  Catholic Church 328
  City Hall 327
  Culture Palace 327
  Farmacia Grozăvescu 329
  Fortress 327
  Hirschl Theatre 329
  Hotel Mureşul 328
  Jewish Quarter 329
  Orthodox Cathedral 328
  Palatul Bohuş 328
  Palatul Neumann 329
  Piaţa Avram Iancu 328
  Piaţa Veche 329
  Red Church 327
  Serb district 329
Arbore 192, 203, 204
Arcuş 455
Armaşeni 452
Armenians, The 212, 249
Arnota 163
Avram Iancu 409
Avrig 468
Axente Sever 471

B
Bacău 236
Baia 214
Baia de Criş 405
Băile Felix 316
Băile Herculane 170
Băile Tuşnad 447, 453
Băişoara 402
Bălţăteşti 229
Banat, The 313
Barboşi 279
Bârgău Valley 437
Bârnova 256
Barnovschi, Prince Miron 248
Bârsa 317
Bâtca Doamnei 232
Báthorys, The 327
Beliş 409
Bihor Mountains 409
Biserica Mirăuţi 212
Biserica Precista 236
Bistriţa 232, 438
Bistriţa, Monastery of 235
Blaj 417
Bogdand 325
Bologa 405
Bonţida 432
Borsec 447
Borzeşti 236
Botfei 318
Brad 404
Brăhăşeşti 280

Brăila 273
Bran Castle 489
Brâncoveanu, Constantin 123, 152, 164
Brâncovenești 443
Brâncuși Constantin 166, 167, 168, 173
Brassaï 484
Brâznic 392
Brașov 477
　Bastionul Țesătorilor 481
　Biserica Neagră 481
　Black Tower 484
　Blacksmiths' Basion 484
　Cerbul Carpatin 484
　Cetatea (the Citadel) 486
　Cetatea Brașov și Fortificațiile din Țara Bârsei (Museum of Brașov Citadel) 481
　Muzeul de Etnografie 481
　Muzeul Județean de Istorie 481
　Muzeul Scheii Brașovului 481
　Piața Sfatului 484
　Poarta Ecaterinei (the Catherine Gate) 484
　Rupea citadel 487
　Schei Brașovului (the Schei District) 486
　Sf Bartolomeu 486
　Tâmpa Hill 485
　Tuchmacherbastei (the Clothiers' Bastion) 484
　Vălenii de Munte 489
　Viscri 487
　Weavers' or Linenweavers' Bastion 484
　White Tower 484
Breaza 185
Brebu 186
Brețcu 454
Brukenthal, Samuel 459, 460, 466
Bucharest 113
　Arc de Triumf 147
　Armenian Quarter 136
　Ateneul Român 140
　Athenée Hilton 141
　B-dul Aviatorilor 146
　Belu Cemetery 151
　Biserica Crețulescu 139

Bucharest cont
　Biserica Doamnei 134
　Biserica Domnească 129
　Biserica Sf Apostoli Petru și Pavel 134
　Calea Dorobanților 138, 147
　Calea Victoriei 133, 138
　Camera Deputaților 150
　Cantacuzino Palace 144
　Capșa Restaurant 138
　Carul cu Bere 132
　Catedrala Patriarhiei 150
　CEC Building 133
　Central University Library 140
　Choral Temple 133
　Chrissoveloni Bank 132
　Cismigiu Gardens 141
　Cotroceni Palace 141
　Curtea Veche 129
　Doamna Bălană 150
　Elisabeta Palace 148
　Faculty of Architecture 135
　Grădina Botanică 143
　Grădina Ioanid 129
　Hanul lui Manuc 132
　Imobil Clara Iancu 137
　K.H. Zambaccian Museum 146
　Lipscani 132
　Mănăstirea Mihai Vodă 149
　Mănăstirea Plumbuita 149
　Minovici Museum of Folk Arts 148
　Muzeul Colecțiilor de Artă 143
　Muzeul de Istorie și Artă al Municipiului 136
　Muzeul de Istorie Naturală 'Grigore Antipa' 145
　Muzeul Național de Arta al României 139
　Muzeul Național de Istorie a României 138
　Muzeul Satului 147
　Muzeul Țăranului Român 145
　Natural History Museum 145
　Palace of the Republic 139
　Palatul Parlamentului 150
　Pallady Museum 137
　Piața Amzei 143
　Piața Revoluției 143
　Piața Universității 135

Bucharest cont
  Senate 140
  Sf Apostoli Petru şi Pavel 149
  Sf Gheorghe Nou 133
  Sf Spiridon Vechi 134, 149
  Spitalul Colţea 133
  Stavropoleos Church 132
  Teatrul Naţional 135
  Telephone Palace 138
  Theodor Aman Museum 141
  World Trade Center 148
Bucium 416
Bucovina 192
Buhuşi 236
Buzău 271
Buzău Mountains 272
Buşteni 182

C

Cabana Turistică Putna 206
Căciulata 161
Câinenii Mici 160
Căldăruşani Monastery 153
Călimăneşti 161
Călimani Mountains 194, 437, 443
Câlnic 470
Câmpeni 404
Câmpina 185
Câmpulung 178
Câmpulung Moldovenesc 217
Câmpuri 269
Cantacuzino, Şerban 123, 142
Cantemir, Dimitrie 246
Carei 323
Carol I 140
Cârţişoara 168
Ceahlău Massif 221
Ceauşescu, Nicolae 51, 113, 114
Cehei 327
Cehu Silvaniei 326
Cerchez, Grigore 126
Cernat 454
Cernica Monastery 154
Cetatea de Baltă 417
Cetăţuia 256
Cheia 489
Cheia Zugrenilor (Zugren Gorge) 195, 221
Cheile Turzii 402
Cheilele Bicazului 221, 447
Chilia lui Daniil 206
Chirpăr 468
Cincu 492
Cisnădie 468, 469
Cisnădioară 468, 469
Ciucaş Mountains 489
Ciucea 405
Ciucsângeorgiu 452
Ciumârna 332
Cleopa 227
Cluj-Napoca 419
  Babeş-Bolyai University 429
  Bastionul Croiţilor 430
  Biblioteca Germană 429
  Calea Moţilor 431
  Calvary Church 431
  Central Reformed Church 430
  Citadel 430
  Colecţia de Istorie a Farmaciei 427
  Franciscan Church and Friary 429
  Grădina Botanică 'Alexandru Borza' 426
  History Museum 429
  Muzeul Etnografic al Transilvaniei 423, 426
  Muzeul Naţional de Artă 424
  Muzeul Naţional de Istorie a Transilvaniei 423
  National Theatre and Opera House 430
  Orthodox Cathedral 430
  Piarist Church 429
  Piaţa Unirii 427
  Reformed Church 431
  Sf Mihai 427
  Str Kogălniceanu 429
  Str Universităţii 429
Cobia 181
Codlea 491
Codreanu, Corneliu Zelea 251
Coman of Iaşi, Dragoş 203
Congă, Ion 223
Copşa Mica 471
Corabia 174
Cornet Skete 160
Corund 448
Corvin, Matei 41, 42, 399, 428
Costache Negri 280

Costești 396
Cotești 268
Covasna 455
Cozia 161
Coșbuc 441
Craiova 171
Crângul Petrești 267
Crapina 280
Crișana 313
Creangă, Ion 254
Crișcior 405
Cristian 470, 490
Cristuru Secuiesc 448
Curtea de Argeș 174

D
Dacian citadels 395
Dacians, The 397
Dadu 187
Dealul Frumos 492
Dealul Mare 186
Dealul cu Melci 409
Dealul Monastery 180
Dealurile Pâclelor 272
Densuș 399
Deva 394
Dintr'un Lemn 165
Dobra 392
Dobrovăț 257
Dracula, Vlad 157, 159, 180, 476
Dragomirna 193, 213
Dragosloveni 270
Drobeta Turnu Severin 169
Durău 221

E
Elizabeta, Queen 185
Enescu, George 144

F
Făgăraș 478, 491
Faraoane 268
Feldioara 487
Feleac 419
Fețele Albe 398
Fildu de Sus 407

G
Gai 330
Galata 255
Galeș 470
Gârboavele Forest 280
Gârvan-Dinogeția 280
Ghelința 454
Gheorgheni 448
Gherla 432
Giumalău Mountains 217
Giurgiu 186
Gojeiești 409
Govora 163
Gurasada 392
Gusti, Dimitrie 147

H
Habsburgs, The 325
Hahnemann, Samuel 462
Hanu Conachi Nature Reserve 280
Hărman 487
Harhoiu, Dana 124, 125
Hațeg 399
Herghelia Lucina 219
Herina 442
Hobița 168
Hodod 326
Homorod 487
Horaița 229
Horea 408
Huda lui Papară cave 403
Huedin 409
Humor 192, 198
Humulești 223
Hunedoara 398
Hurezi Monastery 164
Iancu, Marcel 128

I
Iași 237
   Academia Mihălena (Michaelian Academy) 238
   Art Museum 248
   B-dul Independenței 252
   Barboi Monastery 249
   Barnovschi Church 248
   Biserica Armenească 249

Iași cont
Bojdeuca Ion Creangă 254
Botanical Gardens 254
Casa Dosoftei 248
Casa Ruset 252
Catholic Church 245
Copou Gardens 254
Eminescu Museum 254
Ethnographic Museum 248
French Cultural Centre 254
Fundația Regele Ferdinand I 253
Gate of Hope 252
History Museum 247
Hotel Traian 242
Mănăstirea Golia 249
Museum of Chemistry 255
Museum of Natural History 252
Museum of Old Moldavian Literature 254
Museum of Romanian Literature 254
National Theatre 241
Obelisk of Lions 254
Orthodox Cathedral 242
Palatul Culturii (Culture Palace) 246
Piața Unirii 242
Piați Palatului 246
Râpa Galbena 253
Science and Technology Museum 248
Sf Nicolae Domnesc (Royal St Nicholas's) 248
Sf Sava 249
Sf Spiridon 253
Sinagoga Mare 250
Station 241
Str Anastasie Panu 248
Str Cuza Vodă 252
Str Ghibănescu 249
Teatrul Național V. Alecsandri 252
Town Hall 246
Trei Ierarhi 245, 246, 247
Universitatea Veche 252
Țicău 254
Iclod 432
Ineu 317
Întorsura Buzăului (Buzău Pass) 488
Iron Gates gorges 170
Istrați, Panait 274

J
Jibou 331

K
Kiseleff, Pavel 145
Kogălniceanu, Mihail 255
Kós, Károly 431, 453

L
Lacu Roșu 221
Lacul Brateș 280
Lacul Cinciș 399
Lake Bicaz 221
Lapicida, Andreas 466
Lăpugiu de Jos 393
Lăpugiu de Sus 393
Lăzarea castle 448
Leliceni 452
Lipova 330
Livada 324
Livezile 441
Lotru (Outlaw) Valley 160
Lunca Ilvei 442
Lupu, Vasile 190, 191, 238, 239
Lupșa 403

M
Măgura 272
Mălâncrav 477
Măldărești 164
Mănăstirea Bistrița 163
Mănăstirea Bucovat 173
Mănăstirea Frumoasa 256
Mânăstirea Neamț 224
Mânăstirea Suzana 186
Mărășești 269
Mărăști 269
Mare, Ștefan cel 190, 196, 205, 211, 212, 215, 230, 231
Marginea 202
Marginimea Sibiuliu 470
Marie, Queen 185, 490
Marpod 468
Masivul Bucegi 184
Mediaș 471
Mera 270
Miercurea Ciuc 449

Mihăești 393
Mincu, Ion 127
Miorița 263
Mirăslău 418
Mircea cel Bătrân 123
Mlaștina de la Hărman 488
Mogoșoaia Palace 151
Moigrad 331
Moldavia 189
Moldovița 192, 199, 200
Moneasa 318
Moreni Monastery 260
Movila lui Burcel 259
Mugeni 448
Muntenia 160, 174
Munții Făgărașului (Făgăraș Mountains) 491
Munții Piatra Craiului 490
Munții Vrancei 447

N
Nădașa 444
Narcissus Meadows 452
Negrești-Oaș 324
Negrilești 270
Negru Vodă 178
Nehoiu 272
Nicolești 452
Nicula 432, 433
Nușfalău 328

O
Oaș 324
Obcina Feredeului 217
Odorheiu Secuiesc 448
Olt River 160
Oltenia 160
Oradea 313
Oravița 330
Orăștie 395
Ordâncușa 410
Ortelec 330

P
Padiș Plateau 408
Pădurea Bogății 487
Pădurea Breana 280
Palatul Snagov 153
Paltiniș 469
Panciu 268
Pângarați 221
Pătrăuți 193, 214
Paușa 332
Peleș Castle 184
Petrești 323
Peștera Merești 447
Peștera Meziad 318
Peștera Polovragi 165
Piatra Altarului 318
Piatra Craivii 416
Piatra Fântenele 442
Piatra Neamț 222, 232
Piatra Roșie 398
Pietrele Doamnei 195
Pietroasele 273
Pitești 181
Poarta Mureșului 393
Poiana 280
Poiana Sibiului 470
Poiana Stampei 195
Poienari Castle 177
Ponoarele 409
Potlogi 153
Predeal 489
Prejmer 487, 488
Prisaca 270
Probota 216
Putna 204, 206
Putna Waterfalls 270

R
Rădăuți 193, 206
Rădulești 392
Râmeț 417
Râmnicu Sărat 273
Râmnicu Vâlcea 162
Rareș, Petru 257
Râșca 216
Rășinari 469
Râșnov 490
Rebreanu, Liviu 441
Reci 454
Reghiu 270
Reservația de Arhitectură Vranceană 267

Retezat Mountains 400
Ribița 405
Richiș 473
Roman 236
Roșcani 393
Roșia Montana 403

S

Săcele 488
Săliște 470
Sâmbătă de Sus 478, 491
Sănduleşti 402
Sângeorz Băi 442
Sânmihaiu Almașului 332
Sânzieni 454
Sărata-Monteoru 273
Sarmizegetusa Regia 396
Sarmizegetusa Ulpia Traiana 400
Satu Mare 319
Saxons, The 388
Scorțoașa 272
Sebeș 470
Sebiș 318
Secu 225, 226
Serbs, The 329
Sfânta Ana, Lake 453
Sfântu Gheorghe 453
Sibiel 470
Sibiu 456
  ASTRA Museum 460
  Brukenthal Library 460
  Brukenthal Museum and Library 459
  Brukenthal Palace 460
  Casa Altemberger 466
  Casa Artelor 465
  Casa cu Cariatide 467
  Cathedral 465
  Exposița de Istoria Farmaciei 462
  Jesuit Church 463
  Metropolitan Cathedral 467
  Muzeul de Istorie 462
  Muzeul de Istorie Naturală 463
  Piața Aurarilor 464
  Piața Huet/Grivița 465
  Piața Mare 463
  Piața Mica 464
  Podul Minciunilor 464

Sibiu cont
  Str Avram Ianc 463
  Str Nouă 464
  Str Ocnei 464
  Str Zidului 464
  Turnul Pielarilor 464
  Turnul Pușcarilor 464
  Turnul Sfatului 463, 464
Sighișoara 473
  Biserica din Deal 476
  Casa Vlad Dracul 476
  Pasajul Scărilor 476
  Turnul Cositorarilor 477
  Turnul cu Ceas 474
  Turnul Fierarilor 477
  Turnul Frânghierilor 477
  Turnul Tăbăcarilor 477
  Turul Aurarilor 477
Sihăstria 225, 226
Sihla 226
Sihla Skete 225
Silistea 187
Silvania Region 326
Șimleu Silvaniei 327
Sinaia 183
Sinaia Monastery 184
Slănic 186
Slănic Moldova 236
Slătioara 195
Snagov, Church and Monastery 153
Solca 204
Sona 417
Sovata 445
Soveja 269, 270
Stână 325
Strâmtura 330
Strei 399
Stremț 417
Sucevița 192, 200, 201, 202
Suzană 489
Székely lands 446
Székely villages 451

T

Țara Moților 404
Târgoviște 179
Târgu Bujor 280
Târgu Jiu 166

Târgu Mureş 433
Târgu Ocna 236
Târgu Secuiesc 454
Târlisiua 441
Târpeşti 224
Teiuş 416
Tekelia, Sava 329
Teleajen Valley 186
Ţigăneşti skete 154
Tihuţa Pass 217, 437
Timişoara 336
  Art Museum 341
  Banat Museum 344
  Castel Huniazilor 344
  Dicasterial Palace 341
  Ethnographic Museum 344
  History Museum 344
  National Theatre 342
  Piaţa Libertăţii 341
  Piaţa Unirii 341
  Roman Catholic Cathedral 341
  Serbian Metropolitanate 341
  Str Eminescu 341
  Str Lenau 344
  Teresa Bastion 341
Tismana 168
Tişiţa Forest Reserve 270
Topliţa 443
Topoloveni 182
Tőkés, László 318
Transfăgăraşanu Highway 177, 492
Transylvania 388
Transylvania Heath 446
Treznea 331
Tulnici 270
Turda 418
Turnu Măgurele 187

U
Uileacu Şimleului 327

V
Valcău Citadel 328
Valea Beicii 444
Valea Gurghiului 443
Valea Prahovei (Pravhova Valley) 489
Valea Viilor 471
Valea Vinului 326
Valea Zinelor 455
Vânători-Neamţ 224
Văratec 228
Vatra Dornei 217, 220
Vicovu de Jos 204
Vidra 409
Vinţu de Jos 416
Vizantea 269
Voineasa 160
Voroneţ 192, 195, 197, 198
Vrancea 261
Vurpăr 416, 468

W
Wallachia 155

Z
Zăbala 454
Zalău 329
Zlatna 416

www.ingramcontent.com/pod-product-compliance
Lightning Source LLC
Chambersburg PA
CBHW071932240426
43668CB00038B/1249